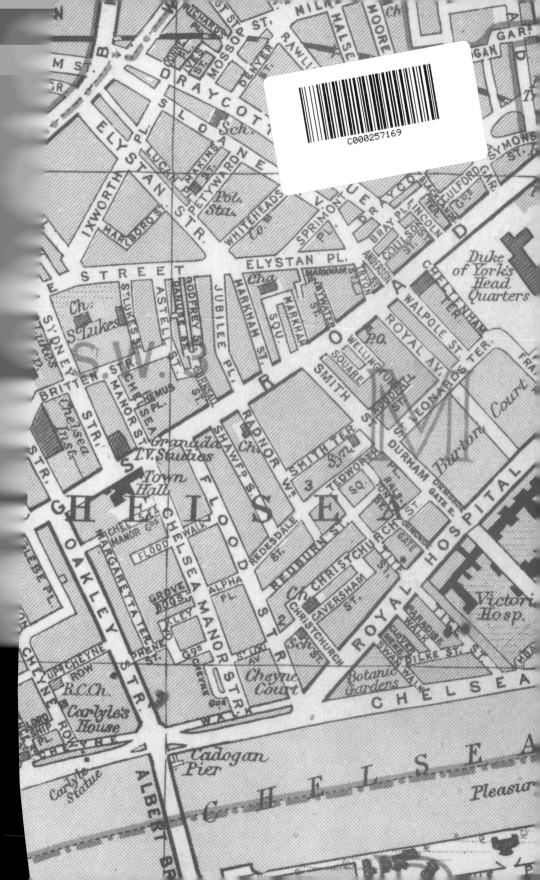

QUENTIN
& PHILIP

Also by Andrew Barrow

The Tap Dancer

The Man in the Moon

ANDREW BARROW

QUENTIN & PHILIP

– A Double Portrait –

MACMILLAN

First published 2002 by Macmillan
an imprint of Pan Macmillan Ltd
Pan Macmillan, 20 New Wharf Road, London N1 9RR
Basingstoke and Oxford
Associated companies throughout the world
www.panmacmillan.com

ISBN 0 333 78051 5

Typeset by SetSystems Ltd, SaffronWalden, Essex
Printed and bound in Great Britain by
Mackays of Chatham plc, Chatham, Kent

Contents

v

CONTENTS

List of Illustrations

Panna Grady

Laurie Lee (*Mary Evans Picture Library*)

Patrick de Maré

Tambimuttu (*McCormick Library of Special Collections, Northwestern University Library*)

Michael Hamburger (*Fritz Eschen*)

Edith Young

John Berger

David Thomson

Paul Potts

Quentin modelling in the 1970s (*Jean Harvey*)

Joan Rhodes

Gordon Richardson

Quentin on stage – four images (*Jean Harvey*)

Quentin in his room (*Derry Moore*)

The fireplace at Beaufort Street, drawn by Quentin

Quentin aged eighty, 1989

Philip aged seventy-one, March 1988 (© *Caroline Forbes*)

Philip and his son Peter, Paris 1975

Quentin at the christening of his great-great-nephew, 1998 (*Michele Crawford*)

Quentin with the author, New York, February 1989

Philip with the author, South of France, April 1991

No mask like open truth to cover lies,
As to go naked is the best disguise.

WILLIAM CONGREVE, *The Double Dealer*, 1694

PART ONE

PART ONE

– I –

East Third Street

I may look all right on the surface but I'm falling apart underneath. My foot hurts. I have a hernia.

QUENTIN CRISP TO ANDREW BARROW, 4 October 1998

There is no uniformed porter, no doorbell or any kind of entry system at 46 East 3rd Street. Visitors have to telephone from the street corner and then make their way across the road to a semi-basement door-way and wait to be admitted. I have been through this procedure before and know the ropes.

As I peer through the glass panels of the front door, I wonder what Quentin Crisp will look like. I have not seen him for eight years and have been disconcerted by recent photographs in which he looks like a little old witch – or would wizard be a nicer word? I do not know what to expect. What do eighty-nine-year-old men look like anyway? Will I find a stick insect?

In the event, it is his feet and legs that I see first as he slowly descends the stairs to let me in. For a moment I wonder if Quentin Crisp, the great stylist, has graduated to the trainers and tracksuit bottoms beloved by octogenarians largely because they are so easy to get in and out of. But no – he is properly dressed in smart black shoes, grey flannels and a tailored grey worsted jacket which I learn later has been given to him by the famous fashion model Lauren Hutton. His only exotic adornments are his coloured neckerchief and the badges on his jacket. He seems smaller, perhaps a little portlier than when I last saw him, but his great beehive of upswept white hair is as buoy-antly bouffant as ever.

I learnt long ago that Quentin does not like to be kissed, let alone embraced – though I once saw Germaine Greer hugging him from behind at a London party without causing him undue dismay. I am excited and heartened to see him again – he is a precious part of my past – but I am not sure we even shake hands before he leads the way in slightly jerky, sideways movements to the second-floor room where he has lived for the last eighteen years.

I have been to this room before, in 1990, but not lingered or quite taken it in, only recalling that the door opened onto a narrow passageway, five or six feet in length, which leads into the room itself. Now I am exposed to the place in all its glory. It is extremely small, as small as a prison cell or hospital cubicle, and so crowded with boxes and packing cases that there is scarcely space for the bed and armchair. Two windows look onto the darkened well of the building and in its gloom the room feels more like a small disused factory or workshop than someone's home. Everything seems to be caked in an oily black debris worse than dust. On the left is a filthy old-fashioned sink with a dirty mirror above it. In the middle of the room there is a small fridge and a TV. On the floor beside the bed is a telephone. On various shelves and surfaces there are discarded kitchen utensils and even a sort of frying-pan on a hob. On the windowsills there are cups and other drinking vessels, including a large brown mug adorned with a sprawling nude male figure of a classical style. I have seen this mug before in London, thirty years earlier, and am amazed that Quentin has bothered to transport it across the Atlantic. Everything else seems to have been accumulated in New York. A bookcase beside the sink is stuffed with useless books which he is too polite or lazy to throw away, and on the floor are dozens of bottles of make-up, fixative and medicine, along with a discarded rumpled shirt such as you might find in any student's room across the world. Only the presence of a bottle of champagne and an unopened bag of luxury groceries give a clue that somebody far from run-of-the-mill lives here.

Quentin Crisp once said of the dirt and dust in his London room, 'It's just a question of keeping your nerve.' To survive in this terrible place on East 3rd Street must require nerves of steel, iron and flint. He also has to cope with the horrified reactions of visitors who do not understand his lifestyle or the strength of his resolve to stay on the bottom rung of society. The police have been called here three times and a few years ago he was dragged off to hospital though there was nothing wrong with him.

Perhaps squalor is, as he has claimed, his natural setting. And perhaps lately the whisky has helped him cope. In the old days when I knew him, he drank Guinness at dawn, even when he was staying with his relations, but now he is sloshing neat Chivas Regal into two mugs, doling out in a rough and ready manner the largest measures I have ever seen. How are we going to sit? Quentin soon settles on the bed, on which a mammoth crossword puzzle is laid out, and I take the armchair, so close to him that, as we squeeze into the available space, our knees keep touching.

My excuse for coming to see Quentin Crisp is to write an article for the *Independent* celebrating his forthcoming ninetieth birthday and the opening of his one-man show in an off-Broadway theatre. But this is not an interview. Like many celebrities, Quentin Crisp does 'the one interview' and says the same thing to everyone. I have heard it or read it all before. The same phrases, witticisms and observations crop up all the time, polished with age. I am not interested in how much he loves America or his impressions of Elaine Paige's dressing-room. I am not interested in his recent appearance on the Charlie Rose TV show, which New Yorkers have been talking about, or how they responded to him in Berlin where against his principles he appeared on a Gay Pride march – 'There was even a gay dog on the parade.' I already know that he has been celibate for half a century and that this is the room where he recharges his batteries and is his 'horrible unique self'. I already know that he longs for a significant, meaningful death, that he believes 'It would be nice to be murdered' and that 'Modern medicine is so unkind that many of us may live to be a hundred.'

Quentin Crisp has been pretending to be old for most of his life. Thirty years ago, when he was not even an old age pensioner, he wrote in *The Naked Civil Servant*, 'To survive at all was an adventure. To reach old age was a miracle.' And many years earlier, he had perceived himself as 'the survivor they hoped they would not find'. Now, at last,

he really *is* old, though he attaches no importance at all to his imminent birthday. Or so he says.

Everything about Quentin's public persona is complicated and contradictory. He proclaims that certain events cause his tears to fall yet
also boasts that he is icily unsentimental. He is a master of the double
bluff. He says he has no secrets and can be read like an open book –
'What you see is what you get' – yet his inner life is wrapped in
mystery. The American academic Paul Robinson has written about
Quentin Crisp's 'comedic aggression directed against himself'. He has
done more for homosexual liberation than anyone on the globe yet
claims to despise the movement and goes out of his way to offend its
leaders, describing them as 'corroded with envy'. In his view, homosexuality is an illness and he wishes he had never been born. He
believes in God but not in a God 'susceptible to prayer' and, as we
shall see, God features a lot in his conversation and even his poetry.
He never says the word 'love' without giving it a mocking twang yet
believes it is his duty to love everybody, to extend his hand in particular
to the unlovable: I have not been in his room long before he is quoting
from St Teresa of Avila – 'We must treat all people as at least better
than ourselves.' Somewhere inside him is a potent moral code, yet it
is masked by a sense of fun.

Over the years, he has inspired innumerable fanciful descriptions.
When I first met him in January 1967 I thought of him as a heraldic
beast and then as an anthropomorphic character out of children's
fiction or even an invention of his old friend and collaborator Mervyn
Peake. He has described himself as 'a stopped clock' and 'a funny old
gentleman'. Michael Holroyd has called him 'a vehicle for delight'.
He is said to resemble 'a retired Latin master' and 'a Persian cat'.
According to the journalist Quentin Letts, he is 'half Margaret Ruther-
ford and half child'.

As always, I want to get behind the façade, engage with him, get
down to brass tacks and the practicalities of his current life. As always,
it is uphill work. He spends a lot of his time travelling about America,
addressing audiences in places like Dallas, Texas, and Phoenix,
Arizona, but when at home spends a lot of time asleep. 'I'm slightly
narcoleptic,' he tells me. 'I fall asleep involuntarily.' He has only to

face the prospect of an afternoon at home and start wondering how he'll fill it before he has nodded off. He acts out the nodding-off process for my benefit. He talks excitedly about the recent death of his agent Connie Clausen, whose body was found in her office, and not at all excitedly about playing Elizabeth the First in the film *Orlando*: everyone raved about this performance but he was concerned only about the weight of the costumes and the corsets which bit into his stomach. He talks bitterly – yes, bitterly – about the Broadway musical about his life that was never made, in spite of the enthusiasm of two impresarios to do it. And he talks about the one-man show that will open on Christmas Day, his ninetieth birthday, and how he will 'cast around to find something to make the audience squeak'.

I ask him about his family. He tells me he has a new great-great-nephew living in New Jersey who has been christened Ian Quentin. I try to talk about our few mutual acquaintances. Does he ever hear from Mr York or Mr Melly? Does he know that Miss Campbell has had a baby? On hearing this last bit of news, he throws up both his hands in a staccato gesture of fake amazement. And then I ask him if he knows that Mr O'Connor, the man who gave him his first radio broadcast back in 1964, died a few months ago. Yes, someone had sent him an obituary in which he was mentioned. I am embarrassed to pursue the topic but I ask him what he feels about Mr O'Connor now. He says, simply, 'Nothing.'

As we squeeze together in that tiny room, I remark on how extra-ordinarily well he looks. His fingernails are dirty and unpainted but his face in the half-light seems to have no lines. He may have been a weak and weedy child but long ago he acquired considerable gravitas. His wrists no longer flap. His face is full of strength, his jaw is steady and he gives an overall impression of firmness, dignity and peace. He tells me this is all a delusion. 'I may look all right on the surface but I'm falling apart underneath. My foot hurts. I have a hernia.' He also has problems with his left hand. But, in spite of these afflictions, he has not lost the actor's ability to 'turn it on'. His gestures remain deft and unhesitant. His haughty demeanour may bear a passing resemblance to his hero Lady Thatcher but his head turns attentively and his concentration on me is absolute. His voice has been said to resemble that of 'a well-mannered tortoise' and he himself has ascribed to it the 'jarring' or 'jangling' quality of a disused or broken piano. Yet it also carries great authority. The actor John Hurt, who portrayed Quentin Crisp on film, said years ago, 'He knows *what* he is going to say, *when* he is going to say it and *how* he is going to say it.' To me, his voice is as full-throated as it was when I first met him thirty-one years ago.

And so are his views. In the last few weeks, he has frightened those following the O. J. Simpson murder trial by saying that killing your wife is 'justifiable homicide'. He has also pronounced that all the women involved in the scandal currently engulfing President Clinton deserve to be 'put together and chopped up like parsley'. Finally, he has gone right over the top and declared that the late Princess of Wales was 'trash' and 'got what she deserved'. These last statements have generated hate mail. From beside his bed he produces a letter saying, 'I now see that you are a bitter, lonely old queen.'

Is Quentin Crisp bitter and lonely? Is he even a queen? On this last point he tells me with some bemusement, 'It's now been explained to me that I'm *not* a homosexual. I'm a *trans*-something.' One suspects that all sexual classifications are quite absurd or irritatingly irrelevant to him. As far as bitterness and loneliness are concerned, I don't yet know the answer.

Anyway, the whisky is working and I am feeling relaxed. Some of the stress and strain of New York is evaporating in the company of this ancient friend from London. After forty minutes or so in this notorious room, we set off for lunch. Quentin puts on a cowboy hat, with brass buttons on it which complement the badges on his jacket, then an overcoat, into which he has difficulty fitting his left arm. As we descend the stairs he winces and whimpers in pain. We then shuffle together to the Bowery Bar & Grill, two blocks away, watched by passers-by who nod and bow to him as if he were a sacred relic – his joke, not mine. He is tired by the time we reach the restaurant and exclaims, 'Very strange!' when his poached eggs and mashed potatoes arrive decorated with chopped-up bits of red and green pepper. And then he says, with a rather surprising hint of irritation, 'There's no butter.' Thanks to the piped music, our conversation is a bit watered down and I am depressed when Quentin tells me there is now a *website* in his honour. He is at his most alert, most dextrous when imitating himself, sending himself up or mocking his own progress. 'When I was young, I was ill-equipped for living. Now I walk into a hotel brazenly and say, "Where's the dining room?" ' At one moment he grabs a spoon and pretends it is a dagger. We end the meal with glasses of amaretto – his idea, not mine – which Quentin says is 'like drinking Italian wedding cake'.

On this rich, evocative and festive note, our conversation ends. Someone has joined us at our table, a man who is going to the cinema with Quentin that afternoon. Quentin's diary seems unwisely full and he, who once loved any sort of attention, seems irritated that this man wants to take photographs. I try to help him on with his overcoat but his bad arm is difficult to manoeuvre and we give up. There is a muddle about which film they will see. Surely Quentin longs to be back in his room, on his bed, asleep? He now seems exasperated, speechless at the man's lack of efficiency. The three of us hobble towards the yellow cab which will take them away. Even now the man is taking photographs. 'No! No more photographs!' Quentin exclaims in almost physical pain. But he gets into the cab without assistance. Now he is sinking back into his seat. As the cab pulls away, he looks snug in his seat but his despairing final words still ring in my ears, '*No! No more!*'

− 2 −

Fontarèches

They make him sound a bit like Tintern Abbey – a
Gothic monument! And I can hear him laughing . . .
I never laughed with anyone as much as I laughed
with Philip. The rest is nothing.

JOHN BERGER TO PANNA GRADY, 11 July 1998

If you take the subway to East 77th Street and head across Central
Park, you will eventually see through the trees a particularly distinguished and slightly forbidding building. It is tall and massive,
constructed mainly of pale yellow brick and has high, pinnacled roofs.
It was built in 1884 and was here long before the others in the
area. It is called the Dakota and according to the writer Stephen
Birmingham is 'New York's Most Unusual Address'.

The cracked paint on the ground-floor shutters and air of gothic
gloom are slightly misleading. Here live and have lived some of the
most interesting if not the richest people in the world. Leonard
Bernstein lived here, so did Judy Garland and Boris Karloff and Syrie
Maugham. In 1980, John Lennon was shot dead at its gate and his
widow Yoko Ono still lives here, gradually acquiring more space at
an estimated million dollars a room. Another long-standing resident
is the actress Lauren Bacall, who has been here since the 1950s.

I do not know who now lives in the third-floor apartment with
four or five windows looking onto Central Park, but in the early 1960s
this was the home of an elegant and demure young woman called Mrs
Grady, then in her early twenties. She had moved into the Dakota on

learning of its well insulated walls and three-foot-thick floors. She wanted to give parties without disturbing the neighbours.

Few people remember Panna Grady today. Her name does not appear in Stephen Birmingham's history of the Dakota, published in 1979. She is mentioned in a caption under a photograph in a book about Andy Warhol but not in the text. But one of the poet Charles Olson's books is dedicated to her and so are a number of fringe publications from the underground press. And there is a page or two about her in Ted Morgan's book about William Burroughs, *Literary Outlaw*. And didn't Mick Jagger write a song about her? It hardly matters. In the early 1960s, Panna Grady was one of the leading patronesses of the counter-culture, certainly the youngest and the most beautiful, with the longest legs. Her apartment in the Dakota was enormous, even by Dakota standards, large enough for five hundred people to pass through comfortably. Writing in the *Sunday Times* some years ago, Anthony Burgess made a passing reference to those evenings as 'literally fabulous' and went on to explain, 'Literally, because the big modern sources of fable were there – Lowell, Warhol, Ginsberg *et al.*'

This is history now – there is no mention of Panna Grady in the most recent biography of Allen Ginsberg – and the woman Mick Jagger may, or may not, have called the Queen of the Underground has not been seen or heard of in New York for many years. Her reign ended suddenly, her court evaporated. In 1965, she fled to England in the footsteps of William Burroughs and on the arm of Charles Olson. For a while she continued her hectic, hospitable life in London – Ginsberg lived under her roof in Regent's Park – and then in the autumn of 1967 she met a derelict writer called Philip O'Connor and disappeared with him to France.

Up to that point Philip O'Connor's life had been hair-raising and his reputation as a madman was considerable. He slapped elderly ladies on the bottom, claimed descent from the kings of Ireland and had fathered seven or eight children by different women. At various times he had tramped around England. In the literary world he was renowned not only for his early surrealist poetry and gifts as an auto-biographer and radio interviewer, but also as 'the Man Who Stood behind the Door and Said *Boo* to T. S. Eliot'. Some found him dreadful. Panna Grady found him irresistible.

Panna Grady and Philip O'Connor never married but they lived together in France for more than thirty years. I met Philip for the first time in 1972 on one of his rare trips to London and was utterly beguiled by him. During the 1970s I visited Philip and Panna often when they lived on the coast near Boulogne but much less often when they moved south to the Avignon area. Their last home together was a small house in a village called Fontarèches, in the area of the South of France known as the Gard. Here on 29 May 1998, Philip O'Connor died peacefully aged eighty-one after a wild and extraordinary life to which Panna Grady had brought a degree of happiness and stability.

Panna now lives at Fontarèches alone, with four or five sheepdogs and a cat or two for company. Her two sons by O'Connor live elsewhere in France, and so does Ella, the daughter from her marriage to a poet called Jim Grady, born when she was living in the Dakota. It is a small, neat house, with one room downstairs and two bedrooms and stands like a lodge at the gate of an old chateau that belongs to a Canadian family whose fortune is said to have something to do with airline food. The fir trees cut out too much of the sun in the winter but make the place cool in the summer.

It is in the summer, a few weeks after Philip O'Connor's death and a few months in advance of my visit to Quentin Crisp in New York, that I have called to pay my respects to Panna Grady. The yard where I once sat drinking with Philip O'Connor is empty. Panna is in the doorway surrounded by barking dogs. When I try to give her a hug, she pushes me away quite forcefully but she is otherwise welcoming. She is tall, slim, wearing a chic woollen dress and her American voice is as soft and wistful as when I first heard it. But, as always, she is distracted. 'I really have to settle these dogs down, Andrew. I really must feed them.'

Inside, I find the house as alluring as ever. The downstairs room, with sink, stove and fridge at one end, is full of tapestries and antique screens. Pride of place is given to the large oval gate-legged table that has come all the way from her family home in Connecticut and which graced both her apartment in the Dakota and her house in Regent's

Park. Upstairs, in her bedroom, there are more treasures – pearl caskets, porcelain vases, snuff-boxes, bangles and beads. These are the remaining crown jewels of a Queen in Exile, Panna Grady's last barricade against poverty and a gentle reminder of the splendour she once knew. On a corner of her dressing-table is a photograph of Panna giggling and glowing at the head of a restaurant table in New York, Burroughs and Warhol beside her. Burroughs has his arm around her, Warhol is responding to a guest across the table.

Panna has no regrets about her change in circumstances or the manner in which she squandered her fortune. 'I had as much as Peggy Guggenheim to start with but Peggy Guggenheim bought paintings and I paid for books to be published,' she says but doesn't explain what happened to the Jackson Pollock she once owned or why she didn't follow through the projects she paid for. She helped a man called Irving Rosenwald start a publishing house which flourished, but admits, 'I didn't follow it up, Andrew, I was too harassed.' Nor does she regret her thirty years with Philip O'Connor or the money she threw away on cars he smashed up and houses he grew bored with, though she does tell me twice that it has cost her ten thousand francs to get Philip into his coffin. She also tells me that she never read Philip's masterpiece *Memoirs of a Public Baby* or anything else he wrote. She didn't have time. They were always moving house. Philip was so demanding. Also, she says, she wanted to preserve the fun of hearing Philip reading aloud from his works. Anyway, whatever she thought of Philip's writing, she saw through it to the person within. As Philip once pointed out, it was poets Panna loved, not poetry. And she's been equally neglectful about Burroughs's books. 'I didn't have time to read properly,' she says. 'But I'll do it now. I'll get a pair of glasses.'

But Panna's love for Philip is undying and has now been whipped up by the public and private responses to his death. On the gate-legged table there are photographs and press cuttings about him, obituaries in all the English broadsheets, the *New York Times* and the local French papers, many of which mention Panna's part in his life and Philip's role in putting the hitherto unknown Quentin Crisp on the map for the first time. My attention is caught by an item from a

Welsh newspaper headed 'A Genius Who Lived Among Them' focusing on O'Connor's five years in a village in Snowdonia, with a girl half his age. 'To me, she looked like a schoolgirl,' a local character, Edgar Parry Williams, is quoted as saying. 'It caused quite a scandal.'

And then there are the letters of sympathy. The writer John Berger comments on the obituaries themselves and goes on to say how much he laughed with Philip, adding, 'The demon in him was very lovable.' A couple called the Blegvads write from an address in Fulham Road beginning, 'Such sad news in all the papers in London', and go on to touch upon the complexity of Philip O'Connor's nature. 'Some of his behaviour was uncomfortable to obnoxious but his preoccupation and insight into the nature of man and society as he knew it were exemplary and make him a noble cause. May the will work its selective effects on his memories and ameliorate his tyrannies.' The actress Anna Wing, who lived with Philip for seven years and bore him a son, writes thanking Panna for making him so happy. Martina Thomson, widow of Philip's closest friend and the man who produced most of his radio programmes, writes saying, 'Surely you are the only being who could have held Philip enthralled ad infinitum?' The bookseller Stephen du Sautoy declares, 'Philip was one of the most extraordinary men I have ever met.' From Imperia on the Italian Riviera, the artist Diana Pollitt writes of Philip's 'red pepper temper' and tells Panna, 'You replaced his mad mother.' From Cumberland, the poet Nick Rawson explains, 'He never became the immobile monolith of accepted letters. He remained within the *lutte*, the skirmishes and sheer fracas of words.' And then there's a letter from Ann Wolff, who long ago made a film called *Captain Busby*, in which both Philip O'Connor and Quentin Crisp acted. 'In a funny way,' she writes, 'I think Philip's spirit had escaped us and that he was too complicated and mercurial for us to catch him and he had slipped away from us.' There are also conventional sympathy cards, two from the remote Welsh village. One is signed 'Aunty Gwen' and the other is from 'Nellie and family'.

Panna's gratitude for these messages and pride in the newspaper tributes are mixed with indignation on Philip's behalf. So many publishers, she says, let him down and not enough people, she says, called on him as he lay dying in the wooden shed at the back of the house. On the last score, I wonder how much he minded. The room where he slept, worked and eventually died was a private place where visitors were usually unwelcome. Philip enjoyed entering and creeping about the ground-floor room at Fontarèches, shouting at its occupants and cooking at the stove, but he needed his place of refuge and in every house he lived had his own private quarters. I had visited him in his various fastnesses and if not rejected at the door had been treated to music from his gramophone or extracts from his journal which he read with far more gusto than he showed at poetry readings in front of an audience.

Panna has made no attempt to tidy Philip's room at Fontarèches though I notice a pile of discarded items outside the door, including the padded white coat with sheepskin trimmings that he had often worn twenty-five years earlier, and the chair with gnarled arms and ancient tacks in which he had sat and roared. Panna calls it Philip's 'throne' and says it may be thirteenth-century – or does she mean Louis the Thirteenth? Inside, the hut or former garage is unchanged. It is a long narrow room, sixteen feet in length and about seven feet wide. In a hollow on the large double bed where Philip died there is an old grey cat with half its tail missing. 'It was always here with Philip,' Panna says. Underneath the desk are a pair of recently dis-carded shoes and near them on the floor a large man-size disposable nappy. Panna grabs this with a humorous gesture. Philip had died of cancer of the rectum and had worn nappies at the end of his life, a completion of the cycle that may have appealed to him in some ways. There is also a shelf of medicines and ointments, mostly with French names, which were used to ease the pain of his final days.

And all around the room there are the bookshelves Philip put up with his own hands when they moved here in 1991 and still crammed with his favourite volumes. Many of these are classics like Cobbett's *Rural Rides* and Mayhew's *Characters*. There are also rows of books by his friends Michael Hamburger and John Berger and Stephen Spender and a whole shelf about Oscar Wilde. There are dullish-sounding ones like *Social Life in Britain from the Conquest to the Reformation* by G. C. Coulton and interesting ones like *The Art of Growing Old* by John Cowper Powys and *Madness and Civilization* by Michel Foucault. Lying loose on the floor is *The Scarlet Letter* by Nathaniel Hawthorne and tucked in tightly somewhere is my own first novel, *The Tap Dancer.* On a high shelf by the door are two bumper volumes of poetry by Charles Olson – Philip had a habit of requisitioning Panna's possessions – and close to his desk are some battered copies of his own works. A first edition of *Memoirs of a Public Baby* is still in its yellow dust-jacket but split open at the spine and covered with his notes. *The Lower View* is here and *Living in Croesor* but there's no sign of *Vagrancy,* the Penguin Special that includes an account of his own time on the road. Like Panna, I have never read any of Philip's books properly and know them best by the blurb and critical acclamations on their covers: I know Dorothy Parker's comment on *Memoirs of a Public Baby* by heart: 'Philip O'Connor, always outside society, saw into it with blinding clearness. As to his writing there can be no calmer word than superb.'

Hanging from these shelves – which also house an urn containing Philip's ashes – or heavily glued onto the wooden walls are familiar pictures and photographs. There is the controversial picture of Philip with his mother, of which more in a moment, and the portrait of Beethoven which hung above the gramophone in the house in northern France where I first visited him. There is a pin-up of Stephen Spender beside his bed and the picture postcard of Charlie Chaplin I sent him a few weeks before his death. Under Panna's instructions I take down or peel off these images to send to Philip's son Peter, who now lives in Japan and was reconciled with his father a few months earlier.

There are also files of papers and letters in various drawers and loose on top of his desk. Philip sold a lot of his papers to American universities – old BBC scripts, submitted synopses and chunks of journals he hadn't tried to find a publisher for. He also sold his letters from Stephen Spender and Quentin Crisp but there are still some here from Peter Levi, Alex Comfort, Jonathan Gathorne-Hardy and other luminaries – and messages of goodwill from the mothers of his children. 'Take it easy,' orders Anna Wing and 'I can't bear you being ill,' writes Maria Scott with whom he lived in Fitzrovia half a century ago. And here is a letter that has arrived since his death from an

unknown fan of *Vagrancy*. 'I know I cannot hope to convey successfully the impact your book has had on me,' his admirer begins
stumblingly, and concludes movingly, 'I write of course as someone
who has lived as a "vagrant" for years at a time.' There are also
bundles of press cuttings about himself and other people. I find a piece
about Quentin Crisp from the *Herald Tribune*, in which Philip's
old sparring-partner is described as 'an international treasure' and
'a master practitioner of public relations and self-mocking self-
promotion'.

Here and there lie fragments of Philip O'Connor's last handwritten
attempts to write something. Some are easy to read. 'Nothing funnier,
Lord, than the prospect of dying,' he writes. 'Lord how funny, how
weirdly funny is the ending of the stupid adventure.' Others are only
scribbles but the few words that stand out indicate that he was still
working away at the themes that had gripped him all his life – 'family',
'mother' and 'madness'.

Panna leaves me alone in Philip's room, where I even attempt a
short snooze on his bed, but soon we are together again and amidst
the barking dogs talking about mutual friends in London she has not
seen since the 1960s and others I do not know but whom she would
like me to get in touch with. 'Oh, it's so dull here without Philip,' she
says suddenly and she is still talking about him and their semi-separate
existences as I start to drive away. Finally, she says pleadingly, '*We
hid from each other.*'

PART TWO

PART TWO

− 3 −

A Terrible Child

Star quality on the stage is indefinable; it roughly means that its possessor has a magnetic, even a mesmeric power which holds the audience immediately and maintains that grasp whatever that performer may be saying or doing. Lauder had that quality to the full.

IVOR BROWN ON SIR HARRY LAUDER,
Dictionary of National Biography

It may seem far-fetched to begin the story of Quentin Crisp with a quotation about a performer he never met, never saw on stage and probably wouldn't have liked if he had. Quentin Crisp had little time for the music hall, though he became a friend of at least one distinguished vaudevillian. But the links with Lauder exist – and links are partly what this story is about. Throughout his life, Quentin was interested in the concept of stardom and in the presentation of himself as a star and, during the last part of his life, he too gave a stage performance of magnetic and mesmeric power. And a century earlier, the two men were also connected by a thin but not entirely negligible geographical proximity.

When Harry Lauder was First Citizen of the Variety Stage, he lived in Longley Road, Tooting, in South London. His plain brick villa, paid for out of pantomime earnings and now distinguished by a blue plaque, was only a few yards away from the house where Quentin Crisp's father was brought up and just across the road from the house where Quentin Crisp's mother spent part of her childhood. Family origins can make tedious reading. Many readers skip those early pages

21

devoted to the ancestors of the subject with which so many biographies and autobiographies kick off, but in the case of such a fanciful and intangible figure as Quentin Crisp, some probing into his background, some attempt to anchor him as a member of the human race seems desirable if not essential.

And this is all the more necessary because Quentin has revealed almost nothing about his background. In his autobiography, he states only that he was born in 1908 at Sutton in Surrey, the youngest of four children, and that his parents lived beyond their means and incurred the attention of bailiffs before any of the children were born. Later on, he reveals that his name was Denis, not Quentin, but he doesn't bother to tell us that his original family name was Pratt, not Crisp.

I do not object to this discretion, the broadness of these brush-strokes or the caricature of 'middle-class, middling, middlebrow' family life that he provides in *The Naked Civil Servant*. In fact, I feel uncomfortable about tampering with the many lacquered images and picturesque pieces of self-portraiture that Quentin offered in all his writings and most of his conversations. Yet this very elusiveness, this jokey gloss on everything is what has prompted me to scrabble away behind the façade and unearth a few facts, however banal they may seem at first glance.

There is not a lot to tell. Quentin Crisp was a product if not an invention of the suburbs. His Englishness is unquestionable and there seems to be nothing at all exotic about his background. In later life he seemed unaware that his mother and father grew up in the same street in Tooting, which is described in a contemporary guidebook as 'a region of villas and nursery gardens, very pleasant and, apart from the common, very commonplace'. Charles Pratt was born in 1871 at Lynton Villa, New Road, Tooting, son of a certain Spencer Pratt, who is variously described as a 'sugar manufacturer' and as a 'traveller to a sugar merchant' and had himself been born in Woolwich in about 1845. Charles Pratt also had a sister, Agnes, never mentioned by Quentin and perhaps never met by him, who will not appear in this narrative again.

By the early 1880s the Pratt family had settled in Longley Road, along with two live-in servants. The house they lived in, double-fronted, white-bricked and on the south side of the road, is still standing today and its name 'Rothsay House' appears written in gold letters in the half-light above the front door. In the front garden, what look like the original zigzagging tiles still hem in the small flowerbeds. From this pleasant enough abode Charles Pratt was sent, like thousands of boys from the semi-prosperous suburbs, to boarding school. In 1884, at the age of twelve, he was despatched to one of the newer public schools, Bloxham's, near Banbury, where he won his football colours and according to the school's records was 'losing finalist in an inter-dormitory fives competition'. He left Bloxham's at the tender age of fifteen in order to become articled to a firm of solicitors.

By this time, or very soon afterwards, a family called Phillips had also moved into Longley Road. Their house, across the road from the Pratts, is also still standing though the gilded lettering proclaiming its name 'Melrose' has almost faded away in the intervening century. The Phillipses, who had previously lived in Holloway, Highbury, and other ancient suburbs of London, consisted of Henry Phillips, who is described as 'a hop factor', and his Lambeth-born wife and four children. According to the 1891 census, these consisted of young Henry Phillips, known as Jim, twenty-one at the time, and grandly described as a 'manufacturing chemist', and three girls, Frances, Katherine and Mabel. In the background, living elsewhere, there was also an Uncle Oram, said to have been a lighterman on the Thames.

I know little of the personalities of Katherine and Mabel, known in the family as Kay and May, or how they spent their early life but have now learnt a lot about Frances Phillips. She did well at school, in spite of disliking mathematics on the grounds that there was only one right answer, and had intellectual and social aspirations and what her son later described as 'a corrected cockney accent'. She got on well with everyone, however, and had close schoolfriends to whom she would write letters for the rest of her life. According to Quentin, his mother had 'a genius for making and keeping friends'. He also made much of the fact that in early adult life she worked as a governess, viewing life from 'the mezzanine floor' between the upper and lower classes and sharpening her social awareness in the process.

One of the families Frances worked for were the Turners, who lived at Tring in Hertfordshire and had a business called Spencer Turner, wholesale haberdashers whose London headquarters had dozens of telephone lines.

Between jobs Frances Phillips must have returned regularly to Longley Road and participated in whatever social activities – tennis parties and the like – were on offer there. In due course, her sister Mabel would marry John Washbourne, whose family lived in an identical house next door to the Pratts, and near the close of the century, Frances became engaged to Charles Pratt, now a qualified solicitor with an office at 46 Cannon Street in the City of London. Their subsequent marriage certificate indicates that Frances Marion Phillips was twenty-six, and Spencer Charles Pratt twenty-eight at the time of their wedding and that this took place on 24 November 1899 at St Mary's, The Boltons, in Kensington. The bridegroom was living temporarily at 53 Drayton Gardens, a newly built block of flats a few minutes' walk from the church.

There is not a great deal to add to these bald details except that Charles Pratt had ginger hair and, then or later, a ginger moustache and that Frances Phillips considered that she had made, by what her son later called 'Lady Bracknell standards', a good marriage. By marrying into the professional classes, 'she considered she had done as well as she could'. The choice of St Mary's, The Boltons, for the nuptials was perhaps an indication of the social pretensions of the young couple. The Boltons, which consists of two crescents of vast white stuccoed mansions, with the church in the middle, was and is one of the grandest addresses in London, much favoured today by the very rich and currently the home of my literary agent Gillon Aitken.

Anyway, the Pratts were never to live in Kensington, or Chelsea for that matter. Their first married home, which I have bothered to visit, was called Westdene on the west side of Beeches Avenue, Carshalton, between houses called Sandhurst and Aviemore. It is an unprepossessing property, in spite of its large bow windows and the communal pathway and hedge which protect it from the road, but Charles Pratt was already living beyond his means. If Quentin is to be trusted, Westdene was soon visited by bailiffs and the Pratts moved on to

4 Kestrel Avenue in Herne Hill, where the Pratts' first child, Phyllis, was born on 10 January 1901, then on to a house called Nethercroft in Grosvenor Road, West Wickham, where a son Gerald was born the following autumn. The family's financial problems remained unresolved and the death of Mr Pratt's father – leaving £413 – did not alleviate matters. On 3 November 1902, Charles Pratt was pronounced bankrupt and the following week faced a public examination in Carey Street.

It is interesting to note that this calamity did not prevent him practising as a solicitor, though it may have accounted for his frequently moving house and office. He was soon in new offices at 73 Queen Victoria Street and in a newly built house called Wolverton in Egmont Road, Sutton. This house is still there today and though now known simply as 52 Egmont Road appears a distinct improvement on the family's previous homes, offering three storeys and plenty of room for an expanding family. Here on 10 November 1907, a second son Lewis was born and, thirteen months later on Christmas Day 1908, lunch was interrupted with the news that Mrs Pratt had given birth to a third son. He was given the names Denis Charles and would be known as Denis until he reached his late twenties and changed it to Quentin Crisp.

This narrative can now be enriched or dolled up or actually distorted by what Quentin has written about his childhood and by what he told me about it in conversations and pseudo-interviews during the last thirty years of his life: I say 'pseudo' because I became an interviewer long before I published my first interview and it could almost be said I was practising on Quentin Crisp, who was a born interviewee. Whenever he spoke or wrote about his childhood he was at pains to emphasize, exaggerate and make jokes about his sickliness. 'I was frightened from the word go,' he told me. A few days old, he caught pneumonia and was 'literally as well as metaphorically wrapped in cotton wool'. For the first twelve years of his life, he suffered from continuous illnesses and spent a lot of time in bed, initially in a cot in his parents' room from where he witnessed 'the long despairing groan' which accompanied his father's sexual climax. Being in bed pleased him. 'It made me feel sacred in some sort of way.' In later life, he boasted that his early ambition was to be 'a chronic invalid' and that he cried 'almost all the time, out of grief and self-pity, all reproach seemed unjust'. When I asked if he was suicidal, he replied, 'All the time. I wished I was dead.' He also had what his governesses called 'accidents', which he subsequently described as attempts to draw attention to himself, exacerbated by his particular susceptibility to 'anal stimulus' and the pleasure of retaining his faeces.

In appearance, he was, he claims, 'a frail, pale, hopeless child'. He was 'very plain', had 'rich mouse hair', 'filthy brown eyes', 'crooked teeth' and was soon to wear spectacles. To this unappealing self-portrait he adds, with the benefit of a sort of hindsight, that he was 'disfigured from birth by the characteristics of a certain type of homosexual person'. He also claims or boasts that he was from birth 'an object of mild ridicule' and 'the wettest of weaklings'. In *How to Become a Virgin*, he explains, 'I was the youngest child and consequently the butt of mockery almost from birth.' This may be so but it was partly his movements, the flutter of his hands and partly his voice, which he described as 'an insinuating blend of eagerness and caution', which apparently inspired people to ask, 'Why is he so feeble? Why is he so wet? Is he ill?'

These lively, semi-comic and oversimplified questions are only Quentin's perception of how he imagined people reacted to his childish self, not what he actually heard them say, and we will meet many more of these self-mocking or self-simplifying projections in the course of this story. This is not to deny that Quentin was a very odd child who may indeed have looked wet and ill. 'I was conspicuously absurd,' he says. 'I went on as though I was a beautiful princess.' When he was not lying flat out and motionless on the hearthrug while his mother and sister sat busily sewing or writing letters in front of a 'threadbare fire', he was swanning around the house in an 'exotic swoon'. Into these games, this world of make-believe involving beautiful ladies and brave knights, he sometimes succeeded in dragging his brother Lewis, but he never ever, he insists, played with any other boys. 'I knew I would get hurt and not win,' he says.

And here we run into the first of many contradictions in the character of Quentin Crisp. Like many superficially inadequate individuals he had considerable inner reserves and his outer drippiness concealed a great deal of pride and haughtiness, assertiveness and an independence which is the opposite of wetness. Even the text of *The Naked Civil Servant* abounds with these contradictions. Describing his life in Sutton, he states that he was far too timid to go beyond the garden gate. Two pages later, he tells us that he thought nothing of going alone to the end of the road and getting a lift off a rag-and-bone man who dumped him on Sutton Downs, two or three miles away. In later life, he could only explain this anomaly by referring to his lust for attention. 'I was a monstrous show-off,' he told me. 'I had this terrible lust for attention, *every* hour of *every* day. I ought to have been an only child. I should have gone on the stage but I was very plain.'

Fortunately, or unfortunately, there was a full household at Egmont Road, a governess and other servants to flatter as well as two parents and three siblings to show off to. Young Denis – his family continued to use this name for the rest of his life – danced incessantly for the servants and made up poetry, which he inflicted on everyone present. Pressed to explain what this poetry was like, he replied, 'I imagine it was romantic, dreamy, sad, pseudo-poetic and *misspelt.*' Other showing-off behaviour included rushing into a room where his mother was talking to a visitor and saying, 'Look, I can stand on one toe!' and if these tactics failed, he had more unpleasant ones up his sleeve – 'I'll cut the tablecloth, shall I?' he once asked – which prompted his sister Phyllis to tell him in later life, 'You were a terrible child.'

How much Mrs Pratt shared this view is difficult to discern. Though lively and chatty and with a gift for friendship, she was herself a pretentious woman, whose way of speaking was sometimes made fun of, especially when she lapsed into cockney by calling her sisters May and Kay 'My' and 'Ky'. Her experiences as a governess had reinforced her class-consciousness. According to Quentin, his mother could spot the difference between real and false diamonds at a distance and she was inclined to speak with 'ostentatious condescension' about 'servant gals' and 'suffragettes'. When people arrived on the dot of three for a tea party, she protested – '*screeched*' is the word Quentin uses – that no one should be so ill-bred as to arrive at the right time. In an interview, Quentin described his mother as very good-looking but in *How to Become a Virgin* he tells us that she had 'a high bridge to her nose, hooded eyes and lips that were made for sucking a lemon'. At Sutton, she kept Pekinese and each week she got two books out of W. H. Smith's Lending Library in Sloane Square rather than the local free library, explaining, 'I don't want my books covered in coffee and blood.'

How much of a conspiracy was there between Mrs Pratt and her youngest child? In many respects, she was a conscientious parent. In later life, Quentin told me that his mother never deceived her children by saying, 'This won't hurt' or 'I'll be back soon', and her initial bewilderment over Denis was followed by years of worry about him. But she also had problems of her own. A frustrated woman with a sociable nature, social pretensions and fashionable ideas, she was restless in the company of her husband and later spent time in various nursing homes coping with the pressures of the marriage. Was the 'exotic swoon' that her son had entered close to her own secret ideal? Quentin Crisp wrote in the autobiographical synopsis submitted to the publishers Jonathan Cape, that he spent his early life dreaming that he was a woman, and adding, 'Either my mother led me into this dream or she sustained me in it.' She certainly seems to have encouraged him to believe that dressing up in female clothes and playing the part of an upper-class woman was, as Quentin puts it, 'a taste we shared'. Or was it just a way of keeping him quiet? And did the social-climbing aspect of her son's 'gauzy internal dream' mean more to her than its sexual ingredient? Certainly Mrs Pratt swung between upbraiding and cosseting him and from time to time she had fits of indulgence, such as buying him a pair of blocked ballet shoes in the vain hope that he might become a dancer. The relationship remains a mystery. When, years later, I asked if he loved his mother, Quentin characteristically sidestepped the issue by replying, 'In the beginning I depended utterly on her. Today I try to love everybody.' But he was frank in admitting that he enjoyed his mother's company – both of them longed to talk – and may have encouraged her in some of her excesses: he remembered begging her as a child to wear gold shoes at a local wedding. Mrs Pratt – known to her family and friends as

'Baba' – was certainly a strong character in her own right and had a cultural influence on Denis which would continue into his teenage years and beyond. 'It could be said,' he remarked magisterially in later life, 'that I inherited something from my mother.' On another occasion, he stated with a certain proud peevishness, 'If anyone shaped my character, I suppose it was my parents, particularly my mother, and regretfully I admit because of them I am invincibly middle-class.'

So what of Mr Pratt? Again, Quentin uses broad brushstrokes to paint a picture of a man who was already exceedingly oblique. In *The Naked Civil Servant*, he tells us that his father was a 'fastidious' man who would dust a chair before sitting down on it and eat a banana with a knife and fork – 'to modern minds a dead giveaway if ever there was one'. Of what, exactly? At other times, Quentin described his father as 'a cypher' and 'a shadow', and adds 'One wished he wasn't there.' According to Quentin, his father was not an authoritative figure, 'just grim' and 'occasionally very angry'. Did he ever hit his youngest son? 'He couldn't afford to. He would have killed me.' In later life, Quentin denounced his father as 'a shyster lawyer, who got money off old ladies', but from the perspective of a child he simply appeared as an excruciatingly solemn city worker, complete with silk hat and ginger moustache, who kissed his wife 'as though she was the Bible' as he set off each morning for the half-hour walk to Sutton station, where he would catch a train to his office in the City of London. In the evening, Mr Pratt had dinner – Quentin calls it 'evening meal' – and then slept, snoring loudly, with the bridge cards still in his hand. At weekends, he retreated to the garage to fiddle about with a broken-down, second-hand car, which was his only outdoor interest besides mowing the lawn. 'He was mechanically-minded but by no means a wizard,' says his son succinctly. Occasionally, he took his family out for a spin, purposeless trips to the surrounding countryside often punctuated by shouts of 'Can you hear a rattling?' Writing many years later to the film director Denis Mitchell, Quentin says of his father's misplaced love of machinery, 'His car was the only thing my father showed any affection for.' But he also acknowledges that his father was the only member of his family who never teased or ridiculed him – 'He went on as if nothing unpleasant had happened' – but adds that this was perhaps because his father hardly ever spoke. In *Resident Alien*, Quentin Crisp also writes that his father had taught him to walk 'in the excruciating armour of self-restraint', thus partly equipping him for his future martyrdom.

But just how accurate are all these impressions? Quentin's sister Phyllis remained devoted to her father, even to the extent of denying that he was ever a bankrupt, and there is a photograph in the family's possession which contradicts the image of Mr Pratt which his son put out. He is tall, good-looking and athletic and wearing tennis clothes. He smiles quizzically towards the camera. Beside him stands his oldest son, Gerald, smiling shyly and also in tennis clothes, and between them in a deckchair sits Baba Pratt, posing prettily under a parasol with her eyes shut.

Quentin admits that his parents suffered on account of his selfishness and seems to have eliminated happy images of them from his mind. 'They were *miserable*,' he says firmly and the main source of their misery was money. 'They never raised their voices. They never had a row. But she was forever asking him for money.' Mrs Pratt had no money of her own and no bank account, and often had to remind her husband as he set off for the City that the coalman or some other tradesman would be calling that day and she had nothing to give them. Denis later noted the arrival of dustmen, postmen and 'other public servants' who came 'knocking on the door and wishing the householder a Merry Christmas until they were given a reward'. Underneath his conventional façade Mr Pratt was, according to Quentin, 'in no sense a realist'. The only thing that kept his parents together – and perhaps binds many couples – was their shared social aspirations. 'Keeping up with the Joneses was a full-time job with my mother and father,' writes Quentin Crisp in his autobiography and goes on to make his famous joke about it being much cheaper to drag the Joneses down to one's own level. On other occasions he remembers how his mother ordered him 'Money is never to be spoken of', how she forbade him to play in the front garden on Sundays and how she dragged her husband off to church even though he had 'no religion'.

Certainly the Pratts did not act as if they were poor. Mr and Mrs Pratt once went on a day trip to Boulogne – their only experience of the

Continent – and regularly took the whole family on seaside holidays to places like Brighton and Bognor where they stayed in rooming houses. 'I realize now how much I hated it,' said Quentin years later. The house in Egmont Road, where they lived until the outbreak of the First World War, seems to have been comfortable and well run, typical of others in this area, most of which had fancy front gates, verandahs – ideal for conversion into a stage for Denis's early amateur dramatics – and boxrooms or attics containing dressing-up boxes full of clothes, sometimes dating back more than one generation. At Egmont Road, there was a 'rug box' in the hall, linen baskets elsewhere and a telephone, used for ordering groceries. There were also Mrs Pratt's Pekinese and there were cats. Quentin's sister Phyllis owned a camera and someone else in the family may have possessed a movie camera: I was told by one of Quentin's nieces that a home movie existed showing Mrs Pratt in bed, surrounded by cats, with her youngest child prancing barefoot in the background.

And of course there were the servants. None of their names will be known until the contents of the 1911 census are unveiled but Quentin remembered a governess named Miss Birmingham: 'She ruled us.' It says something for the Pratts that, whatever their inner struggles, the household presented a united front. Never at this time or at any time in the future were there any feuds in the family and although Denis came in for lots of teasing from his brother Lewis, it did not come, he says, 'in a form that was hard to bear'. When I asked if Lewis was fond of him, he replied simply, 'I wonder.' Occasional visitors to the house also added some amusement. Mr Pratt may have had no friends and his few relations may have made no appearance, but Mrs Pratt made sure that her children kept in touch with her family. Denis met his aunts May and Kay and was 'formally introduced' to his mother's mother, who wore black. Aunt May's husband John Washbourne died at an early age and she was left with a son called Morris to bring up alone. Mrs Pratt urged Lewis and Denis to be kind to Morris when he came over to play but the two brothers decided to give their cousin 'hell', which suggests a certain comradeship existed between them. This was less evident when the two brothers were taken, in matching sailor suits, to a photographer's studio in Sutton. Denis was in his element, 'posing and posturing' for the camera, but Lewis hated the experience, especially when told to hold hands with his little brother. Sadly, those particular photographs have not survived but another picture of Denis's three siblings does exist, in which they look well dressed and well fed. Writing of this period later, Quentin Crisp also makes much of the relationships he formed with various neighbours' children, all girls of course, with whom he played the same rather repetitive game which involved him dressing up in female attire and saying things like 'I am very proud and very beautiful.' More conventional parties, where games involved kissing, Denis approached with great reluctance, avoiding the fray on one occasion by sitting in another room and playing patience with a pack of cards he had 'thoughtfully' brought along with him.

Each Sunday, Denis was forced into the same heavily starched sailor suit and taken along the road to worship at Christchurch, an oppressive Gothic-style building that had gone up in the 1870s and is still there today. When he was a bit older, Mrs Pratt went a great deal further and dolled him up in a green tulle dress and a wreath of roses – was much persuasion needed? – and got him to play a fairy in a production of *A Midsummer Night's Dream* being staged at Sutton Town Hall; his sister Phyllis was also involved and so was a family friend called Miss Benmore. On stage Denis danced himself silly and fought with another fairy for the most prominent place – again revealing some of the assertiveness that lay behind his feeble, tearful façade. 'Fancy my mother allowing it,' he mused later. In *The Naked Civil Servant*, Quentin further titillates the reader with the information that the actor who had directed the production, and on whose knee he had perched, was promptly arrested for seducing one of the boys and was seen on Sutton station in handcuffs.

Life at Wolverton – the name of the house in Egmont Road has a coy flatness without the utter absurdity of those around it which gloried in names like Wyuna, Glenmore and St Columb – seems to have been oriented towards vaguely mind-improving activities. Denis's 'exotic swoon' was hedged in with family prayers, which he says he 'rattled off', and other rituals. He was taught to play the piano but says he had 'no musicality whatsoever' and would indeed profess a

lifelong hatred of music. There was chess, which Quentin Crisp continued to play all his life and with increasing viciousness, and there
were card games. When we met in New York in 1998, he became
particularly animated at the mention of Bolivian canasta and told me
this is 'played with three packs with two jokers each'. But does his
dedication to these pastimes – and later to crosswords, which had not
yet hit England – and his subsequent career bear out his aphorism,
'Those who play games seriously always lose in life'? And how much
did Quentin Crisp owe to his mother's literary interests? According to
his niece Frances, with whose parents Baba Pratt would live in later
life, she was 'extremely well read'. There was her steady stream of
library books and there were the books she read out to her children.
'She read in a "poetry voice" but she read extremely well,' Quentin
recalled, 'partly perhaps because she was made to read the same pieces
so often.' Favoured pieces were *The Lady of the Lake* and *The Idylls
of the King* and these undoubtedly fuelled her son's erotic dreams. She
also read aloud 'quite difficult books' like *Night and Morning* by
Bulwer Lytton, of whom the Pratts possessed the entire works. On
one occasion, Denis would catch his mother dusting these volumes,
taking each off the shelf as she did so. 'I wouldn't do all that,' he told
her, prompting his mother's witty reply, 'I know *you* wouldn't. That's
why *I* must.' In later life, Quentin declared he grew up on the works
of Rider Haggard – but perhaps we are jumping ahead too fast.

In 1914, when Denis was only five years old, the Pratt family made
another of its moves, leaving Wolverton in Egmont Road, whose
next occupant was a certain Brigadier-General Wilkinson, for a rather
smaller house a few minutes' walk away in Cornwall Road. This new
home, in a newly built road on the edge of open countryside, rejoiced
in the rather babyish name Cotlands and was between houses called
Buckhurst and St Ives, all with integral garages and pebbledashed
walls. From here Denis followed his brothers to a private school in
nearby Belmont where he found himself 'the constant object of amused
attention'. By now his brother Lewis was racing around Sutton on a
new bicycle but Denis was becoming increasingly zestless. The First
World War had begun. 'Death was everywhere,' he wrote later. 'It also
floated on the air in the form of Spanish influenza. Even I in my tinsel

tower became aware of it.' He was also aware of the soldiers billeted in various private houses in the area and, in a way he could not quite understand, found them 'emotionally disturbing'.

For most of the First World War the Pratt family seems to have continued its middle-class ways, taking holidays in a rented cottage at Pett on the Romney Marshes, a mile from the sea. With uncharacteristic sentiment, Quentin Crisp later recalled 'the jolly, busy seaside resort of Hastings' and 'the romantic cliffs of Fairlight'. Most days the family carried a picnic to the wasp-infested Fairlight beach. Reverting to his more familiar tone, Quentin tells us, 'I squeaked with feigned delight when I caught sight of the sea', and would later surprise me with the information that he could swim. During these excursions, he also claims that they could hear the guns across the Channel as 'the brave and the beautiful died like stampeding cattle'. Of the war itself he says, 'I remember it all horribly well' and describes it as 'a desperate folly' and 'a horrible affair'.

Eventually, financial worries must have weighed down again upon Mr Pratt. In September of that year, his oldest son Gerald followed him to Bloxham's, where he eventually became captain of the school. School fees and other pressures now forced Mr Pratt to move his family to an even smaller house, called Pemberth, on the other side of Cornwall Road. Quentin Crisp makes much of this 'first defeat in the presence of the Joneses' but says that the only disadvantage of the move from his point of view was there were 'no rooms and presumably no money' for servants. He had lost his captive audience. In this humble new abode, the family lived till the end of the war. Here Denis displayed his taste for danger by begging his parents to wake him up if the Zeppelins came over – they broke their promise – and also experienced 'an inkling of my terrible fate' when he found some men digging up the road outside the new house. Denis was so transfixed by these working-class men and stared at them so hard, that one of them protested, 'Look at him – he's all eyes! Clear off!' with such violence that his companion was moved to say, 'For heaven's sake, Bill. He's only a kid!'

At about this time, Denis also had his first exposure to another happier aspect of his future. As soon as he was old enough not to be sick there, he was taken to the cinema. In a spirit of 'ostentatious condescension' – the second time we have met this phrase – Mrs Pratt accompanied her youngest son to various films at the two picture houses in Sutton. One of these was very small indeed and showed films by Chaplin and Buster Keaton. The other was big and glamorous and called The Futurist. The films his mother allowed him to see were carefully chosen and Quentin said later, 'I got nothing out of it, then.' He preferred the ballet in those days even if part of its charm, or so he claimed, was that one of the dancers might break his neck.

By 1919, Mr Pratt's financial situation must have improved: he was now in new offices at 139 Cannon Street and was able to move his family to a much larger house in Epsom. Number 11 Ashdown Road, which then went under the ridiculous name Wanganni but is today called Heathfield Lodge, is a large three-storey building with six or seven bedrooms, two gates, and tall trees in its spacious garden. In 1919 there was a tennis court, on which even Denis was able to play – 'in a hopeless sort of way' – though the physical grace and co-ordination that came with his mature years were still a long way off. When challenged by two girls with a skipping-rope, he had found he was unable to skip – a disability I remember suffering from at the same age. In this new house, there were servants again – a maid in a black dress served meals – and ten-year-old Denis danced up and down the staircase to entertain them. The only cloud on the horizon was Mrs Pratt's 'nerves'. During the next four years, she went in and out of various nursing homes and hospitals and in her absence the household was run by Denis's sister, Phyllis, now in her late teens. Mr Pratt's presence is again shadowy and Quentin Crisp would issue typically conflicting statements about his father's role in his life. In How to Go to the Movies, he writes of being 'pushed towards boy-hood' by his father but elsewhere he claims, 'My father never took the slightest interest in me or my education.'

With the move to Epsom, Denis also changed schools. In January 1920, he became a pupil at a boys' school called Kingswood House, which had been founded in Ashley Road, Epsom, at the turn of the century. According to local tradition this establishment prided itself on not admitting any boy whose father was in trade and dressed its pupils in red blazers adorned with green piping, and red caps on which the school's monogram was intertwined in green. The school also claims to have had a strong music, art and drama tradition and one of its famous old boys is the artist John Piper, some five years Denis's senior. Closer contemporaries included Desmond Walter Ellis, later an actor, and Austin Duncan-Jones, later a professor of philosophy, who joined the school the same day. Denis's progress in this new environment is hard to evaluate. He was bad at all games, frightened of being hurt, didn't see very well and lacked strength, but these disabilities did not stop him becoming a Boy Scout and even attending a scout camp at Shanklin on the Isle of Wight. In academic terms, he may have seemed 'very bright' but argues that education in those days was 'just a question of memory'. Somewhere inside him lurked a perverted, even violent form of ambition. 'I wanted to *shine*, which was mistaken for a passion for learning,' he told me years later. 'I wanted to be *first* and I wanted to be *praised*.'

It was perhaps in this frame of mind that he wrote the pseudo-jingoistic and remarkably prophetic poem which appeared under his name, D. C. Pratt, in the March 1920 issue of the Kingswood House school magazine.

> Keep up to the mark and don't get slack,
> Intelligence here we ought not to lack!
> Never be feeble and never be slow,
> Girls and women are that you know!
> Sums and French are a bit of a fag
> When you feel you'd rather be having a rag,
> Of course you know this cannot be done,
> Out of School is the time for fun;
> Drawing's the nicest thing in the day,
> Hours and hours at that I could stay!
> Other lessons are not so bad;
> Used up are our brains so when finished we're glad,
> Still it's all right, not too much to do,
> Everyone else ought to come and try too!

There is some outrageous bluffing in these fourteen lines and signs of an obeisance to the school spirit – note that the first letters of each line spell out its name – which seems utterly out of character. His adverse comment on 'girls and women' is comically priggish and disloyal to the woman inside himself, yet the whole poem seems to have the dictatorial quality which coloured some of his later pronouncements. Was it, like so many of his later utterances, a big joke? Or was it a misguided last attempt to embrace boyhood? Only his mention of drawing sounds straightforward and there is an implication that this was an activity he did alone while 'everyone else' was elsewhere. In later life, Quentin Crisp told me, 'I was good at drawing. I could do that from the dawn of history. It's something I knew from the beginning.' His skill with the pencil – he was still only eleven – may have represented a lifeline for him and certainly gave his mother grounds for hoping that her son would one day become an artist.

Kingswood School was run by a certain Revd Kenneth Sandberg who, according to Quentin, ruled his pupils by their nerves. 'When he was not browbeating us, he was kissing us. Both these forms of punishment reduced me to tears.' In the spring of 1920, Mr Sandberg moved the school from its stifling and inadequate premises in Ashley Road to new ones at the top of West Hill, Epsom, which had once been occupied by a girls' school called Tanglewood. Here in the garden during the summer of 1921, Denis and thirty-six other boys posed for a school photograph. The twelve-year-old youth who eventually became Quentin Crisp stares bleakly, haughtily, towards the camera, cap pulled down over his brow. Compared with the smiling, healthy-looking boys who surround him, he resembles an ugly ornament whose small mouth, pointed chin and sticking-out ears give him the look of a sad little elephant, or elf, who is still doing his best to conform. There is no flicker of a smile about his lips or hint of the show-off about his demeanour. Nor is there any flavour of effeminacy about him. At this stage, the future Quentin Crisp was still deeply buried. In later life he said of this period, 'I feigned not to be angry and eventually became entirely free from indignation.'

From what little we know of him, the young Denis Pratt seems to have already led something of a double life. During the holidays, he had glimpses of happiness and excitement, and 'nearly fainted with delight' when his mother took him, sometime in 1920, to see the famous West End show *Chu-Chin-Chow* which had been running for several years at His Majesty's Theatre in the Haymarket, starring Lily Brayton. The show featured live camels on stage and was the first 'adult entertainment' the boy had seen. He was equally delighted to see at this time a film called *The Rift*, starring Pauline Fredericks. At school, there were few pleasures outside the art room though it may have been a consolation that he went home for lunch each day to Ashdown Road. In the classroom he was forced to read *Hereward the Wake* – 'Did you like it?' 'No' – and underwent more of the torture he had already become accustomed to. The staff also tried to score off him, subjecting the 'corrected cockney accent' which he shared with his mother to what he called 'limp ridicule'. In spite of these ordeals, he eventually sat his Common Entrance exam and won what he describes as a very poor scholarship to a public school in the Midlands. His reaction to this small but significant step forward was rather refreshing. Lapsing briefly into the jargon of an ordinary school-boy, he thought to himself, 'Well, that's a relief!'

The school to which he was sent in the autumn of 1922 was called Denstone but is only identified in *The Naked Civil Servant* as 'a public school on the borders of Staffordshire and Derbyshire'. Why the Pratts chose it instead of Bloxham's, where Denis's brother Lewis had recently followed his father and older brother, isn't clear. If Quentin's claims that his father never took any interest in such matters was true, then the school must have been Mrs Pratt's choice – or was the scholarship or 'exhibition' an important factor? The unanswered and unanswerable questions in this book are numerous.

Denstone College had been founded in 1868, on a fine site on top of a hill five miles north of Uttoxeter and not far from Alton Towers, where a famous amusement park stands today. The school, still very much in existence and proud of its past, is built in the Gothic style of what Professor Pevsner calls 'the middle pointed kind' and is devoid of ornament. According to Quentin Crisp, 'It looked a cross between a prison and a church and it was.' The school motto is *Lignum Crucis Arbor Scientiae*, which translates uninterestingly as 'A Branch of the Cross is the Tree of Knowledge'. In 1922, there were 350 boys in the school and the fees were £40 a term. Denis Pratt's 'poor scholar-ship' would have been worth £30 a year, which knocked a quarter off the fees. According to a *Public School Year Book* of that time, all pupils attended gymnastic classes and the school's cadet force competed at Bisley. Arts were not a priority in those days, which the current secretary of the Denstone Old Boys' Association suggests may have accounted for some boys taking them up rather forcefully on leaving school.

Before setting off for Denstone for the first time, Denis had 'a routine fit of weeping' and possibly the last flood of tears or outburst of any form of emotion until the very end of his life. From then on 'the armour of self-restraint' seems to have fallen on him and he somehow managed to cope with all the ensuing humiliations, even claiming that these provided him with a 'dress rehearsal' for the treatment he would receive on the streets of London. 'If I had gone straight from home to adulthood, it would have been like falling off a cliff. At school, you learn how to bear injustice.'

He also learnt how to be anonymous. 'It's a very small entry,' said the current headmaster's secretary on finding the name of D. C. Pratt on the files. Nor are there any surviving school photographs to show him as a teenager. In *The Naked Civil Servant*, Quentin tells us that he spent a lot of his time at boarding school lying low under fire and in a subsequent article in *Vogue* he reveals that he even tried to keep his Christian name a secret 'as though it was a secret vulnerable part of my body'.

He also learnt how to bear being 'half-starved, half-frozen and humiliated in a number of different ways'. Just how much he suffered is hard to tell. 'At public school of course I never had a moment's rest,' he told *The Times* three-quarters of a century later. In his auto-biography, he claims to have been 'very unpopular indeed' and refers to the tiny mark that still existed on his wrist where boys tried to saw through the flesh with a jagged ruler. At night, he told *Vogue* readers, he longed for death and once went to bed with a handkerchief stuffed into his mouth in the hope that he might suffocate. Yet he never tried to escape and never seriously questioned the system that he was part of. Whatever the degree of unpopularity – Quentin Crisp's inclination to exaggerate, bluff and confuse his readers should always be borne in mind – it derived only partly from the wetness and oddness we have already noted. It was also the result of his swottishness. 'I worked hard at lessons,' he said later. 'Or at least hard enough to shine. I was openly eager to take exams.' When the French master announced that Pratt was 'the cleverest boy at Denstone', a very likely claim in view of his eventual triumphs, the other boys sneered and perhaps planned further humiliations.

Looking back on these days at boarding school, Quentin could recall only one friend, and not a particularly close one at that, a boy called Webb who occasionally called on him during the holidays. There was only one boy of this name at the school at this time, a certain Humphrey Gerald Webb, who came from Streatham in South London and would spend all his working life as an employee of the National Provincial Bank, ending his days at a branch in Southampton in 1965. With his other fellow pupils, Denis Pratt 'forfeited all friend-ship' while beadily judging them from a distance. He became par-ticularly incensed by a departing head prefect who 'in the middle of the corniest speech I had ever heard', broke down and said he was actually sorry to be leaving the school. With the teaching staff he had no problems and may have even formed some bonds. The headmaster, Dr Grier, who offered 'a mixture of menace and flirtation', he disliked from the start but an English master named Douglas Laughton, 'tall, painfully thin and very nice' and a cousin of the actor Charles Laughton, won his respect by remarking one hot day, 'This is ridicu-lous. Why don't we go for a long walk?' As walks in the country were never one of Quentin's priorities, his response to this remark is of double interest. Reflecting later on the staff at Denstone, he also said, 'When you look back you realize they were going mad.'

How lonely was he? Did he miss his brother Lewis, now flourishing at Bloxham's where he was due to become both captain of boxing and captain of swimming and something of a star on the school stage? Lewis Pratt's performance as Sir Toby Belch in *Twelfth Night* was said to have got 'a good press' in 1924. And did Denis miss his parents? We know only that at the beginning of each term Mrs Pratt accompanied him to St Pancras Station in silence. 'We hardly spoke,' he would recall later. 'Perhaps she felt guilty. I felt sick.' During his four years at Denstone, Denis received no visits from his parents though this was not unusual at the time and Mrs Pratt doubtless wrote her son scores of letters each term. There were also parcels of tuck from Selfridges department store, which was close to the basement flat at 106 Clarence Gate Mansions, where the family moved in 1924, after a spell in a lodging house in Queen's Gate. This temporary address belongs in this story not because it is near where I live today but because it was here, in the bath, that one day Denis discovered the rewards of masturbation, which he would later describe as 'the only fact of life that I have ever fully understood'.

In his autobiography, Quentin states that by this age he had begun to see sex as 'a weapon to allure, subjugate and if possible destroy the personality of others'. He also claims that he longed to be 'the subject of a school-shaking romance' and 'lure some boy to his doom' but he failed in this ambition, thanks partly to the combination of his physical disadvantages and tin-rimmed spectacles, which formed 'a natural chastity belt'. In *The Naked Civil Servant*, he tells us, 'I think I can say that effeminate homosexuals are those who indulge least in sex acts with other boys at school' and informs us that he went to bed with only one boy during his schooldays.

This incident took place on the last night of one term. Quentin later described the other boy as 'strange' and 'the only coloured boy in the school, a half-caste from India or worse' who was 'hell-bent on having some kind of sexual experience other than masturbation, which he already knew about'. For Denis, 'all that mattered was that I had got into bed with a man', and from this limited point of view the event was 'a great triumph'. For the rest of his schooldays, he was content to lead a voyeuristic role, admitting later that 'the love life of the prefects' was one of his 'abiding preoccupations'. He devotes several paragraphs in his autobiography to a 'brutish and mocking' individual who eventually got beaten by the headmaster in front of the entire school. He describes this 'disgusting' event with uncharacter-istically unambiguous indignation and tells us that his distaste for Dr Grier turned immediately to hatred. 'In our menagerie, our headmaster was the most outrageous gargoyle of them all,' he told *Vogue* readers.

'He walked with a slight limp, to increase the appearance of grandeur, and he was the personification of pompous but cunning cruelty.' Dr Grier, an Old Denstonian himself and father of four sons, later put down his cane and became Provost of St Ninian's Cathedral, Perth, and author of *The Scottish Kalender of Saints*. On his death in 1940, he was described as 'somewhat remote and austere' but a former school chaplain, the Revd C. K. Thacker, would remember him for his 'unfailing kindness and complete understanding of boys'.

During his time at boarding school, Denis Pratt – or is it easier to call him Quentin Crisp? – seems to have succeeded in learning the rules and conforming on many levels. He tells us that he 'splashed about in the mud' on the playing field, without ever going near the ball, and cheered from the touchline with his mouth open but uttering no sound. More remarkably, he also served in the Officers' Cadet Force, properly dressed in puttees, handling a rifle, on occasion commanding the squad, and was eventually promoted to lance-corporal. In academic terms, he initially did well, passing his School Certificate and reaching the sixth form when he was only fifteen. He then gave up, having reached what he describes as 'the limit of my educatability', to the disappointment of his teachers. 'I had a good memory,' he claims, 'but no capacity to reason.' For the rest of his life he would masquerade as a 'dunderhead' and repeatedly claim that he had only 'a crossword mentality'.

Such mock-modesty needs to be taken with the usual pinch of salt and Quentin's boast about his 'crossword mentality' deserves looking at in more detail: the crossword craze had only just arrived from America and the Pratt family had become early addicts. After puzzling all night over a difficult clue, Mrs Pratt once appeared at breakfast and simply announced, '*Porcupine*'. Quentin became a lifelong crossword fanatic, and it is easy to argue that some of his wit, verbal precision, alertness, articulacy and even his emotional detachment may have derived from his addiction to this pastime. It is also very likely that Denis Pratt was far better informed about artistic matters than most of his fellows. During the holidays in Epsom and later in London, Mrs Pratt continued her youngest son's cultural initiation. Quentin reminds us often that his mother had 'mildly highbrow pretensions'.

During the summer holidays of 1925, when Denis was sixteen, she would take him to the Royal Academy summer show, where he would have seen works by William Russell Flint and Henry Tuke. In his autobiography, he writes that 'Lord Leighton's classical mock-ups' were the first pictures he had eyed with real interest. His theatre-going had also become more sophisticated. With his sister Phyllis he had been to see Sybil Thorndike in the title role of *Saint Joan* which had opened in 1924 at the New Theatre in St Martin's Lane, up the street from the theatre where one day he would appear in his own one-man show. He also saw Sean O'Casey's *Juno and the Paycock* and *The Plough and the Stars*, which opened respectively in 1925 and 1926. His reading had now graduated to Rider Haggard and Katherine Mansfield, though he would later say of the latter, 'I now realize she was an excruciatingly feminine writer.' These cultural discoveries were accompanied by further family events. In 1925 the Pratts moved to 9 York Mansions beside Battersea Park, though not actually looking onto it, and were to remain there for two or three years. On 10 June 1925, Phyllis Pratt, now twenty-four, fulfilled her long-term ambition in marrying a clergyman, John Payne, who had been educated at Boston Grammar School and St Edmund's Hall, Oxford, and was soon to become vicar of East and West Anstey on the foothills of Exmoor in what Quentin would repeatedly call 'darkest Devonshire'.

It seems that Denis was allowed time off from Denstone to attend his sister's wedding at St Barnabas's Church in Clapham, South London, at which Mrs Pratt wore a chiffon frock in autumnal colours and Lewis Pratt sang a solo. Whether Denis's heart was in the ceremony is another matter. He later wrote, 'I withdrew my ambassadors from God at the age of fifteen.' At any rate it is unlikely that his absence from Denstone would have been greatly regretted or noticed. During his last few terms at the school, he says he gave up all pretence of work and 'sat in a Nissen hut reading the trashy novels of Susan Glaspell'. And with his schoolfellows he now set out to be provocative, to make a career out of his unpopularity. Deliberately or not, Denis Pratt had become something of a spectacle. 'The other boys pointed me out to their parents. By then, I had given up trying to be a schoolboy,' he says. Already 'hooked on exhibitionism', a phrase which would gain greater meaning in the future, he flopped about the school saying things like 'What is cricket?' Waiting at Derby station with four or five other boys also heading for London, he even started 'jigging about', moving one of those with him to declare, 'My God, you're *dancing*!' At the age of seventeen, his mousy hair went curly and his thoughts about the future darkened. Hearing from the Indian boy about the existence of male prostitutes, he even asked himself bleakly, 'I wonder if I could do that?'

Denis Pratt left Denstone in July 1926 at the age of seventeen. On the last day of that summer term he walked jauntily down the school drive towards the outer world. 'I did not yet know that it was but a larger prison where I would serve a longer sentence,' he wrote later in *Vogue*. As he sauntered by, a boy lying on the grassy verge called out at him, 'You'll be back. They all say they're leaving before they really do.' Denis turned and looked at the speaker coldly but said nothing. Whatever his outer demeanour, he must have felt extremely apprehensive about the next stage of his life. Earlier that term, Mrs Pratt had persuaded her husband to write a desperate letter to the school's elderly classics master, Mr Darwin-Swift, asking what was to be done about the boy. Darwin-Swift had replied that the boy did not have the makings of a scholar but showed some ability to write. His strange suggestion was that Denis should take a course studying journalism. 'I was totally unsuited to this profession,' writes Quentin Crisp in *The Naked Civil Servant*. 'Above all, a journalist must be able to get on with people.' The suggestion did, however, delay what he calls his 'terrible confrontation with the outside world'.

A Comparatively Rare Bird

Philip O'Connor is that comparatively rare bird,
a second-generation bohemian.

ANTHONY POWELL, *Punch*, 3 January 1958

Quentin Crisp may have come from a 'middle-class, middling, middle-brow' background but his mother and father were unmistakably if unsteadily 'upwardly mobile'. The families from whom Philip O'Connor was descended, on the other hand, had elaborate pretensions, if shrouded in a good deal of mystery and make-believe. In the first sentence of *Memoirs of a Public Baby*, Philip proclaims that his mother was 'a Fallen Gentlewoman' and two pages later he is content to repeat a suggestion that his father was descended from the last High King of Ireland.

The facts about Philip's father are hard to establish and his son's attempts to investigate them proved largely unsuccessful. According to Philip's mother, Bernard O'Connor was educated at Downside and Oxford, studied medicine, and early in the First World War was conscripted into service as a naval surgeon only to die at sea a few months later. Downside has a record of a certain Bernard O'Connor, born 1880, who was briefly at the school around 1893 – but neither the Admiralty, Oxford University nor the various doctors' registers are able to authenticate the other claims. If unfounded, they certainly lend weight to the idea perpetuated by Philip's mother that the man she had married was 'riff-raff' and 'a cad'. The portrait of Philip's father that emerges from *Memoirs of a Public Baby* is nonetheless beguiling. According to his wife, Bernard O'Connor had 'a passion for clothes, for travelling, for jewellery and for women – and for cleanliness'. He wore bracelets, a monocle, continually changed his watches and 'always inspected the corners of hotel rooms and raised hell about any dirt he found therein'. He preferred China above all other countries.

It is possible that Philip O'Connor may have injected some of his own pernicketiness into this account. He too very occasionally wore a monocle and he too professed a lifelong love for China, which he never visited. He also informs us that his father was supported by his mother all the time he was with her – another taste of things to come – and 'was frequently and openly unfaithful, bringing his women home'. In an early draft of his book, part of which was published in *Encounter*, there are suggestions, later expurgated, of homosexual activities by his father. And there is the claim, not expurgated, that O'Connor senior would drown in a bucket 'any male child of his issue'. This boast is of course impossible to challenge as it is fairly clear that Philip never met his father, who died or disappeared before he was born, leaving his wife, or widow, to bring up Philip and his older sister Desirée on her own.

Mrs O'Connor was a resourceful and desperate woman, who made equally far-fetched claims about her own background. Born Winifred Xavier Rodyke-Thompson in Limerick in 1889, she sprang from a fervently Roman Catholic family of mixed distinction. It is difficult to substantiate her claims that her grandfather had been born into the Spring-Rice family and changed his name – years later Philip O'Connor tried to broach this matter with the head of the Spring-Rice clan, Lord Monteagle – but perfectly true that others in her family had done well in India, in spite of marrying more than once into Asian families. According to Philip, one of them had become Governor of Bengal, another had won the VC.

Philip O'Connor was proud of his background, claiming to be of Irish-Dutch-Burmese ancestry, even boasting on one occasion that he was 'partly coloured'. He was also proud of his mother's darkish skin, tiny monkey-like figure – she was barely five foot in height – her small hands and feet and 'liquid-oriental' eyes. Whatever her origins – when Lord Monteagle failed to reply, Philip decided that the Spring-Rice family was 'not very noble' after all – Mrs O'Connor was apparently 'distinctly lady-like', showed signs of 'authentic refinement' and had even possessed 'the remains of nice silver before it all went away'. Claims by others that Winifred Rodyke-Thompson had been presented at Court and become a student at the Slade only add to the mystery. After marrying at the age of nineteen, she seems to have operated on two different levels. Philip writes of her 'hallucinated business acumen' and 'infantile irresponsibility'. Apparently, she had quickly embarked on various money-making schemes – later ones included putting slot machines in trams and importing second-hand typewriters from France into Belgium – all of which had foundered, while remaining 'remarkably child-like' in herself and 'devoid of civic consciousness'. Philip O'Connor makes much of his mother's 'infantile giggle' and 'utter lack of British social seriousness'. Shortly before the First World War, Winifred O'Connor had given birth to her daughter Desirée – Philip says that this event took place on a train entering Paris, Desirée herself later stated that she was born in the Paris Ritz, delivered by her father, who was suffering from oyster-poisoning at the time – but these new responsibilities had failed to stabilize her. The war itself, the dwindling of her resources and departure of her husband can have only increased her precariousness.

In the summer of 1916, the threat of Zeppelin attacks on the capital – so exciting for the young Denis Pratt – drove Mrs O'Connor to take refuge at Leighton Buzzard in Bedfordshire, where she found rooms on the very edge of the town. Number 25 Clarence Road is a confusingly tiny two-bedroom, red-brick villa, offering a bow window and other decorative refinements you might find on a much larger house. It was here, on 8 September 1916, that Philip Constant Marie Bancroft O'Connor was born. These names, which he later described as 'reminiscent of a Gilbert and Sullivan opera', are characteristically ornate. So were his mother's subsequent claims that 'the King's physician' assisted at the birth.

Anyway, Mrs O'Connor and her two children were not long in Leighton Buzzard. They soon moved to Pinner in Middlesex and then Yeovil, where Desirée attended a local convent and Philip crawled down the stone steps of their house to offer his beloved toy piano and then his toy train to passers-by. While in Yeovil, Mrs O'Connor founded the Somerset Cigarette Agency and secured a government contract to make an inferior brand of cigarettes to be supplied to the troops.

The fact that she had the resources for these enterprises may owe something to her new friendship with a London character called Robert Haslam Jackson, a man of some means, to whom she had apparently been introduced by her uncle Sebastien, the supposed VC winner, at the time of her husband's disappearance or recruitment into the navy. Haslam Jackson, as he seems to have been generally known, had been born near Barrow-in-Furness in 1880 and was said by Philip O'Connor to have had Spanish-Jewish blood. He had come to London at the turn of the century and become a dandified figure – 'the last fag-end of the Edwardian mashers' – mixing in theatrical and journalistic circles, forming an 'association' with the *Daily Herald* and the *Daily Chronicle* and attending meetings of the Playgoers' Club. He was said to have been a friend of the popular playwright Henry Arthur Jones and a worshipper of Dr Johnson, after whose cat he called his dog. In 1914, Haslam Jackson had moved into comfortable quarters at 3 Essex Court, Middle Temple Lane, and been 'invaded' here by Winifred O'Connor, who would start what was to become a lifelong relationship with him. In *Memoirs of a Public Baby*, Philip O'Connor immediately raises the possibility that Haslam Jackson, rather than the pernickety doctor, was his father, partly on the grounds of his closeness to his mother and partly on the grounds of physical similarity. Photographs of Haslam Jackson certainly bear a resemblance to O'Connor in later life. Philip would talk and write of mannerisms they shared, not least 'a brief upper lip slammed tight on a jutting lower one'. Others have argued that the dates don't fit and such a thing would be quite out of character with what they knew of Jackson. What is incontrovertible is that Haslam Jackson was half-besotted with Winnie O'Connor and willingly and credulously invested several thousand pounds in her unlikely business schemes. At this stage, he could perhaps afford to do so. At Christmas 1916 he was vain and self-confident enough to send out a coloured cartoon of himself, smiling and pipe-smoking, with a *Life of Johnson* in the background.

When the war was over, Mrs O'Connor brought her two children to London where they stayed in a hotel 'with magnificent pillared porticoes' and then in a flat in Cromwell Road which Philip remembered for its 'huge settee', 'embedding arm-chair', 'thick carpets' and 'low luscious lights'. His mother soon embarked on another venture making cheap cigarettes, in a room in Whitehall Court, near the Savoy Hotel, an enterprise which quickly foundered and would lead to Mrs O'Connor suing 'one of the five big banks' and being declared bankrupt.

In *Memoirs of a Public Baby*, Philip O'Connor writes that it was 'probably in 1919' that his mother, sister, nurse and he crossed over by night to France on a rough sea. He does not mention the creditors on his mother's tail or the small weekly allowance provided for her by Haslam Jackson but he describes the whole journey with outstanding vividness: 'the two funnels of the boat dutifully belching clouds of illuminated smoke' and the flat in Paris where he slit open a bright silk cushion to find out what was inside, and then the Hôtel du Louvre, where 'the sheets were silk or at least extremely soft' and where he woke up with his head on his mother's breast for the last time. He also remembers that his mother took a police-whistle with her and a boxful of papers relating to her business battles, two valises and a big trunk containing saucepans, a coffee-pot with an unscrewable handle and the effigy of baby Jesus, whose face had lost its colour by being kissed so much, behaviour which Philip would later describe as 'infantile and idolatrous'.

Eventually the family headed north and came to rest in Wimereux, a seaside town between Calais and Boulogne. This was then a flourishing, rather genteel little resort where many English people stayed, just across the Channel from Fairlight beach. You pass Wimereux on the train a few minutes after leaving Calais and by ship a few minutes before you arrive at Boulogne. Until quite recently, there were people living in Wimereux who remembered men and women in evening dress wandering from the Rue Carnot between the casino and the resort's one or two big hotels. The railway station is high above the town and it was in ground-floor lodgings near the level-crossing that the O'Connors started their life here. Philip recalls these quarters with affection, the muslin-curtained window onto the street, his mother's sewing-machine – had this too travelled in the trunk? – and the first gramophone or phonograph he had known. In the sunny walled garden he was photographed clinging to his mother – or so he claims. The photograph still exists, and was pinned to his bedroom wall at the end of his life, but the woman in it looks more like a sullen servant than the dainty creature he has depicted elsewhere and there is doubt too about the identity of the boy. Much of this narrative is wreathed in mystery and make-believe.

Perhaps like all children without a permanent home, Philip took refuge in his mother's personality, in her trunk and even – a theme he was to return to in later life – in the coffee-pot that always travelled with her. In later recollections, he writes that the world 'already shook with impermanence' and that he felt frightened for his mother in her difficulties, though 'creditors' were still a vague commodity. 'She and I,' he explained, 'lived in a dark cave of fearful cosiness, which fresh air would destroy, in which the sounds and movements of others are hideous.' He also recognized in himself the first signs of a nervous condition shared with his mother. 'I've always been bad-tempered,' he would tell me later. 'When I was three or four I used to have what they called brainstorms. They had to dose me with brandy and milk. It's hereditary. My mother had a screaming, shrieking temper.'

Did the relationship with his sister Desirée, some years older than him, also provide some security? Desirée was 'a very pretty, volatile girl', who had had the dubious advantage of knowing her father, who had carried her on his shoulder and of whom she always spoke with the greatest affection. Up to this point, Desirée had been a 'subsidiary and adoring mother' but in Wimereux she would apparently adopt 'a martial vivacity' and become more interested in acquiring 'frilly dresses and matching knickers' than in looking after her little brother. She would also become her mother's confidante as they discussed 'the difficult tactics of survival'.

After a few weeks in the house by the level-crossing, this strange threesome, with the teenage nurse Dora still in tow, moved to lodgings in Madame Tillieux's 'ruddy' tea-shop in the Rue Carnot. This building is still standing today and still functioning as a *pâtisserie*, with pastries in the left-hand window and jars of sweets on the right just as they were eighty years ago. Shortly after the O'Connors arrived here, the largely unpaid nurse was sent back to England, after dropping Philip from a window and then pulling him out of a hot bath by his hair. A few weeks later, Mrs O'Connor suddenly told her son that she, and his sister, would also be leaving. 'I'll be back quite soon,' she promised.

She did not return for two and a half years. During this period, which haunted Philip O'Connor for the rest of his life, he suffered extraordinary grief and grievous anger at the loss of his mother and 'the embryo of an ideal of delicacy' that she had planted in his mind. He brooded for ever afterwards about his mother's movements – 'only approached in finely articulated music' – and the touch of her hands which were 'like living leaves'. His disappointment when people other than his mother touched him would eventually develop, he writes, into 'a neurasthenic *noli me tangere*'. But he was also to form a passionate relationship with the 'lion-hearted' Madame Tillieux, and with Wimereux itself, which strengthened when he eventually left the town. And while blaming his mother for treating him like a king and then abandoning him with a social class she despised, he acknowledges that she had left him with 'the best woman in the world'. He also claims that these two and a half years of his childhood were the only time during his whole existence when he had a 'normal' or 'regulated' life and when he knew where he was; not a hard claim to believe in the light of his subsequent experiences.

If his mother had 'breeding', Philip says jokily, Madame Tillieux had 'bread'. The proprietor of the *pâtisserie* came from a peasant family in Armentières, near Amiens, and was a war widow with four children – her husband had died in the *trachée des baïonnettes* at Verdun. She supported herself and her offspring by means of her tea-shop, which catered largely for English visitors with a sumptuous range of *gâteaux-bateaux*, Calais cakes and éclairs. Without hesitation, Madame Tillieux immediately and lovingly incorporated young Philip into this 'heavy heaven' – and into her bed. He slept beside her, irritated by her bottom-pinching but reassured by the 'crash' of her urine into an enamel pail. Elsewhere, he describes Madame Tillieux as moving in a comical manner, 'like a badly packed parcel, but a parcel full of strange things never to be discovered by one outside her own family'.

The town and its wide, white beaches – unlike Quentin, Philip never learnt to swim – and the trams that rushed clanging down the Rue Carnot had their particular appeal for the boy. So did the regular routines in Madame Tillieux's three interlocking *salles à manger*. Of the family, his favourite was Berthe, the youngest daughter, who gave him his weekly bath in a tub in front of the cherry-red stove, and from whom he learnt 'bliss – a great sea of bliss in the safety of women' and to whom he devotes many paragraphs of joyful description in his autobiography, best read in the original. His principal playmate and first friend was Pierrot, three years his senior, the younger son, with whom he fished for eels through cracks in the bridge at the other end of the town. In a letter to Stephen Spender nearly three-quarters of a century later, Philip O'Connor mentions Pierrot as one of the boys he loved. He was also passionately fond of the pork butcher's daughter, who lived next door and wore a pink frilly dress. '*Marie-Thérèse, je t'aime*,' he would say, kneeling beside her, but never got a reply.

But Philip's time in Wimereux, the description of which provides some of the most emotional, most evocative writing in *Memoirs of a Public Baby*, went beyond human encounters. Looking back on these years, he sounds ecstatically oversensitive and overobservant. The horizon 'brimmed with tears, an ecstasy of horizontality', and the surface of the river was 'so exactly like laughter as to make one feel laughter at the sight of it'. In Madame Tillieux's third *salle à manger* he first sees beauty, a perfect shape, in the form of a boiled egg: 'its mound slowly undressed of the wavy-edged petticoat of steam, and where the rope-shaped edge of steam left the matt wall of the egg was perfection; and then again where it towered to its final self-enclosing apex'. He also loved the hen that produced the egg and spent a lot of time lying in the hen run in the backyard, even trying to sleep there because he enjoyed the smell so much. He loved the hens for 'their sharp, matronly scrutiny out of eyes like the slits in castles, their eccentric movements expressing an uncompromising thoroughness of purpose'. There was also an old dog, Folette, with eyes 'like old people's', whom he loved to hug.

Other encounters and experiences at Wimereux were less agreeable. Philip much preferred the back of the house to the public rooms where customers excited his fury when he watched 'their big white teeth dipping sheerly into the creams and biscuitry, their lips proudly curve and pensively fold over the sweet crumbles, their cream-coated tongues dart like acquisitive rabbits from red hutches'. And there were more frightening figures in the town: a madman called Cartouche, who liked chasing Philip and Pierrot through the streets, and a crazy old lady, 'like Miss Faversham [sic]', who lived above the Paradis des Enfants toyshop opposite and peeped from her lace-curtained window extending a knowing finger at the children in the street below. Even more frightening were the screams that came from next door, where pigs 'shrieked like babies' as Marie-Thérèse's father slit their throats and let them bleed slowly to death. Philip's worst ordeals along these lines – he hated violence – came when Madame Tillieux's oldest daughter Jeanette entered the *salle à manger* with a cockerel whose neck she had just wrung. Philip, who loved hens more than humans, sobbed and shrieked and cried dementedly. Such constant vulnerability on Philip's part would inspire Madame Tillieux to describe her charge as '*jamais content*'.

During the summer of 1921, Philip got a glimpse of his future when the tea-shop was visited by a tall, shy, slow-moving Englishman with an artificial leg. His name was Albert Joseph Camden Field. He was a civil servant, in his late twenties, apparently on holiday but actually with a deeper purpose in mind which was not at this stage revealed. During his two-week visit to the town, the visitor drank Bass in the bars and saw quite a lot of Philip, took him along the coast to Le Touquet to watch polo, bought him expensive sweets and an expensive pair of shoes. In his company Philip felt 'drugged and exalted' and showed off continuously, marching in Madame Tillieux's yard with a tray on his head and imitating his benefactor when he fanned the sand with his stick before sitting down on the beach. But when this mysterious character eventually returned to England he quickly forgot about him.

The next visitor caused Philip far more confusion. One morning he was playing in the yard, when Madame Tillieux summoned him in to meet an elegant woman dressed in a blue costume with silver threads, a white fox fur and a picture hat. In the paroxysmic shrieking and shuddering that followed, Philip clung to Madame Tillieux and refused to recognize this 'gracious lady' as his mother. Much has been made of this scene – including a highly effective radio play – during which it emerged that Mrs O'Connor and her daughter Desirée had returned to the flat near the railway-crossing and were anxious to claim the boy back. During the next few days, Philip made a series of heart-wrenching journeys between the shop and the flat, and slowly redis-covered his attachment to his mother, her softness, her silks and the aroma of her face powder and eau de Cologne. He also, guiltily or not, entered into a new conspiracy with her. During her two-and-a-half-year absence, Mrs O'Connor had sent no money to Madame Tillieux and, still unable to pay the bill, decided to wriggle out of it by accusing the tea-shop owner of mistreating her child, hitting him and starving him. In this horrible atmosphere, Philip was whisked or stolen away, to spend the rest of his life 'prosecuting an unending hangover from a sojourn in an Eden that time painted in colours ever lovelier as it receded'. Of Madame Tillieux, he would say, '*Elle m'a donné une carte de visite à l'humanité*' and of the town itself, he wrote, 'Memories of twilight in Wimereux return home in a glass of wine; little beans of warmth from the heart's pod pop through the network of nerves to the mnemonic nerve-stations; I inhale accompanied by the sound of the sea in recession, exhale with the sea coming in.'

Mrs O'Connor took Philip first to Calais, where in a hotel near the Gare Maritime she slept 'crucified' between her two children and in the morning regaled them with stories of her romantic past in India and elsewhere. After a few months here they moved to nearby lodgings in a brewery, where Mrs O'Connor again abandoned her son, this time in the care of his sister and a woman called Adèle who gave Philip massive enemas and took him to see John Barrymore in *Dr Jekyll and Mr Hyde*, the transference scene in which gave Philip nightmares and led to him acting out the sequence in front of the mirror. While at the brewery, there was a further visit from the gentle, one-legged Mr Field, who said he would try to find the children's mother.

Early in 1923, she seems to have returned and the family then set off, apparently pushing their belongings in an old pram, towards Belgium. From Ostend, they sailed for England. In *Memoirs of a Public Baby*, Philip O'Connor makes no comments on the actual crossing but has a lot to say about the subsequent journey from Folkestone to London and the 'unusual hushedness and comfort' of the train and the presence of other passengers oddly at ease with themselves yet deeply withdrawn. He has much to say, too, about the bus journey in London. In his autobiography he says that they caught the bus at Waterloo. On other occasions he mentions rolling out of Charing Cross and seems undecided about whether it was a number 1 bus or a 48. He is less ambiguous about the vehicle itself and the 'meaningfully private English curve of its outer staircase and red and black check seats'. In his *Memoirs* he says that they sat on sideways seats and claims – how can he remember such details? – that he spoke in 'rudimentary and guttural English', causing the other passengers to turn and stare, which encouraged or frightened him into further gesticulations of the sort which would soon become a permanent part of his repertoire. At Tottenham Court Road – or was it Charing Cross Road? – they eventually alighted and made their way to a basement in Dean Street, Soho. This foreign, bohemian area at the heart of central London was to feature prominently in Philip O'Connor's subsequent life and his encounter with it at such an early age – he was still only six years old – is highly significant.

The cellar in Dean Street consisted of two rooms and was approached by a smelly staircase. The front room had a large dirty window through which a feeble light entered and from a grating came a continuous rattle of passing feet. In the morning occupants would also hear the clatter of milk cans and occasionally caught snatches of the latest music – 'The Sheikh of Araby' or 'Yes, We Have No Bananas' – from a distant barrel organ. This establishment had recently become the home, or bolthole, of Robert Haslam Jackson. Now in his early forties, Jackson had recently suffered what Philip would call his Fall, losing his money, battling with his creditors and giving up his elegant quarters in the Middle Temple. In these new surroundings, which he shared with his dog Hodge, Haslam was now 'a very dirty man', washing out of the saucepan in which he cooked and rarely, if ever, having a bath, but up on the street he was still 'astonishingly dandi-fied', usually appearing in spats, opera cloak, silk hat and other remnants of his brilliant youth. And in spite of everything, Haslam Jackson was still hopelessly in awe of Winifred O'Connor and easily intimidated by her.

And, in and out of the gloom of the Dean Street cellar, Mrs O'Connor was still preoccupied with her business schemes and still played the grown-up 'in an artful masquerade', mentioning impressive sums like *thirty thousand pounds* in a loud voice as she walked the West End streets. Haslam Jackson responded to her ideas with some admiration, great scepticism and much pedantry. Savage rows often erupted between them. Philip tells us that his mother 'seemed to undress, or split down the middle; and from the chasm a strange shriek would proceed'. On some occasions she would beat Haslam's dog with the back of a brush and Haslam himself would surrender to animal rages, pick up one of his favourite pipes and break it with a yelp, then moan about his vanished fortune. 'Your mother,' he would hiss or roar at Philip and Desirée, and then with greater emphasis, '*Your mother* has got the lot, got the lot, spent the whole sad, sorry, bloody lot!' After such declarations, he would turn in upon himself, 'Poor old Bingo! Poor old, bloody old Bobby Bingo!', which was met by icy reproofs from Mrs O'Connor or threats that she would go and throw herself into the Thames.

The effect of these scenes on Philip was to make his heart race. He had his own troublesome omniscience to cope with, his own 'internal babble'. At the age of seven, he had little sense of his own identity. In *Memoirs of a Public Baby*, he writes, 'I was – and am – like a cup of water without the cup and dangerously flowed into other people's ways of being' and claims he was cruel to people only to stop himself becoming absorbed into them. Besides this, he felt that everyone was his enemy. He missed France desperately, felt 'sensorily under-nourished' in England and had already developed 'a long, long nostalgia' for his foreign past and 'a pretty Anglophobia' which he shared with his mother, who was inclined to talk about 'English pigs'.

Philip estimates that they remained in the Dean Street cellar for about a year, living off Heinz Tomato Soup, Prichard's sandwiches and various home-made snacks. Mrs O'Connor was keen on a sweet-meat made by grinding up coconut, Nestlé's canned milk and cocoa powder. She bought shrimp paste and gingerbread but rarely 'the basics'. Every night, around midnight, Philip and Desirée would be woken up from their perches in the cellar and trotted over to a bug-infested house in nearby Rathbone Place run by a Mrs Meaty – or Mouty – where Mrs O'Connor and her children would spend the night. During the day, Philip's education began at the Notre Dame de France School in Leicester Square, which he would enter through the boys' entrance in Lisle Street, close to where the Prince Charles Cinema stands today.

Philip O'Connor was still only seven years old when this strange and unsatisfactory regime was replaced by one of quite different oddness. One evening in the early summer of 1924, the Dean Street basement was visited by the civil servant with the artificial leg who had twice called upon Philip in France. Mr Field now asked Mrs O'Connor if he could adopt her son. While this arrangement was discussed, Philip claims to have stared with delight at the grey and silver texture of the visitor's coat, his size thirteen boots and aura of freshness. Haslam Jackson looked cordially at Mr Field, while Mrs O'Connor sat crumpled and stunned by the doorway leading to the street. Philip was impatient to be gone in 'the nice new vehicle' that Camden Field represented and screamed to that effect. Only Desirée, who said afterwards that she believed the family should stay together, distrusted Mr Field and disapproved of the plan. There was a brief interlude. Mr Field went off, bought some gumboots for his new charge and returned. Philip then kissed his mother briefly, ignored her tears and set off up the basement stairs in a state of exhilaration and relief to be rid of 'a gathering bric-a-brac of confusion'. Hand in hand, the man and boy set off together through the back-streets of Soho.

— 5 —

The Black Cat

The 'Chat Noir' with its black cat mascot in the window, in Old Compton Street, seems to be becoming more of a family resort in the French style. Men and women go in and sit for hours together, not simply to have some French coffee. It is their parlour. Even the men who lounge across the mahogany bar seem to be there because their homes are uncomfortable. They come to be at home.

STEPHEN GRAHAM, *London Nights*, 1926

Day after uneventful day, night after loveless night, we sat in this café buying each other cups of tea, combing each other's hair and trying on each other's lipsticks.

QUENTIN CRISP, *The Naked Civil Servant*, 1968

Au Chat Noir was one of several café-bars in the back-streets of Soho. Their furniture featured marble-topped tables and a horseshoe-shaped bar of scrubbed wood. They were mostly fantastically named: Roma, the Wooden Soldier, Round the Clock, or prosaically just by their street number. Au Chat Noir had opened on the north side of Old Compton Street close to Wardour Street in the middle of the First World War. By the late 1920s, it had acquired a manager called Mancini, a black-and-white check linoleum floor, ornate mirrors and a fairly dubious clientele that included male prostitutes. According to the writer Stephen Graham, who had been living at 60 Frith Street since 1913, the Black Cat, as it was commonly known, was as much a place for conversation as sustenance. For Quentin Crisp – or Denis Pratt, as he still was – it would prove a place where he could at last begin to be himself.

Quentin Crisp's progression from a respectable minor public school to the mixed delights of a notorious Soho café was fairly rapid. He had left Denstone in July 1926 and in October of that year had started the journalism course at King's College, London, in a mood of increasing anxiety. In his autobiography, he writes that he was beginning to feel 'really uneasy' about the future and 'filled with misgiving' about his sexuality. On one level he feared that he would never be able to earn a living. On another, darker, level he was bewildered to find he had no sexual interest in girls and suspected he was on 'a tiny island' and 'quite unlike anyone else in the world'.

His plight may have been emphasized by the fact that his siblings were now growing up. His sister Phyllis had married her clergyman and his brother Gerald had gone to work for the Asiatic Petroleum Company in Shanghai, where he would marry a woman called Natalie, said to be a Russian princess, and lead a wild life. The only one still at home in the Battersea flat was Lewis, now six foot, red-haired and, according to his younger brother, 'slightly rude to his elders' and 'determined to be an adult as soon as possible'. Mrs Pratt remained nervous and vulnerable. York Mansions was a nice enough address, with an aunt of the actor John Gielgud living upstairs, but Mrs Pratt constantly complained about the sunlessness of the flat and remained extravagant in her habits. 'My father was in debt so she should have spent *nothing*,' tut-tutted Quentin in later years.

However awful he felt in himself, Denis still went through the motions of conforming. He acquired his first suit of his own. He was visited by his schoolfriend Webb, now working for the National Provincial Bank. He took his mother's dog for walks in the park and occasionally 'socialized' with his brother Lewis's friends. And each morning, he took a tram along the Embankment to King's College where he 'dreamed' his way through lectures on journalism by a tall, thin, 'triangular-faced' man called Professor Reed. A different sort of person might have formed useful friendships with some of the people on the same course, who included Joost de Blank, later Archbishop of Capetown, Lord Edward Hay, son of the Marquis of Tweeddale, and Robert Robertson-Glasgow, land-owning brother of a famous cricketing correspondent. But it says something for Denis that he did make friends with a fellow student named Maurice Lovell, who was to join Reuters and lead an adventurous life as a war reporter. All of these former colleagues are now dead. Lord Edward Hay memorably died in the Guards Chapel, when a bomb descended on it in 1944.

One imagines that Denis felt closer to his real self and better prepared for the life that awaited him when in the theatre or cinema. During this period, he saw *The Girlfriend* danced by Louise Brown. He saw Anton Dolin, whom he found 'staggering', at the Coliseum. He saw Florence Mills in the revue *Blackbirds in London*, where she sang a famous song that began 'I'm a little black bird looking for a blue bird just like white folk do.' He saw Pavlova in *The Dying Swan* and was entranced by the way she took her bouquets at the end. He also saw many Hollywood films – which made America seem wonderful to him. He saw the Greta Garbo film *Flesh and the Devil* and explained later that he didn't react at all to the men in the film but swooned over Garbo herself – 'Or, rather, the accoutrements of her beauty, the sumptuous settings, the huge fur coats, the heavy diamond jewellery.' At this stage he claimed to be totally absorbed by every film he saw. But so, he says, was everyone else.

Denis Pratt's inner dream of himself as a woman, partly sustained by these outings, remained in stark conflict with the prevailing moral climate. This was a time when, as Quentin puts it, 'men searched themselves for vestiges of effeminacy as though for lice' and when public or official outrage over books like the lesbian novel, *The Well of Loneliness*, published in 1928, knew no bounds. Of course there were rich, upper-class dandies and ne'er-do-wells who flaunted their sexuality no matter how deviant and there were also individuals like the butcher's son and music-hall artiste Fred Barnes – Quentin Crisp would later describe Barnes as 'the divine image of homosexuality' – who somehow got away with it. But Quentin came from an oppressively middle-class background where there was 'wall-to-wall puritanism' which made him excruciatingly aware of what he calls the 'sin of homosexuality'. In his autobiography, he writes, 'A homosexual person was never anyone you actually knew and seldom anyone you had met', and he later revealed that when he started at King's College even the word 'homosexual' meant nothing to him.

How much Mrs Pratt sustained her son through these lonely unenlightened times isn't clear but she deserves credit for introducing him to a woman who was to represent his first glimpse of the *vie de bohème* – and Soho in particular. This was Cecily Ermyntrude Longhurst, who lived at 84 Charlotte Street near Tottenham Court Road, in a house which belonged to a family of artists and sculptors called Aumonier. Mrs Longhurst, who had worked as a stewardess and portrait model, was an autocratic figure and free spirit and the friendship which she formed with Denis must have made some inroads into his loneliness. For a while, he visited her often, played pontoon and talked about himself and listened to her talking about her lover, whom she met at Victoria Station and who made her insides 'turn over and over'. Mrs Longhurst's mode of speech, and habit of flying from one extreme to another, were to provide a sort of model for the exaggerated form of conversation in which Quentin Crisp was eventually to indulge himself on a massive scale.

Denis turned eighteen on Christmas Day 1926. By now he was becoming increasingly uncomfortable at home and in himself. For the first time in his life, he started to take an interest in his appearance and make the first steps towards 'rearranging' it. This process may have included the forsaking of his tin spectacles and the application of a small amount of make-up, which he could either 'confirm or deny', but it certainly did not have the effect of making him seem full of life. Indeed his mother was now so worried about his listlessness that she decided to take medical advice.

The doctor to whom Mrs Pratt took her son was called Armando Dumas Child. Years later, Quentin Crisp would recall this rather exotic name with characteristic relish and he had good reasons for doing so: Dr Child was to remain his doctor until the 1970s. On this early occasion, the worthy Dr Child, who had rooms in Catherine Street,

Westminster, had only to take one glance at his patient to declare that all he needed was 'a lesson in life'.

In his autobiography, Quentin Crisp says that these words meant nothing at all to him at the time but when boredom drove him to wandering desolately about the West End streets, he at last got an inkling of what the doctor was talking about. 'I learned that I was not alone,' he writes on discovering that there were other men around as strange as himself and if the film version of his book is to be trusted, it was one of these young men who accosted him and later introduced him to the Black Cat.

Quentin has written and spoken a great deal about this café and its inhabitants and his view of it contradicts the more respectable picture offered by Stephen Graham in his book *London Nights*. Quentin is at pains to explain that the Black Cat clientele had no artistic pretensions. It was made up, he says, 'of thugs, low-life queers and effeminate homosexuals'. Among the latter category were a number of male prostitutes. He described these new friends as 'campy little creatures', 'poor wee things', 'really bedraggled' and 'outrageous and helpless'. But though 'as miserable as hell' underneath and full of private tales of woe, they were all immensely cheerful on the surface. They addressed each other, he says, 'in absolutely straight stylized camp', exchanged arch jokes and indulged in 'stylized cattiness' and 'lady-like masquerades' with 'much rolling of blue-lidded eyes'. Cups of tea were made to last for hours and lipstick was famously passed around.

If there is a condescending or somewhat detached tone to these remarks it may be partly because Denis Pratt was cleverer and better educated than these fellow outcasts and came from a different class at a particularly class-ridden time. However much he might like to deny it, he had more in his life. He had Mrs Longhurst to visit in Charlotte Street. He had fashionable books to read in secret. In 1928 he read Evelyn Waugh's *Decline and Fall* and Virginia Woolf's *Orlando* soon after they were published. He called *Decline and Fall* 'wonderful' but said that *Orlando* was 'not one of Virginia Woolf's best', which suggested he'd read her others. He could also draw. One imagines that his friends at the Black Cat were unaware of these refinements or willing to overlook them. 'They forgave me my unfair advantages because I was in the same sexual boat as they,' he writes in *The Naked Civil Servant*. 'I took to them like a duck to ducks.'

In July 1928, Denis Pratt left King's College, London, without a diploma in journalism and his double life began in earnest. On leaving York Mansions he would hurry to the nearest public lavatory and put on make-up. 'I was tinted in those days but not clotted,' he explains, but his new persona was sufficiently shocking to cause his brother Lewis's girlfriend to gasp, '*Did you see that?*' as he swept by. 'Yes, matter of fact I've seen it before,' was Lewis's sanguine reply. Denis hurried on towards the West End where he could be himself. When the others in the Black Cat were not making arch jokes, they were arguing over American film-stars: the distant dazzling permanent icons of the screen. 'I lived in a swoon about one female movie star after another,' said Quentin later. 'My fantasy life was lived chiefly in the cinema.' 'Life was dreary,' he wrote later in *How to Become a Virgin*. 'Only the world of celluloid was rich and full.' Denis Pratt and all the other boys in the Black Cat 'strove to be objects of more and more intense adoration'. They wanted to be like Brigitte Helm or Greta Garbo or Marlene Dietrich and they argued continually about who of these was the most beautiful. They discussed their own make-up routines – 'What do you do with your eyes, girl?' – and talked repeatedly about a possible sex-change operation.

'I would *definitely* like to have been a woman,' Quentin told me years later with great firmness. Had the operation been available, Quentin Crisp would have had it done 'the very next day', or so he asserted. 'Everything would have then fallen into place.' He would have moved to a provincial town – Carlisle was mentioned – and run a knitting shop. 'And no one would have known my guilty secret.' Like many of his claims and pronouncements, this is all too jokey, too hypothetical, to be taken entirely seriously. For one thing, Quentin Crisp would have hated to have 'a guilty secret' and for another, such a decisive step would have entirely obliterated his show-off side. Anyway, it was not to be and when eventually the option did become available, Quentin would be far too confident in his complex new self to give the matter any more thought.

Back in the late 1920s, Denis Pratt had already made enough of a breakthrough by embracing his own effeminacy and throwing in his lot, if only on a part-time basis, with the boys in the Black Cat. In his autobiography and elsewhere, Quentin argued that his effeminacy or femininity was somehow complemented by the thugs who often visited the café. 'They chatted you up exactly as they chatted to girls,' he said when discussing his life story with the scriptwriter Philip Mackie, who eventually turned it all into a film. 'They came in and told the boys how beautiful they were and asked for cups of tea. They were eaten up with curiosity. No girl was as exotic as we were.' The admiration that the thugs offered was in its own way returned. 'We saw in them someone who saw in us what we were,' Quentin explained. Their arrival had 'a tremendous impact' and 'a strong erotic flavour'. 'The dirtier their fingernails, the more desirable,' he added.

With his new chums, Denis Pratt would parade around the West End. They avoided the parks – 'You would have been beaten to death in two seconds' – but drifted down Piccadilly and engaged in banter – 'Darling, you're looking marvellous' – of a timeless variety. From the start he must have realized that many of his friends were prostitutes, spiritual descendants of the painted boys outside Swan & Edgar's who had given Oscar Wilde such a thrill in the 1880s.

Denis's final, inevitable degradation came when he himself went 'on the game'. Looking back on this phase, which he estimated lasted for six months during the winter of 1928–9 Quentin Crisp explained that he never hustled or got arrested though he was constantly told by his colleagues 'You'll get years, girl', a remark which inspired him to add, 'Of course, I was already in prison but I didn't know.' He simply drifted around the West End, got picked up and gladly accepted money – sometimes as little as 7s 6d – for sex in doorways, alleyways and taxis. At the end of his life he told the journalist Simon Hattenstone that he went into prostitution looking for *love* not money, and in the unpublished synopsis for *The Naked Civil Servant* he declares that he looked for love with great persistence in early life. Speculating about the motives of the men who picked him up, he said cynically, 'They don't follow you because you're desirable. They follow you because it can't be wrong', though he added that a few men might be drawn

64

to 'do it' with a homosexual 'because it was so wild'. Describing what actually happened during these encounters, he relaxes into the present tense. 'It is purely a question of abuse – you abuse them. They never take any notice of you at all and they never do anything to you. They merely undo the requisite number of buttons and no more. Because there may be a quick getaway.' Occasionally there was oral copulation but it was much more likely to be 'purely manual labour'. There was usually no dialogue, no flirtation and no compliments. On the contrary, says Quentin, 'Nearly always the situation was fraught with a kind of contempt. I was acutely conscious of this desire to degrade and defile me.' Later in life he described his time as a male prostitute as 'disappointing and disappointed' and confessed, 'Of course I was terribly bad at it, because I was so condescending.'

Quentin is not very specific about other sexual experiences he may have had at the time. He later described his first experience of sodomy as 'like undergoing a colostomy operation without anaesthetic'. To Philip Mackie, he said, 'Homosexuality contains nothing human.' At this stage and perhaps for ever afterwards he saw sex chiefly as a means to an end, as a way of reaching a different life. 'When you're young,' he told me, 'you think of sex as a way, as a door and you imagine that your charm and your sexuality and your great beauty will lead you into the possession of people.' In *How to Go to the Movies*, he writes, 'In youth, one's greatest desire is not for carnal pleasure but for the power that foolishly one imagines may be achieved through wealth, through the protection of an influential keeper and by means of flawless beauty deployed with the utmost deliberation.'

One must not forget the rest of Denis Pratt's life at this time, which appeared to have very little overlap with his West End existence, though he did receive occasional telephone calls at home from one of the least likeable boys in the Black Cat. This young man, nicknamed Thumbnails in *The Naked Civil Servant*, was a postal clerk with mildly bookish, literary pretensions, 'not very camp to look at' but 'invincibly snobbish', and acutely aware of Denis's social advantages. Reluctantly or not, Denis would agree to meet him in Lyons Tea Shops where they would sit 'talking of this and that and planning to write various books, plays, poems or whatever'. Only once did Mrs Pratt ask her son why he never brought any of his friends home and she was apparently entirely satisfied when he assured her she would hate them if he did. Mr Pratt had by now ceased to take any trouble over his son. Quentin recalled that his father knew people at the publishing firm of Hodder and Stoughton – 'but he did not nag them into getting me a job'. In retrospect, Quentin thought this wise. 'If they had said "You can come here and make tea", I would have made it *badly*.'

His mother, on the other hand, still had hopes for him and now clung to the idea that her son could become a commercial artist. With this in mind, Denis had been enrolled in the autumn of 1928 as a student at Battersea Polytechnic. In *The Naked Civil Servant*, he is characteristically self-deprecating about this short-lived phase of his life during which he drew a frog which the principal thought was a piece of drapery, but has much to say about a female student who would remain his friend for the next forty or fifty years. Her name was Pat and she had been crippled with polio as a child and had a metal splint on one leg which made every step forward very difficult. 'Because of her handicap,' Quentin explains, 'she was sympathetic to all deformity and especially drawn to anyone she felt to be worse off than she. I came into this category.' In subsequent conversations about 'the Battersea art student' or 'the crippled girl', as he sometimes called her, he was more gentle and more affectionate than he dares to be in print. He described her as small, fair, blue-eyed and 'infinitely appealing'. That last phrase tells us something about Quentin himself which is hard to square with the icy image of himself he usually put out. It suggests that his emotions were engaged.

During the spring or early summer of 1929, Denis Pratt's curious double life halted. Mrs Pratt's endless complaints about the sunlessness of the Battersea flat had eventually persuaded Mr Pratt to move again – this time to a house in a new housing development outside High Wycombe in Buckinghamshire. Their middle son Lewis had now followed his older brother overseas, taking a job in South America with the Riverplate Telephone Company – Quentin supplied this name with his usual relish – and would in due course become 'a mild success'. Only Denis, an unlikely candidate for an overseas posting, was left at home. He 'could not do otherwise' than go with his parents to their new abode.

This was in Fennel's Way, Flackwell Heath, near High Wycombe, and was the nearest to the countryside that Quentin Crisp, who claimed to dislike flowers and animals, ever lived. The house was called Hillcrest and had four bedrooms, a living-in maid and a gardener. 'Our life now seemed to be luxurious,' was Denis's first reaction to the move but he soon decided that his father had 'abandoned common sense altogether'. The move out of London was Mr Pratt's last financial gamble and beyond his means, though he still attended an office in the City, joining the commuters at Loudwater station in a dark suit and bowler hat but eschewing gloves on the grounds that other travellers might think him pampered.

His youngest son had no such scruples: his mother continued to protect him though she had not abandoned her idea of making him into an artist. Early in 1930, Denis Pratt was enrolled as a student at the art school in Eastern Street, High Wycombe. Now twenty-one, he was already slightly older than the other students and behaved, he says, 'like a genius'. He was allowed to do 'more or less' what he liked and caused a stir with his long hair and long fingernails. In fact, he seems to have worked hard there; the school specialized in furniture design and he learnt how to do 'mechanical drawings' in a 'machine-like way', though he was happiest in the life room, disappointed only by the models' 'lack of daring', a complaint he was eventually to do something about himself.

At home, in pretty, leafy Fennel's Way, life became increasingly hellish, though Denis did manage to read Evelyn Waugh's *Vile Bodies* at this time, later pronouncing it 'the funniest book ever written', and to play the part of a madman in some local amateur theatricals. What he hated was being cut off from London and from perhaps what the Black Cat represented, though he had already tired of his 'very sordid sex life', deciding that sex was 'a dead loss' and he could live without it. It was people that he missed. 'I've always liked people, in spite of the danger,' he said later. 'People are my only occupation.' Instead of people, he had his mother's dogs. Mrs Pratt now kept chows, about which Quentin would later express conflicting feelings. On one occasion he surprised me by saying, 'Chow puppies are the cuddliest things ever', a most peculiar pronouncement from such a lifelong animal-hater, and on another occasion he said of the breed, 'They bite you, snap at you and they're *merciless*.' The truth is that whether he liked animals or not, he was interested in them and observant about them, as his gobsmacked response to a cat drawn by Mervyn Peake will show later.

While taking his mother's dogs for walks in the fields near the house, Denis would look longingly towards London. 'My great fear was that here I might live and die and not matter,' he writes revealingly in his autobiography, which would certainly have been the case if he had changed sex and run a knitting shop. In this state of mind, excursions in the broken-down family car, pointless trips in no particular direction, can have only added to the strain.

So must a visit from the snobbish postal clerk whom he had met in the Black Cat. According to Quentin, this young man, who had grown up in the King's Cross area, could not tell 'the difference between being middle-class and being of high degree' but got himself invited to Flackwell Heath in order to be able to say, 'I have been to a respectable household where they have table mats.' According to *The Naked Civil Servant*, Mrs Pratt made her 'special face' when she saw the visitor's thumbnails, which were broader than they were long.

Whatever the cumulative effect of all this on Denis, it was eventually too much for his mother. After about eighteen months at the new house, she 'went away for a few days', leaving Denis and his father alone together. Quentin Crisp describes this strangely ominous time. 'My father and I got on shakily but, to my amazement, not badly.' For the first time, they actually spoke to each other. At first Mr Pratt asked his son what he intended to do with his life. Later, he declared, '*The trouble is you look like a male whore.*' In gratitude for this uncharacteristic bit of straight talk, Denis promised his father that when he went up to London at Christmas – he would turn twenty-two on Christmas Day 1930 – he would try not to come back.

–6–

The Hut

There is a turning point in the history of an eccentric:
the first time when what he is doing or saying seriously
is greeted with laughter; laughter which indicates his
failure to communicate his meaning; he will thence-
forth speak and act increasingly oddly and hu-
morously.

PHILIP O'CONNOR, *Memoirs of a Public Baby*, 1958

It would be nice to write that as seven-year-old Philip O'Connor and
his twenty-nine-year-old guardian sped through the streets of Soho,
they encountered the painted, or tinted, figure of the young Quentin
Crisp. Unfortunately, the dates don't quite fit. In the summer of 1924,
the Black Cat was certainly flourishing but Denis Pratt was still at
boarding school and his home was in Epsom. In fact it was in the
Epsom direction, or some way beyond it, that the one-legged Mr Field
and his highly strung young charge were now heading.

At Charing Cross Station, they got tickets for Betchworth in Surrey
and during the short journey to this cosy village at the foot of Box
Hill, the economic terrors that had plagued Philip's early childhood
lifted and he 'thrilled' to his guardian's power. The suburban landscape
they passed through offered 'a crinolined chorus of security, sobriety,
sweetness and normality', which reinforced this mood. In his autobiography, Philip O'Connor has a lot to say about the man with whom he
was to live for the next eight years, but furnishes us with minimal
biographical details and no name other than 'Uncle Joseph'. His full
name was, as we know, Albert Joseph Camden Field and he was

actually known by Philip as Uncle Camden. When *Memoirs of a Public Baby* was published in 1958, Philip knew that his former guardian was still alive and made a feeble attempt to disguise his identity. The name Camden Field sounds distinctly patrician, even squirearchical, but he was in fact a Londoner, with 'lower-middle-class roots', according to Philip. Born in East London in 1894, he had been educated at what Philip calls 'a minor public school' and had then lied about his age to enter the army in his early teens. According to the Public Record Office, A. J. C. Field served during the First World War as a private in the 9th Battalion of the London Regiment, and was awarded the Silver War Badge, a medal given to those who were wounded. If Philip is to be trusted, Camden Field was shot in the leg and stomach at the end of the war, and crawled for twenty-four hours dragging his 'semi-detached' limb behind him. After the war, he seems to have found a safe, low-ranking job in the Civil Service, though there is no mention of his name in the *Civil Service Yearbook* and no clue as to which ministry he worked for.

These are the basic biographical facts about his guardian, onto which Philip has pinned a most elaborate and grotesquely convincing set of personal details. His face was 'a shock of childishness' and 'a pudding with implements of needs stuck on it'. A great deal more follows along these lines but Philip never explains how Mr Field had come into his life in the first place or why this shy bachelor wished to take on the burden of bringing up a small boy who was in no way related to him. Philip's extensive descriptions of Mr Field's physical characteristics do not sum up the whole man and it may be reassuring to bear in mind Gabriele Annan's between-the-lines view after reading *Memoirs of a Public Baby* that Philip's guardian was 'a kindly, half-educated and not very bright civil servant'.

We might also ask what Philip, now approaching his eighth birthday, was like at this time. Judging from what he said in later life and from his various writings – all of which have a strong autobiographical content – he seems to have been a highly intelligent, acutely sensitive child. We have already learnt that he suffered from what he calls 'brainstorms' and was easily 'thrilled' or 'chilled' by the people and situations he came across. He already loved the sound of his own voice. He was 'precociously aware of people's characteristics', amazingly observant and possessed, it seems, an extraordinary memory and concern for the past. As he started on his new life with Mr Field, he claims he was not only brooding about Madame Tillieux and his Wimereux life but also thinking about the Dean Street cellar and the constant patter of feet on the basement grating.

Philip's description of arriving in Surrey with Uncle Camden is extremely detailed and full of metaphors. They arrived at Betchworth station at dusk and were greeted by an old porter whom Philip describes as 'a grey, dingy man, as English as teacups held by people on blue-flowered carpets near a bay window'. They then set off together up Box Hill by a chalk path, Mr Field's artificial leg 'slightly thrown forward' and his walking-stick darting out 'like a magician's wand'. Then there's a brief pause, when Field took out his pipe and filled it with Lloyd's Skipper Navy Cut and was soon puffing away 'like a locomotive', the smoke providing further evidence of his power. They were heading for a hut on the most select part of Box Hill, then a famous beauty spot which according to a contemporary *Kelly's Directory* was 'much frequented by picnic parties in summer'. It was a little wooden shack, fitted together with prefabricated sections – Mr Field had built it with his own hands – and measuring twelve foot by eight. Philip describes it as 'a shrine' and as 'a place alone'. Three wooden steps led to its front door and inside was a metal bed, an army stretcher, an effigy of St Anthony, an oil stove and supplies of tinned food, including Nestlé's milk.

In this cosy, primitive, 'religious' atmosphere, Philip and his guardian spent the summer of 1924 and the ambiguous relationship between them sharpened and crystallized. Philip O'Connor writes that he loved Uncle Camden passionately, admired his kindness, his honesty, his simplicity, his bravery, but with equal vigour disliked him and was soon 'openly registering disgust as he murdered apples in his big, many-toothed mouth'. For his part, the slow-speaking Mr Field grew infuriated and embarrassed when the boy finished his sentences for him and failed to adopt his 'doggy egalitarianism'. In response, he retreated into awkwardness and what Philip describes as 'downright ugly smirks'.

In *Memoirs of a Public Baby* and elsewhere, Philip O'Connor has provided us with examples of the pedestrian manner in which Mr Field spoke to him in the hut, which was so arranged that its owner could get things from the cupboard, light the stove and cook bacon without rising from his camp bed. 'Keiller's Marmalade,' he might begin. 'Thick, chunky, bitter. I like thick marmalade, bitter.' Then on opening a can of Nestlé's milk, he might say, 'Milk. Thick rich milk. This'll do you good. Get some hot tea with this in it in your inside and you'll feel better. Cup of char in the morning.' Philip also remembers his own monologues, his pleadings for things. 'Uncle, have you got some? Can I have that? Can you give me that? Oh, please! Oh, please, uncle, I want it!' to which the grumpy reply was 'You always want something.'

In the late summer of 1924, Field and O'Connor returned to London and moved into rooms at 37 Leathwaite Road, off Clapham Common, which were run by a waiter's wife called Mrs Wardlow, who received Philip into her arms with an 'ecstasy' he did not at first share. The tall, thin house is today painted white with an arched doorway, adorned with leafy decorations and a mean rectangle of stained glass in which the number 37 is prominently inserted. From here, Philip was sent to the Winchester House School round the corner in Battersea Rise. This 'dingily select establishment . . . for the more refined children of the district' was run by Mrs Florence Jane Crofts. Rechristened 'Miss Bancroft' in Philip's autobiography, she is submitted to his most savage scrutiny to date. Her face, he writes, 'consisted chiefly of flexible furniture for the expression of public emotions, or a reverent self-arrangement of the draperies of old yellow soul-skin'. Her false teeth were 'large and bluish white' and when she opened her mouth the effect was like 'the sudden self-opening of a piano lid'. And her shoes, he says, were 'extraordinarily long, jutting inward to sharp points at the toe-joints like an old crone's jawbone but flat, and turned severely outwards from the ankle as though in hospitality to the space ahead'.

If he disliked the head teacher, his attitude to most of his fellow pupils was even more intense. Their reading aloud drove him mad with impatience and their hypocrisies made him groan. They were 'almost little institutions, little snippets of ideology'. The only way Philip felt he could get through to them was by acts of cruelty. To borrow modern parlance, he particularly targeted 'a little boy with the unbelievable name of Donald Darling, who appeared to have the unpleasant aspect of combined milk and urine in his face'. He systematically pinched these weaker creatures – how would he have reacted to Denis Pratt? – 'barked tersely' at the girls in the playground as they skipped and was driven to 'trembling excitement' by the sight of their blue knickers. He also devotes a page and a half of his book to his 'first crime', stealing 'with sugar-tong fingers' two pennies from the desk of a little girl called Connie. He soon admitted the offence but condemns Mrs Crofts's 'extreme vulgarity' for telling him that people went to prison for stealing. The schoolwork itself he enjoyed. 'I liked history,' he writes, 'identifying myself at once with all kings, having been brought up to consider myself heir to the Irish throne.'

Outside school, Philip's life followed various paths. At Leathwaite Road, he had a toy train, which ran on a figure of eight, and he grew closer to the landlady Mrs Wardlow, stealing money from her bag and playing with her daughter in a way that the little girl found immoral but which he found 'very delightful'. After a while and perhaps not surprisingly, Mrs Wardlow became vaguely critical or suspicious of the relationship between Philip and his guardian.

It was certainly a strange association. Philip has made various claims about Uncle Camden. He has stated that Field was 'emotionally deprived' and wanted his 'pound of flesh' and something 'to lavish love upon'. He has called him a 'misogynist' and a 'militant atheist'. In an early draft of *Memoirs of a Public Baby*, he suggested that Field was homosexual but removed this suggestion from the published version. In spite of all these insinuations, Philip insists that he loved his guardian passionately and wanted to be alone with him. As much as possible, Field treated Philip as an adult.

They went on excursions together, returning to the hut on Box Hill at holiday times, and on outings in London. Field took Philip to the local Clapham Library, still standing today in all its Flemish Renaissance glory, and he was tremendously impressed by the 'dim din' of the books and decided, as they left, to read as much as possible from then on. Field also took him, in 1925, to the delightful, musty old Shakespeare Theatre on Lavender Hill to see Charlie Chaplin in *The Kid* and *The Gold Rush*. During the second film, Philip cried and laughed simultaneously and left the cinema trembling, 'mad with visions of understanding'. For the rest of his life, Chaplin was in and under his skin, an untold influence and the inspiration for his belief that the clown's art is supreme.

There were also trips to see Haslam Jackson, who had now become the manager of a large marble works on the Walworth side of Kennington just south of the Thames. Temporarily liberated from Mrs O'Connor, who was travelling in France on further business ventures, Uncle Haslam had paid off his debts and was living in a disorderly flat near the works, surrounded by obscure eighteenth-century books, big-bowled pipes, an Egyptian mummy-head and other items which had presumably once graced his rooms in the Temple. Here Philip watched Field and Jackson – his two honorary uncles seemed to be friends – indulging in a mild kind of misogyny, laughing together about the absent Winnie O'Connor. 'Look at us now,' Philip imagines Haslam Jackson saying one Sunday lunchtime. 'The joint sizzling in the oven – the potatoes hissing, going a soft gold-brown; our glasses of Tarragona full, our pipes on fire, the clock gently ticking – Sunday mid-day – what more could a man want? Bring a woman in – rush – tears, things upset. Why? Such is woman's nature.'

Haslam Jackson was wise to make the best of it while he could because Winifred O'Connor would soon return and throw his favourite possessions, opera-hat and cloak, into a back room, sending him into another decline which caused him to lose his will to work, retreating from her casuistry into extreme shabbiness. With Mrs O'Connor came Philip's sister Desirée, now fourteen and 'very bright, brittle, beautiful, passionately made' but also, says Philip, 'as cold as the clicking of a shop till'. The relationship between brother and sister would rapidly develop 'in hatred and sexual attraction'. According to Philip, Desirée was frightened of him because he was 'wild', as well as 'dreadfully common', and he was frightened of her because she represented 'the cruelty of law and order'. These difficulties must have only increased when Desirée was sent to join Philip at Winchester House School.

Philip also remembers being present in the Kennington flat when his mother received a disturbing visit from her stepsister Angela. According to Philip, who thirty years later included the incident in a radio play, the visitor pronounced the flat 'a dreadful appalling slum' and blamed everything on the fact that Winifred was a 'nigger'. In response, Mrs O'Connor called her stepsister 'a buddy, buddy bitch'.

Wild confrontations were already part of Philip's life and he tells us that he ended his Clapham days roaming the streets and forming a gang of boys which would 'stone' another gang on the Common. He announced and half-convinced himself that he was the Prince of Wales incognito and that his guardian had won the VC. Finally, his thefts from his landlady reached the vast sum of half-a-crown, which he stole from her purse and used to buy 'a silly sugar robin in a white sugar cage' which he presented to a particularly hatchet-faced teacher at his school. This theft was quickly discovered and it was roughly at this point that Camden Field decided that he and Philip should leave London and go and live permanently on Box Hill.

In April 1926, they resettled in their tiny hut. Philip was now nine and was to remain here until he was fourteen. Field was thirty-one and presumably working for the same ministry. Philip has little more to add about the hut, except that he and his guardian now built a verandah onto it: woodwork, especially putting up shelves, remained a surprising part of Philip's repertoire into old age. Other adornments to the hut were unwelcome. Cushions were banned and so were some curtains donated by Mr Field's sister. Field explained that he did not wish to clutter up the windows with 'feminine frills'. The food they ate was also notably plain: plain sausages, plain steaks, plain bully-beef. Philip cooked the sausages himself.

For a while, the relationship between man and boy remained 'simple and excellent'. They went on rambles together, taking a picnic tin of sandwiches, looking for flowers and birds and butterflies. They even went to the pub, the nearby olde worlde Barley Mow, where Field would drink a pint or two of something called 'Four X' and may perhaps unwittingly have introduced Philip to the alcoholic pleasures which were to burden him for the rest of his life. In later years, Philip would become a regular frequenter of licensed premises and clearly remembered the Barley Mow at Betchworth as his first public house. Gradually, however, things became more awkward between them and Philip sneered not only at his guardian's eating habits but also at the way 'certain vile vowels' went for 'a toboggan ride' in his throat. Camden Field 'leaned towards working-class directness' yet was 'violently snobbish' in regard to his immediate inferiors. He disliked most of the other hut-dwellers on the hill, whom Philip describes as 'prosperous shopkeepers and a sprinkling of schoolteachers', and would 'hop at the double' past their huts. Women particularly scared him and he took extra pains to avoid them.

From the hut, Mr Field went daily to his job in London and Philip was soon sent to a local school. On 13 May 1926, he became a pupil at the High School in Chart Lane, Dorking, which had been founded in 1892 with the motto *Ora et Labora* meaning 'Pray and Work'. For a while Philip remained 'charmingly obedient' in front of the authorities while denouncing them behind their backs. He had 'a cold eye' for the 'grandeur' of his elders and he would soon abominate the headmaster, A. J. Rivett, even more than Quentin Crisp loathed Denstone's Dr Grier. 'Johnny' Rivett had been headmaster at Dorking since 1912 but, according to Philip, 'had the air and manner of a man-size duckling'. Philip describes him as 'my first proper introduction to British sanitary decadence, the soaped and disinfected decadence of a frightened people', and detected in him 'a most humid gloss of curiously rare vaporous sexuality'. It may be worth noting that when Rivett eventually retired, long after Philip had left the school, he was praised for his 'grace of manner, essential kindliness and shrewdness'. For the other staff Philip had warmer, but more confused feelings. He loved his first English teacher, Miss Allsworth, but flung ink at her timetable and was addressed by her with 'burning cheeks and flashing blue eyes' in front of the class. Of the classroom experience in general, he wrote, 'Schoolmasters' flesh looked like old pastry. You could study it till you felt as sleepy as it.'

During his remaining schooldays, Philip became more eccentric, ill at ease and lonely. He had no role models and his 'total absence of intimate associates or relations' led to what he calls 'living publicly'. His facial expressions became 'increasingly erratic' and 'over-charged with meaning'. He became 'an eternal quibbler', increasingly dreamy and aloof and prone to 'a prattling and feminine imbecility'. Reviewing *Memoirs of a Public Baby* in 1958, Anthony Powell described O'Connor as 'obviously a child of unusual intelligence, whose strange circumstances greatly increased traits already strongly developed in him'. While at Dorking, he also reached that crucial turning-point described at the start of this chapter. He started doing deliberately what he had once done unconsciously or by mistake. One hot afternoon in the art room, Philip tinkled the wooden end of a paint-brush in a glass of water and asked if the sound wasn't delicious. Instead of praising O'Connor for his cheerful turn of phrase, the art master replied that the boy had gone mad.

Around the age of eleven, Philip became a frantic reader, devouring among other things all Dickens's novels: 'His humour convulsed me and his pathos made me weep.' He soon moved on to Stanley Weyman, Harrison Ainsworth, Trollope, Ludwig Renn, Remarque, Thomas Mann, Goethe, Gorky – in fact an almost endless list of authors, some of whom I've never heard of – but very few poets. He liked books he could 'live in for days' like *The Cloister and the Hearth*, the lengthy historical novel by Charles Reade. Inside himself, he claims he was building 'a fortress' out of which he would eventually 'sally forth equipped'. He also claims that this surge of reading coincided with his falling behind with his schoolwork. He had 'obliterated' his education with reading and developed inside himself 'a private pregnancy independent of scholastic nourishment', later arguing that a close connection exists between initiative and delinquency. This is bold talk and in later life he went further, tracing his need to be intellectual to his failure at school, a failure which haunted him for years and which no amount of defiance – in old age he told Stephen Spender, 'I never wanted to be a scholar' – could abate. Anyway, he had by now started writing himself, using his whole body and taking an enormous amount of pleasure or pain in the process. His first self-styled 'early masterpiece', composed in tears, was about the blind girl wandering through the catacombs in Bulwer Lytton's *Last Days of Pompeii*. His first published piece of writing was an article on Dickens in the school magazine, of which no copies survive.

Philip O'Connor's life on Box Hill had various elements to it. At the age of twelve, he went on nature-worshipping walks in the woods. In his own words, he crept, darted about, halted paralytically, mooned over a static water-pond and rasped his throat by smoking 'Old Man's Beard'. He also climbed trees, and up an oak tree one day masturbated for the first time. This practice would become 'a banner of independence' from his guardian but did not have a calming effect. Climbing the hill after school, he felt faint and highly observant at the same time. 'The mere whiff of wind was sensuously delicious, the merest crackle of a twig . . . set my nerves bounding like violin strings.' Later in life, Philip O'Connor wrote and talked about the 'neurotic self-inflation' and 'false individuality' he suffered from in childhood and adolescence. At times, he felt his head might burst like a pumpkin. 'I ached to show that I knew better as though I was in agony to urinate. The word "fool" fastened itself sharply, hissingly on my tongue.'

In appearance and manner, Philip may have been 'a dreamy little lad' – there is a photograph of him in which he looks a healthy little scamp, a far cry from the terrifying picture of Quentin Crisp at the same age – but beneath this façade lurked real aggression. At Box Hill, as at Clapham, Philip formed a gang of supporters. 'I was terribly belligerent,' he told me later. 'I had all sorts of sticks, cutlasses, swords, bows and arrows.' At the age of twelve, he carried a silver shield with a cross painted on it. When many years later a photograph of the youthful Stephen Spender, similarly equipped, reached his attention, Philip responded with great excitement. His gang's preoccupations clearly extended beyond belligerence into theatricals. In his early teens he organized various amateur dramatics on the hill, attended by the whole camp, with himself in the lead role. In one performance, his 'greatest', he writhed and rolled on stage 'in an imitation of epilepsy'.

These social activities caused further friction with his guardian. When the boy returned to the hut, the lonely Mr Field would say jealously, 'I suppose you've been enjoying yourself, eh?' In his autobiography, Philip describes Field as 'a bad giver' who insisted on gratitude, while admitting that he himself – though now confirmed by a Roman Catholic priest in the local town – was incapable of Christian virtues like altruism. 'I could be generously affectionate but would never be so on principle,' he explains, which makes him an exact opposite of Quentin Crisp, who on principle was kind to everyone but never over-affectionate. When Mr Field's artificial leg broke down and the poor man had to struggle up the hill on crutches and in pouring rain, Philip was not sympathetic. When they sat together in the hut, Field would sometimes complain that Philip was not 'there' and Philip became ruder to him, 'vicious as a cat', and mocking him continuously. In later life, he wrote that he found his guardian's grunts and groans 'poetic in their inarticulateness'.

Mr Field was changing in other ways too. With Philip, he was becoming more tactile and these new gestures of affection weighed heavily on the boy. He had also begun to show signs of 'coquetry and coyness' when talking to women. When Philip spotted him holding hands with a woman from Clapham, he saw it as 'a complete betrayal' of his guardian's asocial and misogynistic principles. During these years in the hut, Field also got involved in an assortment of contemporary causes, such as spiritualism, psychoanalysis, and both Fascism and Communism. He was drawn to the latter cause, Philip says, because of its 'order and decency' and because he saw himself as a 'plain man' – a concept that Philip, then and for ever afterwards, found repellent. In his autobiography he writes, 'As an example of the real sewer-soul, the tart-heart, the mashbrain, the scummy-eyed hypocrite, nothing can rival the eminent plain man.'

In spite of this antipathy towards each other, Field and Philip were still very much a couple. They went to the cinema together. They also went on trips to the North of France, visiting Étaples, Le Touquet, Boulogne and Wimereux itself. Here, Philip heard the trams again clanging and screaming down the Rue Carnot and remet Madame Tillieux and her children. Alas, no details of this re-encounter survive but, anyway, it was not the last time that Philip would meet his French family.

By the end of 1930, Field had become exhausted by his nightly climb up Box Hill and decided that he and Philip should return to 'civilization'. Shortly before they left Philip was photographed sitting in the sun on the steps of the hut and accompanied by two girls, much younger than himself, one of whom is showing her knickers. Philip wears flannel trousers with generous turn-ups, a tie but no shoes, and looks sturdy and sane enough, but the photograph is blurred and torn and tells us little more about him or the hut. Field and O'Connor were now to forsake this odd abode, where they had lived for six years, and move to a tiny insubstantial house near a railway bridge in the wet suburb of Raynes Park. After a few weeks or months here, they moved to a flat in Wimbledon Park Parade – number 15a – on the north side of Gap Road in the neighbouring Queen of the Suburbs.

From here, Philip took the train each day to Dorking where his school was soon to be amalgamated with the Girls' High School, moving in July 1931 to new premises in Ashcombe Road. During his remaining months here his work deteriorated further and his nicknames 'the Poet' and 'Philip Augustus' began to suit him more and more. Among the teachers who knew him at this time was the maths master Norman Bradshaw, who is still alive aged ninety-five as I write these words and remembers Philip as 'an extraordinary fellow, very anti-everything, very much a loner, what we call a drop-out'. Mr Bradshaw also recalls that Philip carved a head of someone in chalk, which he considered interesting enough to show to a local artist Richard Garbe, then professor of sculpture at the Royal College of Art.

Philip's new life in the London suburbs had several strands to it and nothing obviously wicked. Keen on the cinema since an early age, he was now 'taking it like a drug in increasing doses'. For the film-star Clara Bow, 'whom in panties for the fourteen-year-old me none could excel', he had a particular passion but it was mainly the 'moronic' male stars, their 'clothes and easy, effective manners' that inspired him. Back at home, in front of the mirror he would make 'a medley of adult faces, judicial, scrutinizing, insinuating, cynical, ironical, portentous-noble, Prussian dead-pan, degenerate-sophisticated faces'. Now, after school hours, he began an acting course at a branch of the Italia Conti School. He says that he was mad about acting and that 'If I had any idea at all of my future, it was in the theatre.' He would soon express dismay at the spectacle of girlish boys playing in *Journey's End* and concentrate on his off-stage performance.

At about this time, Philip began to affect 'a sinful jauntiness of demeanour', using strong tea and his first cigarettes as the 'agents' of his 'increasing debauch'. In later life he described how while in Wimbledon he graduated from Craven As to Du Mauriers. He also watched with interest as Camden Field's commitment to Communism increased and speculates that his guardian was hoping to find in it the warmth and comradeship he had failed to find in him. Philip also got involved, attended meetings of the Wimbledon Communists, but feared that his own 'brilliance' would be swallowed up in this mass movement. At the same time, he reacted to his guardian's steady decency by casting a rebellious glance in the direction of what was to become Fitzrovia. 'I was uncertain in so vulgar a way as to need applause for everything I said and thought,' he later explained, adding, 'Intellectually, I had the attitude of a music hall entertainer, I must get my rabbits out deftly, and get fame in return.' Underlying these desires, this ambition, this antipathy towards society were, he says, 'an aloofness', 'mental aberration' and a strong undercurrent of what he calls 'Messianism' and 'Christ identification'. In one of his less manic moments at this time, he made a half-hearted suicide attempt, by putting his head in a gas oven, on a carefully arranged pillow.

Being back in London had also brought Philip closer to the family that had rejected him. Mrs O'Connor, Desirée and Haslam Jackson had now reached 'rock bottom' in a two-room flat off Westbourne Grove, Bayswater. Here, Haslam slept on a mattress on the floor and took morning walks around the area, wearing slippers, an old grey raincoat belted with string and a pair of spectacles attached to his ears with string. Philip records the details of this 'manifestly sordid' life with relish and regret yet adds that his mother's old *aroma de luxe* lingered on. There were still the old scents and silks, special luxuries and sensory pleasures. There were still the old French coffee-pot, with its unscrewable, bashed-in spout, liqueur chocolates and rare, fat Turkish cigarettes made by Hadjyani-Vuccino – but all was not well. In his mother's and sister's presence, Philip felt gauche and uncouth. Mrs O'Connor had become noticeably fatter – Philip calls her obese

– and increasingly babyish, laughing at Camden Field with 'girlish malice' and calling him 'Camiknickers' when she borrowed a fiver off him. Desirée O'Connor, now nearly an adult and drawn into a semi-fashionable world represented by the Gargoyle Club and famous jazz musicians, spoke again of her brother's 'commonness' and made him writhe in agony.

In *Memoirs of a Public Baby*, Philip writes that he twice failed to matriculate at Dorking High School but the school's records state that in July 1932, two months short of his sixteenth birthday, he passed his General Certificate, gaining distinction in English and Oral French. Whatever the truth of this, his formal education was now drawing to a close. One morning in January 1933, he was waiting for the train to Dorking, when he had 'a funny feeling'. The train duly came in but he ignored it, crossed over to the other platform and took one to Waterloo, from where he made his way to his mother's flat.

–7–

The Fantastic Vehicle

Exhibitionism is a drug. Hooked in adolescence I was
now taking doses so massive that they would have
killed a novice. Blind with mascara and dumb with
lipstick, I paraded the dim streets of Pimlico with my
overcoat wrapped round me as though it were a tail-
less ermine cape.

QUENTIN CRISP, *The Naked Civil Servant*, 1968

This book is a study of two lifelong exhibitionists. We have already
learnt something of Philip O'Connor's youthful giggling imbecilities.
Now we must consider Quentin Crisp's haughty postures as he at last,
aged twenty-two, faced the real world. In Quentin's case, the thing
happened gradually and the form in which he would display himself
was not finally resolved until the year 1933 when he was twenty-four
years old, and even that was not the end of the story. The dyed hair,
for example, came several years later. In *How to Become a Virgin*,
Quentin boasts, 'I always proceeded cautiously' and claims that at no
time in his life had he taken 'a healthy, vigorous action'.

For the period of Quentin Crisp's life between his leaving home at
the end of 1930 and the outbreak of the Second World War, I am
largely dependent on his version, or versions, of events. I have spoken
to one old man who remembers him at his Epsom preparatory school
but know no one who knew him at Denstone and no one who knew
him in the 1930s apart from his niece Frances Ramsay, who was then
a child, and the writer Francis King, who remembers seeing him in
Chelsea streets. I have no doubt that a few contemporaries do survive.

And what about the children of his friends? Or his neighbours' children? Quentin Crisp became one of the sights of London, a Metropolitan Picturesque, fascinating to most children, and the children of that period would only be in their seventies today. But how could I get in touch with them, except by advertising, a degradingly public procedure not guaranteed to bear fruit and which might spoil the semi-secrecy or privacy in which books are best written?

Without other witnesses, I must lean heavily on the sixty-five pages Quentin devotes to this stage of his life in his autobiography and on those precious fragments of information which fell from his lips during my many conversations with him. And, while leaning heavily on these sources, I must also bear in mind that Quentin Crisp was a great teaser, an indefatigable humorist, a master of the double bluff and a pedlar of half-truths masquerading as jokes. He seemed to be so open but his revelations were very much made on his own terms.

While considering his life at this time, one repeatedly wonders how lonely was he, how unhappy, how truly disengaged from other people? The text of *The Naked Civil Servant* reverberates with references to 'friends' and even during his early Black Cat days he knew people well enough to go to their houses and put on his make-up. We also know that he formed friendships as a young man which would last for the next fifty years. Can these dealings really have been as shallow as he makes out and if he really was, as he claims, at the 'losing end' of every friendship wasn't this his own choice? Throughout his life he was socially passive, refused to take any initiative in terms of starting a friendship or keeping it going – and thereby only half-participated in the whole reciprocal process. Those who knew him in later life, including myself, found him 'instantly likeable and sympathetic' yet he repeatedly asserts that he was horribly unpopular, always needed people more than they needed him and that a great many everyday transactions with strangers were beyond him. These self-denigrating claims should be seen in the light of his astounding self-sufficiency from an early age and his rival claim, repeated throughout his life, that he had no capacity for loneliness. In an unpublished interview with the writer Selina Hastings he qualified this by saying, 'I *arranged* to wish to be alone' and argued that he needed to be on his own a lot of the time 'because I'm *never natural* with people'. Early in life he had apparently decided that he needed a room of his own where he could be his 'horrible self' and it was the lack of such a private place that made his first few months in London so 'loathsome'.

When Denis Pratt, as he was to remain for some time, finally left his parents' home in High Wycombe during the festive season of 1930, he headed for the Baron's Court area of West London where the houses remain 'blind with stained glass'. Here his friend Thumbnails – I wish I could replace this grotesque nickname with a real name – had a flat. Denis seems to have had no respect or regard for this class-conscious poverty-stricken young man, whose reverence for 'the highly born' and titled made him wince. There was no sexual connection between them but Thumbnails appeared to be vaguely in awe of Denis, to believe in him in some way, and perhaps hoped to gain prestige in the process. 'Perhaps,' Quentin wrote later, 'he thought that one day something might come of all the talents I claimed by implication to possess.' If this was the case, Thumbnails deserves to be heartily congratulated for such early percipience. Something did indeed come of his friend's curious range of gifts.

But this is moving on. Denis Pratt had scarcely settled in Baron's Court when a telegram arrived announcing his father's death. With his wife at his side, Charles Pratt had died in the local High Wycombe Hospital on 17 January 1931, suffering from cancer of the rectum. He was only fifty-nine but his son said later, 'He must have been longing to die.' According to Quentin, his father was unable to present himself to his wife as a failure and had gone on overspending to the end – 'If he hadn't died, he'd have gone to gaol' – but others in the family reject this view. Quentin's sister Phyllis continued all her life to regard her father as 'the tops' and his niece Frances believes that her grandfather only got into debt on account of paying for his wife's nursing homes. What Quentin really felt about his father's death is a matter for speculation. All he admits to on reading the telegram is his irritation that he would have to go to the funeral. This took place at East Anstey in 'darkest Devonshire', where Phyllis's husband John Payne was now the vicar, after which Denis hurried back to London to continue his battle with the world. His mother would soon dispose of the house at Flackwell Heath and, keeping only enough furniture for her own bedroom, move to East Anstey to live with her daughter and her son-in-law at their pleasant rectory on the foothills of Exmoor.

During those 'long, horrible weeks' in Baron's Court, the unformed and unnamed Quentin Crisp experimented in how he might live. One evening – the scene features in the film of his life – he dressed up in a black silk dress and velvet cape borrowed from a girl he had known in High Wycombe and took the Underground from Baron's Court to Piccadilly Circus. Beside him sat Thumbnails in a dinner-jacket. How Thumbnails owned such a garment when he lived in real poverty was a mystery to Quentin but tells us something about Thumbnails' priorities. The outing was a flop – they had an uneventful drink at the Regent Palace Hotel – and Quentin never again wore drag until old age, when he was persuaded to play Lady Bracknell on stage and Queen Elizabeth the First in a film. At this stage Denis and his 'unlike-able' friend drew far more attention to themselves in the Lyons Corner House in Tottenham Court Road, without dressing up. According to Quentin, the other customers rearranged their chairs and sat watching them, displaying the mixture of hostility and curiosity with which he was becoming increasingly familiar. In this and other cafés, they also resorted to various 'dodgy expedients' to avoid paying the bill. Such unscrupulousness was profoundly out of character for Quentin, who later in life treated everything to do with money as 'sacred'.

Later in the spring of 1931, the two young men moved to a double room – eleven shillings a week each – at 9 Liverpool Street, opposite King's Cross Station. In his autobiography, Quentin describes this new habitat as 'a much more fertile region' than the 'no man's land' of Baron's Court, and joyfully informs us that it was 'loud with the noise of steam trains and lousy with tea shops'. He does not mention that he soon dragged himself away from these attractions and spent two weeks at Barholm in Lincolnshire, where his brother-in-law's father was vicar.

In *The Naked Civil Servant*, Quentin Crisp concentrates instead on a far-fetched and far-reaching incident which took place while he was living in King's Cross. Thanks to the initiative of his flatmate – Thumbnails must be congratulated again – Denis was permitted to partner a speciality dancer in a charity concert at the Scala Theatre in Charlotte Street. He tells us that the audience laughed and applauded his antics to a deafening degree. I don't know the exact date of this event but it must have represented a strange, crazy stepping-stone towards his future frivolities. Does his willingness to make a fool of himself, at the age of twenty-two, in a thousand-seat theatre also tell us something about his need for attention?

Soon after this amusing evening, Denis secured his first job. During the summer of 1931, Mrs Pratt managed to get her son taken on by a large firm of consulting electrical engineers. Employed as a tracer at a salary of £2 10s a week, he was now able to get the room of his own that he yearned for. He found one at 81 Denbigh Street, in 'darkest Pimlico', which had Nottingham lace curtains on the window, 'corned beef linoleum' on the floor and a brass bedstead in one corner. His landlady, Edith Crossman, was 'wonderful'. Later in life he would remark, 'To my amazement I never had an unkind landlady', and Mrs Crossman was wonderful even when Denis's gas meter was rifled by one of his own friends. Also living in the house, which seems not to be standing today, was a woman whose extraordinary name Gertrude Food suggests that she too may have been an embryo stylist. Anyway, Denis was ecstatic to have found a place of his own and to be liberated from the pressures of Thumbnails, of whom he would later talk with hatred. At Denbigh Street, he told me, he would get into bed at night and say, *'Now I'm in bed!'* and wake up in the morning and say, *'Now it's today!'* If Pascal is correct in saying that happiness means being able to sit quietly in a room, Denis Pratt had found happiness.

While in this first room of his own, and working for the engineering firm, he also made a valiant effort to make something of himself on other fronts. He applied to St Martin's School of Art but was turned down by the principal on the grounds that, against all odds, he already had a job. Instead, he took evening classes in life drawing and illustration at the Regent Street Polytechnic. At home in his room he wrote a play about Helen of Troy, and any number of poems, libretti and short stories. He lived in the future and entertained fantasies of being a famous painter, writer or actor. He hawked his manuscripts around but none of them was published and he later confessed, or boasted, that he had 'all the airs and graces of genius but no talent'.

It was also at Denbigh Street that he began to do more work on his persona. In his introduction to the first American edition of *The Naked Civil Servant*, Michael Holroyd writes about the 'fantastic vehicle' of Quentin Crisp, 'fashioned for propaganda and amusement'. There are as many elements to this creation, as many waves and strands and imponderable complications, as there were to his later hairstyle. Up to this point, Denis had merely exploited the innate effeminacy which he claims had been so apparent in him from an early age. While at Denbigh Street, which he occupied until the winter of 1932–3, he took matters a great deal further, progressing 'from the effeminate to the bizarre'. In other words, he became 'not merely a self-confessed homosexual but a self-evident one' and, in the words of a subsequent interviewer, began to project 'a brand image of homosexuality that was outrageously effeminate'. In his own words, he became 'a terrible painted figure prancing through the streets', both beautiful and terrible, like a male ballet dancer in full rig or a curious imitation or mockery of those 'divine women' who meant so much to the boys in the Black Cat and are still 'gay icons' today. Denis Pratt was already an ardent cinema-goer and his study of screen stardom taught him how to transform himself. Of all the current film-stars, Marlene Dietrich, whose film *The Blue Angel* had been released in 1930, affected him most. 'I thought about her a great deal,' he wrote later. 'I wore her clothes, said her sphinx-like lines and ruled her kingdom.'

Yet, though his ambiguous gender and desire to occupy the territory between man and woman remained at the heart of it all, he soon realized that sexual abnormality did not constitute the whole of his difference from other people. The emerging Quentin Crisp defies categorization and there was nothing stereotyped about his performance. According to Professor Robinson, author of a book about homosexual autobiography, Quentin Crisp's effeminacy was 'at once a militant cause and a huge gag'. The Quentin Crisp that emerged in the early 1930s was self-reverential, self-mocking, self-consciously cynical, utterly fastidious and totally perverse – so perverse in fact that even his femininity seems in doubt. Though sometimes mistaken for a woman, he was never a transvestite, never attended a 'drag ball' and was as far removed from the little old lady in the knitting shop as it is possible to imagine. He had embraced the theatrical side of his sexuality. The mannered image that he presented throughout his life was stagey or more precisely filmy, rather than camp. Indeed, he often railed against camp behaviour, which he saw as 'undignified, even hypocritical'. Yet he was a master of the dramatic gesture and during those early days presented an image which, he says, was 'grotesquely grand'. Even those who, he says, 'quite liked' him believed he felt superior to the rest of the world. This may be so – but we need to remember that Quentin Crisp's haughtiness was matched by impeccable manners. He was charming, beguiling, likeable, and, in his own words, 'courteous to a degree unseen in most countries outside the Orient'. He was also utterly reliable – even, he says, 'to the point of being boring'.

And with the make-up and the exotic clothes came a remarkable form of speech. From now onwards, Quentin Crisp would try not to move very far from a dozen or so formal phrases. He repeatedly told people to be 'terribly, terribly gay' and the social banalities which he used to conceal his wit and articulateness would remain with him for the rest of his life. He had already established a jokily formal way of addressing, or referring to people, without using their given names, and would take this old-fashioned practice to absurdly comical or embarrassing extremes. It is all very well to talk about *Mr* Barrow or *Mr* O'Connor but it is quite ridiculous to refer to Prince Philip as *Mr* Philip and Jesus Christ as *Mr* Christ. Yet in stripping us all of our given names he may show a grasp of the absurdity of human identity and the ludicrous labelling provided by names. But this practice was only one aspect of a complete language he created, later branded Crisperanto, which embodied a great deal of wit and a whole philosophy of life in which double-bluffing is a central element. His mother's bohemian friend Cecily Longhurst may have started him off on this tack but the philosophy which he devised during this period is very much his own and was to undergo few changes during the years ahead.

Denis Pratt's final flourish was to change or 'dye' his name. This took place gradually, bit by bit, during these years – for a while he was known as Denis Crisp – and eventually it was a 'committee' of unnamed friends who decided on Quentin Crisp. The name Denis Pratt does not entirely lack piquancy but its conversion into Quentin Crisp is a masterstroke. The name is splendidly dated, fanciful, magical and fastidiously wrought. It is also self-consciously absurd. I think it was G. K. Chesterton who wrote that a good name is a successful name, or words to that effect, and this is what 'Quentin Crisp' ultimately proved to be and we should be grateful that he had the guts to hang on to it. I shall try not to call him Denis Pratt again.

We might well ask what it was all in aid of. What was the purpose behind what Michael Holroyd calls Quentin Crisp's 'strange boxing match with the world' and what caused him to reduce his life to what Professor Robinson calls one of 'affectation and posing'? Quentin himself offers various answers. To start with, he yearned to educate the public, making himself into 'a test case' by 'going to work on all the millions who had never heard of homosexuality'. He also wanted to show that he was not ashamed. He wanted to show that effeminacy existed in people who in all other respects were 'just like home'. Wearing away at other people's primitive hostility gave a purpose to his life but it is also possible that he wished to scorn the world before it scorned him. Up to this point, the humiliation, poverty and loneliness had nearly brought his life to a standstill. Now he began to breathe vitality into all this desolation and, as Michael Holroyd puts it, turn 'his crippling disadvantages into enviable assets'. Yet, there was a lot of playfulness in his nature and at times he certainly felt that he was 'a peacock without a cause'. He also stresses that he had no great choice in the matter. 'I can't be regarded as a saint or a martyr. I did exactly what I had to do.' And then again he says, 'No one forced me into the role of a victim', but this still doesn't give the full picture. We may admire Quentin for exposing himself like King Lear, 'to feel what wretches feel', but he also makes it clear that he was often amused and stimulated by the consequences of his behaviour.

It was said of Marlene Dietrich that her stage act really came alive when she took her applause. Quentin states that he was totally intoxicated with his own existence but he also needed what people would nowadays call 'feedback'. Having made 'a public spectacle' of himself, he lived 'every moment out of doors in a state of feverish awareness', ventilated by other people's curiosity if not animosity. 'I suppose the attention of other people is stimulating to me,' he told me many years later. 'I suppose it's simply the way I am constituted. I really like some perpetual communication, even if it's entirely mute, with the outside world.' Exhibitionism was indeed a drug. It was a game or performance using sexual symbols that was not really about sex. It was also a piece of art. Quentin has described himself as 'a very plain child'. During the 1930s he would transform himself into what many people would call 'a great beauty' and what Philip O'Connor would describe as 'one of London's works of art'. Like other solitary characters, Quentin Crisp used make-up and other forms of self-adornment to give birth to a creature of his own making. Women may know more than men about this particular process, which usually takes place in front of the mirror.

Quentin has also explained that tampering with his personal appearance 'unified' him and, having adopted this 'uniform', the rest of his life 'solidified' around him 'like a plaster cast'. In many senses, Quentin Crisp was now finished. He told Selina Hastings: 'When I was young I had looked for love. I imagined the world would one day recognize my lovability.' He now ceased to pursue the idea of love. He was determined to live alone. Like Joan Crawford, also emerging at this time, he avoided the 'menace of human relationships' by making himself into his own kind of star and like Joan Crawford he had an almost inexhaustible fund of self-discipline with which to apply himself to this task. 'I've always claimed to be an unworldly little thing,' he wrote in *How to Go to the Movies*, 'but I never forgot that Shelley Winters said, "Act girlish but not retarded." ' There was no longer anything wet or weak about him and when looking back to this period he often describes himself as a 'thing' rather than a person, who had now set up a lifestyle where he did not need people. In *The Naked Civil Servant*, he claimed to feel 'a deep-seated indifference about the fate of others' and, when warned that life would pass him by, he declared, 'Thank God for that. We nearly got mixed up in the beastly thing.' And, unlike other outsiders and lame ducks, he did not now or at any time in the future attempt to ingratiate himself with the rich and famous. He preferred whatever society there was to form around him. He said later that he had a vast capacity 'for socializing rather than friendship' and for being happy without any form of intimate commitment or engagement with other people. 'I was alone,' he said on looking back at this formative stage of his life, 'and I had to invent happiness.' Compared with Philip O'Connor and almost everyone else I can think of, Quentin Crisp was to lead an extraordinarily stream-lined existence.

But this is to look ahead to the calmer, more amenable, more sympathetic waters which eventually surrounded him in middle age. Back in the early 1930s, the good ship Quentin, newly launched and freshly, luridly painted and rechristened, had a very rocky maiden voyage. On his first outings from Denbigh Street, he was constantly mauled, pushed around, fingered, threatened, insulted. Mutterings, whistlings and cries of 'Who do you think you are?' soon gave way to actual violence. His face was slapped, his toes stamped on – one of his new quirks was to go bare-footed. 'Nothing can describe the hatred and the terror and the trouble I once caused,' he told an interviewer forty-five years later. 'I provoked the worst behaviour in others.' His strangeness infuriated 'the average man' and excited a pack instinct: it was always groups rather than individuals who went for him. Crowds were created through which the traffic could not pass. Londoners stood with their faces contorted with rage, housewives hissed, and workmen spat as reactions 'passed from startled contempt to outraged hatred'. There were also more positive or peculiar reactions. People told him – mockingly – how beautiful he was and once when he stepped off a bus a man spread a newspaper over a puddle: Quentin walked on it, thanked the man and walked on. And whenever he passed a certain hotel in the Strand, the commissionaire would rush back into the building, take a flower from a vase in the foyer and present it to him.

In his new persona, Quentin Crisp found he was unwelcome in cafés. He later boasted that he was turned out of every Lyons Corner House in London and even the Black Cat banned him, probably following remonstrations from the police. By this time he had anyway grown tired of the Black Cat's monotonous masquerade and in due course the café itself closed in dramatic circumstances. In October 1934, its manager Mancini was charged and acquitted of a famous murder, with the young Quintin Hogg on the prosecuting team.

Quentin Crisp's initial reactions to the uproar he caused are complicated and contradictory. He wanted to have maximum impact but he also wanted his image to be ignored. Later he took a more logical view. 'It is absolutely useless for someone like myself to adopt a peculiar appearance and then *resent* being looked at,' he said. 'This is absolutely daft.' Many people have praised him for his bravery, his confidence in the face of thuggery, and some have even compared him with a Christian saint. Others have suggested that he enjoyed it all and was driven by a form of masochism and it is difficult not to believe that, at least to some extent, he revelled in being so reviled. 'In fact,' he told the scriptwriter Philip Mackie, 'I *didn't* like the uproar. Like all other children who are absolute hell you seek to be loved and admired and when this fails you seek to be noticed, but you don't want to be despised and rejected.' Much later he contradicted himself again, declaring, 'There was even a sense in which I welcomed the animosity of the public.'

Whatever his feelings, his actual responses to aggression were extremely cautious. To start with, he was 'terribly at a loss' and just 'stalked off'. After a while he replied with aphorisms, but never did he attempt to answer anyone back. 'I tried to treat it all graciously,' he explained, 'as though everyone who spoke to me even one sentence were my friend.' On one rare occasion, when a stranger on a bus had ostentatiously moved away from him, he piped up, 'If you like, I will get out at the next stop but even people like me cannot walk everywhere.'

If the young Quentin Crisp was reviled by the populace he went down even worse with his fellow deviants. If he entered a homosexual club or pub, there was a deathly silence, a hushed air of resentment. He was distrusted, disliked and even despised by his fellow homosexuals and this coolness, which was to continue all his life, he found 'wounding in the extreme'. Most other homosexuals seem to believe

that Quentin Crisp presented 'an image of homosexuals being homosexual for the sake of the uproar'. Only a few asked kindly, 'D'you
find it helps?' to which he would reply, 'No, I do it for its own
sake.' It could also be argued that Quentin heartily disliked his fellow
deviants. 'The homosexuals I knew in the Thirties were pseudo-women
in search of pseudo-men,' he says sneeringly. There were of course
several separate universes at this time, quite alien to each other and
held apart by a rigorous class system. Quentin was aware of the
existence of the grand, dandified gay circles of the time – 'All London
gossiped about Stephen Tennant when I was young,' he remarked of
a particularly infamous gay aristocrat – but he was not drawn in this
direction, utterly lacked the social-climbing instinct and appeared out
of tune with the way such people carried on. The homosexuals who
inhabited places like the Gargoyle Club might well have thought
Quentin was 'a scream' but he was having none of it. He preferred
the margins of society. He was a loner, he stalked the streets alone,
with the defensive, haughty bearing that eccentrics assume and never
ever attempted to catch a stranger's eye.

But he did have friends. There were visitors or 'faithful friends' at
the room in Denbigh Street and *The Naked Civil Servant* is full of
evidence of his sociable nature. Friends ranged from the female art
students he had met in Battersea and High Wycombe to male prostitutes he had met in the West End. He has nothing to say about the
latter category except that one of them was called Greta – 'on account
of his reverence for Garbo'. There was also an Irish boy whom he
seems to have met at Marble Arch and who would remain a friend
'for a great many years' and a Scottish friend who was a deserter from
the Seaforth Highlanders. And there was a male model, whom he had
also met in Hyde Park, who brought with him a Polish man with an
unpronounceable name, of whom Quentin was to see a lot more in
the future. This group may, or may not, have formed the 'committee'
that helped him choose his new name.

None of these relationships was sexual. Many years later, he would
speak with terrifying detachment about the Scotsman and the Irishman, who may have often called on him only to borrow sixpence,
which of course he never asked to be returned. 'They were quite cosy,

they were quite nice,' he said cautiously. 'They were terribly worried about being seen with me but they were quite nice otherwise.' And although there was no sexual connection between them, Quentin concedes, 'They obviously appealed to my sympathies', and with these and others he may have enjoyed 'romantic flirtations'.

Since he had come to live in London permanently at the age of twenty-two, Quentin had in fact totally abstained from sex. He now looked back on his time 'on the game' as unbelievably sordid. He had decided that 'Sex is the last refuge of the miserable' and 'a dead loss'. Of homosexual intercourse, he says, 'There tends to be something contrived' and his descriptions of any form of sexual activity are severely clinical. About love, he expressed a similar detachment. He no longer sought or respected it and now feared that if he found it he might get stuck in 'the torture chamber of eternal love'. Masturbation was now his only outlet and later described by him as 'a retreat to the dream within the dream'. Of this practice he explained, 'You know what you're doing and you know what you want' and answered the criticism that masturbation was less satisfying to the soul than sexual intercourse with the predictable retort that by now he had abandoned his soul. Yet he looked back on this period as 'the happy time of my life', explaining, 'For one thing your vitality is so incredible if you lead a life of chastity.' But he quickly qualified this remark by adding, 'Mind you, it makes you intolerable to other people' and went on to confess that he was so full of hysterical energy that he was 'always interrupting people'. A couple called the Van Henglers would declare, 'God save us all from Quentin's terrible vitality!'

It is also very clear that Quentin had not adopted his exotic new image in order to attract men sexually. 'The desire was to fulfil a dream,' he said later, 'not to look younger or more desirable.' On the contrary, he knew that he would have been taken up by men if he hadn't looked 'so awful', but the dream was far more important than sex and sex became not only unnecessary but a contradiction. He wanted to be out of reach and would in future wear heavier and heavier make-up partly in order to be rejected, even to avoid being accosted. Or was it because he was rejected that he went so hopelessly over the top and made himself into what the author Michael De-la-

Noy calls 'such a freak show'? Or, worse still, did he adopt his defensive façade because deep down he knew or suspected that he was not lovable and therefore needed to prevent anyone getting to know him too well?

More than thirty years later, Quentin would tell Selina Hastings, 'I'm not really touched by anything, you know the way other people are touched, by children, small animals, and so on. Other people have got natural feelings and reactions. I haven't.' If this is so, it is not surprising that his relationships with other people were difficult. Talking to Philip Mackie, he explained that though he had learnt how to extort admiration, this almost always came tinged with contempt. He was only attractive, he said, to 'devotees of the exotic' and these sometimes included women. In *The Naked Civil Servant* he mentions that an unworldly cousin of the Battersea student, Pat, had once thrown herself on the floor and professed her love for him. Other more dramatic incidents along these lines would follow.

During these formative years Quentin remained in contact with his immediate family. More distant relations may have said 'terrible things' about him and his two older brothers may have been out of the picture in China and Chile but Quentin seems to have seen his mother often. He saw her both in London, where she took on various housekeeping jobs, and in Devon where she now lived with her daughter. At the end of his life, I asked Quentin how his mother and sister had reacted to his elaborate new persona and he replied, 'My mother took it very calmly. My sister hated it.' This divergence was a natural reflection of their different characters, though both were snobbish. Baba Pratt remained flamboyant and dedicated to the arts and the theatre and, according to her granddaughter Frances, had been 'very fashionable' in her day. Quentin's sister Phyllis Payne loved country life, flowers, her terriers and the Mothers' Union. From time to time, Quentin visited them both at the rectory at East Anstey, got on well with his Oxford-educated brother-in-law John Payne and formed a friendship with Payne's sister Helen to whom he sometimes sent specially designed cards. He also made a special drawing, employing mainly straight lines, of a mongrel dog called Walker which belonged to his young niece Frances. According to Frances, Uncle

Denis was introduced to the neighbours but did not actually attend church. Mrs Pratt must have welcomed these visits. She hated living in a country rectory so far from London and would sometimes express her more general discontent with remarks like 'Why do we never have caviar?'

How Quentin got on in his job at the electrical engineers is something that can only be speculated about. He boasts, 'I never once knew what I was doing' but the fact that he remained employed during a time of severe unemployment, combined with everything we know about his self-discipline and artistic talent, would suggest that he was actually very good at his work. In his autobiography he admits that he became sufficiently self-confident to allow his fingernails and hair to grow longer and it was almost certainly through no fault of his own that during the winter of 1932–3 he was given the sack.

The period of Quentin's self-imposed martyrdom which now followed was probably the grimmest and most dramatic. During the next few months, he kept his nerve and pursued his life of gilded squalor, using make-up, painting his 'rotting' toenails and wearing cardboard in his shoes. Without a job, he was obliged to move from Pimlico to a six-shillings-a-week room in Great Percy Circus in Clerkenwell, again discovered by Thumbnails, and sign on at the local Labour Exchange. He has nothing nice to say about Great Percy Circus and characteristically does not mention that it is a lovely little circus built in early Victorian times on a steep slope near King's Cross Station. He only tells us how he would squeeze out of his tiny attic room onto the roof and try to sleep behind the parapet. He has much more to say about the Labour Exchange in Barnsbury Road where he went each week to pick up his 15s 3d dole money. Several pages of his autobiography are devoted to the men who molested him there and whom he 'feared, desired and sentimentalised' and to whom he tried to appear 'mysterious and aloof'. He was unable to work out whether the interest these men showed in him was due to sexual curiosity or hatred. He also writes at length about a particular unpleasant 'skirmish' in Rosebery Avenue when he tried to escape from a mob by taxi. The taxi driver ordered him out of the cab and he was beaten up in front of Finsbury Town Hall. Finally, he managed to cause some genuine amusement among his attackers by remarking, 'I seem to have annoyed you gentlemen in some way.' This incident might be said to complete Quentin Crisp's transition from the posh suburbs to the gutters of central London, and the bravado that underlies his final retort seems a pointer to his future as a professional entertainer.

During these months, he was repeatedly beaten up in the street and collected small scars he would carry for the rest of his life. And his life was tough in other ways too. He was often close to starving, living off chocolate, milk and bread and in 'a trance of malnutrition' that made his friends predict that he would be 'blown away by the first winds of the winter'. He also received many kindnesses. The manager of the Labour Exchange put his hand on Quentin's shoulder and showed him out by a side door with the words, 'I think you're making things very difficult for yourself, but if it ever gets too much you can come to me and I'll see what I can do.' Such a gesture made Quentin think, 'This is the dawn.' When he fainted in an Express Dairy, the manageress carried him downstairs, fed him with her own hand and told him, 'You're an artist, I expect. You don't always remember to have regular meals.' At a diner-restaurant near Euston Station, another manageress supplied him with food she wanted to get rid of, extra helpings of jam roll, then sat down and watched him eat and told him he was 'a real gentleman'.

In fact, Quentin was unemployed for only a short time. Within a few months his mother had prevailed upon the wife of a publisher she had known in Sutton and got her to nag her husband into coercing a printing firm to employ her son in its art department. Here, again, he insists that he was not a success, though the evidence that he was a good employee and an asset to the firm is overwhelming. He liked its directors, did not share the other workers' 'implacable hatred' of the bosses, executed banal drawings 'with the utmost gusto', worked through the night when necessary and according to the head of his department was 'as meek as a bloody lamb'. He remained employed for four years, receiving regular salary increases, and only left, retiring gracefully, when the business was sold.

Towards the end of his time with the firm, he also published his first book. In *The Naked Civil Servant*, he makes no mention of this achievement, perhaps because it doesn't fit in with the hopeless, downtrodden image he seeks to project and perhaps because there were none of the obvious fringe benefits that come from being published. *Lettering for Brush and Pen* appeared in 1936 and was written in conjunction with a certain Albert Frederick Stuart and produced by Beatrix Potter's publishers Frederick Warne. Most of the work may have been done by Mr Stuart but Quentin Crisp's name was on the cover and the book was still in print thirty years later. It is a serious, solemn, dogmatic little manual, only forty-seven pages long, but it is still a book. In the section on 'Modern Forms' the authors state, 'The word "Smith" written in Roman capitals means nothing but written in Neuland it means something solid and resistant; written in Gill Sanserif Bold it means something very practical with a universal appeal; written in Trafton Script it means something exclusive with an appeal to the eye.'

One wonders if Quentin, still only twenty-seven, but growing in boldness, resistance, exclusivity and appeal to the eye – if not yet universal appeal – presented a copy of this book to his mother, or if the hostile tongues among his distant relations were now partly hushed. Mrs Pratt's only criticism of her son at this time was the frequency with which he changed his address. During his time in the printing firm, he did indeed live in many places, and not always alone. Years later he told me he had once lived with a man who cleared his throat – he demonstrated the sound – at least once every half-minute.

One guesses that his life was expanding a little in many directions. In *The Naked Civil Servant*, he has a lot to say about the Polish gentleman who had been brought to his room in Pimlico and his wife, whose name was Denuta Jurand. In the mid-1930s they lived in poverty in a basement flat in Clifton Road, Maida Vale, and Quentin often visited them there. Denuta Jurand – this name was itself assumed – worked as an artist's model both in art schools and privately for painters like Laura Knight and the Marchioness of Queensberry. Her husband could speak five languages but never did any work. Together they offered Quentin another taste of the *vie de bohème* but he was devastated when he learnt the Polish gentleman had run off with Pat, the art student from Battersea, to whom Quentin had introduced him.

In the aftermath of this drama Denuta Jurand took a two-floor flat above a dentist's surgery at 62 Mortimer Street near Oxford Street, and became a nightclub hostess. Quentin moved in with her and used the services of the dentist, J. Slee Tiffin, in a last attempt to make himself into 'a great beauty'. Slee Tiffin fitted a device to straighten Quentin's two front teeth but when the gadget was removed the teeth 'rushed together again' causing Quentin to state, 'I was back where I started.' While in Mortimer Street, Denuta Jurand took on another lodger in the shape of Hilda Ludlow, daughter of Walter Ludlow, vicar of Dulverton on the edge of Dartmoor, a colleague of Quentin's brother-in-law. During her stay in Mortimer Street, Miss Ludlow, who was a drama student at the Old Vic, caused a lot of trouble in the flat but introduced Quentin to various actress friends who would in due course offer him countless free seats at theatrical events.

By this time, Quentin's attitude towards culture was undergoing a transformation. In later life, it suited him to claim that he had never believed in 'true love or high degree or culture' but up to this date Quentin Crisp had in fact read widely and could converse in detail about *Remembrance of Things Past*, which he describes as 'an almost perfect work of art', and other major literary works. As Professor Robinson points out, the text of *The Naked Civil Servant* is 'festooned with literary and philosophical allusions, from Homer to Sartre' and it also includes a compelling comparison between Michelangelo and Rembrandt. 'Michelangelo,' Quentin writes, 'described not the delights of touching or seeing a man but the excitement of being Man. Every stroke he made spoke of the pleasure of exerting, restraining and putting to the utmost use the divine gravity-resisting machine. His work had the opposite quality to the paintings of Rembrandt, into whose canvases the subjects stumble, broken, conscious of their physical faults and begging the beholder for forgiveness.' During the early 1930s, Quentin had already read all the highbrow art papers at a time when the high arts were taken seriously. He had been to trashy films like *King Kong* but he had also gone, in May 1936, to see Peggy Ashcroft in *The Seagull*. Now, he began to shed 'the monstrous aesthetic affectations' of his youth to make way for 'the monstrous philistine postures of middle age'.

During this time of transition, it is appropriate to note that on 11 June 1936, Quentin Crisp was among the hundreds of people who attended the opening of the surrealism exhibition at the stiflingly hot New Burlington Gallery in Bond Street. In his autobiography he describes how 'orange-faced and vermilion-lipped' he clanked past the surrealist artist Sheila Legge, whose face was covered by a hood of roses and in whose hand was an uncooked pork chop. The pictures on show were, he writes, 'akin to the works to which my mother had directed my attention in childhood . . . Victorianism now put in a perverse form'. Quentin's ambition to become an *objet trouvé* in his own right had already been half-fulfilled.

In 1937 Quentin was still working in the printing firm when he left Mortimer Street and moved to a lodging house at 61 Oakley Street near the river in Chelsea. This was his first home in Chelsea and the first place where he had felt at home. 'Everyone has an Oakley Street phase,' I was told thirty-five years later when I moved into a flat of my own in the same street. By that time, the white stuccoed house where Quentin Crisp had lived was being pulled down to make way for a huge block of flats but in 1937 it was apparently a classic lodging house, filled with actors and other stock bedsitting-room characters. Among them, according to the Voters' Register, were individuals with the stagey names of Keith Baxter, Rhoda Blyth, Pamela Cook, Cedric Jones, Pamela Paulet and Margaret Urquhart, which may convey something to someone. An unlisted incumbent was Estelle Murison, whom Quentin describes as a 'tempestuous actress' and who would later describe Quentin as 'like a character in a Victorian children's story, supernatural, supercilious, all-wise', and a regular visitor to the house was Hilda Lumley, a young ballet dancer of whom there is much to say. Surviving friends of Miss Lumley remember her as 'a stocky little woman' and 'an extravagant creature' who accompanied her words with balletic gestures. Quentin Crisp tells us that Miss Lumley had long golden hair and beautiful arms and hands. He also tells us that she had a 'dream in her head that she was a lady' but adds, 'I've no idea whether she was a lady or not.' More about Miss Lumley and her affectations in a moment.

Of life at 61 Oakley Street, Quentin has said, 'It was very, very cosy, very, very nice.' He tells us that he and the other lodgers ran in and out of each other's rooms 'making tea and talking about our futures'. But he was not corrupted or elevated by this first taste of Chelsea life. Living in the same street were Sybil Thorndike, already a dame, and Olivia Manning, later a famous novelist: Quentin knew neither of them. Down on the Embankment was the Pier Hotel, a haunt of the artist Augustus John: Quentin never met him either. In his autobiography he takes pains to emphasize that he never went to a bohemian party and never got drunk. In other words, he continued to walk alone. On one of his excursions he was spotted by Francis King, then a schoolboy out walking with his mother. 'Don't stare,' ordered Mrs King. 'It only encourages them.'

It was while living in Oakley Street in the summer of 1937 that Quentin made his famous dream-like visit to Portsmouth and attracted a great deal of attention from the sailors. He devotes a whole chapter in his book to this episode, which earned a central position in Philip Mackie's film of his life. Surrounded by benign mariners he walked along the seafront and engaged in an eight-hour conversation, the pleasantness of which would haunt him for ever afterwards and which leaves us with the firm impression that Quentin Crisp particularly enjoyed the company of his intellectual inferiors.

During the same summer, Quentin gave up his job in the printing firm – his salary had reached £3 a week – and became a freelance commercial artist or, in his own words, 'a little man round the corner in advertising'. He subsequently argued that people with a peculiar appearance are drawn to working in the artistic field and also wondered if his peculiar appearance may have sometimes helped him to get work. He states that he had no talent and that advertising itself was 'a disgraceful trade' but he seems to have flourished in it. Those working in Fleet Street and Chancery Lane in the late 1930s would have often seen him in the area carrying his 'arm-splitting' portfolio. In his autobiography, he makes much of his impact on receptionists, secretarial staff and office boys and their reactions of 'stark terror', which he invariably met with 'an air of politeness bordering on subservience', but stresses that he was never bullied or insulted by any of his superiors. Indeed, while the junior staff sent him up 'sky high', the bosses often showed genuine charity. Hostility, he says, only came from those who never spoke to him. Again, he is extremely dismissive of the work he did – catalogue covers, letter-headings, leaflets, book jackets, layouts for advertisements – and claims that he only made a 'fitful income'. Does it tell us more about his earning capacity or about his generous nature that in 1937 he was able to lend someone £10, the equivalent today of several hundred pounds, without giving it a thought?

Quentin Crisp later claimed that he was passing from 'muddled youth to self-confident maturity' during this period but his utterances remain as confusing as ever. He turned twenty-nine on Christmas Day 1937 and argues that from that moment on he no longer cared what anyone thought of him. In the same breath, he declares that he worked 'day and night' at making himself more likeable to other people. He adored strangers, like the sailors in Portsmouth, but he kept in touch with his old friends and had been back to Mortimer Street to a breakfast arranged by Denuta Jurand to celebrate her divorce from the Polish gentleman and her engagement to a certain Major Abbott, whom she had met in a nightclub. In *The Naked Civil Servant*, Quentin gives Major Abbott the unflattering name 'Lord Alcohol' but in conversation described him as 'a darling', adding, 'He even put up with me.'

Having given up his full-time job, Quentin Crisp was also free to slap on more and more make-up and for the first time in his life he began to dye his hair. He chose to make it 'screaming red' and explained that hennaed hair is so malleable that he could 'pile it high, like wire'. He wore different make-up in the daytime and night-time and now painted his toenails and fingernails green, black, gold, mother-of-pearl. At the end of each day, he took off his make-up with great care. Again, one wonders why he was doing all this and again one comes back to the view that it was a form of pre-emptive strike. 'As the whole world rejected me more and more,' he told Philip Mackie, 'the make-up became heavier and heavier because this was a self-evident explanation of the rejection.' This sounds very grim and very sad, but he said these words with immense confidence.

What the fellow inhabitants of 61 Oakley Street made of Quentin's dyed hair and other adornments we do not know but his relationship with the household seems to have been volatile. After little over a year, he gave notice and was almost immediately accused by one of his theatrical landlords of stealing money from another lodger. Anyone who knew Quentin in later life would have found this accusation not just preposterous but comic. Even more hilarious was the subsequent suggestion that he had gone and put the money back.

In March 1938, Quentin moved to 9a Chester Square Mews in the heart of Belgravia, by far the grandest address he would ever occupy and only a few yards from where his sometime hero Lady Thatcher resides today. Here lived the ballet dancer Hilda Violet Lumley, whom I can now describe in more detail, at least from the point of view of her new lodger. According to Quentin, Miss Lumley was 'arty, riddled with culture and believed in true love and high degree'. She also 'spoke posh' and would lapse into a foreign accent at the mention of the ballet, but could not spell. According to Quentin, she misused or misspelt a word a day and throughout their long friendship always got his own name wrong, calling him Quintin. And everything she did was mannered. 'Tea,' says Quentin, 'was poured in this wonderful way.' Thirty years later he was still talking about her but had by then rechristened her Miss Lumley Who Can Do No Wrong.

The maisonette they shared in Chester Square Mews still exists. Quentin describes it as 'a huge barn of a place'. The downstairs workshop was occupied by a firm of house decorators called Meadows & Co. and upstairs was a thirty-foot room where Miss Lumley, who had sustained an ankle injury while working for the Diaghilev company, taught dancing. Quentin was given a room at the back for which his friend bought various items of furniture, including a drawing-board. He does not mention that the actor Valentine Dyall, later famous as 'The Man in Black', lived in the same building.

In spite of their different feelings about culture and class Quentin and his landlady got on well and his exotic presence in this sedate area of central London did not, at first, frighten the horses. He was occasionally stopped by the police but had no problems buying his make-up from the local chemist, who 'understood the whole racket'. At home he stayed discreetly in his room when Miss Lumley was giving a class and even started giving tap-dancing lessons himself, though the amateurish bangings and crashings would cause 'clearly audible curses' from the workshop below. On the downstairs door, he gave himself three names: Denis Pratt, Quentin Crisp and – for some peculiar reason – Lawrence Arkell. The purpose behind this assortment of names is unclear but at least it gave amusement to one caller who, on finding Quentin not at home, declared, 'All the firm were out.'

Under the name Quentin Crisp he was soon to produce another book, this time single-handedly. *Colour in Display* appeared in October 1938 and was a manual on window-dressing, thirty thousand words in length and containing five colour plates. He was paid £60 for his trouble and it was published by the Blandford Press for whom he had often designed dust-jackets. Its title has definite undertones and the poet James Kirkup has suggested that the book holds clues as to how Quentin wished to display himself. Its text is predictably dictatorial but contains a few bits of traditional Crisperanto. He refers to 'the slough of artistic enlightenment' and 'shameful excursions into the world of design' and at one point he asserts, 'Colour is like style. It is only when it is good that one does not notice it.'

The other significant thing that happened during Quentin Crisp's stay in Belgravia was that his seven years of happy celibacy came to an end. On his way home one night he was picked up in Sloane Street by a forty-five-year-old man he describes as 'rather highly placed in one of the ministries' and later portrays as 'infinitely urbane' and 'infinitely cautious'. Why did he embark on this 'very dismal affair'? The only explanation he offers is that he was now thirty years old and that, around this age, 'most people make a few desperate efforts to see if there was anything that they missed out'. Talking about this affair in later life, Quentin said that 'the Man from the Ministry' found his way of carrying on 'a terrible burden' and that this made the whole thing 'slightly sad, pale, wan, forlorn'. A further strain was put on their relationship when Quentin received a visit from the police in response to complaints from neighbours that they could see what was going on in his room. No charges were made but he was warned that the activities that had been observed risked a penalty of seven years' imprisonment. The Man from the Ministry was horrified to hear of this visit but the strange bishop-and-chorus-girl relationship continued for several years.

How Quentin spent the last summer of peacetime is unrecorded. I know that one day he was visited by officials from the Ministry of Employment and, perhaps in an effort to make himself more employable in the event of war, told them he was five years younger than he was. I also know that he spent a week with his sister Phyllis and her family at a rented bungalow at Walcott on the Norfolk coast. To squeeze everyone in, Quentin's brother-in-law John Payne had to sleep in a tent in the garden. One night there was a thunderstorm and Quentin's seven-year-old niece Frances woke up believing that the war had come.

– 8 –

A Frenetic Melancholy

Soon after this, I met Philip O'Connor distributing
leaflets on Putney Common – a quick ready youth
with a fine hungry face and a shock of obsidian curls.
We were both of us living alone at that time, scribbling
poetry in neighbouring streets, so for a while we
visited each other quite often, establishing a defensive
minority of two. To me, he had an adolescent mystery
about him, a frenetic melancholy, like a school-boy
Hamlet; and his poems were the most extravagant
I'd read until then, rhapsodic eruptions of surrealist
fantasy.

LAURIE LEE, *As I Walked Out One
Midsummer Morning*, 1969

Philip O'Connor had left school in January 1933 aged sixteen. His
mother was not particularly surprised to find the truant on her doorstep and may even have been quite pleased by this show of independence. His long-suffering guardian on the other hand was
understandably angry and disappointed. Camden Field had looked
after the boy for eight years and had plans, he said, to send him to
university.

Even now, however, he was apparently willing to give Philip another
chance. The boy said he wanted to become a writer and Mr Field,
who stayed on in the Wimbledon flat until the war, said he would
make him an allowance of twenty-five shillings a week. A room was
taken in the house in Dorking where his English teacher Miss

Allsworth lived, and with her encouragement he started work on what he describes as an autobiography. Miss Allsworth also took an interest in what Philip calls his 'dawning vagabondage' and was only too happy to drive him up to Box Hill and leave him there for the night with only a bar of chocolate for sustenance.

Philip's bizarre character and erratic writing, one may safely assume, flowed into each other. Like other teenagers, he wanted cars, women and film-star's clothing. But he also aspired to be 'an active revolutionary'. At school, he had established himself as a gesticulating exhibitionist with a pathological fear of privacy and messianic tendencies, and his personality now began its 'menacing rise' towards a 'plaster monumentalism' that would stand comparison with Quentin Crisp's carefully created 'plaster cast'. Underneath these 'grotesqueries', he admits to 'a profound maladjustment' and 'a mind like a haystack in a gale, only now and then manageable under a rapidly applied canvas covering, with almost no sense of direction'. This was to remain the case: for the whole of his life Philip O'Connor was 'on the move', without direction and dependent on the ministrations and interventions of others. It is hardly surprising to learn that his first attempts at autobiography were a disappointment to him. When a literary agent suggested that bits of it needed rewriting, he threw it all away in disgust and despair. The failure weighed heavily on him, however, and the long-drawn-out birth of *Memoirs of a Public Baby*, which did not appear for another twenty-five years, is painful to contemplate, though such delays are not unknown on the wilder shores of literary life. A quarter of a century also intervened between my own first attempts at a novel and its eventual publication. Some authors learn their trade very slowly and even then may retain only a feeble grasp of their talent.

In Philip's case, he was now diverted by the illness of his mother. By 1934, Winifred O'Connor had moved into the basement at 20 Cork Street in the West End of London. The building was then known as the Burlington Hotel but a few years later its ground floor and basement became the home of the Redfern Gallery, which is still there today. Philip has written of the 'private shrubbery' of his mother's 'little encampment', which included Desirée and the still tenderly attentive Haslam Jackson. But Winnie O'Connor was now suffering from cancer of the womb and receiving treatment at St George's Hospital at Hyde Park Corner. In a private room there, she told Philip she was getting better and refused to be operated on. She was sent home to Cork Street to die.

In the face of this impending crisis, Philip, now aged seventeen, moved into the basement to be with his mother to the end. Finally, one night, he made peace with her and she told him that a gypsy had predicted he would one day be famous. The following day, 29 April 1934, she died aged fifty-four in the arms of Uncle Haslam, in a pose which strengthened Philip's presumption that there was an intimacy between them. In his autobiography, Philip vulgarly compares the look in his mother's eyes with that of Dolores Costello in the Orson Welles film *The Magnificent Ambersons*. The death certificate was signed by a distinguished specialist at St George's, Dr John Petro, who many years later would be at the centre of a quite different drama, of his own making.

In *Memoirs of a Public Baby*, Philip reports that Haslam Jackson was now hopeless with misery, having been robbed of the most important person in his life. He was very kind to Philip and somehow understood the boy's desire not to attend his mother's burial. This did not take place at Highgate, beside the grave of Karl Marx, as Philip later liked to claim, but in the less salubrious Streatham Common Cemetery in South London. Here the story of Winifred O'Connor might have ended were it not for the extraordinary pressure that her unresolved and undeveloped relationship with her son would exert on him until his own dying day. For ever after, Philip O'Connor would refer to 'my great love, my dead mother' and seek a replacement for her in both men and women.

During the summer of 1934, Philip gave up his room in Dorking and, still supported by Camden Field, moved to one by the river in Putney. Close by lived Madge, an Irish woman who had befriended him on Box Hill. With her, Philip made 'literary talk'. In his own room, he started producing – on Woolworth shelf paper – 'entangled and incoherent' philosophical musings and also verse, composed in a private language consisting of 'a purely phonetic rendering of animal and baby sounds'. While writing this stuff, he often became so excited that his mouth was drenched with saliva. To face what he describes as the 'terrors' of Putney High Street, he gingered up a sense of his own greatness by repeatedly playing Pagliacci's *On with the Motley* on a wind-up gramophone and then pushing, screwing or clenching up his jaw into Mussolinian dimensions before venturing out.

On an outing to distribute leaflets, presumably of his own making, on Putney Common, he met the nineteen-year-old poet Laurie Lee, who had just arrived in London from the West Country. Laurie Lee had a snug room above a café in Lower Richmond Road and, in order to save up enough money to tramp around Spain, was working on a building site pushing barrels of wet cement. One cannot imagine O'Connor in such a role but the two young men got on well. Both were scribbling poetry in their separate rooms. I have quoted from Laurie Lee at the beginning of this chapter and he goes on to say that Philip O'Connor was his first contact with the literary world. When he visited the room above the café, Philip would lie on the bed 'switching his dark eyes on and off' and 'reciting his latest verses in clear cold tones, snappy and rather bitter'. On his part Philip claims that Lee suffered from 'a more sober version' of his own condition and – here comes a typical O'Connor rebuttal – was 'on the trail of professionalism'.

Later in 1934, O'Connor also excited the interest or sympathy of Aldous Huxley, to whom 'in a spirit of vulgar ambition' he had sent some of his poems. The author of *Brave New World*, published two years earlier, had returned O'Connor's offerings with kindly comments and Mallarmé's advice that poetry is written with words not feelings. Philip cannot have liked this advice but the two soon had tea together in Huxley's newly acquired rooms at E2 Albany and later at his studio over a garage in St Albans Place, Lower Regent Street. Huxley, who was then about forty years old, walked round the teenage O'Connor 'as round an object of some interest'. When they strolled together up the Haymarket in the yellow evening fog, Huxley in wide-brimmed period hat suddenly forcefully reminded Philip of his mother.

Other friends and acquaintances at this time were less distinguished. Among them was a dingily dandified homosexual called Arber-Cooke, whom Philip had first met in Wimbledon and who wore a cloak, a sombrero and – echoes of Quentin Crisp – 'much ill-applied cosmetics'. Early in 1935 this man introduced Philip to an odd organization called the Society for Creative Psychology, whose premises at 8 Fitzroy Street were to constitute his first foothold in Fitzrovia – and a distinguished one at that: Sickert had worked in the same building thirty years earlier and Duncan Grant and Vanessa Bell had long shared a studio at the back. Philip subsequently described the society as 'very suspect', claiming that it was largely homosexual and that its members were 'hard-bitten aesthetes, painters and other crackpots'. He might also have stated that they were pioneers, many years ahead of their time, of the practice of group therapy, but Philip was rarely interested in the fuller picture. The 'president' of the society was Basil Beaumont and its 'general secretary' Captain Herbrand Williams MC. In *Memoirs of a Public Baby*, Philip O'Connor has a lot to say about the latter figure, who was a second cousin of Winston Churchill. He had a deadly white, plump face, and a small cherry-red mouth and 'lectured like a soft fondant from the depths of a tobacco-coloured chair, the light arranged with artful discretion above his head'. Billy Williams, as he was known, took an immediate interest in eighteen-year-old O'Connor and let out 'little feminine yelps' whenever he appeared. And though Philip scoffed at the society and its proceedings, he also acknowledges that it encouraged him to take a further dive into 'unconsciousness' or 'automaticism'. It also encouraged him to paint. This, he said, he did 'appallingly'.

To some extent, Billy Williams replaced Camden Field in O'Connor's life. His old guardian had now, he reports, stopped his allowance and 'washed his hands' of him. Philip's sister Desirée had also 'hardened' though she was willing to let him stay in her new flat. Since Winifred O'Connor's death the previous year, Desirée and Haslam Jackson had, in Philip's uncharitable words, 'conspired to better themselves'. In the mid-1930s, Haslam Jackson's fortunes and morale had revived and he had even tidied himself up enough to get involved in a magazine called *Natural Health*, which would be followed by a monthly trade magazine called *Perfumery and Toiletry*. Desirée had worked on both magazines, selling advertising space and enjoying the free samples of scent. Haslam Jackson and Desirée now lived together in a third-floor flat at 7 Craven Hill, an imposing semi-stuccoed building in Bayswater, a few minutes' walk from Hyde Park. Here Philip was given a room, with a mattress on the floor, in return for some household duties which he moodily performed. While washing up he would dream about his mother and trace sad lines in the suds to represent the road in Wimereux he had once walked upon. From time to time, his sister would nag him to get a job or 'trot' him out as a 'freak' to meet her friends. Under these pressures, his resentment was steadily increasing and by the summer of 1935 he had built up a sufficient 'tigerish determination' to break into the gas meter at Craven Hill and make off with the proceeds.

Philip had long wanted to be a tramp: he had enjoyed his nights sleeping rough on Box Hill and his wanderings around London, even when they only consisted of amblings through Mayfair on warm summer evenings. Tramping and his thoughts about it were to become a central feature of Philip O'Connor's life and work, and he would embark on various tramping expeditions in the course of his life.

His five months on the road which began with the gas meter break-in were his first actual experience of tramping and in writing about it he stressed positive aspects. When he set off, he was only eighteen years old. It was summertime. He believed tramping was a pilgrimage, a way of finding his 'true self' and 'the truth' at the same time. He had always, he says, preferred the country to the town – the opposite of Quentin Crisp – liked being on the move, and being liberated from washing, changing his clothes and all the 'gymnastics' of social life. The hunger and wretchedness were part of the appeal. Tramping, he explained, 'pulls one back centuries' and awoke in him the most basic, old-fashioned emotions about food and shelter. In his book *Vagrancy*, O'Connor writes of 'the sheer debauchery of a cup of tea' enjoyed on the road. He also liked and admired his fellow tramps and the 'spiritual finesse' that underlay their grossness. He saw Lear, Tolstoy and Christ in them, symbols of the Holy Pilgrim and the Incorruptible Soul. In tramps, he noted an absence of all 'tartiness', 'meanness of gesture' and other vices of the employed man, and in their company he felt more normal, sharing their dislike of employment and their hostility to strangers to such a degree as to make him a 'natural' man of the road. He was also 'moved and thrilled' by the distance and space that the tramp occupied, the image of 'one man under the sky' and the transformation of the environment from a vagrant viewpoint. While tramping, Philip found that trees and fences became 'loquacious', full of personality, and that houses began to resemble theatrical scenery and their occupants seemed 'jerky and doll-like'. In later life, he claimed that he was 'a chronic physical coward, terrified of brutality, policemen, authorities and dogs', which gives an extra edge of fear to his time on the road: he also boasted that he was sometimes chased by homosexuals. He seems to have had no objection to overtures from other tramps – 'I attempted to comply but the machinery was not suitable,' he writes of one such encounter – but was scared stiff of 'tweedy gentlemen with caps and sports cars'.

In *Memoirs of a Public Baby*, he reveals few of the practicalities of his 1935 tour and only a little of its geography. To start with, he set off for the Surrey hills, the only bit of rural England that he knew and already the focus of those nostalgic longings he felt for all the places where he'd lived. From here, he walked on to Winchester, Portsmouth and Plymouth. The money he had stolen from his sister's gas meter soon ran out but an unidentified 'friend' promised to send him six shillings a week. On this he headed north where from 'some big town' he wrote to Haslam Jackson asking for the fare home. When this reached him, he used it to travel on to Ireland. After a few days in Dublin he began to feel mad, tried to get into a mental hospital but settled for a workhouse and then finally fell onto the mercies of the Salvation Army. Haslam Jackson was again persuaded to send him the fare home and a few days or weeks later he was back in his sister's flat in Bayswater.

These adventures, Philip writes, had augmented his self-esteem but he soon returned to 8 Fitzroy Street and the rather frightening clutches of the lush Captain Williams. Billy Williams's next move was to invite O'Connor to stay with him in Cambridge, where he kept a sort of 'ashram' of young male misfits in the process of becoming medical students. To finalize these arrangements, Williams visited Desirée O'Connor and Haslam Jackson at the flat in Craven Hill. In the taxi taking them there, Philip studied his fat, sensuous benefactor, some twenty years his senior, and his aura of 'erratically luxurious prosperity' and was again reminded of his mother. Desirée O'Connor may have considered Billy Williams a doubtful figure and very likely a homosexual but was perhaps won over by the fact that he was the great-grandson of a duke. It was soon agreed that Philip should spend the next four months with him in a lodging house in some way attached to Peterhouse, Cambridge, and, according to Philip, permeated by sexual oddness.

Philip tells us that his own ideas about sex were 'still vague'. He writes that he had not yet distinguished 'between sexual warmth and affection proper' and as we have seen he had already enjoyed the attention of various male figures, some of whom were homosexuals. For the whole of his life, he seemed to teeter near a sort of sexual borderline but the connection between him and Billy Williams was not so much sexual as a bond between two incurably babyish types. Setting off together by taxi for King's Cross en route to Cambridge, Philip was reminded 'terribly' of going off to France with his mother. Captain Herbrand Williams MC released in Philip a 'social age' of about four. Philip had already done a huge amount of thinking but still felt 'ridiculously infantile'. This was perhaps his most particular quirk and one that he would never relinquish.

But how perceptive was he under this childish disguise? Looking back on Billy Williams, Philip offers us a succulently three-dimensional portrait of an extraordinarily creepy man, but is it any more accurate than the one-dimensional impressions Quentin Crisp serves up of his acquaintances during the same period? We know that the relationship between Williams and O'Connor slowly deteriorated, especially when the older man began to make 'oblique advances', and that on one occasion, Philip fled the Cambridge house in his pyjamas and stayed by a nightwatchman's fire till dawn, but we know less about the more positive aspects of their relationship.

Philip sometimes claimed that Billy Williams rather than Camden Field introduced him to the pleasures of drink but has also acknowledged that he encouraged him in 'the more mature, self-respecting inflations' which were to stand him in good stead later, as well as introducing him to a number of congenial and gifted young men with whom he was to form close, long-lasting friendships. One of these was a medical student called Heinz Wolff, who was both fascinated and frightened by him. Another was Patrick de Maré, who was to become Philip's most long-standing friend and admirer and who is still alive and working as I write these words.

The son of a rich Swedish timber broker, Pat de Maré had in his own words 'everything money could buy'. Born in 1916, he was the same age as Philip and had been sent to school at Wellington and gone up to Peterhouse in 1934 to study medicine, later qualifying as a psychiatrist. On meeting Philip he was bowled over by his looks, his aura of freedom, his real wildness, and more than sixty years later, would speak about him with playful, gushing ease unusual in a psychiatrist. 'He was incredibly good-looking. He was like what you imagine Saint John was like. A beard, long hair – and not all that clean! He really *was* a public baby.' But it was Philip's mind as much as his manner which enthralled him. 'He would come and entertain our group and just talk. And we'd sit entranced. I mean, honestly, when he got going, he was just totally brilliant in his commentary. It was just riveting to listen to him. He was super-articulate.' The only flaw from de Maré's point of view was Philip's obsessive class-consciousness which he describes as 'rather clichéd, actually'. Everything else about him, especially his poetry, was 'pretty authentic'.

The relationship between Philip and de Maré came close to love. 'He did love me,' says de Maré. 'We loved each other in a funny way. There was a warmth between us. We saw eye to eye. We found we were thinking the same thing. We shared the same deep-seated cynicism. I almost gave up medicine and went off with him, bummed around Ireland.' This didn't happen – but de Maré did introduce Philip to his parents who lived in some splendour in Holland Villas Road, West London. 'My mother absolutely adored him. He went up to her at a party in the house and said, "You look like a terrified tit on a frozen wire" and she was overwhelmed, entranced and horrified.' De Maré also remembers that a Swedish maid at the house found a filthy handkerchief under Philip's pillow and was reduced to tears. Writing to de Maré at the end of his life, Philip claimed that the main thing that they had shared in those early days was 'a wild and lovely ignorance of authority'.

Philip's wildness was now his most striking characteristic. Back in London in the summer of 1936 and again living uncomfortably in his sister's flat, he was drawn more forcibly towards the chaos of Fitzrovia and a sort of fashionable madness. Billy Williams had allowed him to sleep sometimes in the society's studio but now began to find him a nuisance and would yelp even louder when he appeared. In private, Philip would launch into furious war-dances and shriek with maniacal laughter. In public, he would perform the 'most pathetic inflations', aping the manners of the cultured classes and discussing books he had scarcely skimmed through with 'blackmailing omnipotence'.

During those summer months he struck out in other directions. He began to give messianic performances at Speaker's Corner and was photographed there in borrowed red trousers and bobbed hair. Like Quentin Crisp, he sought the public's attention and then complained bitterly when people stared at him. He made an exception for a seventeen-year-old Scottish-Greek girl who looked at him invitingly from his Hyde Park audience. They quickly made friends and, in the studio at 8 Fitzroy Street, became lovers. Here they lived together for a while, stealing jam from Craven Hill when things were bad and earning a few pence or shillings by selling Philip's watercolours to a local Fitzrovian junk dealer named Mendelson, who had premises in Rathbone Place off Oxford Street.

Philip was also, inevitably, drawn to the surrealism movement, which was now 'percolating' through London. Condoning lack of technique in both poetry and paint, the movement had an obvious appeal for him, though its leaders, photographed together at the time of the Burlington Gallery exhibition, struck him as 'straightforwardly criminal, from pickpocket-ish to murderous'. Whether he attended the great opening party on 11 June 1936 and thus crossed paths with Quentin Crisp is a matter for earnest speculation.

What is certain is that Philip was getting odder in his behaviour. The relationship with the Scottish-Greek girl had soon petered out and he now wandered about London often not knowing where he was or where to go. When this sense of disorientation became unbearable, he decided to go with his 'cargo of strangeness' to Basil Beaumont, the so-called president of the Society for Creative Psychology. Beaumont consulted Billy Williams and the pair of them then whisked their twenty-year-old protégé by taxi to the Maudsley Hospital in Denmark Hill. Here, Captain Williams went down on his knees, clasped his hands together and successfully begged Dr Walter Maclay to admit his young friend. Philip claimed later to have detected a masonic handshake between the two men. The date of this historic or histrionic event was 21 September 1936.

Was Philip mad? Certainly many people have thought so at different times in his life, though Michael Hamburger, who met him during the war and became a lifelong friend, evades the issue by saying he does not believe in madness. Philip himself claims to have 'dabbled' in madness and spoke obliquely of the 'amateurs in the stalls of this unhappy theatre'. At more flamboyant moments he boasted that he only entered the Maudsley because he had nowhere to live and nothing to eat. Certainly there were times when the Maudsley made him *feel* mad, though he never accepted the label of schizophrenic which was soon given to him. Archivists at the hospital now look upon Philip O'Connor as 'a legend' and share his view that Beaumont and Williams were 'decidedly odder' than himself and part of 'rather a louche crowd' that hung around the Maudsley at this time.

The Maudsley's records are not normally made available but since Philip O'Connor went so 'public' about his time there, this rule has been waived. From the meagre and amateurish notes available, we learn that he was admitted to the hospital on the vague grounds that he 'was said to have been behaving in a peculiar way and his friends were afraid of what he might do next'. He was also said to have made 'no attempt to earn his own living' and to have had 'suicidal tendencies since the age of fourteen'. His condition was said to be 'dirty and dishevelled', with very long hair which he refused to have cut, but in other respects he was apparently 'friendly and co-operative, appearing to wonder why so much trouble was being made'. The only off-note concerned the patient's descriptions of his bodily feelings, which were said to be 'bizarre and abnormal'.

Philip's own accounts of six months in the Maudsley are more exhilarating. He describes it as 'a proper kind of palace for my kind of monarch' and during his incarceration seems to have been immune to the outside world. He makes no mention of the abdication crisis which occurred in November of that year though the same month he did witness the burning of the Crystal Palace from a balcony. On the whole, he was allowed to do as he pleased, particularly painting, drawing, writing and reading, and the pills he was given gave him enjoyably erotic sensations in the throat and elsewhere. He had mixed feelings about the medical staff. He liked a doctor called Hunter, who struck him as 'a decent-seeming fellow, humble' but detested one called Sargeant whom he described as 'bad and stupid'. Those he hated he treated with as much contempt as his features could express – he now had formidable skills in this area – and in the face of their probings developed 'little frills of manic mystery' which, he says, took many years to shed.

The various pencil, charcoal and crayon drawings that Philip O'Connor produced during his stay are not as 'appalling' as he makes out. Even to my untrained eye, they seem stronger and more precise than the wishy-washy embarrassments he produced with such pleasure and good humour in later life. One of his Maudsley pictures consists of an arrangement of well plotted abstract shapes over which he has written the word FOOL in various colours and sizes. He later claimed that a picture called *Apparition* and attributed to Otto Stein, now in the Prinzholm Collection at Heidelberg, was actually drawn by him in the Maudsley.

The most significant thing that happened during these six months was that Philip O'Connor produced his first published poetry. In *Memoirs of a Public Baby*, he claims that writing these verses was far more important for him than publishing them and that they made him feel he had woken from a long sleep and was at last fully alive and modern. Did he send them to Geoffrey Grigson, an editor said to be interested in the 'labours of the mad', or did some third party interpose themselves? Somehow or other, they found their way into the February–March 1937 issue of Grigson's *New Verse* and Philip was astounded that they were taken 'seriously': he places this word, like many others he uses, in inverted commas. In *New Verse* they appeared under the title 'Several Poems' but they were later republished under the title 'Captain Busby'. Many years later these verses – Gavin Ewart calls them a 'surrealist poem which actually worked' – would become the inspiration for a short film in which Quentin Crisp and Philip O'Connor played leading roles.

Philip's time in the Maudsley was later invested with the usual nostalgic conceits but it was not quite such a wonderful interlude as he sometimes makes out. While there, he suffered a nightmarish recollection of Madame Tillieux's daughter Jeanette entering the *salle à manger* at Wimereux with the cockerel whose neck she had wrung. He also spent a lot of time worrying that his sister Desirée, who had technically taken over responsibility for him and whom the hospital authorities had marked down as 'inclined to be excitable', might compel him into a mode of life on his release that would not suit him.

Luckily, this did not happen. When Philip O'Connor left the Maudsley in March 1937, some two months after his official discharge, he seems to have felt a great deal more confident in himself. He even claims that the hospital had transformed him into a grubby, conventional 'intellectual'. Poetry was now his claim to fame and the justification or excuse for his absurdities. A few months later, Geoffrey Grigson, who had paid him thirty shillings for his first effort and expressed surprise that so cynical a writer could be only twenty years old, published Philip's poem 'Blue Bugs in Liquid Silk', which reads as follows:

blue bugs in liquid silk
talk with correlation particularly like
two women in white bandages

a birdcage swings from the spleen of ceiling frowning her soul in
large wastes
and a purple sound purrs in basket-house
putting rubies on with red arms

enter the coalman in a storm of sacks
holding a queenly egg-cup

the window stares and thinks separately her hair impartially
   embankment
to the flood of her thought in motionless torrent
roundly looking the ladies

there is no formula for disruption of pink plaster
or emotions to bandage the dead

Whatever one makes of this clever mixture, Philip O'Connor's arrival on the poetical scene certainly had some impact and, during the next few years, almost all the avant-garde magazines seemed happy to regard him and his startling, misshapen sentences as a find.

Philip says that he took naïve pleasure in everything he wrote, its 'complexity, adroitness, pertinence', but also worked with extreme rapidity, rarely spending more than half an hour on a poem and sometimes not even bothering with a second draft. He shot his efforts off to editors, for whom, according to Stephen Spender, he felt 'a kind of dazed contempt' when they were accepted for publication. Or was it all a smokescreen? Some people see this period as Philip O'Connor's golden age but the quality of his work remains controversial. In later life, the poetry editor Tambimuttu, whose personal life would soon become entangled with Philip O'Connor's, complained that 'no real ocean of thought' lay underneath O'Connor's 'glittering surface'. In his introduction to *Memoirs of a Public Baby*, Spender writes of the goodness and badness of Philip's poems, praises 'the concentration of original observations and vivid hallucinations' but depicts them as 'off-throwings' and 'just cuttings of Philip O'Connor's inner life'. A. T. Tolley, author of *The Poetry of the Thirties*, writes of O'Connor's 'strange unschooled vision' and explains that his 'unusual temperament' and 'weird upbringing' disqualified him from seeing the world as one should if one wants to fit into it, yet describes the poems as 'startling and original' and O'Connor as 'a poet whose work might at first seem as strangely surrealist as any poetry in English'. Tolley concludes by saying that Philip O'Connor's poems suffer from 'limited range of tone' and often seem to be 'the raw material for poems rather than the finished works'. But then he adds that this 'is probably part of the intended effect'.

Philip is much harder on his work than either of these critics. Though daring to describe his poems as 'whispering to God', he downgrades them as 'the mess of my having collided with my head against the brick wall of society's guardians' and as 'a shock-spill of sensations and thoughts in surrealist disarray'. He continued to be surprised that they were taken seriously but grudgingly concedes that some of them contained lines which 'weren't bad'. The fact that he hoped and needed to make money from his poems allowed him to describe them as 'mountebankery' and 'middle-class concoctions'.

This excess of modesty about his poems did not lead him to think that he should undertake any other work or prevent him from feeling 'as wonderful as possible' about his small success. This was now the golden age of surrealism and Philip O'Connor saw himself as 'a legitimate freak in the surrealist school'. During the months that followed his emergence from the Maudsley, Philip played the part of the poet with gusto and remained in 'a state of sometimes shameful invalidism, increasingly nervous and erratic'. Like other insecure individuals, he continued to spend a lot of time looking at himself in the mirror, practising expressions of 'sterling honesty', 'rough nobility', 'luscious disgust' and 'homosexual insinuation'. He then carried his 'fraud-killing scowls' and 'façade-shattering penetration' out with him onto the streets. Does it make the picture more complicated if I add that several of those who knew him at this time shared Patrick de Maré's view that he was also 'very beautiful' and that he accepted this verdict on the dubious grounds that beauty is only a reflection of intelligence? Underneath it all, he confesses, there was 'an immense disparity between what I knew and what I said'.

It is not clear where he lived during the summer of 1937 but the publication of his poems had certainly increased his social opportunities. That streak of vulgarity which had drawn him to Aldous Huxley would soon make him welcome the friendship of the poets Charles Madge and Kathleen Raine, especially when they invited him to stay with them at Grotes Buildings in Blackheath. This illustrious couple were 'very kind' to him – Kathleen Raine called him 'a good devil' – and did not ask him to take an interest in the Mass Observation project then being founded at their home. Instead they suggested that he should go to the local zoo and write about the animals there. The same vulgar streak caused him to gatecrash a party to mark William Empson's departure for China and perform other acts of 'minor literary entrepreneurship'.

For a while Philip kept his distance from women by retreating into 'winsome childishness' – though he saw a lot of male friends like de Maré, not yet qualified as a psychiatrist but soon to have his own studio at 8 Fitzroy Street, and a painter called Gordon Cruikshank, whom he describes as 'the first man I had considerable respect for'. After three weeks with the Madges, he stayed for a while with Cruikshank at Brecknock Studios in Kentish Town and attended surrealist meetings in Hampstead. According to his *Memoirs*, Philip had a violent argument with the obstreperous Belgian artist E. L. T. Mesens, and walked out of a talk by the critic and poet Herbert Read, who was later to become one of his patrons. Sometime that year he also met Stephen Spender for the first time, though he carefully points out he was never a friend 'in the personal sense', and it may have been at this time that he popped out from behind a door or round a street corner and said *Boo* to T. S. Eliot. Philip never denied this story and justified his behaviour on the grounds that the famous poet 'needed taking down a peg'.

Around this time he also met the poet Paul Potts, who needed taking *up* a peg. Potts was five years older than Philip but equally incapable of earning a conventional living – on the day they met Philip had been reduced to living in a basement lavatory – and equally hysterical in his own way. The two men hit it off very well to start with but Philip's initial warmth towards the so-called People's Poet – in an early unpublished draft of *Memoirs of a Public Baby* he admits he loved him – was later obliterated by cruelty. Potts's enthusiasm for Philip lasted much longer. In his memoir *Dante Called You Beatrice*, he wrote, 'He was the first real friend of my life. Until I met him, I had never liked anyone that much before.' According to Potts's biographer Mark Holloway, Paul 'fell in love with Philip'. He wanted someone he could trust and confide in, saw Philip as 'a hopeful field' and would treasure his memories of him. According to Soho veteran Stephen Fothergill, Potts was 'terribly impressed by Philip and loved him deeply'. When I met the impressively dome-headed and famously malodorous People's Poet in the 1970s, he simply said of O'Connor, 'I just fell for him.' We will soon see why the friendship was doomed.

During the remains of 1937 Philip continued to produce and publish poetry, trudge for sixpences and live off doughnuts, tea and Woodbines. From time to time he painted more 'slobbering' pictures which he sold to the untidy Mr Mendelson, tellingly renamed Messier in his *Memoirs*. He also roamed the streets in what he describes as an unconscious search for a female companion. This domestic quest drew him more and more into Fitzrovia which he now saw as 'a national garbage centre' full of uprooted people leading a life of pretence, and 'babies' like himself who prattled themselves 'into worlds of great achievements'.

Fitzrovia has already featured in this book. By 1937, there were innumerable writers and painters living and working in the area – not all unsuccessful – and there were plenty of restaurants, pubs and cafés to cater for their needs. I do not propose to offer a history of the Fitzrovian phenomenon and all its pitfalls, which has been adequately done elsewhere. I only need to record that sometime towards the end of 1937 Philip O'Connor, now aged twenty-one, saw a girl called Jean Hore, then aged twenty-four, crossing Charlotte Street and heading for a pub. In *Memoirs of a Public Baby*, he tells us he immediately followed her – their first words are forgotten – and invited her to the Society for Creative Psychology's rooms at 8 Fitzroy Street where he was then staying.

Will I confuse the reader if I mention that I had a cousin with exactly the same name as the girl in the street, though her surname contained an 'a'? My Jean Hoare was a sporting spinster type with a loud voice. The Jean Hore in this story looked like a young Virginia Woolf and a little like Augustus John's cello-player. Everything about her, writes Philip, was focused or 'sculpted' in her hands, which were 'slim, beautiful, brilliantly articulated, seeking and useless'. They lay 'like forlorn deer on the grass'. These impressions are vividly reinforced by the recollections of Paul Potts, who met Jean Hore a few months later and in a reckless, unreciprocated way, also fell in love with her. 'She looked like Our Lady's younger sister in a painting by Botticelli,'

Potts wrote in *A House with No Address*. 'Her hands were as marvellous as St Francis of Assisi's. She had a face a bit like Shelley and the body of a Chinese empress.' Only her eyes excited controversy. Patrick de Maré describes them as 'anguished'. Philip calls them 'imperturbably serene'.

The details of Jean Hore's past are more prosaic. She was born in Edinburgh on 6 August 1913, daughter of a lawyer who had inherited money. Both her parents had died in influenza epidemics when she was young and she had been brought up partly by her aunt, Mrs Beatrice Thorburn, of Peebles, and partly by a guardian in Edinburgh called Gavin Allardyce. I learnt these facts from the records of St Felix's School, Southwold, where Jean Hore was a pupil between 1927 and 1934. There was also a brother Henry Sinclair Hore, of whom Philip O'Connor never made any mention, and a cousin Colin Cowan, seven years her junior, who remembers Jean not only as 'very kind, very sweet and emotional – and a *real* beauty' but also as 'very disorganized and prone to tantrums'. From Philip's autobiography we learn that Jean had read English and History at Newnham College, Cambridge. Here she was apparently 'a good mixer', who stirred things up. Patrick de Maré who had been at Cambridge at the same time did not know Jean Hore but gathered that she was 'brilliant'. He also claims that she 'had already become very strange before she met Philip'. Anyway, she had left Newnham in 1936, come to London with 'a thirst for life' and set up house in Bloomsbury where according to her cousin she was 'liberal with her favours' and surrounded by people Philip described as 'smart alecs' anxious to help her spend her fortune. From here she had made her way into the more chaotic world of Fitzrovia.

When Philip O'Connor first saw her, he was bowled over. He later confessed that he knew she had money from that first moment. A more compelling factor was that Philip still hungered for someone like his mother and found in Jean a wealth of similarities: 'the authentic refinement', 'an ideal of delicacy' and many other qualities. 'She was as private as I,' he soon discovered. She had 'incorruptible loyalty', no sense of property, a hatred of injustice and a reckless desire to help those in trouble. Her character, he confesses in *Memoirs of a Public*

Baby, dovetailed neatly into his own well established parasitical nature. Her passivity was matched by his 'autocratic bad temper', her eagerness to listen by his compulsion to talk.

Within moments of meeting their lives became inextricably and strangely entwined. After a few semi-chaste nights in the society's rooms at 8 Fitzroy Street, they moved to the studio in the same building which had been acquired by Patrick de Maré and then to a nearby flat. From the outset, Philip makes it clear that there was something odd about the sexual side of the relationship, though he avoids spelling it out and somehow conveys that this abnormality added to the intensity of their connection. He starts by reporting that Jean Hore was incapable of being sexually satisfied and memorably describes her as 'the impotent pilgrim of the orgasm'. He then scatters his account of the relationship with phrases like 'lack of the physical' and 'sexual starvation'. Talking about Jean years later he said, 'Sex wasn't important. It was an obstacle.' Instead of sex – is this what he was saying? – he 'babbled as never before', vomiting his life before her and felt almost overpowered by the realization of his 'incredible misery', 'mean inhibitions' and 'emotional starvation' to date. His first and only task was to protect his new kingdom and separate Jean from her hangers-on, her swarms of other parasites. He also tried to convert her to his mildly communist views and get her to contribute to party funds, though when she suddenly gave £1,000 to this cause, he was said to be 'absolutely furious' about it.

It is highly likely that Philip was also responsible for Jean now kicking over the traces with her family and even severing her connection with Gavin Allardyce, who had acted as her guardian since her parents' death. In *Memoirs of a Public Baby*, where Jean appears simply as *L*, Philip describes dishing out her money like 'delicious dirt'. He overtipped waiters, exercised his new-found love of fine wines and dandified clothing: Jean soon bought him lavender gloves and a yellow waistcoat. From the start, he was apparently determined to sink Jean's 'financial raft' in order that his chaotic private temple should survive. Everything about money – Jean had inherited the modern equivalent of nearly half a million pounds – embarrassed and confused him. He claims to have shuddered at its mention and may or may not have felt guilty about using it to cut himself off from other people and scorn conventional employment.

Whether the relationship gave Philip extra clout with his fellow Fitzrovians is a different matter. He had already had considerable impact on everyone he met, and even T. S. Eliot was said to avoid the place where O'Connor had sprung at him. In the pubs and cafés of the area Philip was regarded both as a menace and 'a real poet'. A man called Peter Murray, later a psychiatrist, who lived at 4 Fitzroy Street, pretended to be Philip's brother and imitated O'Connor's 'rapier-sharp innuendoes'. According to Tambimuttu, who arrived from Ceylon in January 1938 and later became the ringmaster of the wartime poetry circus, Philip O'Connor was 'an idol and model for our circle'. In his memoirs, Tambi describes his first encounter with Philip a few days after arriving in England. Sitting in Madame Buhler's café at the top of Rathbone Place, Tambi noticed 'a hunched-up, sandaled and long-haired figure with intense eyes and pursed lips, his high cheekbones rotating on his tense cobra neck, who surveyed the place like a vinegary monarch, took one peppery look around, and then walked out as casually as he had sailed in'. Writing years later in the *Oxford Mail*, B. Evan Owen described O'Connor as 'one of those odd authors at the centre of a quasi-intellectual cult long before their first royalties have reached the till of the public saloon'.

Within a few weeks or months of meeting Jean, Philip used some of her money to sail off to France, which he still saw as his soul's 'island'. He wanted to see Madame Tillieux again and he wanted to escape the more embarrassing aspects of Communism which were now coming to the surface in London. In the first instance, Jean Hore did not accompany him. Philip says she had 'some emotional parcels to tie up' in London. In *Memoirs of a Public Baby*, he states that he set off alone, via Victoria, Newhaven and Dieppe.

The exact date of his departure and the overall length of his stay in France aren't clear. Nor perhaps are his memories. Later he reveals that he was drunk throughout this period. In various bits of autobiographical writings he says that he left England in 1937, the year that he emerged from the Maudsley Hospital, and that he then lived continuously in France until the outbreak of the Second World War.

How then could he have been seen by Tambimuttu at Madame Buhler's in January 1938? And how could he have published so much poetry and prose in English magazines during this period? The idea of Philip writing his stuff in France and bothering to send it off by post seems highly improbable. It is more likely that his visit to France was shorter than he makes out and that during it he made more than one return trip to London.

All we know is that in the first instance he headed not for Wimereux but Paris, where he found a small hotel in Montparnasse. In *Memoirs of a Public Baby*, he describes a disturbing meeting with a Russian sculptor and engraver named Moissy Kogan, who had been a pupil of Rodin and would later die in a concentration camp. Kogan seems to have challenged Philip O'Connor to grow up, but Philip still balked at this idea which he saw as 'a man's greatest sacrifice'. In an early unpublished version of his book he indicates that he soon felt insecure again, trudging for small change, and was obliged to send telegrams to Jean in London asking for money. He also states that he then returned to London and found Jean looking after Tambimuttu, who had had an accident. 'Her kindness infuriated me,' he writes. 'My furies were high-pitched, prima donna like.' Eventually he got her onto the boat-train and Tambi came to see them off moist-eyed, and had to be 'hustled out of the carriage'. As the train pulled away Philip ordered dinner 'and felt the first movement of the magic carpet'. In this unpublished account, he concludes with the words, 'I was beginning to behave like a much fatter man.'

In Paris, Jean Hore and Philip O'Connor settled briefly in a small hotel in the Rue des Hirondelles, where Philip started buying things 'in great excitement', especially wine and gramophone records, and felt 'as abstracted from my surroundings as I was from myself'. Among others he saw in Paris was a 'tediously flamboyant figure from London' who boasted that he had had five women in the local brothel, and whom Philip later identified as Nigel Heseltine, adding the hope that he might be related to the Conservative politician with the same surname. He also met the poet David Gascoyne, who showed him a typescript of Lawrence Durrell's mildly pornographic novel *The Black*

Book, soon to be published in Paris and which Philip would clumsily review in the winter 1938 edition of the magazine *Seven*.

From Paris, they travelled south to Sanary, near Toulon, where Aldous Huxley had recently had a villa. Here, they rented a studio overlooking the bay and Philip's 'oratory of the second bottle became fully developed in two daily sessions'. Looking back at this phase, he wondered if he was trying to talk away his life, which again suggests he was writing little poetry. He was certainly keen on getting through Jean's money and entering 'some dizzy paradise of maximum expenditure'. He persuaded her to sell her stocks and shares. He bought an expensive car, raced up and down the coast in it, pretending to be a film-star or romantic poet. 'I've always had a car, ever since I was twenty,' he would tell me later, which places a gloss over the years of suffering and tramping that were to follow this temporary opulence. In his autobiography he also tells of his pathological jealousy of Jean and how he felt betrayed when she showed an interest in other people and how tedious he found her trips to the sea. When his 'babbling' ceased, Philip lay beside her like an infant, and claims he used the pain of 'sex-starvation' as a way of eclipsing his sense of chronic unemployment.

In the early summer of 1938, Jean Hore returned briefly to London, apparently in pursuit of another young man, whom according to Philip she loved in a different way. After seeing her off on a night train from Marseilles, Philip went into a lavatory, vomited and then ordered a second dinner. Soon afterwards he visited a brothel where he achieved 'a rudimentary normality', and then overturned the car, the shock of which imposed on him a short period of 'enforced sobriety'.

In Jean's absence, Philip again ran out of money and, unable to get in touch with her, telephoned his sister in London and asked for her help. Desirée O'Connor's life had stabilized further during these months and unknown to her brother she was now engaged to a young solicitor, John Trethowan, whom she would marry on 23 July at St James's, Spanish Place, a few streets away from Fitzrovia. Philip had no knowledge of these events and by now Desirée, who had supported her brother on and off for the last few years, had had enough of him. After consulting her fiancé, she told Philip she could help him no more.

It was the last time that Philip and Desirée spoke or communicated in any way. Their tastes and ambitions had always been different and their lives now totally diverged.

In due course, Jean Hore returned to France and was met by Philip at Boulogne. While in this neighbourhood, he took the opportunity to visit Wimereux and Madame Tillieux, and to use some of Jean's money to settle the long-standing debt incurred by his mother. Madame Tillieux fawned slightly in front of Philip's new gentleman-liness but had not lost her emotional hold over him. Of her children, only Jeanette was 'equal to the occasion'. Next door, the butcher's daughter Marie-Thérèse, whom he had adored, was now 'plump for the French marriage market'.

Jean and Philip returned together to Sanary where they were later joined by Tambimuttu, whose magazine *Poetry London* had now been launched featuring Philip in its first issue alongside Stephen Spender, Gavin Ewart, Dylan Thomas and Lawrence Durrell. According to *Memoirs of a Public Baby*, where he is feebly disguised as 'the oriental impresario', the good-looking Tambimuttu still hung around Jean and his interest in her nearly led to a fight. Tambi was followed to the South of France by Paul Potts, who had become besotted with Jean on her last visit to London, comparing his feelings for her with those of Columbus on first sighting land. Philip describes Potts as 'a great dirty urban creature absolutely immune to sunshine and sea and French graces', but did not feel in the least threatened by him and even argued that Potts rather enjoyed being the 'unsuccessful supplicant' for Jean's affections. Potts later wrote a book about Jean that was rejected by every publisher who saw it and which he eventually threw into the Tiber, beside the Vatican.

Philip's movements are often hard to establish, but at some stage during 1939 he and Jean went off to Italy and Greece, where he tells us they saw Tino Rossi and the Parthenon. Philip wanted to go further east, a lifelong ambition he would never fulfil. Instead, the threat of war brought them back to France though the tension was mounting there too. Talking to Jean in a crowded street in Lyons, Philip was jostled by a secret policeman and asked what he was doing in the city. During that final peacetime summer, Philip tells us that he 'scorched' himself on the cliffs below the old Huxley villa and braced himself for his return to England. Jean wanted them to go to America but he refused. She eventually went ahead of him to London and he revisited the brothels. He then drove north, joining the caravan of 'escaping or repatriating' Englishmen. On the brink of war, he drove from Boulogne to Calais, presumably passing through Wimereux once more. On board the ship taking him and his car back to the country he professed to hate, he remained completely drunk.

-9-

A Wartime Meeting

Every morning seemed posthumous in our eyes, every
night an encounter with all approximations to death.

PHILIP O'CONNOR, *Memoirs of a Public Baby*, 1958

As soon as the bombardment of London began, I felt
totally engaged. When the ground began to shake and
the sky became pink with doom, I could hardly stay
at home. I ceased to go out only when it was necessary
and started to search London for my own true bomb.

QUENTIN CRISP, *The Naked Civil Servant*, 1968

When the hostilities began, Quentin Crisp and Philip O'Connor were
thirty and twenty-two years old respectively. They may perhaps have
crossed paths in Soho or in surrealist circles and they had certainly
inhabited adjacent worlds, but it seems certain they had not yet met
face to face.

The war that eventually threw these two eccentrics together was
greeted by them in quite different ways. Belligerence of a national and
non-personal nature was a new experience for Quentin Crisp and he
could not take the war seriously. He was determined to ignore it as
much as possible. His chief fear on 3 September 1939 – or so he
claimed – was that his supply of cosmetics might run out and
he famously went out and bought two pounds of henna. Years later, he
boasted to George Melly that, having now done his war work, he could
relax. His other immediate concern was financial. For most freelance

artists, it seemed likely all work would cease. The only complete solution was suicide but Quentin tells us that he lacked the determination to take this course – 'Hopelessness was spread like drizzle over my whole outlook' – and settled instead for moving to a cheaper room. Early in the war, he left Chester Square Mews for a room in Callow Street, off Fulham Road. One blessing about this new room was that it was unfurnished and for the nominal sum of £5 his friend and former landlady Hilda Lumley allowed him to take away the bed, drawing-board and other items which she had originally bought for his room under her roof.

For Philip O'Connor, the arrival of war was much more agitating. In France he had looked forward eagerly to the 'deluge' but after hurrying back alone across the Continent, he was in a panic. First he could not find Jean and secondly he was terrified of the expected air-raids. When he found her, they fled to Scotland, but here he found the 'moral coldness' even scarier than the potential bombs. They were soon back in London, and settled in a flat in Mecklenburgh Square, off Gray's Inn Road. In this new context, Philip resumed his well established drinking routines and the 'epileptic exhibitionism' that went with them. He was still obsessed with his 'genius' and regarded it as 'a hot liquor to be expectorated on the world to its advantage'. Attempts to write floundered and he continued to abhor all forms of craft. His words 'streamed together and rolled up in a ball of pregnant inarticulacy'. Stephen Spender later put a generous interpretation on these failures: as a young man, Philip O'Connor was simply 'too clever'.

At this stage, Jean Hore still had plenty of money and at the end of 1939 they moved to the country, renting a large and comfortable house on Box Hill, not far from the hut where Philip had spent a crucial part of his childhood. The constant returning to old haunts is one of the most pronounced features of Philip O'Connor's life and to some extent lessens the effect of so much movement. While there Philip drove in a new and larger car to visit his former guardian, Camden Field, now in his mid-forties and still occupying the same hut. Over a drink in a local pub, perhaps the Barley Mow where they had drunk in the past, Field showed some dismay at Philip's new 'maturity' and some sadness at the lost relationship, but above all appeared reserved and vaguely critical. This may have been the last time the pair met but Philip would remain aware of Field's whereabouts for many years to come.

At the house on Box Hill Philip played with Meccano sets and Hornby trains and 'consistently avoided all sobriety'. At Christmas 1939 they were joined by Patrick de Maré and his half-black girlfriend Val. Years later, de Maré would describe the visit with great enthusiasm: 'A wonderful house, lovely kitchen, marvellous coffee, tons to drink – Philip was usually drunk. They had Charles Trenet singing songs on the gramophone. An incredible atmosphere.' Of Jean Hore, he says, 'She was very attractive, very slim. She gave Val a hundred pounds, just like that. Val was a bit jealous of her.' In his *Memoirs*, Philip confesses that he 'ogled endlessly' at Val but never went any further. His lack of promiscuity was something he often wrangled over.

Back in London, Quentin Crisp took his sex life, or lack of it, calmly. During the first year or so of the war he continued to receive visits from the Man from the Ministry, cautiously preceded by a telephone call – 'He couldn't risk being included in a whole lot of jolly people' – but the blackout now provided other challenges, though not perhaps on the scale he suggests in his autobiography, where he states that London had become like 'a paved double bed'. And along with these new mixed blessings – a total stranger kissed him on the lips outside Leicester Square Underground station – came encounters as violent as anything he had known in the past. At Holborn, he was chased onto the street, beaten up and left unconscious on the pavement. When he revived, he counted his fingernails, felt his teeth with his tongue and then walked home, holding a handkerchief to his bleeding face.

And, there were other blackout encounters which may have had no sexual base at all. One night, around Christmas 1939, Quentin Crisp was 'sweeping along' Ebury Street when his attention was caught by a tall bearded stranger heading in the opposite direction. Normally, Crisp would have sailed haughtily past but on this occasion he broke out of his 'plaster cast' and stopped dead – and so did the stranger.

This turned out to be Angus McBean, the theatrical photographer, who had a studio nearby. A few days later, Quentin Crisp posed for McBean at his large basement premises in Belgrave Road and, with the help of retouching and airbrushing, some of the most memorable and famously beautiful black-and-white images of Quentin Crisp were created. The session took only three-quarters of an hour but the friendship between Crisp and McBean was to last a lifetime. Almost immediately, Quentin seems to have become a part-time member of McBean's entourage. An article by James Laver about McBean photographing the actress Diana Churchill in a restaurant, published in *Picture Post* in February 1940, shows Quentin Crisp reflected in a mirror. Asked to explain McBean's interest in him, Quentin said rather demurely, 'I think he admired my looks.' McBean soon moved to Bath, where his life took an unexpected turn: he was charged with the perversion of minors and sentenced to four years' imprisonment.

A month or so later, Quentin's looks also caught the attention of the artist Clifford Hall, who asked if he could paint his portrait. Then in his mid-thirties, Hall was a distinctive Chelsea figure, who wore a black hat and pointed beard and was 'one of the landmarks of the district'. George Melly describes him as 'a gruff old thing who painted in a limp Sickertish sort of way'. Quentin claims that he was the first artist he had ever met and his home in Trafalgar Studios, Manresa Road, Chelsea, the first proper studio he had ever entered. During the first year of the war, Clifford Hall painted three portraits of Quentin, current whereabouts unknown, one of which may have been in the nude. Some of Quentin's friends claimed that the artist was partly motivated by sexual curiosity but Quentin crossly dismisses these suggestions in *The Naked Civil Servant* and asserts that he was flattered by Mr Hall's attentions and courteous manners, though baffled by his melancholy nature. Quentin Crisp was often 'baffled' by people – or pretended to be. Anyway, he was grateful for the fee Hall paid him, which was the only money he earned at this time.

It may be worth noting that early in the war Quentin Crisp and Philip O'Connor both attempted to join the armed forces – and in Quentin's case the motivations were largely financial. Philip tells us little more than that he turned up at the recruiting office in Dorking and was turned down on health grounds and that his reactions to this rejection ranged from 'secret disappointment' to 'surface rapture'. Quentin gives us a detailed picture of his examination in April 1940 before a medical board in a drill hall at Kingston. His extreme poverty gave him a powerful reason for wanting to enlist and on this occasion he wore no make-up – he could do nothing about the dyed hair – and continued to let the authorities believe he was five years younger than he was. The searching physical examination to which he was subjected would be fully exploited in the film of his life, causing immense distress to the satirist Auberon Waugh, but led to Quentin being given a certificate of total exemption on the grounds that he suffered from sexual perversion. At the time, he felt genuinely surprised by this decision but it's hard to believe his claims that he had now been 'deprived by prejudice of a glorious and convenient death'.

In fact, a few weeks later, in the summer of 1940, his financial fears were eased and his whole life gained a certain gravitas when he found a new and permanent home for himself at 129 Beaufort Street, on the borders of Chelsea and Fulham. This first-floor room in a slightly lacklustre street suited him perfectly and he was to remain here for the rest of the war and long, long beyond. The rent was wonderfully low – only six shillings a week – and there was room for his bed, drawing-board, cupboards for food and clothes and other furniture that had graced his room at Chester Square Mews. To these he would add a typewriter, an aerograph, a crotchety old wireless and in due course many layers of dust. The room measured twelve feet by fifteen, had two large windows looking down onto the street and was heated by a gas-fire set into its original Victorian fireplace. Congenial fellow lodgers included Gordon Richardson, an actor who occupied the bow-fronted room below him, and the house was particularly lucky in its landlady, who lived elsewhere and was later described by Quentin as 'the patron saint of hooligans'.

The name of this remarkable, long-suffering woman was Miss Violet Vereker, known to her friends as 'Vi'. Small, slim and sprightly, she was the daughter of a West Country doctor and devoted to good causes. She had once run a soup kitchen for Chelsea derelicts and now in 1940 was in charge of a hostel for other disadvantaged types on the south coast. Quentin claims that she accepted him as 'one of the hazards of her dedication to humanity'.

Very soon after moving into Beaufort Street, Quentin Crisp felt sufficiently established to install his own telephone. He was assigned the number FLAxman 9398 – his name and number appear in the 1941 London telephone directory – and was soon using this instrument to 'pan the suburbs for a few last nuggets of conviviality', though such behaviour runs contrary to his claims that he never made the running in any relationship and never actually called anyone to see how they were. He was also, he tells us, 'incorrigibly hopeful' about good news that the telephone might bring and was undeterred when he soon began to experience anonymous calls, or 'appointments with fear', to which he responded by repeating in a tired voice, 'What is your name and what do you want?'

Philip O'Connor's number was never listed in the London telephone directory. He was never in one place long enough and had no aspirations towards being settled or established. At the time that Quentin was unpacking his bags at Beaufort Street, Philip and Jean Hore were returning from Box Hill to London and settling in in separate flats, in Fleet Street and Chancery Lane. In July 1940 the bombing of London began. Philip was at first too frightened even to take shelter and when he eventually did so felt profoundly cynical about the new sense of 'community' which surrounded him, which was not at all like the extended family he yearned for. In *Memoirs of a Public Baby*, he writes of the 'awesomely embarrassing manner of comradeship' that existed in the shelter beneath his Fleet Street block and of the 'almost theatrical equality between self-conscious public service workers and their social superiors'. Both sides, he says, were 'engaged in a charade of sentimentality'. Such concerns meant very little to Jean Hore. According to Philip, she was now beginning to show 'symptoms of mental unbalance', jumping off buses in motion, walking into lamp posts and wandering about during the air-raids 'with a fine-cut independence', unabashed by the shrapnel falling around her.

Curiously, that is also exactly how Quentin Crisp behaved when the bombs began to fall, though his state of mind was very different to Jean Hore's. He was in a cottage outside Basingstoke with an actress called Catherine Morley when he heard of the bombardment. His first reaction was to rush home. The camaraderie in the stricken city, that Philip so despised and distrusted, greatly appealed to Quentin. 'Everyone talked to everyone – even to me. The golden age had temporarily arrived.' For the next five years, Quentin walked the streets of London, often bare-footed and always with his red-haired head held high. 'Don't care, huh?' asked policemen sheltering in doorways as he sailed by. In *The Naked Civil Servant*, he claims he longed for death, partly perhaps because it was fascinating in itself. 'For heaven's sake, don't look as though you're enjoying yourself,' a woman said when she found him pausing too long at a bombsite. His determination to ignore the hazards would soon develop into a desire to embrace disaster. Fear was the lure, but luckily for us he never found his 'own true bomb'. Indeed he would soon become a bomb-proof landmark, a reassuring if somewhat ghostly presence amidst the shrapnel.

As we will see, Quentin Crisp had an active war. In the autumn of 1940, he got involved in various ventures centred on a small theatre called The Threshold in Chepstow Villas, Notting Hill. One of the directors of this enterprise was Estelle Murison, the 'tempestuous' actress who had lodged at 61 Oakley Street four years earlier. She commissioned him to write an intimate revue which was never put on and then an 'anti-Pirandello' play, which she later described as 'wholly brilliant and playable', and a drama, *A Man with a Sword*, set in the Trojan Wars, which was also abandoned. These setbacks did not deter him from attending other productions at this minuscule theatre, including the play *Fishing for Shadows*, in which the young Peter Ustinov played an elderly bishop.

On a more humdrum level, Quentin Crisp's lettering skills had now begun to find him freelance work in the booming documentary film industry. For part of the war, he worked full-time for Studio Film Laboratories in Wardour Street. He tells us little about his life in the art department of this firm other than that other members of the staff soon learnt by heart and started to use 'the detestable curlicues with which my discourse was decorated'.

Over in Fleet Street, then the centre of the newspaper world, Philip

O'Connor was also surprisingly active and had got involved with the literary magazine, *Seven*. He had made several contributions to this publication before the war. Now with Jean's money and the assistance of his friend Gordon Cruikshank as 'circulation manager' he took over as *Seven*'s editor and attempted to relaunch it as 'the magazine of people's writing' by getting non-professional writers to contribute. The March 1941 issue carried short monologues by a Waiter, a Commissionaire, a Garage Hand and several children. In his introduction, O'Connor argued that 'people not used to writing make a livelier job of it than the professionals' and went out of his way to condemn 'the lamentable complacency and detachment that artists rapidly achieve, particularly for cash payment'. This was a worthy idea – a forerunner of some of the work that Philip did twenty years later for the BBC Third Programme – but Jean's money had now nearly gone and the next issue of *Seven*, which appeared in July 1941, was the last.

That autumn, Philip and Jean bundled up various portable possessions, which included Chinese drums and a suitcase full of pâté de foie gras, and headed again for Box Hill. This time, as they were now down to their 'last few hundreds', they bought a hut in a wooded encampment off Ashmore Drive. This group of wooden dwellings – on a less prestigious part of the hill than the area where Camden Field lived – is still there sixty years later and still known by the name Ruskin. This was the address for both bride and groom which appears on the marriage certificate for Philip Constant Marie Bancroft O'Connor and Jean Mary Hore. This event took place at the Dorking registry office on 4 December 1941 and was witnessed by Gordon Cruikshank and his wife, also called Jean. What prompted the marriage, which goes unmentioned in *Memoirs of a Public Baby*, is far from clear. Philip and Jean were both in a bad way and he paints a wholly melancholy picture of this long winter together, the dampness under foot, the iron-grey sky and their internal miseries. Philip's 'furious irritability' was now matched by a new self-doubt.

His decision to attend a local Labour Exchange and sign on for a course at a training centre gave him only a brief uplift. For several months he would get up at five in the morning, cycle to a station four miles off and make the long journey to the Handley Page factory in

Cricklewood, North London, where he was employed as an aircraft-part measurer. But his enthusiasm soon wore off. He became 'impossible' in the hut and 'very tired'. One day, his wife started burying their spoons in the garden. Another day, she stood behind him with an axe raised above her head and would have brought it down on him had he not 'caught her wrist nicely'. Soon after this, he guided her with great difficulty to a doctor and thence to a mental hospital. At the hospital entrance, Philip O'Connor claims to have delivered a dramatic speech lasting an hour and a half in which he argued that she owed it to society – 'the society which I had so convincingly vilified' – to get cured. In a state of tortured exultation, Philip tells us that his body then 'careered away like an empty removal lorry'. Back at the hut, he began to sell everything to the local people, the Chinese drums, his wife's clothes, finally the building itself. The next morning he set off by bus to London, causing shrieks of laughter by proposing marriage to a stranger on the front seat.

People may have also shrieked at Quentin Crisp on wartime buses and trains, but his life at 129 Beaufort Street seems to have been entirely free from the gothic dramas and wild reversals which constantly faced Philip O'Connor. At the age of thirty-four Quentin was already styling himself 'a little old man'. At home, he pottered about, always bare-footed, and enjoyed sitting beside his gas-fire. He never bought a newspaper and claims he never read a book. His relationship with the Man from the Ministry slowly petered out though he later told Philip Mackie that this sad, tall, upper-middle-class man had once visited him at Beaufort Street and he had once visited him at his flat in Elizabeth or Ebury Street, which he described as 'a cold, freezing, pitch dark place', on the point of being abandoned. The Man from the Ministry – Quentin soon forgot which one he worked for – was about to leave London and Quentin's life for ever. Questioned about the affair years later, he replied, 'I've never heard of him or seen him and I don't know who he is or where he is or anything.' There were other callers at Beaufort Street whom Quentin may have been happier to see, though he tells us that there was always a vulnerable moment when he opened the front door and he usually took the precaution of first locking his money in a cupboard and then putting the key in another cupboard which he also locked. Money was of great significance to him and another area of his life shrouded in mystery.

Beaufort Street also provided a secure base, from which he went out on innumerable little jaunts. In Chelsea he went to a café called Roma's at 44 Old Church Street – the premises later became a fashionable restaurant known as L'Aiglon – and to the Bar-B-Q at 190 King's Road. In these places he put on a bit of a performance. At Roma's he once offered a stranger a spoonful of his soup, which she accepted, and at the Bar-B-Q he held court and mixed with other local characters who included the artist Mervyn Peake, of whom more in a moment.

He also struck out in other directions, further afield. He often visited his Polish friend and the girl from Battersea called Pat, who now lived 'in sin' at Russell Court in Bloomsbury. He made appearances at the Stamford Bridge Studios in Fulham where residents included John Baker, a stained-glass artist, and the portrait painter Theo Ramos. Mr Ramos remembers these visits well but adds, 'I knew him only as a spectator. But he was utterly polite and friendly and made no allusions to sexual matters.' Early in the war Quentin also visited a basement flat in Earl's Court belonging to the actor Bertram Shuttleworth and there he met Malya Woolf, an actress who was to become a lifelong friend. 'This creature walked in,' she recalls. 'He had long bright red fingernails. I asked, "Don't they get in the way?" and he replied, "I can't do a thing." '

How often he saw his mother at East Anstey isn't clear. His niece Frances, then a schoolgirl, remembers no wartime visits from Uncle Denis, but for part of this time Mrs Pratt seems to have had housekeeping jobs elsewhere. In his final book, *Resident Alien*, Quentin mentions that his mother was staying or working in a large country house in another part of Devon and had to convey a telephone message to Angus McBean's mother, who was living in the lodge and coping with the shock of her son's imprisonment. 'You have nothing to fear,' said Mrs Pratt, 'because I am Quentin Crisp's mother.' According to Quentin, the two women 'instantly pooled their disgrace and became friends'.

Meanwhile, an equally strong bond had been forged between Quentin and one of Angus McBean's closest friends, Esther Grant.

According to her daughter, Esther Grant loved championing the unusual and quickly became a great fan of Quentin and incorporated him into her world. Later in the war, Quentin would visit Esther's house in Gloucester Walk, Kensington, and find her in tears, struggling with her baby son, Luke. 'Go and wash your face! I can't talk to you like that!' he reproved her and when she was out of the room Quentin Crisp had the audacity and know-how to change the baby's nappies. This mind-boggling event, if true, provides further evidence of Quentin Crisp's domesticated nature. In the same house, Esther's daughter Julia Paul Jones, then aged four, remembers sitting chatting on the staircase with Quentin, his painted toenails visible through gold sandals. 'He entered without condescension, in his usual mannered and elaborate conversational style, into my fantasy concerning a stuffed toy elephant to which I had been married for some time before discovering that he was a German spy.' She also recalls that he addressed her throughout, even at her tender age, as Miss Paul Jones, and how, when he finally sailed off down the street, his dark overcoat 'hung and swung from his slight shoulders'.

By now, Quentin Crisp had taken his biggest step forward and become an art school model. He was still working for the Studio Film Laboratories when sometime in 1942 he received an urgent telephone call from a model whom he had known in Oakley Street six years earlier. She begged him to go in her stead and pose before an art class at Toynbee Hall in the East End. 'You're always saying it must be nice to be a model. Now's your chance.' This was both an inspired and an obvious suggestion and from all accounts Quentin Crisp was an instant success in the humble but demanding role into which he was now thrown. The following evening – it would be nice to have a precise date – he put on an old pair of underpants, which he had quickly converted into a posing pouch, and survived a four-hour session in front of ten or twelve art students at Toynbee Hall. In the months and years ahead he was to model in art schools across the land. In *The Naked Civil Servant*, he asserts that this work required 'no aptitude, no education, no references and no previous experience'. He boasts that his physique was nothing to write home about – 'I was undersized in all respects except for a pigeon chest and a huge head' – and all he could really offer was his reliability, though he also acknowledges the 'almost evangelical fervour' with which he tried to force the art students to use their eyes.

Whenever possible Quentin Crisp would present them with 'anatomical riddles'. He rolled on the floor, stood on his head, put one foot on the floor and another on a plinth, hung from beams, held chairs above his head and offered a variety of crucifix poses. These antics and contortions combined the roles of actor and martyr and earned him a reputation as 'the most energetic model in the Home Counties'. They pleased most of the teachers, who were 'almost universally courteous', but he claims they excited 'fury and enmity' among the students, though when fame hit him years later, many would come forward with proud memories of Quentin Crisp as a person and as a model. 'He walked like a king,' recalled Janet Thomas who drew him at Goldsmith's College in the last year of the war. 'He used to come out with some very profound statements.' Another Goldsmith's student Jane Jury remembered, 'He was so exotic. His skin was very white. His hair was red. He looked like something out of the Renaissance.' Many were oblivious to the meaning of it all. 'I didn't know if it was a man or a woman, even when he turned round,' said Marguerite Evans who painted him at Willesden in 1943 and whose oil of him is now in the National Portrait Gallery. Others recalled his conduct in the life room, how he studied a crossword puzzle pinned to the wall while posing and then filled in the answers during the breaks. Several reflected on how, unlike other models, he never walked round the room and looked at how the portraits of him were progressing. This indifference to the end product gives another clue to his character and lack of conventional vanity, at least its more insecure manifestations.

Anyhow, he had now found a job that at last he 'fully understood'. For many years, modelling would represent 'total fulfilment' for him. As the art schools expanded, his reputation spread by word of mouth and he was much in demand. The schools he preferred were the warmest ones and those closest to home but it is difficult to think of any art school in London or the Home Counties that he did not eventually pose in. Perhaps his greatest moment during the war happened when a bomb dropped near Goldsmith's College in Lewisham and blew in the window of the life room. Quentin Crisp continued to hold his pose without batting an eyelid.

Meanwhile, Philip O'Connor had returned to the war zone and the 'terrible' room he had last occupied with Jean at some unspecified address in WC1. From here he continued to attend the Handley Page factory at Cricklewood and got on amiably enough with his fellow workers, while yearning to regain his 'chaos and grandeur'. Eventually he told the factory that he wanted to enlist again, encouraged by the fact that Russia had joined the Allies. He was rejected for the second time but decided to leave the factory nonetheless. In the summer of 1942, Philip bundled up Jean's remaining possessions and sold them to Mr Mendelson and then bounced or crept back into the Soho world. One night in the Swiss Tavern in Old Compton Street, across the road from the site of the Black Cat, he met a young man named Stephen Fothergill, who would feature prominently in his life during the next year or two and who is still alive and very much part of the Soho scene as I write these words. As my story advances towards modern times, these pages will, I hope, become increasingly populated by living links with my two heroes.

A conscientious objector, who had recently come to London after doing war work on a farm near Oxford, Stephen Fothergill had romantic ideas about bohemian life which Soho particularly exemplified. He also describes himself in those days as 'self-centred and half-mad'. On that particular evening he had already spotted O'Connor standing in the middle of Old Compton Street haranguing a bemused passer-by. When Philip entered the Swiss Tavern, they were soon in conversation, though one suspects that O'Connor did most of the talking as Fothergill was and is famous for his observant silence. In *Memoirs of a Public Baby*, Philip gives Fothergill the name Ernest and describes him as 'extremely good-looking' with the kind of face a Russian imperial guard might have in a Hollywood film. Fothergill himself remembers Philip's 'black hair, fierce brown eyes and truculently jutting chin' and claims that he had 'a kind of spiritual beauty, not just in looks'. About his eyes there was 'a hint of the Orient', but Fothergill was also struck by Philip's voice and reported that he spoke with 'a received pronunciation in a determinedly correct manner', a way of speaking which 'contrasted oddly with the unbuttoned nature of his talk'. In his autobiography, O'Connor says, 'We liked each other at once and possibly in a quasi-homosexual way, and certainly because we were equal fools about the world, but felt we had more fun than those who were clever that way.' He omits to say that he put up Fothergill that night, presumably in the room he had once shared with Jean, and asked if he could bugger him. Such a twist is no odder than Quentin Crisp changing a baby's nappy, but whether this bid derived from wartime drunken intimacy, Philip's bizarre nature or a real homosexual ingredient is difficult to know. Philip's own views on the matter would not necessarily have clarified it. Anyway, Fothergill was not phased by these overtures and called on Philip a few days later to talk about books and music.

In the Swiss Tavern a few weeks or months later Philip also met the impoverished young poet Michael Hamburger, then scarcely eighteen and enjoying a 'Soho Period' while waiting for his call-up. The two immediately got on well – 'It was love at first sight,' reports Maria Steiner, of whom more in a moment – and would start a lifelong friendship, partly sustained by correspondence, in which O'Connor's naughtiness sometimes produced a priggish reaction from Hamburger. Of their first meeting, Philip writes in his book *The Lower View*, 'Since I wore the costume of creativity, he naively drew conclusions . . . He probably thought I had something to do with "life" and I certainly knew he had much to do with letters.'

Such magisterial detachment was uncharacteristic of Philip's life during these early years. After rushing around London for many months, much of his life was now spent in Chelsea and in the autumn of 1942, he seems to have had an encounter with 'a sunny little thing' I have identified as Natalie Tartakova, who lived above the Express Dairy in King's Road and was also a friend of Dylan Thomas. In the same building lived a girl called Ann Meo, who remembers Philip as a sort of eel 'weaving about, in a sort of dotty exhilaration, incredibly badly co-ordinated like a *commedia dell'arte* puppet'. After the two-week affair with Natalie he was introduced to a rich, lazy, slightly dour young man, Oliver French, who lived in an upper studio at 48 Tite Street, a Chelsea backwater of distinction. Oliver French is an important and rather elusive figure in Philip's life and his glass-roofed studio is significant for reasons that will emerge later. Philip devotes six pages of his autobiography to his Tite Street life and informs us that Oliver French's face was the most delicate he had ever seen on a man and that his eyes reminded him of his mother. Like Jean Hore and Quentin Crisp, Oliver French delighted in wandering about in the air-raids and was eventually killed when a bomb fell on him outside the Swiss Tavern in Soho. According to Stephen Fothergill, who was also part of the Tite Street circle, Philip was devastated by this event and walked round Soho distraught with misery.

Meanwhile, Philip was paying regular visits to his wife in hospital. He reports that she looked so beautiful robed in white in a padded cell and her face 'an unbelievable rhapsody', that he wept. He would come away from the hospital with a sense of 'the extraordinary purity of insane people' when compared with the disgusting coarseness of the 'cannibals and idiots' of the outside world. After six months he persuaded the hospital to release her and in the late autumn of 1942 they took a semi-basement room in a World's End house run by a landlady who belonged to 'that ancient order of citizens who morally disapprove of insanity'. Jean had changed under the treatment. She now spoke very little, her eyes were bigger, her bones more pronounced, her mind contorted and 'a strange coarseness invested her flesh'. Flickers of life occasionally animated her and Philip worked hard to stir her up, but without success. While here, they were also visited by Paul Potts, who was still preoccupied with Jean and describes the 'near-slum room' they now lived in and Jean's handbag, now old and dirty, through which 'had passed enough money to give her, and the children she never had, a life, a career and a future: it was all gone and so had she'. Looking back on this time, Philip O'Connor dismissed Potts as 'a complex scoundrel' and added, 'He did everything he could to ruin Jean and me.'

They were certainly ruined and the money had indeed gone. In September 1942, Philip submitted some poems to George Orwell, now a talks producer at the BBC, accompanying them with a pencil-written note, which still bears the imprint of his desperation, and concludes 'If you want them, please pay soon, necessarily.' It may have been at the same time of need that Philip waited round the corner while Stephen Fothergill delivered a note to Patrick de Maré's parents in which Philip claimed to be laid up with flu and in need of money for food. 'A fiver was duly extended,' says Fothergill. 'Minutes later we were rolling down to Soho in a taxi.'

Such deceptions played no part in the life of Quentin Crisp, who was slowly proceeding in the Soho direction under his own steam. One evening that same winter, while working at St Martin's School of Art – which had rejected him as a student some ten years earlier – he was introduced to another model named Peter Fisk, a man described as a bookseller and dancer as well as artist's model. Fisk asked Crisp what he was doing after his class, to which he replied in Crisperanto that he was 'going home to have a good cry'. Fisk then suggested that they should visit the Charlotte Street cafés. It was a momentous turning-point. 'If it had not been for this casual invitation,' Quentin writes in *The Naked Civil Servant*, 'a whole world would have been closed to me.' Within a few days or weeks, he had become a fixture of the Fitzrovian cafés and his introduction to the district marked 'the discovery of a new self'. In his youth, he had wanted to reform and to educate. Now, he only wanted to entertain. And for the first time in his life he found he was instantly welcomed and moving among people to whom his homosexuality was 'of no significance whatsoever'. In his autobiography, he states, 'I had met an entirely different kind of people. There were no prejudices and no rules.' He had entered the heart of bohemian London where few of the usual barriers existed. Much later in life, Quentin would cock his head on one side and talk with stagey sentimentality about the time 'when café life began'.

Quentin was drawn to cafés rather than pubs. Within the Fitzrovian community there were many subdivisions, configurations, tribes and coteries, and this is not the place to unravel these incestuous groups and connections. The most obvious division was between what Malya Woolf called the 'pub-ites' and the 'café-ites'. Philip O'Connor has written a lot about the divisions between Bloomsbury and Fitzrovia. Quentin Crisp spoke occasionally of the 'truly great people' like Cyril Connolly, Orwell, Cecil Beaton, the Sitwells and Francis Bacon but declared that these 'divine beings' – does one detect a sarcastic tone?

– kept to themselves and never appeared in the cafés. When I first met Quentin many years later, in a café on the fringe of Fitzrovia, he would reel off the names of the hostelries he had frequented over the years: Tony's, the Alexandria, the Low Dive, the Scala, the Partisan, the Méditerranée, the Coffee An, the En Passant, some of which may have been quite a distance in time and space from Fitzrovia proper. One of the few pubs he visited was the half-timbered Wheatsheaf, where he would sit beside the manorial fireplace and talk to Mrs Stewart, a paper-seller and crossword puzzle expert, but even in the cafés there was a haze of alcohol, an eerie gaiety, a poetical and political ferment mixed with a whiff of 'Soho-itis' or in other words, the disease of drinking and getting nothing done. Quentin Crisp was not the only person who was stimulated by the bombs, by the Blitz, the blackout and the possibility of sudden death, or who would embrace with such zest 'the cult of failure'.

Quentin's degree of zest is worth pondering over. In the film of his life he is depicted as full of life and gaiety and very much in the swing at Fitzrovian gatherings. Malya Woolf, who knew him well during these years, says Quentin was far more likely to stand against the wall and wait for people to approach him and in later life he liked to claim how socially inept he was. But he also admits that he felt at ease in Fitzrovia without ever stopping his performance. 'You're crazy about your entrance,' he was told by someone called Mabs McAllister, and the dialogue that followed his entrances was full of his stock phrases. He had already formed a taste for 'pale grey coffee', one of his standard remarks to strangers was 'Tell me the story of your life', and he usually signed off with the words, 'Be kind and true.' But it is fair to say that he was liked and welcomed in most places. 'I even enjoyed a kind of popularity, which bewildered me at the time,' he said later.

Survivors from this period draw important distinctions between Quentin Crisp and other homosexuals. 'Quentin was one of those few homosexuals who are never catty' is one line. 'Compared with Quentin, other homosexuals were pale shadows' is another. He certainly had impact. The artist John de Paul, who was a schoolboy when he first caught sight of Quentin in the Coffee An, declared, 'I was quite fascinated by the creature' and soon became a lifelong friend.

Others nudged each other and said, 'Who is it?' when they saw him for the first time and were baffled by his hairstyle. On meeting Quentin for the first time a man named Hemingway blurted out that he had already met him in a dream. But for all his phantom qualities, it was generally agreed that he was, in Patrick de Maré's words, 'very, very nice', though some people struggled to find more vivid literary words to describe him, like 'Dostoevskian' and 'Firbankian'.

The inhabitants or daily visitors to wartime Fitzrovia came in all shapes and sizes. The organizers of the Society for Creative Psychology had both fled to Ireland – Billy Williams later qualified as a psychiatrist, inherited money from his mother and died early while Basil Beaumont moved on to Paris and changed his name to Count Ragozci – but there were plenty of other oddities around. Philip O'Connor writes of the 'near-lunatics, alcoholics, tramps, and Dionysians'. Quentin Crisp mentions 'bookies, burglars, actresses, artisans, poets and prostitutes'. There were also young men waiting for their call-up, conscientious objectors, refugees from Eastern Europe, deserters from the armed forces. Quentin describes the whole lot of them as 'hooligans' and among them formed some bonds which would last a lifetime and others that were short-lived. His chief friends, he reminds us, were always women. Among those with whom he would form lasting friendships and who will play a structural role in this narrative are the actress Anna Wing, the variety artist Joan Rhodes, on her way to becoming a celebrity with her strongwoman act, and a refugee from Austria, Maria Gabriele Steiner, whom Quentin described 'as the most beautiful woman in the world'. This alluring creature arrived in Fitzrovia in 1943, taking a two-room flat on the top floor of 12 Fitzroy Street, and first caught sight of Quentin in the Wheatsheaf where he reminded her of the God of Fire from Wagner's *Das Rheingold*. 'I adored him,' she said. 'He was a lovely man. He was very kind. He used to take me to Bertorelli's. We had a marvellous dish there for very little money. I used to feel proud to be with him. I was actually quite in love with him. I used to dream about him.' She was only slightly bemused when it emerged that Quentin had thought she was a lesbian.

It was among these 'hooligans' and in this atmosphere that Quentin

Crisp met Philip O'Connor. The exact time and place are unrecorded and some of their early meetings are as likely to have taken place in Chelsea, where they both were living, as in Fitzrovia. 'I met him in little bits,' said Quentin, whose first and enduring impression of Philip was that he was 'an odd, uncomfortable stick of man, with claw-like hands' and 'a dancing skeleton, only kept alive by gleeful, fiendish curiosity', who could have dropped dead at any second. Quentin was now in his mid-thirties, Philip was eight years younger but appeared to be 'falling apart' and 'as thin as a figure on a crucifix'. According to Quentin, Philip O'Connor's countenance, over which his jet black hair 'hung in sparse ringlets', was 'silvery white', and this 'eroded look' was emphasized by 'the most mirthless smile' he had ever seen and by eyes that instead of gazing were forever 'staring, *screaming*'. On later occasions, Quentin declared that he was 'fascinated and terrified' by O'Connor at the same time and that the predominant impression he gave was of 'evil'.

When they first met, Quentin was fully engaged with his art school modelling. Philip appeared to be doing nothing. 'He fell about,' says Quentin. 'He delivered sentences backwards, spoke in spoonerisms and jingles. I never understood a word he uttered.' According to Quentin, Philip was rude to everyone and his physical gestures were so emphatic that a taxi would stop for him even if it already had a passenger. When they first met, Philip was 'sleeping on a mattress on the floor' – Quentin must have visited the semi-slum, half-basement room in Chelsea – but rumours reached Quentin that Philip 'had been rich beyond the dreams of the Inland Revenue but had given away all his money in handfuls to beggars in public parks'. Quentin was perhaps aware that this money had once belonged to Jean, who now trailed beside her husband on all occasions. Quentin describes her as 'a helpless woman who hardly ever spoke' but adds that he liked her and that in his eyes silence in other people was not a fault. He also acknowledges that Philip had many companions, mainly men, and was 'irresistible to women, no matter how badly he treated them'.

Philip's early and immediate impressions of Quentin were less voluble. He remembers that Quentin lent him £5 at this time and adds, 'one of several lent to me, his was the best'. He later described

Quentin Crisp as a man of great charity, almost a Christian Communist, but shockingly qualified this by adding, 'His bug-like heart wasn't involved in his acts of charity.' He also describes Quentin's appearance and personality as 'works of art' and, long before the media onslaught, spoke of Quentin's career as 'a self-made portrait wittily projected onto the public screen'.

During this period, both men were of course unknown to the wider public, yet in some ways this was a magic moment in their lives. Both occupied hallowed ground, the off-side fringe of society, out of bounds to almost all other members of the intelligentsia. Surrealism flourished during the war and encompassed them both. Quentin Crisp and Philip O'Connor were highly representative and colourful inhabitants of Fitzrovia at its lowest level, significant players behind the wartime scene. They went to the same places and had many acquaintances in common though their reactions to them often differed. Both knew Dylan Thomas. O'Connor describes him as 'a fraud', Crisp as 'a permanently surprised cherub'. Both knew Paul Potts. O'Connor called him 'a faithful and honest liar and kleptomaniac'. Crisp saw him as 'self-doubting, even when viewed from a long way off', and spoke of his 'slightly dead look'. How these and other people reacted to Quentin and Philip also varied. Tambimuttu may have quarrelled with Philip over Jean but he published his poems and idolized him as a person. To Quentin, Tambi was far less welcoming than most Fitzrovians, telling him, 'Don't bother me now!' and 'Get out of my sight!'

Unlike some outsiders, Philip and Quentin were both highly intelligent and painfully self-aware. Quentin says that Philip was 'down to the bone' as far as self-knowledge was concerned and Philip could no doubt repay the compliment. Both were intoxicated with their own existences yet both had experienced extreme poverty and worn other people's old clothes. Both were eccentric exhibitionists and sought to create a stir. Though both had attempted to join the forces, neither of them was particularly patriotic. Philip would make pro-German remarks on the tops of buses. Quentin claimed to be 'neutral' about the outcome of the war and in his writings refers to 'the feast of love and death that St Adolph had set before the palates of the English'.

Both had characters which had set like plaster casts yet underneath the edifices were in perpetual reaction to themselves. For both of them, the paradox or double bluff was, in Philip's words, 'a dialectic of thought' and 'an instrument of work' rather than 'evidence of blocked understanding'. Both were virtuoso conversationalists and indefatigable talkers. Both were capable of listening, observing, and sympathetic understanding yet both gave the impression of talking 'at' their audiences. Underneath their separate performances – comic, colourful, picturesque – lay similar motives. Quentin Crisp and Philip O'Connor both despised privacy and in their different ways sought to share themselves with the world to a maximum degree. 'My person-ality,' Philip wrote later, 'quickly congeals into an unmanageable stock that must, at all costs, be unwrapped, undone, unwound and redistrib-uted to the fields.' Even at the end of his life, Quentin would still express the wish that everything about him should be 'unpacked' and everything known, even the contents of his pockets.

During his saner moments Philip would describe his eccentricity as 'the costume of the sad', a description which Quentin could well have applied to his own behaviour, though others might prefer his subsequent description of himself, complex in its cleverness, as 'a sad person's view of a gay person'. According to Stephen Fothergill, Philip was 'a lonely person with a desperate need to perform' and Philip admits that he sometimes suffered 'the proper punishments of being individualistic, i.e. feeling ugly, lonely and ridiculous'. Quentin did not go this far: he describes himself as 'confused and hurt and hungry' but doesn't mention loneliness and never appeared lonely to those who knew him. On the contrary, he gave an impression of almost impudent self-sufficiency, often flaunting his desire to be alone and live alone. Yet something must have driven both men into their lives of affectation and exhibitionism. Both men sought an audience, yet shrank from human contact and even from human touch. Both found transactions with strangers difficult and claimed to be particularly frightened of waiters. According to John Berger, of whom more in a moment, early photographs of Philip O'Connor show 'a thin man whose eyes accost but whose body looks as if it's trying to disappear'.

As for Quentin, aloofness, fear and real or fake inadequacy were built into his nature.

But here the similarities cease. Philip O'Connor's life was utterly chaotic and untidy and would remain so for many years. He moved around desperately, sleeping on mattresses, borrowing money and spending it instantly, taking taxis whenever possible – 'an absurd luxury' according to his friend Fothergill – and throwing caution to the wind. Such wildness may owe something to Philip's bohemian upbringing, while Quentin's extreme restraint and self-discipline must owe a lot to the 'wall-to-wall puritanism' of his early years. In a sense, neither Quentin nor Philip had really rebelled against his background. Once Quentin had found his 'perfect' room, it would remain his London home for ever: he was still there at the age of seventy-two. Compared with O'Connor's extravagant existence, Quentin's life seems positively restrained, entirely free from emotional attachments or financial burdens. Quentin honoured every commitment, never owed money in his life and was often in a position to lend or give people generous sums. Philip was a famous drunk, with exotic tastes in food, and a passionate regard for Oscar Wilde and Charlie Chaplin. Quentin was famously sober and abstemious, almost oblivious to what he ate and even during the war was boasting about his 'crossword puzzle mind'. In later life he would dismiss Oscar Wilde as 'gross' and Charlie Chaplin as 'nauseatingly sentimental'. Philip was a romantic, poetic, pipe-smoking, footloose figure who had an erotic relationship with everybody and everything. When he found a passage in a book he particularly loved, he liked to kiss it. His poetry, like his personality, was recklessly unrestrained and his emotions often got the better of him. He had a violent temper, he suffered from peccadilloes, he got in a huff, took umbrage. Quentin was famous for his Edwardian manners and stagey courtesies. Philip was rude to everyone, shouted people down and accompanied his quips with imitations of farmyard animals and bursts of childish laughter.

There was also a stark divergence in how the two men earned or attempted to earn a living. Philip O'Connor preferred to live *off* other people – he wrote begging letters most of his life – and made no bones about his parasitical nature. Even his poetical output was halting.

During the war he may have recited or scribbled poetry all day long but his *Selected Poems* contains only three poems bearing wartime dates. In fact he quickly abandoned his factory job and it wasn't until after the war that certain strong-minded women briefly forced him into legitimate employment. Quentin Crisp faced the possibility of destitution at the beginning of the war – and had even considered suicide as an honourable way out – but soon found lettering and design work and this continued after he started working as an art school model. In all his dealings with employers he was utterly reliable and he also found time to make the occasional small bid for the limelight.

His first enterprise of this sort came in 1943 when he wrote a pamphlet and got his Chelsea neighbour Mervyn Peake to illustrate it. The pamphlet consisted of forty-eight 'rather clumsy verses of angerless satire' directed at the Ministry of Labour. Quentin tells us he dashed these off in two afternoons but after ensnaring the co-operation of Mervyn Peake, recently invalided out of the army and then the most fashionable illustrator in England, the book sailed into print. *All This and Bevin Too* was not a great success – when Quentin crept into Hatchards to see how it was selling, the only customer showing an interest in it turned out to be Mr Peake himself – but the connection between the two men has its own pleasing significance. Quentin Crisp's ornate gothic name and matching personality fitted perfectly into the world and imagination of Mervyn Peake and he would become a close friend of the artist's family. Sebastian Peake, then a child, remembers that Quentin was often in the house in Glebe Place and sometimes entrusted to escort him to nursery school, wearing 'open-toed sandals out of which peeped pink toenails'. A second book was commissioned by the publishers Nicholson and Watson, but 'Between the Devil and the BBC' somehow never appeared. *All This and Bevin Too*, which sold for only a shilling, is today a collector's item, worth at least £200.

After this tantalizing episode, Quentin reports that he 'sank back into oblivion' and soon took on a full-time job with a small advertising firm, which designed exhibition stands and display units from tiny premises at Notting Hill Gate. The owner was a small, plump, sandy-haired Scotsman named Kenneth MacQueen and it says much for Quentin's tenacity and patience that he was able to combine this work with his art school bookings and that he would stay in this dull job until the end of the war and beyond, though as we shall see he was sustained by the flood of American servicemen who were soon to arrive in London. And by his triumph at Bow Street Magistrates Court.

Philip O'Connor's life was meanwhile going through further upsets – he describes this period with Jean as 'our dead aftermath' – though he continued to make new friends. One of these was George Mann, an artist who sold his pictures on the pavements of Chelsea, an enterprise in which Philip immediately joined. With Mann's encouragement, Philip also got a job as a fire-watcher in Sloane Square and along with Jean the three of them moved into some studios at the back of 4 Limerston Street, off Fulham Road. These buildings, which could so easily still be there but are now occupied by a modern block, were the setting for further alcohol-fuelled performances. According to *Memoirs of a Public Baby*, Philip tried to stimulate Jean by singing at the top of his voice in imitation Italian and then strutting up and down Chaplin-style. He was rewarded by a few laughs – 'the loveliest gap in the clouds' – and then set off to perform on a more public stage. Dressed in a black silk jockey's cap, he serenaded the Piccadilly prostitutes with a borrowed one-string violin. He also attended auditions for ENSA and the Canadian impresario Carol Levis, who years later would audition the Beatles, and began work on an immense revue called 'The Public Baby', his first use of this phrase, in which he claimed to have involved a girl called Cooper-Willis and his new acquaintance Quentin Crisp, who lived only a few minutes' walk from Limerston Street. When I asked Quentin about this later, he had no memories of it and the project was no doubt soon put aside. Stephen Fothergill, on the other hand, remembers this dire time well. He remembers drinking with Philip in the Eight Bells near Chelsea Town Hall and the Pier Hotel in Oakley Street and finally in the Limerston Street studios where the normally gentle Fothergill became enraged by Jean's 'withdrawn and uncommunicative state, almost catatonic' and threw a glass at her. This created no effect whatsoever but elicited from Philip the comment, 'You could have hit her, you know.'

In June 1944, the buzzbombs began to fall on London and each night Philip and his 'terrifyingly fearless' wife cowered in an air-raid shelter between the studios. 'Every morning,' he writes, 'seemed posthumous in our lives, every night an encounter with all approximations to death.' Closing his eyes during the raids Philip sought 'an apocalyptic vision of enlightenment', encountered door after door and corridor after corridor but never reached 'an Absolute'. After a few more nights like this, George Mann suggested they should all go to his Wiltshire cottage. Here Jean's last trickle of money ran out and Philip claims that he worked for five months on the harvest, while secretly plotting to leave his wife. For two months, presumably during the winter of 1944–5, he then pushed an old man round Salisbury in a bathchair, ignorant of the fact that he was very close to where his estranged sister Desirée was now living with her husband and two small daughters.

That winter, Philip chose a public spot close to Salisbury Cathedral to fly into a rage with his wife and express his 'unwillingness to be with her any more'. There and then he abandoned her – and returned to the studio in Limerston Street, now sublet to Stephen Fothergill. A few days later, Jean reappeared on the doorstep, but he would not let her in and she slept in the air-raid shelter. Philip readily acknowledges his 'incredible brutality' at this time but claims it was only brought about by 'brute fear'. In *Memoirs of a Public Baby*, which more or less ends at this point, he has nothing more to say about Jean and it was left to his friend Patrick de Maré to finish this part of the story. 'I was working at Shenley Hospital,' he explains, 'and lived in a house in the grounds. They came to stay. They'd spent all their money. She was very mad. We had to take her to a big hospital, a very sad journey in a car. Very, very sad.' Philip's last words to Jean were characteristically and unforgivably honest. 'The trouble with you and me, Jean,' he asserted, 'is that you didn't have enough money.'

Later in life Philip confessed that his treatment of Jean was, 'according to conventional standards, very bad', but claimed that he felt 'very honest' and, more doubtfully, that he had stayed with her for some time when there was no money left. Maria Steiner later commented that Philip went through Jean's money 'like a knife through butter' and Paul Potts wrote sneeringly that having spent the whole of Jean's fortune, Philip 'allowed her to be taken away by the parish'. Philip, of course, remained haunted by Jean and paid many flowery tributes to her in his autobiography, describing her as, among other things, 'the most wasted woman or person I know'.

Never at any time in his life could Quentin Crisp be accused of letting anyone down in this way and indeed he would prove to be a far more dutiful son than his two brothers overseas, though he makes no reference to this dutifulness in his autobiography. Throughout his life, Quentin's behaviour was, by conventional standards, very good, and no revelation in *The Naked Civil Servant* echoes the horrifying confessions with which *Memoirs of a Public Baby* is packed. On the contrary, Quentin puts an agonizingly cheery spin on the most unpleasant events and goes completely over the top when describing pleasant ones like the arrival of the American troops in the latter part of the war.

By 1944, there were over a million American servicemen in Britain. Most of them came to London and, according to Quentin, flowed through the capital 'like cream on strawberries or melted butter on green peas'. These visitors apparently had no time for Philip O'Connor – he wrote later, 'The American soldiers looked at me as though I were a freak' – but were thoroughly enchanted by Quentin Crisp. Their easy-going presence seems to have awoken his sexual appetite, which he had been content to let lie dormant, and he writes excitedly of the bodies 'which bulged through every khaki fibre towards our feverish hands'. For the first time in his life, Quentin seems to have taken unqualified pleasure in the attention of strangers and was more than happy to be pursued through the streets, archly observing, 'Never in the history of sex was so much offered to so many by so few.' Some GIs mistook him for a woman but showed no distaste when they discovered he was not, and he later acknowledged that he might represent 'some kind of sexual experience which might not be found elsewhere'. In later life, he described how the Americans would always walk beside him crabwise and never take their eyes off his face while they were speaking. He also explained, 'They were never out to degrade or defile or frighten you and there was never any suggestion that you were lifelong friends.' The sex itself, he said, was 'nearly always sodomy or some kind of oral copulation' but he does not seek to make these activities sound as distasteful as he does on other occasions. He admits that when the streets were thronged by Americans, he lived in an even higher state of constant exhilaration than usual.

To start with, Quentin spread his favours among the many but after a while he settled for a single, unnamed serviceman, who offered him a physical relationship 'without stint and without overtones'. In *The Naked Civil Servant* he goes out of his way to stress that he did not love this man and would never have put his interests before those of his lifelong friends. Discussing this eighteen-month affair with Philip Mackie, Quentin revealed that the man had 'a voluptuous physique', came from Seattle, was a truck driver and had an Italian name. When he visited Quentin at Beaufort Street, he would stay the night. Again he stresses that there was no affection between them. Quentin was as ruthless about love as Philip was about money and when this man ceased to call on him he seems oblivious as to whether he had gone to heaven or New York. He adds that for him these two places were the same anyway, and all his encounters during this period must have reinforced his sense of the wonders of America first instilled in him by early films. By now, he was talking about America as 'the island of the blessed' and claiming that he was, by nature, American and may have even nurtured hopes of living there one day.

The other highlight or major event in Quentin Crisp's life which took place at this time – almost certainly in 1944 – was that, for the first and only time in his life, he was arrested and charged with soliciting. He devotes seven pages of *The Naked Civil Servant* to the incident and it is not surprising that his subsequent court appearance provides a central scene – a 'must' according to the scriptwriter Philip Mackie – in the film of his life. In his autobiography, he explains that an innocent chance encounter with an acquaintance called John Booth Palmer outside the Hippodrome Theatre had led to him being apprehended by two policemen and marched to Savile Row Police Station. Here he was searched, but only stripped far enough for it to be seen that he was not wearing women's underclothes, and had his fingerprints taken – accompanied by ten inky squiggles representing his superfluous fingernails – and waited while someone was found to go bail. His former landlady, Miss Lumley, was his first choice but she was not at home in her new flat at 39 Markham Square, Chelsea. Eventually a friend named Victor Brightmore, whom Quentin describes as an orchestral instrumentalist, was found and Quentin was free to dash through the blacked-out streets to find Mr Palmer – later described as 'nice and cosy and hopeless' – to give evidence on his behalf and to notify his Charlotte Street acquaintances of the exciting miscarriage of justice that was likely to occur.

The following morning, Quentin Crisp appeared at Bow Street Magistrates Court, dressed in black, and surrounded by supporters and admirers, who included his friend Pat from Battersea, still living with the Polish gentleman and working as a shorthand typist, Miss Lumley, Bertram Shuttleworth and his wife, a fellow lodger from Beaufort Street called Miss Beeson and several others. Quentin viewed this event as 'a wonderful, wonderful challenge' and chose to take the witness box to explain that the whole wide world could see he was homosexual and no one looking as he did could possibly hope to solicit anyone in broad daylight. While he was giving evidence, a stranger in the public gallery neatly summed up the whole Quentin Crisp phenomenon by whispering, 'They can't do nuthin' with 'im. He can't 'elp 'isself. You can see that.' John Booth Palmer, who ten years later committed suicide, told the court that he already knew Quentin Crisp and he was followed into the witness box by Hilda Lumley and a string of character witnesses who attested to the irreproachability of Quentin's character. From Mr MacQueen there was written evidence expressing complete confidence in his employee. Eventually the remarkably benign magistrate declared that he was getting tired of this 'recital of praise' and dismissed the case. Quentin later wrote that this was a triumphant moment as he had shown in a court of law that he was 'homosexual and as stainless as Sheffield steel'. Yet, he also wonders if he had ever refrained from any course of action on the grounds that it was 'wrong, illegal or immoral'.

The Not Guilty verdict was of course a disappointment for the police, who subsequently strove to get Quentin banned from the few

Fitzrovia pubs that he frequented. At the Wheatsheaf, the landlord Mr Redvers was accused of running 'a funny sort of place' and when he replied, 'How funny?', the police pointed in Quentin's direction. Protests from friends of Quentin like the painter Frederico Sante, himself a rumbustious figure, who said, 'We can't have this', and the landlord's own protestations that Quentin Crisp had 'never caused a fight or behaved badly' failed to avert the ban.

Was such a distinction ever imposed on Philip O'Connor, who may not have caused fights but certainly behaved extremely badly? At the beginning of 1945, he had returned from Chelsea to Fitzrovia and moved into 48 Maple Street, which is still standing today underneath the Post Office Tower and then belonged to the resourceful Mr Mendelson. Among the other lodgers were Stephen Fothergill, who slept in dirty white tennis trousers on a narrow camp bed encased in an immense mahogany bedstead, and a girl called Bobbie Battersby. Described by Fothergill as 'a fire-eating socialist who insisted on drinking out of a pint tankard', Bobbie had been brought up in Reading and introduced to Soho earlier in the war by a man she remembers for his 'Lord Alfred Douglas lips'. She describes Maple Street as 'a doss house'. Philip moved into the very dark cellar but soon felt sufficiently boosted by an advance from Tambimuttu for a book of poems to be illustrated with his own drawings to begin an affair with Bobbie upstairs, who was then working for the Ministry of Education.

Philip O'Connor and Bobbie Battersby spent six months together in the Maple Street basement. Philip liked Bobbie for, among other reasons, her ability to make triple puns and take risks. Bobbie liked Philip for 'his beautiful one-off mind' and added, 'One of his great qualities was his capacity to bite the hand that fed him, instead of being subverted by it. This is the *essence* of artistic integrity.' Bobbie acknowledges that Philip could be 'nasty on an epic scale' but insists that he 'represented a great deal I aspire to' and which she'd never found in anyone else.

During their time together, Philip briefly wielded the lights at the Bedford Variety Theatre in Camden Town but otherwise, says Bobbie, 'We had no fucking money.' A £30 grant from Herbert Read and his colleagues at the Society of Authors simply gave Philip the chance to get horribly drunk. In the basement, he cooked odd dishes on a primus stove: garlic sausage, powdered egg, baked beans and something Stephen Fothergill called 'beer soup'. It was an odd little household. Fothergill's culinary efforts extended to an omelette made with porridge but Bobbie Battersby claims she was 'utterly undomesticated', determined neither to cook nor sew. One night a v2 rocket fell on nearby Whitfield Street. Fothergill rushed down to the basement, producing an enigmatic comment from Philip, 'That was the devil!' And, all the time, Philip talked about Jean. 'Clearly he was still in love with her,' says Bobbie. 'There was no doubt about that. But who drove who mad I'm not quite sure. They were both psychiatrically disorientated.' One day on the wall of the cellar, Philip saw a three-dimensional hermaphrodite figure in red, green and gold, somewhat resembling Blake's flying Lucifer.

When the war ended, Quentin Crisp had been long enough in his Chelsea room to have discovered that the dust doesn't get any worse after however long it was – he had been there five years now – and Philip O'Connor was still in his Fitzrovian cellar. Bobbie Battersby was now several months pregnant.

The Road to Conformity

I am more sorry than I can say to have to send this back to you, particularly as we took such a very long time to read it and think about it. That long delay did mean, I assure you, that we considered very seriously and carefully indeed the possibility of accepting your book for publication, for – may I say this at once – we have no doubt whatever that it has got very considerable distinction and literary quality. This was the unanimous verdict of several readers. The trouble really is – and I gather one or two other publishers have felt rather as we do about it – that we are convinced that the book would have to be subjected to some very thorough editing, and we feel that we simply haven't ourselves got the time or opportunity to carry it out here. May I send you, though, my most sincere good wishes for placing it elsewhere and assure you again of our regret that we weren't in the end able to accept it for ourselves.

CHARLES MONTEITH TO PHILIP O'CONNOR,
28 September 1955

Philip O'Connor was twenty-eight when the war ended and as 'psychiatrically disoriented' as ever. In a pattern which would repeat itself in future relationships, he marched ahead down Charlotte Street with his pregnant mistress following some distance behind. Bobbie Battersby had her own agonies, feeling torn between Philip and a long-standing boyfriend called Jake. Within a few weeks of the war ending, she had left Fitzrovia and returned to her home in Reading, leaving Philip to have a breakdown in Maple Street. Stephen Fothergill sent a telegram to Bobbie explaining the situation but she did not ride to his rescue. Nor did Philip come to her aid when on 20 December 1945 she gave birth to a baby boy. According to Bobbie, Philip refused to register the birth or play any part in the child's upbringing, though he seems happy or even insistent that the baby be given his own first name.

During the preceding autumn Philip seems to have been adrift – even a telephone box he entered began to tremble – and he appears to have lived in many different places. For a while he stayed at the surgery of the Chelsea vet Anthony O'Neill. Now in his eighties, O'Neill still practises in the same premises in Blacklands Terrace, beside John Sandoe's bookshop, and recalls that Philip occupied a room in the basement and used his typewriter and, in return for these favours, answered the telephone. O'Neill says that it was always difficult pinpointing exactly where Philip's genius lay and he could not 'make head or tail' of his poems. After a few weeks, Philip went off, taking with him O'Neill's typewriter which he never returned.

By Christmas 1945 the arrival of peace had had its impact and Philip noted 'a diminishing bohemian spirit in the air'. During the next few years Philip O'Connor and other rebels retreated into more silent, private worlds, their lively visions shattered or at least reprocessed by the launch of the Welfare State. Yet before he could start off on what he calls 'the halting road to conformity' Philip was to sink even lower, eventually sleeping on a pile of coal inside the old air-raid shelter at the Limerston Street studios. From here he emerged on Christmas Eve 1945 and retraced his steps to Fitzrovia, where he had a chance encounter with Quentin Crisp's beautiful friend Maria Gabrielle Steiner.

Accounts of this meeting are confused. Maria may have been on her way to meet Tambimuttu in a nightclub called the Caribbean or may have actually been with Tambi when she met O'Connor. The volume of Philip's poems that Tambi paid for had, incidentally, not come out and Tambi himself would soon move to New York. One version of events is that Maria there and then offered Philip a bed for the night at 12 Fitzroy Street, or rather the sofa in her kitchen, tucked him up and proceeded to the Caribbean on her own. Another possibility is that she invited Philip to a party the following night in her flat and this prospect made Philip feel secure enough to squander his last few shillings on turkey and Christmas pudding at a Lyons Corner House. What is indisputable is Maria's beauty. I have already mentioned that Quentin Crisp called her 'the most beautiful girl the world has ever known'. Philip would soon describe her as 'an Austrian madonna' and see 'vintage sunshine' in her. She was four years younger than him, very small but strong, with an exciting mixture of pagan, Moravian and Tartar blood. Born into a prosperous home in Vienna, she had come to England in 1937 and been classed as a 'friendly alien'. For a while she had worked as a cook-general and then as an assistant at Mr Saunders's bookshop in Oxford. Here she had been discovered by Sarah Roberts, wife of the painter William Roberts, and been elevated to working with the Bach Choir and modelling at the Slade. According to Philip, her top-floor flat in Fitzroy Street was 'by no means luxurious', but the front door of the building was always open and Quentin Crisp was one of the many who dropped in. At the time she met Philip, Maria was doing little jobs in commercial art, like painting 'plain, cabbagey roses' onto lampshades.

Philip O'Connor once said ungallantly that he only started his affair with Maria because he had 'nowhere to go and she was lonely'. It would be much truer to say that, after his long-drawn-out ordeals at the Maudsley, in coal cellars and lavatories and in the troubled company of Jean Hore, the upper flat at 12 Fitzroy Street represented an encampment of great security and delicate charm, adorned as it was with haunting pictures of lost children, which were and are one of Maria's particular specialities as an artist. When Philip arrived in her life, Maria reports, he had 'very marked features' and looked very like a famous portrait of Lorenzo the Magnificent, though his only adornment at the time was a big scarf. Scarves were a permanent and prominent feature of Philip's wardrobe throughout his life and, if one accepts John Berger's observation, another way of hiding himself from people.

Philip was to remain in Maria's care for three or four years. At the outset she was sternly warned by Quentin Crisp, 'Mr O'Connor won't be able to look after you, Miss Steiner', and she had few expectations of him. 'I knew Philip couldn't work,' she said later. 'He was too frightened to go and get a railway ticket. He used to get very, very frightened and nervous. I remember him shaking with fear at Liverpool Street.' When she told her father, who lived in Dorset, that Philip was too shy to work, his response was explosive but Maria remained indulgent to her lover and concentrated her energies on curing him of a duodenal ulcer by making him drink cabbage and lemon juice. His nervousness persisted, however, and when Maria ducked her head under the water while washing her hair, Philip reacted as if she was committing suicide.

In spite of his protestations, Philip did find occupations. His new attempts to write may have failed – he decided that the licence for his kind of 'surrealist whimsy' had now expired – but when Maria became pregnant he went off to work for two maiden ladies on a farm near Coventry – or was it near Thame in Oxfordshire? Maria herself would continue working until the last moment, painting dolls, and remained phlegmatic. On 21 November 1946, a girl was born and Maria was surprised to find Philip there when she and the baby Sarah – Philip was dissuaded from calling her Tatiana – returned from hospital. 'Nobody leaves gold when they find it,' Philip explained and shortly afterwards astonished Patrick de Maré and others by getting a job in the library at the London School of Economics, cataloguing books that had been evacuated from London, and for a while felt part of 'the family of mankind' even though 'orthodox decency' made him feel 'dishonest'. Others rallied round the young mother. Mervyn Peake's wife Maeve provided baby clothes and Miss Schmidt, the famously bearded boss of Schmidt's restaurant in Charlotte Street, stuffed the baby's pushchair with German sausage. Maria also remembers a strange derelict woman taking a great deal of interest in the new baby and is convinced that this was Philip's wife Jean who she believes was still on the loose in London. Others believe that Jean was by now in the hospital at Banstead, where Philip would visit her for the last time in 1947.

Meanwhile, Philip made further attempts at writing. He sought and obtained reviewing work from the *New Statesman* but suspected that its literary editor, V. S. Pritchett, might have mistaken his 'intellectual air' for 'intellectual achievements' and been beguiled by Maria when she carried his contributions and requests for more work to and fro. In January 1947, Philip submitted five stories to the BBC's newly formed Third Programme, which were rejected, and in the autumn of that year got over his scruples about 'surrealist whimsy' by writing a long and rambling piece of gleeful, malicious prose entitled 'The Meeg'. This appeared in a literary quarterly, *Orion*, edited by Denys Kilham-Roberts, who was one of Philip's supporters at the Society of Authors. How much poetry he published is difficult to find out without going through all the relevant periodicals of the day. Most of the poems in the collected edition are undated and unattributed to a particular publication though Maria believes that Geoffrey Grigson, the first editor to print Philip's poems, had continued to 'look after' him.

In spite of this help and occasional grants of £30 from the Society of Authors, Philip and Maria were often 'miserably poor'. Within days of moving into Fitzroy Street, Philip had pawned Maria's gramophone. He later pawned his overcoat and then sold the pawn ticket itself. In pubs, a few people would stand Philip drinks but the majority avoided him and he often resorted to making roll-ups of other people's fag ends. On Christmas Eve 1947, Philip and Maria went to the National Assistance Board in Kentish Town and banged on the door until they obtained some money.

In spite of these hardships, Maria Steiner tried resolutely to 'achieve' a home with few resources and very little money. She was clever at getting free damaged fruit and vegetables from the Seaton Street market. The traders knew her here and Sarah's pram got piled up with unsold produce at closing time. Maria had her own recipe for muesli, which she had learnt as a child in Austria. 'Philip liked my cooking,' she says, and she enjoyed the bread he loved 'making and baking' but hated his 'beer soup'. In this climate, Philip claims that the 'histrionics' of his youth could not now be repeated at 'as great a length' yet his conduct was often impossible, or simply puzzling. 'You could never tell if he was being serious or just trying to annoy me,' says Maria.

'It was difficult to communicate with him because he was so blistering. He knew how to dig in where I was so vulnerable.' One of Philip's cruder jibes was to tell Maria that she looked like a Viennese whore, but she was equally upset that he was so hostile to her friends and to many of the literary figures in the district. When Dylan Thomas stumbled drunkenly into Maria's house rather than the one next door, which belonged to his friends Edward Clark and Elisabeth Lutyens, Philip barked at the Welshman, 'I'm going to beat you up!' Philip claims that at first he found relaxation and security with Maria but later became irritable, inventing what he calls 'a happy technique of growling like a dog'. Looking back at this time, Maria remembers that Philip could be 'very puritanical'. She remembers him standing on the edge of the dance floor at the Caribbean Club while she was dancing with someone else and muttering, 'You're making a spectacle of yourself.' At home, Philip warned her, 'Everywhere outside this room there are people who would like to destroy us.' 'I felt the room shrinking,' said Maria. 'He made me feel even more confused.' Philip was as possessive of Maria as he was of every other woman in his life. She remembers that he would 'sit on the parapet of the house and watch me with my mother's opera glasses when I went shopping, in case I talked to anyone'. He was also jealous of his own privacy and would sometimes snap at her, 'Be quiet. I'm thinking', though at other times he could be 'very penetrating' and 'would answer when I hadn't actually said anything'. According to Maria, 'Philip talked a lot of nonsense but then said something absolutely amazing. The absolute truth.' He also burdened her with his sadness over Oliver French, and, from time to time, would tease her about Jean. Maria remembers that they once walked past a magnificent Studebaker and Philip said, 'That's the car that Jean and I had.'

Soon after Sarah's birth, Maria says she withdrew from Philip's soul. 'Things got a bit wonky,' she says. 'I got angry with him. I banged a tray of paints down on his head and got him to sleep on the sofa in the bathroom.' Financial pressures added to these problems – Maria had to appear in court for not paying the rent – and they soon decided that Philip should move temporarily to cheap accommodation they'd heard about near Clare in Suffolk and make another attempt at a book. In the summer of 1948 they inspected this place together and, after helping Philip settle in, Maria and her baby returned to London.

The house was called Purton Hall and had been drawn to Maria's attention by an artist named John Grenville whom she had met while working as a landgirl during the war. It was one of the last remaining buildings of a twelfth-century hamlet called Purton Green, which is far from any public road, approachable only across open fields and difficult to describe without sounding as if one is writing a brochure. Too derelict and neglected to be described as picturesque, Purton Hall had once been a small manor-house but was now divided into three parts, surrounded by the remains of a moat and various fruit trees. The only neighbours were Sophie Browne, who had lived in the end part of the house all her life, and Amy Sechell, who lived in an even older surviving house a few yards away. The rent for Philip's bit of Purton Hall was half-a-crown a week.

In *The Lower View*, Philip O'Connor paints a vivid and enviable picture of his life in this isolated ruin, which was in its own way as magical as Maria's encampment in Fitzroy Street – and complementary to it. Though his roots were not rural, he seemed well suited to this primitive setting, entirely devoid of 'facilities', and describes it as 'a place of refuge' from the 'stimulant-clogged city'. He occupied the central bit of the house, cooking on a fire that was large enough to hold three-foot elm logs, and keeping his food warm on an ornate centre-stone that had once graced an arched doorway of a bombed house in Fitzroy Street. Here he 'cosied' voluptuously, supported by a bust of Beethoven and a picture of Michelangelo's *Moses*, with the wind and rain, as likely as not, howling outside.

His solitary routines in this 'hermit's fastness' are carefully, lovingly and self-indulgently described in *The Lower View* and probably provide the best part of this sequel to *Memoirs of a Public Baby*. While here he wrote very little, apart from letters to Maria – in one of which he seems to have begged her not to have an affair in his absence, arguing that a woman's promiscuity does far more harm to the family than a man's – but managed to do a lot of reading. 'Equanimity came with tea and blessings with twilight.' In three-hour sessions he devoured Wordsworth, Conrad, Dostoevski, Gorky, Montaigne, kissing favourite passages and sometimes weeping over them before submerging into the euphoria of pipe-smoking. Michael Hamburger, whose translation of Hölderlin's poems had come out at the end of the war, visited Purton at least once and remembers that one of Philip's pipes had a human head carved onto the bowl.

During the day, Philip sometimes plaited raffia for a shop in London. He also dabbled with gardening, grew a few vegetables and shovelled shit from his earth closet to put on his beans. Dressed in high boots and a plaid-lined cape or opera cloak and supported by a stick, he surveyed his property, counted his greengages and fingered his Blenheim Oranges – a variety of apple – and saw himself as 'monarch of a strange desolation'. Every day he visited the radiantly healthy farmer's wife Mrs Slater to collect milk and sometimes caught a mouth-watering glimpse of her larder, hung with hams, sides of bacon, partridges, pheasants, hares, poultry, cheeses, creams and butters about which he brooded later. Once a week he cycled the six miles into the little town of Clare, registered at the Labour Exchange and collected £2 3s a week in dole money which he used to buy onions, corned beef, Typhoo tea and an ounce of dark flake tobacco. Other excursions took him to the local Greene King pub a mile and a half away in Denston where he liked the Suffolk ale and the landlady Mrs Hourihan told him he would 'make good'. Alone at Purton Hall, he became odder, his solitude thickened and he felt 'shattered' when a book he was reading came to an end. From time to time, he tells us, he emitted 'shrieks of disgust', adopted expressions of 'bestial sensuality' and talked to himself. 'Good evening,' he might say. 'Sit down. I'm making tea; it won't be long. Take your hat off – please do. Are you comfortable? I'm in the kitchen.' His only constant or regular companion was a cat called Tiddles, with whom, he told me later, he had 'relations', using it as 'a masturbation cushion' and then throwing it across the room in disgust.

At regular intervals he was visited by Maria, hitch-hiking from London and imposing her own routines on the place, getting on well with Mrs Slater but 'nicking' Brussels sprouts from her and snatching a rabbit from the cat's mouth which she skinned and cooked. From time to time Philip also broke away from his fastness, cycling the sixty miles to London, especially when money was due from Maria's father. He seems to have spent most of the winter of 1948–9 in London and was certainly there in October 1948 when Aldous Huxley, now a Hollywood scriptwriter, visited the capital. Learning that his old mentor was staying in luxury at Claridges Hotel and being interviewed by people like Cyril Connolly, who reported that the novelist now 'dressed like an Argentinian dandy', O'Connor seized the opportunity to hand in 'a vile piece of paper' to the hotel doorman on which he had scribbled a note to Huxley requesting £5. There is no note of this incident in Sybille Bedford's two-volume biography of Huxley.

While in London, Philip had lent his bit of Purton Hall to Oliver Bernard, oldest of the three Bernard brothers, whom he had met in Charlotte Street and who remembers Philip as cruel and consoling and 'marvellously argumentative'. Bernard mentions his time at Purton in his book *Getting Over It* and describes how he had worked for the farmer, Mr Slater, carting pig manure and fodder beet in a horse-drawn tumbril. It is difficult to imagine Philip performing these tasks, even in a theatrical context.

Philip was back in London the following summer when on 5 June 1949 Maria gave birth to their second child, conceived at Purton Hall, a boy named Peter. This event took place at home in Fitzroy Street, in preparation for which their friend Joan Rhodes had provided a utility bed, Maria's own bed being pronounced too soft by the midwife. Maria recalls how Joan Rhodes – now performing her Mighty Mannequin act in nightclubs – coolly carried the new bed up the stairs on the palm of one hand, Philip panting behind her. Maria describes it as 'a beautiful birth', the sun was shining and Philip was making bread in the kitchen while she was in labour. Informed that he had a son, he then declared, 'A rival!' and declined to look in on the mother and baby and soon afterwards returned to Suffolk leaving Maria to start an affair with his friend Patrick de Maré.

At Purton, he tells us, Philip shrank from most visitors, explaining that they 'dismembered' him, sometimes making him gasp 'in combined ferocity and anxiety', and at other times released in him all the characteristics of the 'village idiot'. On the other hand he was also becoming vaguely aware of his neighbours in the adjacent villages where there was quite a spill-over from the bohemian London he knew. At Denston, living with his wife and eleven-year-old step-daughter Nicolle was John Grenville, who had originally alerted Maria to the existence of Purton Hall and now worked as a copper-beater and silversmith. At Tilty Mill in Essex, Colquhoun and McBryde, Scottish painters and Charlotte Street legends, had set up country quarters. Elsewhere, there were other 'local notables' the proximity to whom, wherever he lived, would often prove disconcerting for Philip.

A less threatening arrival in the area, who was to become a lifelong friend, was the artist Edith Young. Sometime during the spring or summer of 1949, Philip sheepishly called on her cottage for the first time, characteristically 'approaching her door and running away from it simultaneously', full of imaginings that its occupant might have been 'a little nervous of my rumoured wildness'. These embarrassments over, Edith Young, who was some twenty-five years Philip's senior, proceeded to place 'her enormous immovable attention' at his service. She then gave him some delicious Australian fruit cake, which he ate with trembling teeth, and took him to the Greene King pub. Here they soon met most evenings, Edith showing an insatiable appetite for Philip's 'originalities'. In *The Lower View*, Edith is renamed Sybil and Philip writes that she warmed him 'at both ends' and declares that in her company, 'I felt divinely normal, as though I'd swallowed Paradise.' When I asked Maria years later if Philip had had an affair with Edith, Maria said certainly not and added that Philip 'had a horror of old women'.

During this time Philip made further applications – 'Forgive my quaint garrulity' – to the Society of Authors and in an office memo dated 22 May 1950, Denys Kilham-Roberts appears to have persuaded his colleagues to dish out a further £20. 'Poor Philip O'Connor,' he begins. 'He has had serious mental problems at various times in the past – rather like David Gascoyne – and this has made him unfitted for most jobs. Herbert Read, Geoffrey Grigson and I are among the people who have recognized an element of rather crazy genius in his writing.'

Within a few months, Philip's new friend Edith Young had also arranged with her son Michael, a former director of the social studies group at Dartington, that Philip should get a grant and go off and study vagrancy. This he did, but only after a great many false starts which fizzled out at the Greene King pub. It seems that he eventually set off on 10 July 1950 and headed for the Midlands, spending his first night in the open on a pile of grass beside the roadside, 'shivering with terror and cold'. At Ely, he walked around the cathedral until he was shooed away by a little man who said he was out of visiting hours. He then proceeded north in the direction of the Yorkshire home of his benefactor Herbert Read. In *The Lower View* he gives us a vivid account of his journey and reinforces this with further thoughts in *Vagrancy*. In the latter book, he describes the range of emotions he felt on the road: the relief, sense of adventure, depression, stupor, hallucinations, irritability, predatoriness, loss of identity, alienation and 'blissful one-ness with everything and everyone'. On this particular odyssey, he also explains how tramping stretched him out of himself, loosened and lifted him and gave him back the 'breezy, ventilated neurasthenic-messianic feeling' which he'd known in the past. He claims that his voice became weaker and his eyesight sharper. He spotted cigarette ends and scraps of food by the wayside which turned out to be 'nectar'. He complains of feeling tired, lonely and rejected, but says nothing at all about blisters.

As he walked on – he claims to have covered about thirty miles a day – he sensed that his appearance was becoming odder, his eyes wilder. His reflection in shop windows had a wicked air and he saw himself as 'a wild wolverine fellow'. Of the other tramps, none were ever unpleasant to him but he was never quite accepted as one of them, more as one down on his luck than as a natural wanderer. He may have reinforced this impression by adopting a fey manner, behaving absent-mindedly over small change and purchasing what he describes as 'unnecessary refinements'. Yet his speed at spending his Dartington funds, a lot of it on drink, must have placed him into exactly the same circumstances as these more seasoned men of the road. The experience also – as fifteen years earlier – gave him fresh insights into the world around him. Sometimes, this seemed a waste-land of incredible bleakness and society a rat race or dog fight in which free will and self-responsibility played no part. Passing through villages, he was aware of the 'purse-like' expressions on the faces of those he sailed past and the 'crib-cosy' nature of their homes. During his worst burst of hysteria, he was overwhelmed by 'an excruciating perception of the puppet life' that surrounded him.

By the time he reached Herbert Read's lovely honey-coloured house at Stonegrave, near York, Philip was extremely dirty and very embarrassed about his appearance but his host was as gracious as the house, anticipating O'Connor's needs and desires. That night, Philip washed his socks in the bathroom before going to bed. In the morning, there was a small drinks party at the house at which he drank strong gin. Before he left, his host gave him two large cigars to enjoy on his journey. We do not know what Read made of his wild visitor or how he compared with other guests – J. R. Ackerley and his famous dog Queenie had stayed in the house earlier that year – only that he would later declare that Philip O'Connor was 'outside outsiders', or words to that effect.

The visit to this comfortable house nearly diverted Philip from his intended tour round England. Two miles away from Stonegrave, he stopped in a wood and wrote a note to Read suggesting that he become his secretary. Wisely, Read declined and O'Connor pressed on for York, which he found 'distractingly prosperous', and then to Manchester. Here he shared one of his cigars with a busker and spent a night in a stinking reception centre or casual ward, sampling the 'abominable' food. During the small hours he was confronted by various masturbators and in the morning he was delegated to wash the bath. He then wandered on to Liverpool, South Wales and over to North Devon and to Plymouth, where further funds from the Society of Authors awaited him. With them, he bought a pair of jeans – untypical attire for him – and proceeded to Salisbury where he stayed in another reception centre and was asked to clean the lavatory. Had he known he was again near his sister, would he have done anything about it? Anyway he did not linger in Wiltshire for long and by 25 August he had made his way via London back to his Suffolk fastness.

In the autumn and winter of 1950, Philip wrote a number of letters to Maria which tell us something of his concerns at this time. His clothes are 'in rags' – does this include the new jeans? – and the house itself is in such a bad state that even his neighbour Miss Browne is worried about it. He writes of the small sums of money he is hoping to pay to the courts and the larger sums he hopes to get from Dartington, the Royal Literary Fund and elsewhere. He tells Maria that she seemed 'strained and unhappy' on her last visit to Purton and offers to have one or other of the two children to live with him. He also offers to send Maria a box of apples which 'stew deliciously' and says he will try to send an eiderdown, but has nothing to wrap it in. He accepts that Maria's heart is now engaged with Patrick de Maré but continues to express his love for her and the hope that she and the children will come to Suffolk for Christmas. He also complains about Edith Young, who was now in the process of moving into the vacant bit of Purton Hall and threatening to take over the whole place.

In *The Lower View,* he seems more positive about this time and also about Edith Young, who reminded him of his mother. He writes of the 'wealth of cushions' and barrel of Dartington cider she brought with her. Under the influence of this cider and too much beer in the local pub, where they would 'talk the roof off', Philip seems to have decided he would rather write about himself than produce the awaited report on vagrants, for which he had now squandered a further 'advance'. Urged on by Edith Young to 'tell all' about his 'unique experiences', he turned again to his autobiography and for a while the two of them settled into a cosy routine, both together and separate, which seemed to suit him ideally and would be echoed in future relationships. He later claimed that this was a productive time during which the early and best part of *Memoirs of a Public Baby* was written. Inevitably, this was a short-lived experience. At Christmas 1950, Edith Young departed to be with her family and Philip spent the festival alone in the increasingly dilapidated Purton Hall without his family and with only 'a forlorn kipper' on his plate.

He knew that he would not be there much longer and he knew that he must now strike out in other directions. On 12 January 1951 he made another attempt to get into broadcasting by sending P. H.

Newby, a Third Programme producer and novelist, what he describes as a 'tentative, badly typed script'. Howard Newby, two years younger than Philip, wrote back saying, 'The Elizabethan complexity of your prose makes it almost impossible for broadcasting' and goes on chattily, 'The simple direction of conversation is all that is required – otherwise the listener is baffled. What do you think?'

By the end of January, Philip O'Connor was back in London and may have stayed for a while with Patrick de Maré or at least used his new address 1 Upper Harley Street for correspondence. His relationship with Maria Steiner, happily recreated at long distance in later life, was now over though Philip still hung around Fitzrovia and could be heard shouting outside Maria's flat frightening his daughter Sarah. Shortly afterwards Maria took over a studio at 64 Charlotte Street, which had belonged to the artist Denis Lowson. Lowson recalls his first encounter with O'Connor at this time and describes it as 'not the most friendly meeting', and remembers both the timidity of O'Connor's handshake – 'not much authority to the grasp' – and the tartness of his tongue. The two men got on better later.

Philip was also immediately in touch with Michael Hamburger and dragged this sober but supportive friend off to meet Edith Young, who was also in London. Hamburger had been considering going to France as a tutor to a young relation of the French writer André Gide, whom he had met in Sicily the previous year, and suggested that O'Connor should go in his stead. The idea appealed enormously to Philip – the lure of France was great and the illustrious connections with the job must have appealed to his 'vulgar' side – but nothing came of it. For a while Philip wandered around London in the rain, 'collecting odd shillings' and feeling 'far beyond doles and literary grants'. On 8 March 1951, he wrote to Kilham-Roberts at the Society of Authors, saying, 'I'm in a terrible fix, about to be homeless (I can't return to my cottage), moneyless and jobless' and got a reply suggesting that he try Allen Lane at Penguin Books, who apparently had 'a liking for unconventional characters'. A further letter from Howard Newby at the BBC promising to write to him if he could think of some way of making use of Philip's 'services' can have provided little consolation. Instead, he looked 'inefficiently' for humbler work and to his credit soon landed himself a job on the continental telephone exchange near Blackfriars Bridge. Even now he needed help and on Sunday 18 March dropped a note in for Kilham-Roberts saying that he had only 'one shilling tuppence halfpenny' to last him till the following Thursday.

The job itself proved a success and Philip O'Connor would often speak and write of this short phase of his life with pride and affection. He claims that he fitted in well with the other operators, especially a not-so-young Irishman with a monocle whose zeal to take calls some-times caused him to 'scramble the cords'. The immense L-shaped room where they worked was often thrilling. Lights for Paris, Milan and Prague twinkled above their desks and Philip made long-distance friendships with operators overseas. One night he eavesdropped on the Duke of Windsor delightedly telling the Duchess that some school he'd addressed in the North of England 'couldn't have been nicer'. Was he reminded of how on Clapham Common as a child he had claimed to be the Prince of Wales incognito?

In *The Lower View*, Philip writes that he experienced a 'cat-like, cunning cosiness' at being employed and was now able to take a room of his own at 25 Marchmont Street, near Russell Square. He bothers to tell us that this was on the ground floor at the back and that he was sustained here by his coffee-pot, his pipe, an occasional bottle of wine – but no mistress. Maria Steiner visited him, so did other girls, and it was perhaps during this phase that he was taken to the Café Royal by Maria's friend, Joan Rhodes. Philip describes Joan Rhodes as 'tender-hearted' but nothing came of these encounters. Philip's lack of promiscuousness was a lifelong obsession and was almost immedi-ately mentioned by him when he and I first met twenty-one years later.

At Marchmont Street he also did a little work on his book and quite a lot of reading – he mentions in particular *Parables of the Theatre* by Berthold Brecht. He also suffered from fears that his own ideas would 'shrivel away', and perhaps to obliterate these anxieties plunged back into Soho from time to time and got wildly drunk. On 4 August 1951, he was in his cups at a party in Maida Vale following Michael Hamburger's wedding to Anne File. According to Hamburger, Philip ground biscuits into the carpet and slapped some elderly Quaker ladies on their bottoms, causing the bride's father to argue that he should be thrown out, a request that Hamburger refused on the grounds that it would be a bad omen. The following day, Philip telephoned the new Mrs Hamburger, told her, 'Anne, I forgive you' and re-established himself in her good books.

Before the end of 1951, Philip had moved to new quarters on Haverstock Hill. In *The Lower View*, he describes this dramatic development in a section headed 'Conformity Second Stage' and in it relates that he was so excited when he heard of a room to let in 'middle class Hampstead' that he dropped a heavy typewriter on his foot. The room was in a ground-floor flat in a block called Eton Hall and belonged to the actress Anna Wing, who was now in her thirties and has already featured in these pages as an inhabitant of Fitzrovia. A greengrocer's daughter from Hackney, she was already an actress of distinction and many years later would become a household name when she played a 'grumpy, frumpy' matriarch in the original cast of the TV series *East-Enders*. During the war years she had lived at 89 Charlotte Street and made friends with both Maria Steiner and Quentin Crisp. Quentin Crisp had taken her out to dinner in Fitzrovia but her relationship with Maria Steiner was deeper and more complex. According to *The Lower View*, it was Anna's 'truly golden voice' on the telephone which first attracted Philip. When he spoke to her from Marchmont Street he was bowled over by its 'lack of emotional restraint' but reassured by the absence of 'hysteria'. He immediately imagined that this voice could give him security and ensure his arrival as a Man of Letters at last. And in a way, it would.

According to Maria Steiner, there was a provisional meeting between Philip and Anna at the tea-kiosk in Russell Square, not far from Marchmont Street. In *The Lower View*, Philip describes only the doorstep encounter at 70 Eton Hall, Haverstock Hill. He had arrived at the immaculately clean flat wearing 'a grubby duffel-coat' with a 'self-consciously proletarian' Woodbine dangling or jutting insultingly from his lower lip in a manner he had seen employed by Dylan Thomas. He was later scolded for not, on that first visit, offering his cigarettes around but moved in soon afterwards, bringing with him 'a little bag of oddments . . . mostly dirty clothes' which he tried to hide in a cupboard. These were immediately discovered and a prolonged and more general laundering of their owner began. Philip declares that he was 'immensely grubby; foetid with bachelorhood, sour with beer, blocked with tobacco smoke, apathetic with mental self-indulgence'. Anna Wing was an 'enemy of the hidden and dirty'. On my first meeting with her in the early 1970s she immediately asked if I was a homosexual. On first meeting Philip, she began to free him of his 'slime'. He was to spend hours in the washtub where he was bathed 'from head to toe', cleansed of some of his 'psychological oddities' and even of some of the 'immoral' aspects of his writings.

Anna Wing and Philip O'Connor were to spend most of the next six years together. Anna Wing has said very little about this time and in an amiable way has declined to contribute to this book. In an interview with the *Guardian* in 1986 at the height of her soap-star fame she said, 'I was in a terrible tizz when I met O'Connor. He was tremendous, quite agonising in lots of ways.' Philip is naturally more forthcoming. He says that their first year was 'unendurably exciting' and he felt 'completely refreshed'. Even on the humblest, most domestic level, Anna gave Philip a role. 'She organized him, got him to do the laundry. I thought it was very funny,' says Maria Steiner, who had not even attempted to get Philip to do such chores. In some areas he failed, in some he succeeded. On 23 August 1953, Anna Wing gave birth to a son, later named Jon Wing O'Connor, but Philip again found fatherhood difficult and writes that he 'failed dismally' here. Not all duties were shunned. Anna got him to pay maintenance to Maria, and he appears to have been a good stepfather to Anna's son Mark Wing Davey, born in 1948, who remembers this as 'an idyllic time' and describes Philip as 'a terrific father' and 'a terrific cook'. In *The Lower View*, Philip writes that Anna Wing gave him 'such civic papers as I shall ever have' and even the local shopkeepers started treating him as normal. He felt a new confidence and a dawning appreciation that 'Ordinariness is the most exciting prospect open to a human being.'

Along with these positive feelings, Philip soon felt great agitation. The whole 'stage set' of the Hampstead middle class was closing in on him, and Anna and he seemed to be one of hundreds of thousands of other couples, 'dreadful and teeming' in their numbers. He yearned to go off tramping again, supposedly kept a bag packed for this purpose, but in spite of many rehearsals never quite made it. Accompanied or encouraged by Edith Young, who had a flat in Grafton Way, WC1, he did however go on frequent debauches, making new sorties into Fitzrovia which he described 'as a good mud bath' and 'a kitchen of the arts' where all 'hell's cooks' could be met. A more innocent figure he encountered at this time was an art student, Diana Pollitt, who liked him very much and noted 'flashes of feminine gestures in him'. He also paid visits on his old friend Heinz Wolff, and his wife Ann. Heinz Wolff was now a senior registrar at a hospital in Carshalton and felt that Philip 'rather spoiled his image' but Ann Wolff became an immediate fan. 'I got on terribly well with him,' she recalls but remembers that her children, whom he addressed in weird voices, were 'terrified' of him. With or without Anna Wing, he also returned to Purton Hall, which was now sinking into the ground. Here he did some more work on his autobiography and visited old and new neighbours. In 1954 Philip knocked on the door of Clopton Hall, near Poslingford, where the artist Denis Lowson was now living with his wife Annie Mygind, a Danish woman with private means and artistic interests. Lowson recalls how Philip had forgotten their previous encounter and submitted him to the usual doorstep scrutiny followed by a typical double-edged declaration: 'So you're Denis Lowson. I fully expected to have my vomit bowl ready but as it happens I rather like you.' Lowson and Mygind would soon play significant roles in Philip's life.

By the end of 1954, his life had certainly improved on one vital score. With Anna Wing's encouragement he had done some more work on his autobiography and had sent it to Stephen Spender, now co-editing *Encounter*, who was sufficiently impressed by what he read to telephone Philip very late at night – Philip says it was midnight – to tell him how much he liked it. Under Stephen Spender's 'good offices' the messy typescript, with duplicated pages and untidy and illegible additions, had been sent to Roger Senhouse at Secker and Warburg, who had responded by paying Philip £10 for an option on a revised version of the book. During the spring of 1955, Philip had a number of discussions with Senhouse, a noted book-collector and former lover of Lytton Strachey, at his Bloomsbury office and then went away, did some revisions and impatiently awaited the publisher's reactions.

This long-awaited whiff of future success did not liberate Philip from his civic responsibilities or his anxieties about these responsibilities. Now aged thirty-eight, he had enrolled at the Trent Park Teachers' Training College in Middlesex. Writing to Michael Hamburger from temporary lodgings near the college on 12 February he obliquely declared that he was thinking 'of slipping away while I can'. Two months later, on 5 April, he wrote to Hamburger from Eton Hall asking, 'Can you lend me a pound or ten shillings?' In the midst of these troubled times, both versions of his book were returned by Secker and Warburg along with a long letter from Roger Senhouse dated 6 May 1955 which described much of the typescript as 'a tangled skein of words'. The only thing that can have cushioned this blow was that Stephen Spender had now agreed to publish a long extract of the book in the next issue of *Encounter*.

During this period Stephen Spender found himself uncomfortably though valiantly embroiled in O'Connor's life and career, and it is perhaps worth recounting in some detail Spender's role in getting *Memoirs of a Public Baby* published. Spender and O'Connor had met in the 1930s but Philip was at pains to stress that they were never friends 'in the personal sense'. In later life Philip also stressed that he 'loved' Spender but sometimes 'sniped' at him out of 'rankling envy at his social position, superior to mine'. Spender relates that he had found Philip's early poetry 'alive and amusing' and his relationship with him was 'peculiar'. On learning of the Secker and Warburg rejection Spender had immediately sent the book off to Faber and Faber in Russell Square along with a proof of the extract *Encounter* would be publishing. In a handwritten letter to Sir Geoffrey Faber dated 2 June 1955, Spender describes the book as 'a very extraordinary document' and begs Sir Geoffrey and his colleagues 'who are among the very few who care about literature' to have a look at it.

A long silence followed – in August Philip was moved to telephone Fabers to find out what was happening – and it was not until 8 September that Sir Geoffrey Faber wrote to Spender expressing his admiration for the book but saying that editing would take 'weeks and weeks'. On 28 September the book was returned to Philip at Eton Hall with the rejection letter from Faber editor Charles Monteith quoted at the beginning of this chapter. In spite of this setback, O'Connor and Spender remained vigilant. On 11 October, Spender wrote back to Sir Geoffrey Faber saying that his wife Natasha had suggested that the poet Frances Cornford might be the right editor for the book and on 18 January 1956, Philip wrote to Michael Hamburger saying that, having been 'sent down' by the teachers' training college – he had 'failed to make contact with the children' and been pronounced 'temperamentally unsuited to the teaching of children' – he was now free to do more work on 'the Baby'. On 8 April, Philip wrote to Spender saying that he had sent a newly revised version of the book – 'quite coherent, sequential' – to Charles Monteith and wondered if Spender would consider writing a preface to the book if Fabers accepted it.

A few weeks later the book was rejected again. Monteith's letter of 26 April contains a sentence which may strike a chord with other struggling authors. 'I'm afraid we felt that in the general "toning down" process a good deal of the vividness and the vitality of the first version had been lost.' It was at this point that the relationship between O'Connor and Spender became more sticky, not because of the problems with the book – to which Spender remained entirely loyal – but because O'Connor simply saw Spender as another person from whom he could obtain favours. Even before the second rejection by Fabers, Philip had written to Spender proposing that he should advance him £40 to enable him to go and write a book about tramping in Spain. Spender seems to have ignored this request and a few weeks later became more indignant when he heard that while borrowing money for himself, Philip was neglecting Anna Wing and their child. Anna Wing had apparently called on Spender, whom she saw as Philip's major benefactor, and told him that Philip had deserted her.

On 15 May 1956, Philip telephoned Spender from Suffolk and made another request for money. This time Spender put down the receiver and when O'Connor rang again a few minutes later explained why. Philip immediately wrote Spender two letters from Purton Hall accusing him of being 'unjust', 'not caring to enquire into the truth of matters' and suggesting that perhaps his 'reputation' had gone before him. He asked if Spender really thought it was his duty to take on 'unpleasant work eg dishwashing' to help Anna and stated that anyway he and Anna 'have been deciding mutually to separate for some time'. He seems to imply they had already separated and, to make this point or elicit further sympathy or guilt from Spender, adds with some defiance that he would be staying at Bruce House which was then a lodging house for those of no fixed abode. Stephen Spender's own version of this incident appears in his *Journals 1939–1983*. Philip is given the name *A* and the story mysteriously appears under the wrong date, 20 May 1955, which was almost exactly a year earlier.

In fact, Philip was still making some efforts to look after himself, if not after Anna and their child. At around this time and most uncharacteristically he seems to have gone to Scotland and got a job as a cook, only to fall ill immediately, and at the end of May 1956, a week or two after the business with Spender, he wrote to Michael Hamburger from an address in Manchester Street, London W1, saying that he was now working round the corner at a telephone messaging service. He adds grumpily, 'Spender interrupted supplies' and says that he is in 'a bad patch' and needs to be 'put up'. In the same letter he tells Hamburger that he is considering taking a job as a ward orderly at the Maudsley Hospital in order to write a book about mental hospital life. Nothing came of this – or of various proposals he submitted that summer to the BBC. On 16 July, the writer Rayner Heppenstall, who had worked as a radio producer since the war, arranged for Philip to do a 'voice test' for the drama department. This was a failure – Philip's voice was said to be 'neurotic and refeened' – but he continued to bombard the corporation with ideas, among which were programmes on Charlie Chaplin, who remained his god, 'The Impoverished Bohemia of the Thirties', and 'The Househusband'. Supporting the last suggestion, O'Connor wrote, 'I am a writer of forty not at all successful and I am at the moment in the titular position above.' But the proposal was rejected after a pencilled note from one producer to another repeating the voice-test verdict and adding dismissively, 'He can't write.'

Meanwhile, Stephen Spender had remained active on behalf of

Philip's book. During the summer of 1956 he had set about finding the right editor for it. Discussions with Frances Cornford do not seem to have come to much but Spender soon managed to recruit a twenty-six-year-old ex-army officer and schoolmaster, Simon Stuart, who was then teaching at King's School Canterbury and whose background – his father was an Irish peer and his mother a Guggenheim – might have appealed to Philip's snobberies. On 4 October 1956, Stephen Spender sent Charles Monteith at Fabers a sample of the book as rewritten by Simon Stuart, proclaiming it 'a remarkable transform-ation' but adding that Stuart felt he could not continue unless the publication of the book was guaranteed. Two months later, on 13 December, Charles Monteith wrote to Philip O'Connor at Eton Hall, Haverstock Hill, saying that Faber and Faber would now at last publish the book. At this time Philip O'Connor was working at Self-ridges in Oxford Street as 'a kind of porter' and 'very poorly paid'.

Throughout 1957, the book was in production. By the beginning of March, Simon Stuart had finished his rewriting – he cut a lot of abstract passages and generalizations about class and culture – and was able to meet O'Connor and show him his work. Philip character-istically suggested that he should send a copy to Fabers before he had read it but very soon afterwards did read it and on 12 March wrote to Charles Monteith saying that he thought Stuart had done his editing 'very well indeed'. On 21 March, Monteith wrote back agreeing that Stuart had done his work 'admirably' and complaining that some of Philip's 'emendations' were quite illegible and should be done in block capitals. During the next few weeks the full title of the book was agreed upon, though the 'Public Baby' bit had been around for some time. Stephen Spender reread the edited version and submitted his introduction and the book was read for libel. In correspondence with Fabers, O'Connor revealed that he knew his unnamed former guardian was still alive but would not object to how he was depicted. How Philip knew that Camden Field was still alive – he was now in lodgings on the south coast – and how he expected him to tolerate descriptions like 'an uglier man would be difficult to meet' is a double mystery.

All these negotiations took place in writing, and letters between Monteith and O'Connor remain formal and polite – neither of them

Top left: Quentin's brothers Gerald and Lewis, and sister Phyllis, c.1909.

Below: 'A dog is a horrible thing to happen to someone.' Quentin's mother Baba Pratt in late middle age.

Left: 'He taught me to walk in the excruciating armour of self-restraint.' Quentin's father Charles Pratt.

The author outside Madame Tillieux's teashop in Wimereux where Philip was abandoned as a three-year-old.

Philip during his Box Hill days. 'An unusually intelligent child.'

Quentin as a twelve-year-old schoolboy at Epsom, second row, third from right.

'. . . a sad little elephant, or elf, who is still doing his best to conform.'

Quentin, aged thirty, photographed by Angus McBean during the winter
of 1939. 'Mr McBean longed to take photographs as fervently as I desired
to be photographed.'

Philip as a teenager. 'He had an adolescent mystery about him,
like a schoolboy Hamlet.'

Black and white illustration by Quentin, mid-1930s.

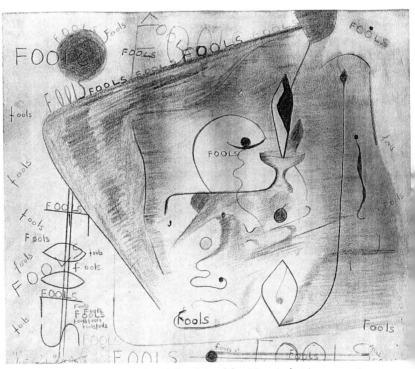

Pencil and crayon drawing by Philip, Maudsley Hospital, winter 1936–7.

Left: Jean Hore in fancy dress. 'She had a face like Shelley and the body of a Chinese empress.'

Above: Philip on the road to conformity, late 1940s.

Below: Maria Gabriele Steiner with her children Sarah and Peter O'Connor. 'She is one of the most beautiful people I have met, an Austrian Madonna.'

Quentin, aged thirty-nine, at Beaufort Street, October 1948, shortly before dyeing his hair blue.

Film-maker John Haggarty. 'The original unobtainable great dark man.'

Jazz singer George Melly. 'Mr Melly has to be obscene to be believed.'

makes use of the other's Christian name – and they do not seem to have met until 5 July 1957 after which Philip wrote to Monteith, 'I enjoyed meeting you and was relieved by your lack of literary bravura.' On this occasion, he may have also met Monteith's assistant Rosemary Goad, who would later recall that Philip 'lit up the atmosphere' in Russell Square and whom Philip himself would describe as 'consistently considerate'.

During the early summer of 1957, Philip also sat for three pencil drawings by Lucian Freud, a Soho acquaintance whom he insisted on calling 'Lucy'. Sittings took place in Freud's home 20 Delamere Terrace in Paddington, and Fabers offered the artist ten guineas to use one of the drawings in the book but Freud eventually destroyed them all. Philip recalled later how Freud, then thirty-four, appeared on the staircase in a towel which scarcely covered his buttocks.

How Philip spent the rest of this year isn't clear. He draws a veil over his relationship with Anna Wing but remained based in her flat. He clearly made excursions elsewhere but the impending publication of his book did not invest him with any form of sober dignity. Stephen Fothergill, who now lived next door to Freud, recalls that Philip would call in after sittings in his usual provocative mood, upsetting some actors living in the house, Bo and Ruby Milton. 'I've forgotten what he said,' says Fothergill, 'but he attacked them in his usual weird sort of way.' He frequently headed further afield and called often drunkenly on Michael Hamburger, who was now working at Reading University, sometimes at four in the morning. 'He did the most dreadful things,' Hamburger recalls. 'The children were terrified of him. He asked, "Where's your au pair girl?" I said, "Oh, she's down in the cellar." I then locked him in the cellar until he had sobered up.'

That year, Philip finally made some progress with the BBC. A letter that he had written the previous September to radio producer David Thomson suggesting that they should meet at the George pub carries a scribbled margin note saying, 'Couldn't make it' but soon afterwards Thomson *could* make it and the two men took an immense liking to each other. David Thomson, who later became a distinguished-looking, short-sighted figure, with a bald head and long untidy grey hair often adorned by a denim cap, had worked on the Third Programme from the beginning and was to become O'Connor's staunchest supporter within the walls of Broadcasting House.

David Thomson's first programme with Philip was a forty-five-minute play called *The Poet Arrested* which was broadcast on 6 August 1957. It was described as 'a brief enquiry into the ethics of the behaviour of the traditional romantic poet' and was probably as complex and obscure as any Third Programme offering at this time. The principal figure in the play is a poet, aged forty, the age Philip had now reached, and he is heard in conflict with other characters, one of whom was played by Anna Wing. To borrow Stephen Spender's words about Philip's poetry, the play reads like the 'off-throwings' or 'cuttings' from his inner life and provides another vehicle for his particular type of wit, originality and self-indulgence. The play was discussed the same week on 'The Critics' programme and said to be 'very well written' and 'full of good phrases' but also 'very pretentious and highfaluting'. Charles Gibbs-Smith wondered if there was 'any real significance or meaning behind the words' and J. M. Richards detected an element of 'rather plaintive self-pity' about the central character.

The next time 'The Critics' met to discuss Philip O'Connor's work would be early the following year when his book *Memoirs of a Public Baby* at last came under their scrutiny, exciting quite hysterical disagreement.

-11-

Accumulating Discontent

The finest, the purest, the most beautiful flower of
unnatural truth is Douglas Vanner. He may be a man,
he may be a woman. He has a blue chin and long
waved ginger hair. His clothes are neither this nor
that. His eyes shine and his smile is delicate, poised
and more than civilised. His wit glitters perfectly and
artificially, from the first greeting 'Tell me the story of
your life!' – to the last farewell – 'But I expect to
suffer!'

ROLAND CAMBERTON, *Scamp*, 1950

On the day that peace 'broke out', thirty-six-year-old Quentin Crisp
– thinly disguised as Douglas Vanner in the novel quoted above –
weaved his way through the West End of London, claiming later that
he did not in the least enjoy the shouting, laughing and singing that was
going on around him. In *The Naked Civil Servant* he describes it as
'that terrible evening' and it was made even more terrible for him
when he was spotted by the snobbish postal clerk he had shared a
flat with in Baron's Court fourteen years earlier and told, 'You look
terrible!'

In spite of all these terrors – he later wondered if the encounter
with Thumbnails took place during the second peace celebrations –
Quentin was to pursue a relatively steady path through the next decade
or two. Philip O'Connor may have been ruled by his heart, by women
and by literary figures he could scrounge off or pin hopes on, but
Quentin Crisp was strikingly independent and free-standing and

whatever hopes he had for the future were hidden by remarks like 'All you have to do is to fill in the gap between the cradle and the grave without getting into debt.' Throughout the postwar period, he resided at 129 Beaufort Street and kept the same telephone number. It was a household of oddities but according to the actor Gordon Richardson, who lived downstairs and sometimes performed parlour tricks with his glass eye, Quentin Crisp was the least eccentric of the lot of them. He paid his rent on the dot, he was never in debt and he never quarrelled with his fellow lodgers. He was now one of the more established incumbents and in due course a little sign appeared beside the middle doorbell saying 'Crisp Two Rings'. Whenever the doorbell rang at Beaufort Street, Quentin would cock his head on one side and listen for the number of rings, sometimes heaving a little sigh of relief or disappointment when he learnt that the caller was not for him.

At the end of the war he was still working for Kenneth MacQueen's advertising firm at Notting Hill Gate and his exotic plumage continued to bring sunshine into the lives of those around him. According to Anne Valery, later an actress and television personality, who worked for the firm during the winter of 1945, Quentin was 'a bird of paradise' and 'just gorgeous', with hair the colour of rubies, heavy-lidded eyes and a voice that was 'sonorous, lingering and utterly non-committal'. And unlike everyone else, he never seemed to 'huddle' against the cold.

And these were certainly cold, grey, dreary times. The word 'austere' is usually used to describe the immediate postwar period and the poverty Philip and Maria experienced was widespread. Writing about his own life, Quentin Crisp is keen to stress if not overemphasize the downhill struggle. In *The Naked Civil Servant* he writes of the horrors of peace. 'Death-made-easy vanished overnight and soon love-made-easy, personified by the American soldiers, also disappeared.' He echoes Philip O'Connor's thoughts about the decline of Fitzrovia and notes how Londoners had now begun to regret their 'indiscriminate expansiveness' during the war. He also writes of his 'accumulating discontent', and claims that he now felt deflated and that even his sense of physical well-being had faded. Lucky or unlucky to survive the bombing, he fears that he had become 'a loathsome reminder of the unfairness of fate': he was still alive and kicking 'while the young, brave and the beautiful were dead'. And when early in 1946 he gave up the job with Mr MacQueen and returned to art school modelling, he would find that the fun was even leaking out of this occupation.

The real story is more complicated. As early as 1945 Quentin had nurtured hopes of going to America – in the summer of that year he wrote to the painter Frederico Sante saying, 'I have a scheme to get my work published there' – but it is also true that his prestige, fame or infamy on the lower reaches of Chelsea and Fitzrovia was growing. Contrary to what he claims, his 'empire' was expanding rather than contracting and the rebuffs he received only added greater velocity to his performance. He had innumerable friends and acquaintances and even as I work on this book, new ones of whom I have never heard keep popping up. His habit of keeping his friends in 'boxes' may have meant that they were mainly unaware of each other. Maria Steiner pointed out that Quentin had 'proper, solid friendships', and Hermione Goacher, of whom more in a moment, explained that he was drawn particularly to 'proper women, mothers, women who had babies'. Obviously, not all his friends fell into this category but he tended to know people on a domestic level.

During the late 1940s Quentin Crisp went and took baths in a house in Margaretta Terrace, Chelsea belonging to a circus historian, Bill Meadmore, whom he had met in Clifford Hall's studio at the start of the war, and whose wife was called Dumps. He also saw a lot of Miss Lumley Who Can Do No Wrong and frequently visited a Chelsea character called Simon Watson-Taylor who lived in another flat in the same house in Markham Square. He continued to meet his art student friend Pat, though she was now grappling with Catholicism and her Polish husband with mental illness. He also saw a lot of Angus McBean, who had impressed him by emerging utterly unscathed from his long prison sentence: he became a regular caller at the photographer's new premises at 53–55 Endell Street, Covent Garden, and even acquired a suit of McBean's, made from cloth ripped off two billiard tables. When McBean's friend Esther Grant and her new husband re-established themselves at a house in New Row, Covent Garden, Quentin soon became a regular fixture at their parties. In

Fitzrovia he continued to call on Maria Steiner at 12 Fitzroy Street though he was somewhat dismayed when she threw in her lot with Philip O'Connor, correctly predicting that Mr O'Connor would never be able to look after her. Friends are the people we get stuck with, Quentin often quipped, but in all these cases – and many more – the arrangement was to everyone's satisfaction.

In spite of these domestic attachments, cafés provided Quentin Crisp with his main playgrounds. Pubs played little part in his life and when years later Christopher Isherwood claimed to have met him in London pubs, Quentin more or less dismissed this idea with the haughty reply, 'Unlikely. I rarely go to pubs.' At this time, he was still banned from most of the Fitzrovia pubs – in 1945 he had told Frederico Sante that his only 'bridgehead' there was The Highlander – and Chelsea pubs never featured in his life. He was much more at home at the Bar-B-Q in King's Road, Tony's in Charlotte Street and the French Café in Old Compton Street. He describes the latter establishment, at the opposite end of the street from where the Black Cat once stood, as 'a human poste restante' whose clients were 'cosy, friendly, poverty-stricken people, ill-equipped to live', many of whom did not look as though they would 'live through another winter'.

In these and other cafés, he chose his table carefully – usually in the window – and raised his performance to new heights. On his way back from modelling in Watford, Willesden or Woolwich he claims to have worked on his repertoire of quips, gags, anecdotes, epigrams and impersonations. His imitations of Barbara Stanwyck and Bette Davis caused delight and he sometimes embarked on imaginary or forgotten creations such as Edith Evans in the role of Cleopatra. Every utterance was polished, elegant and studied, he was very conscious of having an audience and had long ago introduced actorish pauses into his speech. Here, again, there are contradictions: Quentin Crisp claims to have had 'the utmost contempt for the music hall' yet admits that when meeting strangers he was liable to launch into 'a complete cabaret turn'. In *The Naked Civil Servant*, he explains that one of his original objects was to purge his speech of 'the dross of sincerity', but he had now gone far too far and 'robbed it of all meaning'. Some of those who knew him well may have already found his performance repetitive but there were always new admirers in the offing and people went to cafés like the Bar-B-Q and Tony's specifically to see Quentin Crisp and attend his 'little levees'.

Who were these people? Writing in *The World Is a Wedding*, Bernard Kops describes a typical Soho café at this time. In the midst of a gang of 'tearaways, layabouts, lesbians, queers, mysteries and hangers-on, artists without studio or canvas' sits an unnamed but instantly recognizable man with dyed hair: 'He spoke very beautifully and always wore the same upholstered smile. He was gentle and always said to any stranger, "Tell me the story of your life." What's more he listened.' Quentin's ability to listen is sometimes hard to credit but is borne out by the quality of his own imitations and observations. However wrapped up in his own performance and however fundamentally uninterested in other people, especially the rich and famous, Quentin never hesitated to celebrate, glorify and sentimentalize his acquaintances, if sometimes in an exaggeratedly comic manner. We know from his autobiography that lots of people confided in him and did indeed tell him the story of their life. We know that he often begged people, 'Tell me the secret of the universe', and made other extravagant gestures, but he was always able to descend from these rarefied heights in times of need. Anne Valery, his colleague at the advertising firm, states that Quentin became her 'mentor in matters of make-up' and once advised her 'to boil up camomile' in which to wash her blonde hair.

The cast of people who were the recipients of Quentin's wit and wisdom in these postwar years is extensive and many of them are shadowy figures known only by their surname, to which Quentin may sometimes have added some comical handle. In addition to Miss Lumley Who Can Do No Wrong, there was Mrs Godfrey with a Heart of Gold. There was also Mr Warren, Mr Tilley, Mr Pulley, the Real Miss Beeson and the False Miss Beeson and dozens of others, some of whom may have played their part in history. One day he met the famous Marchesa Casati, whose slogan 'I want to be a living work of art' came close to Quentin's own ideal and whose wild red hair, white face and scornful manner matched his own. Casati was then in her seventies and appealed to Quentin as 'a picturesque ruin' and as 'a being of her own invention – not one of any particular sex or time or size or shape'. Another day he was summoned to meet Mr Hill – the gangster who then ruled Soho turned out to be unexpectedly polite – and one afternoon in Chelsea he chatted to Mrs Gardner, an artist's model and occasional film extra who on 20 June 1946 was to die at the hands of the serial killer Neville Heath.

What Luisa Casati, Billy Hill and Margery Gardner made of Quentin Crisp will never be known, but other acquaintances have stressed his 'likeability' and 'super-intelligence', the crudeness or sophistication of his hair dye and his habit of never refusing a meal. 'He would eat seven suppers a day if they were offered to him, recalls David Ball, who met him with Angus McBean. 'He was like a camel filling his hump.' According to Mr Duffey, a regular at the Bar-B-Q at this time, Quentin was 'a very kind man who held court in the best possible manner and always made you feel you were *doing well*'. Mr Duffey also stresses the different images Quentin presented in Chelsea and Soho. 'In his home district,' says Duffey, 'he was unmade up, slightly scruffy, unshaven even.' Philip O'Connor's friend Ann Meo describes Quentin as 'a sort of celebrity' in Chelsea but remembers bus journeys with him to the West End during which his 'squawking' became quite embarrassing. For the impression he made in the West End we should turn again to Roland Camberton's novel *Scamp* where under the guise of Douglas Vanner he appears as 'a masterpiece of decadence' whose real character 'kept itself well out of sight, some-where behind the bright, false smile, the permanently waved hair, the powdered blue chin, the arched back, the slender fangling hands tipped with crimson fingernails and the high-heeled shoes'. Roland Cam-berton, whose real name was Henry Cohen, also writes perceptively of Quentin's conversation, describing 'the meaningless, flippant phrases' which Douglas Vanner uses as 'a formal chinoiserie'. Quentin himself reinforced this view when he explained that many of the 'curlicues' with which he decorated his speech were neither sarcastic nor sincere but simply 'abstract embellishments'.

Others have spotted a dog-like quality in Quentin Crisp, in that he treated everyone the same. Throughout his life he steadfastly avoided a hierarchy of friends and attempted to treat everyone equally. He continued to boast that he was always at 'the losing end of relation-ships' and took pains to avoid anyone getting to know him too well. The fact that he knew some people over a very long period may only reflect the tenacity with which they cultivated or hung onto him. Within his huge circle of acquaintances, among whom thousands of art students should perhaps be counted, certain figures stand out on their own merits or simply by the fact that they have, by chance, come to my attention. Some of these people became Quentin Crisp's lifelong friends. Others, like George Melly, played what might be described as cameo roles in his life.

In the autumn of 1945, the future jazzman was nineteen years old when he came up from Chatham in naval uniform to lunch at the Bar-B-Q with Simon Watson-Taylor, who was at that time secretary to the surrealists' group in England. At another table, surrounded by bohemian admirers, sat Quentin Crisp in his grubby Chelsea mode. After lunch – Melly states that the food there was 'horrible' and 'disgusting' – Quentin invited the young sailor to sit down and tell him the story of his life. On this occasion, Crisp did the talking and Melly sat spellbound. 'In those days I was a screaming gay,' says Melly, but one doubts if this had any bearing on his immediate appreciation of Quentin's character and looks and the courage and authority that underlay them. 'He was very beautiful, but it wasn't a very human beauty,' Melly recalled, puzzling over the various figures in art and literature which Crisp's appearance brought to mind. 'He was like a smaller figure in Richard Dadd, a Shakespearian king, a Beardsley drawing, a character out of Firbank or Evelyn Waugh. He could have been Ambrose Silk.'

Shortly after their first meeting Quentin invited George Melly to see a Rita Hayworth film showing in Clapham, possibly *Gilda*. The bus journey was quite unnerving for Melly, with another passenger shouting, 'Hey, Jack, can't you get yourself a proper girlfriend?' Other meetings took place in Fitzrovia where Melly also noted that Quentin was far more 'spick and span' than in Chelsea, his make-up 'applied with impeccable art' and his table always surrounded by acolytes. On one occasion Melly was astonished to find that these included his highly respectable cousin Pauline Rawdon-Smith. Their paths crossed again soon afterwards at Bill Meadmore's house in Margaretta Terrace, when Melly entered the bathroom to find Quentin lying there 'in full naked glory' and later when the jazzman 'sang himself to bits' at a party in the house, inspiring Quentin's witticism, 'Mr Melly has to be obscene to be believed.' Reflecting later on George Melly's bubbliness, Quentin told me, 'He falls about laughing, he wants to live all the time. It's a kind of generosity – and there seems to be no affectation mixed up with all this gaiety.' Reflecting on Quentin Crisp, Melly said he must have had 'the courage of a lioness' to walk the streets as he did. On a more down-to-earth level, Crisp once gave advice over the telephone to George Melly's mother about how easy it was to cable money via the Post Office, a practicality quite out of keeping with the timid and incompetent image he still tried to project.

Another young serviceman whom Quentin first met in 1945 and who has been said to represent the Unavailable Great Dark Man was John Haggarty, a stridently heterosexual and highly intelligent ex-airman from Rutherglen. Haggarty had left school aged fourteen, served in the marine-craft section of the RAF and discovered Fitzrovia early in the war, meeting Paul Potts in 1940 but missing out on Philip O'Connor and later attaching himself to the dandy Julian Maclaren-Ross, who dominated the Wheatsheaf. Haggarty describes himself as 'a working-class chap' who benefited from the ease of social movement that London offered during and immediately after the war. Haggarty was in his mid-twenties and stood six foot three when he first spotted Quentin Crisp holding court in 'a seedy tea-room', probably Tony's, opposite the old Scala Theatre. 'I never imagined that such a person existed,' he said later. 'He was a great original. He stood out instantly, advertising that he was a remarkable man. I saw him as a Firbankian, orchidaceous figure. I didn't see him as a wee poofter.' The two men liked each other at once. Haggarty saw that Crisp had 'no side' and instantly considered him 'a figure of promise'. Haggarty was also sufficiently confident in his own masculinity to admire Crisp's 'beautiful auburn hair' and 'really feminine flair for make-up'. He was, says Haggarty, 'a very good hair colourist'. He also knew at once that Quentin liked him. 'He had a sort of gaze,' he says. 'Like a friendly dog.'

During the next two or three years Haggarty and Crisp saw each other 'regularly but infrequently'. They walked together in the street, Haggarty towering over Crisp – 'like a battleship escorting a wee boat' – and they went to cafés and the occasional pub, though Quentin stuck to tea or stout. Haggarty says he was 'open' to Crisp and 'extremely friendly and affectionate' to him, as he was to all his friends. The initial fascination that Crisp had exerted did not diminish. Haggarty decided that Crisp was 'all of a piece, the front very formidable but bonded, like rubber and metal can be bonded, to the inner self which nobody knew'. This inner man, Haggarty made vain attempts to discover. 'I tried to probe but it was difficult to get past the barrier of wit and performance,' he says and eventually decided that this inner self was as much a riddle as the universe itself and quite impossible to dismiss, as Quentin was prone to do, with a quip. From the start of their relationship Quentin was 'very welcoming' to Haggarty but 'never dropped his guard, never crossed the line'. He knew from the beginning that Haggarty was unobtainable – and Haggarty quickly learnt that Crisp hated to be touched or in modern parlance was not at all 'touchy-feely'. Even his handshake seemed to lack something, another feature he shared with O'Connor. Never during these years did Haggarty visit Beaufort Street and Crisp never visited, or was invited to visit, John Haggarty's room in Colville Place, off Charlotte Street. Looking back at this time, Haggarty says that he and Quentin Crisp were 'like a couple of birds in Trafalgar Square, strutting around together for a while and then flying off in different directions'. By the end of the 1940s, Haggarty had begun to establish himself as a scriptwriter and film-maker and became engaged in projects which would take him abroad for long periods.

Quentin Crisp does not mention John Haggarty in *The Naked Civil Servant* and in fact gives a very incomplete and one-dimensional picture of his life in the immediate postwar years. He tells us nothing of his family or how they had fared during this period. He makes no mention of his mother, still living at East Anstey, to whom he often still sent money he 'could not squeeze under the mattress' and says nothing of his unmarried Aunt Kay, who spent her whole life working for the epilepsy colony at Chalfont St Peter and wrote poetry she never published, or of his widowed Aunt May, who lived in a rented flat in Streatham. He tells us nothing of his brother Gerald, whose childless marriage to the Russian princess had collapsed before the war and who had been invalided out of the army and come home to take on a rather humble job with the Ministry of Agriculture at Lampeter, declaring that he only wanted to see the 'sane' members of his family. Nor does he say anything of his brother Lewis, flourishing in South America but eccentric enough to attend board meetings wearing his bedroom slippers. According to family tradition, Lewis once wrote a letter to Quentin beginning 'Dear Sir or Madam', though there is plenty of evidence that the two brothers got on well. Whenever Lewis visited England, he insisted on seeing his younger sibling and on one occasion 'bludgeoned' him into having dinner in a smart restaurant where Quentin's appearance caused uproar. Quentin also tells us nothing at all of a historic meeting with his teenage niece Frances which took place, probably at Easter 1946, in the Great Western Hotel, Paddington. Frances Ramsay remembers the event well and recalls that the shock of her uncle's red hair caused a waiter to step backwards and drop a tray of glasses.

Quentin Crisp also wastes few words on his experiences in the art schools of the day, although it is stirring to think of the many hours he must have spent travelling by bus and train to Watford, Willesden, Walthamstow, Southend, St Albans, Kingston, Camberwell and other suburbs of London, many of them similar to the ones in which he had been brought up. It is strange to think of him hovering on mainline stations and then squeezing into railway carriages where he attracted further attention. At Waterloo one day, where Quentin was waiting for his train to set off, a porter threw open the carriage door and said, 'I've just got to ask you this. What do you do for a living?' Quentin replied, 'I'm a model. I'm going to Guildford College of Art.'

His dealings with the art schools were not always harmonious – he stated later that the front office at Camberwell was 'manned by the vilest people on earth', and that Ravensbourne School of Art was 'a cultural borstal' – but he appears to have got on well if somewhat obliquely with most of the teachers. After meeting Lawrence Gowing at Camberwell he was told he was 'a famous artist who paints everything green'. Bernard Fleetwood-Walker at the Royal Academy Schools encouraged him to do quick action poses, hard to hold for more than five minutes. Some of these teachers had already crossed paths with him. John Minton who taught at Camberwell and then at the Central School already knew Quentin from the Wheatsheaf. Christopher Robin Ironside, at Maidstone, and his wife Janey, became friends and had him to dinner at their house in London. Different teachers had different requirements. Mr McCullough at Goldsmith's got him to pose *en arabesque* on a pillar – 'wings optional' – but Claude Rogers at Camberwell and later the Slade wanted him to impersonate 'an ordinary mortal'. For Guy Roddon, who later ran an anatomy class at Goldsmith's attended by Bridget Riley and Mary Quant, Quentin Crisp would wiggle whichever muscle was being discussed. Only one teacher, who worked at Kingston, objected to Quentin's make-up and got him the sack.

The art students who painted or drew Quentin Crisp during this period will have their own memories of him. Those who have spoken to me or already put their memories in print seem to have only good things to say though some seem peculiarly obsessed with the colour of his posing pouches: lilac, gold and red have been mentioned. Others refer to his kindness. Theo Ramos who drew him at the Royal Academy Schools recalls that he brought along a basket of fruit and sandwiches for the students. Many talk about the complexity of his poses. Robin Hurdle who drew him at Camberwell calls them 'masochistic' and Anthony Thorp who did him at the Central School remembered Quentin posing with his hip on the seat of a chair, his legs over its back, one elbow propped on the floor, the other arm pointing. Crisp sums up the situation by describing himself as 'a hated demi-God, part-time sacred, who occasionally became an object of reverence'. He certainly made his presence felt in and around the art schools. Carrie Diamond, who painted him at St Martin's School of Art in the late 1940s, remembers Quentin 'prancing up and down Charing Cross Road in very tight slightly flared trousers' and argues that his eye-shadow and make-up were even more striking than his dyed hair. Mrs Diamond also declared that there were lots of homosexuals around in Soho at that time and they *never* got beaten up. Quentin Crisp 'made bloody sure he was noticed'.

We have already noted Quentin Crisp's chilly relationship with the homosexual community and there was no letting up during this period. The Gateways Club, a famous lesbian haunt in Chelsea, made him welcome and he even once took John Haggarty there, and he appeared at ease when spotted by the poet James Kirkup in a dubious part of the Coventry Street Lyons known as the Lily Pond. But these were the exceptions. He would be turned away by the Rockingham Club, a Soho institution described as the 'closet of closets' where 'top-drawer queers' danced together discreetly, and he would cause 'terrible unease' and 'frozen faces' when he was taken by a woman to a homosexual establishment called the Fifty Fifty Club, but perhaps these rejections belong to a later period. In the 1940s he was still getting enough trouble from so-called 'straight' places. Schmidt's restaurant in Charlotte Street, whose owner was so kind to Maria Steiner, treated him badly enough for him to describe it as 'the most unloving restaurant in the history of the world'. When he appeared at the basement Mandrake Club, its proprietor Boris Watson said, 'Buy him a meal and get him out of here' and even with John Haggarty beside him he did not get beyond the door of the Black Horse in Rathbone Place. Instantly rejected by an angry barmaid, Quentin Crisp uncharacteristically put his hand on his friend's shoulder and said, 'Come away, Mr Haggarty, you will learn, you will learn.' Quentin did not forget such experiences but soon sounded quite boastful when he mentioned these setbacks, as if they added to his significance.

In *The Naked Civil Servant* there is no description of the poverty and austerity which featured so much in the life of the improvident Philip O'Connor, but Quentin confesses that he was dogged by a sense of failure and the feeling that he was sinking into oblivion. He does not mention that in October 1946 he published an article entitled 'The Genius of Mervyn Peake' in a new highbrow magazine called *Facet*. A few months later, in the same magazine, he published an even more learned treatise headed 'Patronage in the Age of Negation'. Both these articles show a depth of knowledge and seriousness almost entirely absent from his café talk, but no lack of liveliness. In his Peake piece he confesses that the drawing of a cat in the artist's portrait of *Mr and Mrs Spratt* shows such genius as to render him speechless. In the article on patronage he argues that the history of art is 'an elaborate striptease act'.

In the summer 1947 issue of *Facet*, Quentin Crisp would perform his own form of striptease in a poem called 'Spring' which goes as follows:

> Spring comes when Spring comes never any more
>   over the barren ploughland of our years
> but we, who always feared the Spring before
>   have found at last an ending to all fears.
>
> When God with knotted winds across the sky
>   scourges the white or weeping clouds of rain;
> or from the bed in which it loved to lie
>   drags by its emerald hair the sleeping grain;
>
> convulses in an agony of birth
>   trees that are old and only long to die;
> or with a 'pox of flowers' infects the earth:
>   these things are like a rainbow in the sky.
>
> If God ordained all this, he did ordain
>   that we who wanted love should be alone.
> We are some kindred miracle of pain.
>   We asked for bread. He gave us precious stone.

There is a great deal in these four verses: paradox, perversity, self-reverence, self-mockery, bitterness, beauty and colour, all of which are crucial and central elements of Quentin Crisp's inner and outer life. The poet and academic Ian Patterson describes this poem as 'a gesture of defiant acceptance of isolation'. It also shows a detailed knowledge of the work of T. S. Eliot, Swinburne and Wordsworth and highlights another difference between Crisp and O'Connor. While Philip often dashed off his stuff without even bothering with a second draft, Quentin clearly put as much 'work' and 'regularity' into this poem as he did into every other aspect of his life. The existence of this poem, published when he was thirty-eight, makes one wonder how many other bits of 'freelance' he attempted during this period. Throughout his life, Quentin Crisp preferred to dwell on his failures and overlook his successes. In his autobiography, he also makes no mention of his two short stories broadcast by the BBC in 1949, both of which merit attention and throw further light on his frame of mind. *Letting a Flat* is about various mechanical human beings, including a housemaid and a policeman. *The Black Thing* is about an undefined black object which haunts a married man and eventually drives his wife to murder him. Both stories were broadcast on the Light Programme but are far from lightweight.

In *The Naked Civil Servant*, Quentin remains resolutely focused on more superficial, personal matters, such as the attack of eczema – 'an allergy to middle age' – which struck him down in the summer of 1948 and would bother him on and off for the rest of his life, and his momentous decision at around the same time to change the colour of his hair. In his book, he states that on Christmas Day 1948, his fortieth birthday, he began the arduous process of turning his hair from red to blue. He tells us that the decision to enter his 'blue period' was partly prompted by a chance remark by a man he calls Lambchop – real name Hugh Pulley – to the effect that he only dyed his hair red in order to appear younger. Since deceptions of this sort had never been part of his style, he decided to change to blue in order to show to the world that he was going grey underneath and not at all ashamed of it. On the contrary, he was determined to embrace his decline with maximum enthusiasm, later explaining to the writer Selina Hastings, 'Remarkably few effeminate men go on looking marvellous.' He was soon branding himself 'one of the stately homos of England' and relishing the remark of his long-standing dentist, J. Slee Tiffin, now working in St James's, that it was not his teeth that were growing old but *himself*.

The 'shaky, transitional state' between the two colours started with Quentin cropping his red hair back to two inches. Many months followed of 'forcing red out and forcing blue in' – this phrase was adapted from a famous soap commercial – and eventually a new lilac-headed Quentin Crisp appeared for everyone to see. He tells us that he felt 'like a Westerner without a gun' and from this moment onwards was 'no longer conspicuously available for sex'. He told his clergyman brother-in-law John Payne that he had 'changed from the Festive Season to Lent'. In the art schools he was asked if he had joined a different brigade and on the streets of London he met a chorus of consternation. 'This piece of lavender came walking towards me,' recalls John Haggarty, followed by Quentin's explanation that he was going to be 'great' rather than 'grey'. A friend of Haggarty called Miss Drury protested, 'Don't do it! Go back, you can be red for longer!' 'Yes, it's dyed but it won't lie down,' he told Joan Rhodes, and Bobbie Battersby's exclamation 'What the *fuck* have you done to your hair?' was met with the explanation that he was planning to grow old gracefully. The spirited Miss Battersby, now bringing up Philip O'Connor's first child with the help of her long-standing boyfriend, replied, well *fuck* that, she would rather grow old disgracefully.

This personal transformation seems to have coincided with Quentin's increasing disenchantment with modelling, the profession which a few years earlier had given him 'total fulfilment'. At the end of the 1940s he got a full-time job in the art department of the publishers Harrap and Co. In his autobiography he tells us that he got this job through answering a newspaper advertisement, which again suggests a certain capability or assertiveness on his part. He also tells us that the firm's premises at 182 High Holborn had an atmosphere as 'undisturbed as that of a St James's Street club'. Here, in this 'rest home for retired gentlefolk', he luxuriated for two and a half years, always clamouring for work but scornfully dismissing everything he did. When he eventually announced he was leaving, the response of his immediate boss – 'You swine!' – tells us that he had become a valuable member of the team, and the response of the managing director Walter Harrap – 'I just want to say how tolerant I think you've been' – suggests that he had almost become a beloved icon in this old family firm. These examples of respect and kindness need to be weighed against the atrocities he suffered at other times.

He does not in this instance provide details of his salary, but his relative affluence showed itself in various ways. In the early 1950s he was able to arrange for his mother and his niece to rent Miss Lumley's flat at 39 Markham Square and he called there every evening, usually leaving £5 on the mantelpiece for the next day's food. He also brought friends to the flat, including Mr Duffey, who offers a vivid picture of Mrs Pratt, now in her seventies. 'She was a wonderful little creature, like a bird,' he recalls. 'She was a very keen card player and she would reprimand her son, saying things like "Denis, behave yourself!" ' The other indication of Quentin's solvency was the fact that he could now take time off to write a short satirical novel. *Love Made Easy* was, alas, a complete flop, rejected by every publisher who saw it and a disappointment even to Miss Lumley, who declared, 'I wish you hadn't made every line funny. It's so depressing.' In his account of this endeavour, he refers to 'the pathetic parcel of greatness' that lay around in his room for the next few months.

Quentin Crisp's account of his life during the 1950s is as sketchy and jokey as ever, though certain major and minor incidents stand out, usually undated, and the general drift of his life is vaguely visible beneath the surface. One of its most stable elements was 129 Beaufort Street and one suspects that very little changed here apart from the coming and going of different lodgers. The Voters' Registers for this period provide us with some of their names, or versions of their names. Some are classic Voters' Register names like Wilfred J. Kesterton and Mabel E. Pledger and give no clue as to the character of the house. Others, like Wanda Manners-Howe and Valerie Leaf, have a more Chelsea-ish feel. There were never less than eight or nine under the roof and some of them stayed for years. Many were never mentioned by Quentin Crisp but a select few featured prominently in his conversation and writings. Ursula Beeson, who had been a character witness at Quentin's court case in 1944, lived at the house from the middle of the war until the end of the 1950s and was elevated to legendary status as 'the Real Miss Beeson', as opposed to 'the False Miss Beeson', an American acquaintance named Irene Beeson whom he had met in the Bar-B-Q. Other lodgers are distinguished only by their deeds or misdeeds. One of them was a woman with 'a lust for rows and reconciliations'. There was also a lady railway porter and a girl who sold Quentin 'a wonderful gold American watch'. And downstairs of course there was always Gordon Richardson, now graduating from repertory work to making brief appearances as doctors or clergymen in the films of the day.

Quentin Crisp gives a firm impression of his steady home life during these years. While Philip O'Connor fled from one domestic settlement to another, cosy though they often were, Quentin stayed put in his dusty, dirty Chelsea room, leading just the one solitary life with few encumbrances. He liked, and needed, to be alone. He drank Guinness at breakfast, he did the crossword and he attended to his correspondence. His letters were laid out in a distinctive pattern, each new paragraph beginning at the point where the previous one had ended. He drew a circle round the dot on top of the 'i's in Quentin Crisp and even letters to his family signed 'Denis' or 'Uncle Denis' ended with his adopted name in capital letters. His commitment to his invented name was now so great that a letter addressed to him as Denis Pratt was returned by another lodger, marked 'not known here'. And even when he was not engaged in these activities he was entirely content to sit simply breathing, blinking and, if the eczema got too bad, *scratching*. Home was the place where he could be himself and if the menacing telephone calls became unbearable he could take the receiver off the hook. He sat in a bucket seat someone had extracted from a motor-car. His cupboards and suitcases were full of clothes he might need sometime in the future, but he preferred to wear a filthy dressing-gown at home. He had few visitors and many of his acquaintances seem to have visited him only once. Those that did visit his pictureless bedsitter went away with vivid memories of it. The painter John de Paul, who had met him in Fitzrovia during the war, was surprised to find four volumes of Dickens under his pillow, apparently put there to keep his hair in place while he slept. De Paul also states that the dust in the room 'glowed like jewels'. Maria Steiner remembers an enormous mirror and others recall that Quentin provided them with a page of *The Times* to sit on but that the dust itself never invaded his own person. Quentin himself explains that he would 'jump in the air' to put on his trousers. As Professor Robinson points out, Quentin Crisp had 'no interest whatsoever in domesticity . . . He lived in perpetual squalor and never learned to cook.'

As we know only too well, Quentin did no housework but he did change the bed linen once a week in case it got so dirty that the laundry refused to accept it. For food, he was about to discover a grey-coloured food-substitute called Complan, invented for invalids, containing all the essential vitamins and available at chemists, whom Quentin found so much easier to deal with than butchers or green-grocers. He was capable of living on Complan for months on end, with or without the approval of Dr Armando Dumas Child, who had been his doctor since the late 1920s. Complan would remain a much flaunted part of his diet into the distant future and his addiction to this fuel-like substance draws further attention to the slightly inhuman if not mechanical aspect of his character. John Haggarty reinforces this impression by describing Quentin Crisp as 'creaturely' and his Beaufort Street room as 'a cave or eyrie from which he made sorties into the world'.

During the 1950s, Quentin made many excursions. He went often, sometimes twice a day, to the Forum Cinema at the top of the street and to other picture-houses elsewhere. He describes the cinema as 'the forgetting chamber' and went there to 'revive the exotic dreams of my childhood'. He claimed that if he was ever found unconscious in the street, all that would be needed to revive him would be 'an injection of celluloid'. Most of the films he saw were mainstream events but he lets slip in *Resident Alien* that he also loved the highbrow movies of Jean Cocteau. He went out in pursuit of work, food, paraffin for his room heater, and often for pleasure but never in search of sex or love. In Chelsea, he continued to fascinate people in the street. The writer Simon Gray, then a schoolboy, remembers him drifting by and a lady called Gwen Otter, who lived in Margaretta Terrace, responded to the same vision by murmuring to her young companion Willie Landels, later an artist and magazine editor, 'The English have improved lately.'

In his own neighbourhood, Quentin's mixture of respectable and unrespectable friends included June Churchill, gauzily glamorous daughter-in-law of the then Prime Minister, who had a particular penchant for effeminate men and once declared that she wanted to sleep with 'the queerest man in the room'. The Chelsea artist Theo de Rose painted him and Quentin himself produced a good portrait of Peggy Thorburn, daughter-in-law of the noted bird-painter. And of course he made friends with families and their children, not just individuals. 'Hello Quentin,' Simon Watson-Taylor once greeted him. 'Where are you going? Don't tell me. You're going to tea with one married woman and supper with another. It's *disgusting*.' During this time he saw a lot of the Mervyn Peakes and a particularly hospitable couple called the Dennerhys who lived at 7 Elm Park Gardens. On 31 December 1951 he attended a New Year's Eve party at this address wearing green make-up and a long, flowing green scarf given him by the students of Walthamstow School of Art, which suggests that he continued to do modelling work while employed by Harraps. Eve Dennerhy 'really loved' Quentin, and her painfully thin husband Denny, who had served as a flight lieutenant during the war and always wore an RAF blazer, 'really liked' him though he disagreed quite violently with what he said and was 'mercilessly teased' by Quentin in return. Theo Ramos's wife Julia remembers that Quentin stuffed himself with cucumber sandwiches at these parties and was shunned only by a highly respectable male couple called Keith and George, who wore Savile Row suits. More new friends came via the art schools and included the painter Penelope Makyns, who met Quentin when he was working at the Byam Shaw School of Art. Miss Makyns went often to Beaufort Street and played chess with Quentin and later took her husband, the future Lord Harvey of Tasburgh, to the squalid room. At a subsequent private view of Penelope Makyns's work, Lord Harvey recalls that Quentin Crisp was mistaken for the wife of the French Ambassador.

In Fitzrovia, or what was left of it, Quentin pursued a similarly active life on a dusty level of bohemian society left uncharted or obscured in most contemporary memoirs. In *The Naked Civil Servant*, he writes, 'By the early 1950s, the inhabitants of Fitzrovia had come a long way, all of it downhill, from the happy time.' He continues his lament, 'The whole *vie de bohème* was passing without hope or warning', but then confusingly acknowledges that the old bans on him had lifted like mist and a man had even been asked to leave the Coach and Horses in Greek Street because he made fun of him. Employing what seems like the royal 'we', he writes, 'We could at last walk majestically in our natural setting.'

Some of Quentin's old acquaintances and courtiers were flourishing. Some were not. His art student friend Pat was now a nun in France and her Polish husband in a mental hospital in Epsom, where Quentin felt obliged to pay him time-consuming regular visits. Other acquaintances were dead, though death had no dominion over Quentin Crisp. In November 1953, he was sitting in the French Café in Old Compton Street when a distraught stranger rushed in announcing that Dylan Thomas had died. Sickened by this display of emotion, Quentin piped up, 'Was he a relation of yours?' – the only bitchy remark he ever admitted making. Many more friends had left 'the reservation' and settled further afield. Philip O'Connor was now being scrubbed clean on Haverstock Hill. Maria Steiner was living with a structural engineer called John Scott and bringing up her expanding family in Camden Town, though occasionally using Quentin's services as a babysitter – her son Peter O'Connor recalls the 'gloved hand' on the gatepost. And Joan Rhodes was now famous, performing feats of strength in places like the Palladium and Metropolitan Music Hall, but still able to lure Quentin over to her flat in Belsize Park with the promise of roast lamb.

As some of these people faded away, new ones entered his life. Among them was Barbara Markham, who ran a dressmaking business in Covent Garden and was proclaimed by Quentin to be 'the greatest trouser-taperer in the world'. Dressing as he did, mainly in other people's discarded clothes, her services were much needed. Mrs Markham remembers taking the tail off a shirt for him and other tailoring tasks, but she also accompanied him to cinemas and cafés. 'He concentrated utterly on you,' she recalls. 'He never looked over your shoulder.' Another person enthralled by Quentin's manners who saw him a lot at this time was Philip O'Connor's friend Oliver Bernard, who firmly refutes the idea that Quentin didn't engage in normal conversation. 'He listened a lot before he embarked on a lecture and he was a great observer,' says Bernard, who saw in Crisp 'an innate inner puritanism' splendidly at odds with his rather cold exterior beauty and 'all that eye make-up and stuff', which seemed to carry an aura of the French court under Louis the Fourteenth, Fifteenth or Sixteenth, Bernard wasn't sure which. 'In a way, it disguised him,' he says. 'Underneath, he was much more ordinary, less exotic. I don't think he liked his ordinary self.'

Was it anything to do with this suggested dislike of his ordinary self that thrust Quentin Crisp at the age of forty-three into the strangest relationship of his life? Sometime in 1952, in the Alexandria café in Rathbone Place, he met George Taylor, who was about twelve years younger than him. In *The Naked Civil Servant*, Quentin seeks to minimize the libel risk by placing this encounter in the middle of his account of the Second World War and by giving Mr Taylor white hair and the name of Barn Door. Taylor was massively built and worked as a porter in a Soho market. Quentin later described him as 'marvellously handsome' with 'a built-in nose' and 'ludicrously manly' but also as 'a poor wee thing'. For some reason, Quentin took George Taylor home with him that night and a relationship began that would last for nearly four years. Quentin has explained that Barn Door was an 'active sodomite' but added that sex was not a significant factor in their relationship.

What other bonds can have existed between such different men? In his book, he does not explain but in conversation with the scriptwriter Philip Mackie he made it clear that he was motivated by a form of kindness or compassion. He wanted to give George Taylor, who had been 'pushed around' by everyone he had ever met, a sort of 'kingdom'. On a part-time basis, Quentin became his slave – and at the same time treated him as if he was a boy of eleven. 'I went through the whole domestic racket, taking his clothes to the cleaners and giving them back to him the next weekend.' He even attempted to tidy his room to please him – 'He thought if I had a nice tray to put the tea cups on all would be well and all would be different' – and cooked meals for him. Quentin's friends were horrified and confused and saw Quentin's companion George Taylor as 'big, heavy and boring'. Miss Lumley said, 'I've never understood your relationship with him.' Mr Duffey believes that Quentin was in awe of Taylor but adds, 'We didn't approve of him. In fact, all Quentin's friends resented him. He wasn't a Quentin person.' John de Paul describes Taylor as 'a gentle giant' but says Quentin treated him like 'the Prince of Wales' and would ring up at short notice and cancel a game of canasta on account of some last-minute demand from this new friend.

Though Taylor only visited Quentin at weekends, they became another spectacle on the streets of London. Taylor would walk several yards behind him, making faces and sometimes removing his false teeth. They sat separately on buses, Taylor upstairs and Crisp in his preferred place downstairs. At a distance, Taylor would try to make fun of Crisp, but when they sat together in cafés, he would sometimes grab his friend's hand and make embarrassing declarations – 'Mr Crisp and I have been together for four years' – and then burst into snatches of opera or imitations of Winston Churchill. At home in Beaufort Street, Quentin claims he was driven increasingly neurotic and 'spinsterish' by the ensuing disarrangement to his room and even boasted that he would 'burst into a fit of weeping if the kettle was not facing due East'. Quentin's niece Frances recalls that her uncle 'moaned like mad' about Mr Taylor. Reflecting later on the affair, Quentin writes that it at last taught him that there was no Great Dark Man and that 'even under an exterior as rugged as a mountain range, there lurks the same wounded, wincing psyche that cripples the rest of us'. Alas, we do not have George Taylor's account of the friendship or his reactions to Quentin's subsequent fame. We know nothing about what happened to him afterwards, except that he got married, or how exactly the affair ended. According to Quentin, the crucial moment came when one Easter he told Taylor that he needed to visit his mother.

Mrs Pratt seems to have been the only person in his circle who welcomed Taylor into her son's life, even to the extent of sending birthday cards to him, which perhaps shows how close mother and son had stayed to each other. During this period Quentin wrote enough letters to his mother to justify his joke that one of the advantages of dying is that you would never have to write to your mother again. In 1950, Quentin's sister Phyllis and her husband had left darkest Devonshire and moved to Buckinghamshire, where John Payne became vicar of Twyford. Mrs Pratt came with them and much preferred the magnificent old vicarage near London, though her health was declining. Baba Pratt was a prodigious letter-writer – she still wrote letters to girls she had been at school with in the 1890s – and though she had very little money, was always friendly and sociable. She had made friends quickly with Angus McBean's mother and had stayed with her in London. Though she had never stepped over the threshold at 129 Beaufort Street, she had met many of Quentin's friends and she and Quentin had been to stay with Denuta Jurand and her new husband Major Abbott at Angmering-on-Sea in Sussex. In 1953, Mrs Pratt had a hip replacement and afterwards needed a wheelchair. A few years later she moved with the Paynes to Calverton Rectory near Milton Keynes, where Quentin continued to visit her, sometimes driven there by his niece Frances who by now had a job in London. During one such journey, Frances knocked down a dog with her Austin 40 and her uncle coolly responded, 'One less dog!'

When staying at Calverton, Quentin was permitted his usual Guinness at breakfast but then seems to have retreated to his mother's ground-floor bedroom. 'He sat in her room *all* the time,' says Frances. 'He came to see *her*.' There is also a photograph of Quentin and his mother sitting outside in the sun playing Scrabble together, Quentin in short sleeves, keeping the score. At the end of his life, Quentin said simply that he had enjoyed his mother's company. She talked about the books she had read in the past, sometimes muddling their plots, and about people she had known in Sutton like the Benmores, the Aldridges and a certain Muffet Maude. She also discussed her marriage to Quentin's father. 'I never loved him,' she said. 'But you hated him enough to marry him,' retorted Quentin. 'Well, there was that,' she replied. From time to time, she would ask if he was still out of work but the full extent of her influence on and involvement in her son's life remains a mystery. What did she think of the person he had become? Where had her own theatricality, well formed more than half a century earlier, originated? And what would she have made of her son's own special bit of 'living theatre' at Beaufort Street?

Life in what its most long-standing resident Gordon Richardson called 'the Madhouse' had continued throughout the Barn Door years. In the summer of 1955, a serious, stern and brooding note was struck when a cluster of guests from one of Mr Richardson's parties made their way upstairs and called on Quentin, who was in the process of dishing up bacon and eggs for George Taylor. Among the visitors, who carried glasses of sherry, was the then unknown Harold Pinter. The twenty-four-year-old repertory actor surveyed the scene through thick horn-rimmed spectacles and later told Quentin that this was the moment at which he first felt inspired to write a play. The performance two years later of his first work *The Room* certainly bears out this claim. According to its stage directions, this is set in 'a snug, stuffy, rather down-at-heel bed-sit with gas fire and cooking facilities' and 'an aura of self-containment'. This description fits Quentin Crisp's Beaufort Street room to a tee. Writing about this encounter at the end of the century, Pinter remembers the complete silence of Mr Taylor, who never looked up or spoke a word. More mysteriously, he recalls that Quentin Crisp's hair was *blond*.

The Voters' Register for 1956 records the arrival at 129 Beaufort Street of a certain Belinda Carlyon. Without mentioning her name, Quentin Crisp devotes two pages of his autobiography to this flamboyant figure whom he describes as 'the richest and noisiest girl in the world' and as 'a true friend'. For a while she occupied the back room on the same floor, sharing it with a boxer dog and its owner, and on various occasions she took Quentin on hair-raising spins in her low-slung sports car which made him 'squeak' with delight. More significantly, she also introduced him to the small and somewhat unconventional design firm in Soho, where he was soon to find permanent employment. Between 1956 and 1960, Quentin worked for Manhattan Displays on the top floor of 16 Greek Street, making display units, hand-painted stands, trays, containers and other gadgets and gimmicks to encourage sales. He had long been looking for 'a sitting-down job' that would yield a change from 'the agony of posing' and he now found himself answering the telephone – he was sometimes mistaken for a woman – making cocoa, typing letters, filing, and playing Scrabble with his employer, who was an American. Of the work itself, he has little to say other than that he once painted the faces of four thousand dolls and almost as many pigs. He was helped with the dolls by his friend Mrs Markham and when working on the pigs, for use in butchers' shops, he endeavoured to put a different expression on each of them. While thus engaged he spotted his old friend George Melly from the window and summoned him upstairs to see what he was doing. Melly recalls the expressions on the pigs' faces as 'very extraordinary indeed'. How many of these pigs survive in butchers' shops today? And would one recognize them as Quentin Crisp's handiwork?

This job did not keep Quentin out of the art schools but it did keep him on the move. He remained a powerful presence on the streets of Soho and Chelsea where he attracted new waves of admirers and detractors. Julia Ramos remembers seeing him posing for Fulham Road football crowds by reclining on a chaise-longue outside another shop belonging to junk dealer Mr Mendelson. Alfred Hecht, who had a picture-framing business in King's Road, remembered Quentin as 'a bloody nuisance' but withdrew this opinion when he became famous. Countless others saw him but never spoke to him, but recall that he 'created amazement wherever he went'. According to Jane Miller, who later became his editor at Jonathan Cape, 'Quentin's head was always in the air. He wasn't soliciting your interest. He didn't want anyone to react.' According to David Ball, who had met Quentin with Angus McBean ten years earlier, he reinforced this impression by walking extremely fast. 'You could never catch up with him. Angus and I used to watch him from the 14 bus. All the way to Knightsbridge. Then of course Bunny Roger took over.' The career of the rich, dapper and eccentric Mr Roger, another sight for sore eyes, deserves to be charted elsewhere but does not seem to have ever overlapped that of Quentin Crisp.

In 1958 the household at 129 Beaufort Street was further enriched by the addition of John Ransley, a young man who knew something about odd institutions, being the son of the Governor of Wakefield and then Wandsworth Gaol. He took over the second-floor front room immediately above Quentin, became a light in Quentin's life and remained a friend for more than forty years. Ransley confirms the impression that Quentin's life was solitary, with no lovers coming and going, and recalls that Quentin would often come upstairs and warm himself in front of his fire and meet his friends. At this stage the household seems to have been as relaxed and bohemian as any in Chelsea, thanks partly to the benign influence of its owner Vi Vereker, who lived in Oakley Street but called frequently bringing Vim and toilet paper. During the late 1950s, Quentin was in and out of everyone's rooms and often attended parties at Gordon Richardson's downstairs. Here he saw more of Harold Pinter and also met the young actors Ronald Harwood and Paul Bailey who would both emerge as writers. Harwood remembers that Crisp was wearing 'a voluminous open-necked shirt with a Peter Pan collar, purple baggy linen trousers and open sandals', had 'exquisite hands which he used exquisitely' and spoke 'as if he had just woken from sleep'. Paul Bailey remembers pleasing Quentin by telling him that he was like a character out of a Firbankian novel but being somewhat unimpressed by the 'dodgy truisms' that fell from his lips, to which the only possible response was to laugh. Bailey also recalls a party at Richardson's where Quentin was upstaged by 'an ancient queen' who announced to everyone, 'I think you should know that I was Oscar Wilde's last lover.' Quentin's lifelong venomous attitude towards Oscar Wilde cannot have helped matters. Upstairs at John Ransley's he met other friends including a girl called Hermione Goacher, of whom he was to see a lot in the next few years.

Hermione Goacher was the daughter of the Shakespearian actress Wendy Seymour and when she first met Quentin in 1960 was living in Cheyne Court, Royal Hospital Road, with a maid to look after her. She confirms that Quentin was 'a very concealed person' and 'a secret reader' and, like other people, she remembers 'I never touched him, I never kissed him' but her view of him contradicts the more familiar view in that she did not think of him as at all peculiar. 'His hands were a bit Jane Austen but I didn't think of him as unusual in any other way.' When Quentin called at Better Books in Charing Cross Road, where she worked, other members of the staff gasped and mentioned his name but she had no idea that he was already well known in Soho circles. She also contradicts the usual view, particularly perpetuated by Quentin himself, that he hated nature. 'He *loved* flowers,' she says, 'they were the *only* thing he loved.' She also recalls that far from being oblivious to the taste and appearance of food and in spite of his dedication to Complan he loved fancy treats. In his room, Hermione recalls, Quentin served 'very pretty croissants with marzipan in them'. He also adored meringues. In fact, says Mrs

Goacher, he adored all food 'except cucumbers', which may surprise all those who saw him wolfing down those sandwiches at Chelsea parties.

These impressions – Hermione Goacher's close encounter with Quentin and Jane Miller's more distant view of him as a character on the Chelsea streets – suggest that by this time Quentin Crisp had reached his 'glorious peak' and had done so without tangible achievements of any sort. It was in this mode that on 24 September 1960 he attended the wedding of Esther Grant's daughter Julia Paul Jones, whom he had known since she was a child, to the actor Nigel Keen, which took place at St Paul's Covent Garden. At the reception afterwards at Angus McBean's house in Gibson Square, Islington, Quentin was photographed by McBean talking to the bride's father, then an employee of the British Standards Institute. Quentin wears no buttonhole, but he looks supremely confident in a conventional dark suit, loose-fitting cream shirt and loosely knotted tie. His shy, charming, conventional-looking companion and their delight at being photographed together show the happy bond that could exist between Quentin and the ordinary world. History does not record how Quentin got on with the bride's formidable aunt Guinevere Hunter-Tilney, who later became an adviser on dress to Margaret Thatcher. At her niece's wedding the future Dame Guinevere drew attention to herself by saying, 'Throw rice – it hurts more' and at the reception she made an impromptu speech in favour of capital punishment.

In his memoirs, Quentin makes no mention of this happy party – nor does he mention his mother's death earlier in the year. On 31 March 1960, Baba Pratt had died at Calverton Rectory, at the age of eighty-six. Family matters do not feature in later pages of *The Naked Civil Servant*, though readers of that book would surely have been interested to know what happened to Mrs Pratt and some might even have been glad to know that she left her entire estate of £718 18s 2d to her daughter Phyllis. Her death, nearly thirty years after that of her husband, had little effect on the course of Quentin's life though it was at about this time that he gave up his job at Manhattan Displays and returned to full-time modelling. Predictably enough he presents this move as another backward step, though it provides one of the most dazzling passages in his autobiography. 'I fell back into the oubliette of art,' he writes. 'In this Havisham twilight, I was grimly at home. About me there was something of the dusty elaboration of her mouse-nibbled wedding cake. So here, propped up on some rickety Victorian chair, I sat silent and, I hope, apparently resigned – an ashy clinker from the long dead fires of bohemia.'

The early 1960s also saw the first flickering flames of Swinging London, though these did not yet light up the life of Quentin Crisp. He was now a 'battery model' working in the art schools and privately for small groups and individual artists. His poses were less daring than in the past though he was still much in demand for portrait classes and responded to them 'with grace and gratitude'. From time to time, he even made flamboyant attempts to get more work, delivering by hand a fancy, beautifully hand-scripted letter to the painter Guy Roddon, who had a studio a few yards from Beaufort Street, in which he begged him to tell the world that he was still posing. At about this time, Roddon considered using him as Christ in a fourteen-part Stations of the Cross but decided he was 'not quite right' and asked him instead to model the various Daughters of Jerusalem.

Quentin spent the rest of his time stalking about, nose in the air, and being noticed. The young actress Susannah York, who occasionally saw him in the King's Road and describes him as an 'elf', confesses she would follow him at a discreet distance – 'You wanted to protect him,' she explains – but others were more assertive. Outside a King's Road pub, the Chelsea character David Litvinoff, who was said to work for the property racketeer Rachman, proclaimed that Quentin Crisp offered 'the best conversation in London'. Quentin still made regular trips to the cinema but did not always like what was on offer. *Psycho*, which he saw in 1960, convinced him that Alfred Hitchcock, whom he had long admired for his message that no one is ever safe and that terrible events can even happen in grand hotels, was now on the way down. He may have had similar feelings about himself. During the Cuban missiles crisis in the autumn of 1962, he embraced the possibility of obliteration in a nuclear war with typical enthusiasm. By the following summer, that particular opportunity had passed and

Quentin Crisp, who was now fifty-four years old, wondered how he would fill the rest of his life. Not for the first time, he noted that he had 'exhausted all the potentialities of my character'. On 12 August 1963 he was sitting in his room and dressed in his usual filthy dressing-gown when the doorbell rang. He listened carefully for the distinctive number of rings then scampered downstairs to open the door to someone he had not seen for fifteen years. Out on the street stood Philip O'Connor.

— 12 —

Begging Letters

As you may know he is an odd character, with a wary hostility towards anything savouring towards the Establishment and prone to trail his coat if he thinks he can get a rise out of anybody. On the other hand, he has, I think, a very shrewd judgement and considerable fluency. It would be rather a gamble having him on The Critics; but if The Critics may be considered oysters, Philip O'Connor would be the grit that might produce some pearls.

DOUGLAS CLEVERDON TO PEGGY BARKER,
1 January 1960

Philip O'Connor's autobiography *Memoirs of a Public Baby* had been published by Faber and Faber in January 1958. The book was priced at eighteen shillings and had a yellow dust-jacket designed by Berthold Wolpe on which the title and name of the author occupied most of the available space. The blurb on the first edition stated that it was 'both an extraordinarily frank self-revelation and a distinguished piece of literature' and promised that the book would be 'long remembered'.

The book was dedicated to Anna Wing and carried a note from the author thanking 'the Hon. Simon Stuart' for his work in 'imposing a chronological order and generally editing an extremely untidy narrative'. There was no photograph of the author but in an introduction Stephen Spender describes him as 'small, lithe, dark, concentrated and totally absorbed in being Philip O'Connor', 'absolutely the genuine article' and 'part angel, part demon', who somehow offered body and spirit 'a blessed new chance'.

The book was an instant success in critical terms. Cyril Connolly gave it his lead review in the *Sunday Times* and wrote of O'Connor's 'acutely conscious and contemporary sensibility'. In the *Observer*, Philip Toynbee described O'Connor as 'a writer who can transcend the tired prose styles of our time' and praised him for his 'humour and humility, combined with a proper ferocity'. In *Punch*, Anthony Powell acknowledged the author's unusual gift of 'being able to write coherently about the incoherent'. In *Encounter*, Peter Levi marvelled over the book's 'Rabelaisian force of phrase' and 'the immediacy of it all' and in the *New Statesman*, John Raymond called it 'the most excitingly literate personal confession that has appeared since Genet's *Journal d'un Voleur*'.

One of the few notes of dissent came from the lady novelist E. Arnot Robertson on 'The Critics' programme. Spluttering words like 'turgid', 'abnormal' and 'schizoid', she dismissed *Memoirs of a Public Baby* as 'a very juvenile picture of a man who seems to be out to shock all the time'. When another member of the panel, the writer David Sylvester, began to speak of the book's 'tremendous maturity and the moral stature of the man coming through', Miss Arnot Robertson interjected in a high, loud voice, 'Good heavens!' and 'I'm just amazed!' and reasserted her claim that the book could only be of interest to a psychiatrist or a nurse.

I do not need to emphasize that the book had already had a very long history and would cast an even longer shadow over the rest of the author's life. Considering that he had been working on it since the 1930s, his exhilarated relief over its successful publication is entirely understandable. He later explained that he wrote the book for a mixture of reasons: 'elements of exhibitionism, self-pity and the wish to make some money' and also, 'to give vent to certain hatreds that had prevented the smooth course of certain loves'. In his postscript, he claimed that he had partly written it to 'worm' his way into the 'graces' and 'heart' of society. Many writers have been similarly motivated and in Philip O'Connor's case these ambitions were for some time partly realized.

In the wake of the book's publication, Philip found himself marginally more popular, more in the swim but never quite lionized. He said later that he could never cope with the 'literati', but publishing types now took him seriously and made themselves available to him. John Calder wrote saying he didn't mind being telephoned late at night or early in the morning and in Soho Philip ran into elevated figures like Brendan Behan, though he later declared that beside the Irishman's 'careless rapture' he felt like a 'careful rodent'. At about this time he also made friends with the young John Berger, then in transition between being an artist and a writer. Berger says he is 'not a good historian' and he and O'Connor may well have 'rubbed shoulders or even exchanged a glass of wine' at some earlier period. Whatever the truth of this, Berger's first and presiding impression of O'Connor was the way in which he seemed to be trying to disappear all the time. Berger finds further evidence of this trait in *Memoirs of a Public Baby*. 'Its outspokenness is oblique, almost furtive, as if addressed not to the audience but to somebody standing in the wings.'

Among his old gang in Soho, Philip O'Connor became 'a deity'. According to Maria Steiner, those who had often crossed the road to avoid his requests for money now declared, 'We always knew there was gold there.' According to Stephen Fothergill, Philip 'would bathe in the warm glow of success' for the next few years and Ann Meo would go as far as to describe him as 'more or less recovered'. From Paul Potts came a more complex reaction. Potts had written to Philip at once and congratulated him on the book's 'huge success' but was actually disappointed by it, having hoped for different things from the man he had once loved more than anyone. In *Dante Called You Beatrice*, Potts describes running into Philip during this heady time. Philip had just come out of a bank and had lots of money on him and was even carrying his famous book. Potts had only a letter on him saying that his last manuscript had been lost in the post and would brood over this unhappy meeting, made more painful by the fact that Philip's new patron Stephen Spender had just rejected a bunch of his own poems and the fact that Philip O'Connor hadn't given him a halfpenny.

It is worth noting that *Memoirs of a Public Baby* did not become a bestseller and was rejected by all the paperback firms. On 27 January 1958, O'Connor wrote to Michael Hamburger, 'Sales are bad – eight hundred and fifty in the first two weeks; the accountant very much doubts they'll reach five thousand, which I'd hoped for.' Many letters were exchanged with Fabers on financial matters, not least the fact that Philip had quickly run up a bill of £30 by having copies of the book sent to all sorts of people, including Charlie Chaplin, care of United Artists. Yet in spite of these disappointments – 'Good reviews didn't sell the Baby,' Philip would remark in later life – the book's fame spread and unknown to Philip even reached the Salisbury home of his sister Desirée Trethowan, whose two daughters were now at school. It is unclear whether Desirée read any of the book, in which she is given her real name and fairly viciously portrayed. Years later I would learn that she had 'nearly had a heart attack' over the book but made no attempt to take action against her brother, who remained entirely ignorant of his sister's marriage and whereabouts. Whether the book reached the attention of Philip's former guardian Camden Field, now aged sixty-two and living at 64 Marine Parade in Brighton, remains a mystery. Field is unnamed in the book but would have instantly recognized the extended portrait of himself. His views about his one-time protégé's unexpected success would have been fascinating to learn.

The publication did not bring stability or stuffiness to its author's life – in fact it seems to have had the reverse effect. During the spring of 1958, Philip seems to have been in as much turmoil as ever. At the end of January he wrote to Michael Hamburger, 'I've been on a three day bender & have arrived safely (I think) home again; hope in the course of this I've done nothing to annoy you.' It may have been during this particular bender that the writer Peter Vansittart was summoned with Philip Toynbee to go and rescue, or at least inspect, Philip's comatose figure lying under a table in the Soho restaurant Le Jardin des Gourmets. Such lapses were frequent – and created mixed reactions among his friends. The BBC producer David Thomson, himself a keen drinker, was more tolerant of them than Michael Hamburger, to whom Philip wrote of his continuing 'cultural insecurity' and in response to Hamburger's gently expressed admonishments, begged him, 'You shouldn't take the circus too seriously.' Looking back on this period Philip has described how vodka held him up 'while I exploited the last shreds of grandeur attending the publication of my little book'. Alas, the process of trying to dine off the *Public Baby* was to continue for the rest of his life. 'He always expected more,' said Ann Wolff – but on 8 May 1958, he was thrown into understandable exhilaration by a telegram from Rosemary Goad at Fabers saying that the *New York Times* needed a photograph of him to accompany a feature-review in its literary supplement and that six thousand copies of the book had been ordered by the British Book Centre in New York. In a letter to David Thomson a few days later, Philip wrote of his subsequent 'piggeries around the Caves de France' which had 'much upset' Anna Wing. Getting home to Eton Hall after these debauches he received 'the first black eye in our connubial blisstime'.

On the other hand, Philip had now met the radio producer Douglas Cleverdon, best known as midwife to Dylan Thomas's *Under Milk Wood*, and got on well with him, even if progress on a new radio play was 'very, very slow'. He had also done some reviewing for Terence Kilmartin at the *Observer* though admitting, 'I shall never be a good or acceptable reviewer', and was also bucked up by laudatory late reviews for the *Baby*. In the *London Magazine* of April 1958 the critic Francis Wyndham wrote that O'Connor's writing 'sustains a high pitch of almost feverish sensibility' and in *Isis* the following month, the undergraduate Michael Horovitz praised the book for 'its total absence of backhanded ingratiation' and unlike other reviewers and editors found no fault with the book's surviving philosophical passages, describing them as 'lightning sharp but nakedly conceived'. According to Horovitz, half the charm and brilliance of Philip O'Connor lay in the fact that he 'cannot bring himself to theorising without laughing at the idea'. Early the following year, O'Connor would visit Oxford at Horovitz's request, lecture to the Poetry Society and enjoy the 'excellent food and drink' laid on for him.

During the summer of 1958, Philip continued to lead a wild, fluctuating existence. On 10 June, he wrote to Faber and Faber from Reading saying that he was 'on a short tramping holiday' and had run out of money. He asked for £5 to be sent to the nearest poste restante but the following day he returned to London in a panic and collected the money from the Faber office. By 25 June, he seemed to have made another attempt to toe the line and had again found work with a telephone answering service, doing all-night duty, but by 17 July he was off the rails again. That night he got himself onto the platform of the ICA in Mayfair where he was meant to be giving a talk called 'Self Limited' but was too drunk to get any further. According to Peter Vansittart, Philip then attempted to read from the works of Gorky but couldn't manage this either.

Philip's relationship with Anna Wing was now very delicate. He was still living part of the time at Eton Hall but keener than ever to be on his way. According to Maria Steiner, Philip was 'swollen-headed' and 'straining at the bit' and making jokes, using 'a knotted sheet' to let himself out of a window of Anna's ground-floor flat. In *The Lower View*, he tells us he was keen to set off round England interviewing 'cultural workers' and 'fortified mandarins' for *Time and Tide*, whose editor Martin Shuttleworth had shown an interest in his writing. As always, there were several false starts and panic-struck returns to base. In *The Lower View* he tells us he purchased 'a thin scraggy animal' called a Cyclemaster but fell off this machine as he 'puttered' down Charing Cross Road and was sucked into a zombie-like exchange with a stony-faced onlooker. 'The road is slippery,' volunteered the stranger. 'Yes, it is,' O'Connor replied. Such banal exchanges always inspired a great deal of agonized thought and emotion in him.

His first interview in the series was with Stephen Spender in the *Encounter* office in the Haymarket and is more interesting for the atmosphere that surrounds it than for its actual contents. In *The Lower View*, where this dialogue also appeared, Philip complains that Spender always left him feeling 'tongue-tied' and 'ridiculously public' and that the conversation that 'should be, never is'. In spite of these drawbacks or handicaps, Spender boldly describes himself as 'perverted' and moments later declares that he is suffering from 'the Change of Life'. Unfortunately O'Connor does not ask what he meant by these phrases.

At the end of July 1958 Philip O'Connor left London on the repaired Cyclemaster and headed for old and new haunts in Suffolk without telling Anna Wing where he was going. As he pedalled out of London, two packs slung over the back wheels of his motorized machine, he writes, 'the literary vapours rolled off with the alcoholic ones'. He claims that he was tired of being 'an interesting person' and tired of being 'operatic' in his 'vacuum'. In *The Lower View*, he tells us he spent three lovely weeks in Suffolk. His first port of call was the Grenvilles at Denston who had been responsible for his move to Purton Green ten years earlier. He also describes how John Grenville's copper-beating activities aided the calming-down process but he makes no mention of Grenville's teenage stepdaughter, Nicolle Gaillard-d'Andel, who was working in a crafts shop in Clare and with whom he now fell in love. After a few days with the Grenvilles, he moved on to Denis Lowson and Annie Mygind at Clopton Hall, Poslingford, and on 8 August wrote to Faber and Faber asking them to send a copy of *Memoirs of a Public Baby* to Miss Gaillard-d'Andel at her shop. A few days later he wrote again to Rosemary Goad saying that his new address should be given to 'no one (including Mrs O'Connor)'.

Whatever turmoil he was going through at Clopton, he apparently behaved very well as a guest. 'He was very abstemious and disciplined, almost monk-like in his room. He was pretty meticulous. He didn't throw his clothes about,' recalls Denis Lowson. 'We played chess in the evenings. He liked Annie's food. But his going to pubs. That was a bore. He would come back very sloshed.' Drunk or not, Philip used this time in Suffolk to go and interview the composer Alan Raws-thorne, himself a famous drinker, the poet Edwin Muir and Frances Cornford, whose dusty names masked formidable talents.

At the end of August, Philip returned to London where he was received by Anna Wing with immense generosity – 'arms opened, forgiveness eternal, liberty unbounded' is how he puts it. Soon he set off again, this time for good, but in an even more tortured state. On 3 September, he told David Thomson that he was 'emotionally torn' and asked, 'Do you know this condition? Extremely painful and most uninteresting.' He says nothing of his son Jon, now five years old, or his stepson Mark, or of Anna Wing herself, who was devastated by Philip's final departure and later declared that it took her fifteen years to recover from the affair and, more obliquely, that she had learned the dangers of moral rectitude from him. She eventually found consolation in Quakerism, in her two children, and in her own distinguished acting career. With typical cold-bloodedness, Philip would write later that he had stayed with Anna until he could 'afford' to leave, or, in other words, had the confidence to break loose from the 'nurse-mother-wife' combination that he always needed. He made the transition, he says, with a mixture of daring and fear and with some awareness that he was still 'a toddler of forty-two'.

Along with Anna, he also gave up his Cyclemaster. In early September he set off in Denis Lowson's Hillman to see writers further afield. The idea was that Lowson should sketch these people while O'Connor chatted to them. Their first stop was to see Michael Hamburger at Reading University. In *The Lower View*, Philip says little about Hamburger's books and translations but proclaims that his old friend possessed 'a nice cleavage (which could be put to coy uses) between his nature and his culture', that he was 'precociously bent in letters' and had 'a very tender soul sometimes to his considerable embarrassment'. Even more interesting to Philip was 'a delightful little pub' a mile away from Hamburger's house, where there was copious Worthington E.

Lowson and O'Connor drove on to North Wales to see eighty-six-year-old Bertrand Russell. In *The Lower View*, Philip writes that 'inspired intelligent timing' had allowed him to miss Russell's letter to the *Time and Tide* office saying that he couldn't see him. In the event, the aged philosopher could offer only a half-hour interview, which O'Connor approached smelling of beer and with a heightened sense of his own 'disorderly mind', 'deficient education' and 'vulgar respect for worldly attainment'. The brief meeting went well enough, however, and O'Connor was impressed by the 'cool precinct' of Russell's verandah at Plas Penrhyn, which overlooked 'a fine peaceful sweep of mountain landscape', and came away with 'an exhilarating picture of the durability of the mind'.

From here the two men drove on to Herbert Read's house in Yorkshire, which Philip had last visited as a tramp eight years earlier. Once again, the interest is more in the atmosphere around the interview rather than in the stilted words that were exchanged – Philip notes the mint julep they drank on 'a fine clerical lawn' and the presence of some 'remarkably intelligent-looking children' – though Sir Herbert's final observation that the only realizable aim in life was to create what Eric Gill called 'a cell of good living' is worth pondering over.

Before the end of the summer, Philip was back in London and seeing more of John Grenville's nineteen-year-old stepdaughter Nicolle, who was now doing a secretarial course there and whose effect on him he describes as 'a blaze'. The exact circumstances of their elopement are vague but her character and personality seem clear-cut. Nicolle Gaillard-d'Andel was uncomplicated, unliterary and unspoilt. She was practical and well balanced and had beautiful neat, rounded handwriting. She loved animals, plants and children. John Grenville describes her as 'very self-contained, very able to cope with adversity and very independent'. Philip would later write that 'the lines of her character are as simple as a good Matisse drawing and her eyes deep enough to travel the world in' and may have also been attracted by the fact that she was half French. Maria Steiner describes Nicolle as 'lovely' and says, 'I think he genuinely loved her.' According to Philip's letters, their cohabitation began in the middle of September 1958. By the middle of October they were settled in Edith Young's flat at 59 Lamb's Conduit Street and leading a semi-secret life. From here, he wrote to Michael Hamburger, saying, 'Life's remarkably serene – & sober – with my child-wife.' Writing later of this time he expressed his good fortune to become attached at the age of forty-two to a girl of nineteen. He describes the whole development as 'a happy reminder that I was not dead'.

It would be wrong, however, to consider that even during these early days everything ran serenely. According to Maria Steiner, Philip and Nicolle were 'desperately short of money' and whenever he had some, Philip would plunge back into Soho and make a fool of himself. In December 1958, Laurie Lee and the playwright Frank Norman were wandering through Soho when Lee spotted his old friend from Putney whom he hadn't seen for twenty-five years. According to Lee's biographer Valerie Grove, Philip was in bombastic form, and announced that he had just been in 'the madhouse' and ended the encounter by saying, 'Anyway, Laurie, you're better than Louis Mac-Neice. And I couldn't say lower than that, could I? Well, man, God bless you.'

During that winter, Philip's finances remained desperate and were not eased by £25 from Faber and Faber for an option on his new book, or by the work that now started at the BBC on his play *He Who Refrains*, produced by Douglas Cleverdon, with music by Alan Rawsthorne and with Philip himself playing a small part. On 21 January 1959, Philip wrote to Cleverdon from Lamb's Conduit Street, saying, 'I'm in a serious financial crisis. Do you know of any hack work, donkey work I could do?' On 4 March, he wrote even more desperately to Michael Hamburger asking, 'Can you lend me any money?', mentioning that Anna Wing was now putting pressure on him to support their son and signing off, 'Let me know by return please.'

Nicolle was now pregnant and Philip was growing increasingly sick of London which he saw as 'paramountly a centre of buying and selling'. He argued that this was 'a disgusting operation to any normal person . . . a grotesque distortion of one's true feelings'. For a while they considered returning to Suffolk and caretaking Clopton Hall for the Lowsons, but Philip reckoned that 'the old parcel' of himself had lain too long in those parts and he now yearned to be free from past associations. In early April Philip learnt that a cottage in which he and Denis Lowson had stayed in North Wales was available for 7s 6d a week. This property had been rented by a friend of Edith Young called Ruth Elias and had been empty for six months.

Once the arrangements to go there had been made, Philip felt liberated and 'the city bowled along chirruping'. He later described their exuberant departure and journey westwards. 'We packed *pianissimo*, scooping our possessions into winged cases,' he wrote. 'We left Paddington (a destination-sucked tunnel of glamour) *crescendo*: landed *vibrato* on the still platform at Penrhyndeudraeth.' His account of the scenery and atmosphere that surrounded them on arrival is equally vigorous and full of wild comparisons. The scenery is as he imagines northern Persia and the air is Grecian, only colder.

The village of Croesor, to which they were driven by a taxi driver 'with an expression like a winking rose', is a dark and lonely place, some five hundred feet above sea level and some two hundred and fifteen miles from London. Croesor's population was then about fifty, and it consisted of a collection of cottages and farmhouses dominated by an immensely ugly chapel. The house to which they were heading was, and is, a lean-to attached to this building and still goes under the name Ty Capel. According to Denis Lowson, it was 'an awful, neglected holiday home, disturbingly unclean' and 'a place where you feared there would be odd things under the bed'.

In the book that he later wrote about the village, Philip describes the cottage's disadvantages with relish: slate floor, damp walls, dark kitchen and the overall feel of 'an undertaking business at the bottom of the lift shaft', but he also mentions its 'outstanding compensations'. From the kitchen yard you could see the sea, five or six miles away, and just above the house there was a little 'plateau' where they could 'take' tea in good weather. They would stay here at Ty Capel for six months, thriving on their financial crises, enthralled by the music from the adjacent chapel, appalled by the constant rain but going for long walks together in the enfolding mountains, bathing under a waterfall in the river and getting to know and be known by some of the local people, many of whom still live there today. To start with, they were seen as 'intellectual interlopers' and Philip must have struck the villagers as particularly odd. 'He dressed rather funnily when he came here,' said Tudur Owen. 'Long, long coat down to here. Black hat. I didn't converse with him at all. And he was very, very *secretive* when he first came here.' Others remember Philip and Nicolle returning from shopping expeditions, Philip walking alone ahead, his pregnant girlfriend following him carrying the shopping. Philip also found time to cast vicious backward glances at the 'sordidness, the gnashed *brio*, the epileptic and cerebrating hilarity' of his London acquaintances. In letters to Douglas Cleverdon at the BBC, Philip stated that things were 'a little bit difficult . . . though pleasanter in general than London' and there were inevitable requests for money, or more specifically, cash. 'Cheques most difficult to cash here – always a personal favour – and my bank is still unapproachable.'

On 7 May 1959 Philip sent the manuscript of *The Lower View* to

Faber and Faber, where it was greeted as 'a real old hotch-potch'. A few weeks later, Philip explained that he had sent in the manuscript 'prematurely' but by then the familiar editing process had begun. Simon Stuart, now teaching at Stowe and working on a book of his own, turned down this task which was given instead to twenty-five-year-old Julian Mitchell, on the point of coming down from Wadham College, Oxford. On 26 June, Mitchell wrote to Charles Monteith at Fabers describing *The Lower View* as 'a most remarkable book' and adding, 'My admiration for O'Connor's honesty and refusal to deceive himself grows greater every time I pick up the MS.' This was all very well – but did not ease the author's 'painful and delicious' poverty. Philip would later claim that his only source of income during this time came from reviewing for *The Times Literary Supplement*. There were many frantic telephone calls between Croesor and the paper's assistant editor, Arthur Crook, who, in his attempts to be reassuring, joined the long list of people who reminded Philip of his mother.

These financial worries may have been heightened or perhaps temporarily upstaged when on 3 July Nicolle gave birth to a girl in Bangor Hospital. This happy event was preceded by dramas – wrong numbers, the ambulance breaking down on the way to hospital and being repaired by another motorist – but the baby was 'a very well made production' and given the name Allaye and expected to grow up speaking Welsh. To this expanding household were soon added a dog called Monty, aged fourteen, and a cat called Toto. The arrival of the baby also established O'Connor and Nicolle as part of the Croesor community, but the lease of the cottage was running out and though it was likely they could get another one in the village they decided to move the whole ménage to Suffolk for the winter.

At the end of September 1959, Denis Lowson's wife Annie Mygind drove Philip O'Connor and his new family to Clopton Hall, which she and her husband were now in the process of vacating. Here Philip and Nicolle would spend a productive six months. Part of Philip's time was spent working on the script for a short film the Lowsons were making called *Circus at Clopton Hall*. This would feature Annie's children by an earlier marriage and an imaginary circus in a barn. The wry and wistful qualities of this enterprise were reinforced by Philip's words, which were spoken in the film by the young actress Vanessa Redgrave, who had already made her debut at Stratford in *A Midsummer Night's Dream*. Philip remembered working on the film with great affection, describing it as one of the happiest times of his life. He was also preoccupied with the preparation of *The Lower View* for the printers and the sorting-out of its libel potentials. Maria Steiner wrote to Philip on 12 September, saying, 'Write whatever you wish about our being together in Fitzroy Street', but Anna Wing was initially more cautious. She had already been in touch with Fabers about money matters – Philip had still paid nothing towards his son's upkeep and she was considering briefing a lawyer – and she had also been disconcerted by Philip's new radio play *He Who Refrains*, which was about a man so misunderstood by his wife that he leaves her to seek a young girl.

In spite of these hesitations Anna Wing eventually approved everything Philip had written about her and Charles Monteith wrote thanking her for her 'extremely generous attitude'. In November Anna wrote to Philip wishing him 'success and God speed'. Fabers' lawyers had also wondered if Philip might offend Michael Hamburger by doubting the 'spontaneity' of his sorrow but on this point Philip was confident, writing wittily of his old friend, 'I *cannot* believe you would sue poor, tiny, effete, insignificant, ineffectual, subnormal philip for libel, can I?' The lower-case initial letter to his name may have helped to mollify Hamburger, if this were needed, and the book was now formally accepted for publication. In January 1960, Philip would receive a cheque for £75 from Faber and Faber for the full rights to the book.

During that winter, Philip seems to have consolidated his position at the BBC and had further dealings with both Cleverdon and Thomson. Both these men were supportive, tried to get his expenses paid quickly and liked his ideas. Among those he submitted were an enquiry into 'The Quality of Joy', 'The Backgrounds to Creative Personality' and a programme on the thesis that the heart is part of the mind. These had mixed responses. Without disputing O'Connor's ability 'to heap words together' and 'write with alarming speed', some people at the BBC found his proposals 'odd' and 'very incoherent', and there were comments like 'I fear I don't connect with this at all' and 'This is not at all my cup of tea.' Commissioning him was held by many to be 'a pretty dubious gamble' but some programmes were commissioned and broadcast. On 20 October 1959 Philip travelled to London from Suffolk – his first-class rail fare and overnight expenses were covered by the BBC – to have lunch with Douglas Cleverdon and discuss his programme 'The Letter', which was eventually broadcast on 26 November. On another visit to London he stayed with David Thomson at 22 Regent's Park Terrace and wrote later apologizing if he had strummed for too long on their piano. On 1 January 1960, Douglas Cleverdon sent the memo from which I quoted at the beginning of this chapter, in which he begged Peggy Barker, producer of 'The Critics' programme, to use Philip as a regular member of the panel. Miss Barker's response is not available, nor is it easy to visualize Philip's life had he advanced down this path. But even without this boost, Philip O'Connor now believed his future looked more promising than his past.

Meanwhile he pursued other chances. Early in the New Year he heard that the Olympia Press were contracting for his meanderingly surrealist novel *Steiner's Tour* and on 19 January he was in London for a lunchtime meeting at the Mermaid Theatre with Bernard Miles, who had expressed an interest in an O'Connor musical play. 'I'd have to be (and most advisably) very sober,' he told Annie Mygind in advance, but in the event Miles placed a bottle of brandy 'within easy reach' which he claims may have 'over-liberated' his style. Back in Suffolk, O'Connor trudged through the snow to post a further letter to Annie about a magazine he hoped to found on the lines of his wartime production *Seven*, with Herbert Read, Stephen Spender and his new friend John Berger as contributors. Another letter mentioned a possible trip to India by 'mini-bus' or 'micro-bus' but most of his correspondence with Annie simply concerns 'shocking' finances, income tax, debts, powerful creditors and insurance stamps.

In April 1960, Philip, Nicolle and Allaye returned to Croesor, having secured the tenancy of a cottage, in a row of three, a quarter of a mile outside the village. The block was called Bryn Hyfrid and Philip and his family were to occupy the middle part for the next few years. The cottage on one side would soon be acquired by Edith Young, whose interest in Philip was undiminished, and who would use the place during the summer and holiday times, while on the other side lived Nellie Jones and her children whom Philip was to raise to legendary status. He describes his new home as 'a near-slum' – there was no bath, no fridge, no telephone – but praises the environment that his landlord Clough Williams-Ellis, then in the process of building the seaside town of Portmeirion, had created around it. The mountains were closer than men, he tells us, and he had already established a pattern of going for long walks by himself. Just behind the house there was another mountain stream with a pool in which they could bathe. There was also a house up the hill belonging to 'an absent business type' where they could take baths and where Philip would sometimes go to work in peace. One of the only problems about the place was the weather. Even in the summer, everything was 'wet and wilting' as one grey damp day followed another.

A fragmented picture of life in and out of 2 Bryn Hyfrid emerges from Philip's book *Living in Croesor*, from his letters and from the memories of his children who grew up there. Allaye recalls the sound of Philip's typewriter upstairs and the fact that he was 'an early adherent' of the scarf or polo-neck. Philip did a lot of cooking. He mentions hash made of corned beef and boiled bacon served with dandelion leaves. He tried brewing his own beer and when he could afford it, he got wine from a shop in Penrhyndeudraeth. Nicolle was patient and long-suffering but often tired. She was a shrewd reader but, according to Allaye, did not attempt an intellectual relationship with Philip, who went off on remedial walks alone in the mountains, noting, 'The nonsense in oneself walks quietly out of the premises; yet a time comes, sometimes, when one's grinning mask, replete with grinning phrases, stares down at one from an accommodating configuration of rock.' Nicolle gave him his freedom and was often lonely as a result.

Although this would prove the most productive stage of Philip O'Connor's life – he produced children, published several books and made numerous contributions to the Third Programme – it was also a time of almost continuous poverty. For the only time in his life,

Philip was the sole breadwinner and his letters from Croesor are full of references to severe financial conditions, accompanied by requests for help and protests about fees and advances that have not arrived. Debts pile up while the coal runs out. 'I have £1 exactly,' he writes to Annie Mygind. 'Not exactly, a few shillings one way or the other.' From Rosemary Goad at Fabers he requests thirty shillings owed to him. 'I'm living on disaster's doorstep and could use the resulting ten pints of bitter.' Other letters refer to being 'in a very bad financial mess again' and 'in a temporary but very bad financial bog'. Eventually there was a vast grocer's bill and the need to find £150 in rent or face summonses and eviction. Even his benevolent landlord is railed against: 'Clough W-E is as hard as senile nails now and acquiring local fame through more than one triumphant eviction.' At other times, he manages a wry smile. 'Future looks black, but it usually does,' he writes to Michael Hamburger. And informing Annie Mygind of a rare spell of good weather, he says, 'The sun's giving a golden glow to all the bills lying around' and he enjoys this joke enough to repeat it in another letter two days later.

The letters which Philip wrote from Croesor are characteristic of those he wrote all his life. He was a prodigious correspondent, sometimes writing twice in one day to the same person. Most of his letters are crisply, clinically, though not always accurately typed and spotlessly laid out on pristine paper, sharply folded. During the years ahead, he remained loyal to the format he had established many years earlier. The first impression his letters create is attractive and graceful, even when they contain daunting slabs of prose. Typing errors are part of the fun and often an excuse for further wordplay. Only the contents could dismay. Philip's letters from Wales may have contained philosophical ramblings and innumerable bits of 'surrealist whimsy' but they also, almost invariably, asked people to do things for him. Shameless requests for money – often for £5 and sometimes for as little as ten shillings – featured among exhausting enquiries about subsidies, fundings, advances, outlets and fresh backing for his new magazine. The overall impression is of a struggling author and drunkard with his back against the wall. Even in those days, Philip constantly complained that people did not reply, yet on the whole his correspondence *did* bear fruit. Annie Mygind sent him innumerable large and small sums and made further loans against publishers' advances, which may never have been repaid. She also sent him a blanket. Michael Hamburger sent clothes, which Philip would describe chirpily as 'utterly refined and a credit to their wearer (me now); they fit me, I think, now to meet you in London, something I dreaded in my previous shabbiness. The *raincoat* has a sensitive & introvert air, but the *overcoat* is typically the camouflage which the sensitive introvert places over himself.'

The correspondence between O'Connor and Hamburger often drifts away from Philip's worldly needs into pleas for greater tolerance, lengthy attempts to justify his compulsion to do what Hamburger called 'the circus', sometimes shifting the blame for these performances onto Hamburger's own sobriety. Occasionally Philip admits he is a nasty piece of work – 'I fail to doubt that I shall be an unpleasant old man' – and at other times pretends he is a reformed character – 'I'm a delightful person now, smooth in speech, splendidly well-behaved, with a genuine hilarity often quite infectious' – and jokily tells Hamburger to inform his wife of 'my new found sobriety, my grievous sense of responsibility and my admiration for grace and order in a household'. In response to these sallies, Hamburger dashed off quick stylish replies, sometimes throwing in remarks like 'Overwhelmed with work and chores' but winning praise from Philip for his handwriting which apparently showed 'the consolidation of earlier delicacies: fern fronds'. To David Thomson, he offered fewer of these niceties, on one occasion simply writing, 'Just a note to thank you for commendable toleration of routine excesses.'

Throughout his adult life, letter-writing was one of Philip's ways of expressing himself, second only to speaking, and may have appealed to him partly because it did not need a publisher's approval or suffer from the dangers and compromises associated with getting published. Philip was a prolific and continuous writer, who needed more than just books to write and was usually at his desk in the upper front room at Bryn Hyfrid by 5.30 each morning. The actual process of writing was for him 'like self-surgery – getting something out with a sharp instrument'. And, while in Wales, he claims to have begun to love the instrument itself. 'It gets stronger and sharper; if it's very sharp, it penetrates deeper.'

Philip also wrote letters to lure his friends into visiting Croesor and here a refreshingly practical note entered his correspondence. He told Michael Hamburger that the best train was 'the 10.10 am from Paddington known as the Cambrian Express' and urges him to bring 'rubber or waterproof boots' and 'some *good* coffee'. To Annie Mygind, who had now broken up with her husband Denis, he wrote urging that she should come down 'sooner or later' and 'before the summer's ended' and offering her Edith Young's empty cottage next door where she would not have his 'morning frost' to cope with. Such visits would be followed by retrospective comments and enquiries. To Hamburger, he wrote, 'Hope you didn't get depressed here. It's rained ever since', and to Annie Mygind, he wrote almost identically, 'It was fun your being here and I hope you didn't get depressed.' Both would return in due course.

There were various other callers. Nicolle's mother and stepfather came and stayed next door and there were intermittent visits from Edith Young, who had first told Philip about Croesor. When Edith was not preoccupied by a visit from her son Michael, whose book *The Rise of the Meritocracy* had now been published, she and Philip would 'sail down' to the local pub, just as they had in Suffolk ten years earlier.

The pub in question is still standing, a mile or two outside the village, and is officially known as the Brondanw Arms but locally as the Ring. Philip praises it for its lack of the 'neo-bucolic jollity' that he'd found in the Suffolk pubs and its lack of class feeling. In it, he was unable to dance but he did 'represent a jig'. He describes the Brondanw Arms as 'the point where Croesor meets the world'. It was also the place where he met up with various men friends who lived part of the time in the area. The principal and perhaps only members of this group were a surgeon named Kenneth Bloor, the writer Jeremy Brooks and the literary critic and sports writer Christopher Wordsworth. In *Living in Croesor*, Philip describes Wordsworth as 'a connoisseur of life' who knows that 'the tidbit by the wayside'

– Philip had sampled it often enough – 'tastes better than the presented banquet', but the friendship soon perished.

With the other two men he got more closely involved. He went fishing with Bloor in the Penrhyn Estuary – 'Caught nothing, thank goodness' – and told Bloor's wife Giovanna, daughter of a Nobel prize-winner, that she reminded him of his wife Jean and asked her to visit him when he was dying. The Brookses saw a lot of Philip in Croesor, where they had had a home since 1953, and also put him up at their house in Kentish Town, North London. Jeremy Brooks had admired Philip's poetry since he was a schoolboy and described him as 'a dedicated alchemist in pursuit of gold', and Eleanor Brooks loved Philip's 'naughtiness' and 'the sheer brilliance of his chatter', especially in the early morning when his streams of consciousness were at their best. Jeremy Brooks eventually grew impatient of Philip, and Philip took care not to call too often at his house by the river. To the others, he described Brooks as 'a local enemy of mine (I've made him that way)'. Another local character, with whom he did not drink or socialize, was Showell Styles, Arctic explorer and author of more than a hundred books, who still lives at Porthmadog and is now in his nineties. According to local people, Styles disliked O'Connor intensely, and reputedly put him in a detective novel called *The Death of a Weirdy*.

Philip's behaviours and costumes certainly had an impact on the neighbourhood. His arrogant bearing was noted. So was his swinging walk, his slight stoop and his cloak and boots. On meeting new neighbours, Philip tells us, he 'discharged en bloc my creaking London "interestingness" while inwardly wincing at this macabre dervish in garrulity'. Only with a reporter from a local paper was he un-characteristically quiet, coming across as 'slight, mild-mannered and bespectacled' and vehement only in his reported ambition to get out of the British Isles. All this time at Croesor he nursed the desire to go and live in France, though he continued to prefer his new neighbours to the 'miniaturely damned' of his London acquaintance.

Soon after returning to Croesor in April 1960, Philip O'Connor got to know many of the local people a great deal better by making a radio programme about the village. The most significant and closest of these was Nellie Jones, who had lived next door since the late 1940s and now had five children by different fathers. Philip tells us that she looked and lived like a gypsy in 'zestful confusion' and praised her way of standing talking in her doorway and the security that emanated from within. Across the valley lived the Williams brothers, the only drinkers in the village, whose house was 'the most home-like' Philip had ever seen and seemed to have grown round them 'like a suit of clothes', just as the building itself had 'been grown around by the mountain'. Other colourful, magical people lived in the main bit of the village, beside the chapel. One of them was known as Auntie Gwen, who possessed eyes 'of unmatched purity . . . breath-taking in their first impact . . . 'the clearest and deepest of pools'. And then there was Mrs Morgan, the schoolteacher with whom Nicolle had already formed a bond, 'chattering like a small stream accompanying a deep river to the seas of matrimonial *sagesse*'. Between Philip and Mrs Morgan the recorded dialogue was more stilted, her answers more assured than his questions.

P.O'C.: Do you punish them all, Mrs Morgan? How do you punish them, I mean?
Mrs M.: Well, I never get the occasion to punish them.
P.O'C.: You don't really?
Mrs M.: No, not really. They're very, very good children.
P.O'C.: No thrashing?
Mrs M.: No thrashing, no.
P.O'C.: You don't stand them in a corner?
Mrs M.: No, never.
P.O'C.: You don't give them extra lessons – nothing?
Mrs M.: Never.
P.O'C.: They like – they actually like—
Mrs M.: They like school.
P.O'C.: Good heavens!

The programme was broadcast on 29 June 1960 to a mixed reception. According to an audience-research report some listeners found O'Connor 'a delightful interviewer, agreeable, unconventional, intelligent and sympathetic'. Others declared that he was 'silly and embarrassing', 'inclined to condescend and patronise' and had 'tire-some, nervous mannerisms'.

None of these comments surprises me, nor does the chaos sur-rounding Philip's visit to London the following month to interview his old friend Paul Potts. Potts's book *Dante Called You Beatrice*, from which I have already quoted and whose libellous passages Philip claimed to have 'nobly' passed, had now been published. For a ten-guinea fee, it was arranged that O'Connor should conduct a seven-minute interview with Potts on a BBC programme called 'World of Books'. This encounter was much looked forward to – even Charles Monteith at Fabers had expressed excitement about the men 'having a go at each other' – but it is clear that Philip was hopelessly drunk at the recording on 15 July. In a letter to David Thomson, he explains that Potts was 'on his best (paralysed) behaviour, shusshing everything I said to him'. To the 'World of Books' producer, Philip wrote apologi-zing for his 'rather jolly condition at the recording' and offers as an excuse the fact that he had met 'some happy people that lunchtime'. A man named Owen Leeming writes back that he is 'endeavouring' to edit the interview – what a pity there is no transcript of the original recording – followed a few days later by a letter from R. E. 'Dick' Keen explaining that the interview was 'not suitable for broadcasting'. Philip then wrote defiantly and not altogether truthfully, 'I haven't conversed with Mr Potts for many years and did dread one of those stilted exchanges that sometimes occur in such broadcasts.' He had clearly chosen to forget his meeting with Potts outside the bank two years earlier. Brooding over the affair later, Philip wrote dismissively of Potts's 'schoolgirlish poems and watery prose' – he had originally stated that parts of the book were 'very good' – and Potts himself went as far as to accuse Philip of climbing on his bandwagon.

All this time, Philip's mentors at the BBC strove away on his behalf. In September 1960 David Thomson was moved to send a memo to P. H. Newby, head of the department, criticizing the average interviewer for adopting 'conventional attitudes and styles' and arguing that 'readers of *Memoirs of a Public Baby* would like to hear Philip O'Connor on any subject that concerns him'. Douglas Cleverdon praised the 'rat-like, scurrying voice of the inner monologue' that was evident in Philip's work and others like Neil Crichton-Miller spotted a 'certain primitive originality' in O'Connor's approach, 'that is at once rich and rare'. On his part, Philip would claim that making documentaries for the Third Programme had 'great therapeutic value' for him, robbing him of some of his Anglophobia and forcing him into an engagement with the world that he had never hitherto experienced.

With David Thomson, he became particularly engaged. According to Philip, Thomson was 'absent-minded, gentle, naïve and charmingly eccentric in manner', perhaps even more so than O'Connor himself. But he remained highly professional and would prove later with his autobiographical books like *Woodbrook* and *Nairn*, published after he left the BBC, that he was also a genius. Without Thomson's patience, loyalty, skills, experience and taste for Philip's offerings and affection for his working methods, O'Connor would have quickly lost his foothold in Broadcasting House. As a rule, Philip got bored with his projects and it was only Thomson's perseverance that saw them through. A great friendship – and drinking companionship – had also grown up between the two men and when he was in London Philip would call often at 22 Regent's Park Terrace. Martina Thomson remembers the exhilaration with which he would arrive, announcing, 'I've got a taxi waiting. Can you pay that off?' then sleep on the red downstairs sofa. In due course, Philip would pronounce this household 'the nicest settlement I've ever come across'.

During this period, Philip's career as an author also hung by a thread. In the autumn of 1960, *Steiner's Tour* was published in Paris without much impact on the British market in spite of a specially commissioned cover by Ronald Searle. In November it was followed in and out of the bookshops by *The Lower View* which described his life with Maria and Anna and included his interviews with the bigwigs already mentioned. Judging by his letters to Annie Mygind and David Thomson, Philip had now decided that this was an 'odd book', 'a bit scrappy' and that the interviews in it were 'not too jolly', if not in fact 'bloody awful'. He was, nevertheless, predictably upset by the 'stinking' reviews that poured in from many directions and marvelled, 'Wonderful how quickly one can fall from grace.' In *Punch*, R. G. G. Price perceived a 'vaguely menacing tone' to the book which 'gives way to gusts of clarity and humour'. In the *New Statesman* Simon Gray may not have annoyed Philip unduly by describing the book as 'a curiosity, an eccentric mixture of social, literary and philosophical analysis, intensely personal statement and a tantalising minimum of autobiographical information', but he was 'astonished and downcast' by Rayner Heppenstall's attack in the *Observer* on his 'slovenly prose' and was moved to write a letter to the paper in protest. He also objected to being described elsewhere as a 'character' and argued, 'I'm not lovable enough for drowning in the soft bosom of the public.'

The worst review of *The Lower View* was in the *Sunday Times*, written by John Coleman under the heading 'Portrait of a Failure', and would inspire a supportive but truthful letter to O'Connor from his mentor Herbert Read. 'Your whole attitude to life is marginal,' wrote Sir Herbert. 'You are a "beat" in the sense that you don't belong anywhere, least of all to Mr Coleman's world of values. You don't belong to any kind of establishment in this country, you're not even an outsider because there seems to be no inside to be outside – you are like Genet in that respect, but you must therefore not expect praise or respect or any kind of success. Coleman's mustard goes with roast beef and not with your game.' O'Connor described this letter as 'not warm, but explanatory', but accepted Sir Herbert's verdict and would often boast in later life that Herbert Read had pronounced him 'outside outsiders'. The idea of Philip O'Connor becoming a member of any form of establishment is unthinkable – especially a broadcasting one. At the end of *The Lower View* he takes a convincingly contemporary swipe at 'the buffoon personality of TV . . . the hippopotamus with a pea-sized brain and the soul of a cash register', whom he had no desire or ability to emulate.

From his workroom at Bryn Hyfrid he did however pour out ideas for books and radio and television programmes, many of which overlapped. To David Thomson in particular he submitted proposals for programmes on 'Laughter', 'Laziness', 'Drink', 'Patriotism', 'Mental Illness', 'Outsiderism', 'Vagrancy' and other ideas closer to home. One suggestion was entitled 'The Fear of Behaving Oddly' and proposed focusing on those who have 'felt mad' and tried to behave 'normally', drawing parallels between 'creative' and 'mad' behaviour. Another offering was 'Writing and Smoking', which promised to explore the effects of smoking on 'mentational manners' and even 'style, breathing changes, accelerated heart beats'. It says much for the Third Programme that many of his ideas were seriously considered and several of them made it onto the air. The 'Drink' idea quickly fizzled out but 'Vagrancy' would develop into both an impressive radio programme and a paperback book.

In April 1961 Philip O'Connor began a month-long tramp, staying in Salvation Army hostels and other doss-houses and interviewing their incumbents. He was accompanied part of the time by the photographer Roger Mayne – 'a very fine fellow' – and by a BBC recording van. He warned Michael Hamburger that if he reached his home in Reading 'only the better crusts will be accepted'. Looking back, he admits that he did the tour in 'as much comfort as I could' – the BBC were later faced with a 'terrible' £32 bill for a hired car – but compromised to the extent of wearing carefully torn trousers which caused consternation to the staff at Manchester's Midland Hotel. In the same city, he enjoyed enormous sandwiches in the Mechanics Arms outside the gates of Strangeways Gaol and annoyed his Croesor acquaintance Mrs Bloor, whose husband worked in the city, by grabbing her cooking sherry and downing the lot. He later reported to Hamburger that the trip had been successful – 'despite intoxicants' – and that he had really smelt 'the underworld, which is still going strong, as I suspected'.

Back in Croesor, Philip faced the imminent expansion of his family. That spring he wrote buoyantly to Hamburger, 'O'Connor the Sixth is being lobbied in Infinity. She launches in July.' In June he wrote again, 'Pre-natal tensions are awful. I confuse myself with the foetus', but on 30 June 1961 he became a father for the sixth time when his son Patric Bryn O'Connor was born in Pwllheli General. A devil for making his life more complicated, Philip also acquired a new dog, when a nurse at the hospital gave him a black Labrador to replace the elderly Monty. He called it Clough, after his landlord. Within a few weeks he was complaining to Annie Mygind, 'I was mad yesterday, with both children screaming and Nellie's chorus outside' and begging her to send earplugs.

He also made a number of trips to London. In March that year, he had been present at the National Film Theatre when *Circus at Clopton Hall* was shown to the press and public. In the early autumn he was there again, lunching with the publisher Anthony Blond on 5 October to discuss a book on dirt and indecency, and meeting the satirist Peter Cook who had just opened his Soho club, the Establishment, with much publicity. In mid-October O'Connor reports that Cook was rehearsing a five-minute sketch of his. One of the actors involved was John Fortune, who recalls that no one on stage had any idea what they were doing, but O'Connor himself sat shrieking with delight in the audience.

Meanwhile Philip had successfully persuaded the documentary film-maker Denis Mitchell to make a programme about Croesor. In the spring of 1962, Mitchell came down with a film crew and made a television film called *The Changing Village*, using Philip as front man. Mitchell was by then one of the most celebrated men in his field but this particular production wasn't very good, according to his wife Linda, who remembers watching the filming with little Patric O'Connor on her lap. Philip wrote later that he had consumed 'much liquor' during the visit and had insulted Mitchell, who had become cool towards him. Other brief television appearances followed when Philip's book *Living in Croesor* was published that autumn. This received mixed reviews. In *Punch*, R. C. Scriven described it as a book the intellectuals will quarrel about and the intelligent will consider. In *The Times Literary Supplement*, the reviewer stated that Croesor had obviously been good for O'Connor but whether he was good for Croesor was up to the locals to say. In his acknowledgements, Philip mysteriously adds 'Esq.' to the names of all the local men who had helped him.

And so this rollercoaster existence continued. Philip battled on with his book on *Vagrancy*, which would eventually become a Penguin Special, and was no doubt excited by the success of his radio programme on the same subject which was broadcast on 20 May, receiving the best audience response figures he had known. Among those who heard the broadcast was a certain Mr Francis Kendall-Husband who was very keen to get in touch with O'Connor, claiming that he had had a very wide experience of the subject of vagrancy. A few weeks later, at the end of June, Philip boasted that he had made a disgrace of himself at the Portmeirion Festival, dancing and singing on the stage and putting his head inside someone's trombone – or does he mean tuba? In September 1962 he told Martina Thomson that the situation was, once again, black. Four months later, Philip was again facing 'momentously awful' financial problems and mentions a debt of £159 to a grocer, who would allow this to go still higher and even permit Philip to interview him for a radio programme while the debt was outstanding. By 12 March 1963, Philip and Nicolle were 'in mild financial euphoria' having paid off all their debts – the grocer looked astonished when his bill was paid and David Thomson may have been a bit astounded to get back his £36. How they were able to do this is a mystery – had Annie Mygind or some other benefactor suddenly intervened? – but the following day, 13 March, they were even able to take delivery of a 'serviceable unbeautiful' car. Was this the vehicle in which Philip and Michael Hamburger would give a lift to two Jehovah's Witnesses, at whom Philip shouted, 'I am Jehovah and I don't want any witnesses!', leaving the two ladies to trudge off in the rain?

During the spring and summer of 1963 there were several significant family events, some of them sad. In April, Philip received a visit from his twelve-year-old son Peter, of whom he had seen very little. Peter would later describe it as 'a nightmare' and remembers how his father shut himself in his workroom at Bryn Hyfrid, shouting that he was a genius. After this visit, Philip wrote guiltily or guiltlessly to Peter's mother Maria Scott, as she had now become. 'I'm afraid we're not very alike you know – I don't find communication at all easy.' During this time Philip was also finally going through a divorce from his wife, Jean, now in the Bangour Village Hospital in West Lothian and said to be of 'incurably unsound mind'. The divorce became absolute on 2 July and one of the conditions was that Philip should pay £25 15s a year to the medical superintendent at the hospital. Three weeks later, another chapter ended. On 22 July, his old guardian, Albert Joseph Camden Field, died in Redhill Hospital aged sixty-eight, though this event did not come to Philip's attention and he was unaware of it even ten years later – and equally unaware that his guardian had continued to occupy the hut on Box Hill till his death. The final happier event of that summer was that at St Pancras Registry Office on 7 August, Philip O'Connor and Nicolle Gaillard-d'Andel got married. Again, he does not make a fuss about this event in his letters, or explain why they chose to get married at this moment, though the divorce from Jean must have had something to do with it.

Philip's presence in London was not surprising. His star was now slightly in the ascendant at the BBC and in June that year he had been commissioned to make a series called 'London Characters'. He would be paid twenty-five guineas per interview and his voice would be edited out of each fifteen-minute monologue. It was up to him whom he chose to record. On Monday 12 August 1963, he decided to pay a visit, out of the blue and without any appointment or preliminary telephone call, on Quentin Crisp at 129 Beaufort Street.

The Surprise of the Week

I have a hunch about this. I daren't send you the
photograph of the author as a young man, but take
my word for it, it is quite stunning, alluring and
beautiful in an only mildly sickening way. It inevitably
prejudices one slightly in favour of the manuscript.

TOM MASCHLER TO MICHAEL HOWARD,
3 December 1965

Quentin Crisp has described Philip O'Connor's visit to his room three
times in print and at least once in a tape-recorded conversation. In all
these accounts he stresses the unpredictability of the visit. According
to Quentin, Philip O'Connor called on him 'quite by chance', after an
absence of fifteen years. Quentin tells us that he was 'sitting innocently'
beside his 'asthmatic' gas-fire – even in August? – and 'staring aimlessly' at his feet when the doorbell began ringing. He had then hurried
downstairs and found Philip standing 'rather sheepishly' on his doorstep. 'He found me *in*,' he said later. 'If he had found me *out*, I don't
know whether he would have bothered to come back.'

In one account, Quentin tells us that Philip looked 'somewhat
redeemed; that is to say he was a little thicker and mentally he was a
lot clearer'. In another account, he says that Philip looked the same
as before: 'Disraeli ringlets still hung over a brow not merely pallid,
but incandescent with moral decay. His eyes were still as bright as
those of a sex maniac and his smile was as mirthless as the hilarity of
a skull.' Anyway, it was Philip's character rather than looks that
seemed to have changed: 'He now wanted to get things done – an

ambition absolutely forbidden in the southern confines of bohemia which he used to frequent.'

Quentin Crisp found Philip O'Connor's presence on his doorstep 'mildly surprising' but invited him in. After a few 'pleasantries' – an odd word to use in the circumstances – he learnt that his old acquaintance now worked for the BBC's Third Programme, which, according to Quentin, was then thought to be 'highbrow to the point of being a joke'. In *The Naked Civil Servant*, Quentin reports that Philip told him he was making a programme about eccentrics and Quentin claims to have responded, 'What's in it for me?', again an unlikely turn of phrase. After feverishly walking up and down for a while, Philip asked if he might go and get a tape-recorder from his car, or taxi, outside. He returned with a machine 'as big as a gas meter', squatted on the filthy carpet at Quentin's feet and pointed the microphone at him, urging him to say 'something about life and death'.

Eventually the tape ran out and O'Connor seemed satisfied by what he had got and left almost immediately. He returned four days later, accompanied by David Thomson, to record a few more 'peroratory phrases' and that was the end of the matter. In the BBC archives there is a note of Philip's expenses over those two days. On 12 August, he claimed £3 for luncheon, drinks and taxi fares. On the 16th, he claimed £1 5s for unspecified sundries and £1 for a taxi fare. Philip later described the interview as 'the best impromptu or prepared recording I have made', but during the long delay between the recording and the actual transmission Quentin wrote a letter to his friend Joan Rhodes describing it all as 'a wild idea in the head of Mr O'Connor'.

The programme was eventually broadcast on 28 February 1964, when it became the first in O'Connor's series of 'London Characters'. Entitled 'A Male Artist's Model', it began with a few words from Philip emphasizing the difference between Quentin Crisp's public life as 'a work of art' and his private life in an undusted Chelsea room. 'His message to the housewives of England,' said Philip, 'is that after four years the dirt never gets worse.' In the monologue that followed, Quentin repeated many of the jokes and phrases that he had invented long ago and which were later to work their way into his autobiography and even his stage show. The fact that many of these appear almost verbatim shows what a polished set-piece he had already created and perfected. In the broadcast he talked about 'the ungovernable rage' he flew into when he realized his mother's love had to be divided between her four children and about the 'overdose of exhibitionism' he had been able to take. He said that being an art school model combined being 'a martyr and an actor' and was 'the only job where I understood what I was doing'. He stated that he came from a time when 'men who wore suede shoes were under suspicion' and that the only purpose of life was 'to make a mad dash between the cradle and the grave'. To the latter aphorism he would later add, 'without getting into debt'. Less familiar and more revealing was the part of the monologue where he spoke of the danger all eccentrics run of becoming completely disconnected from the outside world and the difficulty of 'protesting your sincerity to people who believe you to be totally flippant and affected'. As far as I know, he did not address this problem area again, certainly not in his books or stage show.

The broadcast went down very well and did credit to both O'Connor and Crisp. In *The Listener*, Arthur Calder-Marshall described the programme as 'the surprise of the week' and summarized Quentin Crisp's plight with the sentence, 'In order to save his self-made beautiful self he has had to lose other people.' Characteristically, Quentin did not listen to the programme, but among those who did was the publisher William Kimber, whose instant reaction was that Quentin Crisp should write a book. When weeks or months later this off-the-cuff remark reached Quentin he showed uncharacteristic assertiveness by telephoning his admirer, whom he had never met, and asking if the rumoured remark was true. Mr Kimber, best known for publishing military histories and the like, replied that it was and told Crisp to write a two-thousand-word synopsis of his possible autobiography. This Quentin quickly did but it proved to be a false trail. In *How to Become a Virgin*, he tells us that Kimber was 'frightened' by the synopsis and wrote back a courteous letter masking his fears with the rather far-fetched claim that if his firm published the book it would be 'bombarded from all directions with libel suits'.

The door that Philip O'Connor had unwittingly opened mercifully remained ajar. In the spring of 1965, Quentin Crisp told his Kimber 'tale of woe' to a trainload of art teachers bound for Maidstone College of Art. Among these was Maidstone's vice-principal Bob Caine, who immediately declared that Quentin could do better than Kimber and promised to introduce him to a literary agent he knew. This was Donald Carroll, a Catholic Texan, who had recently set up as an author's representative. Within a few days, Carroll had telephoned Quentin, summoned him to his flat in Putney – Quentin made the journey on the 14 bus – and persuaded him to write a few chapters that could be added to the synopsis.

Quentin appears to have spent part of that summer working on the book, oblivious to other events and distractions. On 12 June 1965 he was not present at the party – in a marquee on the lawn at Calverton Rectory – following the marriage of his niece Frances Payne to Peter Ramsay, who worked for Walls Ice Cream. 'I've been to several family funerals,' he explained. 'I draw the line at weddings.' He was less indifferent to or more intruded upon by the fact that 129 Beaufort Street was now undergoing external redecoration, inspiring him to write skittishly to Joan Rhodes that 'wicked men with steel erections' were now scaffolding the house.

By the autumn of 1965 the sample chapters were finished and Donald Carroll decided to submit the whole package to the publishers Jonathan Cape, along with some of the photographs taken of Quentin by Angus McBean twenty-five years earlier. In a covering letter to the firm's managing director, Carroll promised that Quentin Crisp would 'provide the story that surrounds the image'.

At this time Jonathan Cape was still an independent firm with semi-stately offices in Bedford Square, across the road from Fitzrovia, and its managing director Tom Maschler was a thirty-two-year-old 'whizzkid' or 'young meteor' of the emerging Swinging London, who hadn't been to university and rode around the city on a Lambretta. On 3 December 1965, Maschler wrote to his fellow director Michael Howard expressing his interest in the submitted written material – 'There is something about the style, slight as it is, that intrigues me' – and adding, 'I daren't send you the photograph of the author as a young man, but take my word for it, it is quite stunning, alluring and beautiful in an only mildly sickening way. It inevitably prejudices one slightly in favour of the manuscript.' He was also aware that Carroll had submitted the same material to Secker and Warburg and was quite sure they would take it if Cape didn't. The outcome of these deliberations was that on 15 December Jonathan Cape signed a contract with Quentin Crisp paying him £100 to finish writing the book. Quentin reputedly used part of his advance to have his tweed overcoat relined by his friend Mrs Markham in a beautiful shade of lilac.

During the next six months Quentin wrote the rest of the book in chunks, delivering them to Donald Carroll who eventually carried the completed manuscript to Bedford Square. Writing later about this historic moment for the *Los Angeles Times*, Carroll recalled a disconcerting encounter with the author Desmond Morris, who was emerging from Maschler's office after delivering the manuscript of *The Naked Ape*, leaving Carroll wondering how Quentin's book could possibly hold its own with this obvious bestseller. A few weeks later, in late October 1966, Quentin himself was ushered into Tom Maschler's stately first-floor office, noted for its supposed Adam ceiling, and came away declaring that Mr Maschler was a fabulously glamorous figure 'who showers you with hot sequins as he talks'. This preposterous description is another example of the way that Quentin Crisp inverted the truth and, as Peter York would point out in *Harpers & Queen*, was far more true of Crisp himself than of Maschler.

In due course, the unnamed typescript was handed over to a part-time editorial assistant, Jane Miller, who had joined the firm in 1963 at a salary of £7 a week. Mrs Miller was already well aware of Quentin Crisp's existence, having seen him often in Chelsea and Fulham. Since 1960 she and her husband Karl Miller, soon to be editor of *The Listener*, had lived in Limerston Street, a few minutes' walk from Beaufort Street, and a few years earlier Jane's mother Ruth Salaman had painted Quentin when he modelled for a private painting class. When she met Quentin face to face for the first time in December 1966, Jane Miller felt faintly intimidated. 'I was very shy. We were both very shy. I pretended I didn't know anything about him,' she says, explaining she was thirty-six at the time and 'a stuffy little blue stocking'. She had known plenty of homosexuals at Cambridge and was 'quite easy' about it, but Quentin Crisp was 'another kettle of fish'. She saw that he was 'very beautiful' but there was also something 'fastidious' and 'squeamish' about his persona. He had 'a physical and psychological timidity' and occupied 'a sort of cocoon' around him. In spite of these reservations, she says she became very fond of him and would like to have known him better. For his part, Quentin Crisp describes Mrs Miller as 'a beautiful woman whose eyes forever held an expression of dismayed surprise'.

For convenience, Jane Miller would work on the book with Quentin at 26 Limerston Street rather than her basement office in Bedford Square. Mrs Miller recalls that the house was overrun with children and that her husband, between jobs on the *New Statesman* and *The Listener*, was often there too. Talking to me later about Mrs Miller's domestic responsibilities, Quentin advanced the comical and distorted opinion, 'She's got a husband to feed and three children to hit.'

As far as the book was concerned, Jane Miller knew at once she was on to 'a very good thing' though she saw it as 'in many ways very decorous and not a tremendously shocking book' and even recognized in it 'a *Cranford* quality', and perhaps it was for these reasons that it was turned down by two American publishers to whom Maschler sent it. Harper and Row rejected the book on the grounds that 'the writing seems less than sparkling' and Fred Jordan at Grove Press declared, 'None of us are terribly excited . . . It's much too English and repressed for what it purports to be.' Mrs Miller also reports that there was a lot of editing to do. 'I worried about his mannerisms and tried to wean him away from some of them. Occasionally he resisted me. He was not at all grand about his talent but was adamant about his *Mr* and *Mrs*.' Quentin was not prepared to break his lifelong habit of never using anyone's given name – a few seem to have fallen through the net – but described Mrs Miller as 'infinitely patient, never making the slightest emendation to my typescript without consulting me'. In conversation with Philip Mackie, he later expressed surprise that Mrs Miller had never heard of the playwright Rodney Ackland whose name he had mentioned in connection with the Oakley Street lodging house. In Jane Miller's view, the book remained far from perfect. 'He doesn't have a perfect ear, does he? There *are* hiccups. The wit doesn't always come off. But who am I to quibble?' Another publisher's reader declared that the punctuation in Quentin's original typescript was 'often slapdash and sometimes definitely wrong'.

On the matter of the book's title there was fierce disagreement. Quentin Crisp wanted to call the book 'My Reign in Hell', though he admitted that these were 'paperback words', and always seems to have regarded *The Naked Civil Servant* as a mistake, creating 'bewilderment if not fatal misunderstanding' in the minds of book-buyers. Other titles considered were 'A Senile Delinquent', 'The Monasteries of Bohemia' and 'A Room Without a Door'. Quentin was attracted to the last one on the grounds that it gave some idea of the 'narrowness and squalor' of his life – but eventually *The Naked Civil Servant* won through and, on the G. K. Chesterton principle that a good title is a successful title, seems to have been the right long-term choice. After several years and a great deal of work by Quentin himself, this chosen title became hugely successful or at least well known across the world.

As the book edged its way towards publication, Quentin's public and private life went on very much as before, though the world itself was changing. He continued to model in art schools 'from dawn to dusk'. He continued to see his surviving relations or at least write letters to them. At Beaufort Street, lodgers came and went. In April 1964 John Ransley had departed for America. Other sympathetic figures arrived in the shape of Jean Cooper, Peter Hirst-Smith and, at a later date, Ralph Noyes, great-nephew of the poet Alfred Noyes. Out on the street at this time he saw Maeve Peake supporting an unrecognizable old man, who said, 'Oh, look, there's Quentin!' Soon after this Mervyn Peake went into hospital for the last time. Meanwhile, in King's Road, Chelsea, a permanent party had begun which Quentin felt he looked as if he was trying to gatecrash. He was even stopped by the police to see if he had any drugs on him – and then simply dismissed as mad. 'By an unlucky chance,' he writes in *The Naked Civil Servant*, 'the symbols I had adopted forty years earlier to express my sexual type had become the uniform of all young people.'

The more the pop music world and fashion trade adopted effeminacy, the more Quentin Crisp quite literally lost face. He describes himself during this period as 'a stopped grandfather clock' and 'the oldest teenager in the business' whose eyes now hung 'like an impending avalanche over the cheek-bones'. An art student, Victoria Gillick, later a family rights campaigner, remembers drawing him at Maidstone at this time and confirms, 'He was frankly disgusting and his body was quite literally going to pot.'

During this transitional waiting period he saw old friends and made new ones, though some of them may have cast a more critical eye over him than in the past. The writer Jeremy Trafford, who met him for the first time in 1966, remembers how his initial fascination with Quentin as 'the epitome of the *vie de bohème*' faded a little when he became aware of his 'coldness' and the fact that he was so 'hooked on the plaudits of others'.

Was Quentin's attitude to people also changing? When questioned by Jonathan Cape's libel lawyers about the character he had called Thumbnails, who was 'presumably still living', he responded savagely that his old flatmate had been 'a common informant and made thousands of pounds out of it' and 'must know the law well and would do anything to make money'. But his attitude towards Philip O'Connor had certainly mellowed. He now spoke of him with respect and awe, expressed admiration for *Memoirs of a Public Baby* and often acknowledged the way that Philip had opened the door for him onto a new profession. At the beginning of 1967, he agreed to appear in a film based on Philip O'Connor's poem 'Captain Busby'. Before the work began, the director Ann Wolff invited Quentin, whom she had never met or heard of, round to her house in Reddington Road, Hampstead. Mrs Wolff remembers opening the door to a beautifully coiffured figure and recalls how, instead of giving him tea from one of her usual kitchen mugs, she stretched out instinctively for her mother's best porcelain tea service.

The filming of *Captain Busby*, in which Philip O'Connor played the principal role and Quentin was dressed as an admiral, took place on a provincial railway station in May 1967. One evening after filming, Quentin made his way to Seven Dials in Covent Garden where there was a café with the skittish and insinuating name As You Like It. Here over a pale grey coffee or lukewarm orange squash, he spoke about Mr O'Connor and the movie to a pale young man with heavy rimmed spectacles.

-14-

A Crazy Flying-Machine

Although the man has got a lot of talent, he is personally so impossible to work with, verging as he does
on the borders of shrieking insanity, that in the end I
dropped the whole thing as it was too hot to handle.

JONATHAN MILLER ON PHILIP O'CONNOR,
11 February 1965

After recording Quentin Crisp in his room at Beaufort Street, Philip
O'Connor's life had continued on its erratic, controversial and quirky
path. He remained productive and provocative, acquired some fine
new feathers in his cap but often felt desperate, and praise for even
his finest achievements was always accompanied by admonishments.

In September 1963 his Penguin Special entitled *Vagrancy* was published to a typically mixed reception. The book carried a dedication
to Annie Mygind 'who distinguishes between man and property', and
a foreword by the writer Jeremy Sandford, who declared that what
followed could be read 'as the strange but revealing outpourings of
one who has been through that world and escaped'. In it, Philip
O'Connor remains on the side of the tramp especially in his incapacity
to handle 'the perversities of social life as we know it', and expresses
the belief that in at least some cases the tramp may be able to use the
typewriter, as he had, to escape his predicament. Reviewing the book
in the *New Statesman*, the future Poet Laureate Ted Hughes accused
the author of 'rancour and overstatement' and described O'Connor's
prose as 'a crazy flying-machine pieced together out of psychologist's
and sociologist's and phrenologist's jargon and driven by an irate blast

of rhetorical poetry'. The best part of the book, said Hughes, was O'Connor's account of his own tramping: 'He can write well about himself, his words run smoothly and his remarks have weight. His description of the mental changes that followed him on his quitting society is a piece of truly awful knowledge.'

Whatever its strengths and weaknesses, *Vagrancy* certainly reinforced O'Connor's reputation as a man of the gutter. At the end of September 1963 he had a timely meeting with the young writer Heathcote Williams, then working on the *Transatlantic Review* and soon to publish his own book on the vagrant speakers in Hyde Park, who would become one of his champions in later life. *Vagrancy* also did him no harm at the BBC, for whom he would record further 'London Characters' and a new series called 'I Remember'. By 20 May 1964, David Thomson felt sufficiently enthusiastic to write a long, passionate memo to his superiors at the Third Programme begging that O'Connor should have a regular contract. 'He is one of the quickest workers and most prolific in ideas,' he began and went on to praise Philip's 'unusual knack of getting people to say what they deeply mean – to bare their hearts so to speak' and to describe Philip's technique as 'a welcome relief from the John Freeman type of approach' – a reference to the aggressive television interviewer who had reduced several of his subjects to tears. The memo concluded in the manner of a school report, by stating, 'Technically, he is now skilled in the use of midget and ficord recording machines and in rough pre-editing', and 'He always sends in his work in good time and is meticulous about schedules.'

This pleading came to nothing but Philip continued to make programmes and submit more ideas for programmes from his workroom at Bryn Hyfrid and often travelled long distances on assignments closely linked with his own character or experiences. His most significant trip during this period was to Wimereux, the French seaside resort where he had spent part of his childhood and which had haunted him ever since. In November 1964 he went there to research an autobiographical one-hour radio play, *Return to Wimereux*. It was his first visit to France for twenty-five years and according to the BBC archives he ran up expenses of 1,222 francs, partly on entertaining 'aged friends' from his childhood, who included some of Madame

Tillieux's children. Madame Tillieux had died but Philip's visit to her grave would be incorporated into the play, which also featured his mother, his sister Desirée, Uncle Haslam and one of Madame Tillieux's hens, whose part was played by Philip's oldest daughter Sarah, now a budding actress aged eighteen. Anna Wing and Martina Thomson were also involved. In the play Philip describes this return visit, which lasted six days, as 'the most exciting brief period I can remember'. He found the *pâtisserie* unchanged, jars of sweets in the right-hand window, the same kind of cakes on the left. Across the street the toyshop Paradis des Enfants was still in business. Only Madame Tillieux was missing. Philip learnt that she died in 1945 at the age of seventy-five, her mind unbalanced by the suffering under the Occupation. In the play, which was broadcast on 5 May 1965, Philip made a further link between his past lives by burying in the sand an apple that had come from Purton Green, which indicates that he sometimes returned to those old haunts. In a hopeful gesture towards a more sober future he also threw a bottle of cognac into the river, aware that for him alcohol 'subdues the intelligence that deals with contemporary actuality'.

During the spring of 1965 Philip was also involved in another subject close to his heart, a study of 'Laughter', on which he worked for a while with the new television 'talent' Jonathan Miller. The two men did not get on well together. On 8 February, O'Connor wrote to Miller, 'I gather from David that our last encounter impressed you unfavourably. Apologies: I'm variable.' On 11 February, Miller wrote about O'Connor and the laughter project in an internal memo, noted at the start of this chapter. No doubt, it hadn't helped that a recording of the eminent Sinologist Arthur Waley talking about laughter had come out completely blank.

Meanwhile Philip's life in Wales had become increasingly difficult. In letters from Bryn Hyfrid to Hamburger and Thomson, he writes of his desolation and says he is waiting 'for the end' and an 'exit order' from his landlord. His BBC earnings did not begin to cover his outgoings and he says he is even seeking other employment – 'what, I don't know, being so undesirable'. He describes the atmosphere at Bryn Hyfrid as 'pretty hell', and following the birth of his daughter Rachel in March 1964, complains that there is 'no room' in the house, adding, 'I fall asleep as soon as I arrive and rage to keep awake.' Other problems are 'too dark to write about – *terrible*'. By January 1965 these had driven him to leave Bryn Hyfrid and take a room in a farmhouse called Brondanw Bach, near the pub. On 22 April, he reports to Michael Hamburger that domestic matters are more stable and adds, 'I think if the "troubles" hadn't arisen we might well have wandered away from each other.' In the same letter he states: '£2.18.0 stares me in the face' and asks Hamburger to send him some money by return post. Hamburger obliges, but adds strictly, 'I shall need to have the money as soon as you can repay it.'

A few days later Philip, Nicolle and their three children left Croesor and moved to the Moat Farmhouse, Broxford, Suffolk, where Nicolle's mother and stepfather John Grenville were now living. In one letter to Hamburger, he describes this as 'dreadfully near to Nic's parents'. In another he states that they are actually 'camping with Nic's parents' and adds, 'I am not happy.' On 3 June, he tells David Thomson that the palmist Mir Bashir has predicted another year of difficulties and then 'fame and success' at the age of fifty. On 25 July, he is in low spirits again, declaring, 'Circumstances aren't too good at the moment.' One day his son Patric fell out of a window, annoying him when he was working. Another day he went off to see his old friend Oliver Bernard in Norfolk and was asked by Oliver's son, 'Why are your teeth so green?'

One of the results of these ups and downs is that on 7 September 1965 Philip O'Connor went on the wagon. At his forty-ninth birthday celebrations the next day he drank only lemonade and on 1 October he reported to David Thomson, 'I am a complete abstainer from alcohol', explaining that he was now 'absolutely bored with drink' which he claims had left him 'sensorily under-nourished' and repetitive in his work. On 4 November he was able to lecture about vagrancy to the Cambridge Sociology Society without the usual dramas, but at the end of that month he again tells Thomson that the situation at Moat Farmhouse is 'very unpleasant' and that he fears 'an explosion'. From its archives, it appears that all this time Philip was also submitting ideas to the BBC and having them seriously considered by

Third Programme producers. In April 1965 he had suggested a programme on 'Motoring Accidents' and in July he had submitted a proposal entitled 'Permutations of Competitive Salvation', which a BBC reader dismissed as 'academic twaddle masquerading as profundity'. The same month, a new name appears in the BBC files, a certain C. F. O. 'Toby' Clarke, who notes, 'I do not know O'Connor personally but I am told he can be brilliant but is somewhat difficult and that Thomson handled him well.'

In January 1966, Philip O'Connor had another chance to prove his brilliance when he was commissioned to make a programme about circus clowns, working and retired. Work on this project started with a hiccup when Coco the Clown 'postponed recordings' in London, but Philip was soon off to Billy Smart's in Birmingham to interview on site a clown called Smartie. During one of these excursions he started drinking again, downing ten pints of beer on 4 February, but he seems to have re-embraced sobriety soon afterwards. The programme was broadcast on 3 April and in it Philip asked Coco the Clown, 'Are you at all sensitive at being laughed at in private life?' to which Coco replied, 'Very much so.' While working on this project he had also made progress with a programme on 'Success', to be produced by Douglas Cleverdon. And on 26 March he wrote to David Thomson suggesting a programme on 'Parasites' and included with his proposal the order: 'Lend me £5 again.'

In April 1966 Philip and Nicolle moved again, this time to a small thatched house in a village called Lidgate, near Newmarket. The house was called Brookside on account of the ditch that divided it from the road. According to John Grenville, this may have seemed 'a poor man's house' after Moat Farm, which was 'rather grand', but Philip wrote cheerfully enough to David Thomson on 20 April saying that they had all settled into their new home, which was warm and had 'lots of hot water which, to the underprivileged as we must regard ourselves, is a boon'. To Michael Hamburger he wrote in an equally truculent mood, saying, 'Michael, now, how do we stand, Man to Man?' and providing his own answer, 'Excellent, excellent.' A week later he was feeling far from excellent and told various correspondents that he and Nicolle were down with jaundice, their eyes the colour of egg yolks. During this illness, Philip read Boswell and pronounced him a 'very lovable man'. On 22 May he wrote to Hamburger of the revelations yielded by sobriety: 'Having been sober for eight months has allowed me to look at my life in a certain way for the first time; it seems to have been extraordinarily stupid, untidy, incredibly uncalculated, like a mad man's.' This was all very well but sobriety did not bring money. Later that month he warned David Thomson of 'a financial crisis imminent within a week' and his literary agent, A. P. Watt, wrote to the BBC about his latest programme: 'I gather from Mr O'Connor that it would be a considerable convenience for him to have the first half of the fee now due.' He also regretted making a contorted reply to the offer of a loan from the publisher Tony Godwin and now had 'to grovel in the dust & twirl my fancy waistcoats' to remind him of his kind offer.

During the summer of 1966 Philip became increasingly disappointed by his sobriety. 'I still seem to offend people, even without drink,' he wrote to Thomson in July after an encounter with Philip Toynbee's American wife, and by the end of August was sufficiently upset by 'prescriptions' about how he should behave from Michael Hamburger to stand him up in London and boast afterwards that he had done so deliberately. Drunk or sober, he also started work on his programme on 'Success'. On 7 September – on the eve of his fiftieth birthday – he interviewed Sir Michael Redgrave at a house in Knightsbridge and later in the autumn tackled Malcolm Muggeridge, Philip Toynbee and John Berger, all of whom, aided and abetted by Philip, expressed suspicion of worldly achievement. While thus engaged, Philip himself made a brief attempt to ape conventional success by appearing at Crockford's Club in a suit borrowed from David Thomson to be photographed as a contributor to a book Anthony Blond was publishing about London. At the same time he was bombarding the BBC with further submissions and requests. On 17 October 1966, he wrote to Douglas Cleverdon from Lidgate saying, 'I'm in the usual chaos' and asking, 'Can further expenses be gathered for the current programme?' On 30 October he wrote to radio producer Hallam Tennyson, volunteering to take mescaline and be tape-recorded at the Maudsley Hospital. A few days later, he was once again in need and wrote to David Thomson, 'Can you send your apologies for not being able to oblige an old friend with the loan of a bob? I'll tell God and report his remarks to you.'

Meanwhile, interest had been stirred up in the possible publication of a book of Philip O'Connor's collected poems. This idea had first been suggested by Robin Skelton, then an assistant professor at the University of Victoria, British Columbia, whose relationship with O'Connor and admiration for his work stretched back many years. In September 1966 Skelton presented the idea to none other than Tom Maschler at Jonathan Cape, who was at that moment awaiting the arrival of Quentin Crisp's completed autobiography. Maschler already knew *Memoirs of a Public Baby*, describing it as 'one of the most moving and true and good books I have read in a number of years', and may have been won over in favour of publishing O'Connor's poems by enthusiastic letters from the critic Francis Wyndham and the poet B. S. Johnson. On 26 September Wyndham wrote to Maschler, 'I hear that you might be going to do some Collected Poems of Philip O'Connor – & this is just to say that I hope you do as I think he is very good.' On 4 October B. S. Johnson wrote in more detail: 'O'Connor seems to me to be one of the best poets of the Thirties but the most underrated. I think he is an original, an innovator, and know of no one with his doggedness in working out metaphors and making an image work like hell for him. This leads to density, but not to obscurity: though it may take several readings to understand a poem fully.'

Once again, all Philip himself seemed concerned about was his 'frightful financial position'. On 7 February 1967 he signed a contract with Jonathan Cape for a measly £50 and two days later met Tom Maschler in the same stately office where Quentin Crisp claimed to have been showered with hot sequins a few months earlier. Philip later wrote to Maschler saying he had enjoyed meeting him and informing him of the 'regular and impending crisis' that he was facing. Earlier the same month he had written to Michael Hamburger complaining that BBC work had practically dried up, informing him that he had applied for training as a probation officer and adding, 'Can you send me any old clothes?'

In spite of these handicaps he was able, later that spring, to persuade his friend Ann Wolff to make a film of the poem 'Captain Busby' which he had written in the Maudsley thirty years earlier. Mrs Wolff agreed to this suggestion and considering the surrealist and fantastic nature of this poem decided 'to do it straight', employing no fancy camera work. She also discussed the project with Bruce Beresford at the British Film Institute, who could not 'make head or tail' of the script but trusted Ann Wolff enough to provide modest funding. In due course Philip approached Quentin Crisp and invited him to appear in the film along with another lodger at Beaufort Street, Peter Hirst-Smith, David Thomson's wife Martina and one or two others. Filming took place in May 1967 partly in London and partly at the then deserted Betchworth railway station on the edge of Box Hill – another instance of the way Philip habitually retraced his steps and the fourth time that Box Hill had featured significantly in his life. It was at Betchworth station that Philip and his guardian had first alighted forty-three years earlier.

The short black-and-white film that resulted shows Philip at his most exuberant, stagily dressed in tail-coat, spats, monocle, and grasping a pair of sugar-tongs. To David Thomson, he explained that he aimed to play the title role in 'deadly-comic kind of Dr Caligari' mode and his doll-like movements certainly underlined what he called the 'pedantic orthodoxy' of a character not far removed from his own. Quentin Crisp comes across as more masculine than feminine, 'quite butch' according to one observer, in heavily epauletted admiral's uniform and three-cornered admiral's hat. Ann Wolff reports that during the filming Quentin was protected by his fellow lodger Peter Hirst-Smith, who played a porter. At lunchtime Philip and the rest of the cast went off to the local pub, but Quentin announced, 'It's easier for me to stay here at the station.'

On 4 July 1967 Philip and Quentin were both present at the National Film Theatre when the fifteen-minute film was shown to a large, culture-conscious audience. According to Ann Wolff, *Captain Busby* had a 'tiny success' and benefited from a prevailing surrealist boom, but nothing would ever satisfy Philip, who later attacked his friend for not making the film more successful. This was not uncharacteristic behaviour for Philip at any time, but during the summer of 1967 a bitter and turbulent streak ran through his life. On 22 July he wrote a wild letter to Michael Hamburger about marriage: 'Probably you have both become crucified by Grim Truths, Hard Facts, Bitter Realities and other nails sold by the weight . . .' On 26 July, he wrote to Ed Victor, then an editor at Jonathan Cape, complaining about an Allen Ginsberg performance at the Roundhouse which they had both attended: 'I hope you hated it as much as I did.' To Michael Hamburger, he says he felt very sick after this event and adds desperately, 'Lately I've felt as though I was falling to pieces. The struggle to keep the family and to write begins to seem impossible and there's nothing I can do to earn a living.'

By this time Philip's domestic life had certainly entered a dark phase. His children by Nicolle prefer to draw a veil over the relevant events, referring only to 'lots of bad stuff'. On a trip to meet Philip at Broadcasting House, Nicolle found that he had already spent the whole fee for a programme at the bar. More programmes were commissioned, notably ones on the Sue Ryder Homes and the Simon Community which would show Philip at his best, but he rightly sensed that his tenuous connection with the BBC was weakening. During that year he had submitted a drama script called 'Excessive Wonder of Life' which had been accepted and in due course broadcast, only to be dismissed by new figures at the Third Programme as 'a piece of preposterously over-written pointlessness which serves no purpose', said to show O'Connor at his silliest. Other suggestions, such as programmes on 'Hell' and 'Violence', were flatly rejected and his mentor Douglas Cleverdon, now facing retirement, told Philip: 'I am now more of a broken reed than ever.'

There were still bright moments in O'Connor's life. Working on his *Selected Poems*, due out the following spring, must have given him some satisfaction and on his way to London in early August he paid Alan Rawsthorne and his wife Isabel a memorable visit at their cottage near Thaxted. The composer had promptly cracked open two bottles of what he called 'a very modest little wine' and his wife had 'stormed off' to her studio. The pleasures of such moments quickly evaporated, however, and on 1 September Philip wrote to David Thomson saying,

'I can't come to London because I've no money' and told him he had applied for a job in Budapest, working for the new *Hungarian Quarterly*.

By now, after nearly nine years together, Nicolle had had enough. On 16 September 1967, she finally threw Philip out of the house at Lidgate and he set off for London with one small suitcase. He would later argue that he had 'half-engineered' this ejection. In London he seems to have headed directly to writer Jeremy Brooks's house in Bartholomew Road, Kentish Town. During the next few homeless days he was also seen at Michael Hamburger's new London home, 34a Half Moon Lane, SE24. Ann Wolff remembers finding Philip here, lying on the floor and kicking his heels like a baby, saying, 'I must have a woman!' and 'I don't know what to do!' He was also at Half Moon Lane on Monday 2 October when the telephone rang and Michael Hamburger answered it to hear a soothing, female American voice asking him to come and have a drink that night in Regent's Park. Hamburger explained to the caller, whose name was Panna Grady, that he had somebody with him, another poet. Without hesitation, Mrs Grady urged Michael to bring his friend along.

PART THREE

– 15 –

Panna Grady

Materially I have everything I ever wanted: house,
land, trees, circumstantial tranquillity. My workroom
is being built. I have also the most beautiful and intelligent woman I have ever met, including Jean, to whom
I feel as near. And yet – because I have lived too long
in England? – I am frightened.

PHILIP O'CONNOR TO DAVID THOMSON, 14 July 1968

The beautiful and intelligent woman who was to rescue Philip
O'Connor was born Panna de Cholnoky on 20 September 1936 at
Grove Lane, Greenwich, Connecticut. Her father, Dr Tibor de Cholnoky, was a plastic surgeon of aristocratic Hungarian origins. Her
mother was American, the heiress to a steam-engine fortune. Later in
life, Panna would remember her father as an impatient, autocratic
perfectionist, who specialized in cosmetic cancer operations, especially
reconstructions of the breast. When she was old enough to watch him
in the operating theatre, she was awestruck by his swift, deft gestures
with the knife.

Her early childhood was happy and secure. The Grove Lane property ran alongside the home of the first President Bush – famous names
dominate the first few pages of this chapter which has been compressed
from an article I wrote for *Vanity Fair* – and the two families were
constantly in and out of each other's houses. Panna remembers her
own home for having 'such a calm, such a luxury'. There were chiming
clocks in every room and five live-in servants, headed by a deaf Negro
butler named John, who rolled the butter in front of you. Panna grew

up without a sense of the existence of the poor. 'The majority of people in Greenwich lived as well as each other,' she said later. 'You didn't imagine the world was different.'

Like George Bush Snr, Panna de Cholnoky attended Greenwich County Day School and then the Abbot Academy. At the age of seventeen she became a boarder at Wellesley College, Boston, where her favourite sports were fencing, riding and tennis. Holidays were spent in Switzerland or Bermuda. One year she went on summer camp with Laura Rockefeller, whose parents Laurence and Mary were old family friends. When she was eighteen Panna 'came out' as a debutante on New York's Austro-Hungarian circuit. Along with her friend Elvira Esterhazy and twenty other girls she was formally presented to Prince Otto von Hapsburg at the Plaza Hotel. A photograph exists of Panna on this occasion, in a white dress with a sash and white gloves and accompanied by her father in white tie and tails. Panna looks amusing and bemused but her life had already been touched by sadness. When she was only thirteen, her mother had died of cancer and her father had remarried. Looking back on these days, Panna claims to have felt an inner need for another sort of family.

She was soon to find this. In 1955 her privileged and somewhat restrained upbringing came to an end when she moved to Berkeley, California, began to study psychology and became exposed to the San Francisco poetry renaissance. The world of the 'beats' beckoned her. Her unusual beauty, fabulously long legs, intellectual sparkle and generosity with the fortune to which she now had access made her an irresistible figure on the Berkeley campus. Her distinctive redwood house on Mosswood Road eventually became the setting for her first literary party. This was organized for her in 1959 by the writer William Stine, attended by Allen Ginsberg and had, as guest of honour, Stephen Spender, on leave from his duties at *Encounter* for a six-month professorship at Berkeley. 'It was very charming that he could come,' Panna said later.

In 1960 Panna returned to New York to study acting at the Berkhof School. She rented a top-floor apartment in Bank Street in the West Village and, though always abstemious herself, quickly fell in with some of the great drinkers of the time like Jason Robards and Delmore

Schwartz, who were patrons of the nearby Cedar Bar and White Horse Tavern. She later described this time as 'the beginning of the end', but occasionally her past intruded. Knowing of her acting aspirations, an old Greenwich neighbour, investment banker Eustace Seligman, invited Panna to lunch with his friend Greta Garbo. 'It didn't work out,' Panna recalls. 'I was a pest to her. I kept asking her questions. Eventually Eustace asked me to please not stop her between the pool and her bedroom.'

The 'big break' with her past came when she married the poet and heavy drinker Jim Grady and on 10 June 1963 had a baby by him. The relationship did not last long but as far as her family were concerned Panna was now 'beyond the pale'. By this time she had also fallen out with her West Side neighbours. 'I served drinks after the bars had closed. They told me I must choose between my friends and my home.' She had chosen the former and in order to entertain them in the style they demanded had paid $42,000 for a seven-room apartment in the Dakota building on Central Park West, famous for its insulated walls and three-foot-thick floors.

Between 1962 and 1966, Panna Grady lived here with her daughter Ella and entertained constantly, sometimes round a gate-legged table that had come from her family home in Connecticut and sometimes on a much larger scale. Her apartment overlooking the park was big enough for five hundred people to pass through comfortably during an evening. Among those who did were William Burroughs, Andy Warhol, Allen Ginsberg, Anaïs Nin, Viva, Lillian Hellman, Marshall McLuhan, Maxine de la Falaise, Jasper Johns, Susan Sontag, Anthony Burgess, Yoko Ono, Tom Wolfe, Robert Lowell, George Plimpton, Philip Roth, Norman Mailer, John Wain and hundreds more. 'Half the people there didn't know I was giving the party. I wasn't on display,' Panna said later. 'I always wore the same dress. I didn't feel qualified. I always felt I was just a handmaiden who was there to serve. Most of the people knew each other already so I didn't even introduce them.'

Norman Mailer declares that it was impossible to know where to place Panna Grady on the hierarchy of New York hostesses, only that he met people at her parties he could not meet elsewhere. Part of the magic was in the mixture: East Side, West Side, Uptown, Downtown, Crosstown mixed together, young hopefuls mingled with towering greats. 'Literally fabulous' is how Anthony Burgess described those evenings. Invitations went out by mail. Panna Grady always used the same familiar innocuous picture postcard called Lilac Hedges. Not everyone who came had an invitation. 'When I was trying to close it down, there would often be eighty people at the gates downstairs clambering to get in.' As the night drew on, the chaos would mount – but Panna seemed to enjoy the dramas. She was equally easy-going about furniture which got broken or stolen and the clothes and jewellery that disappeared from her closet. 'People had more use of it than I did,' she says today. 'Anyway, you feel wanted when people steal from you.'

Panna's generosity was immense, in emotional as well as material terms. 'She gave and she gave and all she asked in return was the company of artists,' wrote Ted Morgan in his biography of Panna's then best friend William Burroughs. Exactly how much she gave is uncertain. Panna herself mentions the figure of $500,000 – the equivalent of how many millions today? – and possibly it was a good deal more than that. Very little of the money was spent on herself. The day she bought a hundred hats – 'They all looked so good. I couldn't decide' – had cured her of that sort of silliness. Instead, she spent $17,000 putting on someone's play in a theatre whose name she now forgets and gave a British poet a blank cheque which he filled in for several thousand dollars. For a while at any rate, Panna Grady could have claimed to be the banker of the beat movement. She paid for Herbert Hunke's journal to be published. She helped finance a magazine called *Fuck You* edited by someone called Ed Sanders. She paid for Tambimuttu's festschrift for Marianne Moore's seventy-seventh birthday. And she was equally generous with her apartment: she had Tambi himself, weak on Bourbon after fifteen years in New York, to stay there for three weeks and she lent it to Andy Warhol and moved out while he made a film called *Poor Little Rich Girl*. 'I gave him the key,' Panna said later. 'If you agree with someone to make a film, you can't start meddling.' So determined was she not to be a nuisance, Panna never even asked to see the finished film. In one of his autobiographical writings, Warhol simply said of Panna Grady, 'She seemed to adore the drug-related writers in particular.'

Such open-handedness can be partly explained by Panna's extra-ordinary goodwill. She saw the best in everyone and was almost incapable of making an adverse judgement. She was apparently so unaware of her own charms as to believe that money was the only bond between her and the artists she knew. 'Money made me feel essential. I had more effect on people's lives.' She was also reckless. 'I didn't think of having a future,' she explains. 'I was a bit hectic. I didn't imagine I'd outlive it. My mother died very young. One of my sisters died young. I really thought I wouldn't live long. I imagined that five years hence I would have cancer.' In those days she never foresaw the possibility of remarrying or having more than one child to look after. 'I didn't see the men around me as family men, as husbands. They did not inspire the idea of marriage. Most of them were homosexuals.'

One of the men she did have an affair with was the English novelist Nicholas Mosley with whom she travelled across America, and one of the few men who never sought to take advantage of her was William Burroughs. Burroughs and Panna had first met in Boston, introduced by pioneering hippy Timothy Leary, and she had been mesmerized by his courtesy, his looks, his humour, his delicacy and his air of remote-ness. According to Ted Morgan, she became so fascinated by Burroughs that she was prepared to buy information about him, paying $50 to $100 a time according to the quality of the story. She also tried to lure him into her life by giving parties for him.

In the spring of 1965, she gave a huge party in Burroughs's honour which so many people attempted to gatecrash that Panna reluctantly told the doormen to stop letting people come in. This resulted in a broken arm for a latecomer named LeRoi Jones – or was it the doorman's? – and upstairs there were further dramas. Asked to confirm or deny a rumour that an avant-garde poet had urinated into Norman Mailer's pocket, Panna says simply, 'Yes, I suppose it came to that.' The night was only saved by Allen Ginsberg playing his finger cymbals and leading everyone out like hypnotized sheep. A less successful event was the dinner Panna arranged for Burroughs to meet Andy Warhol.

This took place in the El Quixote restaurant beside the famous Chelsea Hotel. 'They did not get on,' Panna modestly recalls. Uncouth behaviour by a member of Warhol's entourage caused Burroughs to leave halfway through the meal, Panna in pursuit.

Soon afterwards Panna decided that life at the Dakota had 'got out of hand'. She had 'too many friends' and her reputation as the softest of soft touches had earned her the unsavoury nickname 'Pan of Gravy'. Her decision to sell her apartment coincided with William Burroughs's departure for London. In October 1966, she decided to follow him to England, accompanied by the Black Mountain poet Charles Olson and her daughter Ella, now three.

Panna Grady and Charles Olson spent that autumn in a rented flat in Mount Street, Mayfair, which Olson liked on account of the proximity of the Connaught Hotel. Here Panna often entertained, giving dinners for ten or twelve people and invariably picking up the bill. Her London circle rapidly expanded to include the Labour MP Tom Driberg, who took her to Annabel's nightclub and a party at Jonathan Cape's, and the antique dealer Christopher Gibbs who took her to Finch's pub in Fulham Road where she could meet some artists. Through Gibbs, Panna also met the writer John Michell, and visited him often at his flat in Notting Hill. Michell remembers that Panna had style but 'seemed unloved' and at the same time 'suspicious of potential suitors', and explains that this was a 'time of acid and experiences of all sorts'. Meanwhile, Panna's friend Yoko Ono had also arrived in London and in November 1966 had met John Lennon for the first time in the Indica Gallery.

In January 1967 Panna Grady and Charles Olson – then in his fifties – moved to rooms at 17 Hanover Terrace overlooking Regent's Park, which was full of literary and artistic associations, past and present. Feliks Topolski lived there, so did Harold Pinter, and a hundred years earlier Charles Dickens had finished writing *Great Expectations* at a house in the same terrace. For the next six months Panna Grady continued her lavish lifestyle and remembers that Olson's odd hours made family life rather difficult: Olson would get up in the evening just as Ella was having her supper, and wanted his lunch served at one o'clock in the morning. Olson's subsequent disappearance – friends advertised for him in the *Herald Tribune* – is another story and by then Panna had anyway taken a ten-year lease of 2 Hanover Terrace and moved in with her child, a cook and a maid. This large white-stuccoed house, with marble staircase and walnut-panelled floors, would provide an even more gracious setting for entertaining than the Dakota and was soon adorned by the gate-legged table from Connecticut and various lavish antiques, chairs covered in silver leather and any number of inlaid cabinets, which Panna bought from Christopher Gibbs. During the summer of 1967 there were many people in and out of the house. The top floor was taken by Janet Hobhouse, teenage daughter of a New York friend, and the mews house was intermittently occupied by Allen Ginsberg. His fellow beat poet, Alex Trocchi, recently released from prison, was another frequent visitor. There was also a sick dog in the house, sick enough to require the attentions of the Chelsea vet Tony O'Neill, who has already appeared in this story.

It was in these surroundings and amidst these distractions that on Sunday 17 July 1967 Panna Grady gave her last great party, one of the few events she arranged that got written up in the newspapers. In the *Evening Standard* the young reporter Jonathan Aitken, whose own life would prove equally eventful, argued that Mrs Grady deserved 'the Nobel Prize for generational peace-making'. That night Burroughs, Ginsberg and other New York cronies mingled with international types like film director Pier Paolo Pasolini and distinguished Londoners of varying vintages such as Mick Jagger, Robert Conquest, Lord Goodman, Harold Pinter, Professor William Empson, Peter Brook and others described by Aitken as 'the weirdest weirdies'. The evening ended when a fight broke out between two poets and the police arrived. All the ministrations of Professor Empson, author of *Seven Types of Ambiguity*, were needed to send the forces of the law packing.

Meanwhile, demands for Panna's money were increasing. One morning she was found behind her desk with a cheque book while a queue of hopeful hangers-on formed in front of her. 'People came to me with their sad lives,' she explained later. 'I had too many pressures on me to help people out. I was aware of too many people who needed money. You can't pick and choose. A lot of it *did* seem wasted. It did get to the stage that I was simply and finally paying for people's drugs.'

It may have been in this frame of mind that on 2 October of that year, Panna Grady telephoned Michael Hamburger, whom she had met during one of his visits to New York, and asked him and his homeless friend round for a drink. Panna is uncertain about the exact sequence of events and believes it was Hamburger who telephoned her that day. At any rate the subsequent arrival of O'Connor and Hamburger on the palatial doorstep of 2 Hanover Terrace can be presented as a historic and catastrophic event. Both the visitors were mildly famous as writers. Hamburger had already written or translated several dozen books and was not at that time saddled with the fame of being the brother of the millionaire publisher Paul Hamlyn. Philip had produced only five books – his *Selected Poems* were still in production – but his works had all made their mark or ferocious scrawl across the hearts and minds of the better-educated English readers. Panna loved all writers and poets and yearned to be connected with bohemia. Her own memories of her first encounter with Philip O'Connor are clear-cut: 'He was leering through the grille. He looked at me over his glasses in the most significant manner even before he had got through the door. He had nothing, no suitcase, no money, no home.' According to Michael Hamburger, Philip then behaved as abominably as ever, bullying and insulting Panna from the start. 'D'you call this vodka?' he exclaimed in protest at the non-Russian version she offered him. Hamburger became increasingly embarrassed but when he told Panna, 'I'll take him away', she protested, 'Oh, no. I think he's wonderful.'

Eventually Michael Hamburger set off on his own, leaving Panna Grady and Philip O'Connor to start the relationship which was to preoccupy them for the next thirty years. That very night Philip also began to throw the hangers-on out of the house and the following morning, or soon afterwards, he put his demands on the table. He wanted a home, a motor-car, enough money to start a magazine and other material things. All of these Panna was more than happy to provide and, in spite of these demands, soon told a friend, 'I think he loves me for myself.' For Philip, Panna was 'a beautiful ghostly figure in search of an identity, quite lost in England – they were so greedy with her'. To what extent she also reminded him of his mother was never quite clear. For Panna, Philip was the ultimate bohemian, the genius, the great oddity she had failed to secure in New York.

Over the next few days Philip had encounters with several of Panna's friends and many more of her hangers-on. He met Leslie Fiedler, author of *Love and Death in the American Novel*, and Alexander Trocchi and called unaccompanied on William Burroughs at Duke Street, St James's, announcing himself as 'Panna Grady's terrible husband' and questioning him about his social rank. Back at Hanover Terrace he reputedly upset Yoko Ono when he pulled the hair away from her face to see who she was and caused horror to the critic John Wain, who went upstairs and was sick on the carpet when he realized that Philip and Panna were 'together'. Wain predicted that the relationship would last eighteen months, no more. Philip explained later, 'I didn't want all those creeps to be there.' Panna doesn't accept this description of her friends – 'They may have been unsavoury to him but they all had characters' – but acquiesced as he cleared the house and shouted at a man named Hollingshead, 'In the name of God, go!' A lesser man might have tried to ingratiate himself with a new patroness by praising her other friends but O'Connor was, as we know, made of strong metal.

On the other hand, he did not presume to impose much of his past on Mrs Grady and none of his seven children were at this stage presented to her. A few old friends who did call at Hanover Terrace were startled by what they found. Ann Wolff was staggered by the lavishness and mentions the Persian rugs on rollers which were used as curtains and other exotic decorations – 'all hers and all priceless' – and David and Martina Thomson were equally disconcerted by the chairs covered in silver leather and an atmosphere 'altogether too grand'. The Brookses, with whom Philip had been staying on the day he met Panna, felt 'dropped' though recalled that Philip had visited them in Kentish Town boasting, 'The maid brought us breakfast in bed this morning.' Eleanor Brooks wondered what to do with the pathetic little suitcase Philip had left at the house. Philip told her to give it to Oxfam. Eleanor opened it before she did so and found it full of bills Philip was hiding from Nicolle. It also contained a silver cup, which had possibly once belonged to Philip's mother. Mrs Brooks could have hung on to this but, disgruntled by Philip's aloofness, disposed of it as he had suggested. He was less dismissive of other property and, within days of meeting Panna, even made a day trip to Suffolk to pick up various possessions that were scattered about. Driven by Panna's friend John Michell in his Talbot Sunbeam, Philip called at various pubs, picked up various items and perhaps settled some bills. Michell remembers only that it had to be done very quickly and that O'Connor was 'very manic' and 'very jabber-jabber'.

This was a short-lived phase. Philip O'Connor was desperate to get away at long last to France and Panna now declared that she had finally lost her appetite for social life. 'I had always wanted to live in France again but I never had the courage to live there alone,' Philip said later. On 17 October 1967, only fifteen days after their first meeting, Philip and Panna set off with Ella in a safari car they had bought from Feliks Topolski's son Dan. Panna remembers simply turning the key of the front door at Hanover Terrace and seems unaware of the tides of bemusement and confusion that this sudden departure caused. 'Oh yes,' said Philip's friend Denis Lowson, 'we heard how he'd met Panna and whisked her out of her phoney London set.' Even Michael Hamburger seemed slightly put out by the suddenness with which his two friends had 'buzzed off' together to France. From Panna's side of things, Christopher Gibbs expressed a certain amount of dismay that this remarkable young woman had gone off with a 'derelict', and Allen Ginsberg wondered how Panna could stand Philip's continuous 'prattling', though admitted the same question could be asked of himself. And there was also disgruntlement from Tambimuttu, now back in London and hoping that Panna Grady would finance the relaunch of his magazine *Poetry London*. For the second time in his life, Tambi had been romantically upstaged by Philip O'Connor.

Philip was now fifty-one years old, Panna was thirty-one and Ella was four. Together they crossed to France and then headed south to Seillans, near Grasse, recommended by Leslie Fiedler. Here they stayed for a week or two at Le Mas du Vieux Moulin but found the terrain very bleak and dry. At the beginning of November they moved to Brittany, where Panna took a year's lease on a house called Le Châtelier on the dramatic Cancale peninsula overlooking Mont St Michel. On 4 November Philip wrote to David Thomson offering to come to London to finish work on the Simon Community radio programme but ordering him to tell no one of his new address. On 9 November he wrote to Tom Maschler at Jonathan Cape thanking him for a pre-publication copy of *The Naked Civil Servant*, which had been sent to him at Quentin Crisp's request and adding that he 'much liked it'. He also mentions his 'liverish disposition' and the effect of pastis on his bowels. That winter he gave a copy of *Memoirs of a Public Baby* to Panna Grady and signed it 'en amour'. By the end of the year Panna was pregnant.

Early in the New Year Panna and Philip went to America for a few weeks. Panna went on ahead with Ella, Philip would follow at the end of January, after spending a few days in London during which he did some work with David Thomson on the two outstanding radio programmes. He eventually flew to New York, sitting next to the wife of the eminent American writer Ed Dorn whom Panna already knew. In letters to David Thomson and Michael Hamburger, Philip declares that he loathed New York and hated America – 'have never been as depressed by an environment' – which reminded him of Wimbledon blown up. While in New York he met Ginsberg and Mailer and complained later about Ginsberg's moist handshake, but enjoyed Mailer's champagne at the Algonquin Hotel. He found the poet and sociologist Paul Goodman 'ineffably pompous serious *à l'Américain*' but liked Maurice Girodias, who vaguely commissioned him to write a book about money. They had then driven to Charleston, South Carolina, which was better, though Philip continued to tut-tut about the 'doomed, damned country' he was in. On 26 February 1968 he wrote to Michael Hamburger from West Hampton, Long Island, listing his dislikes and enclosing £50 which he owed him. The following day Panna and Philip left Ella with her father and sailed for Cherbourg on board the SS *France*. Philip had his typewriter on the deck and still acted the part of the professional writer. He was still in touch with the BBC and his *Selected Poems* were due out the following month from Jonathan Cape.

Philip was back in Brittany when this book was published on 7 March and he did not seem particularly interested in how it went down, though he arranged for copies to be sent to his children and to people he admired like Stephen Spender and Herbert Read and other acquaintances at out-of-date addresses, which were subsequently returned to Jonathan Cape marked with the words 'gone away' or 'not known'. The critical response to the book was both varied and inspired. Several reviewers described Philip's poems as 'meaningless' and 'going nowhere' and in the *London Magazine* Peter Bland accused O'Connor of mistaking fickleness for wit and claimed that his poems 'nearly always vanish up themselves'. There were also comments about O'Connor's 'knockabout slapstick act with rhyme', his 'welding of free rhythms into a concise imagery that carries both the observation and emotional reaction to it' and his way of allowing 'words to adhere to images like iron filings to a magnet'. In *Country Life*, Richard Church praised O'Connor's 'vagabondage way in a world increasingly standardized' and called it 'a singing pilgrimage'. None of these comments, many of which seem relevant to Philip's whole personality as well as to his poetry, appear to have registered with him and in his correspondence at this time he refers only to a 'horrible' review in the *Observer* by Ian Hamilton who dismissed Philip's outpourings as 'sour and dour'.

Unboosted but undeterred by this reception, Philip and Panna spent the early summer of 1968 at Cancale and also took some time off to visit England together. The mews house at Hanover Terrace was still in Panna's name and they may have stayed here for a day or two before setting off for East Anglia, where they saw Alan Rawsthorne's wife Isabel and had a late night in A. L. Morton's library at Clare. They then headed for Wales, stayed in the Royal Goat Hotel at Beddgelert and visited Croesor, where Panna met Philip's old neighbour Nellie Jones. They also began to look for a permanent property in France and soon found a farmhouse at Saunerie near Manzac-sur-Vern in the Dordogne.

By the end of June 1968 they had settled here in some discomfort.

The house had a tower, white-painted shutters and several acres of land around it, including orchards, but no lavatory. In letters to David Thomson, Philip writes that the place is as peaceful as Purton Green, set in a quiet valley with woods and streams, and states that a workroom was being built for him. Looking back on this move, Panna makes light of the expenditure, saying simply, 'Yeh, yeh, I had money to spend.' Soon some of the fine furniture arrived from London – the rest was sold back to Christopher Gibbs – and more was acquired locally, including a very old chair with gnarled arms which would become Philip's 'throne'. In a letter to David Thomson dated 12 July Philip declared, 'I tread my twelve acres masterfully, keeping a smart lookout for Poachers, Gypsies and all sorts of Vagabonds that they Trespass not on my land.' On 20 September this domestic magic kingdom must have felt almost complete when Panna gave birth to a baby boy in the Périgueux Hospital. He was given the name of Maxim, which was also the second name of his son by Bobbie Battersby born twenty-three years earlier. Soon after the event, Philip telegraphed David Thomson: 'Get silver spoon.'

That autumn Philip and Panna should have felt secure. Philip was a creature of routine and judging by his behaviour on other occasions one imagines he quickly settled into various domestic rituals: certainly he took over the kitchen and was soon telling friends, 'I cook nearly French.' But, looking back on this time, Panna Grady says that she had no sense of a future together. Philip's protestations of love were invariably followed by threats to leave her. In the letter to David Thomson quoted at the start of this chapter, Philip says he now has everything he ever wanted but still feels frightened – and the fear made him drink. One of the problems was that Panna's money had not only liberated Philip from the need to 'scribble' and to try to earn a living or 'scrounge for sixpences'. It had also given him the freedom or opportunity to drink as much as he wanted. 'Philip was wild,' Panna recalls. 'He drank seventeen double pastis one afternoon. He was out of his mind. He would go off for a few days. I bought him this. I bought him that. He had money to throw around in the bar. He gave tips of a hundred francs.'

Philip's letters to David Thomson confirm the fix he imagined he was in. 'We achieve total love in bed and total misunderstanding out of it,' he had written on 19 July 1968. At other times he puts it in other ways: 'Life is not easy with my beloved' and 'My love of her prevents total collapse.' During this time he seems to have made half-hearted attempts to leave Panna, counted these attempts and boasted about his love to David Thomson. 'I try to leave her everyday and fail everyday.' At other times he calls Panna 'a cow' and writes of her 'inexhaustible provocation of my temper'. Panna's money also provoked Philip into various unseemly postures. He soon used some of it to pay a firm to establish his aristocratic ancestry, without any success. On several occasions he sent postcards to Thomson only to boast of the particular vintage he is drinking at that moment and asking, 'Am I the fellow you knew?' When Thomson retorts that Philip is going 'the way of the rich' and makes a joke about Panna's Rockefeller connection Philip is overcome with indignation and takes pains to stress that Panna is now on the brink of poverty. 'I find that P's money is nearly all gone,' he writes back and even claims, 'We're in a very bad financial crisis – can't take money out of England.' Perhaps in lip-service to these smokescreens, he bothered to submit a note of his expenses to the BBC for work he had done the previous year. He also mentions more than once that Panna has enabled him to settle his Welsh and Suffolk debts and that he has passed quite a lot of money on to Nicolle, whom he still misses.

Philip's links with the mothers of his children remained potent. They all forgave him, they all respected him and, now or later, they all expressed gratitude to Panna Grady for taking over responsibility for the impossible man they loved. Nicolle was still only twenty-seven when Philip left her and would stay on with her three children in Lidgate, banishing photographs of Philip from the house but never speaking slightingly of him. Anna Wing and Maria Scott saw a lot of each other and brought up Philip's children conscientiously and capably, as well as getting on with their own lives. In due course, Maria got a job with a charity for the blind and her husband John Scott, who had already emerged as a lexicographer, would produce a groundbreaking dictionary of structural terminology.

During the remainder of 1968 and 1969, it is difficult to see what

Philip did other than get drunk, often on pastis. Panna mentions the particular bar at St Asher that he inhabited, where he threw her money around and from where she would sometimes rescue him. She also mentions his trips, his brief disappearances, some of which, like his visit to John Berger at nearby Bonnieux, had a legitimate purpose. Several years earlier Berger had agreed to edit Philip's journal and this undertaking had been mentioned on the jacket of his *Selected Poems*. Berger recalls sending Philip 150 edited pages but declares that Philip 'wasn't very encouraging' and the project fizzled out. Philip also made occasional trips to England, hating it more and more, but finally completing work on the two outstanding radio programmes. His last programme was on the Simon Community, and would be transmitted on 19 March 1969, showing Philip at his most effective but nevertheless marking the end of his broadcasting career.

By this time he was facing the consequences of his higher level of drinking. In January 1969 a doctor told him that if he continued at this rate, he was only two months away from cirrhosis of the liver and only two years from death. A few weeks later, he reported that he was now 'watering' his liver, taking sedatives, and was allowed only two glasses of champagne a day. He also told David Thomson he was thinking of taking a recuperative week in the seaside resort of his childhood.

On 4 May Philip wrote to David Thomson beginning, 'You'll be astonished to hear I'm in Wimereux' and went on, 'I face the sea, typing this, upon the sand on which I played as a boy. Imagine that! *L'éternel retour*, this time with a bad liver!' He had taken a room in the Hotel Speranza, where he liked the lady proprietor, and though complaining of 'the hordes of people who weren't here in 1922' was now looking for a place in the town where he and Panna could live. On 27 June he wrote to Thomson from a house called Clair de Lune, explaining, 'We're buying this villa, so well-named, and are going to let the two ground floors. It's enormous & very solid & on the quieter part of the beach.'

The house, which would become Philip's and Panna's home for the next six years, was built by a Belgian architect in either 1902 or 1908 – the fancy numerals on the front of it are difficult to decipher – and had steps leading down from it onto the sand. With its pinnacled roof and dormer windows it looked like a small slice of the Dakota building but was in fact one of the largest houses in the town. In due course Panna would pile her sumptuous furniture into the top two or three floors leaving the two ground floors untouched, but there was still space in the house for them to lead semi-separate lives. The move did not, however, improve Philip's health and part of his first few months in Wimereux were spent bedridden. In November 1969 he was admitted to an expensive clinic, La Métairie, at Nyon near Geneva. From here he wrote to David Thomson, 'No need to pity me – I've always liked hospitals and this is the best I've been in. Medical and nursing staff excellent.' While here he was at last dried out and then filled with an allergy to alcohol. He dreamed he was in a holiday home for elderly Boy Scouts and refused to have gossamer wings sewn on and he also claimed to have written twenty thousand words a week in his journal. His time in the clinic was enlivened by visits from John Berger, and he told David Thomson that he yearned to meet another neighbour, Charlie Chaplin – 'Can't you do anything? Be so nice.' On 4 December, he wrote from the clinic to Stephen Spender saying that he was 'disintoxicated and metabolized' but could not believe he would not need alcohol when he came out.

On 13 December he was discharged and wrote that day to Thomson from the Hôtel Vendôme in Paris stating that he had finished the cure and had to take pills to stay off the drink for a year. On Boxing Day he wrote again from Wimereux saying he had 'jumped straight from hospital into flu, which with 30 pills a day to keep drink away, doesn't make life rosy'. The next phase of Philip's life certainly had thorny patches and his life with Panna on the upper floors of Clair de Lune was rocky. During these years Philip spent a great deal of time drinking and despairing. Photographs showed him looking prosperous and chubby and quite a different character to the dancing skeleton of the war years, but inside he seems to have felt a lot of the old turmoil. Two months after leaving the Swiss clinic, he was back on the bottle after a trip to London and full of confusion about Panna. At some point he says: 'It all seems to be breaking into a madhouse' and at other times he reports, 'A little calm has arrived.' He protests that he can't work and is getting iller and iller. 'Old age is nearly arrived,' he states on 27 July 1970 and adds, 'Death a certainty, may come *any time*.' He calls Panna a 'beast' and a 'pythoness' but says he can't stop loving her.

In spite of these worries and his poor health, Philip and Panna went off with Maxim for a holiday in October 1970 in Eastern Europe, travelling via Verona, Trieste and Vienna into Hungary. In Budapest they stayed in the Hilton or Intercontinental Hotel where two-year-old Maxim wandered onto the bandstand and was shooed away by the orchestra. Outside in the street, Philip was dismayed by the dirtiness, ran a disapproving finger along a dusty window-ledge and after less than a day in the city insisted that they leave. Another drama awaited them in Yugoslavia where they got lost in the mountains and ended up in a private hunting lodge, full of sportsmen with guns. Wherever they went, Philip sent a trail of attractive, expensive picture postcards to David Thomson on which he scribbled brief messages about the state of his liver and the superficiality or otherwise of the latest bottle of wine he had drunk.

One of the root causes of Philip's discontent was his lack of work. From time to time he made feeble approaches to the BBC. On 9 July 1970 he had sent a letter beginning 'Dear Sirs' and explaining, 'I am not in touch with re-organized radio so send the following to the BBC generally' and the following February he sent several pieces to the radio producer George MacBeth accompanied by a note saying, 'I nearly presume you won't like these', to which MacBeth did indeed respond with 'disappointing news'. Another letter to the Corporation simply gave his address as 'France' and it soon became obvious that the whole BBC features department as he had known it no longer existed.

Sometimes in pursuit of work and sometimes only to get away from 'terrible things' at Wimereux, Philip went on other trips and behaved recklessly. On 16 September 1971 he was alone in Switzerland and, perhaps after seeing John Berger, took a taxi from Lausanne to Geneva, running up a bill of 112 Swiss francs. Unable to pay, he was obliged to seek help from the British Consul, who contacted the Society of Authors in London on his behalf. Hearing that Philip had then left on an early flight to Heathrow, George Astley at the society commented, 'This man is a rogue.' On trips to London, he stayed in hotels like the Glendower at South Kensington and in the houses of his friends. Annie Mygind now had a small house in Stewart's Grove, Chelsea, and Philip stayed there on his own during the early summer of 1971, breaking the plastic attachment to a curtain rail and cooking lunch for his eighteen-year-old son Jon Wing O'Connor, whom he later described in a letter to Annie as a 'nice child'.

Back in France in June 1972, Panna made another attempt to wean Philip away from the bottle by getting Denis Lowson and his new wife Marja to take him off her hands for a while. Apprehensive about this plan, the Lowsons drove Philip through Brittany and tried to prevent him having a drink. They survived Chartres without alcohol but by the time they had reached St Malo, Philip was getting 'increasingly crotchety and difficult' and Denis realized they were 'denying him his pleasures'. The Lowsons parted amicably from Philip and returned to England leaving him to drive back to Wimereux alone. At the end of the month he had a bad car crash, telling David Thomson, 'Nobody hurt – but if the fine isn't paid I go to prison.' A few weeks later he was banned from driving for three years.

Philip remained restless and discontented. On 30 July he asked Annie Mygind how much it cost to live in London in 'a cheap but not horrible room' explaining, 'I doubt if I can continue to live here much longer.' He then typed underneath this handwritten scrawl, 'This is quite untrue.' He was back in London on 24 August staying at the Glendower Hotel, and on 27 September he wrote to the Society of Authors from Wimereux stating that he needed £50 to return to England, explaining, 'The arrangement by which I have been living in France has come to an end' and adding, 'I am also in very bad health.' At the end of October he was in London again, partly thanks to Annie Mygind who had given him some money to do a series of interviews which might lead to writing a new book about the class system. During October and November he stayed in a hotel in Onslow Gardens and in Annie's house in Stewart's Grove and could be seen around the streets of London with a cheap tape-recorder slung over his shoulder.

Into this machine, he delivered a long, jerky, highly theatrical and upbeat monologue about his past, present and future. 'When you talk to yourself you become very spooky-spooky,' he said, revving himself up. 'You become *a little bit mad*.' On the tape he practises his voices, his accents, his giggles and cackles. He puts on the genteel voice with which he would talk to the police when he was tramping but admits, 'My upper-class voice was always a bit shaky.' He also puts on the childish voice in which he spoke to his guardian nearly half a century earlier in their hut. He says that he has no real voice, only the silent one he uses when he is writing. He also expresses enraged despair about his private life and 'this wandering from one to the other'. He growls and spits into the machine that he is 'sick of the bloody complications' and wants 'a clear straight road'. He longs to have enough security to enable him not to drink excessively. He expresses fear and dread of returning to Wimereux. He says he finds his daily discourse with Panna 'horrifyingly remote' and declares: 'It is more healthy to live alone than to live alone with someone else.' He asks himself, 'Do I think I am a crook?' and 'Do I want to live alone?' and 'What am I going to do?'

PART FOUR

– 16 –

Show Business

Dear Andy Barrow, I am sorry to tell you that the
Bull's Head are not pleased with your work & have
asked me to replace you for the rest of the week.
Will you kindly then finish there on the Wednesday
night . . . Sonny Gross for Harry Gunn Asscs Ltd.

SONNY GROSS TO ANDREW BARROW, 26 January 1965

I was born on 5 November 1945 far away from Fitzrovia on the
outskirts of the North Country town of Lancaster. The house, where
my father was also born, is still there today but its garden has been
chopped into two or three: other people's homes now stand where
our tennis court was and in the paddock where our pony lived. The
original house built in about 1900, and still called High Bank, bears
comparison to innumerable villas that sprang up at the same time in
the suburbs of London. One of its features is a large pebbledashed
porch, above which there is a sort of balcony, and from a back
bedroom it may still be possible to see the mudflats of Morecambe
Bay.

I have happy memories of High Bank, which actually belonged to
my grandmother: my parents were only living there thanks to the
upheaval of the Second World War. My father was away most of
the time working for the Board of Trade in London and leaving the
task of bringing up five sons – I am the fourth – in the capable hands
of our mother. My childhood was happy and secure – I think I used
the same words to describe Panna Grady's upbringing – and the
undercurrents of competition between the five brothers never got

seriously out of hand. Indeed, we may have been specially bonded together by my father's peculiar tyrannies and the apparent distance between him and my mother.

I became more aware of this gulf and the odd divisions within my father's character as I grew older and we moved to the South of England. Here my mother ran the house and garden. My father came home at weekends, clambering out of his dapper city suits into uncomfortable tweeds and corduroys, kept in mothballs when he wasn't wearing them. Dressed in these overweight garments he attempted to play the country squire but his conversation remained focused on London life and in particular, or so it often seemed, its theatrical aspects. The life my father led during the week was that of a respectable bachelor but in the evenings he liked nothing better than to drop in at the Metropolitan Music Hall on Edgware Road.

In my father's old engagement diaries, I find that the word 'Met' features often, usually accompanied by the name of an artiste he had particularly enjoyed. At the Metropolitan there was also a bar where patrons could meet the artistes and it was here he had bought Max Miller a drink and got into conversation with a variety artiste called Joan Rhodes. In the mid-1950s, Joan Rhodes was more of a supporting act than a star but she was also a famous woman. Her feats of strength on stage – she bent ten-inch nails and tore up telephone directories – were much talked and joked about and her blonde good looks fascinated men and women. In May 1955 a portrait of her by Dame Laura Knight was shown at the Royal Academy beside Annigoni's portrait of the Queen. My father had attended the opening of this show on 4 May and that night and again later in the week had gone to see Joan Rhodes performing at the Metropolitan Music Hall. On one of these occasions he had been introduced to her at the bar and made the bold and unusual suggestion that he should take her to the Hampstead Golf Club and see if her strength could be applied to his favourite sport. She accepted his invitation and two such outings took place, the details of which elude me. The friendship soon petered out gracefully but my father continued to talk admiringly of Joan Rhodes for many years.

My father's interest in theatrical matters infiltrated the whole family and gave him an angle on life which was at variance with his other interests and concerns. At odd moments he would tap-dance on the kitchen floor. Once he had slipped on something while he was doing this and couldn't help smiling when he found it was a banana skin. Another time he had faltered while showing off in this way and declared, 'Oh, my God, I nearly went down on my back then!'

How much effect my father's showbiz affectations have had on my own life is hard to say. My teenage years were relatively happy but at boarding school I had been marked down as an eccentric and played up to this image. I did not think I *was* mad but I felt sure that with my pale face and spectacles and unruly hair I *looked* mad – and I had already begun to make wild gestures of independence. On 1 September 1960 at the age of fourteen I had walked the whole way from Lancaster to the village of Dacre in Cumberland, where my other grandmother lived, covering a distance of fifty-seven miles in about twenty hours. I was also attracted to eccentric, solitary people. In my grandmother's village and within view of her garden there was an old farmhouse known as Dacre Castle. When I was fifteen, this imposing building, a one-time border fort, had been rented by a man named Frere, a former herald, an unhappy bachelor with a haughty manner, who lived beyond his means and wore belted tweeds. For months I was infatuated by this fish out of water, who came from a very different world to the one I knew, and my younger brother Jonathan and I even compiled a scrapbook about him which I still possess. Had Philip O'Connor or Quentin Crisp lived alone in the castle – I cannot resist this digression – I would have gone even madder with delight, partly on account of the shock effect their presence would have had on the neighbours and my own family, whom I then saw as invincibly stuffy. Thanks to his compartmentalized nature, my father was able to look upon theatrical types like Joan Rhodes with real regard but had only sneering contempt for upper-class misfits like James Frere, whose circle – I digress again – would later turn out to have included Panna Grady's friend John Michell.

What my father made of my own half-crazy decision to attempt a career on the stage is also hard to say. Some people may suspect that I was a junior member of a large family trying to draw attention to himself or wonder if this bid wasn't an attempt to capitalize on the inherent eccentricity I mentioned earlier. At any rate my father was initially encouraging, and when in January 1965 at the age of nineteen I went back to Lancashire seeking work as a stand-up comic, he had thoroughly entered into the spirit of the thing. 'Jolly good luck at the Bull's Head Hotel next week,' he had written to me after I had obtained my first professional booking in a Manchester pub. 'By the way, artistes do not drink with the customers until after their last act. I hope your digs are fixed up.' A few weeks later – my week at the Bull's Head had not been a success – he had written, 'We hear you are still in Town and will not be on the Coast for the present.'

Those who wish to know more about my eccentric father can read my novel *The Tap Dancer* where he appears under the thinnest possible disguise. Here I must continue the story of my own odd life. For the next thirteen months I moved around the Midlands and North of England seeking work as a comedian. I often got 'paid off' – in other words, given half my agreed fee and told not to return – and even when my act had gone reasonably well there were people who warned me I had 'a lot of deaths to die'. Twice I spent the night on a railway station and I survived one weekend living off bread and chocolate. Meanwhile, I worked with other comedians, singers, ventriloquists, male and female strippers and innumerable drag acts: such was my ignorance of life in general and sexual matters in particular that I sometimes thought these were real women. One evening I found myself on the same bill as a comedian named Reg Grey. He was billed as 'an outstanding attraction' and I was delighted to see him pulverizing the audience, taking tumultuous applause and then joining my table and hurling a cigarette at me in a careless gesture of triumph. For a while Reg took me under his wing – I got on better with him than I had with most of my school contemporaries – and sometimes he gave me lifts in his silencer-broken Austin A40. As we drove between Derby and Stoke-on-Trent he pointed out that we were passing through 'the cradle of so-called traditional comedy'.

By the spring of 1966 my theatrical fever had to some extent abated. The crazy confidence and egotism of youth had dwindled and I had begun to come to my senses though no alternative life or career suggested itself to me. I spent most of that summer in London, living in a glass-roofed studio which belonged to one of my older brothers in Tite Street, Chelsea. During the day and night-time I hung around Soho, which had exercised an eerie fascination over me since my early teenage years. During exeats from boarding school, my brother Jonathan and I had hurried to the area behind the bright lights. My interest in this part of the West End had been revved up by an old book called *London Nights*, bought by my father in a second-hand shop, which told of café and theatre bars, some of which stayed open round the clock. These seemed to have gone, but I soon ran into surviving Soho characters, among them an eccentric antique dealer or junk merchant called Mendelson, who now ran a shop in Berwick Street and barked as you entered his crowded emporium, 'Yes, sir, what can I sell you?' I got jobs in the area – I worked for a while at Selfridges – and, like many other young men, aimlessly wandered around the streets. It was in these circumstances that I met Reg Grey again.

My comedian friend was then in his late thirties and still a big hit in the northern clubs but indignant about his inability to break through into television, which he blamed on the conservatism of the 'showbiz moguls' and the phoney London 'in-set'. Though he disliked London, he felt obliged to visit the capital in search of more sophisticated work, calling upon theatrical agents and producers and playing tape-recordings of his act. My own career having ignominiously fizzled out, I briefly took up my friend's cause and on 26 May 1966 had even played one of his tapes to a BBC producer called Douglas Cleverdon, who treated me with immense courtesy and listened patiently to a cracklingly inadequate recording of Reg Grey's act, after which he politely enquired, 'Does he use a mike?'

During West End excursions with Reg, he would take me to the haunts of his past. One of these was a café in Monmouth Street, off the upper part of Shaftesbury Avenue, which went by the exaggeratedly cosy name of As You Like It. At first glance there was nothing unusual about this place. Then you noticed the posters of famous film actresses on the walls and the fact that several of the male customers were wearing make-up. Everyone seemed delighted when Reg arrived. 'They think I'm God,' he said and there were gasps and then bursts of laughter as he mocked and reproved the regular customers. 'Smile at them and they smile back,' Reg explained. 'They can't afford to offend you.'

In due course Reg went north again, where he eventually changed his name, appeared quite often on television and even made a record which went to number thirteen in the hit parade. Without his exuberant presence to counterbalance the exhilarating oddness of the As You Like It, I did not at first feel like going there on my own but after a while I had taken the plunge and found my feet, learning the names or nicknames of the regular customers and having my presence acknowledged by the lively young proprietor Barrie Stacey. During the rest of 1966 I went there a great deal – and so did my brother Jonathan. While I listened to their conversations, my brother sketched the other customers on a paper napkin, sometimes murmuring, 'Keep still, you bastard.'

The As You Like It stayed open very late at night, but after a certain hour would-be customers had to ring the doorbell to get in. Almost everyone knew each other and almost everyone was in show business or, as the proprietor explained, 'on the fringes of the show-business world: backstage, front of house, resting'. The fact that their lives were even more precarious than my own was a comfort to me. A few of them were witty – I remember an out-of-work comedian entering the café one hot afternoon and remarking, 'Is there any need to wear mink underwear in this weather?' – several of them were bookish, a great deal better read than myself, and many of them knew a great deal about films and the lighter side of contemporary theatre. Several worked as dressers in West End theatres and took their intimate relationship with the stars fascinatingly for granted, and when occasionally famous figures like Jane Asher and Long John Baldry appeared in the café they caused very little stir by their presence.

What the other customers made of me is another matter. A few of them were aware of my bid to go on the stage and the fact that I now nurtured hopes of becoming a Man of Letters. One afternoon an old lady who sold antiquarian books and usually sat by the door surprised me by asking in a loud, sharp voice, 'Getting the proofs next week?'

and one busy lunchtime the café's owner Barrie Stacey turned on me and said, 'You're *mad*. As mad as a hatter.' This struck a painful chord but I answered back, 'What kind of madness? These things are classifiable you know', to which he thoughtfully responded, 'I don't know. *That's* interesting.' A few minutes later he had passed my table, grinned at me and added, 'There's money in madness.'

The café was certainly a haven for some very unusual individuals, people off the rails or addicted to something or other, eye-catching figures in the no man's land between the sexes. One such figure, who was a dresser at the Royal Opera House, wore a woman's hairpiece on his head and a bewitched expression on his face, and drew the comment from the out-of-work comedian who frequented the place, 'Seven more operations and he'll be a man.' Such people fascinated me and I was soon inspired to ask Barrie Stacey who was the most extraordinary of all his customers. Without hesitation, he mentioned someone called Quentin Crisp. This strange and rather ridiculous name was utterly unfamiliar to me but carried an odd aura and seemed loaded with possibilities.

– 17 –

Beaufort Street

Mr Crisp is not only a remarkable character – candid,
acute, and brave enough to face the uttermost impli-
cations of his scepticism – he is also a brilliantly
entertaining talker who is conducting a continual
exasperated dialogue with the God he has rejected, in
revenge no doubt for his own rejection by an unfeeling
world. It is this reluctantly theological basis to his talk
which gives it its exceptional pungency: he is one of
those atheists who are in love with the God they think
they hate.

MAURICE WIGGIN, *Sunday Times*, 12 July 1970

I first saw Quentin Crisp on the afternoon of Monday 16 January
1967. By now, I had a job in an advertising agency down the road
from the As You Like It and often called there after work. On that
particular day, Quentin was sitting towards the back of the café, at a
table with two or three people around him. He was wearing silver
sandals with high heels and a blue duffel-coat with brass buttons,
purely decorative, round the hood. His pale blue hair was piled up
into those bouffant waves and curls that hundreds of feature-writers
would soon struggle to describe.

On this first encounter, his voice, which the *New York Times* would
later describe as 'pitched desperately in the quicksands between confidence and despair', may have had even more impact than his
demeanour. He was talking about a Christmas card he had received
which the donor had tampered with, so that Father Christmas was

'*blind* with mascara' and '*dumb* with lipstick'. I soon learnt that these overemphasized phrases were a long-established part of Quentin Crisp's repertoire. On this first occasion, I did not speak to him, but I heard most of what was going on. I think Quentin may have asked for some orange juice 'not hot but not cold' which I would learn was a variant on his usual 'pale grey coffee', and at one moment the out-of-work comedian stamped his foot and screamed out in response to some witticism, 'Isn't it a beautiful classic line?' That week Quentin was working at Maidstone College of Art, and there was a reference to getting up every morning at six and 'sandwiches cut at dawn'. When he eventually left the café, he said, 'See you on a different day' and finally 'Be kind and true.' And as he passed the window his head was held high and he was smiling.

During the spring of 1967, I saw and spoke to Quentin Crisp often in the café and became more acquainted with the complications of his character and appearance. His face was both masculine and feminine, noble and ignoble, imperious and depraved. His hairstyle was like a charlady's or a duchess's. There was something utterly archaic about him yet he had the effect of a tonic. He described himself as a self-confessed, self-evident homosexual, yet was not remotely limp or insinuating and spoke without a hint of a lisp. He was also very good at hamming it up. A lot of what he said seemed to be in inverted commas and whenever possible he addressed the café as a whole. 'I've always wanted to have a nervous breakdown,' he intoned during one of those early encounters. 'I've always wanted to lie on the floor and say "Take me home".' Although he was only fifty-eight, he already saw himself as 'an eccentric old gentleman' and spoke of his own death with exaggerated relish: 'When it all ends, I'll get into my coffin and I'll sleep.' His pronouncements at the As You Like It were accompanied by old-fashioned catch-phrases and stock responses. 'That's nice,' he might say – and 'This is true' and 'I'll say' and occasionally, 'That's very gay!' He sometimes spoke of 'the sweet bye and bye' and when he finally took his leave would always declare, 'Be kind and true!' One of his favourite words was 'cosy' and he often referred to things that happened 'many long dark years ago'.

Like others in the café, he spoke often about Hollywood films of long ago. One afternoon he mentioned a film called *Metropolis*, which he said had 'no reference to real life' and in which tea is drunk 'as if it were poison'. Another day he talked about Jane Russell – 'her hair like boiled snow' – and slipped into an impersonation of some star of similar vintage – 'I guess you multiplied someplace where you should have divided' – to the delight of those around him. He also talked about 'Mr Hitchcock's downfall' and described his recent offering *The Birds* as 'a really reckless film'. I listened to this film stuff with growing interest and the contrast between these self-confident opinions and the run-down surroundings in which they were voiced provided a new kind of frisson.

The As You Like It, Quentin explained, was 'the last of the layabout cafés' and the latest in a long line of such places he had known. He reeled off their evocative old-fashioned names, and also mentioned a restaurant called the Star in Old Compton Street, which I would discover had once been a haunt of Rimbaud and Verlaine. The As You Like It had won its inclusion in this grand tradition because it was the only café left in the West End where, Quentin said, you could linger over a cup of tea the whole afternoon.

The other customers there treated Quentin with respect, screeched at his witticisms, thumped their feet on the cracked linoleum floor and praised him for his 'very high critical faculty'. When he was not present, their comments were more qualified and even Barrie Stacey confessed that his first reactions to Quentin were negative. 'I hated him on sight,' he said and, though now admiring him greatly, added, 'You've got to be careful with him or he'll scare away normal trade' – and it was perhaps in deference to this point of view that Quentin did not take his customary window seat. One of the part-time waiters had also responded '*Must he?*' when he first encountered Quentin, and one of the young men who laughed loudest at Quentin's jokes said afterwards, '*He's had it.*' Another admiring fellow customer argued, 'Quentin's got to stick to the poofy areas of London. He can't go down the East End of an evening.' Yet the interest in him was great and his movements were charted and his visits proclaimed. 'Quentin Crisp was here all yesterday afternoon. You missed him,' said Barrie Stacey, making me feel I had missed a free trip to the theatre. 'The

Crisp was in, holding court,' I was told another day. 'He's just come from art school. He was dressed in silver lamé.' Sometimes I asked, 'D'you think Quentin might be in later?' and got the reply, 'He might be in, yes.' 'Is he ever in late at night?' I persisted. 'No, he goes to bed at nine.' I was impressed to learn that Quentin Crisp lived in Chelsea but Barrie Stacey quickly qualified this by saying, 'Beaufort Street is rather tat.' Others informed me that Quentin Crisp planned, sooner or later, to commit suicide.

In the advertising firm down the road, where I worked as a trainee copywriter, I was excited to find that some of my colleagues also knew about Quentin Crisp. One of the designers remembered painting him in art school. 'He used to stand holding a chair above his head with one hand for a whole morning.' One of the art directors had worked with him at Harraps fifteen years earlier. 'He wore lipstick, make-up, nail varnish, but he could draw – I'll say that for him.' Then a copywriter named May Turner chipped in, 'He was the man who said the dust doesn't get any worse after ten years. His catch-phrase was "Be kind and true".' When I reported the last contribution back to Quentin, he mused for a while and then said darkly, 'Miss Turner . . . owes me three pounds.' In the office the following day May Turner said, 'I couldn't enjoy being a fan of Quentin's. I was simply after the price of a meal. I was thinking on the Circle Line this morning, I hope I wasn't too hard on him yesterday.'

In the café, and doubtless across London, Quentin's natural grandeur was now reinforced by the news that he had a book coming out the following winter, his autobiography. The details he sketched in added to the glamour of the enterprise and lent prestige to the café itself. He was under contract to Jonathan Cape and had been paid £250. The firm's managing director Mr Maschler was 'a man of astonishing glamour' and his editor Mrs Miller 'a sweetie'. According to Barrie Stacey, the book was about Soho – 'That's all he knows about' – but according to Quentin the book was about sex. He had already taken the precaution of warning his relations about it and told us with some glee that his niece had responded, 'We never expected it to be cosy.' With what I would discover was typical false self-effacement, Quentin made out that he really had nothing to say. 'I have been nowhere. I have lived in the same room for twenty-seven years and I have never met anyone famous.'

In May that year Quentin acquired further lustre when he regaled those present in the café with the information: 'I have been making a movie.' He explained that a certain Mr O'Connor who had once interviewed him on the radio had now asked him to take part in a film, and that the then Minister of the Arts, Jennie Lee, 'scatters money around like confetti for people to make experimental movies'. The film was based on one of Mr O'Connor's poems and was currently being shot on the platform of a one-line railway station in Surrey. Mr O'Connor, Quentin explained, had written a book about 'the mechanisms of the outsider' called *Memoirs of a Public Beggary*. I noted the title down wrong but I did not forget the name of Philip O'Connor which, like that of Quentin Crisp, seemed full of possibilities. My own aspirations to be a writer were growing and the uncharted seas I was embarking on needed beacons of light and hope.

Part of the early appeal of Quentin Crisp for me was that he was a writer. My one-time hero Frere had also written a book but this had been a slapdash affair called *The British Monarchy at Home*, cheaply produced by a minor publishing house and containing very little auto-biographical detail. Quentin's book was apparently *all* about himself and was soon to be published by the famous firm of Jonathan Cape with the much-talked-about Tom Maschler at its helm. I had an exaggerated sense of the philistinism of my background, where artistic activity had a dubious reputation. One of my older brothers was a painter, but his work then struck me as very conventional. The fact that my mother's cousin had been the calligrapher Edward Johnston, responsible for the lettering on the London Underground system, did not carry the weight it should and the career of my great-uncle Douglas Hoare, who had been the joint author of several plays produced in the West End, seemed to have only caused sniggers among his relations. His play *Lord Richard in the Pantry*, starring the comedian Cyril Maude, had opened at the Criterion Theatre on 11 November 1919 and run for 576 performances – but Uncle Douglas had later died in poverty. There was a lot of ground to be made up and Quentin Crisp,

highly articulate and authoritative in spite of his faded façade, pointed
the way ahead.

The first views Quentin advanced on literature were characteristically extravagant and melancholy. He praised a book by someone
called Ethel Waters which began with the line, 'I never was a child',
and he was highly critical of most modern fiction, especially those
'absolutely hopeless, fatuous, sententious novels about the raising of
an eyebrow'. As I got to know him better, I became aware that he
inhabited a specialized bohemian and artistic world of slightly antique
cosiness. He talked about books that had been famous in the past,
such as *Scamp* by Roland Camberton, about the works of Mervyn
Peake and about the artist Christopher Ironside, with whom he occasionally went to supper in Kensington and who was apparently in the
habit of 'falling about laughing'. I also soon learnt about Quentin's
own earlier books, the titles of which only reinforced the archaic aura
of his invented name. I purchased a copy of *Lettering for Brush and
Pen*, which was still in print after thirty-one years, and I summoned
up *Colour in Display* at the British Museum and marvelled over its
five colour plates. Looking back, I realize that Quentin Crisp's artistic
and professional life and the worlds inhabited by my own less philistine antecedents may have overlapped. He must have been well aware
of Edward Johnston's role in the history of lettering and he may
conceivably have been taken by his mother to see one of Douglas
Hoare's comedies. And though he and my father were notably unalike,
they were almost exactly the same age, my father only eighteen months
older than Quentin, both born in the reign of Edward VII and carrying
with them some of the attitudes and disciplines of that era. The fact
that Quentin was, like me, the son of a qualified solicitor was another
as yet undiscovered link between us.

During those first few months of our acquaintanceship, I saw
Quentin only in the café and never by prior arrangement. On many
occasions Barrie Stacey triumphantly informed me that I had just
missed Quentin, that he had been there all afternoon or every day
earlier that week. I remember that one sunny day he wore a kind of
racing-driver's sunshield and on another day I presented him with a
large box of Black Magic chocolates I had been given by the advertising

firm – an odd gesture on my part perhaps partly inspired by Quentin's feminine aura. For a while I shrank from a close encounter. Once I left the café soon after him and found myself walking behind his great bulbous hair-do as he proceeded towards Shaftesbury Avenue, but did not feel comfortable about accosting him in the street. A few minutes later, there was a heavy downfall of rain and I wondered how he would have coped with this act of nature.

My interest in Quentin Crisp was shared to some extent by my younger brother Jonathan, who still attended the café and sometimes took girlfriends there. We were both excited to find that Quentin's name and address were listed in the London telephone directory. The existence of this telephone number and his use of the initial Q rather than his full first name lent him a temporary ordinariness as well as emphasizing that he was quietly but firmly established as a Londoner. Neither I nor most of the others who came to the As You Like It were listed in any telephone directory. Soon afterwards, my brother and I visited Beaufort Street and agreed that it was 'rather tat', but noted the longish flight of steps to Quentin's front door and the generous proportions of the windows. On a second visit we climbed these steps and found the handwritten instructions 'Crisp Two Rings' beside the doorbell. We had then peeped through the letterbox and seen a neat pile of letters on a small hall table. We also noted the presence of the stately Forum Cinema at the top of the street. Driving past the house a few nights later we saw the curtains being drawn on an upper floor. The thought of this espionage embarrasses me more today than it did in 1967 and anyway I then shared the experience with my brother. Looking back, I recognize that my early excitement about Quentin Crisp was accompanied by a certain amount of sniggering and bemused amusement.

Shortly after 'casing the joint' in this way, I telephoned Quentin and heard for the first time the long-drawn-out '*Ohhh-yes?*' with which he responded to all callers. On learning my name, he said with equal emphasis, 'Tell me *everything*!' and speedily agreed that my brother and I should visit him that afternoon. As we drove to Beaufort Street a few hours later, my brother suggested that Quentin Crisp would now be 'frantically getting tea ready'. This was a joke:

we both knew that there was nothing 'frantic' about our host and 'tea' was hardly something he would need to get 'ready', yet the remark reflects the slightly patronizing and quizzical way in which we both viewed him.

The first-floor room which he showed us into that day in June 1967 was not yet famous, but it lived up to my expectations. I noted the bed, covered in dark and heavy material, the gas-fire, the paraffin heater, the telephone, two chests of drawers, the television, the old-fashioned artist's drawing-desk that Edward Johnston might have worked at, and a suitcase on top of a clothes cupboard painted with the name 'Crisp' and the address 129 Beaufort Street. Dust and grime may have clung to every surface but the overall effect was neither unpleasant nor forbidding. Two large windows onto the leafy street provided ample light and there was also an Angle-poise lamp over the desk. The room was entirely devoid of pretension or decorative additions. No pictures hung from the picture rail and there was no sign of any book. The only volumes I could see were the neat stacks of old telephone directories at either end of the mantelpiece. Between them was a scatter of documents, old invitations and old Christmas cards, some of them possibly dating back many years.

Quentin was half-dressed and bare-legged in an old dressing-gown but entirely at ease in this attire, completely welcoming and completely in control of the situation. I would later become familiar with his words of welcome: 'Rush in, sit down, flop about on the bed' and his offer of 'pale grey coffee' or 'old toast'. Quentin took the chair or bucket seat with his back to the window and talked that day about *The Well of Loneliness* and writers 'who wrote out their fundamental dream' and then about the American novelist Edmund Wilson, whom he praised for having 'no style at all'. After an hour or so we left and Quentin saw us out with his words: 'Call again. *Incessantly.*'

We called again often – though my brother's visits to Beaufort Street would eventually tail off: when a few months later I proposed a visit to Quentin he said ungallantly, 'I was bored stiff last time we went there.' Perhaps I had more to learn from these encounters, which added ballast to my limited knowledge of life. My brother was already making his way in the world and was less in need of Quentin's guidance, less in awe of his knowledge and experience. I was now twenty-one, Quentin was fifty-eight and seemed to me to have immense authority and self-confidence as he viewed the world from this bed-sitter to crown all bed-sitters.

Quentin was as polite in his room as he was in the café. When I asked if I could smoke, he responded: 'You *eat* as many cigarettes as you like. I will give you an ashtray. Would you like a cup of pale grey . . .?' His repertoire had become cosily familiar. Cosiness was indeed part of his appeal. I grew accustomed to his amazingly dirty dressing-gown, the dirty white shirts with their flapping collars, the glimpse of short grey underwear and the bare legs ending in what he would describe as 'the misshapen plinths' of his bare feet. I grew accustomed to the incongruously grand mug adorned with a sprawling male nude from which only he drank. I also grew accustomed to the taste of powdered coffee, often accompanied by slightly rancid milk, which during the summer months he kept on a windowsill. Never at any time did this calculated seediness and aura of world-weariness rob Quentin of his effervescence, and in spite of the ghastliness of the clothing he wore at home and his 'avalanching' cheeks, his hair always seemed buoyantly well combed. When occasionally we watched television together, he sat like a cat, loving every moment, his eyes half closed and contentment spread over his face. Again and again I felt I was in a glowing, confident, cultured presence, but when he spoke his words were sometimes surprisingly down to earth and out of character. 'This woman is a terrible bore,' he confided when a particular pop-star appeared on the television screen. I later decided that his self-assurance derived directly from his solitariness, his apparent lack of dependence on other people and perhaps from his suffering. Whatever its origins, his confidence came with an aura of greatness, true haughtiness, a heroic persona which was in many ways enchanting and, in spite of all the oddness, in no way ridiculous. His movements were also beautifully co-ordinated, like a furry animal's, though never in the least furtive. There was something hamster-like about him as he moved snugly about his cage of a room and put himself pleasingly at the disposal of his visitor.

Quentin's conversational style at home was more intimate and more attentive than the hectoring tones he tended to employ in the café. His utterings were a lively mixture of irony, self-mockery, poetic licence and down-to-earthness. He was, as he would say on innumerable occasions in the future, 'horribly articulate'. Almost everything he said had been said before. Long before the age of fifty-eight, he had worked everything out. As I noted earlier, he was particularly at ease when speaking in inverted commas and continually used the catch-phrases and clichés of other people to make his point. From time to time, he adopted mock indignation – 'Rubbish! I'm a genius!' – or other people's oversimplifications – 'It's all right. You'll get by' – to explain some complex aspect of self-image and survival. Even when he spoke of himself – 'I've got things taped. I'm OK for the moment' – or other people's attitudes towards him – 'Oh for heaven's sake, he's a mass of affectation' – he lapsed into a hackneyed style which might have come out of an old film. And he used equally familiar phrases – 'Was he speaking to me? Oh! He's gone now!' and 'Who the hell is she – or is she nobody?' – to dissect the minor dramas of everyday life. None of these are expressions which Quentin would have used first hand, but in their second-hand use they played an integral part in any conversation or discussion in which he was involved. He was a solitary performer who observed, processed, regurgitated and turned to his own elevated use the banal words of others. The use of such phrases injected extra bounce and comedy into his discourse and was reinforced by physical gestures of great dexterity. Talking of his work in the art schools, he said, 'There's nothing worse than a model who . . .' and then pretended to slump into sleep.

I soon discovered that he was at his most alert imitating or poking fun at himself. Mentioning the Chinese philosopher Lin Yutang, he bowed his head on his folded arms in a mocking posture but caught my eye as he did so as if to point out how ludicrously he himself was behaving. His vocabulary was often chosen to blur as well as emphasize his meaning and perhaps primarily to entertain. A simple word like 'squeak' was a particular favourite but lethal in the use he made of it: 'If a plane I was in suddenly dived towards the earth I would cry and pray and *squeak*.' His vision of himself and his own frailty was charming as well as comic and often wide of the mark. 'How is dreary old Quentin?' he once jokily suggested people might be asking. Inaccuracy, oversimplification and reversals of the truth were often the basis of his distinctly slapstick wit. His comment on the domestic life of his editor Jane Miller – 'She's got a husband to feed and three children to hit' – beautifully illustrates this point and he himself neatly summarized the technique when he prefaced one of his remarks by saying, 'I'll have to make this absurd to get my meaning across.' And even when responding to something I had said, he would fall back onto politenesses polished with use, such as 'Well, well. How amazing!', which made it quite clear that he wasn't in the least amazed.

Quentin's desire to be 'totally revealed' allowed me to pepper him with questions, which he answered patiently. He told me a few things about his background. He described his reassuringly middle-class origins and said he had been to a minor public school in Staffordshire. He told me he had a brother-in-law who was a clergyman. He had lived in his room since 1940 and never attempted to clean it, though he did send his sheets to the laundry once a week. I asked why he didn't use the launderette and he replied, 'I don't think I would be able to understand the machines.' His hair, he said, was 'bone-dry by nature' and only had to be pressed into position. He dyed it every three weeks and then lapsing out of character described the process as 'such a fag'. At home, he liked lolling about in his dressing-gown and wearing the least restricting clothes possible. 'First of all, I like it, I find it easier. Secondly, I suffer from a skin allergy so I try not to wear any clothes which fit me tightly.' He began each morning by drinking Guinness – 'to shorten the day' – and described this beverage as 'a drug, a soporific'. He also banged on a lot about Complan, the food substitute for invalids off which he was quite happy to live for weeks on end. On top of these mundane details, he flung more fanciful claims. He stated, 'I never actually spend money', and boasted that he didn't go to restaurants because he was frightened of the waiters. 'I'm socially inept, in a grand way,' he explained, though even in these days before he had entered the limelight this was hard to believe.

During my early visits to his room, I tried to find the frame of mind behind these attitudes and behaviours. Time after time, Quentin reiterated his desire to be 'totally accountable'. He said it would worry him very much if anyone thought he was unreliable. 'I seek to be known by heart,' he explained. 'I want people to see everything in my pockets. I long to be accepted for myself on all fronts.' He had merely 'settled' for the person he was and did not seek to be cherished by anyone. He told me he felt 'cosy'. At home in Beaufort Street he did not sit around wondering, 'How can I get out of all of this?' He told me he liked spare time: 'I breathe and I blink. I am never bored, never restless. I live in a perpetual daydream. In my life, I am writing a perpetual novel.' He said he never did anything on impulse and had complete control over his primary reactions: 'If I noticed your fly-buttons were undone from north to south, I wouldn't start laughing.' On the state of his health, he was more confusing. Though still two years short of sixty, he already depicted himself as 'an eccentric old gentleman' and as 'an old man of feeble physique', yet also asserted that he had enjoyed good health almost continuously since people ceased to look after him. 'I am never ill,' he told me. 'I will live for ever.' When I asked if he had ever been to hospital, he replied, 'Never, I'm glad to say. I would really *hate* to go to hospital.'

I soon learnt that Quentin disliked or pretended to dislike nature, flowers and grass and had no desire, as he put it, lapsing into double inverted commas, 'to go for a jaunt in the country'. But nothing was ever quite as he claimed: I learnt later that he spent a week during that summer staying with his old friend Angus McBean in Suffolk and he also paid occasional visits to his sister and brother-in-law who now lived in a clergy retirement bungalow at Fleet in Hampshire. All excursions from Beaufort Street were anyway invested with drama. One day he told me, 'At about five o'clock, I shall spring like a greyhound from my trap into darkest Wimbledon.' Another day he revealed that he had been taken to a foreign restaurant – 'I ate Indian food and I wasn't frightened' – and clearly he relished every moment out of doors as much as he did indoors. Very occasionally he let slip some unadorned truth, stating for example that he disliked the people who sat outside the King's Road pub, the Chelsea Potter.

I also found that Quentin's circle extended far beyond Chelsea and Soho and into distant regions of English life. His conversation was full of the names of those he knew and his habit of never using anyone's first name reduced or elevated everyone to a sort of shabby villagey gentility. He talked about a Miss Lewthwaite, a Miss Mac Murray, Mrs Dennerhy and Miss Lumley Who Can Do No Wrong. He talked about his doctor, his dentist and his landlady Miss Vereker. He talked about going to dinner with someone he described as 'my only rich friend' and about Mr Richardson, the actor who lived downstairs with whom he sometimes met a young man called Mr Bailey. In June 1967, I learnt that this was Paul Bailey, who had just produced his first novel *At the Jerusalem* to widespread acclaim, and I was immediately inspired to take my own copy of this book to the shop where the author was working and get him to inscribe it. Quentin talked a lot about his friends and their goings-on, with frankness and occasional bemusement. He told me that someone he knew was 'a fully paid-up member of the Higher Faith' and that someone else was a 'minimum-risk person'. Another friend was 'frivolous but not light-hearted' and had 'the nerve to teach art appreciation'. He spoke of people who 'almost always have a cold' and others who 'didn't look . . . terribly well'.

I soon realized that Quentin Crisp pursued none of these friends but simply sat back and felt vaguely amused by whoever bothered to approach him. Usually he understood his friends but occasionally they behaved in ways that prompted him into saying with a hint of peevishness, 'And this I find so strange.' He conveyed these daily dramas to me vividly and sometimes told stories to his own disadvantage. One day, a woman had approached him in the street and said, 'You look to me like a sad person' and urged him, 'Cheer up love!' to which he had replied, 'I'll try!'

During our early conversations Quentin and I talked often about the other people in the café where we had met. His veneration for the As You Like It and acknowledgement of its sacred position as 'the last of the layabout cafés' did not blinker or sentimentalize his view of its incumbents. Of a young man there who claimed to look like Laurence Olivier, Quentin commented, 'A person *less* like Laurence Olivier is hard to imagine. He has a spooky, twitchy attitude towards everything.' Of the out-of-work comedian who sometimes harangued us, he said, 'He is a typical compère. Even when you meet him in real life you feel he is trying out his patter on you.' For the café's hard-working and slightly manic proprietor Barrie Stacey, he had only admiration: 'Mr Stacey loves stage gossip, stage people, stage events. He's mad about stage people. He's much madder about actors than he is about food.'

During my visits to his room, Quentin also talked at length about Soho characters he knew, or had known. He talked about the gangster Billy Hill, the jazz singer George Melly and the playwright Frank Norman whom Quentin had known before his success with *Fings Ain't Wot They Used T'Be* and who now looked 'more and more self-assured, more and more prosperous'. He talked about Joan Rhodes, whom he had known 'since the beginning of time' but whose stage performances he had never witnessed. He talked a little about the poet Paul Potts – 'He never seems pleased with anything. He always looks so worried' – and a great deal about the poet and interviewer Philip O'Connor.

It was O'Connor's outsider status, as presented and described by Quentin, that particularly appealed to me, but I was also aware that he was enough of an insider to have played a significant role in Quentin's recent life. The *Captain Busby* episode was now concluded – Crisp and O'Connor had attended the showing at the National Film Theatre – but Quentin had not forgotten that Philip O'Connor had given him the broadcast three years earlier which had led directly to him writing his book. Like the comedian in the café whom Quentin had described as a natural compère, he had the knack of making everyone sound significant. His account of the 'frisky unaccountable' man for whom a taxi would stop even if it already had a passenger was irresistible to me and was soon reinforced by a reference to O'Connor in a booklet called *Bluff Your Way in Literature* by Martin Seymour-Smith. Here I learnt that Philip O'Connor had been part of the surrealist group in the 1930s and had later emerged as 'a highly effective off-beat radio interviewer and the author of a good autobiography, which it is rather with-it to say you have read'. After digesting these claims I pressed Quentin Crisp for more details of his old chum. He told me that Mr O'Connor might turn up on your doorstep dressed as an admiral and that he might do something 'really outlandish, like committing a murder'.

At that stage, I did not seek out a copy of O'Connor's book *Memoirs of a Public Baby* though I now knew that this was its proper title, nor did I try to find out when I might catch a broadcast by this off-beat interviewer. In the summer of 1967 Philip O'Connor was – as readers of this book will know – going through a crisis of his own, and I was also preoccupied with my own ordeals in the advertising agency and elsewhere and more inclined to mope about them than seek fresh pastures. Regular doses of wit and wisdom from Quentin Crisp provided my life with some of its brighter moments.

Quentin had a great deal to say and much to teach me. 'I have views on what is glibly called Life,' he told me. Many of our conversations revolved round happiness and love. Quentin told me that happiness came from within and that he was happier than most people he knew. He considered that most people were in torment about their relationships with other people. 'I am by nature happy and relaxed,' he told me and as we approached Christmas 1967, remarked, 'Those who are happy all the time have no need for jollity.' He told me there was no such thing as long-term bad luck. He defined self-pity as 'feeling badly treated by the world' and warned me, 'Moping is a bad thing and it can lead to more moping.' If you can put your problem into words, he argued, it no longer exists. The idea of 'love' he utterly dismissed and emphasized his distaste for this idea by pronouncing the word with a mocking twang. He also mocked people who said things like 'You don't really love me' and 'Why don't you love me?' and 'When will true love come to me?' In answer to the last question, he said decisively, '*It never will!*' From time to time, he spoke vehemently about the virtues of standing alone, 'not as a last resort but as a very viable alternative'. To these cold-blooded comments, he added the thought 'If love means anything at all, it means extending your hand to the unlovable' and he confused the issue further by quoting from D. H. Lawrence to the effect that sleep should be shared. Some conundrums remained beyond his grasp: sometimes he would simply say, 'This-I-can't-explain' and on one occasion he said of life itself, 'I don't understand it in any way.'

Most of his snatches of wisdom or philosophy had been thought out long ago and even the divulging of them had become polished with use. I took my share in relatively small helpings, often interrupted him when he was speaking, made patronizing noises, or changed the subject. Yet each visit to Beaufort Street had a beneficial effect on me. When I decided to telephone or call on him, I was often in low spirits, but once in his company, sitting opposite him beside his gas-fire, I felt revitalized and re-engaged. Quentin was utterly consistent and dependable. If I called at some late hour, he might have a stern expression on his face as he opened the front door, but I don't remember him ever turning me away or behaving as if he had better things to do.

He was, of course, sometimes diverted by telephone calls while we talked. Some of these callers Quentin knew well and when they asked how he was he would tell them, 'I've gone on living in spite of everything' and when they asked if he had somebody with him, might reply, 'I have indeed. So I won't tarry for long.' Some were people he liked. Others he pretended to dislike. 'That was a certain Miss Pierce,' he said cheerfully, and then less cheerfully, 'That was a Miss Gosnell' – pronouncing this name with jokey distaste and adding, 'who has already called four times today.' Some callers sought appointments with him to which he willingly agreed. 'I'm free in the daytime,' he told one person. 'But at nightfall I go to Hammersmith. My name is on the middle bell. You ring it twice. Take no notice. See you then.' During one visit, a man telephoned and asked Quentin if he still 'entertained' to which he replied, 'Not very much now because I'm much older.' Sometimes he described his other visitors to me. One of them was a famous Chelsea battle-axe, Dr Rachel Pinney, who was apparently 'a woman who pretends to know everything about every subject'. There had also been 'a strange young man', who had 'mercifully' given up calling. One Saturday morning we were more agreeably interrupted by the sound of the milk-float outside. 'I must go and buy a lot of milk,' said Quentin Crisp. 'You sit there in amazement.'

At the end of 1967 the publication of *The Naked Civil Servant* was imminent and, for the first time, Quentin showed signs of nervousness, though in my eyes he was acquiring another level of greatness. Early in the new year, I bought an early copy of the book at Better Books in Charing Cross Road and found it elegantly produced, bound in purple cloth with silver lettering and printed on paper which I would discover later had been allocated for an autobiography by the actress Elizabeth Taylor which had never materialized. The dust-jacket featured three photographs of Quentin Crisp in different postures. On the front and back cover, one of Angus McBean's 1939 photographs was split with an untouched-up one taken in modern times by a photographer named Simon Dell. On the spine, a full-length picture portrait taken by Peter Hirst-Smith, his fellow lodger at Beaufort Street, who had also appeared in *Captain Busby*, showed Quentin looking perky and amusing. In the blurb, the publishers describe the author as 'unsparingly truthful about himself', praise his 'bravado and intelligence' and 'crusading spirit and inevitable cynicism', but make an enticing reference to 'night-long conversations' of which there is no mention whatsoever in the book. The notes on the author state that Quentin Crisp had lived in the same room in Chelsea for twenty-three years, when twenty-seven would have been more accurate, describe *The Naked Civil Servant* as his first book, when in fact it was his fourth – but accurately conclude with the information that the book 'grew out of a 1964 broadcast with Philip O'Connor'.

I opened it on the last page and when I read its final line – 'I stumble towards my grave confused and hurt and hungry' – a lump formed in my throat at the thought of Quentin's heroic and plucky life and my good fortune to have got to know such a rare and now famous individual. The book also moved many of its reviewers. Michael Holroyd would later state that the critics 'buried the book with respectability', though one or two off-notes were struck. *The Times Literary Supplement* deplored 'the arch and jaunty style' in which it was written and in *Punch*, Quentin's Chelsea neighbour B. A. Young said that the book was 'full of self-pity'. With or without these comments the book went into the bestseller list. News of its success also reached my office and I saw people carrying it in the street. In the café, Quentin Crisp's fame ruffled no one and the worldly proprietor Barrie Stacey declared, 'He wants to get another book out quickly while the public still remember. They forget so quickly.'

While all this was going on, and perhaps partly inspired by Quentin's example and partly by Paul Bailey's novel, I had been using all my spare time to write a book of my own. By the end of January 1968 I had dashed off an autobiographical novel, featuring my father, my colleagues at the advertising firm and even some of the characters at the café, though not Quentin himself. It was an extremely sloppy piece of work, but I was keen to send it off to a potential publisher as quickly as possible and without further thought sent it to Jane Miller at Jonathan Cape, mentioning the name of Quentin Crisp by way of introduction. At the end of February, the manuscript came back to me, together with a letter from Mrs Miller, saying that though my prose was 'graceful' and I had 'perceptive and original insights', it was 'not ready yet for publication'. The letter ended: 'I'm sure you will write a good book soon and I hope you will let me have a look at it.' This was a bitter blow, but I was not convinced that the book was entirely worthless. I decided I needed further advice and opinions and gave the manuscript almost immediately to Quentin Crisp.

When I telephoned him a few days later, he began chirpily, 'I've read the book' but immediately made it clear he was not over the moon about it. He spoke of the content being 'so slight', what seemed to be 'errors of style' and other faults. 'Anyway, I will go into all this when I see you.' The following Sunday, 10 March, I went to his room and he told me that since the book was 'not about climbing the Andes' it needed to be word-perfect. There were many grammatical errors, typing mistakes and areas which had left him thinking, 'I *suppose* that's what he means.' He praised the descriptions of the weather and the narrator's 'enthralment' with other people but said that most readers would want more revelation. He urged me 'to pull away that veil, to expand and describe more' and at the same time to write 'in a more leisurely way'. This was frank and valuable advice but difficult to follow through and, when I next met him in the As You Like It, I said, 'I've given it to another publisher, without alteration.' He replied, 'That is naughty', but was sympathetic about the ordeal of waiting for news and how to occupy oneself in those circumstances. 'You feel you can't do anything but wait.' For the next few months I would send the unaltered book out to every publisher and literary agent I had heard of, all of whom would return it with rejection slips or stereotyped letters of refusal unadorned by even the most qualified praise.

Meanwhile Quentin's bandwagon had begun to rumble, or lurch, forward. His book slipped off the bestseller lists but people in my office continued to talk about him. Whether they wished to meet him or not was another matter. One weekend I took an American colleague to Beaufort Street and questioned him afterwards about the visit. 'You quite respected him?' I asked. '*Naah*,' he replied. 'I've got no reason to respect him. It's not enough that he's a nonconformist.' The same man had taken an instant dislike to the As You Like It, declaring, 'I don't want to go to that coffee lounge ever again.' But in spite of these reservations, he occasionally ribbed me about my famous friend, pronouncing his name in compressed Americanized style as '*Quen'ncrisp*', which seemed to convey some recognition of Quentin's orthodox decency or what might today be described as 'blokishness'.

As the months went by, my own book got forgotten and my life in the advertising firm became more oppressive. Quentin's life, on the other hand, seemed as exciting as ever. One afternoon, I dropped in at the 'coffee lounge' and found him talking about an artist called Mr Hailstone, who had engaged him to model the figure of Sir Laurence Olivier for an oil painting. This controversial portrait, in which the actor appears in an open-necked shirt and loosely knotted tie, with one hand at his face and the other on his lap, now hangs in the bar at the Garrick Club, but might be said to have more in it of Crisp than Olivier.

Later in the year, I called at the café and found Quentin talking about a film-maker called Mr Mitchell, whom he had been to see in a rented flat in Pont Street, Knightsbridge. 'I was there for *five hours*. I couldn't get him to say a single sensible thing.' He went on to describe Mr Mitchell's approach as 'bogus' and 'fatuous' and seemed ignorant of the fact that Denis Mitchell was then a famous figure in television documentaries and unaware that he had made a film using Philip O'Connor a few years earlier. Further discussions followed at Beaufort Street and, early in October, Denis Mitchell returned with a production team. Quentin would later report that a generator had chugged away in the street and sound technicians had squeezed into the bathroom as he was filmed walking barefoot round his room, sitting in his chair, lolling on the bed and uttering familiar statements, to which Mitchell's man-to-man interjections would act as a counter-balance. The half-hour film, the first Mitchell had shot in colour, would not be broadcast for many months but in the meantime a friendship developed between Quentin and Mr and Mrs Mitchell – and between me and the Mitchells.

In the autumn of 1968, I was made redundant by the advertising firm and now had time enough to pursue my obsessions. From this new wilderness I had written to Denis Mitchell at his Pont Street flat offering my services and was rewarded with various lunches and dinners but no suggestion of an offer of employment. During the remainder of 1968 and throughout the following year I saw Denis and his wife Linda often. Mitchell was a cosy, relaxed middle-aged figure with a neat hairstyle and a paunch. He had kind eyes and made everything seem effortless, especially when he swept up one's empty glass for refilling. As soon as his film on Quentin was completed he was off on other projects which included a film about an unlikely friend of Quentin, a Commander Drage who lived in Sheffield Terrace, Kensington. Mitchell told me he was interested in good, saintly people with something to say.

Quentin Crisp fitted into this category. 'But the sadness is, he's finished himself,' said Mitchell. 'He can't get *any better or worse*.' One day the Mitchells reported that Quentin had telephoned them out of the blue. 'Obviously an SOS call,' murmured Mitchell. I vigorously disputed that Quentin would ever expose himself in this way, but Mitchell was determined to see Quentin Crisp as an ordinary mortal, even to the extent of offering him a cigarette. 'I'd rather die!' Quentin had replied.

Whenever I visited Beaufort Street I now encouraged Quentin to talk about Denis Mitchell. 'Mr Mitchell spreads the gospel of the worthwhileness of ordinary people,' he began, and went on to describe Mitchell's calculated policy of self-effacement, which he suggested stemmed partly from politeness. As so often, Quentin's descriptions incorporated words in inverted commas. 'Mr Mitchell longs for you to feel at ease – "Come in, sit down" – and be having a nice time. He wants to coax you into revealing yourself.' On another occasion he briefly stepped out of character and said with a hint of disapproval, 'They both drink a great deal.'

During this phase of my life I also spent more time at home. I now lived across the road from the Tite Street studio and wandered between the two rooms of the new flat in a rather desultory way. It was in this mood that on 19 March 1969, I happened to turn on the radio and heard part of a programme about the Simon Community, a charity for drug addicts. A heroin addict was speaking about her life to an interviewer with a timid, hesitant voice. She was talking about her complicated dealings with the Home Office. The interviewer interrupted her, 'Of course it's all like being in a funny play, isn't it, and you can't get hold of the scriptwriter?' 'Yes, it is,' she replied. 'It's rather frightening,' commented the interviewer. 'It is very frightening,' admitted the addict. 'Very frightening, yes,' repeated the interviewer. At the end of the programme I learnt that the interviewer with such a sympathetic, understanding voice and who offered such a gush of fresh air was Quentin Crisp's old friend Philip O'Connor.

I needed more heroes to illuminate my path. Quentin Crisp's world was more interesting than anyone else's I knew and had already 'produced' Denis Mitchell. I now stretched out for Philip O'Connor by telephoning the BBC and asking about his whereabouts. My first attempt to do so was thwarted by a woman who said, 'Our freelance department don't have a note of his name. I don't think he can be doing any work for us any more', but I pressed on with my enquiries and soon afterwards received a telephone call from the secretary to a radio producer called David Thomson. She told me that Philip O'Connor now lived in France. She told me to write to him at the BBC – 'if you'd like to' – and my letter would be forwarded. This seemed out of my reach and the distance between me as a member of the public and Philip O'Connor as a broadcaster too vast to negotiate. This division was emphasized when my friendship with the Mitchells began to falter – Mitchell had said somewhat tersely, 'You haven't even *begun* to grow up' – and they moved their base to a village in

Norfolk. But I continued to see Quentin and in the spring of 1970 attempted to involve him in the events which now overtook my family.

Earlier that year my younger brother Jonathan, now twenty-two years old and unlike me already making a name for himself as an artist and writer, announced his engagement to a wild and beautiful girl whom he had known for only a few months. One day he had taken his fiancée to 129 Beaufort Street and had coldly reported that Quentin Crisp had 'lost his effervescence'. In spite of this visit he had subsequently sent Quentin an embossed invitation to his wedding at a fashionable London church, scribbling on its reverse, 'Yes, Quentin, please come.' Everything was going wonderfully well when, at the height of their euphoria, only two weeks before the wedding day, in broad daylight, my brother and his fiancée were killed in a car crash.

I was completely unhinged by this event, but when I telephoned Quentin and told him about it he was stalwart, kindly though not at all sentimental, and even boldly stated, 'We never grieve for the dead.' A few weeks later I invited him to lunch at the new flat in Tite Street. I asked him to bring a loaf of sliced bread and watched from the window until I saw his bouncy silhouette appear at the top of the street with his shopping under his arm. During lunch, of fish fingers, at an octagonal table overlooking Sir Christopher Wren's Royal Hospital, I told him that, days before his death, my brother had completed an absolutely brilliant novel and that I hoped to live for ever off his talents. He mocked me for all this and even said that if *his* brother had died leaving an unpublished manuscript he would have burnt it immediately. In due course I showed Quentin my brother's macabre book and he commented: 'Your brother looked healthy, happy, natural. He could have played head prefect at Eton. They all adored him at the As You Like It. But everything else about him is extremely odd. Not faintly odd. *Extremely odd* – except in appearance. He's the *opposite of you.*' At any rate, the wedding invitation, headed 'Mr Quentin Crisp', would remain on the mantelpiece at 129 Beaufort Street for many months, even years, to come.

I was still disoriented by this tragedy when, on 6 July 1970, Denis Mitchell's film about Quentin was at last broadcast, the first of a series of portraits by Mitchell which would fill Granada TV's *World in*

Action slot during that summer. By this time, I had become almost as fascinated by Mitchell as I was by Crisp and his own contributions to the film were as memorable as many of Quentin's polished pronouncements. 'It's all a bit dirty, Quentin,' Mitchell declares at one point and 'Silly question, but did you say you were happy?' and 'Friendship, Quentin. Do you value it?' and 'Do you believe in anything?', to which Quentin Crisp revealingly replied, '*Not really.*' Finally Mitchell seems to be almost jibing at his subject when he tells Quentin that he has 'no drink, no sex, no money, no nothing really'. According to Quentin, Denis Mitchell wanted to emphasize his sad, wasted life and to present him as a 'poor wee lonely little thing' but the film was extremely well received. Writing in the *Sunday Times*, the TV critic Maurice Wiggin described the broadcast as 'the moment one waits for, the moment which seems to change one out of all triviality' and went on to offer the highly perceptive comments quoted at the beginning of this chapter. Quentin seemed happy enough with the film but expressed astonishment that neither the newspapers nor Granada Television had made any reference to his book *The Naked Civil Servant*. Nor did Jonathan Cape make any attempt to capitalize on this piece of free publicity. When I asked Quentin about his publisher's disinterest, he said, 'Mr Maschler is always friendly, almost bordering on matey, but he obviously doesn't want me to write another book.'

The broadcast seemed to have little effect on Quentin's life but he remained resilient. In the autumn of 1970 he started talking about a Mr Haggarty, whom he had known in the late 1940s, and who was now apparently interested in making a film of *The Naked Civil Servant*. With this name was soon linked that of a Mr Mackie and in November Quentin told me that he had been summoned to Mr Mackie's flat behind the Strand to talk in detail about his life. I learnt later that in the midst of these discussions, Quentin had spent Christmas with the Mitchells at Great Massingham in Norfolk. Here he had declined an invitation to the village pub but been happy to meet Granada's managing director, Denis Forman, who was shooting pheasants nearby and arrived with a brace under his arm. In front of Mr Forman, Quentin had remarked of his host's films: 'Mr Mitchell likes it sad', to which Mitchell had replied, 'I like it the way it is.' The

Mitchells gave him a first-class ticket for his return journey. Back in Chelsea he had lunch with a friend in Glebe Place and met the actress Fenella Fielding. When I asked him what she was like, he replied, 'She's actressy but she doesn't clobber you with it.'

My own visits to Beaufort Street continued on an irregular basis though I sometimes wondered if Quentin was tiring of my company. When I telephoned him, he responded chirpily, 'How are you today?', which seemed to carry the implication that nothing could have changed in my life. When I made an appointment to see him, I sometimes detected a curtness in his tone as he said, 'That's all right. Come then.' My father's jokey observation 'Andrew mixes mainly with bed-sitter and boarding-house people' still had some truth to it and though my life had expanded a little in the wake of my brother's death, I found I still needed the solace, security, stimulation and escape that Quentin Crisp provided. Looking back I wonder if my visits to 129 Beaufort Street, with their formalized structure, were a bit like visiting a psychotherapist or psychoanalyst. Quentin never lost his authority and managed each visit like a piece of clockwork, though there was rarely any limit to the time he had available and one evening we talked until the room became almost completely dark.

Our conversations covered much of the same ground as before, while occasionally adding new verses to the canon. Quentin expressed real hatred for Oscar Wilde and real dislike for the new Prime Minister Edward Heath and his 'exaggerated laughter and awful affectations'. He told me he couldn't stand the 'invincible amateurism' of the satirist Peter Cook but had inordinate admiration for the villainous Kray twins: 'They ruled the world and enjoyed themselves. Their crowning achievement was to get caught.' In the midst of this viciousness he surprised me by saying how cuddly chow puppies are, but reaffirmed his hatred of animals a few days later. Talking to me on the telephone, he suddenly exclaimed, '*A cat!* A horrifying cat has just come into the house! I must get it out! And *quickly!*' In spite of these alarms, he seemed content with his lot and appeared to have no inklings of his future celebrity. From time to time he mentioned Mr Haggarty and Mr Mackie but he did not take the idea of a film of his book very seriously. Other people's films, even ones he hated, excited him more.

He described *Death in Venice*, which he saw in the spring of 1971, as a 'crashingly boring film' with 'a lingering shot of everything'. Its star Dirk Bogarde, he said, was 'such a drip' and he expanded on this by adding, 'There's something so awful about his face – this not-quite-cooked look about the lower half of his face.'

During this period I had continued my struggle to get something published and in September 1971 eventually succeeded in getting an article accepted by *Punch*. This long-awaited event in no way constituted the break I was hoping for and Quentin's jubilation that I now 'ruled' *Punch* merely rubbed in my disappointment. I needed to explore other fields and a few weeks later conceived the idea of doing an interview with my father's old acquaintance and Quentin's old friend Joan Rhodes and perhaps then selling the story to the literary critic Francis Wyndham, who was now an editor at the *Sunday Times*. On 18 November I visited Miss Rhodes's flat in Belsize Park and got her to talk abut her life as a variety artiste. We did not talk about Quentin Crisp and when I mentioned my father it was not clear from her response whether she remembered him at all – or only too well. And when in due course I told my father, who had now moved to the Isle of Man, that I had been to see Joan Rhodes he seemed surprisingly uninterested. Perhaps his interest in London life was contracting just as mine expanded. The interview was anyway rejected by Francis Wyndham, with an effusively apologetic letter in which there were many typing errors.

This failure to connect coincided with a minor family development which perhaps belongs to this story. Earlier that autumn, one of my older brothers and his family had moved into a house in Priory Walk, a few hundred yards from 129 Beaufort Street. When I told Quentin this news, he said he passed Priory Walk 'incessantly' but couldn't think where it was. The proximity of my brother to Quentin enabled me to call there on my way to family dinners – or at least to notice in passing whether his lights were on or off. There were other minor consequences. One day I was spotted by my brother's au-pair girl as I made my way to Quentin's room. 'She now knows about your secret life,' said Quentin, dramatizing the incident. Another day I told Quentin that my sister-in-law had annoyed her husband by refusing to give a tramp some bread. 'And of course she's *right*,' he said, taking her side. 'Because he'll be *back*.' The difference between the two households, the tidy smartness in my brother's house compared with the exhilarating murkiness of Quentin's room, continued to fascinate me and it amused me to think of such different heads on such different pillows at night.

In May 1972 I made my own move, into the basement of a house in Oakley Street, Chelsea, unaware that thirty-five years earlier Quentin Crisp had lived in one of the houses now being demolished across the road to make way for a block of flats. Later that year I would find a better foothold in journalism as a contributor to *Harpers & Queen* – to the distress of some of my friends who urged me to stop writing such 'rubbish' and get back to my 'own stuff'. My world expanded and I made more friends. One of these was a girl called Niki Trethowan, who was extremely hospitable and asked me to parties in a spacious mansion-flat in Kensington where I more than once met an exceptionally tall and distinguished-looking man called Gillon Aitken, later my literary agent.

During this period, I still saw Quentin Crisp from time to time but our social lives no longer overlapped – Barrie Stacey had closed the As You Like It the previous autumn, putting a notice in the window saying he hoped all friends would stay 'in close contact' – and at 129 Beaufort Street our conversations took a new turn. In a delicate and kindly way, Quentin accused me of 'a faint heartlessness' and 'an absence of lichenous growth' round the edges of my relationships, what he called 'a lack of fuzziness'. He said of me: 'There's only stones, there's no moss or weeds.' Without sounding at all touchy about it, he accused me of 'scoring off' him and 'getting at' him. I knew this was partly true and in retrospect can only marvel at his patience with me. On another occasion he told me how wrong it was to consider oneself superior to other people. These were the kind of eye-opening helpings of the truth you might get from a shrink, but they were delivered with charm, wit and nothing high-and-mighty or hostile on his part. I was chastened by his remarks but also flattered that he dared to be so frank with me.

I continued to visit him regularly after these admonishing words were uttered though he was still slaving away in the art schools 'from dawn to dusk' during term-time and I was preoccupied trying to find fame in glossy magazines. This would prove only an episode: I was not cut out for that sort of work, though my 'faint heartlessness' surely equipped me well for it. I remained restless and unengaged. From time to time I telephoned Quentin in the hope of learning something interesting. On 13 November 1972, I telephoned him for no particular reason and learnt that he had received a visit that morning from Philip O'Connor.

-18-

Cross Purposes

He remains unchanged over the thirty years, a man of
anachronistic integrity, calculated generosity, witty
and intelligent in a way his own; and that, maybe, is
why he has decorously eschewed the larger personality
cult. He is a self-made man who has perfected his
handiwork outside the media and the media, maybe,
like to do all the work themselves: today, editing,
filming, televising become the determinant shaper of
the commodity – mere man – in which they deal. He
is islanded by the intelligence which enabled him to
become what he is before the market became aware
of him.

PHILIP O'CONNOR ON QUENTIN CRISP, November 1972

Philip O'Connor's second visit to 129 Beaufort Street was as impromptu and unplanned as the one he had made seven and a half
years earlier. On this occasion, he also brought with him a tape-
recorder, but he did not now have a radio programme in mind and
anyway his relationship with the BBC had expired long ago. The
ostensible purpose of his calling on Quentin Crisp was to get him to
contribute to his uncommissioned book on class.

The cassette on which their conversation is recorded, about forty
minutes in length, is on my desk as I write this chapter. It does not
offer any exchanges of a sensational nature but it effectively illustrates
the way Philip and Quentin spoke and shows the two men in their
true semi-superficial colours. Quentin does most of the talking and

Philip's interjections are accompanied by the *tick-tick-tick* of Quentin's alarm clock and the occasional scratching sound of Philip striking a match to relight his pipe. Close to the beginning of the tape Quentin hands Philip a mug of coffee and invites him to help himself to sugar.

Both men sound very peculiar. Quentin's voice is extremely exuberant, strident, staccato, alternatively pleading and despairing. It also has a nasal quality and there are quick coughs, minor throat-clearings and self-confident *ums* and *ers* as he gathers momentum, hits the right word. Philip's voice is softer, delicately deferential and impatient at the same time. At one moment he sniggers or snuffles politely. At another, he makes bored or dismissive noises and changes the subject. Throughout the discussion, Philip sounds pleased to be in Quentin's presence – he pronounces the name Quentin in a fussy, detached, rather French manner – and Quentin himself sounds delighted to be given yet another chance to express his opinions, talk about himself and climb on his high-horses. At no point does their dialogue touch upon mutual acquaintances or past events.

A lot of the time the two men seem to be getting on well, even laughing together in the matey manner you might expect from two men who have known each other for nearly thirty years. At other moments they seem at cross-purposes, Quentin pursuing well aired themes or lapsing into polished set-pieces with titanic conviction and relish while Philip battles away to make an obscure point of his own. Throughout the dialogue, both men seem utterly confident and Philip shows little sign of the insecurities which were engulfing him at this time. Each man seems more interested in what he is saying than in what the other has to say. Over and over again, Quentin echoes, agrees with and repeats almost verbatim what Philip has just said.

The conversation starts clumsily about the class system but gets livelier when Quentin describes his modest circumstances.

P.O'C.: You earn six pounds a week?

Q.C.: About an average of six pounds a week.

P.O'C.: But d'you live on that? Just that?

Q.C.: And I live on that.

P.O'C.: Good heavens! You give me hope.

Q.C.: So this is a message of hope?

P.O'C.: It certainly is.

Q.C.: My rent is twenty-five shillings.

P.O'C.: Oh, that's wonderful isn't it?

Q.C.: And – *um* – I wear other people's clothes and I eat other people's food. Or I eat Complan.

You sense that Quentin has been here before, many times, and that Philip is employing the techniques he perfected for the Third Programme. He fails however to take up the point about Complan. Quentin's dependence on this bland food and vitamin substitute had long been an element of his fame, almost a feather in his cap. Instead of pursuing this gastronomic point, Philip now confesses that he too, in a more obvious way, is 'a kept man' who longs to be 'promiscuous'. Quentin replies that Philip will need 'a lot of stamina' and 'boundless humility' to be promiscuous.

P.O'C.: Mine isn't boundless yet, is it?

Q.C.: I don't know whether your humility is yet boundless.

P.O'C.: I doubt it!

Q.C.: If it isn't, you may fail. In total promiscuity.

From here the conversation moves on to love and Quentin launches into one of his set-pieces employing the tone of voice he might have used to address a large audience. Love, he has decided long ago, is not a good idea. 'I think love has genuinely turned out to be a mistake. If I were asked what the main causes of the downfall of the world were I would certainly list love as one of them.' He then takes a familiar swipe at the envy-ridden society in which we live and proceeds entertainingly and provocatively, 'Now I know that sex has got nothing to do with love but – *um* – they are both a mistake.' He then ignores or overrules Philip's muttered objections and goes full steam ahead. 'What can you say of love?' he asks. 'I mean there's a negative sense in which, by consent, I love everybody. I would do a little – very little, because of my limited circumstances – to help them. I would give them a fake reference, write a letter trying to get someone to employ them, lend them half-a-crown, give them a cup of coffee, let

321

them have a bath in my house – or in *this* house, shall we say? And this, I would say, is my token of love. Anything more I cannot understand.'

Soon they are debating sex again.

P.O'C.: One can't live without sex though, Quentin.

Q.C.: Well, actually, I've got terrible news for you. You can!

P.O'C.: I know. I've done it. But it's uncomfortable. In the early period anyway.

Q.C.: But, also, if you only want orgasms you don't need other people.

P.O'C.: But if you want good orgasms you need other people, I find.

Q.C.: I see.

P.O'C.: I mean a good orgasm involves you totally, you see.

Q.C.: Yes, I see.

P.O'C.: It refreshes the brain for one thing. It washes it.

Q.C.: I see. Well, I'll try to think of the situation in this way because evidently there must be something in this racket or else people wouldn't go on about it.

P.O'C.: Of course not.

Here, Philip's 'Of course not' is almost a non sequitur, comic in its inappropriateness and mild pomposity, and all Quentin's polite and half-hearted protestations of 'I see' and 'I'll try to think of the situation in this way' are utterly unconvincing. He has thought out his position long, long ago, and is not going to budge an inch: his assurance is impregnable. His final offering on the subject is that, in his experience, a man's sexual 'processes' do not alter between the ages of twenty-four and sixty-four.

The next topic the two men tackle – or on which Quentin holds forth – is society. Here Quentin offers more chunks from his repertoire: 'Stand where you are and wait for society to form round you. And it will!' and 'Never go to a party that is numerically bigger than your personality.' These observations draw bored noises from O'Connor and an attempt to change the subject by getting Quentin to define his social class. Soon, Quentin tellingly reveals that he struggles to bridge the class barriers 'by putting on a perpetual performance with all classes, so that they look upon you not as their equal but as their court jester.' He goes on, 'You must do your perpetual music hall act so as to nullify your fundamental class.'

Later, the topic changes to survival and warfare. In even more hectoring tones, Quentin Crisp declares, 'You cannot live except at the expense of others. This you have to realize. For me to sit down in this terrible, broken-down room is to occupy several square yards that other people in the world are waiting to get their hands on. And this is territory that I must defend.' He goes on to add that he must also defend his body and even mere personality at the expense of other people. 'We are all in the murder business,' he concludes, drawing an off-beat response from Philip O'Connor.

P.O'C.: We can smile our way out, Quentin.

Q.C.: We can smile our way out. This is what we do. I clown my way out. Other people smile their way out. As for the humility racket—

P.O'C.: Well, some people love their way out.

Q.C.: Some people love their way out. This is very dangerous.

P.O'C.: Is it, Quentin?

Q.C.: Yes, it involves people in a different way.

Quentin longs to say more about the 'humility racket' and confesses that there must be something wrong with it. O'Connor interjects that he doesn't know the word 'wrong'. He only knows the word 'ugly'. Quentin agrees half-heartedly and adds, 'Beyond the word "ugly" is the word "inefficient".' O'Connor responds, 'And beyond "inefficient" is just death. Clumsiness. Death through clumsiness. Through stupidity.' Quentin then embarks on a polished set-piece on death. 'Now, of course, I'm at an age where as long as death is not uncomfortable it is not unacceptable. There have been people who have said to me, people of my own age, "Oh, I couldn't bear it! I would die! I haven't done hundreds of things yet I intend to do, or hope to do." Well, I don't feel like this. If it's cosy, I accept it. I only don't want a violent death.'

A quarter of a century later – this story is far from finished – Quentin Crisp would dramatically reverse this final statement and had indeed already coined his joke 'It would be nice to be murdered', and he must not forget that he had spent part of the war searching London for his 'own true bomb'. But now it was left to Philip O'Connor to quiz him about his earlier ordeals on the streets of London.

P.O'C.: Have you ever been beaten up or anything?

Q.C.: Yes, I have been beaten up often. Very seldom badly. About two or three times in a lifetime badly. So that I was bruised or cut or whatever.

P.O'C.: Very frightening?

Q.C.: It's very frightening. You are in the presence of some incomprehensible force. You find yourself being attacked by people who have never spoken a word to you. You only turn round and think 'Why are they so close to me?' and you're hit.

P.O'C.: And there's no way out of this?

Q.C.: And there's no way out of this.

P.O'C.: Not any degree of clowning or anything? Nothing you do?

Q.C.: Well, when you're young you have only your looks to get you out of it. When you're older you can try clowning. And lastly you have your humility.

P.O'C.: Oh, that might make them fiercer, don't you think?

Quentin Crisp ignores this interjection and carries on vehemently, 'Never fight back!' to which Philip O'Connor says, 'Oh, no, no, no, no!' This final response by Philip gives him the air of a man of the world, an experienced if slightly timid survivor. It is on this note that the tape ends and one imagines that Philip O'Connor left Beaufort Street fairly soon afterwards. He would later write the notes printed at the beginning of this chapter, but the book on class was never completed. The two men never met again.

-19-

The Public Baby Man

Get him out of here!

ISOBEL STRACHEY TO ANDREW BARROW,
16 November 1972

Although Quentin Crisp may have had mixed feelings about Philip O'Connor it was with real jubilation that he told me later that day that his old sparring partner was in London. For the second time, I felt driven to get in touch with the man whose voice I had heard on the radio and this time I did not get fobbed off by a BBC secretary telling me to write a letter. Instead I was provided with David Thomson's home telephone number and when I dialled these digits I was greeted by an encouragingly relaxed and dreamy-sounding man quite unlike those I had met in advertising or elsewhere, who did not seem at all put out when I asked for Philip O'Connor's number. 'Hold on,' he said, 'I'll get it.' Minutes later I was dialling the number of a hotel in South Kensington.

Philip O'Connor was summoned from his room and answered the telephone on a landing. His voice was soft, almost feminine in its timidity, but when I asked if I could meet him, he asked in a sharp tone, 'Why?' I mumbled something about his radio interviews and he agreed to meet me for lunch later that week. Either he or I suggested that we should meet at Finch's in Fulham Road, then the haunt of various artists and writers.

I was meant to be having lunch on 16 November with my friend Niki Trethowan but postponed it. I arrived in good time at Finch's, well aware that I knew very little about Philip O'Connor other than

325

what Quentin Crisp had told me and what I had read in Martin Seymour-Smith's *Bluff Your Way in Literature*. I had found none of his books in Foyles and had not read a word he had written. But I did not have to wait long before my vague and hopeful ideas about him could be tested against the real man. My first impression of Philip O'Connor was disappointing. He was not obviously eccentric, indeed he fitted well into my idea of a standardized BBC personality and even had a tape-recorder dangling from his shoulder. I had visited Broadcasting House more than once and had observed 'the BBC type' in various situations. Horn-rimmed spectacles and a polo-neck jersey were part of the look, combined with a neat haircut and suede shoes. With his rounded, baby-like head, Philip O'Connor looked like a trendy vicar but within minutes I sensed the hysteria behind the façade and the angry wet-lipped zest half-disguised by his man-of-the-world aura. I must have also discovered within minutes that he was an enthusiastic drinker.

We were not long at the Finch's bar but even while we were standing there he had given me a taste of his repertoire. When he hissed or laughed with merriment, his hand went to his mouth: I learnt later that this crudely oriental gesture was meant to cover his blackened teeth. Within minutes of our meeting, he had mentioned his mother, Charlie Chaplin, the woman he lived with called Panna Grady and the fact that he had not had an orgasm for three weeks. After a while we went off to a French restaurant nearby called the Bistingo, one of a popular chain which probably no longer exists. Here in a downstairs room, against recorded songs like 'Those Were the Days, My Friend', our conversation became more chaotic. Philip O'Connor soon lapsed into verse, declared, 'I haven't a chance/Because I won't dance/In the arc lights' and made other lacklustre pronouncements, such as 'I'm the gorilla that smiled at the baby' and 'I'm going to ring for the Virgin Mary/She'll turn up all hairy.' I preferred his more straightforward utterances. 'Got a cold?' he politely enquired at one juncture. I imagine we drank two bottles of wine. I reluctantly paid the bill.

In the middle of the afternoon we set off for Oakley Street. I noticed that Philip walked with a sort of slinky elegance which made his pale brown overcoat flap like a tail-coat. When we reached the house in which I lived I did not show him down to my basement but rang the main doorbell and introduced him to my landlady Isobel Strachey. I noted the way that Philip instantly made himself at home in the house, slinging his tape-recorder over the pegs where Isobel hung her coats, uninvited. This impression was soon reinforced by his request for whisky with his tea and very soon my landlady was whispering or hissing at me: 'Get him out of here!' Isobel Strachey had started her married life in Charlotte Street, as the wife of a nephew of Lytton Strachey, and had a few acquaintances in common with Philip O'Connor, but their lifestyles did not in any way overlap.

I then remembered I had a party to go to, a book launch of some sort, and decided to take Philip with me by taxi, but by the time we reached Theobald's Road I had become disenchanted by my companion and the party's lack of glamour rubbed in my disgruntlement. One of the straggling figures there knew O'Connor already, called him 'the Public Baby man' and protested to me that he was still doing his 'Public Baby act' and that he ought to grow up. By this stage I felt so fed up that I left Philip at the party, full of resentment about the amount of money I had spent on him, primly telling myself that I hated chaotic days and reproaching myself for getting drunk with a stranger I might never see again.

Early the next morning, he regained some of the lost ground when he telephoned me and spoke in the quiet, fragile, precise, almost pernickety voice he had used when I first spoke to him. Of the people at the party where I had abandoned him, he said, 'I suppose they get a little bit of warmth from clinging to each other.' We arranged to meet the following week. This second meeting, on 21 November in another South Kensington pub, went better. Philip endeared himself to me with the remark 'Most people are insufferably dull!' and showed me a list of those he would be interviewing for his new book. I was flattered to find my own name included among figures like Alexander Trocchi and Nicholas Mosley. Though his hold over me had now tightened a little, my old life continued. That night I attended another party at Niki Trethowan's and noted the presence of my hostess's formidable mother. I drag in this information for structural reasons which will eventually become apparent.

Two days later, I had another date with O'Connor. This time he had invited me to dinner at 5 Stewart's Grove, a cottage in a narrow street off Fulham Road, which was the home of his friend Annie Mygind, who was away. It was the first time I had seen Philip in a domestic setting – and he had added to its charms by laying a table for two and preparing a delicious meal, one dish of which was an endive salad he had made earlier in the day for Alexander Trocchi: I noted how utterly phlegmatic Philip was about the Scottish writer's failure to turn up for lunch. He had also cooked some veal and with it served a brand of Beaujolais called Les Courtiers. A huge bunch of bay leaves hung from the low ceiling, though this refinement was an indication of Annie Mygind's tastes rather than Philip's. On the shelves which lined one side of the room were most of Philip O'Connor's books, none of which I had seen before and which carried enthusiastic notices by critics I had heard of like Cyril Connolly and Philip Toynbee. Some of them showed photographs of O'Connor in earlier times and all of them seemed to be autobiographical. There was also an up-to-date stereo system on which he put a work by Shostakovich, whom he described as his favourite composer. His questions flattered me – 'D'you fuck a lot? D'you like fucking a lot? D'you push in hard and come out all sensitive?' – as did his observation that I was 'a collection of fragments stuck together by the glue of Must Get On'. When he sat opposite me after the meal, I felt soothed and stimulated by his presence and by general pronouncements like 'Possessing is the opposite of loving' and 'To describe is scholarly, to point is scientific.' Eventually the wine ran out – he suggested I went and got some more, adding the excuse or explanation, 'After all, I *am* an alcoholic' – and so did the oil in a hurricane lamp, which he showed impressive practical skills in quickly getting going again.

I returned to Oakley Street at about midnight, feeling invigorated by this extraordinary new friendship and ready to approach my other engagements with more energy. These included, the following day, another meeting with the Trethowans. On 24 November, I had dinner in the kitchen of Mrs Trethowan's flat in Eaton Mansions on the corner of Sloane Square. I think there were only the three of us present. I must assume that I talked a lot about my new friend Philip O'Connor but cannot recall how either mother or daughter reacted.

Early the next morning Philip telephoned me and suggested that I returned to France with him. Though he did not spell out the reason for this peculiar, sudden invitation, I gathered it owed something to the complexities of his relationship with Panna Grady. I could not agree to this plan but suggested that we had lunch on the day before his departure at Otello's, a Soho restaurant, which had already played a part in my life. I had first been there with my mother during the school holidays and with my brother Jonathan and I had been there most recently with a friend called James Graham, who had upset the waiters by demanding yet another carafe of wine and had eventually been physically guided, if not actually carried, off the premises. Celebrations with Philip O'Connor began calmly enough with him describing Otello's house wine as 'very, very bad' and replacing it with an order for Ruffino, which he described as 'excellent – it always is'. Under the growing influence of this, he told me I reminded him of someone called Oliver French, whom he had known in Tite Street during the war, and said flatteringly, 'I rather admire your enquiring capacity, *mon petit cousin.*' He also teased me by saying, 'I pretended not to know your name just then' and warned me, 'To be sure of anything is to be a cretin.' He also had more to say about Panna Grady, particularly her underwear, which he compared to water-lilies and which inspired him to boast, 'It's as long as Bardot's, the suspender to the pantie.' He also declared: 'All my life I've cried wolf and all that turned up was a little fox terrier.' Towards the end of lunch he came up with the idea that we should visit his friend David Thomson, who lived in Camden Town. During the taxi journey there Philip suddenly seemed to sober up, giving precise instructions to the driver. 'Yes, it's right here and then left and then right.' He also excited me by saying, 'We may get waylaid by David, who drinks an awful lot', and adding subversively, 'You can get a very good Beaujolais from the pub opposite.'

I remember little of that first visit to Regent's Park Terrace except that David Thomson was extremely welcoming, his eyes twinkling behind heavy prescription lenses, as he showed us into the large and pleasant house where he lived with his wife Martina and their three sons. I recall chiefly the affection and familiarity between the two men, as they danced around each other, combined with moments of distance or self-protective withdrawal by David Thomson, in spite of his generosity with the red wine. I would soon learn that since retiring from the BBC three years earlier Thomson had worked diligently and successfully as an author whereas Philip during the same period had written very little besides his journal and published nothing since his *Selected Poems*.

Later Philip and I returned by taxi to Stewart's Grove and I met Annie Mygind for the first time. Annie was Danish and had a helmet of white hair and a comfortable manner, which was echoed by her surroundings. Philip had said of her earlier, 'These women are so difficult if you don't sleep with them' but soon they were squabbling together playfully. 'D'you think I don't want to be wrong?' proclaimed Philip with jokey defiance. 'D'you think that's not my favourite position?' On her part Annie provoked Philip by denying that she had been generous to him in the past and meeting his claim 'Twice in my life you have put me afloat' with the words, 'When? When?', to which Philip replied, 'In North Wales. Oh yes you did. Oh yes you did.' When the idea of eating something was discussed Annie ticked him off, by saying, 'You're always thinking of yourself. I'm thinking of Andrew.' As the night wore on, Philip talked more about Panna Grady, saying, 'I'm in love with this – thingummy' and telling me in a more slippery manner, 'You don't know people like me, *mon ami*. That's why we live abroad with our Panna.' Hostility to England bubbled away continuously in Philip's cauldron. 'D'you know what terrifies me about the English?' he asked. 'The dumb look. The first reflex after the dumb look is to attack.'

With these impressions spinning in my head and a sense of Philip's charms being reinforced by the charms of David Thomson and Annie Mygind, I returned to my basement flat with further vigour and self-confidence. I had not yet come across Stephen Spender's assertion that Philip O'Connor 'offers body and spirit a blessed new chance', but was already experiencing something along these lines. I felt optimistic.

I felt that at last, at the age of twenty-seven, I had made contact with the real world and had something to offer it.

The following day, I mused over the fact that Philip O'Connor would now be crossing the sea to Wimereux and perhaps already reading my brother's book – I had forced the unpublished typescript on him – and went and sought out the elderly antiquarian bookseller who had frequented the As You Like It and asked her to find a copy of *Memoirs of a Public Baby* for me. This she quickly did, ringing me a few days later to say that she had found a first edition but apologizing for its cost. 'It's forty-five bob,' she told me.

– 20 –

Wimereux Weekends

It's always you scholarly-looking fellows
who drink a lot.

PHILIP O'CONNOR TO ANDREW BARROW, 14 January 1973

Letters and cards between me and Philip O'Connor were exchanged. His first postcard dated 29 November 1972 and sent from Wimereux was double-edged: 'Don't forget to call – your brother's book no good.' It was followed by an undated letter from a rented house at Le Beausset, near Toulon, stating that they would be home at the end of December and ordering me, if I visited, to bring Annie Mygind's tape-recorder and my own.

I did not intend to heed this request when I despatched a postcard saying that I would come over for the weekend of 6–8 January 1973. I was excited by the plan and the unlikeliness of the whole friendship. The prospect of the Continent, its pull and romance, thrilled me and my appetite for a different sort of foreignness sharpened. As I stepped onto the cross-Channel ferry, I noted the refreshing colour of the sea and the presence on board of assorted travellers, several of whom looked as if they were on solitary ego-trips like me. A middle-aged man in an Old Etonian tie, dark glasses and shepherd's cloth trousers caught my attention and, after a few glasses of beer, I got into conversation with him and even volunteered, 'I'm going to stay with the writer Philip O'Connor.' 'Are you a writer?' he asked politely. '*Yes!*' I exclaimed and when we parted he added the friendly words, 'Perhaps our paths will cross again.' In this cheerful state I arrived at Calais and I was only marginally put out that there was no sign of Philip

O'Connor or Panna Grady at the dock. Quentin Crisp's remark that Philip was utterly unpredictable played on my mind, but I remained hopeful that this was only a minor hitch. Still excited, I found the way to Calais Ville station and got a smooth, snug train that would drop me off at the coastal resort of Wimereux. Unpossessively, I slung my small suitcase onto the rack and bathed in the sensation of escape and being unfollowed.

Within half an hour I had arrived at the town where I now knew Philip O'Connor had spent a crucial part of his childhood and where he had been living for three years. The train comes in to Wimereux at its highest point: most of the town is spread out between the railway line and the sea. Into these streets I plunged, quickly locating the Rue Carnot if not the actual *pâtisserie* where Philip had once lived. I then went in search of the Rue Jeanne d'Arc and found it beyond the church and across the river – the river in which Philip had fished as a youngster – in the most easterly part of the town. I soon found Clair de Lune, a large house squeezed between others, with a back door onto the street and a more elaborate and stately front facing the sea and giving directly onto the deserted sandy beach.

The house appeared completely shut up and shuttered. The dustbin at the back door was empty and through the glass panes of the front door I could see only a darkened uncarpeted staircase leading upwards. In many respects the house was like others in the town, with lots of woodwork and balconies facing the sea. Right at the top of its façade were two moons, one smiling, one sad, the name of the architect and an unreadable date. The ground-floor verandah was scattered with sand.

I wondered what had happened. Were Philip and Panna Grady even now meeting me in Calais? Had he got my card too late – or simply changed his mind? Could he be on a drinking stint in Paris? Could he even be back in London? Whatever the cause of his absence, I decided to bide my time and stay in Wimereux for the weekend to give him the chance to turn up. I also decided that I would not book into a hotel until dusk. For the rest of the afternoon and early evening I sauntered about the town with my suitcase, paying regular trips to the seafront to see if a light was now on at Clair de Lune or smoke rising from a chimney, but on each occasion the house seemed darker and blacker.

I eventually booked into the plainest hotel in the Rue Carnot and after a wholesome set dinner went to bed listening to the voices in the bar below, the rattle of the pinball machine and the buzz of motor-cycles outside. The next day, I resumed my perambulations, sat in different bars, returned with hangdoggish regularity to Clair de Lune and pondered over the wording of any message I might eventually leave on the doorstep. I did not ask anyone if they knew Monsieur O'Connor and I doubted if any of the inhabitants of the town wondered what I was up to. As another night descended, I listened to the cold, splashing, invisible sea and wrestled with feelings of gloom and folly as Clair de Lune became a more and more inanimate hulk, inside which it was hard to imagine Philip's lively existence. On Monday morning 8 January, I left a note on the doorstep expressing an eagerness to return at once if summoned by telegram and left Wimereux by the same route on which I had come. In wintry blackness I eventually took the boat-train from Folkestone to London.

Two days later a telegram from O'Connor arrived at Oakley Street, beginning 'SORRY CONFUSION' and promising to meet me the following Saturday at Calais. Weird though it was to repeat this travel experience so quickly, I duly set off for Wimereux again, carrying the same suitcase, wearing the same brown suit and entirely confident that this time Philip O'Connor would be waiting for me at the dock. He was there before I had started looking for him, and wearing a padded white coat with a sheepskin lining. On later visits he would behave oddly at the dock, putting out a little finger when I extended my hand, causing a clumsy collision of flesh, but on this first occasion he seemed almost affable as he led me to the car in which Panna Grady was waiting. Panna was a more familiar type than Philip, thirty-nine years old, almost plump, girlish, and now pregnant with their second child. During the journey to Wimereux, she seemed subdued, happy to let Philip do the talking and to go along half-heartedly with what he said. From the back of the car I studied her and Philip studied me. He told Panna that I had 'a sulky Italianate face' – no one has ever said such a thing before or since – and she acquiesced. Was their son Maxim in the car – or at home with Panna's daughter Ella? Anyway, we were soon all together on the luxurious upper floors of Clair de Lune.

Could any of Philip's earlier homes have competed with the luscious oddness of those rooms overlooking the sea? Into them had been squeezed magnificent furniture and furnishings Panna had acquired in London: draperies, tapestries, cabinets and gnarled antiques and overlapping layers of Persian carpets bearing motifs which reminded me of some of the rugs in my father's house. No structural alterations had been made to the house and its varnished wood walls studded with old-fashioned light switches provided a suitably austere contrast to its contents.

The main room, where most of the dramas were played out, was the third-floor dining room, which had a full-length dormer window set into the sloping ceiling through which the sea in its many manifestations was visible and audible. The main piece of furniture was a marble-topped octagonal table, around which were arranged slender ebonized chairs with brass adornments. There was also an ancient chair with tubular arms in which Philip sat and held forth, his offerings combining with those of the sea and the many bits of music that he swept on and off a modern gramophone. On various shelves and inside a cabinet there were books. The first title I spotted was *Seventeenth-Century France* by a certain G. R. R. Treasure, who ten years earlier had taught history at my boarding school and found me 'infuriating'. There was also a large privately printed green leather volume called *The Stones of Land's End* by John Michell, which listed 'Panna Grady, Wimereux' as a subscriber for two copies. Some of the books were particularly interesting for the handwritten inscriptions on their end-papers. One volume was inscribed 'Panna with love Tom Driberg Feast of the Holy Innocents 1968' and another bore the words, 'For Panna and Phil, love Alex Trocchi'. Adjoining the dining room and also overlooking the sea was the kitchen, of which more in a moment.

On the same floor overlooking the back-streets of the town was Philip's bedroom. This was a holy place, a temple with luscious lights – am I lapsing into his own kind of language? – which featured a fur-covered double bed beside which lay an array of pipes, bowls or platefuls of ash, as there were in every room he used, and various medicaments like earplugs and Vichybiline tablets. There was also a lavatory on this floor, the only one in the occupied part of the house, and from the landing another door led to a rickety staircase which gave access to the attic where Philip painted or typed at another grand old table under a roof where the tiles rattled in bad weather. In due course I would retreat to this room and sit at Philip's desk and adopt the postures of a Man of Letters as well as making occasional forays into his waste-paper basket.

On the floor below the dining room, Panna Grady slept in a room full of antique screens and Venetian mirrors, which she would soon share with the new baby. Next door was her daughter Ella's room, spartan and unpretentious by comparison and showing the signs of a sturdy, normal, American schoolgirl's nature. Ella was now nine years old. Her half-brother Maxim was four and shared another room on the same floor with a television and lots of large fluffy toys. The room to which I was assigned was another floor down, larger and plainer than those above and furnished mainly with fitted pieces of furniture which had come with the house, including a large oil painting set into the wall showing two men in cavalier dress drinking beer at a cloth-covered table. Here I felt closer to the sea and the wind which rattled the shutters, but could often hear raised voices from the floors above.

I soon realized that Philip and Panna had fallen into a way of living which would never really change and that a lot of Philip's domestic ritual and rigmarole followed a pattern established many years earlier with other partners, and perhaps Maria in particular. During the next three years, I would spend many weekends at Clair de Lune, now fused into one memory and one experience. The days might start with the cry of the new baby – born in the spring of 1973 and given the name Felix – or perhaps with the sound of Philip descending the uncarpeted staircase to go out and buy croissants. An hour or two later, Philip might enter my bedroom and go straight into some intimate speech, without preamble. One morning he woke me up with the question, 'Are you very intelligent?' Eventually I would ascend the two floors, place myself in the dining room and wait for action. Philip, up and about for ages, would be in a very uncertain humour, talking to himself in the kitchen – 'God I can't stand it!' – or carefully performing some private task like carrying hot water to his bedroom. Whatever he did at this hour was accompanied with gasps of 'Oh!' and 'Ah!' and 'Eugh!' and sometimes, unexpectedly early, the pop of a cork. He was always spruce, with his hair swept back, but he tended to wear the same clothes every day, which always included a roll-neck sweater. Sometimes he wore slippers, a cosy sandstone colour, and I heard him shuffling about in them. He took his domestic duties very seriously, especially making Panna's breakfast, wrapping the coffee-grinder in his corduroy coat so that its buzzing did not wake her too soon, reheating her croissants and arranging her tray carefully. Trays played an important part in his rituals.

My presence put extra pressure on him and drew many hostile or double-edged responses from his lips. 'Well, well, well. Fancy having you to show off to again. I suppose you want me to cook your damned breakfast?' 'I've got to get your damned breakfast. That's what I hate doing', and even 'Would you like to go before breakfast?' Sometimes he avoided me altogether by staying in his bedroom, from which I might hear only a disdainful cough. He might then emerge very fast, see me and say, 'Oh hello. Good God' to which I might respond, 'I hope you slept well', a remark which he would either answer seriously – 'No, I wake at two now' – or utterly rebuff with some cleverness like 'Give me a cliché from a fucking liar.'

I soon learnt to play along with this nonsense and might march upstairs, clapping my hands and saying, 'Right, now, breakfast please, as soon as possible!' or equally provocatively, 'Have you had breakfast yourself?' to which he once responded, 'What a curiously obliquely slanted question.' With more sighs and gasps he then set unstintingly and meticulously about his tasks and eventually a formal tray would appear in the dining room, containing croissants – sometimes slightly burnt – jams, honeys, and some kind of cooked dish, eggs poached or otherwise, speckled with pepper and sometimes accompanied by ham, all served on slightly chipped plates of great charm. Coffee was the great centrepiece and the accompanying milk – kept warm on asbestos-type discs on the plain little gas stove – but my compliments about it were usually met with some disinterest: 'Pardon? Good coffee? Oh good.' And only rarely with self-satisfaction: 'We make good coffee, don't we?' Coffee was drunk from a handleless bowl and during many of my visits accompanied by the sight and sound of wind and rain batting against the window and by further comments or abuse from my host. When I jokily suggested that my eggs should be 'sunny side up', Philip replied, 'What a disgusting remark!' and he used the same adjective to describe French attempts at marmalade. English marmalades also disappointed him and inspired knowledgeable pronouncements: 'Oxford, you know, has gone off in the last five years. It has become ostentatiously harsh.' Long after breakfast was served, he would fish for further responses to his domestic efforts – 'I think you're regretting the bad bacon and egg that were served this morning. It takes a long time to recover from a bad breakfast' – but I was always more than satisfied and quite bewildered by the quality of his cooking and its delicate presentation.

Philip did not share my breakfast though he often settled beside me while I ate it, sometimes asking questions like 'What now, little man?', but sometimes diverted by Maxim's arrival on the scene, with whom he exchanged grown-up greetings – *'Bonjour, monsieur'* – while I gazed at a Sealink Ferry making its way across the Channel with smoke sometimes pouring horizontally from its funnels. Philip would have been out shopping at the earliest opportunity and after serving Panna's breakfast he would harangue, cajole or sweetly gossip with her in the room below. I was amazed by how quickly things I told him got passed on to her. His own physical needs were met by elaborate and piquant mid-morning snacks. I sometimes found half-abandoned tea-trays in the attic workroom and noticed on one occasion that he had bitten into the bread in an odd way.

These delicacies echoed his mother's snacks which I had now read about in *Memoirs of a Public Baby* and reflected the 'shrimps on a silver dish' which had featured in one of his early poems. They involved anchovies, salami, home-made meat paste on toast, *croque-monsieurs* or ham sandwiches made with raw onion or garlic – 'Ham by itself is too sickly' – and were accompanied by thick black Earl Grey or Twining's Prince of Wales tea – 'They call it the burgundy of teas' – which he made in a large enamelled metal teapot. When I asked for the secret of one of these brews, he said, 'There's no secret. It was done with full publicity' and then, 'You silly fellow!' I was sometimes invited to participate in these little treats, to nibble raw onion. 'D'you want one of these?' he said, offering me a miniature pancake. 'Y'see, they won't keep hot. They're nice, aren't they?'

With these snacks came wine. 'I start drinking at half past nine,' Philip announced, consulting his wristwatch with fake alarm. 'I'm not late, am I?' He drank simple red wines, Beaujolais Villages, in single and double bottles. One morning he pointed at a single bottle of St Émilion and said, 'That's all I'm allowed. They're very, very hard, these people', though actually he had whatever he wanted and Panna's protests about the 'two monster bottles' he brought home and consumed every day washed over him. He drank from a large blue space-age mug, explaining, 'I think this sort of rough wine should be drunk out of pottery. The lips of the vessel control the speed of the quantity that comes into your mouth.' His first gulps were often accompanied by cries of '*Ugh!* I hate alcohol', and protestations that bouquet was of no importance to him. 'All I bother about is the damned taste of the muck.'

I did not start drinking as early as Philip but my own glass, or mug, would be brimming before noon, causing my host to observe, 'I envy you your youth that you can still drink with a sense of excitement.' He was always generous at refilling my glass though his first offer of a drink each morning would be couched in comedy. He once offered me a tiny thimble of wine and remarked, 'Liberty Hall!' and then asked wickedly, 'Would you like a glass of boiling rum?' Another morning he stuck two fingers into the corners of his mouth, stretched it into a funny fake smile and asked in a strangled voice, 'Would you like a drink?' More amiably, he greeted me with a gurgle of a laugh when I entered the kitchen and said simply, 'It's next door.'

Sooner or later he would become involved in the preparation of lunch, classical music playing on a radio channel which included long bursts of applause, and, instead of an apron, he put on a silk coat of Chinese invention. These culinary processes may have begun cheerfully – 'I thought I would make a moussaka actually' – but never ran smoothly and his lack of progress would be marked by screams, shouts and self-indulgent sighs. 'I'm so tired of cooking,' he began. 'You see

I get so . . . I *loathe* cooking. All this damned cooking. I have to be drunk to cook. Let me drink a little, then I'll cook.' He might then slop more wine into the blue mug and feeling perkier explain 'I always drink a bottle of wine while I'm cooking', and when I entered the kitchen I would often notice a bottle slightly hidden among the utensils. '*My God!*' he exclaimed one morning. 'It's 11.20! The fowl should be in the oven!' Then he might talk to himself: 'You ask them to get cheese and what happens automatically? They don't get cheese.' Once I heard an unexpected cry of delight at the discovery of a new bottle on the kitchen table. 'Oh, isn't that nice of her. Dear little Ella. I didn't think she would.'

Philip O'Connor's relationship with his common-law stepdaughter was complicated: Ella sometimes went shopping for him but did not always buy what he wanted. 'Did Ella get olive oil?' he asked Panna one morning. 'No, because you called her a pig last night,' Panna replied. 'But pigs love olive oil,' he retorted. Every morning, and evening, these declarations and accompanying screams and louder music built up into a crescendo. One day he opened the fridge and caused an avalanche of its contents, Évian bottles and much else bouncing across the floor. He stood there shouting and roaring, his arms raised with his fingers pointing upwards. Most of such animosity was directed at Panna. He shouted her name constantly but when she called for him he howled back ferociously, '*I'm cooking!*' Often I heard him shake open a drawer of cutlery, then make a further cry of 'Panna!' and 'I'm getting a bit sick of this!' To these tirades Panna might yell back with the baby Felix in her arms, 'Oh, Philip, for heaven's sake. Nobody asked you to do anything!', but Philip had other tricks up his sleeve and excelled himself by speaking in a pantomime voice: 'They've put soup in the coffee pot!! Aaaagh! *Aaaaaaagh!!*'

While these dramas were going on, vegetables would be steaming on the stove. Philip would be beating the *pommes purées* and exhilarating aromas would be coming from the oven, the most exhilarating I had yet encountered. As the mealtime grew closer, Philip would try new ways of attracting Panna's attention, sometimes speaking in a very soft voice, 'Panna, can you come up?' and sometimes shouting full-

throatedly and enunciating every word separately, 'Panna! Will...
you... please... come... up!'

Usually Philip would provide more food than was needed and serve
it temptingly on assorted deep-rimmed dishes, with coloured napkins
and the battered English silver that Panna had acquired on some
earlier occasion. Annie Mygind had told me that Philip's cooking had
improved over the years, and surely even those who found Philip
tiresome and tedious would have relished the wholesome and delicious
taste of his roast chicken? But before these tasty dishes were served
and in spite of Panna's 'We'd better eat, Philip, huh?' there was often
a further fuss. 'What a dreary table,' Philip might declare, blaming
American table-laying habits. 'Panna, that table looks like a pig-sty.
This hideous table... looks like a pig-sty... total lack of harmony.
For five years I've tried to teach Panna to lay a table... I say, this
table is filthily laid.' Then came a further admonishment: 'At least
turn the knives inwards.' If Panna was still not present there would
be a further crescendo of cries – '*Panna! Panna!! Panna!!!*' – and
when she and the baby eventually appeared, a much softer appeal:
'Panna, can you serve people?'

A critic of my first novel *The Tap Dancer* accused me of employing
too many lists, which is perhaps a journalistic habit, but I cannot
resist mentioning some of the dishes that Philip O'Connor served
during my visits to Wimereux. I have already mentioned roast chicken,
which he carved before it reached the table and which he usually
stuffed with sausage meat and accompanied with sadistically well
whipped mashed potatoes. He made 'as good a spinach as you'll find
in any rest-or-rant'. He disliked sardines unless they were 'fresh and
boiled in fat'. He made excellent cassoulets. He liked steaming things
– 'steamed sausages are quite possible' – and used a lot of soy sauce,
which in those days came only in a bottle with a fancy Chinese label.
His salads were aromatic, but he could not make cakes or tarts – 'God
the Fifth can't make cakes!' – though claimed to be quite good at
bread and rolls. His chips had improved – 'They used to be pretty
bad' – and the best sausages, he said, were those stuffed with truffles.
His final verdict on his cooking was that he preferred Panna's – 'Mine's
a drinker's cooking' – and he was almost entirely self-taught. The only

recipe book he'd ever used was the Countess Morphy's *Cookery of All the Nations*, which he claimed contained the words 'When the rice was slightly burnt, the natives jumped for joy.' Years later, I owned a copy of this book and searched in vain for this cherished line.

Meals were chaotic. Maxim's non-appearances were respected by his father, who said, 'Perhaps Maxim won't be eating. He doesn't sometimes.' Ella was usually there, sometimes exciting some of Philip's most schoolboyish rudeness – 'You yourself have never opened your mouth to make a sensible remark so don't tell *me* to shut up' – but after more than five years together, Ella had learnt how to hold her own and when Philip had something particularly lewd to say would simply make a clucking sound and did not seem troubled when he referred to her 'greed' and called her 'the fat little one'. Philip himself ate very little and what he did eat he consumed ungreedily, sticking his tongue out fastidiously between morsels. 'Cooks are notorious for their bad appetites,' he explained, and 'I don't like eating when it interferes with talking.' His pipe and wine got most of the attention. 'Don't take my blood away,' he protested when Ella shifted his wine glass half an inch across the table and he often lit up his pipe between courses. In his own funny way, he enjoyed observing my table manners. '*An'ew*,' he began, carefully mispronouncing my name by omitting its two central consonants, and then '*Andrew*,' correctly pronounced, 'when you put the instruments of eating back on your plate don't make the angle too wide.' As each meal got going or reached its conclusion, Philip relaxed into his old gnarled throne and Panna took control of the domestic operation, asking, 'Is there anything more I can do for you?' and sometimes presenting a sumptuous flan from the *pâtisserie* where Philip had lived as a child. 'Are you through, Philip?' was coarsely met with 'I'm not through with your interruptions!'

By this time, Philip was well into the oratory of the second or third bottle. 'I have to drink two bottles to go through the performance of caring for you,' he declared and on several occasions we faced a wine shortage. Occasionally he slipped me money to go and get more with the words, 'Now then my dear friend . . .' At other times I only had to go as far as the kitchen to be greeted by Philip with the words, 'I'm glad you've found it. Could you invite me to a little?' I sometimes presented him with a bottle of wine I had bought on my own. 'We'll open that in a couple of hours,' I might say. 'A couple of minutes,' Philip would reply. In the resulting haze he would cast further backward glances at the meal we had eaten. 'Was the lunch cooked all right? Was the chicken all right?' Then his feet might go up on the table and he would say, 'So, therefore, if you drink at the right times, life isn't too bad', and click away at his pipe with a cigarette lighter.

I could have said more about his pipe earlier. I learnt that it had been a feature of his life since early adulthood, part of his armoury and another addiction. He now smoked a French tobacco called Caporal Export which came – still comes – in a brown-and-red packet. Pipe-smoking was central to his life. He spoke of its effects, the rewards of a 'pipe think' and what he described as 'a click in the diaphragm, a twitch, a subliminal twitch'. He now had many pipes: one of them was very fat, one of them was a foot and a half long, and one of them had a human head on its bowl which had been with him since before the war and had once belonged to the Uncle Haslam character he had written about in *Memoirs of a Public Baby*. During our conversations, and sometimes against the background of the buffeting wind, he dug mercilessly into the bowl of his current pipe with a penknife. On my second visit to Clair de Lune in May 1973, I started borrowing a pipe from Philip, using the same tobacco, enjoyed its various effects and formed a habit which has remained with me spasmodically ever since. 'Tobacco, please,' I often rapped out at him and when on a subsequent visit I said this seconds after my arrival at the dockside he remarked, 'You get down to it quickly.' Sometimes our supplies ran short. 'Do you realize,' he asked me one evening, 'we're out of tobacco, matches, and friendship?'

Further uplift – or madness – came from music. Philip worked his gramophone hard and swept records on and off the Grundig turntable. His range of records was well loved and well worn. Of one particular favourite, he said, 'D'you realize I've played this record so many times, it's practically unrepresentable, it's so scratched and tortured.' He played a lot of jazz, gypsy violin and Hungarian dances. He played 'Mac the Knife' sung by Louis Armstrong and 'Don't Get Around Much Anymore' by Duke Ellington. He played 'J'Attendrais' by

Charles Trenet which he had known since the 1930s, and 'Hit the Road Jack' so loud that it could be heard by people on the beach. And he often joined in with the lyrics. When Frank Sinatra sang 'I like to lead . . .' Philip eclipsed him with ' . . . *when I dance*' and when Sinatra warbled, 'I would work and slave my whole life through', Philip heckled, '*I wouldn't.*' He also offered 'corny French' in the form of Édith Piaf and explained, 'When you get to my age you see such wonderful things in corn and so little in the opposite.' He might then contradict himself by putting on a classical piece and proclaiming, 'It's going to put an end to your tittle-tattle, this music.' It certainly didn't silence *him*. Playing Mahler, he commented, 'Orchestration! Rawsthorne couldn't master his strings like this chap! Nobody could do it! This is courage!' Playing Suite Bergamasque, he said, 'Anything of Debussy's goes well with the sound of the sea' and when listening to a Bach cantata, he said, 'It forgives all sins. It's a kind of blessing. I always think of Panna like this.' Then he went off at a tangent, 'I can't live without her! I can't live without people who appreciate Bach. I call this a bit of triumph.' Replacing Bach with another record, he said, 'This is Rachmaninov. And this is the world's greatest pianist, Horowitz. Look at it. Look at his tender playing. And this is his face.' The record sleeves showing the composer or performer often excited him even more than the music itself. Looking at a photograph of the pianist Richter, he enthused, 'It's a tramp's face. All good faces are tramps' faces because they haven't found a good enough dwelling place. Except Clair de Lune.'

For Beethoven, whose portrait was pinned above the gramophone and whose dark looks sometimes reminded me of my brother Jonathan, he reserved his wildest superlatives. 'You listen to this. This is his Ninth. You'll never find anything cleverer than this. This is why I like Beethoven. His brain was a cathedral. Beethoven's the only friend I've ever had. Beethoven was a comfort to the wounded soul. He's been through everything we've been through. And made a success of it! Imagine all that suffering . . . made musical. D'you know Beethoven was one of the most bad-tempered men who ever lived? He died of anger. All his life he was in a fury. Beethoven couldn't stand humanity. It smelt. He expected the world to be a Garden of Eden. And it wasn't.

And he never forgave it. This is the most poignant passage in Western music. He puts up the question, from Monkey to Man, was it worth it? And he *doesn't* answer it!' Playing Beethoven's last quartet, Philip declared, 'I don't think you can do more than this' and then added, 'Of course I know nothing about his sex life. I suppose he was one of the most accomplished masturbators of all time. It's a possibility. Don't despise possibilities.'

Some of these comments applied more to himself than to Beethoven, but washed down with wine and accompanied by hissing laughter and the roar of the sea, were themselves a form of performance. And as always such seriousness was rapidly followed by irreverence. 'Which piece is this?' I asked later during the Beethoven concert. 'One of his fucking pieces. You can't tell one from the other,' Philip replied, and sometimes he grew tired of music and put on instead an old crackling record of John Gielgud reciting from Shakespeare. This he played at full blast, pronouncing the actor to be 'the best speaker in the world, the Western world'.

Listening to Philip O'Connor's own speech, with or without the backing of music, the sea, and screams from other members of his expanding family, was my principal preoccupation during these visits. Philip, like Quentin, had a lot to say and his manner of speaking itself deserves scrutiny. He made noises as well as words. His voice had a wide range. At one end of the scale, he was quiet, frail, discreetly pouting, utterly gentle. At the other, with or without alcohol, he was a roaring monster or monkey, laughing, spitting, shouting and screeching. As a rule he raised his hand to cover the 'ancient ruins' of his teeth but in his boldest moods he bared his fangs, fully revealing their gnarled stubs and giving extraordinary shapes to his mouth. When he laughed at his own jokes, the laughter went on and on, hitting different peaks of cackling, and he occasionally interrupted himself with a jokily self-reproving expression. After dinner, his reper-toire of words and noises reached an even higher level of shouted cleverness, and the laughter and shouting continued when he left the room to visit the lavatory across the landing. 'I love these noises I make when you appear,' he said on his return. 'You give my mouth such fun.' Maxim also found it fun and sometimes imitated his father's laughter, but Panna was often moved to protest that he would wake the baby. 'Don't shout! Why do you shout so?', and even 'God, it's hideous the sound you make, Philip.' Under this sort of pressure he explained that he laughed out of embarrassment and was terrified of being taken seriously. And occasionally he issued a warning that a new laugh was on its way – 'Here we go! The Widow Rawsthorne!' – explaining that the composer's wife had an even wilder way of expressing merriment. 'Don't make it too loud,' pleaded Panna Grady.

Philip's choice of conversational topics was erratic and unpredictable. He said things out of the blue, like 'Do you like the word *duke*?' and began his sentences quirkily, with words like 'In my profession, which is the clergy . . .' He pronounced words daintily, made observations on his own speaking style – 'D'you notice when I'm being a little inaccurate I have an American accent?' – and sometimes criticized the way I spoke. 'You say the word *I*, which I like to be like a razor-blade, like *Oi*.' Though his face often wore a look of integrity, concentration and sometimes formidable calmness, much of what he said only made sense in surreal terms. 'My cleverness comes from pain, window pane,' he said with innocent delight, and 'I am fifty-five and very nifty.' He could switch from fury to gentleness and the other way round at the drop of a hat and when interrupted by Panna or me, might shout, 'I haven't finished my sentence!' Sometimes he would try the other tack and say, 'You didn't hear the full stop', but even when he seemed to have finished making his point, he would suddenly start up again – '*But! But! But!*' – and go off at a new tangent.

What did we talk about? Many of his outpourings appeared facile ironies – 'I can't stand anyone who's not a fool. They're dangerous.' 'Those who fight evil are utterly suspect' and 'Problems are invented, you know. You can see that from babies and children.' Other outbursts were sentimental in the extreme, even when they contained elements of self-knowledge. 'What I hate is pain and cruelty. I want a world where children can be happy. I want to make people kinder. I can't stand cruelty. I've got so much of it in myself and I can't stand it' was followed by 'All famous writers are orphans looking for a family. The only family they have is the public. They hunger for the family. This explains all writers and painters.' The latter observation was one of his most familiar and his quest for the human family a lifelong preoccupation borne out by the title of his autobiography, though somewhat at odds with his attitude towards the human race. 'Humanity is loathsome,' he told me one weekend. 'It does ugly things . . . all this stupidity, all this complication . . . they can't face the tremendous issue of simplicity.' Then he added, 'The eyes of humanity are a couple of hard-boiled eggs sometimes.' In the face of all these sweeping generalizations, I yearned for the more personal, human side of Philip O'Connor and was touched when he told me: 'I've got an incredible habit. When I find a good passage in a book I like to kiss it sometimes.' On the same theme, he asked me, 'You like books, don't you? I mean, physically?'

Yet polemics, histrionics and sweeping statements, backed by passion and fuelled by alcohol, occupied him much of the time. As already noted, his attitude towards England was particularly savage, and from the way he talked one almost forgot that he was born there and had spent most of his life there. His comment, 'You see I hate England. I hate the English', had little substance to it and he made the dubious claim that had he stayed in England he would have become a 'personality' and boasted, 'It was that from which I fled.' He said he never felt at home in London, 'though Suffolk and Wales seemed better', and appeared to disown the whole country whenever he mentioned it. Sentences began 'In fact there was a minister in your House of Commons' and 'Your creepy island has got into the Common Market', and he employed the same dismissive tone even when describing the British painter Crome as 'one of your best'. According to Philip, 'The only good sentence Hitler ever perpetrated was "I would like to see the end of England." ' All this hostility to his country of origin may have been a joke or a tease or a veiled attack on me but it bubbled away most of the time and produced some odd outbursts. 'We don't want any of your filthy foreign foods!' he yelled at one point. 'We're Englishmen! We eat each other!' On another occasion, he explained, 'The English are always pushing each other into gutters and off cliffs. Panna's the only person I like!' As on other matters, he claimed that Panna shared his views. 'We hate the English. We hate their bodies. So lumpy.'

Parallel to this hatred of the country across the Channel ran his love for, or grotesque sentiment about, the East. 'Everything is changing,' he would pontificate. 'I think the decline of the West is a dead cert now.' His old Communist sympathies clung to him and he argued, 'There wasn't a single Communist country in the world when I was born. And look at us now. We're resisting the inevitable. Take this Solzhenitsyn. D'you know his book sales are beginning to decline already?' Here he slapped the arm of his chair triumphantly. 'Shall I tell you what the truth about Russia is?' he then began temptingly, but had nothing more to say other than 'So obvious. So obvious.' I soon learnt that Philip had never been further east than Hungary, but the unknown orient fascinated and infected him. It was also to some extent in his blood. He often mentioned that he was partly Burmese and there were certainly times when he looked like a Buddhist monk. There were many oriental trappings at Clair de Lune, most notably a Buddhist statuette with its hand raised to its mouth, which looked like a household god, imitating its master. At peaceful moments, Philip asked, 'Is it interesting to find yourself in little Peking?' and tried to beg me to go east. He predicted that my great-grandson would be chairman of the Peking Town Council and recalled that Charlie Chaplin loved Japan and had had a Japanese valet. At times of stress or disgruntlement, he declared, 'But I shall be leaving you all soon ... Bombay ...' Part of the attraction of the East may have been sexual. 'D'you know in China, after the dessert, they have these little boys who run up and down interesting the mandarins' penises?'

Sex featured often in our conversations, or rather, in Philip's shouted or whispered monologues. He saw the topic from various angles and even made national distinctions. 'The English take their sex lives so fucking seriously,' he told me, and on another occasion, 'Frenchmen have a holy horror of impotence', and then, lowering his voice a little, 'D'you know the best lovers in the world are the Russians?' Of his own sex life he spoke often. 'The older I get,' he declared, 'the more I like sex. What they call sex.' He praised and proclaimed the quality of his erections – 'even when I'm in my deepest cups' – lamented that the orgasm was 'so pitifully short in duration' and explained why homosexual activity was out of the question for him: 'The aperture is minute especially for a man of my dimensions. Tom Driberg has a very small one, I may tell you. I have a large one. *Of Arabic dimensions.* That's what I was told by one of my ladies. No, it is actually uncomfortably large. It is actually enormous. No buttocks could entertain it. No Servant's Entrance.'

He made more sense when he spoke about love, but here too he flew to extremes. He shouted at the top of his voice, 'Beauty is unpossessable, whether it be a woman or a ripe fig', and then, in a calmer voice, explained, 'You only cling when you're uncertain. People who really love each other are completely independent. People who really love each other have so little need to be together that they remain together.' Declarations about love and sex often fizzled out. 'Sexual love can be—' he began portentously and then said, 'I forget.' Another conversation ended with the declaration: 'Oh, I'm so clever. I wish I could sleep with myself.'

Philip O'Connor was well aware of his ability to exhaust people with such self-centred silliness. He said of himself, 'I am one of the most tiring people going', and 'I'm the sort of man who, if he was crying, would immediately squeeze an onion into his eye.' His self-assessments were often comically boastful or inaccurate. 'After all,' he said at one juncture, 'I am an extremely unimportant person, aren't I?' At another moment, he spoke of his 'excruciating intelligence' and proclaimed, 'I'm one of the most clever men alive, as a matter of a fact.' His semi-professional babyishness underlay much of what he said. All his life he said he had played 'babykins'. He had also liked to appear 'a whimsy-wheezy drunkard'. But then explained, 'It's only my social self that's so childish. In bed I'm as old as the hills.' And he was not content to leave the matter there. 'I'm getting old, aren't I?' he pressed on. 'I must be one of the oldest people in the world.' Then he added, 'My greatest achievement is not to change. I wake up feeling the same as I did when I was five years old.'

It was always a relief when some seriousness or unembroidered truth came through. One weekend he confessed that his writing had got 'horribly mangled on account of the drink' and said how much he hated being over-excited. 'This awful business of inflation, being above the ground – it's killing. It's only in a condition of ordinariness that you get your bright sparks.' But these were rare moments. Most of the time Philip seemed to be wrapped up in a comic vision of himself, proud that he wasn't a shopkeeper – ' "He wasn't a shopkeeper." Put that on my tombstone' – and displaying a jokey snobbery about his ancestry. When I questioned him about his moral character, he retaliated, 'Me a criminal? Coming from generations of justices? We used to dish out punishments. I still do.' When I asked if he felt any guilt about anything at all, he shouted back, 'None whatever! Good God, no! I've felt dirty, sloppy, never guilty. All guilt is humbug!' He argued that conscience was only 'fear of police, parents, authority, an exalted form of cowardice'. He claimed to have 'no natural obedience, no natural respect, no natural disrespect either'. When I asked him if he'd felt ashamed of anything he had done, he replied, 'No, no, no, no, no. I don't feel responsible for myself. Those who feel responsible for themselves are in the madhouse.' Perhaps so – but he was also prepared to use the madhouse as an escape route. He spoke with affection of his time in the Maudsley Hospital and one weekend he mentioned that he still owed £600 to an English court and explained, 'As a last refuge I could always get a certificate of lunacy.' When I asked if he was, in fact, a schizophrenic, he replied, 'Only usefully', then added in his flat man-of-the-world voice, 'No, I'm not actually, clinically.'

During these visits to Wimereux, I must have realized that some years back Philip's career had ground to a halt. In practical, concrete terms he rested heavily on his laurels. Every so often an old poem of his resurfaced in a new anthology – in 1973, a poem called 'Writing in England Now' appeared in the *Oxford Book of Twentieth Century English Verse*, edited by Philip Larkin – and from time to time he made a bid to get *Memoirs of a Public Baby* filmed or televised. I soon heard no more about the book on class which had supposedly brought him to London in the autumn of 1972. Panna tolerated this state of affairs, remarking with good humour that Philip had only earned £2 in the last five years.

Philip occasionally expressed a desire to be 'well known and established' and to lead 'a comfortable upper-class life, for a few years' but on the whole seemed content with his lot. The humiliations that

publishers and others had dealt out to him did not disturb his composure or air of self-importance. Nor did they diminish my interest in
him. Part of the lure of Philip O'Connor and Quentin Crisp was that
they were cobwebby figures whose finest hours seemed to have
occurred long ago. Somehow Philip had retained his interest in words
and delight in his own writing even though none of it was being
published – and he spoke with utter conviction about the writing
process. 'Being a writer,' he claimed, 'is nothing to do with writing well.
No writer writes well.' Of his own career, he said, 'I bathed in life
and dried myself on the typewriter.'

The distinctions between poetry and prose inspired further sweeping
judgements. 'Prose is addressed to idiots,' he said. 'The essence of
poetry is the questioning of reality.' In justification of his way
of dashing off poems, without editing them, he claimed that Yeats had
said that a poem that takes ten minutes to write is better than one
that takes thirty years. Both poetry and prose – all of it dashed off –
were employed in the journal which had now diverted him for several
years and which John Berger had once been editing for publication.
He spoke of his journal with affection. 'I'll read you a couple of pages
tonight from my philosophical garden,' he might promise. Some of
this stuff he described as a 'soufflé', other bits as 'more wodgy'. Buried
in these great incomprehensible chunks from which he read with great
exuberance were many sweetnesses, little gems and happy phrases.
'I love my writing,' he hardly needed to tell me. 'I think that's what's
wrong with it.' His object, he said, was to 'elucidate the apparent
nonsense of my life' and 'to tell them what I know'. But words, he
complained, were 'a medium of endless qualification', and 'When I
try to explain I become incomprehensible.' His frustration that writing
was not scientific made him try harder and moved him to contradict
himself endlessly and even cast aspersions on his only famous book.
'The *Baby* was too simplistic, ingenuous and naïve,' he declared, and
contradicted himself again by saying, 'I haven't done any writing that's
given me pleasure.' But minutes after such an utterance he might
change his tune completely and say with total conviction, 'So you see,
Andrew, in all our misery we are not unhappy.' And then detach

himself from the worries of writing by saying, 'All I want is to live with the woman I love until I die.'

He talked more about the past than the future. He talked of his family background, though his knowledge was sketchy and unreliable. 'There was a Burmese wife involved. Later on there was a marriage to a Lascelles. I hired an agency, genealogists, but they found nothing. In 1830, a Spring-Rice went to Burma . . .' Philip told me that he was born in Leighton Buzzard, and that he attended Dorking High School from nine to sixteen, but couldn't stand the sort of education offered. He had no idea whether his father was still alive, ditto his sister, his guardian and the Uncle Haslam mentioned in the book. He had an address for his first wife Jean, who had gone mad, and was now in a hospital in Scotland. He had tried suicide twice as a child, at fourteen in a gas oven and at seventeen in a river. He talked about the gypsies he met on the road and how they always had wads of money on them. 'I was an awful fool when I was young,' he told me. 'I hated familiarity, back-slapping, the coarseness of it.'

One morning he read out the long poem he had written in the Maudsley Hospital which had been made into a film. He also told me about the glass-roofed studio in Tite Street, Chelsea, where he had lived during part of the war and which I soon realized was the very flat where I had lived when I first came to London in the 1960s. He spoke affectionately of his house in Suffolk, its walnut tree, its moat and its strontium-yellow door. 'I grew my own carrots and lettuces. And I had a lovely little tree of pippins.' He used to love interviewing – 'I get too drunk now' – and talked at length about his last visit to the Rawsthornes in Suffolk. 'The chops were burnt and there were stacks of Beaujolais bottles around. Together they were like bacon and eggs. The thing sizzled. The wittiest couple I have ever met. They made life worth living. I wish the Widow Rawsthorne would call on us. I invited her and she turned a deaf ear.'

He also told me about Panna when he first met her – 'She was a sort of honeypot for everyone' – and about his former wives and girlfriends. One of them had declared, 'No baby of mine will ever eat tomato skin' which had enraged him. 'She hadn't even bothered to look in a medical dictionary. The harm tomato skin can do, by the way, is *nil*.' I asked him how he had avoided making payments to one of his ex-wives and he replied pompously, 'By the presentation of my honest face in the courtroom, sir. The magistrate said, "Pay a shilling a week in arrears." He knew a tartar when he saw one. I brought the house down with my impeccable courtroom behaviour.' Recollections of this event caused him to go into another reverie about his family connections. 'No, no. A lot of my family were lawyers, barristers, judges and whatnot. Yes, we have a judge in the family. Mr Justice O'Connor. He's still on circuit. Lots of us are in law. One of us died recently. General Sir Arthur O'Connor. I saw his widow on the ship. A porter was saying, "This way, Lady O'Connor." ' When I asked him if he had been in love with Anna Wing, he replied, 'What an extraordinarily rude question. What an unpleasant man you are!' And he then made a disapproving policeman-like cough to Panna and said, 'We're going to get rid of that fellow. We don't like you.' Moments later, he changed his tune, said '*Merci*' when I pointed the bottle at his empty glass and announced, 'I'll read you the end of *Wings of a Dove*.'

Philip often gabbled away about his favourite authors, film-stars, artists. For Henry James, who apparently had been to school in Boulogne, he had a lifelong affection, announcing, 'I'm reading James again' and identifying with him in little ways. 'James was terrified of laughter and the bark of dogs.' Trollope he described as 'another chap you don't finish with' and Dickens 'spread the great message of harmlessness'. For more minor and more contemporary figures he had no time at all. At the mention of Evelyn Waugh, he flapped his hand dismissively and said, 'He was no good.' V. S. Pritchett, he said, was 'a total idiot – George Eliot would have cleaned the lavatory with him'. Henry Moore was described as 'one of the world's worst sculptors, a complete charlatan' and John Betjeman as 'a fucking Tinkerbell, no poet at all'. When I asked why he considered Anthony Powell 'negligible, negligible', he replied, 'Because he doesn't mean a word of it.' When I praised Michael Holroyd's biography of Augustus John, I was met with even more explosive splutterings. 'It's appalling, absolutely appalling,' he told me. 'It's pedestrian, utterly pedestrian.'

Showbiz figures were more warmly received. Cecil Beaton, he said, had been 'dazzled by life'. Ken Russell seemed to be 'a funny sort of vulgarian' and he introduced me to the name of a famous film-maker called René Clair, who apparently concentrated on 'the flap of a jacket tail'. The most exciting person in films was Orson Welles. What about Chaplin? I asked. 'Chaplin wasn't a person. He was a clown.' When I then expressed interest in whether Chaplin was a pleasant man, he responded in his man-of-the-world voice, 'Oh, I shouldn't think so. Of course not.'

The richest and most intriguing field of discussion concerned Philip's and Panna's own circle of friends and acquaintances. He spoke often of the Widow Rawsthorne, whom I only knew as the subject of a famous triptych by Francis Bacon. He talked about Alan Sillitoe who had recently visited them in Wimereux and about an artist, Edith Young, whose son was the famous social historian Michael Young. He talked about someone called Patrick de Maré, whom he had apparently known since he was seventeen and about Stephen Spender and Aldous Huxley. Panna talked with equal enthusiasm about her friends in New York, produced a letter from Tom Wolfe and declared that Maxine de la Falaise was 'even more beautiful than Isabel Rawsthorne'. Both Panna and Philip admired the writer Heathcote Williams, now famous in London, and from time to time Panna talked about William Burroughs, to whom she had recently sent a pot of caviar which had constituted his entire Christmas lunch. For David Thomson, who seemed to be his best friend, Philip had unqualified admiration and respect, though this panegyric included references to Thomson's 'rat-like head' as well as to his 'totally unpretentious, genuinely limpid prose'.

And then of course there was Quentin Crisp, who had introduced me to Philip in the first place. When I asked him who was the most interesting man he had ever met he replied without hesitation, 'Crisp', but I soon detected a slightly condescending tone in even his use of this simple surname. He remembered Quentin's charitable acts but claimed that his heart was not engaged. He told me that Quentin was not concerned with the truth: 'He only reads the headlines, the advertisements.' Quentin's lifestyle and circumstances marked him as mildly inferior in Philip's eyes. He spoke of his room in Beaufort Street as 'that infernal cupboard' and said with relish, 'I once saw his grey thighs. He was wearing off-white knickers. His legs were the colour of cold suet pudding. In that beautiful room of his. Nescafé on the hob, I daresay.' Though Philip acknowledged he had launched Quentin into 'a little bit of his world' his tone remained slightly sneering. Out of the blue he once asked me, 'Are you going to Crisp's funeral?' and one of his many unfinished sentences began, 'I'm afraid our friend Quentin . . .'

At intervals during the day Philip and I gave each other space. I occasionally retreated to my bedroom. More often I went upstairs to the attic room. It was the quietest place in the house, though the full effects of the sea were magnified by the window in the roof. The tap of rain or shaking of the wind combined with the smell of oil paint and the whiff of old pipe smoke, and the presence of forgotten snacks – half a currant biscuit on a Chinese plate – created a cosy atmosphere. But, though Philip O'Connor was a purposeful-looking man and often spoke in a businesslike way, there was no real suggestion of work in progress.

I spent quite a lot of time here alone under the roof, cut off from the cries of 'Tais-toi!' from below and not always tempted downstairs by a fresh splurge of classical music or even by the pop of a cork. And though there was usually nothing in the typewriter, there were other things to read in various open boxes. In a file of letters from publishers I came across one from Charles Pick at Heinemann, beginning 'I enjoyed meeting you very much', and another from the literary agent Herbert Van Thal, saying, 'I was absolutely delighted to hear from you, and even more delighted that you would like to come to me to have your literary affairs looked after as I was a great admirer of *Memoirs of a Public Baby*.' Nothing had come of these gushings – and other correspondents were far less complimentary. One publisher had written, 'I can't at all take your long abstractions. I always feel the utmost relief when you get down to the concrete again, if only by some fine image.' Though I had now established that Philip had published nothing new for several years, I learnt that he had found an outlet for his unpublished pieces at the University of Texas. In a catalogue of the material which the university's library had bought from him over the recent years were items with enticing titles like 'Untitled Work on his Return to France', 'Uses of Loneliness' and 'The Secrets of Naughtiness'.

In another file, there was a sad letter from his ex-wife Nicolle, from an address in Suffolk – 'I'm rather broke, if you can send anything to help' – and an even sadder one from Maria Scott, mother of his children Sarah and Peter: 'I think Sarah minded that you never wrote to her for her wedding. Was it because you had no money? It didn't matter, Philip. She just wanted a goodwill message.' Even more touching was the entry in his address book for his first wife Jean: 'Villa 11' at a hospital in some Scottish village I'd never heard of.

Sometimes, while I was engaged in these studies, Philip O'Connor would start mounting the flimsy staircase and enter the attic in a dramatic and accusatory manner. His attitude towards me included elements of jokiness, rudeness, understanding, mockery, flattery and cruelty and he would switch between these attitudes in the course of a short conversation. On the lightest level, he concentrated on my foolishness and many of his remarks were double-edged. Even at the station, he might greet me with 'You are such a fool . . . You are so stupid' and in the course of a Wimereux day he might scream at me, 'You fool! You funny little boy!' and, within earshot, ask Panna 'Where's that halfwit?' and 'Won't it be interestingly amusing not to have Andrew here again?' In my company, he declared, 'You need educating, you milky-mouthed little wretch' and, in a vaguely complimentary way, 'You may be the most utter fool I ever met.'

He might then embark upon a sort of flattery, stating in various different ways that he liked me. 'I like you very much as a matter of fact', or 'I like you. Very much', were followed by the reasons why he liked me. 'I like you because you're a fool, in the Dostoevskian sense of the word. You're not corrupted', and then, a fresh thought striking him, 'That's why I like you. You remind me of Bangkok, Thailand, Shanghai.' As far as I know, there is nothing oriental about me but the delicacy with which he pronounced these place-names gave some authority to his observation. He also declared, 'I like you because you're *familiar*.' He referred often to our first meeting. Remarks like 'When I first saw you I knew that you knew me' and 'I'm more yourself than you'll ever be' were hard to follow, but I agreed that Philip and I might have had a 'common unplacement'. On other occasions he said that I was 'Old English', 'very Dickens-like' and 'a nice fellow' who reminded him of Pilgrim in John Bunyan. Even these compliments seemed tinged with double meaning. 'You have no fundamental hostility,' he pronounced. 'And that comes out in your hands, which are like two well bred vultures.' And Philip was not averse to asking, 'Would you mind knowing me until I die?' And 'Do you like me?' When I answered in the affirmative, he looked at his watch and said, 'Then in that case—' Was it more wine he wanted or some other favour?

All this attention was heart-warming and through it filtered a kind of encouragement. 'You're quite a lover, aren't you?' he asked and 'Isn't she lovely? Don't you know she's beautiful? That girl of yours? More than that, she's got character.' When I first met Philip and when he spoke these words, I had no girlfriend but went along with the fantasy and was sustained by it. 'D'you know you're in love?' Philip persisted. 'With whom?' I asked. 'With no one,' Philip replied. 'That's why you can have another drink.' Later he said, 'You need a strong woman with a sense of humour and above all she must make fun of your *greed*.' On another occasion, he asked, 'Have you ever been entangled in any homosexual—?' but did not finish his sentence and early on in our friendship he had said, 'We met at the right time. We'd both been bottled long enough, laid down long enough.'

The relationship often mystified him, however. 'Why do you come to see an old man across the sea?' he asked, and then, 'I don't know why you've got to know us. I don't know why you visit us. I don't know why you go snoogling up in my studio. Haven't you got enough data now?' Another time he said, 'If your father had loved you, you'd never have got to know me.' There was some truth in this but exposure to my father had also taught me how to deal with eccentricity, even given me a taste or affection for it. It's too corny to describe Philip as a father or even an older brother substitute but undoubtedly Philip and Panna together provided me with an expanding alternative family, an exotic haven, intellectual uplift, some insight into literary life and into myself: 'You like me,' said Philip 'because I tell you the truth.'

Philip was also my first serious drinking companion after James Graham, and his natural, automatic generosity with wine and food was seductive. This generosity was matched by my own neediness. 'The truth about you is you're a baby,' Philip pronounced on one of my earliest visits. 'Now a baby of twenty-seven is a little bit off.' How much I understood Philip O'Connor is another question. 'Don't be too sure about anything about me,' Philip warned at one moment. At another, he said, 'You begin to understand old O'Connor?' and later, 'You go through a curious facsimile of understanding me.'

In a way, the relationship between me and Philip *was* physical. All his movements, his exits and entrances were calculated, self-conscious and comic – and I responded to them in kind. I never saw him off guard or fully relaxed – as I occasionally had seen Quentin Crisp – though he could go through the motions of relaxation and ease with aplomb. He walked round me just as Aldous Huxley had apparently walked round him forty years earlier. Once he had suddenly sat down very close to me and asked, 'Have you ever spoken to anyone man to man?' and then looked at me over his spectacles and out of the corner of his eye. 'Few people survive my investigation,' he told me. Another time he entered my room while I was still in bed and after his initial 'Are you very intelligent?' had done an Inspector Maigret act for my benefit. He had examined my bedding and looked into the pockets and even the crutch of my discarded trousers and at my wristwatch. '*Two* jewels,' he tut-tutted.

In *Memoirs of a Public Baby*, Philip had shown that he had an overriding interest in people's physical appearances and I had come under his sharpest scrutiny. My demeanour, he said, gave the impression that I had been 'half-starved of love, understanding and respect' and that I had been 'left alone' all my life. He also encouraged me to take a good look at him. 'If you looked at me well enough I could be relieved of the chore.' One weekend he asked, 'Do you observe that I'm not beautiful?' and soon afterwards began to tamper with his lack of beauty by growing a beard. 'I've got such lines of meanness, misery and disgust,' he explained. 'The beard covers them.' At the start of the process, he announced his beard was going to be 'like an American president's, almost an imperial' but when Panna observed that it still had no shape, he retorted, 'I can't stop stroking the damned thing.' The beard made him look older, rather than younger, and more ferocious when he shouted his refrains.

With Quentin Crisp, I was never more than an interviewer or a feed. With Philip O'Connor, I was seduced into doing a double act. 'We could have played Laurel and Hardy,' Philip proclaimed and on another occasion as I filled my pipe with his Caporal Export, 'Now you're looking like Sherlock Holmes robbing Dr Watson of his tobacco.' When I challenged him, 'You don't keep to your contracts, do you?' he replied in his tut-tutting, businesslike voice, 'Always, yes, meticulous.' And then he added, 'We've got beyond, at nearly sixty, tit-for-tattery' and 'I'm practically impossible to insult, I'm far too squirmy.' One weekend he went at me with a large pair of red scissors, snipping the air, and announcing, 'Isn't it funny to be humans together? Later we'll be dead.' Another weekend, he pronounced, 'You're lower upper-middle. I've finally graded you. Genetically – you must learn this word – I'm *royal*.' Once I asked him, 'You've never been decorated, have you?' and once he began a conversation with the words, 'What have you been doing lately?' and added, 'You see, I'm beginning to speak like an Englishman.' Equally out of the blue and often after a long pause came pronouncements of a more surreal nature. 'I wouldn't presume your scrotum was made of leather. I would at least subscribe chamois to it.'

Occasionally I told him about my life in London, and about my father and began one conversation with 'I've been thinking of all the things you've got in common with my father', to which he quickly replied, 'Such as hatred of you!' When the wine became too much for me and I started talking about the progress of a current hangover, he accused me of issuing bulletins about my health and added, 'I thought that was my prerogative.' When I said with studied pomposity, 'Thank you for your friendship, Philip', he swallowed it whole and shouted immediately for Panna. 'Thank You For Your Friendship! An English remark I've just collected!' Then, in regular waves, came the usual qualified doses of flattery. 'Do you like us? We like you. A bit.' And 'You don't seem to have the brute in you. And you compensate by being greedy, mean and all the things that we know so well.' And into all this were mixed occasional comments about my life in London – 'Have you still got that awful unroasted hen living upstairs?' – and snippets of advice about my work for the glossy magazines. 'Why don't you get hold of Getty? He lives in Guildford.' The idea that the oil millionaire lived *in* rather than *near* Guildford betrayed a comic disdain on Philip's part for the residential arrangements of the rich.

Philip's remarks about me sometimes had a darker, more serious hue, which may have overlapped or eclipsed Quentin's comments about my lack of 'moss'. One weekend he told me, 'You'll die miserably. Someone you love will be horrible to you. You'll become socially impossible if you live. You need to plug into the world. You have no real rapport with people.' He often spoke cruelly about my impending departure – 'I'm glad you're going tomorrow' – and made cold asides to Panna – 'We won't have him again' – followed by 'Have you got a corkscrew, *chérie*?'

I have said very little about Panna Grady – and even less about her daughter Ella. Perhaps this is because Ella was still only a little girl and perhaps because she spent a good deal of time away, sometimes in America visiting her father, and perhaps because even when she was present, she kept her distance from Philip, whom she was still learning how to deal with. Panna, on the other hand, was always present or within earshot during most of our conversations and her attendance, sometimes dressed in a billowing pale purple dressing-gown, which inspired Philip to proclaim, as she entered the room, 'Mother Russia!', was crucial. Without her, Philip could not have coped. The house and everything in it belonged to Panna. She paid every bill, bought all his clothes and had even got him a whole set of new teeth, now partly covered by his beard, and already deteriorating: 'He blackens them with his life, his foul mouth,' Panna explained. In every sense she propped him up and gave him the freedom to do as he liked. They were not in each other's pockets. Their relationship, their love affair, was pursued at long distance: there was a huge amount of talk from Philip about love but few public embraces except as a kind of jest. From Panna's point of view this was what she wished. 'One isn't responsible for his good humour,' she explained. 'It's self-perpetuating. It makes for a nice independence. If a man comes to you to make him whole, it's dreary.' But however detached from Philip she may have been, she monitored his conversations very carefully and sometimes interjected from downstairs, 'Yes, Philip?' or more fiercely, 'What you are saying is *totally untrue*.' She remained beguiled by his mannerisms – 'He pulls down his spectacles and gives me these intellectual looks' – and when I asked if she believed in God, her response was to make a gesture at Philip and say, 'Yes, there he is!'

And Philip, of course, talked a great deal about Panna and idolized her in his own way. 'She and I are in love,' he confided. 'We have the same tastes, points of view.' Another time, he said, 'Panna's the only person I care about. And d'you know why? She reminds me of my mother.' And then, again, 'She's the cleverest woman I've ever met. She's so clever she can wear her stupidity like a pearl on her neck.' And 'If there's one person who knows that the art of living is giving it's Panna.' In a more explanatory mood, he added, 'She understands me with her hands, her screen-like hands. Her hands are like Japanese fans. There's nothing like love, Andrew Barrow. It makes life possible.' More calculatingly, he explained, 'I think the intellectual rewards of fidelity are so great few can take them. If you can survive the boredom, you'll find something honey-sweet the other side.' In a conspiratorial tone, he also asked, 'You haven't seen her legs properly have you? They are the best in the world.' He also said, 'I'm trying to write on her knickers but I can't get them into the typewriter' and more perversely, 'I'd love to see a beautiful boy's prick going into her.'

At other less enchanted times, he spoke of a permanent 'look' in Panna's eyes and seemed to relish the idea that she might lead a double life. When she spent rather a long time closing the shutters of the dining-room window, he asked, 'Was he there?' At one of his wilder moments, he exclaimed, 'She prefers Tom Driberg to me! She prefers Alex Trocchi to me! She prefers Maxim to me!' One weekend, he complained that there was no heart or hearth at Clair de Lune: 'I'm not happily married. She's like a castle. I wait for the portcullis to ascend. So I can walk in her chambers.' He occasionally talked of being bored, of leaving her, even of living in London again. 'D'you know every day I plot to get away from her? And, every night, before I go to sleep, I decide I won't.' At other wild moments he reinforced this decision, shouting, 'Panna and I will never leave each other. We'll always be together. Always! Always! Always!'

Philip rarely allowed Panna to speak, but when she got the chance I was touched by the generosity of her views – 'Ugly men are nice' – and her frankness about the famous men she had been to bed with. When Philip would permit it, she ministered to me, called me 'Baby-doll' and talked with sad zest about party-giving in London and New York. 'You need a lush woman to give a reception.' She also produced her old notebooks and gave me an address for William Burroughs in London and the telephone number for the poet and editor Michael Horovitz. She talked about antique dealer Christopher Gibbs, the writer John Michell and other Londoners I'd heard of. During these conversations, Philip would get increasingly impatient and a full shouting-match between the two of them might follow, in which Panna held her own. These spats never lasted long and were often followed by gentle overtures from Philip, like 'Shall I cook supper, my beloved?' and 'Will you marry me?' An hour or two later, after further scraps and reconciliations, we might adjourn to the television room downstairs in which Maxim also slept. One night here, Philip ignored Panna's remark, 'They've found oil in the North Sea', but responded to her announcement that there was a film on TV with Marlon Brando playing Julius Caesar and John Gielgud playing Cassius by saying, 'What can I play?' Later, on the sofa covered with toys, on which Maxim often slept instead of his bed, Philip would make assignations with Panna: 'Are you coming to bed with me tonight?' or 'Are you coming up tonight? I'll kill you if you don't.' Usually I would retire long before anyone else and from my own room on a lower floor I would listen to the sound of the sea mingled with declarations of love, intimate pleading and the crying of children upstairs.

I have probably given the impression that these weekends in Wimereux were spent entirely in the hothouse of those upper floors at Clair de Lune. In fact there were many outings. Sometimes, if I stopped him on the staircase, I would join Philip on his first early excursion of the day. He usually shopped alone and never with Panna – 'I don't like to be seen out with her as a matter of fact' – but responded amiably to my company. He walked very slowly, even when it was raining, hunched and suspicious with his large umbrella held aloft, which somehow made him look like someone out of an oriental print. 'You're taller than me, aren't you?' he remarked. 'Much taller,' I replied. 'Not *much* taller, don't be stupid,' he retorted. He eyed the passers-by in a twitchingly hostile manner. 'I don't know who could love the Northern French,' he said. 'I'm nearly dead with boredom. Their sophistication consists of loafing, casting meaningful glances, slit-eyed nonchalance.' 'Who's that bastard?' I asked, playing along with him. 'Police spy,' he replied. He then continued, 'I'm thought very odd in this town. I didn't fit into England. I don't fit into France. Where will I fit in? The cemetery?' Then he pulled himself together and said, 'Well, will you come with me into this shop?'

Once in the butcher's or greengrocer's, he chatted happily with the shopkeepers, making them laugh and screech and somewhat under- mining his protestations that he hated the shopkeeper mentality. He showed me the hairdressing salon in the Rue Carnot where some of his watery oil paintings were on sale, then a funeral director's bearing the inscription 'Pompes Funèbres Générales' and other shops that he said had been there half a century earlier. Finally we entered the *pâtisserie* or *salon de thé*, also named *pavillon des gourmets*, where he had spent those crucial years. We sat down in the darkened middle parlour, smoked our pipes and eyed our surroundings. According to Philip, everything was the same as in Madame Tillieux's day, the same cakes and sweets in the same windows, the same plasterwork on the ceiling and the same doors leading through to the inner private salon where he had once been thrilled by the sight of a boiled egg. Today I wish I had asked him for more, for every sacred detail, every unpub- lished memory.

Later, mid-morning expeditions involved or ended with a visit to a bar. Here Philip ordered a special beer that came from a cupboard behind the counter and was dressed in silver foil like champagne and may have come from Belgium. Sometimes this was not available and he had to settle for a French *bière de luxe*, which he allowed me to finish for him. 'Yes, you may. It is filthy. French beer's like sucking a pissing cock.' And he added, 'The only beer I don't dislike is draught Guinness. It soothes and encourages.' With or without alcoholic satisfaction,

Philip relaxed. 'Actually this is the jolliest of cafés. For short periods.' Looking at a notice on the wall, I observed, 'There's a party here on Saturday night', to which Philip replied, 'Always, but I can't take my grey locks to it.' Then he cast his eye around at the other customers and after engaging with the barman declared, 'It's only in bars that I'm really appreciated. You should see me in an English tea-shop. I sweat with fear.' He also turned his attention to me, asking, 'Explain how you are able to speak so vividly, vivaciously, charmingly, wittily?', and when I needed to relight my pipe handed me his lighter with the kind of gracefulness that might accompany a gift. When I tried to get involved with others at the bar and referred to Philip O'Connor as my father he said nothing to start with, but remarked later, 'You could well be my son as a matter of fact.' These sessions were never prolonged and were sometimes satisfactorily cut short by Panna's arrival. On one occasion we moved on to the Atlantic Hotel, where Philip declared, 'Let's have an aperitif on the terrace. Then I'll dabble with chicken. I could do the chicken interestingly.'

Some afternoons there were longer excursions into the rolling countryside behind Boulogne. Before Philip regained his driving licence, these trips involved Panna as the driver, Maxim and little Felix but never Ella. On the point of departure Philip might suddenly sound like any father, shouting 'Camera!' as we got into the big bouncy Citroën, and add to the sense of normality with other harmless sentimental remarks, like 'The air's much cleaner than it is in England. That's why I really like France. Everything's much cleaner.' One of the places we visited was Pittefort, where there was a small chateau, a church and a bar, but other signs that teasingly reminded me of England: cattle in a meadow, roses in the walled garden behind the bar. Panna and Philip were more interested in the chateau's owner. 'The Marquis de Picolay,' said Philip. 'It's a very old family. It goes back to Henry the Fourth. Henry of Navarre. Oh yes, we know this.' They also knew about a recent party at the chateau, for the christening of the Marquis's granddaughter, with guests in Bentleys. Interest in such details combined oddly with their extraordinary reclusiveness at Clair de Lune, but in the walled garden behind the bar family issues dominated. When Philip's youngest child Felix, hardly a year and a half, began to pull up newly planted flowers, Panna exclaimed, 'Look, Philip, look!' 'Exactly, I know,' Philip replied without a glance in the child's direction. He was more interested in complaining about another customer, 'What an ugly person!', encouraging Panna to protest, 'Why d'you bother to look at ugly people?' 'Because they look at me,' Philip replied.

When Philip got his licence back, he and I went on these rural ramblings on our own. 'I'm going to take him round my beer circuit,' he told Panna. 'Will you stay out? Back for tea?' she replied with housewifely self-effacement. The excursion, he said, had become a compulsion, taking in Pittefort and other villages. 'D'you know I do this practically every day? Isn't it awful?' In darkened rural inns he upbraided the ladies behind the bar and remarked, 'It's never changed, this Frenchness, and it never will.' Somewhat to my surprise I found I drank faster than Philip, but when he stopped the car on our return journey to Wimereux and remarked, 'I think I'll have a little something in here', I stood in front of the door of the roadside bar and tried to prevent him entering. 'Don't do that,' he told me. 'Anyhow it's against the law.' The tour often ended at the tiny Café de la Gare at Wimereux where we drank *eau de vie* to further protests from Philip. 'All my enemies are here. All my enemies have moustaches.'

During these weekend visits I sometimes went out alone on the streets, brief excursions on my own initiative or perhaps to get more wine for Philip. On winter nights, the greyness and the dampness, the barking dogs and the motorcycles tearing around corners only served to emphasize the strange inner warmth of Clair de Lune. A lot of the houses were empty and the whole town was a bit like a stage set, but the smell of fires and wood smoke indicated that all was not quite as dead as it seemed. Sometimes I wandered onto the beach and looked up at the semi-darkened façade of Clair de Lune and was delighted by the beacon of light from Philip's kitchen. In the summer, at the height of the day, I made the same trip though the beach was now crowded with children on slides and swings in a fenced-off area called Le Mickey Mouse Club. This summer invasion under his windows was 'hell' for Philip though his children enjoyed the beach and I did too. One hot weekend I swam in the sea and glanced back at the house to see the white-jacketed shape of Philip O'Connor watching me from an upper window. Exhilarated, I would return from these outings and climb the uncarpeted staircase at Clair de Lune to be greeted by the smell of delicious cooking, loud classical music on the kitchen radio and a proposal from Philip – 'Let's have a quarrel.'

Philip O'Connor and I did not quarrel but by the summer of 1975, I was aware of a deterioration in our relationship. On my part, I had started to feel judgemental about him. For all his domestic finesse and dexterity in the kitchen, he seemed unable to build a home, an organized life. His spiky fastidiousness was grounded in chaos. During the summer months, he also had to contend with the lodgers to whom Panna let the lower two floors. When one of these men appeared one day on the upper floor to pay a shy social call, Philip screamed that he would call the gendarmes. When there were lodgers, I had to sleep in the bosom of the family, either in Ella's room if she was in America or in Philip's studio upstairs. Proximity tightened the net. Meanwhile, a neighbour had begun building a garage at the back of the house. 'God, that fucking noise!' Philip screamed. 'The ramparts are crumbling! People are beginning to stroke each other's buttocks!' In his workroom I found a terse note from Lawrence Durrell discouraging him from buying a property in the South of France. And I also felt uneasy about the way the children were being brought up. One evening I found Maxim asleep on a bed upon which also lay a bagatelle board while Felix tore round the room being fed After Eight mints. And into this disorder Philip had not hesitated to introduce a dog. This large and amiable puppy was a sheepdog named Nico, whose wagging tail swept objects off the table. It was often in the kitchen gnawing at bread and barked often if not continuously. One weekend, I screamed, 'This is a madhouse.' Half an hour later, after further diversions, Philip replied, 'This, by the way, is *not* a madhouse. A madhouse is where everything is swept under the carpet!' Then early one morning I heard Panna trying to be sick. Further off, I heard a cock crowing or some wailing beast.

During the daytime, the shouting and bad temper got worse. Cries of '*Panna! Panna! Panna!*' drowned or mimicked the thud of the sea and there were further cries of 'God, I can't stand it!' If Philip was merciless to Ella, even when she looked after the children – 'Don't make him cry, you stupid fat fool!' – he was soon savage to me. For a while I put up with this onslaught, this rejection, aware that his mood might change at any moment into something much nicer. It usually did improve but not enough to prevent me wondering what I was doing there. My last visit to Wimereux was on the weekend of 15 November 1975. I stayed only one night and would not invite myself there again. Nor was I invited.

Oakley Street

I'm still nervous anyway after a man called O'Connor author of a long ago best seller *Memoirs of a Public Baby* came to my house and ran at me, lunging with his cane and shrieking that I was the ugliest woman he had ever met.

EMMA TENNANT, *Burnt Diaries*, 1998

I will now describe how my life in London had been enriched by my friendship with Philip O'Connor – and how my urban struggles were ameliorated by the intellectual grandeur or pretension of my life across the Channel. Some of Philip's zest had immediately rubbed off on me, and infected by his exuberant attitude towards the opposite sex I had begun a love affair with a married woman who lived near Victoria Station and with whom I often stayed on my way to or from the boat-train. I had also acquired some of Philip's mannerisms and habits and in my basement flat in Oakley Street I hung up his paintings, cooked his kind of food and let out some of his gasps as I did so. While my landlady pit-pattered about upstairs, I smoked Philip's pipes and dug into the same Caporal Export tobacco.

My weekends in Wimereux had taught me a lot about bohemian life and, rather surprisingly, I would run into quite a few of the people in London whom either Philip or Panna had mentioned. In Portobello Road, I had quite literally bumped into Alexander Trocchi, who after a few warm words said, 'I must dash', and crashed into someone else. At a party in Belgravia, I had met the tall and imposingly highbrow figure of Nicholas Mosley, who had touched upon his affair with

Panna Grady in his novel, *Impossible Object*. I had also met Tambi-muttu and visited the one-room flat in Cornwall Gardens where he seemed to sleep in frilly women's sheets. A proposed pub-crawl with this now venerable long-haired figure had ended before we had reached our first pub, when a policeman confronted Tambi with the words, 'Haven't you had enough?' In the French pub in Soho, I met the large and oppressive figure of Paul Potts, who told me he had fallen in love with Philip but added, 'I'm so *un*queer you can't believe it.' When I boasted to Potts about my friendship with his old friend, he had said grumpily, 'I didn't know you were *all tied up* with him.' I had gone home to read one of Potts's books, which included the lines, 'I was so lonely and hurt. Everything I had loved in my life had turned me down. I was so ugly I screamed with fright at the very thought of myself.' And after getting drunk at James Graham's wedding at Clar-idges, I had called at Heathcote Williams's flat in Notting Hill, still wearing my tail-coat, and told him that I was Philip O'Connor's son – a proposition which he took completely in his stride.

I had also paid Annie Mygind impromptu visits in Chelsea and encouraged her to talk about our friend across the Channel. She described and imitated the gurgle in his throat as he drank wine – 'a great gulp of air goes down with it' – and mentioned his 'penetrating poetic analysis of life situations'. She also declared that Philip was 'a complete baby' and prophesied that he would never grow up – 'I think I can guarantee that' – and declared that his way of making friends with people was to tear them to pieces – 'He's not torn *you* to pieces, has he?' Sometimes she asked me about my own private life – 'Got a girlfriend?' – and once when I rang her doorbell, she appeared at an upper window, shook her head as if she was very tired and told me to telephone the next day.

Wherever I went I would talk about Philip O'Connor and was often pleased with people's responses. In the *Encounter* office, the managing editor Margot Walmsley declared that Philip O'Connor was 'under-estimated in every way'. In the French pub, a man called Bryce McNab described O'Connor as 'the one who got away' and at a literary party a publisher named Smith declared, 'He's drinking himself to death over there, isn't he?' Over cocktails in Hanover Terrace, a few doors away from Panna Grady's old home, the writer and film-maker Andrew Sinclair told me that Philip O'Connor had been inspiring people for twenty years, but over lunch in the French Club in St James's, the author Jonathan Gathorne-Hardy said that Philip sounded more interesting to *hear about* than actually *meet*. Even when I did not talk about him I was reminded of his existence by other hunched-up arrogant figures on the streets of London and even by the despairing sigh of a decorator who was working on the outside of the house where I lived.

I also, of course, talked often about Philip O'Connor to Quentin Crisp. When I asked Quentin what our mutual friend across the Channel might be doing at that very moment, he replied without missing a beat, 'Drinking and despairing.' He also said, 'Mr O'Connor's not a completely organized man but he's got endless, almost inexhaustible vitality.' He spoke of Philip's ability to 'discard the past' in terms of responsibility for others and made a comparison between O'Connor and Paul Potts, to the latter's disadvantage. 'Mr O'Connor lives in a sort of dream but he can bounce forward. Mr Potts lives in a horrid fantasy about women and their attractions. He would be a *hopeless* interviewer.' Quentin also volunteered that Philip and I were 'made for each other'.

Be that as it may, I also talked and thought a lot about Wimereux, which from my London perspective seemed a magical, secret place across the Channel. In an old guidebook I learnt that 'the pig and rabbit thrive in close confines in Picardy and the frog prospers in its ponds and marshes'. Most of those I spoke to seemed to have no knowledge of the place but a few people responded warmly. A child psychiatrist, David Shaffer, told me he knew Wimereux well and had even stayed at the Atlantic Hotel where I had had cocktails with Philip. Niki Trethowan mentioned that her grandmother had often visited the town before the war, and more unpredictably my father recalled visiting Wimereux as a Cambridge undergraduate in order to play golf, remembering it only as a 'sandhilly place'.

A much stronger and more personal link between Philip O'Connor's world and my own was also established when I was telephoned out of the blue by his son Peter. Infused by Philip's spontaneity I suggested that he came round to my flat immediately and an hour or two later he swung through the door wearing a hat that his father had given him. Peter O'Connor was twenty-five-years old, four years my junior, and had his father's concentrated looks combined with gypsy curls which he complemented with a waistcoat and scarves. Peter told me, 'My father wasn't around when I was a child. I only met him three or four times. I just remember him pushing my pram, going to the National Assistance.' He told me he had only recently made contact with him and had visited him in Wimereux. 'When we met at Boulogne, his lips were quivering. He was very nervous.' During dinner in a Chelsea restaurant not far from the one where I had first had lunch with Philip, Peter said, 'You think he's great, don't you?' and 'I expect you think I'm a pale version of my father.'

During the next few weeks and months, I saw a lot of Peter O'Connor and received the benefit of his own wisdom. He mocked me for my snobbery – 'When you see someone famous you stiffen like a whippet on a leash' – and introduced me to Carlsberg Special – 'It's very nice. It will make you very happy' – and to various members of his family. I visited his small vivacious mother, Maria Scott, at her house in Crouch End where lunch was served on a staircase, each participant tucked into a corner of their own, and late one night we called together on Anna Wing at her flat near Broadcasting House. 'Peter who?' she asked from behind her locked door before admitting us in her short nightgown. Then she gushed at us, asked me if I was a homosexual and showed me a photograph of Philip taken some twenty years earlier grinning at his typewriter with the look of a wild dog on his face. During the months ahead, I felt privileged to meet different figures from Philip O'Connor's past and present and also took the step of introducing Peter to my married friend, whom he later described as looking like 'an over-bred Afghan hound'. As my friendship with Peter deepened, our frames of reference broadened and he was soon able to remark, 'I notice my father's occurring less and less in our natter.'

This might have been so, but neatly laid out letters had arrived regularly from Wimereux, tightening the links between me and Philip. Some of these responded to my suggestions that I should visit on such and such a weekend. Others contained requests for things like Henry James's *Princess Casamassima* and new needles for his stereo system. There was also a far-fetched request that I should use my 'sleuth's avidity' to try and track down a man called Leonard Lowndes who had once been the lover of his sister Desirée. If I found him, Philip wanted me to ask him if he knew anything about the current whereabouts of his sister whom he had not seen since before the war. There were also bits of news, like 'Ella returns to the States in July' and more dramatically, 'I'm five weeks on Vichy.' These letters would be flipped down the inner staircase by my landlady with the announcement 'Philip O'Connor!', causing me to leap from my bed. Once she called out 'Easter egg!' but I found a parcel from France containing fresh supplies of Caporal Export.

There had also been visits from Philip in person. However much he professed to hate England, he made the crossing at least once a year. Sometimes he telephoned as early as seven o'clock in the morning to announce his surprise arrival. Sometimes he materialized unannounced on my doorstep at an equally early hour and disappeared again with another flick of his tail. During these visits he stayed at the Grosvenor Hotel at Victoria Station or more obscure places elsewhere, all of which, even the humdrum Ashburn Hotel in Cromwell Road, I immediately saw in a new light. In London he wore an overcoat with a brown velvet collar and sometimes carried his typewriter and a walking-stick. He also brought his pipe, tobacco and eau de Cologne. These brief reappearances in his old battle zone were a kind of performance, invested with an air of detachment or old-fashioned leisure. He spoke of an old porter who had leapt forward to assist him at Victoria Station, saying, 'Willingly, sir, I'll carry your baggage', and 'This way, sir, how nice to see you again. Not like the old days, is it, sir?' Philip claimed this man would guide him through the crowds and help him onto the boat-train. 'He thinks I'm an old gentleman. He thinks I am rich. We have played many roles.' Was it the same porter who had once declared, 'You're a happy man, sir', and been enlightened by Philip to the effect that jollity was not the same thing as contentment?

The purpose of these visits was not easy to discern. When I asked what he was doing in England, he replied, 'I'm suffering from a dirty handkerchief and catarrh' and sometimes he found things to praise in London, like the Selfridges windows which one Christmas were given over to scenes from Dickens. He told me this without mentioning that he had once worked at Selfridges and without me revealing that I too had once worked at the Oxford Street store. Was seeing old friends like David Thomson and Annie Mygind one reason for his visits? Sometimes he stayed with these friends and sometimes he quarrelled with them. When Annie Mygind told him, 'You're getting a bore' and refused to lend him money, he responded, 'Fancy *bothering* not to lend me £10', and a stay under her roof produced the lament from his hostess, 'I was woken by him creeping around at five past six in the morning.' Another night, these two old friends had gone to the Chelsea Arts Club where Philip got very drunk and according to Annie, 'slunk off into the night'. A visit to David Thomson's house in Camden Town was preceded by an upsetting visit to the lavatory at the nearby Edinburgh Castle pub. 'The seat was absolutely slimy,' Philip reported. 'There was no paper. It was the dirtiest thing that's ever happened to me. I had to wipe my bottom with my handkerchief and, just to revenge myself, I put my handkerchief into the cistern.' At Regent's Park Terrace, David Thomson had then biffed Philip on the jaw after he had said something insulting about Martina, and Philip had gone off in a huff, declaring, 'I shall not call on you again. Never, never, never.' He had also gone on other abortive missions. He had arranged to meet the publisher Anthony Blond at the Reform Club and quickly became impossible; he had telephoned Tambimuttu but found him still in bed; and he had called on the writer Emma Tennant at her home in Elgin Crescent, where she was editing the magazine *Bananas*, and caused the rumpus described at the start of this chapter.

Philip often ended up drunk in my company too. He started cheerily, pouring down wine very fast or smacking his lips as he took his first gulp of Guinness, warning 'I shall soon be too hilarious for propriety.' One evening together ended in a pub in Hampstead, where the barmaids refused to serve him and bit their lips in preparation for another outburst of his wit. Philip had then stood out in the street shouting and screaming for a taxi in a sore-throated voice. But there were also sober moments when he continued to quiz and speculate about me, as well as calling me 'You little wretch!' and saying, 'Don't you dare climb up our Wimereux stairs!' His own feelings about Wimereux sometimes became more hostile in his absence. 'Oh, I hate the place,' he said, 'I know absolutely nobody in that awful town, just shopkeepers', and 'I don't feel at home anywhere.' But at other times he talked about getting back to 'my harbour in life' and said of Panna, 'I've found my mate. I've been looking for her for thirty years', and, with odd detachment, 'I took a mess and made out of it my heart's desire.' At wilder moments he again enthused, 'I am never leaving that woman. *Never! Never! Never!*'

On only one occasion was Philip accompanied by his mate. On 19 July 1973, she had come to London with Philip for one night, stayed at the Grosvenor Hotel and momentarily re-entered the world she had abandoned six years earlier. That evening she and Philip gave a dinner at the Connaught Hotel attended by William Burroughs, Allen Ginsberg and Alex Trocchi. I did not know of the visit until the following day when Philip rang at 7.30 a.m. speaking in his usual timid telephone voice and invited me to lunch that day at the Vendôme in Dover Street. Here I found Panna, Philip and the Thomsons. After a while we were joined by the fashionable psychiatrist R. D. Laing and his new wife Utta. Laing ordered a double Pernod. I drank a lot of white wine. Later that afternoon I called drunkenly at the studio in Tite Street where I had lived in the 1960s and where Philip had lived during the war. After listening briefly to my outpourings, the current occupant said simply, 'Now, leave.'

During this period I suffered many such setbacks. I can only re-emphasize how Philip O'Connor helped frame my life, providing a yardstick with which to measure my experiences and a counterbalance to my father, who across the water on the Isle of Man sometimes put on a domestic performance which matched O'Connor's – 'Would you like a glass of port, Barrow?' – and cast an equally beady eye on the London scene. Among my father's fellow expatriates, I was interested to meet a retired farmer, Captain Thirkell Price, who spoke warmly of Peter O'Connor, whom he had met in Scotland during his footloose

Anna Wing. 'An enemy of the hidden and the dirty'.

Nicolle Gaillard-d'Andel in the yard at Croesor. 'Uncomplicated, un-literary and un-spoilt.'

Philip in Wales, early 1960s. 'A mind like a haystack in a gale, only now and then manageable with a rapidly applied canvas covering.'

Panna Grady. 'A beautiful ghostly figure in search of an identity, quite lost in England – they were so greedy with her.'

Laurie Lee, poet and autobiographer.
'A more sober version' of Philip's
condition.'

Patrick de Maré, Philip's lifelong
friend and admirer. 'I really do think
he was a genius.'

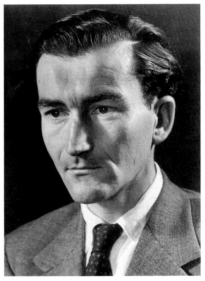

Tambimuttu, romantically upstaged
by Philip more than once.

Michael Hamburger, prolific writer
and translator, said by Philip to
possess 'a nice cleavage (which could
be put to coy uses) between his nature
and his culture'.

Edith Young at a tea party.
She encouraged Philip to 'tell all'
about his 'unique experiences'.

John Berger. The only art critic Philip
could read.

David Thomson. Philip's long-
suffering radio producer.

'The People's Poet' – Paul Potts shortly
before his death in a fire.

Joan Rhodes, the Mighty Mannequin, friend of Quentin, Philip and the author's father.

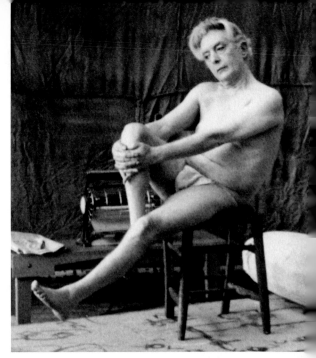

Quentin modelling in the 1970s. 'The only profession I have ever understood.'

Gordon Richardson, actor and fellow lodger at Beaufort Street.

Clockwise from top left: Quentin on stage at the King's Head Theatre, Islington, 1976 – explaining, pleading, recoiling and reading.

Quentin in his Chelsea room. 'A curtain-raiser for the *Rocky Horror Show*.'

The fireplace at Beaufort Street, drawn by Quentin for the author, mid-1970s.

Quentin aged eighty in New York, 1989.

Philip aged seventy-one at the relaunch of *Memoirs of a Public Baby*, March 1988.

Philip and his son Peter, Paris 1975.

Quentin at the christening of his great-great-nephew Ian Quentin Crawford, 1998. 'Don't let the name give you any ideas.'

Quentin with the author, New York, February 1989.

Philip with the author, south of France, April 1991.

days: 'A very romantic figure. Yes, a gypsy. We write but we haven't heard from him. Is he all right now?' While staying on the Isle of Man, I also attempted to read *Memoirs of a Public Baby* properly and was bemused when I found my father had appropriated the yellow-jacketed book and placed it beside his own bed.

My life in London remained fragmented. Though indulged by my married friend, I was often at a loose end and needed further diversions. Among others I still saw was Niki Trethowan, who continued to ask me to parties in the Knightsbridge and Chelsea flats she occupied in quick succession and at one stage shared with a pet rabbit. In return I occasionally asked her to lunch in Oakley Street. She was happy to descend to my level, but on one occasion the meal ended prematurely with the clump of her formidable mother coming down the area steps to pick her daughter up. To Niki and everyone else I met I continued to babble obsessively about Philip O'Connor – and I even gave her one of his paintings. The next time I visited her flat I was surprised to find the picture propped up in a place of honour.

My weekends in Wimereux had also offered a healthy contrast to the journalistic treadmill which now took up a lot of my energy. Much of my time in London was spent interviewing famous and not-so-famous people on a variety of pretexts. Some of these encounters were fiascos. The young Earl of Pembroke threw me out of his Kensington flat after a few minutes because I had done no homework for the interview and had not even taken the precaution of looking him up in *Who's Who*. Others were more long-suffering. On 8 September 1975, I went and interviewed the famous journalist and restaurant-reviewer Quentin Crewe in another Kensington flat. During the course of our conversation, he told me that he was beginning to get rather rattled by the growing fame of another man with a similar name.

PART FIVE

-22-

A Figure of Affection

I see your point about Crisp. Part of the appeal is that
he *wasn't* Oscar Wilde, but only a neighbourhood wit
and character. But the actor who will do Crisp properly must be a great virtuoso. Do you agree? He must
tear your heart and emotions to shreds while at the
same time making you laugh. But I think it can be
done in the film medium superbly well.

SAM ROSENBERG TO JOHN HAGGARTY, 21 August 1971

I must now retrace my steps and write about the rest of Quentin
Crisp's life in the late 1960s and early 1970s without dragging myself
too much into the story. The 1960s had ended on what he makes out
was a typically hopeless note. He would later write and talk about
'the long dark years' between the publication of *The Naked Civil
Servant* in January 1968 and its televising in December 1975. Throughout this period, Quentin chose to deny there was any bandwagon in
his favour and plays instead upon the negative aspects of his situation.
In the closing pages of his autobiography he had confessed, 'I am the
survivor they hoped they would not find – something too broken to
be restored by active life but not quite ready for decent burial. My
lips still move.'

In keeping with this dismal image, he had played down his first
television appearance, at the time of the book's publication. Unwit-
nessed by me, he had been interviewed on 11 January 1968 on a
programme called *Late Night Line Up* and asked about the 'oddities'
of his appearance and domestic routine. He was also unforthcoming

about a sit-down lunch for seventeen people which had been held in the book's honour at Schmidt's in Charlotte Street – a restaurant he professed to hate. I learnt later that he had worn a white silk tie and dark shirt and perched on the shoulder of Joan Rhodes for a photograph. His old friends Mr Duffey and Mr de Paul were among those present, so were Miss Leaf, who had once lived at Beaufort Street, and a Miss Lizzie Lemon, who was a painter. The names of the others, all of whom had paid ten shillings to be present, elude me. These celebrations did not last for ever and early the following year Quentin would write to his friend Hermione Goacher, 'It seems that my literary career has come to an end', explaining that an American publisher, Stein and Day, had rejected his book and several ideas for television plays had been returned to his agent Donald Carroll. Soon he would have no agent at all – Carroll moved to Texas – and even the book itself would go out of print.

Always prone to comic, ironic exaggeration, Quentin Crisp made out he was now in 'the winter' of his life. He had told me that his energy was much reduced and boasted, 'I'm now on the way down.' To Hermione Goacher he wrote bravely, 'I go on as though nothing unpleasant had happened and work in the art schools as before', but it was difficult for his friends not to feel some disappointment on his behalf that more had not come of his book.

Though family affairs were of little concern to him, it is worth noting that some of his relations were also on the way down – or out of the picture altogether. On 15 September 1968, his brother Lewis died in South America at the age of sixty, leaving two daughters, Denise and Elaine. On 23 February 1969, his brother-in-law John Payne had died at Fleet in Hampshire; and the following winter Quentin would spend some time with his sister Phyllis while she recovered from a hip operation, belying his incompetent image by helping her dress and getting her meals. Phyllis Payne was still recovering from the shock of her brother's autobiography and the horror of learning that he had been a male prostitute. The reactions to the book of Quentin's older brother Gerald, now living in a cottage at Mere in Wiltshire and either then or earlier doing part-time work for the National Trust at Stourhead, are not recorded.

Several of his friends were also ailing. In the late 1960s, Angus McBean had also had a hip operation and Quentin had been to stay with him in Suffolk, again partly in order to help look after him. McBean now lived in a moated Tudor mansion called Flemings Hall, near Debenham, the grandeur of which caused Quentin to start laughing out loud when it first sprang into view, though even he can hardly have been unimpressed by this fine fifteenth-century mansion with its lovely staircase and splendid rooms. During his week-long stay at the house, which he nicknamed 'Radclyffe Hall' and 'The Well of Loneliness', McBean's other helpers Norman Kelvin and David Ball took him on an improbable jaunt to see the oldest barn in Suffolk – Quentin horrified its owner. A more suitable diversion was having the ballet dancer Sir Frederick Ashton to dinner. According to David Ball, Crisp and Ashton sat opposite each other beside the inglenook fireplace looking like 'a pair of Staffordshire pot dogs'.

Among his circle of old friends in London, there was now a strange falling-out. During these years Quentin continued to see Denuta Jurand whom he had known since the 1930s and the crippled art student from Battersea, who was now working at the British Museum and whom he had known since he was a teenager. He also saw Mervyn Peake's widow Maeve and Mrs Dennerhy, both of whom were still neighbours in Chelsea. Only with Miss Lumley Who Can Do No Wrong was there now some friction. Increasingly overbearing in old age and perhaps more accurately described all along as Miss Lumley Who Can Do No Wrong *In Her Eyes*, the former ballet teacher had recently moved across the river to Putney and was said to be capable of drinking a whole bottle of whisky with a friend. Still brooding about the furniture she had sold him for only £5 at the start of the war, Miss Lumley wrote a letter to Quentin in 1970, accusing him of growing bored with her, and when they met in person had silenced him by declaring, 'Oh, Quentin, you're such a bore!'

This incident seems to have been an isolated one. During these years Quentin's popularity grew and he made many new friends. In 1969, his friend Hermione Goacher had gone to live in 'darkest Devonshire' but had introduced him to her friend Annie Wignall, who lived in Brechin Place, South Kensington, and would have him to many parties and dinners. At one of these events an eccentric fellow guest had asked, 'Can I tread on your toes?' to which Quentin had responded with delight, explaining, 'Nobody throws stones at me any more.' This might have been so, but the publication of *The Naked Civil Servant* and the broadcasting of Denis Mitchell's film about Quentin had certainly released another wave of hostile, violent or contemptuous telephone calls to Beaufort Street. Some were genuine cries for help but most of them were bizarre. At half past five one morning he was telephoned from Glasgow and asked if he would accept a call from someone pretending to be Mr Mitchell himself.

On the other hand his fame had also caused old friends to resurface. One of these was a Charlotte Street acquaintance named Colin Davis who telephoned and said, 'Come at once!' and bought Quentin 'a huge great meal', explaining, 'It's in return for all the cups of tea.' Another was Anne Valery, who had worked with Quentin in the advertising firm in the mid-1940s and since then established herself as an actress and stooge, most notably as Miss Bracegirdle to the comedian Ted Ray. In about 1970, Anne Valery ran into Quentin in the street and started asking him to parties at her home in Waterford Road, Fulham. Here he always sat in the same chair near the fire, was 'absolutely charming' to everyone and only thrown when his hostess asked him during a dinner party what his real name was. He had further fun with John de Paul. Around this time, de Paul remembers walking with Quentin down King's Road and seeing Rudolf Nureyev and the choreographer Roland Petit approaching along the pavement. 'I thought "Who's going to win?" But Quentin knew *exactly* what was happening and walked past them imperiously. They both looked back with their mouths hanging open.' News of *The Naked Civil Servant* had meanwhile reached Harold Pinter's attention and in the autumn of 1970 Quentin attended a party at the playwright's home in Hanover Terrace, almost next door to the house where Panna Grady had lived three years earlier. Here, he noticed his book prominently displayed and met his old friend Anna Wing, rubbed shoulders with Sir John Gielgud and told Feliks Topolski, who had drawn him some years earlier, 'I am able to utter the famous line "Do you recognize me with my clothes on?" ' At the same party Crisp asked Pinter, 'What do your plays mean?' and Pinter responded 'Mean?', employing an inflection that Quentin described as 'usually reserved for exclaiming "A handbag?" ' Pinter had then added, 'They are just what those people said on that day.'

The book and the Mitchell documentary also re-alerted John Haggarty, who had spent much of the last twenty years making films overseas, to Quentin's existence, and on 16 October 1970 this old friend from the 1940s telephoned Jonathan Cape to find out if the film rights to *The Naked Civil Servant* were available. Haggarty then visited 129 Beaufort Street for the first time and found Quentin more or less unchanged – 'still slightly jesty, still slightly flirtatious'. A few days later Haggarty introduced him to Philip Mackie, who had run the drama department at Granada TV. That winter Quentin Crisp visited Mackie's flat at 1 Buckingham Street off the Strand and had the first of three tape-recorded conversations with Mackie and Haggarty about his life and times. Mackie then set about writing a script to which he would give the slightly oppressive title *I, Quentin*. There were many delays and rejections but during the months and years ahead Haggarty would discuss the scheme with his photographer friend Sam Rosenberg and Mackie would twice renew his option on the rights at £250 a time. Added to what he had already got from Jonathan Cape, Quentin soon calculated that he made 'almost a thousand pounds' – he mentioned this sum with immense relish – from what he described as 'this – um – project'. In November 1971 Crisp talked to Mackie on the telephone, urging him to 'send the whole thing up'. For a while there was talk of the female impersonator Danny La Rue taking the leading role, an idea Quentin approved. The screenplay continued on its rounds. In October 1972, David Chasman, vice-president of United Artists, turned down the project, explaining to Haggarty that the company had lost its shirt on a movie about the transsexual Christine Jorgensen. Mackie had meanwhile oriented the project towards television but, after three rejections by the BBC, was said to be very disheartened and drinking heavily.

For a while it looked as though Quentin's career had ground to another halt. He had now written a book on style, a subject on which he had many ideas, but this had been returned by Jonathan Cape 'as quickly as if we had been playing badminton', and though this book was accepted in August 1971 by the small independent publisher Cecil Woolf, husband of Quentin's friend Malya Woolf, many months would pass without any sign of it going into production. The acquisition of a new agent in the rounded shape of Richard Gollner, who saw himself as more of a 'distant counsellor' than a pushy businessman, had no immediate impact on Quentin's career.

In domestic terms his life went on much as before though his peace was still disturbed by telephone callers offering phoney invitations to strange parties where there would be 'lots of lovely boys', and by even weirder visitors to his room. One of these was a young man who 'looked like a *Sunday Times* clothing advertisement' and quickly asked Quentin if he still 'did a bit of spanking and that'. Another was a 'falling-apart man' who arrived one afternoon from Putney. 'Above all he was lost,' Quentin said. 'He wanted us to be friends and for me to understand his soul. He wanted me to say, "I too am broken. Isn't it awful?" ' At midnight the man had returned to the house but been rebuffed on the doorstep by a firm *'Out!'* from Quentin. 'Because I'm nice to him, he thinks he can fall on top of me,' he explained. 'If he'd gone into any pub in Putney he could have got into conversation in ten minutes.' When these or other callers mentioned sex, Quentin tried to react as if it was something he had heard of long ago.

His routines at 129 Beaufort Street remained unchanged. He kept the gas-fire on in the summer and ate what he could buy from the milkman. In March 1972 he had acquired a better television set but hung on to the old one. The machine was often on when I called, sometimes with the sound turned down. He was sometimes waiting for a film. 'What I want is movies, movies, movies,' he explained and 'I'm wedded to narrative content.' He often got up at six, explaining, 'In a rooming house if you want to have a bath you must have it before anyone else would want it.' He then added the matter-of-fact detail, 'I can shave in here', which is interesting only because such humdrum utterances rarely fell from his lips.

Another reason for getting up early was that he was still much in demand as an art school model. 'I am working like a fiend,' he wrote to Denis and Linda Mitchell during the fuel crisis of March 1972, 'and under great hardships.' He explained that the electric fires had been locked away at St Albans College of Art and the following term he was equally hard at work at the London School of Printing at Elephant and Castle, though claiming this institution had no need for a model and that he was employed only as 'a kind of status symbol'. In the autumn of 1974, he was back at St Albans, declaring, 'I have been sold so deep into slavery that I now work even on a Saturday till five o'clock.' Quentin's letters to the Mitchells are uncharacteristically signed off 'Love' or 'Love to you both' but have a slightly plaintive quality which comes out in the rather feeble jokes he felt obliged to make. At Easter 1971, he had written 'Crisp is risen...' and on Christmas Eve 1974, he declared, 'I shall be running from turkey to turkey on the fatal natal day.'

There was a purpose behind this correspondence. During the early 1970s, Denis Mitchell conceived various projects for Quentin, one of which was that he should write a series of fictional letters to great figures of the past and present, and had even advanced him various sums of money to start on this work. Quentin was half-hearted about this idea, which he saw as a stunt, but was grateful for the money: he had turned sixty-five at Christmas 1973 but owing to the early mix-up about his age that he himself had initiated in the 1930s could not draw a pension for several years. In one letter to Mitchell he states that he is 'anxious (to the fringe of lunacy) to deliver something'.

One way Quentin tried to repay Mitchell's kindness was to offer him 'a rogue's gallery' of possible characters for TV films. A potential subject was the writer Jean Rhys, who had apparently written Quentin a fan letter after reading *The Naked Civil Servant*. In a letter to Mitchell, Quentin wrote that he was anxious to avoid 'an illicit relationship' with Miss Rhys because it would oblige him to read her novel *Wide Sargasso Sea*, but knew through a friend that she was currently staying at an address in Belgravia under an assumed name. Later he suggested a Mr Clarkson, a Mrs Pick and 'a certain Miss Dick who lives in Brighton and wears a monocle'. The fact that Quentin knew of these people gives us some idea of the extent of his secret kingdom. He also put forward Joan Rhodes, whom he described as 'an enchanting person', and this last suggestion seems to have been the only one that Mitchell took up. In November 1974 Miss Rhodes was filmed in her basement flat in Belsize Park and at one point is seen playing Scrabble with Quentin, who utters the remark, 'Those who play games seriously always lose in life.' I watched the broadcast on Christmas Day 1974 with my parents on the Isle of Man, blushed when Quentin Crisp appeared on the screen but was again surprised that my father showed little interest in the woman he once talked about so much and had twice tried to teach to play golf.

If Quentin Crisp had, up to this date, lost in life, things certainly picked up for him soon afterwards. The least significant event of the eventful year of 1975 was the publication in March of *How to Have a Life Style*. This book had been in the hands of the publisher Cecil Woolf for nearly four years and only appeared in print when Quentin had started asking for it back, thinking that perhaps Denis Mitchell might make use of it. Partly through my efforts, some of the book had been published several months earlier in *Harpers & Queen*, earning Quentin far more for a double spread than Woolf had paid him for the whole book. In critical terms the book was mainly ignored, though Paul Bailey described it in the *Observer* as 'the most chirpily aphoristic do-it-yourself manual' he had ever encountered, while protesting at its shoddy presentation, printing errors and the dreary illustrations which accompanied the text. When I telephoned Quentin about the book, I was surprised to find that he shared Bailey's anger on this score – though he may have used this disappointment in order to cling on to his current sense of failure. Earlier that spring he had written to Mrs Goacher saying, 'Like you, I have no news; we live and we work and we hope and we die', thanking her at the same time for a gift of a handkerchief into which he promised to 'cry tears of the largest and most expensive kind – like the heroine of Mr Wells's novel'.

So far so bad, but in April 1975, his luck changed at last when he learnt that Philip Mackie had sold the script of *The Naked Civil Servant* to Thames Television. The director Jack Gold had received the screenplay through the post and proclaimed it 'the best script I've ever read'. After years of delay, things then moved very fast. At the end of that month, Quentin Crisp was collected from Beaufort Street by taxi and taken to the studios at Teddington to meet Jack Gold and the actor John Hurt, who was to star in the ninety-minute film and would later speak of 'the complete joy' he experienced on reading the script. Quentin Crisp later described this occasion as 'the turning-point of the tide against which I had been swimming for more than sixty years'. I asked him afterwards how he had dressed for this historic event and learnt that he had worn a white shirt, black jacket and grey trousers. 'And shoes?' I had asked. 'Yes, *shoes*,' he replied, perhaps exasperated by my curiosity, but I had pressed on and enquired, 'What about make-up?' to which he had calmly replied, 'I wore a tiny line of make-up along the eyelid, a tiny amount of lipstick. And then I just powdered my face.' The days of heavy mascara, gold eye-shadow and bare feet were over. So was the hostility that he had encountered so often in the past. Everyone at Thames Television was 'friendly and businesslike' and Hurt and Crisp had got on well from the start. 'Mr Hurt has the same tired eyes,' Quentin said later. 'He holds his head back to save him the bother of opening his eyes.' Lunch was served in a special dining room – 'There was a canteen which we passed with curled lips' – during which Crisp keenly acquiesced to every proposal.

'I want what you want' was to become one of his catch-phrases during the remaining part of his life, but Philip Mackie was moved to write him a letter after this meeting – 'as if I were fearing for my image', Quentin said – and also to inform him that he had never seen anyone as keen to play a part as John Hurt. A few days later, Quentin Crisp dined with the thirty-five-year-old actor and his 'true love' at their home in Flask Walk, Hampstead, but again offered no suggestions on how he should play the role. Hurt volunteered, 'I have no intention of merely giving a vaudeville imitation of Mr Crisp' and later claimed that he avoided seeing too much of Quentin at this time 'because I didn't want it to be a mimic thing, an impersonation'. He did, however, listen to the recordings that Mackie had made in 1970 and later told John Haggarty, 'You were the third voice on the tapes.' In due course Quentin was taken to a firm of wig-makers in New Burlington Street so that an exact replica of his current coiffure could be made for Hurt to wear in the film's closing sequence. In the event five different wigs were made for the actor and Crisp himself was recruited as 'technical adviser', though this simply meant that he appeared four times on the set – 'Of course I never said anything.'

While the filming or editing was going on, Quentin took another significant step forward when he was invited to give a series of lunch-time lectures at the King's Head Theatre in Islington. The idea of this show had been dreamed up by an impresario called Richard Jackson and consisted of Quentin sitting on the stage and delivering what he described as 'straight talk from a bent speaker'. His audiences were small – on one occasion there were only three people present – but he won critical approval. In the *Observer*, B. A. Young, who had described *The Naked Civil Servant* as 'full of self-pity', wrote that Quentin Crisp was 'not only a genuinely amusing man but a pretty wise man' and 'there is a great deal of sense about his frivolities'. During its three-week run I twice attended the show and on one occasion Joan Rhodes was photographed with Quentin outside the theatre. I remember that Quentin put on dark glasses and a hat as he crossed the road to the bus stop.

What did he feel about the fame, the respectability and the public affection now creeping up on him? In September of that year he told me, 'I'm interested, I've perked up' but added that he was too old for 'the big time'. In the next few months he would go along with all that was offered, however, while steadfastly refusing to climb off the bottom rung of the ladder in every other respect. His drive to be known, to rule the world, did not include a desire to change his material circumstances. In his own way, Quentin Crisp was as uncompromising as Philip O'Connor: both men were incurable eccentrics, utterly incapable of giving up their outsider status.

On 10 December 1975, a week before the screening of *The Naked Civil Servant*, there was a press preview of the film at the Thames offices in Euston Road. The car sent to collect Quentin from Beaufort Street was late, so he missed part of the film and the solemn announcement at the beginning that the Independent Broadcasting Authority had ordered that the line 'Sexual intercourse is a poor substitute for masturbation' be replaced with the remark, 'Wasn't it fun in the bath tonight?' I had gatecrashed the event and sat through the film nervously, mildly perplexed by the slight distortions of the Quentin Crisp I knew, but elevated by the triumphant march at the end. When it was over, the film's producer made a short speech which included the head-spinning words, 'Mr Crisp is here.' At the reception afterwards, he was there indeed, looking very spruce, his hair wonderfully combed, and wearing a blue chalk-striped suit I had never seen before. I spoke briefly to John Hurt who told me that the film 'would make one or two people a lot happier'. Hurt, Crisp and Philip Mackie went off to lunch together.

A week later, on 17 December, the film was broadcast by Thames Television as a 'Wednesday Special'. Quentin Crisp described it as 'a saga of depravity', praised John Hurt's 'immense tact' and wrote later that had he not been personally involved, he would not have watched the film 'in a million years'. Homosexuality, he explained, was a subject he had long ago ceased to be interested in. His sister Phyllis, now seventy-four years old, watched the film with her daughter and son-in-law and protested that the furniture in the family home hadn't been arranged in that manner. Of the film itself, she said, 'What an awful thing!' The public and critical response both to the programme and to Quentin Crisp as a person was, on the whole, immensely favourable. Writing in the *Sunday Times* Peter Lennon declared that Crisp's 'confrontations with the world were a kind of tragic parody of normal confrontations' but in the *Guardian*, Nancy Banks-Smith stated that the film justified the existence of television. The education-alist Lord Wolfenden, who had been partly responsible for the change in the law against homosexuals, described Crisp as 'articulate, intelli-gent and amusing' and the playwright Robert Bolt praised the way the film brought out 'the tenderness of the individual against the cruelty of the crowd'. Speculating later about reasons for the film's success, John Hurt said, 'I think the whole business of the unloved, all those rather grey and difficult areas, seemed to touch a lot of people.'

In *How to Become a Virgin*, Quentin Crisp would write that the film changed him from 'a despised outcast' to 'a figure of affection' and that from this moment on he received 'a subtle blend of curi-osity and forgiveness' from the public. He was only mystified that

Jonathan Cape had again made no attempt to capitalize on 'the tidal wave' of publicity that flowed from the film. *The Naked Civil Servant* was never reprinted in its highly distinctive and distinguished original format.

The publicity for Quentin Crisp as an individual had already begun with a one-page profile by Peter York in the December 1975 issue of *Harpers & Queen*. Peter York, later branded a 'style guru', began cautiously by writing about 'someone called Quentin Crisp' but went on to describe him as 'a lemur who has been taken to Elizabeth Arden', who had set about 'polishing, heightening, and lacquering the presentation of self'. In the week of the broadcast the *Sunday Times* Colour Supplement had run a much longer piece in which the journalist Mark Amory expressed bewilderment that a bachelor noted for his style would live in such appalling conditions. On the day after the screening, Quentin was interviewed by Mavis Nicholson on her afternoon TV show and other media invitations poured in. On 20 December he attended a party at the writer Margaret Drabble's house in Hampstead, which he described as 'stuffed with geniuses'. Here, he was rushed, or pushed, across the room to meet television personality Melvyn Bragg and later confronted by the playwright John Osborne with the words, 'You've made sure that young man never gets a good part!' – a prediction that would prove ludicrously wrong, as John Hurt would never look back from that point onwards.

During those heady days Quentin was suffering from a bad leg – looked after by a 'tame doctor' across the street who had replaced Dr Armando Dumas Child whom he had known for more than forty years. In spite of this affliction, he remained on top of the world yet not too busy to attend a party given by me on 23 December in my brother's Chelsea studio. Among my guests were June Churchill and Peter O'Connor, both of whom had known Quentin much longer than I had. Among those meeting him for the first time were Niki Trethowan and a pinstriped civil servant, brought by another guest, who showed himself to be unexpectedly courteous to the guest of honour, talking to him very directly without fawning or sneering. One of my guests whispered that she would prefer not to be introduced to Mr Crisp, but Peter O'Connor told me afterwards that Quentin was the only person he had enjoyed talking to. Later, Quentin himself declared that Peter was like his father: 'the pallor, the dark hair, the brightness'.

Quentin Crisp's bandwagon was rolling at last. During the next few weeks, months and years, his image was built up by interviews and photographs, television and stage appearances. 'Photographers come almost daily,' he soon told me, and interviewers followed. Quentin was a 'natural', he smiled and posed effortlessly and he welcomed personal questions. Interviewers struggled to describe his style and the colour of his coiffure. Peter York had written of its 'pompadour curves and waves'. Another interviewer said it was 'woven like spaghetti'. There were references to his 'jewel-encrusted fingers', his voice like 'a ruined piano' – wasn't that one of his own phrases? – and his 'witty, willowy charm'. His room 'at the brackish end of Chelsea where it commingles with Fulham' was described as 'a grotto of dun shades' where the mantelpiece was 'stacked with old telephone directories'. To each interviewer Quentin said much the same thing, repeatedly picturing himself as 'a funny old gentleman' and 'a professional failure' and as 'a shallow personality' who was 'horribly articulate'. He frequently made the joke, invented years earlier, about overacting at the end of the run, and would go on making it till the end of his life. The interviews were accompanied by photographs in which he looked affable, convivial, resigned, haughty – and his haughtiness extended to an indifference about how he was written about and how he appeared. 'I don't think he'd like this shot,' said a photographer ignorant of this aloofness. 'I slipped on the wide-angled lens without him noticing.'

Quentin was well aware that this moment of glory – many reporters described him as 'a hero' – might not last for ever. To me he confided, 'I expect to be forgotten soon. I expect people to say, "Quentin Crisp? Wasn't he one of the Great Train Robbers?"' Some people were already confused about him. An admirer asked if Quentin had had a series named after him and on a radio chat show, the presenter Monty Modlyn said, 'Lets have that record again, "Yiddishe Momme". I'm sure, Quentin, you'd like it too?' to which Quentin replied, 'Yes indeed.'

Quentin's new level of fame generated further attention from

strangers. Anonymous telephone calls had passed from 'tittering contempt' to 'growling anger', to which Quentin responded by laying
down the receiver and letting his tormentors carry on. He also had at
least one letter a day from a complete stranger. Some correspondents
aired their own problems. Others wrote believing that Quentin was
lonely and miserable. To a girl who offered her services as cleaner and
housekeeper, he wrote back that he needed to be alone to recharge
his batteries. Among unwelcome visitors to Beaufort Street was a French-
man who made overt propositions and virtually chased him round
the room.

He was also accosted in the streets. A local shopkeeper who asked,
'How are we bearing up under our fame?' got the reply, 'Don't expect
me to cut my wrists!', and in Shepherd's Bush a lorry-driver stopped
his vehicle, got out and said, 'So you're Quentin Crisp. I've got the
hang of it now.' Taxi drivers got particularly over-excited. 'I've been
waiting for this,' said one awestruck cabbie. 'You can forget your
money for a start. But would you sign this for my wife? She's never
going to believe this!'

He also received more invitations, social and professional. Events
and personalities began to crowd in on him – so that 'inner development' was no longer possible, but he liked being lionized and tried to
give 'good value'. One day I heard him telling a caller, 'One a.m.
I can manage. If I stay up much later, it would all end in tears.' He
accepted invitations from comparative strangers. The ballet critic
David Dougill – 'whoever he may be' – took him to performances at
the Coliseum and the Royal Opera House and the novelist Edna
O'Brien dragged him to his first Beckett play. He was taken to a
fashionable restaurant called Trattoo by someone connected to the
West End show *A Chorus Line*, transported there and back in a car
'as long as Charing Cross Road'. He was invited to a party given by
Harpers & Queen features editor Ann Barr, who said before the event,
'They'll all be thrilled to death if he comes.' I was present on this
occasion and found myself not so much thrilled to death as startled
by Quentin's strange presence among my colleagues. He also gave
more lectures. He told students at the Royal College of Art 'what a
mistake the visual arts are' and he alienated a homosexual group in

Luton by telling them not to be so militant. This latter theme would play an increasingly large part in his repertoire.

In March 1976 he returned for a further lunchtime season at the King's Head Theatre and this time played to packed houses. He made light of this 'lark', telling Hermione Goacher, 'I am filling in the Easter holiday haranguing the multitude in a back room behind a pub in Islington.' I went to the show with June Churchill, who drove Quentin and me back to Chelsea afterwards where I was briefly overcome by an unexpected wave of depression on account of the grimness of his room. On 29 March, Mrs Churchill returned to the King's Head with her eighty-three-year-old friend Lady Diana Cooper, who had starred in the West End when Quentin was a child. At the end of the performance Quentin Crisp asked this illustrious old lady, who wore 'a huge black hat' as if she was 'in mourning for Ascot', whether she had understood him and she snapped back, 'Yes, partly.' The show had now been extended for a further three weeks, which Quentin survived in spite of a bad attack of laryngitis which affected him in early April.

At the end of the month, Quentin surprised me by telephoning out of the blue and, speaking in a sumptuously rich, gurglingly buoyant voice, asked me if I would like to come with him to the theatre the following week. In the course of our friendship Quentin telephoned me only twice and this call was inspired by the fact that an actress who had seen his lunchtime show had given him two free tickets to a musical comedy called *Happy as a Sandbag*. On the appointed day, I picked Quentin up in a taxi and we travelled to the West End with the driver wondering which celebrity he had on board. 'I know you,' he told Quentin when we got out. 'Bin on the boards, haven't we?' I noted the speed and confidence with which Quentin bounced into the theatre and across the foyer and the minor incident that then took place when we took our seats in the front stalls. A woman beside Quentin gave him a hard stare and then changed places with her companion. I also remember that Quentin's head was raised throughout the performance in trance-like fascination with the events on stage. Afterwards we briefly went back stage – Quentin knew this was expected – to pay our respects to his actress friend. I then suggested a visit to the French pub in Dean Street but he turned this down and we took the bus to Chelsea from Shaftesbury Avenue. We travelled on the upper deck for some reason and Quentin remarked, 'I've grown out of the theatre. I'm like your father.'

A few weeks later, on 12 May, I was walking down King's Road after a dinner at my brother's house in Priory Walk in honour of my father, when a voice said, 'Hi!' Quentin Crisp had materialized like a sprite by the wayside: tiny, neat and effervescent. I walked back on my tracks with him to his door – he walked much faster than me – and as we hurtled along he told me he had had lunch that day at the *Punch* table and met Lord Goodman. On this occasion, he told me with some glee and exaggerated concern, this famous old lawyer was looking '*very* ill', but when he spoke of the encounter a few days later he put a different, less truthful gloss on things, intoning that Lord Goodman was '*amazingly* interesting', an unlikely proposition from Quentin's perspective. 'Did you speak to him?' I then asked. 'I'm not sure I did,' he replied, the truthful tone returning.

The same month Quentin Crisp left England for the first time. Aged sixty-seven, he went to Scotland to address the students of St Andrew's University. He told me later that he had been content to sit up all night without a sleeper, arrive in the morning, speak for two hours and later take a train home also travelling through the night. This was one of the first of several visits to universities, all of which impressed on him that undergraduates were now incredibly courteous and pleasant. He would be equally well received this year on the campus at Hull, where he'd been invited by a student called Jeremy Trevathan, who happens to be the publisher of this book. Trevathan remembers driving out into the country with Quentin to show him a local beauty spot, an odd excursion for a man who later claimed that the world would be better concreted over.

In spite of all these new activities – and extensions of his kingdom – Quentin continued modelling in art schools when the work was offered and would occasionally adopt the old dramatic poses. Carrie Diamond, who drew or painted him again at this time, suggested that he wanted to show he could still 'cut the mustard' and he was also prepared to sit for smaller groups and individual artists. Zsuzsi Roboz, who painted him in 1975, recalled that Quentin Crisp insisted on taking off his clothes in spite of having what she described as 'a very, very bad figure'. At St Alban's School of Art, he would sit for a bust by John Mills, who had known Quentin for thirty years and found him 'absolutely charming and devastatingly intelligent'. Several years later, the bust was auctioned for charity at Sotheby's and acquired by the restaurant owner Anthony Worrall-Thompson.

He also continued during this active time to see old and new friends. He was regularly lured over to Joan Rhodes's flat in Belsize Park and he saw a lot of the young writer Peter Ackroyd who was living nearby in Chelsea. In a piece in the *Sunday Times*, published in May 1976, he describes going to the cinema with Anne Valery and her friend Hattie Jacques, star of the *Carry On* films, and marvelled afterwards how Miss Jacques had made no reference in the whole course of the evening to 'any film she had made or would have made if only . . .'. He went to play chess with an 'itinerant flower-seller' who lived in Putney and to visit another old acquaintance in Brockley Heath, 'which is miles from everywhere'. He attended a play by John Haggarty put on in a Leicester Square basement and designed its programme cover. And he attended June Churchill's parties in Cornwall Gardens, sitting demurely on a sofa surrounded by immaculate foreign queers – until Mrs Churchill decided he was so successful he no longer needed her patronage.

It was strange that in spite of being so active he always managed to be at home at Beaufort Street when I called out of the blue. His room was infamously unmodernized and he continued to give his telephone number as FLAxman 9398. The other lodgers, he said, 'mostly take me for granted' and made no reference to his fame when they passed on the stairs. In the old days, he had often sat around in other people's rooms but now he knew no one in the house. Gordon Richardson had moved to Islington and Ralph Noyes to Oakley Street. Both kept in touch with Quentin and, when I met Mr Noyes in King's Road, he expressed delight with his friend's progress. 'Things have very much woken up for him recently,' he said. 'I mean he's coming to a gay group I belong to. He's very much in demand for that sort of thing. Me? No! I'm just a civil servant.'

I did not always find Quentin in good heart when I called. One day I found him agonizing over a letter that someone had failed to forward to him. He had even been to an address in Hampstead trying to retrieve it, without success – and would write later of the 'diabolical cruelty' of those involved in this prank. Another time I found him upset about a stray cat on the staircase, stabbing at it through the banisters with his latch-key. Both episodes throw light on the darker, more troubled side to his nature, but on most occasions he was his usual effervescent self, lying back in his armchair, utterly relaxed in his dirty dressing-gown which lay in such a way as to expose most of his buttocks. Somewhat contradictorily, he told me he still sat around 'a hell of a lot' though just recently he had had 'very little spare time'. Our conversations ran on the same lines as before. Of Philip O'Connor, he now said, 'I think he's cruel and he looks cruel but he's not as cruel as he looks. He looks *fiendish*.' And when I said that Philip was very interesting, he replied, 'Everybody's interesting.' We moved on to religion and he said, 'I'm not a Christian. I do hope death will be the end.' I asked about his earnings and he said he gave extra money away to his nieces. I asked him if he felt mature or immature and he replied, 'I suppose I am immature for all time. I undertake no responsibility of a long-lasting nature. I would say I am not sufficiently strong. I would fall apart in the end if I had to look after an invalid.' More flippant questions and lighter topics followed. I asked if he could drive a car, to which he replied, 'Not a thing. I can't even ride a push-bike.' I told him I had just eaten a quail's egg – my life was looking up – and he responded, 'How grand! I've never eaten a quail's egg.'

During one of our conversations, we were interrupted by a gentle tapping on the door. 'This could be trouble,' was Quentin's first reaction and I wondered if a fan had got into the house, but the visitor turned out to be his long-suffering and saintly landlady Miss Vereker. In correspondence at this time, Quentin had mentioned that Miss Vereker had recently begun to find the house too much. Earlier in 1976 a boyfriend of one of the lodgers had broken into a gas meter. Miss Vereker had offered to pay the Gas Board the stolen money and had refused to call the police. 'She has no higher opinion of them than you or I,' Quentin told Mrs Goacher. In a letter to the Mitchells, he said he had even tried to rally the other 'inmates into buying the house jointly' but added, 'This I couldn't manage.' On this particular occasion Miss Vereker showed her innocence by very politely asking Quentin if he wouldn't mind tidying his room a little – she spoke of dust and lurking germs. Quentin had accepted her admonitions but added jauntily, 'I'm very healthy on it, for my age!'

Though I saw a lot of Quentin Crisp during 1976, my relationship with him remained superficial and I remained as ignorant as ever of many aspects of his life. He did not tell me that his sister Phyllis had died that summer or that he had helped nurse her at the end of her life – though the experience may have informed his remark about the strength needed to look after an invalid. While working on this book, I learnt that he had told Hermione Goacher of his sister's death and in response to Mrs Goacher's words of sympathy, had become completely silent for four minutes. There are very few windows onto Quentin's soul, but this was one of them.

My interest in Quentin Crisp had grown since the moment I first met him and I still saw him as a source of knowledge about how the world worked, and I felt increasingly tender-hearted towards him and full of admiration for the way he had walked backwards into the limelight. Some of my friends did not share my enthusiasm for him – or indeed my equal admiration for Philip O'Connor. When I played a tape-recording of Quentin to a friend who had become a barrister, he responded, 'What a dull little man! A *brave* man but what a dull man!' Philip O'Connor's friend Annie Mygind was even more vindictive when I mentioned Quentin Crisp – 'I regard him as very sick.' Among Quentin's own circle, there were also some negative responses. His wartime acquaintance Stephen Fothergill already disappointed by 'all the whinging' in The Naked Civil Servant, ran into Quentin in the Caves de France in Soho. 'He seemed terribly ill at ease. I walked him down to a bus stop and left him.'

Many of those I introduced to Quentin seemed to like him, though they sometimes teased me about the friendship, referring to 'your pal Quentin'. One day during the summer of 1976 I had told the photographer Derry Moore, 'Put your trust in me' and taken him to

Quentin's room. He had returned on his own and taken some remarkable photographs, one of which caught the sitter under his television screen featuring at that moment an elaborate clock-face, for all intents and purposes, the famous stopped clock with which Quentin had proudly identified himself. That same summer, I gave another party in my brother's studio after which a group of us including Quentin Crisp, June Churchill, the literary agent Caroline Dawnay and the writer Jonathan Gathorne-Hardy had gone to a restaurant in Fulham Road. Here Gathorne-Hardy treated Crisp with remarkable robustness, sloshing wine into his glass as if he was a heavy-drinking man like himself and finally getting the men present to split the bill. Quentin had chipped in his fiver with perfect grace. Out on the street afterwards, Gathorne-Hardy shouted a final salutation to Crisp – *'Ahoy, there!'* – as he turned for home.

In August the good ship Quentin sailed into a new one-man show at the New End Theatre in Hampstead. Here he delivered his monologue on style and after an interval answered questions submitted in writing by the audience. I attended the show on 21 August with Peter O'Connor, who submitted a question more interesting to the readers of this book than to anyone present on that occasion. Soon Quentin was reading out Peter's question, which he had pulled from a hat. 'Can you furnish us with any memories of the late Philip O'Connor?' I have forgotten his reply and recall only that he registered and queried the suggestion that his old acquaintance and occasional sparring partner was dead.

A month later, Quentin was one of the attractions at the Edinburgh Festival delivering his one-man show at the Heriot-Watt Theatre. From here, on 6 September, he made 'a mad dash' to London to record a television show with John Hurt and the guardian of public morals, Mary Whitehouse. The programme was chaired by the American chat-show host Dick Cavett and was intended to prepare American audiences for *The Naked Civil Servant* which was due to be shown in New York that winter. As part of this process, Quentin was soon visited at Beaufort Street by the former Mayor of New York John Lindsay, to record an interview to be broadcast at the same time as the film. Crisp later described Lindsay as 'effortlessly sociable' and reports that he made no comment whatsoever on the room 'out of sheer politeness'. When Lindsay asked Quentin if he was planning to come to America, Crisp responded, 'What about my sin?' Lindsay overrode this worry while warning Crisp that he would have to promise not to overthrow the American government by force. The interview would later be shown on a programme called 'Good Morning, America', and was watched by eleven million viewers.

In November, *The Naked Civil Servant* blazed across American TV screens and was watched by more than a million New Yorkers. Michael Holroyd arrived in New York a week after the showing and found that everyone was talking about it. The film would go on to win every possible award and accolade, but Quentin Crisp would draw gasps of amazed indignation from his audiences in London when he revealed that he had only made £17.50 from the show. Money was not one of his priorities. In August that year he had written to his niece Frances about the money his sister had left him, saying, 'I certainly do not need it now.' Yet, here again, there are the inevitable complexities. He was now paying £2 a week for his room. 'If the rent was raised to £12 a week,' he told me, 'I simply wouldn't be able to pay it.' He may have been paid only a pittance for his appearances, but his expenses were paid and his income and spirits were a good deal higher than in the past. Following a visit to Northern Ireland at the end of November where he said he had hoped to get shot – 'I jumped up and down in front of the soldiers but they ran away' – he wrote to Denis Mitchell, 'As you surmise, I have had the most astonishing time. I have become a fashion to an almost ludicrous extent.'

He had also become a fixture on the social scene and now numbered among his friends the oil heiress Olga Deterding, who was then giving parties in a Mayfair penthouse. 'I adore Miss Deterding,' Quentin was soon crooning, 'I can hardly live without her.' During the months ahead he appeared often in Miss Deterding's three-floor apartment, adding antique sparkle to the gang of jet-setters and journalists who made up the guest list. He never stayed late and he had sometimes left before I arrived.

Yes, I, too, had become part of that insanely star-struck circle and in March 1977 would mark my commitment to gossip and snobbery by signing a contract, drawn up by Gillon Aitken, to write a book composed of deadpan snippets of society tittle-tattle drawn from old newspapers. I was not entirely at ease with this task, but enjoyed the research in the Colindale Newspaper Library and occasionally telephoned Quentin for information about movie-stars of whom I had not heard. As my life blossomed and I made the same movement from outsider to insider status that Crisp and to some extent O'Connor had made, I also yearned for the off-beat grassroots world I had once inhabited and, in particular, regretted that the 'layabouts' café' where I had first met Quentin had long since closed its doors.

By this time *The Naked Civil Servant* had at last appeared in paperback and gone back into the bestseller lists and a new hardback edition had been published by the independent house of Duckworth. In February 1977, Duckworth had also produced the novel for which Quentin had failed to find a publisher twenty-five years earlier, *Love Made Easy*, which was described in the blurb as 'an extravaganza' set in a 'tatty London . . . recovering from wartime shortages and blackout morality'. Quentin Crisp would make no bones about the fact that this book proved an international flop, securing bad reviews even in New Zealand. In the *Observer*, Lorna Sage described it as 'pretty awful' and 'a wet romp'.

This was a predictable hiccup. During 1977, while I was slaving away on my book, Quentin was working on a new novel, for which he had received a £2,000 advance from Methuen. This was *Chog*, a story about the relationship between a dog and a prostitute and their horrific progeny, which I will discuss in more detail later. He was also caught up in an ever-expanding social life. One day he attended a party given by Annie Wignall at which the rival star guest was the actor Kenneth Williams. The two celebrity guests, who had more than a little in common, apparently held court in separate rooms. Quentin was also in demand as a literary critic, reviewing regularly in *Punch* and writing perceptively in *Gay News* about his old friend George Melly's autobiography and the 'limp stiffness' of the singer's hands.

Quentin Crisp had also spent quite a lot of the summer of 1977 making discreet arrangements to go abroad – or at least to be able to go abroad if he was invited. He now at last changed his name officially from Denis Pratt to Quentin Crisp and for the first time in his life – he was sixty-eight – acquired a passport. This took 'a lot of doing' and was greatly helped by the manager of his local Lloyds Bank, who used his own penknife to trim Quentin's passport photo. He had also entrusted the bank with some of his surplus money. Hitherto, he had kept all his funds in a Post Office account, giving away any surplus to his relations.

By the end of September these arrangements were in place when *The Naked Civil Servant* was published by Holt, Rinehart and Winston in New York. The author was not present for the transatlantic launch but the book carried a preface by Michael Holroyd introducing Mr Crisp to American readers. Holroyd had not then met Quentin Crisp but rightly described him as a remarkable character whose 'gaunt and mincing figure' was 'full of stamina and wrapped round with cunning and iron politeness'. Still in London on 24 September, Quentin lunched with the film-star Arnold Schwarzenegger, who was publicizing his film *Pumping Iron,* and the actress Caroline Langrishe who was also apparently on the crest of stardom. The event, which took place at San Lorenzo's in Beauchamp Place, was arranged by the journalist Duncan Fallowell and written up by him with great verve in a magazine called *De Luxe.* During the course of the meal, Quentin told Schwarzenegger that he would love to go to America but needed a proper invitation – in other words, someone to pay his fare – and still had to get a visa. He also remarked, 'I was waiting to rule the world ever since I was born.'

About a month later, Quentin Crisp crossed the Atlantic for the first time. He flew first to Toronto, where he had been invited at short notice following the broadcasting of *The Naked Civil Servant* on Canadian television. He spent only a day and a half in the city, appearing on various radio and television stations. He then flew on to New York. Here a large and bulky airport official examined his passport carefully and then asked quietly, 'Is it nice to be vindicated at last?'

– 23 –

Such a Forgotten One

> I would like to write to Panna Grady and thank her
> for looking after this magnificent character, for keep-
> ing him alive, preserving him and protecting him from
> the stupidity of society. She must have suffered. But
> she suffered for love.
>
> BOBBIE BATTERSBY TO ANDREW BARROW,
> 28 September 1999

My last visit to Wimereux was in November 1975. I had made the
mistake of getting drunk on the Hovercraft and was exhausted and
hung over by the time I reached Clair de Lune. Philip O'Connor had
immediately exploited my weakness, shouting, 'Get out! Go back to
England!' and 'Oh, you're so dull!' I put up with this onslaught, aware
that his mood often changed, but when this didn't happen I was
forced to admit that something had gone wrong with our friendship.
Travelling home the next day, I retaliated by beginning to feel fed
up with Philip and angry about his whole domestic set-up and his
relationship with the indulgent and long-suffering Panna Grady. Back
in London, I told Peter O'Connor that I had had my fill of his father
and shortly afterwards Peter received a letter from Philip saying he
had 'cut the links' with me.

The process was soon marked by letters. On 8 January 1976 Philip
wrote saying he was seeking advice from the Society of Authors on
how to restrain me from using any material I had 'snooped/appropri-
ated' over the previous three years, repeating the threat in red biro at
the bottom of the letter. I wrote back politely asking which manuscripts

he had in mind, but got an unspecific reply on 17 January, ending, 'En fin, we're quite sick of the isle's exports – *quite* sick, and are taking precautions.' This letter arrived in the same post as a postcard stating simply, 'My adventure isn't finished.'

For a while I tried to convince myself that this break with O'Connor was a good thing, that he was too bizarre to identify with, that I needed more normal heroes and that I ought to be more preoccupied with the new life that was at last unfolding for me in London. Such reasoning didn't quite work. During the next few months I missed Philip and his world, Wimereux and the whole Cap Gris Nez. I missed the way he would materialize in the sunlight at the station, his generosity, his fussiness, even his anger. I thought about him a lot, I smoked the pipes he had given me and still cooked dishes in my Oakley Street basement which were vaguely inspired by his cuisine. Philip was still my mentor and the separation from him caused me anguish. There is an ugliness to all estrangements and I had set my heart on remaining a loyal and devoted friend to Philip O'Connor until he died. I felt a similar commitment to Quentin Crisp, but here my heart was not engaged in the same way and the links were flimsier.

Anyhow, Philip's life was changing, and he had other plans. In March that year he and Panna paid a visit to a pretty but not wildly fashionable part of the South of France called Gard. Here they bought a house in the village of Flaux, between Avignon and Uzès. Panna then returned to Wimereux, leaving Philip on his own in the new house. On 27 March, Philip wrote from here to Annie Mygind saying he expected to be there all summer and, on 8 April, he temporarily forgot his hostility to me by writing in praise of the social life in the area and the excellence of the local wine. His letter concluded with the unflatteringly worded invitation: 'Maybe your wormy head might whitely appear over the garden gate, prospecting for free mutton and baths of wine.' His first visitor proved to be Annie Mygind, who reported that Flaux was a tiny village and that Philip's new house was 'a large hovel'. She also spoke of the existence of a friendly and sociable neighbour, Tony Daniells, whose house outside the village and half-hidden in the uncultivated terrain known as the *garrigue* was the 'nerve centre of the English colony'. Panna Grady had been the first to pay her respects at this bachelor's paradise, asking, 'May I bring my husband?'

It is a relief to record that Tony Daniells took an immediate liking to Philip – 'because he was so straight' – and during the years ahead was never offended by him. When Panna left for Wimereux, she had asked Daniells to 'look after' Philip and he would take his duties seriously, even to the extent of digging a hole in Philip's garden for him to use as a lavatory. Philip became a regular visitor at Daniells's secluded home, often arriving at unsociably early hours and sometimes opening the curtains of Daniells's bedroom and asking, 'Are you buggering someone?' Tony took these intrusions in good heart but added, 'If I did have someone with me, the curtains would be swept aside and this figure would come in spluttering and they would be horrified.' Philip also 'drowned' Tony in 'the facts of his life', just as he had done with Jean Hore and everyone else he had known, telling his new friend that he had been a tramp, that he had been in the Maudsley and how he was really Burmese. Daniells noted that Philip spoke 'good erudite French'.

It's unclear how long Philip stayed alone in Flaux that year. His plans were always flexible and so apparently was his resolution not to see me. Early in the morning of 30 May 1976 he called at Oakley Street and spoke with excitement about his new home. He described Tony Daniells as his new 'bosom friend' and listed some other 'notables' who had homes in the area. The writer Daphne Fielding shared a holiday house with Lady Diana Cooper in Uzès, then there was Lawrence Durrell, the Duchess of Montesquiou, various 'faggots' and his old patron Stephen Spender. The following day, I visited Philip at the Glendower Hotel, South Kensington, where he was staying with Maxim, now seven years old – 'Just wait till you have children!' – and who seemed to take my presence for granted. With the hotel staff, Philip was already engaged in repartee and telling them, too, the facts of his life. 'Are you English?' 'I'm Irish-Dutch-Burmese.' 'Oh, I say!' 'I used to be a tramp. I used to put on an upper-class accent . . .' During the taxi journey to Victoria Station, Philip protested, 'I hate everything nowadays. It's horrible, frightening', but gave off an air of well-being, self-respect and self-confidence. He was travelling very light and again Victoria Station was invested with his lightness.

On 1 July, Panna, Philip and the rest of the family finally made the move from Wimereux to Flaux. I did not see Philip again for more than two years. During this time, he established himself in his new corner of France as a drunken eccentric. Sarah Harrison, an English girl living in the area, who became one of his staunchest admirers, first encountered him lying or crawling under a table in a café in Uzès, but saw him as a 'hoot' and found him 'liberating'. Being with him, she explained, 'relieved you of the necessities of social conventions, but if he sensed you were feeling down he would eat you like a vampire'. He was often said to be aggressive and offensive. 'Oh, my dear!' he addressed an American neighbour famous for his ill-fitting dentures, 'Where *did* you get those teeth?' Approached by other people in the street, he shrank from contact. He did not salute people in the Mediterranean style and when Sarah Harrison called out, 'Hello, Mr O'Connor!' she made him jump.

Many of Philip's new neighbours naturally thought him a drunken bore. Daphne Fielding, whom I met later in London, admitted that he had 'already created a stir' but considered him 'dotty'. Others like Lawrence Durrell had long been aware of Philip's reputation and, jealous of his time and pestered by his fans, begged Tony Daniells not to invite O'Connor at the same time. In spite of this embargo, the two men would meet several times at Daniells's house, with disastrous results. On one occasion, Durrell had tried to escape O'Connor by retreating to the lower part of the garden but O'Connor had followed him there. 'D'you want a fight?' Durrell had asked, and been persuaded by his daughter to leave at once. Daniells had also reintroduced Philip to Stephen and Natasha Spender, but the Spenders and their friend Alison Hooper had run off, with Philip hurling particularly personal abuse. Daniells was unflustered by these incidents and said simply, 'I've got used to my friends not liking each other and anyway I like monsters.' He also got used to the 'screaming, orchestrated teamwork' that Philip and Panna provided when they called on him together, Philip's questions about life and death clashing with Panna's talk of Manhattan. Panna's belief that it cost £3,000 to give a party seemed particularly comical to Daniells, who entertained with great generosity without appearing to spend money.

On 8 September 1976 Philip turned sixty, but his advancing years did not bring maturity. During that autumn he brooded over his disconnection with Stephen Spender and wrote various letters to his old mentor which focused embarrassingly on what he perceived as their different social worlds. On 3 September he had written, 'I know you don't like me – naturally, I'm not charming – but I think you fairly distinguish people from their books, at least to the extent of not judging one by the other.' He attempted to revive the old Spender – more indulgent to him? – by adding, 'When I met you at Tony's, I didn't have the impression that you had fundamentally changed.' The only fairly close and 'notable' neighbour who had time for O'Connor and visited him at Flaux was John Berger. Reflecting later on these times, the art critic described Panna as 'a wonderful woman' and Philip as 'a wonderful cook' and 'a considerable connoisseur of wine'. He also recalled, 'I don't think anyone made me laugh more than Philip – the outrageous comparisons – I used to play along with him.'

Berger also drank along with him – not that Philip needed any encouraging. Within a few months of settling at Flaux, Philip's consumption of the 'lethally cheap' local wine reached a dangerous point and he soon told Michael Hamburger that he had almost stopped writing and painting. On 3 March 1977 he was found shouting for Panna in the middle of the village, blind-drunk and apparently unable to get himself the few yards home. It was a dramatic and terrible scene, for which I had seen various rehearsals in Wimereux and London.

Philip was confined to bed for several weeks, cared for by a certain Dr Laffont, who at one point summoned three-year-old Felix O'Connor, and told him to go and say goodbye to his father. Felix remembers this as one of the few times that his father appeared without his usual layer of comic defences, behind which he kept a lookout on life. By 6 April Philip had made a partial recovery and was well enough to write to Michael Hamburger reporting that the doctor had told him he was in the advanced first stage of cirrhosis. 'If I don't stop drinking the liver will bleed in a year's time.' His letter concluded wittily, 'You are of course responsible for this, having introduced me to an unfailing supply of liquor.' Later that summer he wrote equally perkily to Hamburger, saying, 'I have been asked to do Languedoc for a Shell Guide – imagine: "Reaching the summit after a somewhat weary climb one arrives at the grey escarpment on Mont Pucelle, defended in the 9th century by Sir Michael Hamburger and Lord O'Connor (the latter's title bought with a loan from Sir M.H.)".' Typically enough, this project came to nothing but Philip remained frightened enough of dying to keep off alcohol and within a few months also relinquished pipe-smoking. He wanted to 'clean the works'. A letter he wrote to David Thomson that autumn bears a big red wine stain, but clearly this was Thomson's, not O'Connor's.

I had not heard from Philip during this period. On 3 November 1977 he broke his silence by writing that they were now poor, living on 'a well paid English secretary's salary' and again enquiring, 'Will you ever tell me the point of your investigative activities? Are you planning a quest for corvo'connor? If so, the corpse will smell before you're able to do it. I may live a long time, having been teetotal for eight months.'

The following March he responded politely to a letter from me asking for a packet of Caporal Export and telling him about Quentin Crisp's latest success. On Quentin, he reflected, 'Interesting to think that – in a way – his previous life was a sort of stage training. He must think: I haven't been wasting my time. Maybe he'll have a comfortable old age, in his method of discomfort. Yes; and I think much of value ends up in performance.' The letter ended with a formal invitation to come and stay and offered old-fashioned and rather muddled instructions about how to get there. 'Cheapest way is via Paris, rail to Avignon, where I could meet you; expensive and quicker is air to Nice (or maybe Montpellier or Nîmes – I don't think so but am not certain. Montpellier is nearer than Avignon). Or maybe Le Havre makes the journey shorter – not much though – Cherbourg?' A few days later a *petit paquet* flew down my basement staircase containing three pouches of the desired tobacco. It was typical of Philip to send far more tobacco than I had requested. In further letters that spring, he referred to himself as 'such a forgotten one', stated that he never now went to Paris, that he had started yet another book and that the local colony thoroughly disliked him.

I arranged to visit him in the summer of 1978. Philip asked me to bring a large jar of Marmite and four Rachmaninov piano concertos. I took the train to Avignon arriving on the afternoon of 3 August. Philip met me in a white Maserati Citroën, which sounds grander than it was. He spoke in the voice of pernickety weariness that I had first heard on the telephone six years earlier. With him was his suntanned and amiable neighbour Tony Daniells, who had established an easy rapport with him, laughing at his jokes and sympathizing with his view. It was the first time I had seen Philip 'on the wagon'. Without drink and pipe he was the same but politer. The house to which they drove me was as humble as Annie Mygind had described it, though possessing a small grassy courtyard, with a large gate that was held shut with a heavy chain and unused padlock. Facing it was a field of luscious vines and then the rougher and wilder *garrigue*. From the nearby church and the *mairie* two bells clanged each hour.

Inside, the house was unexpectedly spacious. I was given Ella's room on the ground floor. Panna's daughter was said to be flourishing, going to school in Uzès each day by scooter and now on holiday with her father in America. Panna had her own room, full of her treasures, and Philip had a suite consisting of his bedroom and a large improvised studio where he painted, listened to music, ate or abandoned his snacks. From the enclosed garden, you could hear his music and sometimes see him fully engaged preparing a canvas. The children, Maxim now nine and Felix five, both wore expressions of contentment and I was soon walking them up to the *garrigue*, stopping only when Maxim decided that it was enough. I asked Maxim if he would like to be a farmer. He said no, he wanted to travel, mentioning Japan and China, echoing his father's dreams. There was also the sheepdog Nico with its curly tail and slightly absurd, smiling mouth. And a cat, which purred a little too willingly.

Onto this pleasant environment, held together by Panna's maternal instincts, Philip had imposed his own regimes, odd hours and bursts of bad temper. His face was still graced by its beard, but he was well groomed and self-pampered, his remaining hair sleekly swept back –

'I have all the superficial vanities,' he once told me – so that the overall impression or illusion was of a brisk, competent Man of Letters, a well respected left-wing writer or even a retired Great Train Robber. Whenever possible, he kept in the shade and wore a white polo-neck, white socks, sandals and slightly flowing, faintly oriental linen jackets. To protect himself from the sun, he carried a comedian's red umbrella.

I soon learnt that, as always, he spent a lot of his time alone. He got up very early and drove the seven kilometres to the picturesque town of Uzès, where coffee and a croissant at the Esplanade Café absorbed the whole of the small pension he now got from the Society of Authors. From my bedroom I might hear him departing, his muffled curse, the rattle of the gate and the sound of the car. At other times I heard nothing: he was capable of moving with great stealth. On his return from shopping, he sometimes sat in the car for a while, a habit he shared with my father. Then came snippets of news, such as the death of the Pope or the fact that we had been invited to dinner at Tony Daniells's that night. Then, the pattern established in Wimereux, or perhaps earlier, was repeated. With painstaking care he would set about making Panna's breakfast, his self-consciously fastidious arrangements accompanied by his cries, wails and groans as the rest of the household woke up. Eventually I would hear the clunk of Panna's breakfast things as Philip carried the tray aloft. Then came one of those private sessions when Philip passed on information to Panna, especially filling her in on anything I had revealed. 'I was sorry to hear your mother had died,' she said later one morning.

Philip would then retreat to his upper suite announcing his presence there with the music, the same pieces he played in Wimereux, which poured from the open window. I remember visiting him in this private place and finding him lying in ecstasy on his fur-covered sofa listening to some concerto. 'I've come to visit you,' I said smiling. 'Oh, don't, don't. I'm awfully fussy,' he replied in a quiet voice. 'Okay, okay,' I said, backing away.

Once or twice during my visit, I backed away completely by walking into Uzès, getting drunk on my own and walking back under the first great starlit skies I had ever seen, reaching Flaux as its two clocks were clanging midnight. Philip was by then in bed but Panna was still up, in the kitchen, pampering me with extra food, home-made yoghurts, goat cheeses from the local farm. Detached from Philip, she was very talkative in her own right, especially about her Manhattan friends and those she had met during her whirlwind months in London. Her generosity encompassed everyone, even my father. One night she had asked me about his early life and learning that my father's younger brother had died as a baby, explained how such a shock might have had the effect of making him withdraw emotionally, severely hurt. I am ashamed that these thoughts had never occurred to me and indeed were soon forgotten afterwards. Talking to Panna, I felt privileged and honoured. She might wear the same dress every day but her style, delicacy and taste did not tire. Only when Philip was around, or within earshot, did she become subdued. Philip's irritation with other people's conversation was boundless and expressed with cries of 'Shut up! Shut up! Shut up!' which were delivered in the staccato tones employed by kabuki actors. To these protests Panna would murmur with a hint of mockery, 'Disturbs the evening, Andrew. Disturbs the evening. Mustn't talk.'

By the end of my trip – I succeeded in staying eleven days, the longest I would ever spend in Philip's company – I had met several of his neighbours and paid several visits with him to Tony Daniells's secluded paradise on the other side of the village. Tony was indulgent and kind to Philip and everyone else, though his manner was some-times scolding. The two men were at ease with each other. When Philip broke a strut of one of Tony's chairs neither of them showed distress about it. And Tony showed no embarrassment when Philip questioned him closely about a young man shortly to visit him from England. 'Do you love him?' 'Yes.' By this time, Philip was beginning to celebrate my own impending departure, making remarks like 'This voice will be silenced for ever on Thursday', but when we eventually stood together on Avignon station, he said, 'Come again' and suddenly produced one of his old pipes as a going-away present. 'You *are* a funny little man,' I said, and set off for England with an idealized view of the way Philip lived.

The truth was hard to get at. Philip remained on the wagon but his career did not pick up. Back in London, my newly acquired literary agent Gillon Aitken declared at a dinner party that Philip O'Connor would never write another book. The media which had embraced Quentin Crisp entirely shunned Philip O'Connor. Did he care? Quentin had now moved on to a world stage, while Philip played to smaller and smaller audiences: Panna, Maxim, Felix, Ella, a scattering of neighbours including Tony Daniells, the odd shopkeeper in Uzès, John Berger and the handful of old friends to whom he wrote regularly. He may have been flattered by a letter from Laurie Lee saying, 'I always remember you as of special importance to us all' but took great pains to prevent the world beating a path to his door. He corresponded happily with some of the former women in his life, but none of his children were made welcome. Those that did appear were, according to all accounts, cruelly treated.

During this period I received dozens of letters from Philip, sometimes two in the same post. They were usually neatly typed in the format he had established long before I had met him. They looked exciting, especially at first glance: great blocks of prose, full of quotation marks, brackets, explosions of poetry and pretentiousness. I liked their feel, was always excited to hear from him and their arrival bolstered my fragile image of myself as a Man of Letters. I cannot claim to have read them very carefully. The letters had both an uplifting and a depressing effect. Philip used heart-sinking phrases like 'subliterary arrivistes' and then made exciting references to books he was reading, like Thomas Szasz's *The Manufacture of Madness*. They contained both flattery and insults. References to my stinginess and the typescripts he liked to believe I had stolen in Wimereux 'now valued by an impartial arbiter at three thousand pounds' were followed by a statement that he would like to see me again 'in measured quantities'. There were also bits of news: the dog Nico had killed the kittens, the *pâtissier* in Uzès had bought one of Philip's paintings for his parlour, it was too hot, it was too cold and there were impending financial difficulties. He asked often about Quentin Crisp – 'Do you see him?' – and complained constantly that people, including myself, did not respond to his letters or requests. He cursed the English or 'the islanders' and fumed furiously about 'the rudeness of these people', adding a ferocious line of exclamation marks. Several letters referred to my first book *Gossip*, which appeared in the autumn of 1978. He described it as an 'anti-snobs pornography' but added with cool condescension, 'I don't think it's a waste of time – odd facts you've dug up, quite comic things.'

I also visited him each year. I was back in Flaux in the spring of 1979, this time with a girl who came close to representing the 'strong woman with a sense of humour' that Philip said I needed. While staying in a cottage in the village, I received a telegram, gently delivered by Felix, telling me that my father, whom I had ended up loving very much, had died on the Isle of Man. When I started to tell Philip this news he interrupted me with the word, '*Dead.*' He was equally assertive in letters after my visit, saying, 'Marry that girl!' but still puzzling, 'I can't make out why you continue to communicate.'

Although I was busier now and soon at work on another book, I still had a special place in my life for Philip O'Connor. I still bought up copies of his *Memoirs of a Public Baby* whenever I spotted them in second-hand bookshops and still saw in myself an O'Connorish element which I tried to balance with the more practical and ambitious side that Philip loved to mock and abuse. How much Philip understood me I do not know, but I was flattered by his occasional attempts to do so and not at all displeased when during a visit to Flaux in April 1980 he suddenly and excitedly proclaimed that I was the White Clown – or in other words the tall circus performer with the powdered face who never smiles. In London I also got more involved with Philip's friends and family. I had seen a lot of Peter O'Connor who in July 1980 published a novel called *The Happy Elephants* which Bernard Levin made his lead review in the *Sunday Times*. I had also been to a party at Anna Wing's house in Brighton and seen her son Jon Wing O'Connor, now a schoolmaster, swinging through the door carrying a tall potted plant. In the London Library, I had bumped into David Thomson and walked down the street with him, beguiled by his bald head, battered gymshoes and the lively eyes that sparkled behind his thick spectacles.

I did not know at this time that Philip was meanwhile firing off letters to Thomson and others, which often contained derogatory material about me. To David Thomson he pointed out that my name rhymed with 'marrow, sallow, tallow & fallow' and to Michael Hamburger he wrote more viciously, 'Beware of Andrew Barrow. He's taken much more from my waste-paper basket and maybe elsewhere, and tapes – abused confidence. I think he thinks he'll do a sort of *Quest for Corvo* book on me.' For the record, it may be worth repeating that I had at that time no thought of writing about O'Connor – or Quentin Crisp for that matter – but Philip often tried to promote the idea in this roundabout way.

His letters at this time are full of more blatant attempts to promote his own career. In the late 1970s he had acquired Quentin Crisp's agent Richard Gollner and soon had five unpublished books, two plays and 'various oddments' going the rounds. Via Anna Wing, who had played a small but memorable part in the film of *The Naked Civil Servant*, he tried to interest Thames Television director Jack Gold in a dramatization of *Memoirs of a Public Baby*. He had also asked Heathcote Williams to write the screenplay but received a tactful and amusing reply, saying, ''Twere best your own strings plucked it', and 'I cannot think you would approve of the kind of nappies I found for your *Baby* but I don't mind taking it for a walk occasionally.' He also sought an editor for his journals – John Berger's efforts ten years earlier had failed to please him – which now ran to at least half a million words. Some of his letters contained great chunks of his journals, written at five in the morning.

Other letters struck a more down-to-earth note. He mentioned the summer heat – forty degrees centigrade in the shade – his prolonged sobriety, his current reading matter, his old sparring partners like Paul Potts and Tambimuttu, and the enemies among his new neighbours. To Maria Scott he revealed with glee that the film-maker Mai Zetterling had taken 'an instant dislike' to him though he got on quite well with her husband David Hughes. He expressed frequent displeasure with his surroundings. To Michael Hamburger he wrote, 'We're thinking of moving to India in four years' time', adding, 'I don't really like the occidentals & no doubt may dislike the Orientals and die misanthropically – still I'm grateful for my illusions.' 'Everything's bad,' he wrote to Annie Mygind, just as he had twenty years earlier from North Wales. To Maria Scott, he wrote of 'the dear old poverty slowly returning', and finally he would inform me that they were 'on the rocks we've been envisaging for the last two or three years'.

At the end of October 1980, the situation was so bad that Panna felt obliged to take a job in the village, cleaning the schoolmistress's apartment. Philip made a great song and dance about this dramatic comedown and news even reached the Society of Authors that the once affluent Mrs Grady, goddaughter of a Rockefeller, was reduced to doing cleaning, but Panna herself was keen to emphasize that she saw nothing demeaning about the work – her closest friends as a child had been the servants – and anyway the crisis was soon over. A few months later, she was visited by her goddaughter Janet Hobhouse, soon to make her own mark as a novelist, who came away delighted by 'the marvellous new pastoral picture' that Panna presented. With Janet was her friend Victoria Rothschild, to whom Philip took a particular liking. The two girls later invited Philip and Panna to the house in St Tropez where they were staying.

Some slight uplift, spiritual rather than material, may have also been provided by the publication by Sidgwick and Jackson of a slim volume of Philip's poetry. The book was called *Arias of Water* and was edited by a faithful admirer, Stephen du Sautoy, whose father had been chairman of Faber and Faber. It contained some forty or fifty poems that Philip had written at Flaux since going on the wagon. One of them was called 'Mother' and recalled how her 'fat body' had 'waltzed in our slum'. Others were the usual incomprehensible mixture of fine phrases and careless dottiness. One poem referred mysteriously to 'Quentin Crisp and the silent majority'.

The book's publication necessitated a visit by O'Connor to London in the spring of 1981. By this time I had married the strong woman with a sense of humour and a flat I had recently bought in King's Road, Chelsea, was unoccupied. Philip stayed there during his visit, made himself at home and was cooking bacon and eggs when I called on him. He had other things on his plate: three poetry readings to do and friends to visit or ignore. On 4 March he lunched with David and Martina Thomson at Regent's Park Terrace, but seemed otherwise to avoid them. 'I think he was punishing us for not letting him sleep on the red sofa,' Thomson noted later in the diary part of his book

In Camden Town. 'He always did sleep on it in the old days but I wrote to say it would make me too nervous now. You have to surrender the whole morning to him.' Another day he called on Tambimuttu in Cornwall Gardens but found his old rival for Jean Hore's affection had become 'a horror' stinking of cannabis and waiting to go into hospital. On 5 March he did a reading for the Cambridge Poetry Society, organized by the poetry don, J. H. Prynne, and talked to undergraduates he found 'bright'. The next day I was present at the Poetry Society in Earl's Court Square in London where he did another reading in a very rapid, mellow voice which prompted the blind poet John Heath-Stubbs to tell him to speak up. According to David Thomson's diary, the small audience was fascinated by O'Connor but he never looked at them. Instead, grumbled Thomson, he 'keeps his head down and rushes along at high speed'. Afterwards there was a small dinner in a local restaurant attended by Heathcote Williams, my wife and myself and a few others. Philip ordered three small mullet but gave two of them away.

A few days later – during which he managed to visit Edith Young at her new home in Totnes, Devon – I saw him off at Victoria Station. I noted that he had worn exactly the same clothes every day and that his magic, which sprang from his concentrated approach to life, still lingered. He wrote later to Michael Hamburger, 'London was horrible and I hope never to return . . . The only person I truly liked was Heathcote Williams.' Thanking me for the stay in my flat, he wrote, 'I was a little saddened by your pleasant behaviour to me because I think it may be the beginning of a slow illness' and repeated, 'I shall never come to London again.' The book of poems was a failure. According to the *Irish Times* it had no ideas in it and it managed to sell only 177 copies, which Philip gleefully or ruefully compared to the 35,000 sale of Ted Hughes's latest volume. I had my own disappointment at that time. A book I had written about the Church of England had also failed to sell and had been described by Philip's old friend from Wales, Christopher Wordsworth, as like 'an over-long sermon, more numbing than stinging'.

Yet in spite of Philip's lack of public prestige I remained dependent on him and protective of his spark of genius. Part of his magic derived from his utter isolation from media success and the charm and oddness of the private world he had created with Panna. 'We like very few people,' Philip said at this time. 'We don't even like each other very much sometimes.' When I bowled odd questions at them, like asking Philip if he and Panna had ever danced together, I was met by 'Mind your own business!' Panna's unexpected happiness in this rural setting was another influential factor. Philip described her contentment as 'a lighthouse across the wastelands of desolate cheer'. And anyway, it was a wasteland that Philip protected with defiant daily routines, as keen to hang on to his obscurity as Quentin Crisp was to give it up.

I could not keep away for long. In April 1982 I set off to visit him again, this time bringing my wife and baby daughter, Lauretta. Driving south, I noticed that my appetite for my monkey-faced old friend was building up again and this time I would find his growls, bark and hisses echoed by the real-life menagerie that Panna had installed at the house: birds, rabbits, cats, ponies and the lively presiding dog Nico. I enjoyed the visit, especially meeting Panna's daughter Ella again, who after a seven-year gap had emerged as a beauty, but learnt later – biographical research has some of the penalties of eavesdropping – that Philip remained ambiguous about me. 'Andrew Barrow's been here & child & wife,' he wrote to Annie Mygind afterwards – 'I can't like the fellow. He really is sleazy. With some pathos, I suppose, and baby appeal. But really—'

Oh dear, oh dear. And nor did Philip share my exalted view of the place where he lived. Noisy neighbours upset him and his lifelong restlessness had not abated. In the summer of 1982, they decided to sell the house at a loss and move to a watermill at Pont-des-Charrettes in a wooded valley below Uzès. 'Idyllic,' he told David Thomson, 'except for the noisy motors roaring across the bridge dividing our garden.' Philip would occupy the old machine shop. Panna's bed would lie behind a screen in a salon overlooking the river. By November 1982 they had completed the move and Panna would reflect that the chestnuts, poplars and willows that now surrounded them were as splendid as anything Central Park had to offer.

-24-

International Celebrity

I long for New York like a bridegroom for his bride.

QUENTIN CRISP TO HERMIONE GOACHER, 5 June 1980

Quentin Crisp first visited New York in October 1977, aged sixty-eight. He stayed there for only two and a half days but over the next four years would travel frequently between England and America. During this period he kept on his room in London and I occasionally telephoned him here, but could not always keep track of him as his career and reputation advanced on an international scale.

On his first visit to the city of his dreams, he was the guest of Michael Bennett, impresario of *A Chorus Line*, who was interested in buying the stage rights to *The Naked Civil Servant*. As he was driven by Rolls-Royce from the airport, Quentin claims that he stretched his arms out of the window at the skyscrapers 'like a child beholding a Christmas tree'. He later wrote that every single man on the sidewalks reminded him of the American soldiers he had met in London during the war.

For two nights he and his agent Richard Gollner were put up at the Drake Hotel on the Upper East Side and taken round the town by Mr Bennett. On his second evening in the city, Quentin was taken on a whistle-stop tour of the various theatres in the Schubert Group – a show featuring Victor Borge impressed him most – and then given dinner at Sardi's where he claimed later there was 'more waving, more squeaking, more embracing than anywhere else on earth'. The following morning, Mr Bennett called at the Drake and presented Quentin with a large American flag, which he wore like a college scarf on his return flight to London and which would later provide his room in Beaufort Street with its only adornment.

That winter, Quentin's reputation in England was boosted by the third showing of *The Naked Civil Servant* on television and by his appearance at various London parties. One of these was a dinner given by me on 5 November, also attended by the writers Germaine Greer and Philippa Pullar, who argued vociferously, leaving Quentin silent and upstaged. He said later that the two women had 'brought out the worst in each other'. I was at the time bogged down writing my first book and saw little more of him. Was I faintly bored by his new international life, the gush about Sardi's and famous people who sounded much less remarkable than Miss Lumley Who Can Do No Wrong? On 3 December 1977, I noted Quentin's presence at Olga Deterding's penthouse, but did not speak to him.

During these weeks he was also heavily involved in the editing of his novel *Chog*. In November he had handed over the typescript to Eyre Methuen, inducing what can only be described as extreme queasiness among the staff. A publisher's reader wrote, 'I was unprepared for the bleakness of a horror story', and argued that there was a danger of the reader 'being not merely depressed but bored by the dearth of sympathetic characters'. In New York, the literary agent Connie Clausen, who had now become involved in Quentin's career, stated, 'The characters are almost identical in their misanthropy. There is not a single redeeming feature in any of them.' The only way of cheering up the text, the publishers agreed, was to have illustrations and during the next few weeks several artists were approached. Ronald Searle was 'the obvious candidate' but didn't like the story enough to do it for pleasure, and suggested the book would have as much curiosity value if Crisp illustrated it himself. Edward Gorey was also considered and John Glashan, who claimed to be 'heavily committed', also suggested that Crisp should do it himself. Finally the task fell to a student of Ralph Steadman called Jo Lynch. The fact that most of these potential illustrators already knew Crisp personally and were aware of his skills as an artist is itself significant.

While this matter was being resolved, Quentin took another sudden step forward. Early in the New Year he was booked to do his one-man show at the Duke of York's Theatre in St Martin's Lane, just down the street from where the As You Like It had once stood. The impresario Richard Jackson, who had mounted the show at the King's Head in Islington, had seized upon the sudden availability of the theatre following the collapse of a play called *Spinechiller* starring Sian Phillips. Typically, Quentin took this development very calmly, including a visit to the empty auditorium with Brian Rix, director of the company which owned the building. 'I shouldn't think we'll do more than fill the stalls,' he told the *Evening Standard* on 20 January, 'but if it makes people happy, I'll flounder along.'

He did much better than that. The opening night, on 30 January, was packed with admirers. As always, he climbed onto the stage from the auditorium, quite as dramatic an entrance as from the wings. The monologue he then delivered was exactly the same as at the King's Head. During the interval, he mingled with the audience and signed books, even had a drink. In the second half he answered questions from the audience. On the opening night, Joan Rhodes greeted me in the bar. So did Quentin himself, who looked on the crest of a wave. The only unhappy face was, by his own admission, Cecil Woolf, publisher of Quentin's book *How to Have a Life Style*. 'I sat through the first night *fuming*,' he said later. 'Quentin had ridden roughshod through the contract by using whole chunks of the book. He had given the performing rights to *me*.' Others must decide if this indicates a ruthless streak in Quentin Crisp or an oversensitivity on Mr Woolf's part. At any rate the two men remained on speaking terms, Crisp merely once asking Woolf, 'Are you still in a huff?'

After the opening performance, Quentin's new friend Olga Deterding gave a party in his honour in her penthouse and the following day there were ecstatic reviews in all the papers. The *Guardian* pronounced Quentin 'a tonic and a delight' and explained, 'You go in expecting a show and come out having met a remarkable and very likeable man.' The *Evening News* attributed to Quentin 'the slyness of a naughty cherub' and described his show as 'without doubt the most extraordinary entertainment in London'. In the *Evening Standard*, Milton Shulman wrote that Quentin Crisp looked like 'an old actor in some Victorian melodrama', and added, 'He delivered each word as if it were on the end of sugar tongs.'

An Evening with Quentin Crisp ran at the Duke of York's for the next four weeks – and for much of this period Quentin showed his astounding stamina by continuing to model at Camberwell School of Art during the day. Sometimes he was driven to and from the theatre but on many occasions he made the journey on his own by bus. These journeys were not devoid of incident. Waiting for the bus one evening, he was approached by a gang of youths, who shoved him off the pavement and threw his hat in the gutter: an odd degradation for someone whose name was in lights in the West End of London and a startling reminder of the humiliations of the past.

At the theatre almost everyone was friendly and each night there was prolonged applause when Quentin wandered onto the stage. It was a relief to discover that he had not buried his genius with his success. His performances got better and better. His voice got louder, without extra effort, his timing was perfected and the whole performance was so informal that when the audience laughed unexpectedly at some piece of Crisperanto, he was not above asking in a puzzled tone, 'Why are you laughing?' The relaxed quality of the second half gave the audience a chance to see him thinking on his feet. For some of those present it was also a chance to air their concerns about him. One night a woman asked if his view of style wasn't 'a bit archaic' and she rubbed this in by saying, 'I used to see you in the King's Road years ago and I thought you were archaic then.' Quentin simply turned to the audience and said, 'It's true. I *am* archaic', producing another roar of laughter. The only hint of real hostility came from the occasional militant in the audience furious that there was no mention of homosexuality in the performance; Quentin's opening remarks about his show being a 'straight talk from a bent speaker' and description of himself as 'a sad person's idea of a gay person' only upset the activists further. But no one could deny him his triumphant wave at the end as a dinner-jacketed theatre manager finally ushered him back stage.

The show was attended by many old friends from his past and other acquaintances who had admired him from a distance but been too timid to get close to him in public. Among the former category were Oliver Bernard and Stephen Fothergill, both of whom said they had heard it all before. It would be nice to report that the Man from the Ministry slipped into the theatre one night or at least was aware of his former lover's success. Quentin did receive a visit from Angus McBean and his friend David Ball, who also noted that he was churning out the same old stuff, polished up. On 3 February Harold Pinter was there with his 'lady love' and took Quentin to dinner afterwards, during which a stray remark from a fellow guest that the world had accepted Quentin at last drew the comment from the playwright: 'About time too.' Another evening an over-medicated friend of my landlady found himself sitting next to the Poet Laureate John Betjeman – and disgraced himself by falling asleep.

But the show was a huge success and brought Crisp to a new audience. People who had never hitherto heard of him came up from the provinces to see the show, his name was mentioned at dinner parties across the capital, and even my cleaning lady joked that Quentin Crisp got his dust from Fortnum and Mason. I saw the show a second time on 24 February and found the audience full of faces I had never seen before. From time to time I telephoned Quentin and asked him how it was going. He said he was tired by the students who came and questioned him before each performance and revealed that he kept his eyes shut for several minutes before going on stage so that they looked 'wet and dark' when he eventually came on. Early in the run he also told me he had not yet received a single penny for the show but was perfectly happy to carry on – 'providing I don't have to *pay* to appear at the Duke of York's'. Years later, Mr Jackson told me he was paying him £500 a week, but Quentin had other things on his mind. His sights were set on returning to America. He also appeared loved and cherished by backstage visits from a stream of celebrities. One night the *Dad's Army* actor John Le Mesurier had entered his dressing-room with such a lugubrious expression that Quentin wondered if he was going to give him the sack. Another day the actress Elaine Stritch had summoned him to her bedside at the London Clinic and said, 'Just get 'em to like you.'

Quentin did not get the sack and he had already got his audience to like him very much indeed. After a few weeks it was announced that 'the much acclaimed Quentin Crisp' would be transferring to the Ambassador's Theatre on 27 February. He was replaced at the Duke of York's by John Gielgud in a play called *Half-Life* by Julian Mitchell, who has already featured in this narrative as the editor of Philip O'Connor's book *The Lower View*. Up at the Ambassador's, famous for its long run of *The Mousetrap*, Quentin gave the same performance but for technical reasons was obliged to enter the stage from the wings. Here he continued to play to full houses but perhaps fearing a run of *Mousetrap* proportions, reflected, 'I can't go on appearing at the Ambassador's for ever.' The show ended its West End run on 17 March and Quentin then made a series of appearances in provincial theatre, some of which were arranged by the indefatigable Barrie Stacey, at whose café I had met Quentin eleven years earlier. I learnt later that Crisp and Stacey travelled to and from many of these dates together in someone's car, getting Quentin back to Beaufort Street in the small hours, which he much preferred to the ordeals of staying overnight in a provincial hotel.

Many of these provincial performances attracted other figures from Quentin's past. The actress with whom he had stayed in Basingstoke at the time of the Blitz resurfaced in Newcastle under the name of Mrs Reed. Angus McBean and David Ball saw the show again in Norwich, and in Exeter Hermione Goacher materialized with a bundle of clothes for Quentin that had belonged to the young Lord O'Hagan, a cousin of Lytton Strachey and former page to the Queen. In Bristol, the audience included Esther Grant and Barbara Markham, whom he had known since the 1940s, and also his niece Frances, now living with her husband Peter Ramsay at Cheltenham. After the show, Frances approached her famous uncle and was coolly treated by him. 'I could have been *anybody*,' she said later. 'He did not show any interest in me. I was very upset.'

On 31 May 1978, Quentin wrote to Hermione Goacher, 'I rush all over England and even Wales, returning home at dawn having slept in the car.' He added, 'Audiences are remarkably polite' and 'I enjoy myself enormously.' This new busy life at last forced him to give up art school modelling though he continued to pose for photographers. That year, Quentin would sit for a memorable portrait by Jane Bown, who caught him preening himself beside his blackened kettle at Beaufort Street. He would also pose completely nude for a drawing by the artist R. B. Kitaj, who had lived across the street in Elm Park Road for the past twenty years and often admired Quentin at a distance.

This portrait would later be exhibited at the Tate Gallery and hailed as 'a lesson in the anatomy of melancholy' but, when I visited Quentin during this period, I found him full of bounce and gumption and looking unbelievably youthful at sixty-nine. To me, he seemed remarkably self-sufficient and ecstatic about everything. 'I want to be infinitely present,' he said. 'I like perfectly simple ... *fame*.' When I asked him to explain, he said, 'I want to be photographed at airports. I like to be liked.' Sometime earlier he had written to Hermione Goacher, 'When I die it will be in all the papers', and now that fame had come he was making the most of it. He appeared often on radio and television, sometimes introduced as 'self-confessed eccentric Quentin Crisp', and he made some vitriolic contributions to the newspapers including a memorable attack on contemporary music. In spite of his abhorrence of many aspects of modern social life, he accepted all invitations and sometimes packed several events into an evening. On 3 June he was marked down as 'Late Arrival' on the guest list for yet another party in Olga Deterding's penthouse, but arrived in time to chat to other publicized figures like Lady Diana Cooper and Margaret Duchess of Argyll.

On 20 June he left for what he claims was a rather unsuccessful tour of Australia, appearing in every major city except Darwin. He feared that the Australians would find him 'particularly revolting' but, though he was mobbed at airports, the tour was a 'disaster' in terms of ticket sales and his 'unfailingly courteous' promoter suffered what Quentin describes as 'a staggering financial loss'. On 25 August he was back in London. Within ten minutes of his return I telephoned him at Beaufort Street, which I feared gave the impression I had been telephoning him incessantly during his absence. He laughed and told me not to worry and by then must have got used to being pestered. It was around this time that two policemen called on him and informed him that a respectable middle-aged woman from the North of England had been so disturbed by the spectacle of Quentin Crisp's loneliness that she threatened to murder him and then 'do away' with herself. He confidently advised the police to take no action.

On 16 September I had a picnic lunch with Quentin in his room, bringing along tomatoes, peaches, a slice of Brie and Guinness, and it may have been on this occasion that he remarked, 'A sensitive tomato. It doesn't like to be cut.' He told me he had not been out at all since his return from Australia, except to appear in further provincial theatres. I realized I no longer had a flood of questions to ask him and there were times that day when our conversation dried up. A few weeks later I called on him again, this time bringing the proofs of my book *Gossip*, which I hoped he might review somewhere. On 3 October I returned to his room to pick up the proofs and read Quentin's review, which to my slight disappointment would appear in *Gay News* rather than *The Times*. This time I attempted to enliven the proceedings by wearing a blue suit and silver tie but Quentin was already in effervescent form, sitting opposite me looking as fresh as a daisy and praising my book for all it was worth. It was only a short visit but there was time for at least one anonymous phone call. When I left, he shot down the Beaufort Street stairs in front of me with the agility of a ten-year-old. I walked away with the proofs of my book in an envelope and noticed that the smell of Quentin's room clung to them for several days afterwards.

I wondered when I would see him again. Or indeed if I would ever see him again. On 7 October he flew to America, staying first at the Chelsea Hotel in New York, where his brief visit was enlivened by the murder of his fellow guest Nancy Spungeon by the Sex Pistol star Sid Vicious. Later that month he went 'whizzing round' the United States speaking with melodramatic emphasis on radio and TV shows in Chicago, San Francisco, Los Angeles, Boston and elsewhere. He was accompanied throughout by his agent Richard Gollner, whom some Americans seemed to think was the Barn Door character from *The Naked Civil Servant*. On 31 October he made his first paid appearance in America at the New Wharf Theatre, New Haven, Connecticut. Here *An Evening with Quentin Crisp*, staged by the impresario Hillard Elkins, ran for two weeks, during which Quentin would uncharacteristically watch the punters arriving at the theatre from his hotel bedroom window. In mid-November he returned via Washington to New York, where he was put up at the famous Algonquin Hotel amidst talk that Mr Elkins was now in 'serious conversations' with the pop-star David Bowie about a musical based on Quentin's book. To stir up interest, Crisp began to attend events in New York. One night he attended a party at the Waldorf Astoria in honour of the actress Bette Midler. Posing with Quentin as he showed off to the camera, Miss Midler murmured, 'That's right, baby, do the whole bit.' Another night, he had dinner with Condé Nast editor Leo Lerman and the English writer A. L. Rowse at the Café des Artistes. Here the waiters made such a fuss over him that A. L. Rowse felt upstaged and after Quentin had departed asked grumpily, 'Who was that woman?'

On 20 December 1978 he opened at the Players Theatre, Mac-Dougal Street, making his usual entrance by walking straight up the aisle onto a stage adorned only by an antique chair and a pot of ferns. The critics, he wrote later, were amazingly kind to him, perhaps on account of the fact that he was 'a foreigner, an outcast, an old man and alone'. In the *New York Post* Clive Barnes described the show as 'heartrendingly enjoyable' and 'an evening of comprehensive humanity'. In the *New York Times*, Richard Elder praised Crisp's 'valiant and original mind' and described him as 'the message in the bottle'. Like all admirers of the show, Elder particularly delighted in the second half when Quentin answered spontaneous questions from the audience. 'His mind becomes a pleasure to watch as it works within the confines of his answers.' The eleven-week run which followed was literally lit up one night by a fire at the theatre during which Quentin characteristically remained on stage while the audience hurried out.

During the day he wrote syrupy book reviews for *New York* magazine – 'The cover of this book alone is enough to make you long to buy it' – and rubbed shoulders with other guests at the Algonquin, including a Congressman from Minnesota who approached him over breakfast. He also did what people nowadays call 'admin'. Writing to Bob Wooding, his editor at Eyre Methuen, on 9 February 1979, he declared, 'I expect to be in New York more or less for ever but must return to England to say goodbye to my room.' The following day he moved into a less famous hotel, the fictional-sounding Middletowne

Hotel on East 48th Street, where he read the proofs of *Chog*. On 22 February he recorded his one-man show in front of a conscripted audience at New York's Columbia Studios. He then went again to California where he did his show, stayed in a Beverley Hills hotel with Mr Gollner and was entertained by Hillard and Judy Elkins at a house 'made entirely of glass' and by David Hockney at his studio overlooking the ocean. With uncharacteristic straightforwardness, Quentin would later describe Hockney as 'a truly original artist and a fascinating and lovable human being'.

On 3 April Quentin was still away from England when Mrs Thatcher 'ascended the throne', but was back in London a few days later amidst press reports of his 'spectacular series of successes' in America and further talk of David Bowie appearing in a musical based on his autobiography. During that summer I saw little of him and when I spoke to him on the telephone was disappointed by his artificial and rather phoney manner. I knew nothing of his movements, but learnt later that he had addressed a publisher's sales conference on 11 June, appeared at Bournemouth on 1 July and at the Royal Shakespeare Theatre a week later. On the afternoon of Sunday 12 August I rang the doorbell at 129 Beaufort Street and found Quentin at home. I can remember very little of what we talked about. I may or may not have told him that my father had died that spring but we certainly discussed the death of Olga Deterding, who had choked to death the previous New Year's Eve. In his book *How to Become a Virgin* he writes, 'I cannot say that I ever expected to become a close friend of Miss Deterding but when she died – I was sorry.' This comes as a slight relief after his statement in *The Naked Civil Servant* that he had never heard of anyone dying without experiencing a thrill of pleasure.

In September 1979 *Chog* was published by Methuen. Though Quentin described the book as 'a deliciously disgusting fantasy', the widespread apprehension about the project seems to have been justified. The book was published without much publicity – I didn't notice its appearance myself – and the reviews were mixed. In the *Daily Telegraph* Martyn Goff described *Chog* as 'a black fairytale, quickly and expertly told . . . a gothic horror'. But in *Punch* Quentin's old Soho acquaintance Jeffrey Bernard wrote, 'I tried to work out what disgusts Quentin Crisp so much but gave up after a few seconds. 'The human race, I suppose.' In the *New Statesman*, Andrew Motion went deeper, describing the book as 'sick' and claiming that in it, Quentin Crisp mourns 'the absence of love' and mouths 'his dislike and distrust of the world'. Many of his friends were equally shocked by the book, though a few may have been reassured to learn that their friend had not mellowed in the least. In Japan, where it was listed as a children's book, *Chog* sold an alarming eighteen thousand copies.

Later that autumn Quentin spent three days lecturing at the University of Alberta and the following spring he was back again beside Mr Elkins's pool in Los Angeles and apparently swanning around at Hollywood parties 'thronged with celebrities'. I was now preoccupied with another book and travelling on my own account. I went to Japan, Spain and France – where I received further helpings of Philip O'Connor's wisdom. I learnt later that Quentin's life was not quite as easy as it appeared and that saying 'goodbye' to his London room took some doing. His devoted landlady Miss Vereker had now sold the house to a man who politely asked Quentin if he could pay six guineas a week. 'I'm being fleeced,' he moaned to Hermione Goacher's husband and to Hermione herself he complained that he had to get his teeth renewed and pay £450 to the Ministry of Pensions, who had accused him of 'not taking due care to avoid over-payment'. In response to these grumbles, Mr Goacher tried to persuade him that six guineas a week was a very fair rent and from her home in Devon Mrs Goacher embarrassed him more than once by sending money. On 5 June 1980 Quentin wrote to her declaring, 'I am quite frightened by the cascades of money falling out of Devonshire' and explaining, 'I am not starving so you must never send me any more money, welcome though it is.' In the same letter, he reasserted his determination to settle in America – 'I long for New York like a bridegroom for his bride' – and added that he now had a lawyer helping him with his immigration arrangements.

Later that summer he crossed the Atlantic again and after a spell in a Californian 'sea lodge' found temporary accommodation on New York's West 14th Street in a room belonging to the Church of the Beloved Disciple, a religious homosexual organization run by an old friend of Angus McBean named Johnny Noble. He was here when I visited New York for the first time early that autumn and on 26 September I met him in the Algonquin Hotel and bought him a drink. He looked extremely well but again I found I had little to say or ask him and realized that I had only arranged to see him for old time's sake. The most interesting moment came when we left the building together. Almost immediately a man on the sidewalk shouted '*Quentin Crisp!*' Someone else asked for his autograph and another stranger took a photograph. A few days later I bumped into him again in a restaurant where he was surrounded by fawning English people who made my heart sink.

The following spring I was abroad on honeymoon and Quentin was still away from London when Miss Vereker, 'patron saint of hooligans', died at the age of eighty-five. In her later years 'Vi' Vereker had refused to discuss her famous lodger, whispering that her father, long since dead, was in the next room and adding, 'He's a doctor, you know.' In the middle of April 1981, Quentin at last returned 'to pack his bags', a process that would take him five months and be interrupted by further brief visits to America. On Whit Monday he made a day trip to Atlanta, Georgia, to sign copies of his new book *How to Become a Virgin*, a sequel to *The Naked Civil Servant*, after which he promised he would put a stop to 'this literary nonsense'. Later that month, the actor Derek Jacobi, who was a friend of one of Quentin's 'spies' in New York, brought back a bundle of letters that had arrived for him at West 14th Street. In London, Fenella Fielding took Quentin to meet Jacobi back stage and pick up the letters, one of which contained the magic Green Card which would permit him 'to dwell forever in Manhattan'.

During his last few months in London, Quentin Crisp appeared in his one-man show at the Mayfair Theatre – Anne Valery was present the night he was severely heckled by a member of the audience – and said farewell to some of his friends and relations. In August he dined with Annie Wignall and Denis Goacher, now living together in South Kensington, and told Hermione Goacher that he had had 'a wonderful evening'. The same month he visited his niece Frances Ramsay in Cheltenham, travelling there by coach, and was snapped on the verandah wearing an old brown jacket and sandals, while scrutinizing a newspaper. Beside him sat the Ramsays' son, Tim, who mimicked his great-uncle's pose. Quentin commented afterwards that Mr and Mrs Ramsay went in for 'standard of living'.

Meanwhile, he had submitted himself to a number of farewell interviews. To Stephen Pile of the *Sunday Times*, he declared, 'Tell them I am in love with America. It is a land of perpetual summer where happiness rains from the sky. And the British have become embittered.' To another reporter he explained that living in Beaufort Street for so many years was like wearing old clothes, but he was leaving it with no regrets. To Stephen Pile he said finally, 'I shall leave the room as if I had never been here. I shall wipe the slate clean. And that will be very nice.'

The Times states that Quentin Crisp left on 13 September. The *Guardian* says that it was 12 September. On whichever day it was, Richard Gollner called at Beaufort Street and found his famous client throwing stuff into a dustbin including some of his own drawings. When Gollner protested, Quentin gave them to him instead, along with a portrait of him painted in 1936 and the chess set with which the two men had often played. Other possessions, including a whole trunk of linen and bundles of clothes he would never use, were already on their way to New York. Quentin would also take with him the mug adorned with the homoerotic figure resembling himself. A few hours later neighbours waved goodbye from their windows as he finally turned his back on the room that he had occupied for the last forty-one years. In a taxi crammed with his possessions, he was driven to Heathrow Airport from where he flew off to live for ever in New York. He was now seventy-two years old, the age at which many people enter 'a twilight home'.

Medieval Gate-Keeper

I am now, like yourself, an elderly gent, overbooked,
burdened and committed but I will do everything possible for your magazine. When I hear the literary fire
bell ringing I stagger to my feet like an old fire horse.

SAUL BELLOW TO PHILIP O'CONNOR, 15 August 1990

Quentin Crisp was already installed in a cheap and horrible room on
New York's Lower East Side when Philip O'Connor and Panna Grady
moved into their rambling old mill in the beautiful valley of Pont-des-
Charrettes. Both were isolated locations in their own way: Quentin's
murky abode remained the dressing-room where he could be his 'horrible self' and from where he would saunter out to further triumphs,
whereas Philip's picturesque new home was another castle in which
to barricade himself, firing off innumerable letters to the outside
world but hardly connecting with it and making very few personal
appearances.

To a large extent, Philip O'Connor's life stood still and like many
old people – he was sixty-six when they moved into the Moulin – he
spent a lot of his time looking backwards or inwards. He remained
sober, however, and his daily routines in the new house would follow
an even more rigid pattern. As always, he got up before dawn, stalked
up the path into Uzès to go shopping and returned to prepare Panna's
breakfast with the usual fuss and bother. Eventually he would carry
the neatly arranged tray to her fur-covered bed overlooking the river
and begin his first oratorical performance of the day. Yet, even inside
the mill, Philip's life was hedged in with further layers of privacy:

Felix O'Connor recalls how his father's inner sanctum at Flaux had been approached through a series of doors, one of which jammed, and a similar 'accordion' existed at the Moulin, culminating in a door with a stiff steel bolt, also inclined to jam. Panna and Philip kept very different hours and rarely ate or did anything else together. When not preoccupied with her children Panna would tend the irises, daisies, valerian and jasmine that grew on the banks of the river and sometimes wade up to her waist as she cleared the water of debris, while Philip marched around his property in long boots, erupting with fury when a motorbike roared over the bridge. One afternoon during his first summer there, he had found a Canadian couple swimming naked in the river and boldly invited them into the house. 'But we've no clothes,' protested the couple, who were called Linda and Phil. 'That doesn't matter,' Philip replied. To these passers-by, O'Connor seemed like 'a medieval gatekeeper, collecting tolls', but they soon began to enjoy his 'habit of bantering vociferously on about things not usually mention-able in polite society'. Such moments of sociability were rare. Most evenings, Philip would go to bed at eight o'clock, locking his door and putting in earplugs.

Inside this inner fastness, he wrote letters and his journal: after a while, the letters and journals would fuse together, recipients some-times getting a block of journal instead of a letter, or a letter that lapsed into the sort of philosophical ramblings that filled his journal. He wrote in much the same style to everyone, some letters running to eight hundred words or more. He described himself as 'a remorseless windbag' and 'a garrulous old man'. To his oldest friend, Patrick de Maré, he wrote, 'I'm an awful letter writer', and wondered, 'Maybe if I were more published, I'd refrain.' To the poet Ian Patterson, of whom more in a moment, he would write, 'Correspondence is the only form of publication left to me', yet he consoled himself with the thought that he now had 'the liberty to write what I want with no danger of publication', or in other words, 'to write what I like and not what the phantom reader might'. But his letters were still full of requests, some attempting to breathe life into his career. He sought information about publishers, he asked correspondents to make enqui-ries on his behalf about any number of things. Early in the 1980s he stated, 'Really my bloody career is over' but he still sent out ideas or synopses to everyone, some of which seemed to get lost in the post or at the publishers'; he rarely kept copies. For a while he was in correspondence with a publisher in Moscow. He mentions and mis-names, perhaps deliberately, a certain 'Robert McCrumble' at his old publishers Faber and Faber. He continued to think about getting *Memoirs of a Public Baby* republished or filmed. He wrote to Denis Mitchell about a TV adaptation, wanting John Hurt to do 'the grown-up part' but expressing interest in playing 'the funny old man' himself. At one point he seems to have confused the film director Jack Gold with the literary agent Richard Gollner, who was still circulating his work in London.

On one level these letters make heavy reading – and one wonders if anyone read them carefully. Wading through great tracts of agitated thought, one longs for less abstract material, for trivia, for personal detail. It is a relief when Philip tells Patrick de Maré that he has bought 'a beautiful Alfa Romeo small estate on the never never' or even mentions that the roof leaks and the septic tank is overflowing. It is also a relief when he writes about remote figures from his past, about his 'repressedly homosexual guardian's touch' or Madame Til-lieux, 'whom I loved as I love (good) bread', or makes some robust prediction about his future: 'We'll kick the bucket soon.' Yet on another level, even the most philosophical of his letters contain some-thing precious, unique to O'Connor, some fragment of self-deflating candour, some enlightening playfulness, or petulant reworking of a word or sound pattern, however lost the idea behind it. Or some reference to the active and reckless life he had now exchanged for the sober and sedentary life of a letter-writer. Or some sudden warmth, as when he thanks Michael Hamburger for sending him his latest published work and comments, 'Your book is lovable, like yourself.'

A hostile, even nasty tone is more common. Belligerent references to Tambimuttu had continued for forty years and did not cease when Tambi died in the summer of 1983 after a drab last few years. Philip also awaited the death of Paul Potts with cruel keenness. And he continued to savage the best-known English writers whenever he could, now describing Michael Holroyd as 'some idiot biographer',

Peter Ackroyd as 'a clever idiot' and Anthony Powell as 'a failed novelist'. Writers, he says, are 'a nasty tribe' and he's glad he remained outside it, 'however perforcedly'. He even refers to Quentin Crisp as a 'foetid resurrection' and accuses him of being 'incredibly vulgar' by calling him a 'hooligan' in *How to Become a Virgin*, which he dismisses as 'an atrocious booklet'. Sad though this sounds, one must remember that Philip O'Connor had thrived on hostilities all his life: he would explain to Ian Patterson, 'I think enemies usually provide the walls of one's fortress.'

Philip's letters may show him up as a compulsive crosspatch, but he also used correspondence to perpetuate or revive old friendships. He had not seen Maria Scott for twenty-five years – she feared his cruelty in person – but they continued to carry on an amiable and unemotional relationship by post. Philip praised the short stories Maria had started writing, called them 'very good indeed' and urged her, 'Carry on, my dear, you're on a good path.' When Maria heard that Philip was thinking of writing a book about clowns, she wrote about the famous ones she had seen in her youth: 'I saw Grock, I also saw Pallenberg and Karl Valentin, who was the greatest.' In November 1983, the death of Philip's stalwart supporter and patron Annie Mygind – I had lost touch with her – prompted Philip to write with untypical fondness to her son Martin. 'I loved her as one might love the "northern lights",' he wrote. 'I had some of the best times of my life with her . . . Good luck and inherit her bright lights.' This generous, graceful letter was followed by cruder, semi-begging ones as Philip quickly added Annie's son to the list of those who might in some way be able to help him. He also gleefully informed other correspondents that he had learnt from *The Times* that Annie Mygind had left the tidy sum, especially for those days, of £346,000.

During this period Philip wrote many letters to me, the arrival of which always gave me pleasure, partly because I was still excited to have a friend living abroad. These were variously addressed, 'Child', 'Kreep', 'Boy', 'Barrow', 'Old Man', 'Barrow Andrew' and 'Barrow of London'. Many letters contained complaints that I had not replied to his last one and almost all contained requests. He asked me to collect a typescript from publisher Marion Boyars, to find out about an editor called David Profumo, who was apparently a fan of his, to get a copy of Ford Madox Ford's *Memories and Criticisms* and, not for the first time, a new gramophone needle, now costing £36. He also asked for old clothes and often mentions with gratitude a pair of my father's shoes that I had given him during his last visit to London and which were the only ones that could accommodate his bunion. He wrote often about money, referring to 'the sink of penury' he and Panna were in and his troubled relationship with the bank: 'The cashier rushes to the manager as soon as I appear.' One letter began with the bold words 'Can you send me two thousand pounds?' and in another he wonders if he could make some money suing Quentin Crisp for the libellous remarks in his 'frightful' book. There are various cruel or hostile notes. 'You remain rather silly,' he told me and he also expressed 'sorrow' that David Thomson and I sometimes met in London – 'I smell no good therefrom' – and says, 'Yes: I'm dropping my very few remaining English friends.' He warns me, 'Others enjoying my dislike are doing very badly round here' and once again enquires, 'Why do you creep around my life? Have you a posthumous biography in store?' On a kinder note, he sometimes sent me tobacco and made gentle enquiries after my 'little mites' – my son Nicholas had been born in September 1983.

I did not stay at the Moulin but I occasionally visited him there during this period, bringing my wife and children. These encounters lacked the euphoria of my solo visits ten years earlier but I found Philip still provided an excitingly undiluted and invasive intimacy which no one else I knew had offered. He was also kind to my children. To my daughter Lauretta he gave a Bounty bar, the coconut contents of which perhaps reminded him of the sweetmeats his mother had once prepared. After a few munches and with her mouth still full, Lauretta had said unapologetically, 'I don't like it', but when he asked her, 'Why do you like me?' she replied more tactfully, 'Because you're so handsome.'

Felix O'Connor, who was still a child at the time, has described Philip's appearance when he stepped out of his fastness: the 'extreme tension' of his lips, their 'fierce compression' and 'dead-drunk babyish curl', and the way in which he still remained partly hidden, his head 'fixed on a curve' and his words 'paralysing the gaze of others'. In July 1985 he took his complicated persona all the way to London for his daughter Allaye's wedding to a young doctor. This trip was accomplished with a certain stealth – he complained that his new passport photograph made him look like a 'bomber' – but he saw his old friends like Thomson, de Maré and Rosemary Goad, stayed with Ann Wolff at Eton Villas and saw quite a lot of his children, extending what Mrs Wolff described as 'immense charm to those he knew least well'.

I was not involved in these family activities but met up with him on 11 July in the BBC pub called the George. Here I found him leering at me from a seat by the door, a muscle pulsating furiously in his cheek as I approached, but when we set off together through the streets he seemed happy, mellow and cool. We came to rest in an Indian restaurant in a basement in Percy Street, Fitzrovia, where he simply ordered 'a curry' accompanied by 'flaky yellow rice' which arrived in little dishes which could have come from his own kitchen. He was still not drinking but I needed three Coca-Colas to keep me sparkling. I then walked with him to Cambridge Circus, where he said goodbye and slipped away without a backwards glance.

Three days later he was back in the South of France and secure in his steel-locked fortress, licking his wounds and telling correspondents, 'London gets worse and worse.' The following month he had further cause for chagrin when he learnt that Tony Daniells had excluded him from a dinner for Stephen Spender on account of his tendency to be 'too aggressive'. Philip's feelings about his old mentor were always complex and the correspondence between the two of them was marked by extreme politeness and patience on Spender's part and by embarrassed affection and bouts of touchiness from O'Connor.

In the autumn of 1985 these tensions got much worse when Rosemary Goad unwittingly sent Philip a copy of Spender's newly published *Journals* which included a description of the telephone encounter in May 1956 which has already featured in this narrative. Though Philip was not referred to by name, he was enraged by Spender's criticism of his begging activities and fired off at least two letters to him saying that the piece was 'quite disgusting' in its 'moralistic priggery' and informing him: 'You have got what the English lovingly call the bare facts wrong.' He explained, 'I did not leave my wife – we were unmarried.' And Anna Wing was 'a working actress & quite comfortably off'. He went on to reprimand Spender for his 'absurdly "uptight" view of what you consider parasitism' and to argue, 'No one has ever suffered from my "borrowing" ' and 'Certainly I kept my first wife after she tried to kill me (for which I never criticized her).' This lively tirade of self-justification continued with O'Connor accusing Spender of sniffing at the 'philosophizing' which he claimed was 'the best and whole meaning of my life'. His final point was that he was not as Spender had described him 'anti-bourgeois', but 'non-bourgeois'. In response to this lengthy lament – was Quentin Crisp right in saying that Philip was never self-pitying? – Stephen Spender wrote a longish letter of apology, which O'Connor promptly sold for £40 to the antiquarian bookseller Bertram Rota – and later apologized for selling: 'I was short of cash then. We're better off now.'

The relationship between the two men muddled on, however, and Philip told Spender in a subsequent letter, 'For a reason mysterious to me you remind me of my mother', and went on, 'This mother of mine is, I suppose, my real hallucination. I've seen her everywhere.' In April 1987 Philip wrote, 'As you continue not to reply, my letters will peter out', but didn't keep up this threat. In July Spender wrote to Philip, 'Like you I have a feeling of time running out' but said he would be happy to write a new introduction to Philip's autobiography if anyone wanted to republish it. In August Philip and Panna went over to lunch with the Spenders in their garden at Maussane-les-Alpilles where a bit of film was shot of the two men talking, only interrupted when Spender leapt up to answer a telephone ringing inside the house. Spender's life was undeniably sociable – and he used the back of one of Philip's letters as a makeshift diary, noting appointments with 'Jeremy Fry' and 'Brendel'. One wonders if he knew these people half as well as he knew O'Connor, whose career owed so much to him. On 13 March the following year, Philip kept the ball rolling by complimenting Spender on his novel *The Temple* and unburdening himself of some of his own sexual uncertainties. He mentions 'the healing touch' of several wives and continues, 'But I understand "too well" love of beautiful boys, not men "perhaps". I was in love with Pierrot, aged four, in Wimereux, with Pat de Maré when we were both seventeen, with Cruikshank, with whom I edited my wartime magazine, with Oliver French anarchist son of a Glasgow millionaire.'

By this time Philip had lost two of his staunchest, most beloved friends. In 1987 his old mentor Edith Young, with whom he had lived and drunk in Suffolk and Wales, had died aged ninety-five. Her son Michael, now Lord Young of Dartington, would later despatch an antique plate that Edith had left Philip in her will. 'She had a marvellous eye for such things and always managed to pick them up for a bargain.' And in February 1988 David Thomson died aged seventy-four, prompting what Philip described as a 'sugary' obituary from Seamus Heaney. Already very frail, Thomson had paid a final visit to France the previous autumn, meeting up with Philip in Vaucluse.

Meanwhile, he had acquired a new friend and admirer in the form of poet and academic Ian Patterson, whose comments on Quentin Crisp's poetry I quoted earlier. In the spring of 1987, Patterson had been on holiday in Uzès and heard by chance that Philip O'Connor, whose early published work he knew well, was living nearby. On their first meeting O'Connor had beguiled Patterson by asking, 'Why do you lie?' and then presented himself as a 'virtuoso conversationalist, very interesting and perceptive about people'. They met again when Patterson rented Tony Daniells's house in Flaux and for a while letters flew from Philip's typewriter to Patterson's home in Cambridge, to which on one occasion Patterson responded robustly, 'Don't be so damned testy.' At around this time Philip also had a 'friendly reconnection' with Anna Wing, now a household name and face in England as the old granny in *EastEnders*. At the end of December 1987 Anna Wing had met Philip and for the first time Panna Grady near Carcassonne. She had offered 'almost overwhelming benevolence' while carefully withholding her telephone number. A less easy visit was from Ann Wolff, director of the *Captain Busby* film, who jolted Philip by telling him that he was getting cut off in France and was forgotten in England. Panna had leapt forward and assured him that Ann was talking nonsense.

Whether or not this was true, Philip's name became marginally better known the following spring when *Memoirs of a Public Baby* was at last republished in England. The keen young publishers Fourth Estate, who were hungry for new books and the previous year had even produced an esoteric stocking-filler of my own, were persuaded by me and others to take on the task. In his promised new introduction Stephen Spender proclaimed the book 'a Chaplinesque comic masterpiece', described Philip O'Connor's alienated world, the 'trickiness' of his act and his supreme understanding that making 'avoidance of pain the criterion of happiness anaesthetises large areas of consciousness'.

The long-awaited republication of his best-known book gave Philip a reason for visiting London, for the last time, again without Panna. On 19 March 1988 there was a party at L'Escargot in Greek Street, only a stone's throw away from the Dean Street cellar where O'Connor had spent part of his childhood. Stephen Spender allowed his name to be used as 'host' and the event was attended by a mixture of hangers-on and old friends. Anna Wing was there, now at the height of her new fame, and so were other members of the family, including Peter and Allaye. Maria Scott characteristically stayed away though she had nothing to fear from Philip O'Connor, who was on his best sober behaviour and had even shaved off his beard. Panna's old friend Nicholas Mosley was there – so were the Hamburgers, the Jeremy Brookses, Ann Wolff, Michael Horovitz, Martina Thomson, Gavin Ewart, Patrick de Maré, Ian Patterson and the vet Tony O'Neill. The author Andrew Sinclair and his wife Sonia Melchett brought a touch of mainstream glamour. I was abroad but sent two of my older brothers instead. The event received a brief mention in the *Evening Standard* and the book was favourably reviewed in the *Observer* by the faithful Paul Bailey, who described it as 'strange and rather wonderful' and 'the perfect book to read in Mrs Thatcher's Britain'. He also quoted O'Connor's description of his father as 'one of those men cursed with an imaginative esoteric morality of their own' and wondered if this could be applied to O'Connor himself.

I returned to England on 31 March and invited Philip to spend the following weekend at the house where I was now living in Sussex. On the Saturday morning he appeared on the live radio programme 'Loose Ends' promoting his book in rather a querulous voice, and being stopped by the chairman Ned Sherrin when he started to name Captain Herbrand Williams as the man who had tried to seduce him before the war. I met him later that morning at Lewes station. The visit went well. A few people came to lunch including my mother-in-law and a neighbour called Mrs Spencer. Philip immediately noticed a spot on Mrs Spencer's cheek and asked, 'Cancerous?' and was later pronounced by Mrs Spencer to be 'frightfully affected'. With my mother-in-law, whom I had always found extremely easy-going, he got on far worse, wincing with pain in her company, saying nothing, turning his back to her and sitting as far away as possible. With two girls staying in the house, an American and an Indian, both in their twenties, he got on swimmingly, chatting with them like three students together, making them laugh, being calm and rising to the occasion. The Indian girl, Vaneeta Saroop, remarked to him, 'You seem fascinated by human anatomy.' He also got on well with my own children and with a newly acquired Cavalier King Charles puppy whom he fondled affectionately.

The photographs taken on this occasion show O'Connor looking good at seventy-one years old, chubby and unlined: my wife pointed out that he had had an easy life during the past twenty years, protected from anxiety. That night he went to bed early but made a memorable reappearance in the kitchen, completely silent, opening the fridge door like a magician and getting things out for the bedroom snacks that were an essential part of his life. The following day I proudly gave him £20 to cover his first-class fare back to London.

I saw him again the following week, when he gave a reading at Bernard Stone's bookshop in Lamb's Conduit Street, introduced by his old acquaintance Laurie Lee, who described O'Connor as 'the first true poet I ever met' and 'a unique creative character' who had had 'a liberating effect' on him. Lee also informed Philip, 'You've weathered the years better than I have' and spoke admiringly of his 'nine children and doctor's order not to drink'. As usual the reading that followed lacked the fire that Philip put into his private performances, and the following day he returned to France, never to visit England again.

At the end of that year he was re-established in his private fastness at Pont-des-Charrettes when news came that his oldest daughter Sarah, now in her early forties and the mother of two children, had been killed in an accident in a Bristol street. Philip and Sarah had remained estranged over the years – a recent visit by Sarah to the Moulin had failed to resolve their difficulties – and Philip's reaction to her death was characteristically detached. He gave further evidence of this coolness by devoting only one short paragraph to the tragedy in a long letter he wrote to Patrick de Maré after Christmas.

In the spring of 1989 it was also in sad circumstances that I paid another visit to the Moulin. My marriage was beginning to break up and I was preoccupied with this drama and my failure, not unconnected, to publish a revised version of the novel I had dashed off more than twenty years earlier. I also spent two brief spells in New York that year, seeing Quentin Crisp and visiting the offices of W. W. Norton, who were to publish an American edition of *Memoirs of a Public Baby*. In the run-up to this event, Philip anticipated that Quentin, now an established figure in New York, would help to promote the book and told Patrick de Maré that he might even appear on stage with his old friend, whom he patronizingly described as a 'professional homosexual' and whom, he said, he 'would not have chosen, but the fates have'. In spite of this attitude, Philip had written to Quentin under the assumption that the American media were at his fingertips and on 21 January 1989, Quentin had written back saying, 'It was nice to hear from you' and stating that he was perfectly willing to appear with him on any television channel in the United States but adding, 'I do not have the power to cause this to happen. I am entirely a victim of fate; I go on whatever television channel I am told.' In a heart-warming postscript, he had added, 'Commend me to Mr Barrow if you still see him . . .'

The book eventually appeared in November 1989 without Crisp's recommendation but garlanded in praise from some of America's greatest writers. Panna Grady's old friends William Burroughs and Norman Mailer led the chorus. Burroughs wrote of O'Connor's 'unique personality' and Mailer declared that the book offered 'a wit, intensity and originality of perception that comes near to surpassing all comparison in contemporary writing'. Joseph Brodsky, Saul Bellow, Arthur Miller and Richard Wilbur followed suit, Wilbur commenting,

'O'Connor is that rare thing, a superbly talkative *isolato*.' It says much for the vigour of the W. W. Norton editor Rose Kernochan that these quotes were obtained but, though they impressed Stephen Spender, they did not inspire good reviews. Writing in the *New York Review of Books*, Gabriele Annan said that reading *Memoirs of a Public Baby* was like 'trying to swallow the contents of a cement-mixer a quarter of an hour after it has been switched off'. Though she admired O'Connor's 'sadistic honesty about himself', she protested that 'the trouble with drunks and madmen ... is that they are terribly boring'. O'Connor would later comment that the book had fallen 'flat as a cowpat' in America.

Meanwhile, he had been ill. In the autumn of 1988 he had complained of 'terrible spots'. In the early summer of 1989, he had a prostate operation at a hospital near Chamonix in the Haute Savoie. I telephoned him there and found him perky and over-excited, his voice quite different as he told me he was now in his 'monkeyhood'. I wondered if this jollity was the effect of medication, but learnt later that after twelve years of sobriety he was drinking again. Who or what had started him off again isn't clear – Panna blames an English visitor – but by the time he went into hospital he was already off the wagon and when John Berger visited him on his motorbike bringing wine it was too late to turn back.

During his new phase an incident occurred which may or may not be blamed on alcohol. In the spring of 1990 the Hamburgers visited the area, staying with the quiet and reticent poet André du Bouchet, in the Drôme region of France. Philip and Panna were invited over for tea, which ended in disaster. Philip told du Bouchet, 'You haven't suffered enough', which resulted in the poet turning the table over, smashing everything and prompting Panna to produce her chequebook and try to pay for the damage. Du Bouchet wrote to Philip later that he had not aimed the table at anyone in particular – 'It was a general discharge' – and Philip wrote to du Bouchet, 'The colour of your tea – Lapsang Souchong – was not too strong to blend with – O harmony – the colour of my trousers.'

Earlier that year Philip heard – and was possibly sustained by the news – that Paul Potts had died in London. On 25 January a pipe belonging to the seventy-nine-year-old People's Poet had set light to his bedclothes and after ordering the firemen to leave, Potts had perished in the smoke. Philip's attitude towards Potts remained complicated even now. He continued to complain of treacheries committed by his old friend, but wrote several friendly letters about him to Mark Holloway, who was working on a book on Potts. We know anyway that, like Quentin, Philip had a tendency to celebrate the deaths of those he had known and almost no capacity to mourn anyone other than his mother.

By this time Philip had got involved in a new project, which was to start another magazine of his own. It was nearly fifty years since he had produced his wartime magazine *Seven* and he had often discussed with friends like Annie Mygind the possible funding of a new one. On first meeting Panna Grady in October 1967, the thought of her backing a magazine was uppermost in his mind. Now, at last, when Panna's fortune had almost evaporated, he started work on a magazine he would call *The Rambler*, recruiting his old gang of surviving literary friends to help him – and some new ones. He wrote to British left-wing politicians Michael Foot and Tony Benn, to Dr Alex Comfort whom he had known since the war, Yehudi Menuhin and many others, most of whom seem to have responded zestfully to the invitation to contribute. From Chicago Saul Bellow wrote on 15 August 1990, saying that at the time of the *Baby* relaunch he had done 'everything possible to rouse American readers from their lethargy, decay and hebetude', and again promised to do 'everything possible' for the new magazine. 'When I hear the literary fire bell ringing I stagger to my feet like an old fire horse.'

While work was proceeding on the first number of *The Rambler*, Philip and Panna left the Moulin, which they were now trying to sell, and moved back to the North of France, settling at St Cast on the Brittany coast. Here they had bought, or rented, a small pavilion tucked away off the Rue du Sémaphore with a henhouse in the garden in which Philip could do his writing and editing. With them went the old sheepdog Nico, whom they had acquired during their last year in Wimereux. At the end of August 1990 I visited St Cast with my son Nicholas, now six years old. We stayed in a hotel recommended by

Panna, where Philip made his first appearance while we were having breakfast on our first morning. It was a dramatic entrance, heightened by the hat and coat and wrapped-up look, particularly odd at the height of summer, and drew an excited cry from my son: 'There's Philip O'Connor!' Nicholas did not at that time share my enthusiasm for Philip, perhaps feeling threatened by his eccentricity and vaguely sensing that here was a rival for my attention.

During the visit I became aware that Philip was drinking again, though not yet on the mammoth scale he had previously enjoyed: it would be a mistake to blame the patchy quality of the first issue of *The Rambler*, which appeared in December 1990, on this fact. The magazine was cheaply, shoddily produced and typed by various hands, often the authors of the pieces themselves, and ran to sixty pages. It included contributions by John Berger, Maria Scott, Alex Comfort, Michael Hamburger, Harry Fainlight, Peter Levi, and Philip O'Connor's distinguished solicitor Ambrose Appelbe, whose firm had handled his two divorces and whose other clients included the murderer Christie. There was also a contribution from André du Bouchet, who had forgiven Philip enough to send him a poem, and various reprinted pieces by Stephen Spender, Aldous Huxley and Oscar Wilde. Prominent in this mishmash was a blurred photograph of Quentin Crisp and the typewritten words, extracted from a letter Philip had already sold, saying, 'Thank you, dear Mr O'Connor' and 'I am delighted that you have gone on living.' The notes on contributors included the inaccurate information that Quentin Crisp was born in Croydon.

By the time the magazine appeared, Philip and Panna were back in the south again, renting a small, modern furnished house near Uzès, whose only adornment seemed to be a protruding turret. I felt obliged to visit them in this new ivory tower and did so in April 1991. I could not delay seeing Philip indefinitely, nor could I let our friendship peter out in some careless way. I also derived security from the fact that my friendship with Philip and Panna had lasted longer than my marriage. Both seemed well, though Philip, now white-bearded and bleary-eyed, looked increasingly bizarre and Middle Eastern and the house itself the anonymous sort of place you might rent if you were on the run from Interpol. All the time I was there Philip kept a cap tightly pulled down on his head, indoors as well as out, supposedly to cover some red spots on his scalp. He kept this on when I took them both to a restaurant in Uzès, where he drank an aperitif and two or three glasses of wine without becoming unruly. During my visit he talked about the past, mentioning that his house on Box Hill had been rented from a certain Sir Benjamin Brodie, who happened to be a cousin of my grandmother, and thus stumbling on another link between us. At the end of this visit Panna drove me to Montpellier airport, weeping about her goddaughter Janet Hobhouse, who had died of cancer a few months earlier.

While living in this rented house – I had not penetrated his workroom for which he had naturally chosen the top of the turret – Philip's drinking got much heavier. According to his son Felix, now seventeen, Philip was soon imbibing on a spectacular scale, as if suffering an epileptic fit or engaging in a race between himself and the world, a battle between his private perceptions and the blanket bombardment from the increasingly pervasive media. Felix also describes his father as a man who 'constantly breathed language' and who 'ceaselessly changed subject and opinion so that breathing can hardly be distinguished from language'.

Later that summer, the family moved again, along with Panna's furniture, to a small two-bedroomed cottage in the village of Fontarèches, a few kilometres north of Uzès. The house, which included a wooden lean-to garage, where Philip would install his bed, throne, books and workbench, had been bought for them by Ella, now flourishing in a law firm in Paris. Thereafter Philip would refer to Ella as his landlord: 'I'm buying a hat suitable for taking off in her presence.'

Here he worked on the next number of *The Rambler* and here he received various letters from a man named Christopher Thompson, who was a cousin of his mother and something of a genealogist. From him Philip learnt that his sister Desirée, whom he had not seen since 1937, had died in London only four years earlier leaving a husband and two daughters. Philip soon passed this news on to me and with his encouragement I telephoned Mr Thompson at his home in Carshalton. He told me that in 1938 Desirée O'Connor had married a solicitor called John Trethowan. One of the daughters was married and lived in Somerset. The other lived in London and was called Niki. This information startled me. Readers will know that for the past twenty years I had known a girl called Niki Trethowan – generous, pretty and fey – and had met her smart, sociable mother more than once. The dawning realization that this formidable woman, who counted the oil millionaire Paul Getty among her friends, was Philip O'Connor's long-lost sister caused me enormous excitement and established another connection between our two very different worlds.

The revelation also caused me bewilderment. On first meeting Philip O'Connor, I had chattered obsessively about him to almost everyone I met, sometimes eliciting responses like 'He sounds like someone more interesting to hear about than actually meet.' Niki Trethowan had received her fair share of this stuff but, though she had accepted one of Philip's paintings and once remarked that her grandmother had visited Wimereux, had never attempted to reveal her side of the story. On the other hand, had she instantly exclaimed, *'But he's my uncle!'* I would have almost certainly thought she was joking.

– 26 –

Resident Alien

The English treasure their indignation. They used to
stare at me and say: 'Who the hell do you think you
are?' It was terrible. But here they all accept me. The
Americans think that the English treasure their eccentrics. They treasure their *rich* eccentrics and that was
my sin. I was middle class and eccentric and that is
not permissible.

QUENTIN CRISP, *Hello*, 13 August 1994

I cannot offer any surprises about Quentin Crisp's relations. Though
his new home in New York and worldwide fame brought him closer
to his family, especially those who lived in South America, and some
of his relations would even visit his tiny room on Manhattan's Lower
East Side, he continued to follow a path of utter singularity and
increasingly eminent isolation.

The room into which he moved in the autumn of 1981 was a
dreadful place. It had been found with the help of John Ransley, who
had once lived in the room above him in Beaufort Street – Quentin had
many helpers or 'spies' of this sort – and was on the second floor of
46 East 3rd Street. Like many New York rooms, it looked onto the
well of the building. The sun never shone through its windows – yet
light from it at night disturbed another resident across the well so
much that Quentin felt forced to undress in the dark after evenings
out. The room had a sink but no fireplace and its heating was never
adequate. There was a hotplate of some sort but no bathroom: to the
end of his life Quentin Crisp would share a lavatory and shower with

five others on his floor. There was also no desk: for the next eighteen years, he would use the bed as his table. There was a telephone but no doorbell or entry system for the building: callers would have to telephone from the street corner and he would then go downstairs and let them in.

Most people in their seventies would find such deprivations intolerable but, though Quentin now confessed to liking hotels, he would have been uncomfortable living permanently in sleek or streamlined surroundings. Over the years his only complaint about his new home was that it was cold. In letters and articles, he describes working curved over the typewriter he had brought from London, wrapped in blankets with only 'my claws sticking out like a large mole'. The only thing he admitted missing about his room in London was its famously 'asthmatic' gas-fire. What he felt about leaving all those warm friends, some of whom he had known for many years, is a matter for conjecture. Years ago in London, he had told me, 'I'm not longing to get out of all this', yet he had now made the move of a lifetime.

In his room on East 3rd Street, Quentin continued to be his 'horrible unique self', which often meant sitting around doing nothing. 'I breathe and I blink. I am never bored. Never restless,' he repeated to more than one interviewer. He also wrote letters. He replied to every letter he received and then destroyed it. Occasionally he announced that he was using a particular day for 'writing letters', which has an old-fashioned almost Edwardian ring to it. He also passed his time doing the crossword, a habit to which he had been addicted since the craze hit England in the 1920s. 'I become very shaky if I am deprived of the opportunity to solve at least two puzzles a day,' he explained. 'To me they are the aerobics of the soul.' His hunger for this form of mental exercise was sometimes so great that he would search the dustbins at East 3rd Street in pursuit of a discarded newspaper which might contain a crossword.

Quentin had no complaints about his neighbours or the neighbourhood. Members of a Hell's Angels gang lived in the block, the house was managed by a drag queen and even an incumbent who started putting dead mice under his door did not incur his wrath. The rundown area of New York suited him very well and was later described by the writer John Walsh as 'the dunghill upon which the Quentinal orchid flourished'.

It was also the base from which Quentin Crisp would exercise, expand and exploit his celebrity. During the next few years I saw him only when he came to London and often not even then. We had no close friends in common and I would learn of his activities and pronouncements mainly through the media. My own life was fairly full – I soon had two children to look after and more books to write – but Quentin seemed busier than I was. He had already published his book *How to Become a Virgin* and in the autumn of 1981 he followed it with *Doing It with Style* which he had written in collaboration with Donald Carroll, his former literary agent. This book lacks the confident solo voice of Quentin Crisp, but the two men had fun promoting it on a three-week coast-to-coast tour of America, during which they sometimes shared a hotel room. Carroll later reported that Quentin was as 'bald as an egg' on top and when he slept his remaining hair was 'all over the place' but carefully reconstructed by himself every morning, sometimes inadvertently using Carroll's toothbrush to touch up the dye. Crisp noted later that Carroll never complained about his 'terrible snoring' and there are photographs of the two together at the Chateau Marmont Hotel in Los Angeles looking very contented, Quentin's right leg tucked up on the sofa. Some nights, says Carroll, the two men sat up all night talking. Quentin never initiated these dialogues but would hold his own with vigour. During one of these conversations Quentin apparently declared that he would rather go without mascara than split an infinitive.

These first few weeks in America had a bitter-sweet quality. The artist Patrick Hughes, who was living in New York at the time, remembers that Quentin was 'terribly happy' in spite of wearing galoshes to cover the holes in his shoes, and the playwright Ronald Harwood, whom he had met years ago in Beaufort Street, remembers Quentin blowing a kiss to him in Madison Avenue. Did these friends also know that Quentin was ill? That winter he told at least one correspondent that he was suffering from 'appalling rheumatic pains', doubled up in pain and unable to walk, and if he was to make any more stage appearances it would have to be done from a wheelchair. John Ransley recalls that Quentin needed hospital treatment – an outcome he dreaded – but it was against all his principles to complain and he handled these new ailments with the same discretion with which he treated his long-standing skin problems, which were to get a great deal worse in the years ahead.

From now on his life had a watered-down quality. He spread himself thin. He appeared on television, attended major and minor social events, was photographed and interviewed. He told people he was in 'the smiling and nodding racket' and it brought him into contact with other celebrities of varying hues. Wearing an expression of 'fatuous affability' he joined a gang of 'gibbering and twitching' people on the 'champagne and peanut circuit'. He travelled in purring limousines – or by bus. One day on the bus he heard someone ask, 'Who the hell is he?', prompting him to say when he got off, 'I'm sorry I wasn't anyone.' At the Whitney Museum, he met Andy Warhol, whose only words were 'We must be photographed.' Later he had lunch with Warhol, Baby Jane Holzer and the British pop-star Boy George who described him as 'the life and soul of the party'. On a return visit to the Algonquin Hotel, he met Douglas Fairbanks Jnr and over cucumber sandwiches at a certain Mrs Mason's he met Panna Grady's friend William Burroughs, who remarked, 'What is worth having is worth fighting for' to which Quentin replied, 'What we can only retain by force, we should try to do without.' He also met scores of others whose surnames may or may not mean anything to the readers of this book: Mr Kooder, Mrs Branagh, Mr Vincent, Mr Sting, Mr O'Horgan. Quentin Crisp's name and number soon appeared in the Manhattan telephone directory and he was able to boast, 'I receive calls all day and all night.' He made little distinction between his new acquaintances. Some were glamorous and fun-loving like the nightclub hostess Nell Campbell, others were utterly seedy or deeply dodgy. He accepted all invitations with gratitude and almost always turned up, even when he was feeling tired. Later he would write about the 'kind invitations' he had received from 'kind friends' and the 'truly memorable occasions' he had attended. When the chat-show host David Letterman asked if he minded 'all the weirdos' having his telephone number, he bounced back, 'I'm the weirdest of them all.'

His fame grew. A letter addressed simply 'Quentin Crisp, New York, America' reached him at East 3rd Street. Publishers asked him for pre-publication quotes for their books. Strangers asked for money, which he often provided. A man from Shreveport, Louisiana, asked him for a dust-jacket he had designed to which Quentin replied that he had discarded this sort of thing years ago. Only when a fan asked for a lock of his hair, did he put his foot down firmly, replying, 'At my age, I haven't got so much hair left I can afford to distribute it to strangers.'

He made many much publicized pronouncements. His repertoire still included a lot of the old jokes he had been using for the last forty or fifty years – but he constantly added new ones. As always he gave a performance, instead of engaging in a conversation, and talked principally about himself. He described himself as 'a shallow and horribly articulate personality'. He declared, 'I was a loser. I still am – but it's become a profession.' He claimed that he had no spiritual side: 'I am not a metaphysical person. I find it hard enough coping with real life.' He portrayed himself 'as unchanging as a stuffed bird, but not as silent'. He made sex sound increasingly distasteful, expressed increasing disinterest in the taste of food – 'I like food to be the same texture and taste as oneself' – and professed more and more indifference to nature. 'I don't like leaves, I don't like blades of grass. I need steel and glass and cement – all the things which are inanimate and don't threaten me' and 'I eagerly await the day when the world will be a vast slab of concrete like a global Grand Central Station.' He continued to proclaim that he had enough dumb friends without pet animals and with comic succinctness added, 'A dog is a horrible thing to happen to anybody.' Asked if he was ever unhappy, he replied, 'There are times when I'm neutral' and when people suggested that his 'sickeningly ingratiating image' contained 'another angry self waiting to burst forth', he responded, 'What little you see of me is all you're likely to get.'

One of the great new topics on which he held forth was America. Just how easy the transition from London to New York had been for such a man of habit is hard to guess, but any pain he may have experienced at the upheaval would be concealed for the rest of his life under layers of evangelical pronouncements about the wonders of America and particularly New York. Though he would complain about the 'oven-like heat' of the city in the summer and the coldness of his room and the ice and snow in the streets in the winter, he continued to call America 'the promised land where everyone is your friend'. He may have disliked bubblegum – 'Imagine you had to sit up all night to invent this filthy stuff' – but he often mentioned the humanity of the US police and the friendliness of others on the street. He spoke often of some policemen who had stopped him only to enquire how his new show was going and of the black man on Third Avenue who had exclaimed, 'Well, my, you've got it all on today!' And though he claimed to worship Mrs Thatcher, he spoke of the increasing fierceness of the English and of the treatment he had received at their hands. In England, he claimed to have been 'miserable'. In America, he was 'happy'.

In the country of his choice he was much in demand on many levels. Within a few months of his arrival in New York he found a new outlet for his wit and wisdom when he was invited to review films for the magazine *Christopher Street* which served the city's gay community. Though he sometimes expressed the desire to do the same work for a bigger and richer paper, a warm relationship sprang up between him and *Christopher Street*'s editor, Tom Steele, who would become one of his most regular companions in New York. In 1982 they saw *Tootsie*, starring Dustin Hoffman, and thereafter attended previews fairly regularly in screening rooms, preview theatres, playhouses and cinemas 'like expensive padded cells' where they sat in armchairs 'as luxurious as a feather bed'. Tom Steele later described cinema-going with Quentin Crisp as rather like going to church – 'It was almost a holy ritual.' The reviews that Quentin produced were invariably witty, but also showed a sharpness and aggression absent from the rest of his life, where tiredness or politeness reduced him to uttering platitudes. The fact that Quentin soon began to play small parts in films himself may have given him further insight into the movie business.

During his first year or two in New York he also acted in two plays. He appeared as Lady Bracknell in the Soho Repertory Theatre production of *The Importance of Being Earnest* and as an elderly Lord Alfred Douglas in a play by Professor Eric Bentley called *Lord Alfred's Lover*. In the latter venture, which was staged in 'a dim basement' on Second Avenue in December 1982, he sat on the edge of the stage reading his lines from a book. Both ventures seemed to him to be 'stunts' and in the programme notes for *Lord Alfred's Lover*, he anticipated that he would bring disgrace to the American theatre. He was much more at home speaking his own words in his one-man show, which he was soon performing all over America.

I do not have a record of all Quentin Crisp's stage appearances, but can state that during the 1980s he appeared in San Francisco, Los Angeles, Seattle, Austin, Detroit, Key West, Chicago and Minneapolis. He also ventured over the border to Toronto where another immigration official apparently said, 'Vindicated at last, eh?', to which he now replied, 'You're too kind.' In the autumn of 1982 he flew to Sweden, which he described as 'a mistake'. He also lectured on cruise ships going to places like Ochos Rios, Nassau and the Cayman Islands. Whenever possible he travelled with only hand-luggage and preferred to sleep on planes rather than stay overnight. But sometimes he had a long run to contend with. In September 1983 he appeared for four days in a small theatre in New Orleans and then returned for the third time to Chicago, where he appeared for a month at the Ivanhoe Theatre. Wherever he went he caused a stir. In San Francisco he received bad notices after declaring, 'Every theatre-goer throughout the world is a middle-class, middle-aged woman with a broken heart' and in Chicago he was repeatedly asked about his underclothes. Writing to Hermione Goacher, he said that he was having great fun but was very tired: 'I must now make these journeys alone whereas once I was provided with a "roadie" who made all the decisions for me.'

These travels occasionally brought him in touch with people he had not seen for 'huge stretches of time'. Somewhere or other he met a woman called Francesca whom he had not seen since the early 1930s. He found these old acquaintances 'calmer' while he himself had become 'more feverish'. Over Christmas 1983, he spent a week or two staying with Donald Carroll and his latest wife in Los Angeles.

'It was the happiest I've *ever* seen him,' Carroll recalled later. 'He had a glimpse of happy family life and showed affecting clumsiness as he tried to fit in. He asked me how he should give a present to my eleven-year-old son. He did not want to disgrace himself.' Writing about this time in a subsequent tribute to Quentin, Carroll wrote, 'One couldn't avoid the suspicion that he was having fun of a type that he had thought closed to him.'

Between these excursions he consolidated his position in New York. During the summer of 1983 he had spent six sizzling weeks at the Actors' Playhouse on Seventh Avenue, where his one-man show was entitled *How to Make It in the Big Time* and inspired Reuters News Service to dub him 'the Powdered Messiah'. Early the following year, he trudged through heavy snow to the same theatre. 'I must concentrate on my wages,' he told Mrs Goacher and admitted that these were 'by English standards . . . high'. Quentin's finances were in fact now good enough for his English pension to mount up untouched in a London bank account and for him to repay $7,000 to Hutchinson for a book that he had not delivered. Thanks to the auspices of John Ransley he had also found a woman at Hutton's on Wall Street to help him with his investments.

In spite of his comparative affluence, he felt obliged to return to England from time to time. When in London he stayed at the Chelsea Arts Club, a few streets away from Beaufort Street, and occasionally at Joan Rhodes's flat in Belsize Park, where she gave up her bedroom for him. His first return visit was in May 1984 in order to appear on television with Molly Parkin. 'She was fine,' he told Mrs Goacher. 'But the programme was one of the most ill-conceived and under-rehearsed items ever – as bad as the cable programmes in America.' In spite of this fiasco he was back in England a few weeks later to promote his new book *Manners from Heaven*. This was his ninth book, if you include his pre-war and wartime publications, but was mysteriously written 'with John Hofsess' and in spite of many flashes of brilliance does not read like pure Crisp. People are given their full names and the text is dolled up with quotations from Wittgenstein and Thomas Carlyle, grumbling comments and minor obscenities. The previous autumn, Quentin had explained to Mrs Goacher that he no longer really wrote his books. 'I speak them and other people type the tapes and organize the material. It saves me a lot of bother.' Though dismissive of the book, he attended a crowded promotional party at the Soho Brasserie on 21 June 1984, attended by Christopher Bland, who had met Quentin several years earlier with Harold Pinter and was now the chairman of Hutchinson, along with assorted journalists and the inevitable TV crew. Afterwards there was a dinner for him organized by Molly Parkin at which the seventy-five-year-old guest of honour felt tired. 'And they *knew* I was tired,' he said afterwards.

On 26 June I met him at the Pan Bookshop in Fulham Road where he was signing books and took him out to a late lunch at the Hungry Horse. Here the waiter and waitress were extremely friendly to him, as befitted the sweet old man that he had become. I remember nothing he said, only his clothes: galoshes over his shoes, a rather cheap velvet jacket, rather tight trousers and a shirt open at the sleeves. On our way back to the Chelsea Arts Club, where he was staying, I spotted Francis Bacon rapidly proceeding along the other side of the road and wished afterwards that I had forced a meeting between the two men.

The following day Quentin Crisp was interviewed by Adam Mars-Jones at the Institute of Contemporary Arts: a recording of their conversation is now in the British Library. On 30 June he appeared at the Brighton Dome; on 2 July at the Duchess Theatre in London; and on 3 July at a theatre in Bristol, though these performances were poorly promoted and attracted audiences which the publicity woman at Hutchinson later described as 'tiny'.

He was back in the British Isles the following year, opening at the Gate Theatre in Dublin on 22 April 1985 'on the stage where Mr Welles once stood'. This was a triumph and he was offered dates in Cork and Limerick which he was too tired to accept. During the run he was also picked up by Desmond Guinness and Penny Cuthbertson – 'We're star-fuckers,' said Cuthbertson – and went to lunch at their stately home near the city, Leixlip Castle. A fellow guest was the writer John Michell, who has already featured in this narrative as a friend of both Panna Grady and my childhood hero James Frere. 'It was a stately lunch,' Michell said later. 'Quentin was a stately man, as you know. A real gent. A professional. The rest of us are amateurs.'

Quentin's distaste for his homeland grew but his links with it would prove difficult to break. Kind friends sent him Bovril and Germolene, which were difficult to get in New York. In the winter of 1985 he heard that the National Portrait Gallery had purchased a portrait of him done in the war. 'Your news fills me with amusement,' he wrote to the artist, Marguerite Evans. 'The whole idea of my becoming a fragment of English history after the way I was treated there is a source of amazement to me, but I cannot say it lessens my hatred for England.' In December 1985 his New York room was visited by the British television personality Russell Harty and soon afterwards he appeared by satellite on a television programme about his old friend George Melly. I felt sorry when I missed these broadcasts, but if I deliberately watched out for them I was often disappointed or even embarrassed by what I saw. I had heard it all before. On the other hand I could not quite give him up. Quentin was my only world-famous friend and I enjoyed boasting about how often I had visited his Beaufort Street room in the days when he was more or less undiscovered.

During these years, Quentin made new bonds with his family – on 5 July 1986 he attended the wedding of his great-niece Michèle, granddaughter of his brother Lewis, at a church in New Jersey – but showed remarkable indifference to the fate of anyone he had known in England. On 15 July he replied to a letter from Mrs Goacher saying that he did not know if the actor Gordon Richardson, who had lodged below him all those years at Beaufort Street, was alive or dead and even expressed some vagueness about the fate of his saintly former landlady Miss Vereker. According to writer Jeremy Trafford, Quentin was not prepared to 'lift his polished finger' to help old friends who had been generous to him in the past, and when he learnt of the death in March 1985 of Miss Lumley Who Can Do No Wrong, his response was 'jubilant'. This indifference about those he had known was underlined by his constant vigorous and obsessive declaration that he hoped never, ever, to return to England.

But return he did. Whenever some impresario or television producer offered him a show in London he found it impossible to say no. He was back in May 1987 for a season at the Donmar Warehouse in Covent Garden which he promoted on the Terry Wogan TV show, after which he toured England, appearing at Richmond, Lewisham, Sheffield, Cambridge and even the Theatre Royal, Bath, where I had attended the pantomime as a child. Though he wrote later to Mrs Goacher, 'I was glad to find the British are becoming nicer – more American', he also declared, 'I really think that this most recent visit to England must be my last; I really did become extremely tired towards the end of it.' Later that year he wrote to Marguerite Evans, 'Of all the places on the face of the earth, England is the one that I wish to visit least.'

In October 1987 he wrote to Mrs Goacher about the stock-market crash. 'Wall Street has fallen apart. I tried to remove my money from Mr Hutton before disaster struck but was unable to do so. Like W. C. Fields, I "didn't want a return on my investment, I just wanted my investment returned".' Perhaps it was partly because of this setback that he agreed to return again to London the following autumn. In September 1988 he was said to be paying 'a final visit' to England on the eve of his eightieth birthday. He played to further packed audiences at the Donmar and made more chat-show appearances though he had no book to promote. On 28 September I was present at a dinner in his honour at the Chelsea Arts Club, also attended by the singer Bob Geldof and the painter Patrick Hughes, who had considered having Quentin as his best man at his recent wedding. Another artist, Maggie Hambling, sat next to Quentin but told me later that she had never met him before and never saw him again afterwards. During this visit Quentin was taken to the nearby Queen's Elm pub where he met Mervyn Peake's son Sebastian, whom he had known since he was a baby. He continued to ponder over his status. Writing to a certain Mrs Watkin he declared, 'I find it amazing that I have become a sort of national monument when I consider the treatment I received from the English when I lived there.' This was a theme that he would repeat and expand upon, never acknowledging that the whole world was changing and that he had helped to change it.

In February 1989 I visited New York without an overcoat. The following day I hurried through the snow to Macy's department store and bought a tweed garment made in Ireland. In this lacklustre garb I visited Quentin and had lunch with him in a café near the room, which he clearly did not wish me to see. The waitress smiled at him with real affection. He ordered a turkey sandwich and washed it down with two glasses of Guinness. Later he put two large lumps of sugar and two little beakers of cream in his coffee and slurped noisily over the first sip or two. Again, it was his appearance I particularly noted: more and more magisterial, if not regal, with his hair dyed – or sprayed – pale lavender and gold rings on his strong-looking hands. He told me that his current life involved a lot of 'smirking' and 'simpering' and that he didn't feel he was 'winning' until he came to America. He told me he'd recently been on a television panel of elderly homosexuals. They had been asked if they still had a sex life. Quentin had replied, no, not for fifty years, and shared his amusement with me that an ancient lesbian on the panel, much older than him, had said, 'Yes.' We had later walked to the Post Office on 11th Street. During our stroll together, Quentin Crisp was constantly recognized but no one actually spoke to him.

I returned to New York in June 1989, partly to escape the matrimonial problems which now assailed me. That month Quentin offered to take me to a party given by his friend Mrs Mason, with whom he had once met William Burroughs. I met him at East 3rd Street and during our journey standing up on a crowded bus he showed me that he had now translated the layout of New York into his own language, making remarks like 'Hudson Street is what happens to Ninth Avenue when all is lost.' I was more surprised when another passenger shouted, 'Get a haircut!' and when I asked if he had heard this, he murmured in a puzzled tone, 'Someone was annoyed.' Getting off the bus near Mrs Mason's apartment, I was again surprised, this time by the speed with which he rattled along the crowded sidewalk. The party was small and embarrassing and my heart sank when Quentin immediately went into a performance.

During the 1990s Quentin's life continued along these lines. He told Mrs Goacher, 'I'm too old for world travel' and 'In old age I really love doing nothing', yet he remained active on many levels. He struggled on in his increasingly grimy room, dictated more books, received more publicity and whizzed around doing his one-man show. As far as things in England were concerned, he appeared more affected by events like the end of Mrs Thatcher's 'acid reign' than by the death on 4 June 1990 of his friend Angus McBean, but it would be unwise to assume he was only interested in events he could make jokes about. In April 1990 I took my children to New York for the first time, stayed in the Gramercy Park Hotel and saw Panna Grady's dandified friend Tom Wolfe on the sidewalk. I wondered about introducing Lauretta and Nicholas, then aged eight and six, to Quentin but decided against it, though the encounter might have been illuminating. After the children had returned to England with their mother, from whom I was now separated, I stayed on to interview Quentin about his new book *How to Go to the Movies* for the *Daily Telegraph*.

On 16 April I picked him up from East 3rd Street and this time got a brief glimpse of his room, noticeably smaller and darker than his London one, though Quentin himself, as I later wrote in my piece, seemed in spectacularly good health. As we climbed into a taxi an onlooker shouted, 'God bless you, sir' to which Quentin responded with a semi-regal gesture. I wanted to 'bulk out' my interview by accompanying Quentin to a film preview. The movie we saw that afternoon was called *Strapless*. Quentin sat through it motionless and sphinx-like, his hands clasped at his lips as if in prayer, his hat at his feet. At the end I asked him if he had enjoyed it. 'Not really,' he said in an uncharacteristically flat voice. 'It wasn't about anything. Nothing happened. There was no movie.' He then told me that earlier in the year he had gone with Tom Steele to see *The War of the Roses* – and dozed off after a few minutes. Someone had then tapped Mr Steele on the arm and said, 'I think your father's gone to sleep.' Mr Steele claims to have replied, 'He's not my father, he's my lover.'

I will talk more about *How to Go to the Movies* later. Unlike some of his recent publications this was written rather than dictated by Quentin and, though it contains many contradictions, has a great deal to tell us about him, perhaps more than any book he wrote. In my interview I concentrated on superficials and followed instructions from my editor, Miriam Gross, not to let Quentin bang on about wanting to die. This had now become one of his themes and would play an increasingly prominent part in his repertoire in the years ahead. Growing old had been one of his favourite topics since long before I met him and as long ago as the late 1940s he had described himself as old. His physical deterioration, or jokey version of it, had featured frequently in *The Naked Civil Servant* and *How to Become a Virgin*, and on hearing of the death of his friend Annie Wignall in 1982, he had remarked, 'What could be tidier than to die suddenly?' Later he would argue, 'Death is the *least* awful thing that can happen to anyone.' During the late 1980s he had referred to his energy being very limited and postulated, 'I've said all I can say' and 'I am on overtime.' His face, he said, now looked 'as if it had been gnawed by rats', and he explained, 'As time goes by, we begin to look like airline food – a good imitation of what we used to be but dehydrated.' In March 1988 he had told Hermione Goacher, 'I'm falling apart, but slowly', and the same year had informed Marguerite Evans, 'As telephone operators say in hospitals, I'm doing as well as can be expected.' On the eve of his eightieth birthday, he had confidently announced, 'I reckon I must die in the next year or two and indeed I hope to do so.' Yet he could not be sure of it and was soon complaining of the cruel way modern medicine kept people alive. And the idea of life *after* death was even more unwelcome than old age: 'The one thing I would not wish on my worst enemy is eternal life.' In one of our earliest conversations, he had boldly stated, 'I am never ill. I will live for ever', but he now contemplated his demise with a certain relish and had started longing for what he called 'a significant death', adding to his old jest 'It would be nice to be murdered' the words, 'Indeed, to be the victim of a grisly murder.' On a desert island, his luxury would be a 'vintage bottle of arsenic'.

It was difficult to know the real state of his health. Shortly after my visit to him in 1990 he wrote, 'I am now so old I spend half my time asleep.' To others he mentions spending most of his time 'dozing'. He also refers to 'awful lumbago', toothache, and the perennial problem of eczema. Somewhere he mentions that he has rubbed his eyelid so badly he has given himself a black eye, and from 1988 onwards he had increasing problems with his left hand. During this final decade of his life he would sometimes repeat a remark by a Fitzrovian acquaintance, Mrs Davis, 'Old age is not for cissies.' But he also took trouble to avoid disaster. In his book *Resident Alien* which told of his life in the early 1990s he confesses to ducking out of Baroness Sherry von Kober Bernstein's birthday party at Club 53 on account of bad weather. 'I am frightened of the snow,' he writes. 'Like many people of my age, I dread slippery or uneven surfaces; if I were to fall and break even the smallest bone, it would never mend.'

His other great preoccupation and one of his lifelong interests was the folly, as he saw it, of gay activism. In the early 1980s he had upset an audience in Chicago by referring to the AIDS obsession as a 'fad'. In *Manners from Heaven*, he or his ghost-writer referred to homosexuals 'dropping like flies' from the disease – hardly the kindest image. He was fond of referring to sex as 'a mistake' and could be merciless when describing homosexual activity. 'Passive sodomy is an addictive habit that leads to the abandonment of all reason,' he writes in *How to Go to the Movies*. 'No one who practises this vice can count on living happily ever after, or even long after.' In the old days, Quentin considered that he had represented 'the whole of homosexuality' to the outside world. Now he saw himself as 'a minority within a minority'. We have already seen that he had lost all interest in the issues addressed in *The Naked Civil Servant*. Now he explained that he no longer believed in a two-sex world – 'When Jan Morris had her operation it was in reverence for a two-sex world' – and saw no need for people to declare their sexuality. When a man in the audience in Boston had asked if he should tell his mother he was gay, Quentin had replied, 'Never tell your mother anything!' which had prompted the man's mother to pipe up, 'I'm with you. I don't want to know.'

Of the Gay Liberation Movement he now said, 'I don't feel I'm part of it somehow' and he doubted whether it had enabled people to lead more creative lives. What he chiefly objected to was not the cause itself, but the stridency of the campaign. He was appalled at 'all the marching, protesting and grumbling'. He argued that gay people were 'mad about their rights' and 'corroded with envy'. He was particularly opposed to the idea of 'gay marriage' and declared, 'Wild, pink horses would not make me turn the adjective "gay" into a noun.' His relationship with the homosexual community got chillier as it went on. He was accused of jumping *off* the bandwagon he had helped to start rolling. Ever since early adulthood, Quentin Crisp had given homosexuality a bad name. By the start of the 1990s he was distrusted, disliked and even despised by the gay community in New York and elsewhere. Later in the decade, the gay rights activist Larry Kramer told the *New York Times*, 'Quentin Crisp has never fought for us or the cause. He's been fighting for himself.'

Quentin would doubtless have agreed wholeheartedly with this comment but it is also worth noting that he did, from time to time, appear on gay marches and the like. In 1990 he took part in a gay parade in Seattle, being driven through the streets in an open car, while suspecting that those on the sidewalks were asking, 'Who the hell *is* he?' He would later attend a similar event in Berlin. 'It was nice but slightly absurd,' he said later, and perhaps the presence of the 'gay dog' on the parade diffused the solemnity. He was also bemused to learn that there was now a Quentin Hotel in Amsterdam.

His kingdom expanded in other directions too. He met a mixture of new celebrities, from the American novelist Edmund White to a certain Countess Klent-de-Boen, who on Christmas Day 1990 threw a party for his eighty-second birthday in an upper room at the El Morocco Club. He also held sway over a band of mediocrities to the despair of some of his older, closer friends like his one-time agent Donald Carroll, who expressed surprise that such an intelligent person, the best-read man Carroll had ever met, should live in 'such an intellectual desert' and surround himself with 'such morons'. The less simpering side of his nature was expressed in the memorably spiky film reviews he now began contributing to the *Guardian* back in England. Of the actor Peter Sellers he would write, 'Nothing can conceal from the camera that there was something thoroughly unpleasant about him, something diabolical.' And he continued to perform his one-man show. Setting off on a mini-cruise out of Key West, he told Mrs Goacher, 'I shall be imprisoned with my audience for five days with no time off for good behaviour.' In the winter of 1990 he appeared at the Alice B. Theatre in Seattle and in due course would make a remarkable appearance in front of three or four thousand people in New York's Central Park. In that particular audience was the English drag star Bette Bourne, who later invited Quentin 'to meet a lot of noble queens' over dinner at his New York apartment.

'Inevitably Quentin took over,' Bourne reports. 'There were some complaints afterwards.' These face-to-face clashes with homosexual society had long been part of Quentin's life.

During these years he had also been in demand as a film extra, playing small parts in a number of productions, sometimes ending up on the cutting-room floor as in *Fatal Attraction*, and at other times getting star billing as in *The Bride*, in which he played a laboratory assistant alongside his friend Sting. This English pop-star would also involve himself in a film about Quentin called *Resident Alien* which opened at the Manhattan Cinema on 18 October 1991. Later that same autumn all these ventures into celluloid were eclipsed when Quentin Crisp was offered the role of Queen Elizabeth the First in a film based on Virginia Woolf's novel *Orlando*.

The film's director Sally Potter said later that she had never considered anyone else for this part, explaining that she saw Quentin Crisp as 'a living pun' who would throw light on Queen Elizabeth's famous comment that she had the mind of a man inside the body of a woman. From the very start Quentin seems to have disapproved of the project, but as Sally Potter points out, 'One had to decode the fabric of what he was saying' and 'He was always saying one thing and doing another.' She saw Quentin not only as a living pun but also as 'a living dialogue with himself and everything around him. Nothing was ever what it seemed or what he said it was.' In the winter of 1991, he was faced with the ordeal of being measured for wigs and costumes and underwent a medical examination for insurance purposes by a Dr Besnon on the upper reaches of Seventh Avenue. 'You're worth a lot of money to somebody,' remarked the doctor, to which Quentin replied that he was only doing it for the money. In England, this inspired piece of casting caused a stir, but when the Elizabethan expert A. L. Rowse was consulted about Crisp's suitability for the role, he forgot that he had met him in New York several years earlier and huffily declared that he had never even heard of Quentin Crisp.

With great reluctance, or so he claimed, Quentin flew to England on 9 March 1992 to do the filming and was greeted with inevitable cries of 'I thought you were never coming back', though he saw none of his friends, not even Joan Rhodes. At the Chelsea Arts Club his room was too small for him to try on his elaborate costumes and his dressers had to find another one along the corridor. A few days later he was moved to the Bush Hall Hotel near Hatfield House, where most of the filming would take place. Quentin said later that he was utterly unprepared for the role and simply stepped into the costume and said the lines just as he had in *Captain Busby* twenty-five years earlier. Each day or night – some of the filming took place at four in the morning – Quentin would be attired in a costume consisting of a corset, a bustle, a quilted petticoat, another petticoat and an outer skirt. His face was voluptuously over-rouged and on his head he wore a huge red wig surmounted by a tiara. 'The experience was absolute hell,' he said afterwards. 'My costume weighed almost as much as I do and I wore a corset so tight that it blistered my stomach but I had to do it because of the money.' Nonetheless the performance he gave was exquisitely underplayed, perhaps his crowning achievement, and Sally Potter was staggered by his professionalism and his ability to catch 'the hidden layer of sadness, longing or melancholy', pronouncing him 'a great tragedian'. On 29 March he flew back first-class to New York, 'heartily glad that it was all over' and not at all interested in discussing or being praised for his acting ability.

In his last published book *Resident Alien* which would appear in 1996, Quentin gives us a fairly vivid account of his life in the early 1990s and makes as much of his sufferings as his triumphs. I did not visit him during this period but I sent him my novel *The Tap Dancer*, which had at last found a publisher. 'I am fearful of what all your fierce brothers will say,' he wrote back after reading a few pages of this thinly disguised family saga. I also telephoned him occasionally, though I never had much to say or ask. Sometimes his line was busy. Sometimes there was no reply. On one occasion he sounded drunk or exhausted. Once I telephoned him by mistake in the middle of the night, confusing his number with that of Philip O'Connor in the South of France. The following day I rang to apologize but he made light of my folly and his interrupted sleep. Whenever possible, throughout his life, he endeavoured to sound perky and welcoming on the telephone, instantly turning on keenness – '*Tell me everything!*' – no matter how he felt underneath.

In the spring of 1993 he often felt ill. On 27 February he wrote to Marguerite Evans, 'I am now very ill, have lost my voice and become almost totally deaf . . . I shall make no more movies.' It was perhaps at this time that Sally Potter visited him at East 3rd Street, bringing various provisions, and, going down on one knee, told him how much she loved him and thanked him for his contribution to her film. 'He was hideously embarrassed at the display,' she wrote afterwards. 'It was a nightmare for him. He seemed to like the soup though.' Other highs and lows followed. In the autumn of 1993 he was interviewed by Naim Attallah for his magazine the *Oldie* and told him frankly, 'Homosexual intercourse is often actually painful, sometimes uncomfortable, sometimes nasty.' A few weeks later, three policemen, mysteriously alerted by a well-meaning friend, burst into Quentin's room and bundled him off to hospital, even though there was obviously nothing wrong with him. At the local Catholic hospital he was treated like a serious casualty, flung onto a wheeled stretcher and then onto a bed. Here, a Filipino nurse stripped him of his clothes and the bandages he now habitually wore round his ankles in his fight against eczema, and then emitted a shriek of glee when she confused his underwear with diapers.

Why Quentin should have allowed this incident to take place is beyond comprehension and one is left wondering whether he has given a full account. Apparently the doctor who later examined him said, 'You sure do go with the flow', and yet even someone as passive and anxious to please as Quentin Crisp would surely have refused to go through this charade unless he was really ill.

That Christmas he seemed in better spirits, receiving a case of champagne from Naim Attallah, and on Christmas Day itself, his eighty-fifth birthday, he was recruited to deliver 'An Alternative Queen's Message' to British television viewers from a suite in New York's Plaza Hotel. Though the programme showed Quentin waving idiotically from a horse-drawn vehicle beside Central Park, the content of his message was utterly unfrivolous and unfatuous and chiefly concerned with ridding the world of envy, one of his favourite themes. He said later he had only agreed to appear in this absurd stunt if he was allowed to say exactly what he wanted.

The remaining years of Quentin's life would be spent apparently longing to die, never losing his nerve, meeting strangers who 'haven't heard it all before' and doing what other people wished. He also submitted himself to further publicity: in 1994 he received the ultimate accolade, or disgrace, of an interview in *Hello* magazine, posing in a slightly ill-fitting but spotless white suit, possibly provided for the occasion, repeating all his oldest jokes but adding, 'I welcome death.' The same year he was interviewed on Staten Island ferry by the British entertainer Julian Clary, who reported afterwards, 'Whatever the question, he would swerve round it and set off on his anecdotes ... all about how he loved New York and set-pieces he'd done in the theatre ... He was enjoying himself but I felt sad afterwards.'

Sooner or later he was bound to be invited back to Europe and equally bound after token protests to accept the invitation. In the spring of 1995 he visited Vienna which, like Sweden, he described as 'a mistake'. Later that year and in 1996 he once again touched down on British soil. I did not know about these visits until I started writing this book and still remain confused about some of the dates. One visit was to promote a brand of Scotch whisky named after him and to attend, against his better instincts, a Gay Pride event in Scotland. On 23 June 1996 he addressed an audience in a café in Edinburgh. A subsequent visit was to promote his new book *Resident Alien*. This was another dictated job in which he professed to have no confidence. 'My publisher disapproves of me altogether,' he told his old friend James Kirkup. 'They only printed the book reluctantly.' The book carried an introduction by Donald Carroll, who rightly praised Crisp's 'almost alchemical wizardry in converting seemingly lacklustre truths into lustrous *aperçus*', but there is less wit than usual in this final volume, which overflows with 'fatuous affability' and oddly un-Crisp-like words and phrases like 'hilarious' and 'sincerely grateful'. Reviewing the book in the *Daily Telegraph*, Lynn Barber regretted its 'lack of emotional engagement'. Those who met him at the Chelsea Arts Club during these final visits to London also felt that Quentin Crisp was fading out. To the journalist Miles Chapman, who had seen him often in New York, Quentin seemed 'almost gaga', and the art dealer

Richard Salmon found him 'completely blank ... he wasn't there at all.'

But Quentin was now eighty-seven and these were *off-stage* encounters. Given an audience, he perked up immediately and became as spiky and saucy as ever, and he had quickly risen to the occasion when taken out to lunch at the Ivy in June 1996 by Paul Bailey and his English publisher Helen Ellis. Deadbeat and jet-lagged, Quentin had immediately ordered what Bailey describes as 'a very, very large vodka' and was soon on top form. Lunching at the same restaurant were Lady Antonia Fraser and the novelist William Boyd, but Harold Pinter's wife and Quentin Crisp rather surprisingly exchanged no greetings.

In America in the late 1990s Quentin actually overcame his frailty, now aggravated by the limited use of his left arm, and enjoyed a kind of renaissance. Following the death of his agent Connie Clausen, his affairs had to some extent fallen into the hands of a former English policeman turned theatrical agent named Charles Largo, who had relaunched Quentin's one-man show and sent him off on the road again. Some years had now passed since Quentin had talked about style, and one of his relations was recruited to type out his monologue from an old recording, so that he could relearn it. Some of his new audiences in Dallas, Texas, and Phoenix, Arizona, noted the rather 'parroted' quality of the first half of his performance, but during the second half when he answered questions he was as spontaneous as ever and his whole stage presence and the waspishness of his remarks were enhanced by his fragility. On stage and in occasional newspaper articles he spoke or wrote with immense brio about the real old age that had at last engulfed him. 'I never dreamt I would live as long as I have,' he declared, 'but here I am, a slightly grisly sight, tottering about the Lower East Side of Manhattan.' He was also in demand as an 'extra', in spite of his earlier protestations that his movie-making days were over, and appeared in a number of film commercials. He modelled jeans for 'Mr Levi Strauss' and promoted perfume for Calvin Klein, and seemed quite equal to the occasion when he fell to the floor of the limousine taking him to the latter shoot. Here his idle question, 'What does it all mean?', was wisely kept on the sound track.

His lifestyle at East 3rd Street where he now paid $350 a month for his room remained the same, though the grime mounted around him and he continued to use his bed as a desk. 'Everyone is worried about it,' he told the *New York Times*, and old friends like John Ransley nagged him to leave this hell-hole. 'But I'm now fully acclimatized,' he told Hermione Goacher, 'and haven't the strength to leave.' As he had often explained, he understood the furnished life and disliked change. He still took his washing to a Chinese laundry on First Avenue, still did the crossword vigorously and the only change at home was to drink whisky rather than Guinness.

He also wrote a lot of letters, now in longhand since his left hand had packed up, replying to everyone who had written to him or even sent a Christmas card. Some of those he wrote to, like Joan Rhodes, he had first met fifty or sixty years earlier in Fitzrovia. And in these letters he often made references to other figures from the distant past who still seemed to be living. His friend Anne Valery would point out, 'Soho casts a long and possessive shadow', and Quentin was bound by good manners rather than his heart to respond to every overture he received from the past. A few of his letters are signed off 'Love Quentin'. All are studiously courteous, but bad-luck stories and cries for help are met with firm advice. To a woman he had known for half a century who had been thrown out of her home, he wrote sternly, 'You can begin the process of enduring your fate. I sincerely hope you can adapt yourself to your new circumstances.' Occasionally he expressed confusion about his own circumstances – Mrs Goacher did not keep some of the sadder letters she got from him at this time – but usually he managed to make jokes about his life. In February 1998, he would tell various correspondents – like Philip O'Connor, he tended to share his jokes with several people – that technicians from Madame Tussaud's had moved him to a hotel and set about him. 'Whether I am to appear in the Chamber of Horrors or not, I do not know.'

From time to time, he made new pronouncements or repeated the same old joke. He still told people he was in 'the smiling and nodding racket' and reissued his declaration about 'filling in the time between the cradle and the grave without getting into debt'. He described money, fame and wisdom as 'the booby prizes of the elderly' – which may perhaps contain an implicit admission that he himself was now comfortably off. He also admitted he was losing his grip – 'The more desperately I try to shock the more hopelessly routine my act becomes' – but there was nothing new about this self-denigration and he could well have made the same observation in the 1930s. Perhaps the most striking feature of his current life was that he had few battles left to fight. Above all, Quentin needed to have what Michael Holroyd called his 'boxing match with the world'. He now sometimes spoke of himself as 'neutered' and almost seemed to search around for enemies. Aside from England and the English, one great target remained, in the shape of the Gay Liberation Movement.

During these years, he enjoyed telling people that he had angered the gay community in America but been accepted by the real people. The AIDS holocaust had, like the Second World War, left him again in the unpopular position of a survivor and perhaps increased his self-loathing and sense of his own sterility. During these final years, he took pleasure in again attacking gay icons like Oscar Wilde, whom he described as 'a gross human being trying to enter English society', and he was more than a little amused when he learnt that a performer masquerading as Quentin Crisp at the Edinburgh Festival had been beaten up in the street. In the spring of 1997, he backed a call that gay babies should be aborted – and on 17 February of that year his photograph appeared in *The Times*, captioned 'Often wished he had never been born' and followed by a news story in which Crisp was quoted as saying that he had been 'unhappy about his sexuality since he was six years old' and was sure that the world would be a better place without homosexuals.

All this may have been part of the 'inner dialogue' to which Sally Potter referred – more than tongue-in-cheek, more than irony, but still very difficult to decipher. His pronouncement following the death of the Princess of Wales in the summer of 1997 is equally incomprehensible and reprehensible. What did he mean when he declared that the Princess was 'trash' and 'got what she deserved'? Was he trying to cause excitement or pain? Was the remark aimed at the millions of homosexuals across the Western world who doted on her? Or was it simply an attack on a fellow exhibitionist and icon – and thus on himself? The pronouncement was certainly one of his most hard-hitting and tasteless and, as I mentioned at the beginning of the book, it generated hate mail.

As Quentin entered his ninetieth year, he worked harder than he had for years. Charles Largo, whom he always described as 'the Policeman', sent him off to do innumerable shows in places like Cleveland, Ohio, where he played to packed houses. He also received visits from various old friends, though some of these came away feeling rather sad. One day he had lunch with the English agony aunt Virginia Ironside, whose parents Christopher and Janey Ironside had been among his staunchest friends in London. 'I got the treatment,' said Virginia later. 'He went into auto-pilot.' Tod Ramos, whose parents had also known Quentin in the past, found him depressed and nervous and wondered if he'd now become disenchanted by New York: 'He'd got the cream and decided he didn't like it.' Tod and Quentin went for a walk round the Lower East Side and witnessed a screech of brakes and a near-collision which left Quentin 'visibly shaken'. Other long-standing friends from England like Malya Woolf were sorry that Quentin, once the most generous of men, now expected everyone to pay for him when he went out. But there were other, happier, encounters. Quentin saw John Hurt whenever he was in New York and had attended the premiere of Hurt's film *Love and Death in Long Island*, which he marvelled over. He also had several meetings with a young English publisher, Matthew Thomas, who was writing and taking photographs for a book about Soho and its survivors. On one occasion Thomas helped Quentin to buy a surgical undergarment for the hernia that was now developing, but also noted with amazement the way Quentin 'shinned up the stairs' at East 3rd Street.

During these years Quentin's relations had also rallied round. His last surviving sibling Gerald had died in the spring of 1983, aged eighty, leaving Quentin in the unlikely role of patriarch. He had happy visits from his niece Frances, whom he addressed as Mrs Ramsay in letters but never to her face, and from his two nieces who lived in South America, Denise and Elaine. With Elaine's daughter Michèle Crawford, who lived in New Jersey and whose wedding he had attended in 1986, he formed a particular bond though Michèle was realistic about its inevitable imbalance. 'I really think I'm of no importance to him whatsoever,' she told the *Sunday Times*, 'but he is of great importance to me.' This was probably true but Quentin was sufficiently involved with this branch of his family to attend, on 1 March 1998, the christening of Mrs Crawford's third son, who was given the name Ian Quentin. Quentin was photographed with his great-great-nephew on his lap but told the baby, 'Don't let the name give you any ideas.'

One suspects that, like many very old people, he had good days and bad days. As he approached his ninetieth birthday, Quentin submitted himself to various interviews by English journalists who presented a much grimmer and graver portrait of him, though some of them were beguiled by his icily unsentimental brain and remarks like, 'I'm hollow.' The writer John Walsh, who had seen him in 1997, was particularly shocked by the extent to which Quentin had allowed a certain kind of society to form around him. Protesting about the 'awful people' he hung out with, Walsh asked, 'Why can't you tell them to get lost?' Quentin's reply, 'Oh, I couldn't possibly say a thing like that', prompted Walsh to brand him 'a hopeless naïf'. In 1998, the journalist Quentin Letts told *Daily Telegraph* readers that his namesake was 'an old man, skinny and shivering and somehow, for all his bluster and repartee, really rather sad'. More devastating was Letts's observation that Crisp was 'not happy in the slightest'. Dominique Nabokov, who photographed the famous room on East 3rd Street at this time, later complained that Quentin 'refused to go away ... usually I like to work when the subject is out ... it made me very nervous ... it was very difficult'. Another visitor to the room was Simon Hattenstone from the *Guardian*, who had been publishing Quentin's cinema reviews for the past eight years. The two men had had 'a night on the town', with Quentin 'done up to the nines'. The following day Hattenstone called at East 3rd Street to be greeted by 'a shocking apparition'. Quentin's short dressing-gown showed off 'impossibly skinny legs and a trail of weeping sores'. His toenails were like 'whelk shells' and this thin hair was 'wrapped around his head in sad circles'. But after a few minutes, Hattenstone reports, the shock subsided and Quentin looked 'more beautiful, more delicate than ever'.

It was in the wake of these interviews that, after an absence of eight years and still several weeks short of his ninetieth birthday, I paid my last visit to Quentin Crisp.

One of Shakespeare's Fools

I expect to die soon, unless a Balinese dancer aged
thirteen, complete with yacht and rickety throne arrives.

PHILIP O'CONNOR TO MICHAEL HAMBURGER,
13 March 1995

Towards the end of their lives, Quentin Crisp and Philip O'Connor
both got closer to the families from which they had emerged. In Philip's
case he made friends with several of his estranged children and went
some way to making it up with the family of his sister Desirée, whom
he had not seen since before the Second World War. The discovery
that I had known his sister quite well and been friends with his niece
Niki for more than twenty years continued to astonish me, but Philip
saw it as further evidence of the 'familiarity' which I had apparently
given off when we first met in 1972.

Following the discovery of the link, Philip exchanged a number of
letters with his surviving brother-in-law John Trethowan, now in his
eighties. Introducing himself as 'Desirée's delinquent brother', he
described himself as 'an ancient Stalinist and a present Gorbachovian,
and ineffectual propagandist of what I call Christian Communism' and
as 'a post-Communist Taoist anarchist'. Of his late sister he said, 'We
were never friends' and went on to write as fiercely about her as he had
in *Memoirs of a Public Baby*. 'My sister was a horrible combination of
social arrivisme and factitious morality and she was much against my
mother's genuine bohemianism.' In spite of this ferocity Philip
welcomed the idea of family warmth, quoted from Ray Charles, 'It's
cold outside', and even confided, 'Life has been difficult but not by

Auschwitz standards.' He also confidently predicted, 'We'll never meet.' On his part John Trethowan was studiously courteous, sending best wishes from his family, adding, 'I always felt rather sorry that Desirée had no contact with you' and furnishing Philip with the information that Desirée had died in 1987 and been buried with her mother at Streatham, and that Robert Haslam Jackson had lived with the Trethowans until his death from cancer in 1944. John Trethowan firmly rejected the idea that Haslam Jackson could have been Philip's father: 'From what I knew of RHJ, I cannot conceive that he was involved.'

During the next few months Philip spoke several times to his niece Niki on the telephone, pronounced her 'amiable' and 'sharp' and expressed a mischievous desire to meet his great-niece Camilla, 'if she's pretty'. From time to time I would also encourage Niki to write to her uncle, send a birthday card or visit him in person, though I stopped short of offering to accompany her on such a mission. I also introduced Niki to her first cousin Peter O'Connor, though the two may already have met at the party I had given some fifteen years earlier in honour of Quentin Crisp. On 17 October 1991 Niki brought her daughter Camilla to the studio in Eldon Road, Kensington, where I now lived, and met Peter and his fiancée Hideko. A week or two later, Niki attended a party in Islington to celebrate Peter's wedding and met various other members of her family, including Anna Wing, who had now retired as grandmother in the TV series *EastEnders*.

Meanwhile at Fontarèches, Philip wrote off to friends like Michael Hamburger expressing his excitement at the sudden discovery of 'a horde of maternal relations' in whom he recognized or expected to recognize 'the Burmese giggle' that I had already spotted in both Nikki and Peter. Among his newly discovered cousins was Patricia Portoleau, who lived in Paris and was to visit Philip several times in the South of France. Sixty years earlier, Patricia's father and aunt Pauline had visited Haslam Jackson's flat in Kennington and ticked Mrs O'Connor off for living in such a slum, but Patricia Portoleau was enchanted by her eccentric cousin, particularly his 'language', and had him to stay at her holiday flat in Marseilles.

Looking back and making connections with the present was deeply embedded in Philip O'Connor's nature – especially during these secluded years. When in June 1992 I sent him my novel, *The Tap Dancer*, he declared that its hero was 'a parody of Victorian authority and a toothless old dog, with a hint of senility but still barking' and 'very like Uncle Haslam'. His mother, he added, had a horror of the sort of middle-class people I wrote about and much preferred the slum-dwellers. He also spotted elements of 'faded gentility' and 'mothball fragrancy' in the book, and claimed that my 'queer attachment' to him was partly on account of his 'class superiority' and my sidelong respect for his 'dusty but dustable social profile'. I did not bother to reply that my attachment to him owed a great deal to his actual dustiness and his real eccentricity as a Man of Letters, and nothing at all to a sense of his mother's 'social delicacy'.

Philip O'Connor's final years were full of such misunderstandings – and attendant tantrums – but in his own way he remained productive. Unable to drive because no one would insure him, he spent more and more time in the tiny encampment at Fontarèches. In the converted lean-to garage in which he slept and worked, he laboured away on further editions of *The Rambler* and other projects. Letters flew thicker and faster off a series of slightly dysfunctional typewriters, full of insults, wit, wisdom and touchiness but above all requests. But his endeavours were not entirely unrewarded. In 1991 a French edition of *Memoirs of a Public Baby* appeared, selling a respectable two thousand copies. An Italian edition was also sold for £2,500, although this never appeared. Thanks to Saul Bellow, the winter 1991–2 issue of *Bostonia* carried Philip's 'Letters to my Son', earning him $800, and in the same magazine Bellow described O'Connor as 'an intriguing writer, a special case' who gives the impression of 'boundless eccentricity and wilfulness'. According to Bellow, O'Connor is 'the lost child who still takes part in the deliberations of the mature man' and who 'has never been willing to tone down or expel the first knowledge of the kid, the full preconceptual state which society makes it its business to abolish'.

In December 1992 Philip produced the second issue of *The Rambler*, containing the same mixture of contributions from Peter Levi, Stephen Spender, Michael Hamburger, John Berger and me. In letters to friends,

Philip boasted that the magazine contained 'typing errors galore' and told Michael Hamburger in particular, 'Believe me, I didn't even bother to look through it.' Stephen Spender, whose poem 'Tom's A-Cold' had been included, wrote saying, 'Of course the mistakes did not matter' but Peter Levi wondered if O'Connor wasn't suffering from 'that special fury which makes the politics of little magazines so lively, so narrow, and so short-lived'.

While working on the third *Rambler*, Philip also managed to get a volume of his journals published by the Tuba Press, a small publishing house run by an expatriate neighbour named Peter Ellson, whose wife Barbara Norman had been a noted Fitzrovian figure and a friend of both Crisp and O'Connor. The production of this volume, which was called *Egocide*, was no easy business, Ellson soon preferring to meet Philip in a bar rather than on home territory when they discussed editorial matters, and its publication towards the end of 1993 was to cause a row between Philip and his staunchest friend John Berger. Hearing that the book had been completely and predictably ignored by the critics, Berger had written an enthusiastic and inspired review for the *Guardian* and prior to publication had sent a copy of this to Philip. The review began 'I don't want to put down or write up this man. I would like to try to get beside him, to recognize him. It's not easy', and went on to state that O'Connor's 'crazy, crazy' book offered 'a striking view of the world we live in' and to hail the author as the 'direct descendant of Shakespeare's Fools and Clowns and the ones driven mad or playing madness in Shakespeare's theatre'. O'Connor, he wrote, had inherited from these characters 'the same lèse-majesté, the same gift of juggling the claims of the powerful, the same devious-ness, the same nonsense, the same risk, if turned out of the Court, of being locked away, and the same tricky play, both cunning and naïve, with words'.

Philip's reaction to the piece could not have been predicted. According to Panna, his first response was to weep with gratitude and she had telephoned Berger to say that they both thought the review was wonderful. Hours or days afterwards, Philip completely changed his mind, became violently hostile to Berger and even wrote to Stephen Spender, 'The most horribly obtuse and patronizing review of my

Egocide is to appear in the *Guardian*.' Philip's objection was that Berger had simply stressed what a funny man he was and said nothing about the philosophical content of the book. Angry telephone calls between Philip and Berger followed, Berger at one stage expressing anger that Philip was angry, with the result that the review, which would have done Philip great and much needed credit, was obediently withdrawn by Berger. Philip continued to simmer with rage and told everyone that he had now severed links with his distinguished friend. A second volume of journals would appear two years later under the irritatingly quirky title *Life after Dearth?* and led to a quarrel with the publisher Peter Ellson, who protested at Philip's bullying attempts to make last-minute alterations when the book was already in production.

Berger and Ellson were not the only people Philip quarrelled with. A letter from Peter Levi to Philip contains the line, 'I have no idea what you have against John Berger and Michael Hamburger, both of whom I view serenely', which suggests that yet another old friend had somehow incurred Philip's wrath – but that particular rumpus blew over quickly and Philip was soon writing to Hamburger, 'My reason for living is a flower, a sunset, a love, an art, a prayer called a poem, a rose, a scent, a taste, a musical thought – is anything.' His dealings with Pat de Maré were also placid – 'We'll be two wonderful old men soon, unless our wives put a stop to it' – and he failed to annoy my old friend Jonathan Gathorne-Hardy by asking him to return a book which he had sent him. 'Do you make a habit of giving presents and asking for them back?' asked Gathorne-Hardy. 'The copy is elaborately and kindly inscribed to me but, if you really do need it or that is your habit, I'll of course return it.'

With the faithful Stephen Fothergill he also found fault. In the summer of 1994 Fothergill had written a short portrait of Philip, possibly for publication in the *London Magazine*, and had conscientiously submitted the typescript for Philip's approval. As with Berger's article, Philip's first reactions were friendly. On 18 June he declared that the piece was 'harmless'. On 19 June he wrote again, pointing out 'some errors of fact'. On 8 July he wrote a further friendly letter after having drunk 'two bottles of the local' and half a bottle of champagne given him by his daughter Allaye, who was visiting. This letter was signed off 'Bon soir, my dear Stephen' but was followed by yet another letter dated 24 July in which he completely changed his tune. He now denied that Panna's income had ever been 'substantial' and warned Fothergill that he was in danger of 'tittle-tattling scandal-mongering' and signed off 'Gossip is disgusting.' Like Berger, Stephen Fothergill decided not to publish the piece – and would not even include it in his book of reminiscences *The Last Lamplighter* published after Philip's death.

Philip's professed disgust of gossip – he often branded me a 'gossip-monger' or worse – may have been revived by a misplaced identification with Stephen Spender, who had recently confided in him about a biography 'some muckraker with the soul of a gossipy housemaid' was doing of him 'entirely against my wishes and despite my violent protests'. Philip's relationship with Spender had been going through the usual ups and downs. In 1991 Spender had written, 'The fact that you like my poems means a great deal to me and I often think of this', but Philip was soon cross with him for not responding to a new set of demands. 'Presumably you've been too busy to reply to my last letters,' he wrote rudely on 9 January 1994. 'May you manage to do so soon?' A few months later Spender had written tersely, 'I am eighty-five and have not been well, have a large correspondence to deal with and no secretarial help in doing so. Please excuse me for being a bad correspondent.' With or without this apology Philip soon felt sufficiently mollified to stick a photograph of his aged mentor beside his bed.

In fact neither Spender nor O'Connor were well and Spender had only a year to live. In the early 1990s Philip had made various references to his own declining health, telling me in various letters, 'I am not well' and 'I am fairly ill', and at the age of seventy-seven he had written, 'Get your obituary ready.' Among the afflictions he complained of were rheumatism, bronchitis, ulcers, lumbago, toothache and 'awful spots'. He also claimed that cirrhosis was threatening again, but short periods without alcohol were followed by attempts to drink a litre of Côtes du Rhône a day. To Patrick de Maré he reported on 25 June 1992 that he was 'yellow and sensitive under the knee of the left leg', and added, 'If amputated, will cook with sage and onions and come to dinner.' A few months later he told de Maré, 'I am honoured by illness', mentioning two attacks of bronchitis. To Michael Hamburger he complained of loss of memory – 'but the doctor has given me some pills for that, unfortunately' – and on 13 March 1995 he told Hamburger, 'I expect to die soon, unless a Balinese dancer aged thirteen, complete with yacht and rickety throne arrives.' To Diana Pollitt whom he'd known in London in the 1950s he wrote, 'Yes, I'm an ill old man' and moaned on, 'What a life! We're absolutely broke. I try everything to earn some pence, in vain. I've become incomprehensible in my writing.' When Pollitt eventually visited Philip at Fontarèches, she came across 'an old man, a stranger'.

In the spring of 1995 he managed to produce a fourth and final issue of *The Rambler*, which concluded with an editorial note to the effect that unless an eccentric came to the rescue this issue would be the last. Unoccupied, he then plunged into a mysterious new crisis – or state of mind – that is difficult to get the hang of. The previous June one of his letters to me had mentioned 'a possible separation' without going into details and in October 1994 he had made a strange joke about being 'airlifted out of here by the RAF'. Now on 19 March 1995, he wrote a telegram-like letter to Patrick de Maré saying, 'Get me out of here and I suppose it would have to be back to England. I can't give you details here and now – ill, upset, old fears – I need some kind of being looked after – existence impossible as I am now.' Four days later, he sent me a handwritten letter saying, 'Please contact de Maré and RLF to get me back to the UK.' Over the page he had scrawled, 'I'm in a very bad way – beaten up & alcohol.' On 26 March he wrote again to de Maré, 'It is essential for my health I return to England: there's a local madman here, dangerous – whole situation a mess. Can you contact the Royal Lit Fund people? I can't travel alone.' A postscript gave my name and address and that of his daughter Allaye, now living in Highbury, and added the information: 'She has a Volkswagen mini-bus for luggage.'

In the eye of this storm, neither Pat de Maré nor I contacted each other, but I told a representative of the Royal Literary Fund that on no account should Philip be encouraged to leave the safe haven Panna

Grady provided. In any event the crisis blew over and soon was eclipsed by a more serious health problem. On 8 December 1995 Philip wrote to de Maré that he was soon to enter hospital for the removal of a polyp from his colon. While he was awaiting the results of his tests, Philip received a visit from his twenty-one-year-old granddaughter Jane Monson, whose mother Sarah had died in an accident seven years earlier. In her account of this visit, Jane describes Philip O'Connor as drunk, watching the television with the sound off, cursing England, swinging his cane, smirking, cackling, reading aloud, sniggering grotesquely, never stopping talking and hounding her round the house so purposefully that she considered locking her bedroom door. On the day she arrived, Philip was summoned to the telephone and told that the polyp was cancerous. Jane recalls that Philip was back 'on stage' again within hours of this news.

During the next few weeks Philip was in and out of the hospital at the nearby town of Bagnols in extraordinary high spirits and behaving outrageously, snipping intravenous tubes with scissors hidden under blankets and obliging the nursing staff to handcuff him to his bed. Evidently escape of one sort or another still appealed to him. On 16 February 1996 he asked Patrick de Maré to make 'dulcet enquiries' about 'retirement homes for old writers', adding, 'I think it is very possible that if I do survive I shall want to leave my beloved, preferring as always, not life but my poor scribbling.' By the end of April, following another operation and radiotherapy at a Montpellier hospital, he had calmed down again, acknowledging his dependence on Panna and revealing that the Royal Literary Fund had now added £3,000 to his pension. Earlier appeals to the Society of Authors had also borne fruit. It says something for Philip's industry that during this troubled time he managed to produce a new book of poems, entitled *Thinking of Li Po*, which was published in January 1996 by an enterprising young admirer in London, Patricia Scanlon. During negotiations with Miss Scanlon, Philip had proposed marriage more than once.

That year I made a plan to visit Philip O'Connor on the eve of his eightieth birthday and bringing with me a girl to whom I was also in the habit of proposing marriage. Philip and I had corresponded regularly and he had written, 'You should come for us to have a last glance & sniff at you', followed by an appeal that we should meet 'pre-posthumously'. Below the turbulent surface of our relationship there was further off-stage friction and he had continued to take what he described as a 'King Leary view' of my social performances. In 1993 I had offended Philip by calling him an 'alcoholic genius' in the *Literary Review* and he had told Michael Hamburger that since the critical success of *The Tap Dancer* I had become 'absolutely distant'. In fact I remained loyal, infatuated, indulgent and exhilarated by the prospect of grappling again with the man who had guided and inspired me through my early adulthood. In the middle of August 1996, my would-be wife and I stayed with Tony Daniells in his private paradise at Flaux and drove over often to Philip's dog-infested enclosure under the fir trees at Fontarèches. Here Philip remained 'King Leary', switching more than ever between rage and gentleness and incorporating other literary characters like the Ancient Mariner into his act. He wore white and his unkempt beard, outsize dark glasses and the straw hat that had replaced his winter cap kept his face so hidden one could only focus on what he called 'the cathedral' of his mouth. Like Quentin Crisp, he was now to some extent on 'auto-pilot' and was perhaps too wrapped up in himself or too pickled in the local Châteu de Bastet even to make the insulting personal observations which had once been his speciality: during that visit he offered me no insights about my intended wife nor did he comically foul-mouth me to her as he might have done in earlier times.

I saw him alone and in company. One afternoon, Panna's gate-legged table from Connecticut was dragged out into the courtyard for a large lunch party attended by Felix O'Connor, now twenty-three years old, Tony Daniells, who had remained attentive to Philip over the years, Ella Grady and her Italian husband – Philip had not been invited to the wedding – and by Panna's sister who was visiting France with an adopted oriental daughter in her early teens, with whom Philip had immediately struck up a bond. Philip was often absent from the table and at one juncture he told me, 'I don't like the way you look at me. You look at me as if you think I'm going to die.' At the end of my stay I drove over to Fontarèches alone to visit him for the last time. I found him in the same white garments, dark glasses and straw hat, seated in a shady corner of the yard at a small table on which Panna had placed flowers. Here he intermittently raised his glass and shouted a ferocious, barbaric toast to Russia, at the top of his voice and with a great deal of self-mockery. '*Russ-kaia!*'

I did not see Philip again, though he lived on for nearly two years. I rang him fairly regularly at Fontarèches and heard him sighing and gasping as he made his way up the uncarpeted staircase to the telephone. Sometimes he sounded lucid and gentle, at other times he was crazily and boisterously uncommunicative, drunk or drugged. I also received letters from him, full of requests, along with predictions that the end was nigh and praise for the French medical service. He focused on the idea of his death with a sharp eye, and approached the final drama with what Tony Daniells described as 'a giggle, a laugh and a shout'. In Saul Bellow's magazine *The Republic of Letters* he wrote, 'Imagine my posthumous amusement: the stars look down at a possible reader of these last farewells. Who does he think he is?'

All this while, he was angelically sustained by Panna, by regular visits from Maxim and Felix and by the gathering round of other members of his extended family. The birth in Tokyo of Peter's and Hideko's daughter in March 1997 gave him the spiritual foothold in the East he had always yearned for. Meanwhile his daughter Allaye had carefully and long-sufferingly rebuilt her relationship with him. In May of that year, fearing that Philip had little time to live and now divorced from her husband, Allaye moved into a flat in Uzès in order to be close to him. Her two children were 'wary' of their grandfather but did 'some quite funny impersonations of him' and Allaye reports that, though she still had rows with her father, he always telephoned afterwards, apologized and invited her to tea. Distraught about a love affair, Allaye had called on Philip at three or four in the morning and he had been more than equal to the occasion. 'He was completely reassuring. He took me in his arms, made me a cup of tea. He was very strong.'

In June 1997 he returned to hospital to be fitted for a colostomy bag but remained robust in spite of circumstances which Panna described as 'discouraging', and later in the year he started to receive twice-daily visits from nursing staff. He got on well with these ladies and they agreed to let him go on sleeping in the large old bed in his hut. One of his last visitors from England was his old friend Denis Lowson, but he continued to receive letters and messages from other figures from his past. The Chelsea vet Tony O'Neill, still occupying the surgery where Philip had stayed in 1945, wrote offering sympathy and complaining of 'a few agues' of his own. Anna Wing sent cheery cards and Maria Scott wrote boldly, 'I find your being ill intolerable.' In January 1998 Peter O'Connor visited Fontarèches and made peace with his father and told him that he loved him. 'It lifted a weight off me,' Peter said later, and Philip told Panna that he had never parted with someone on such good terms. On 23 January Peter wrote to his father, 'Maybe we'll meet again. I hope so.' Even now Philip did not give up. He wrote and talked as much as ever and amazed his doctors by combining his medicines with three bottles of *vin du pays* per day. He also continued to fuss over grants and pensions and on 18 February 1998 was rewarded with a cheque from the Royal Literary Fund for £4,180.

In the late spring of 1998 Philip decided that he had been captive at Fontarèches for too long and arranged to visit Uzès for a last solo bar crawl. Panna drove him into the town and watched anxiously from a discreet distance, but Philip gave up the venture after only one stop. He also received visits from some of his neighbours – though not as many as Panna would have liked. One caller was Sarah Harrison, who had first encountered Philip twenty years earlier under a café table, and she noted that though he was very weak he got out of bed to find *Seven Years in Tibet* for her. A less generously treated visitor was his Welsh-born son Patric, now thirty-five, and living part of the time in France. Resuming his old monstrous form, Philip had shouted at Patric through the gate, 'Fuck off, you creep!' and then added for good measure, '*Mediocrity!*'

But on the whole this was a time for making peace with people. In April he wrote a last letter to Patrick de Maré. The letter was typewritten but full of mistakes. In it he reflected, 'Amazing the conceit illness gives one! The self-importance! The humble gratitude, politeness, gentleness! The authoritarian bully disappears; one's a humble little fellow en fin.' He went on, 'I've gassed my way through this small world of mine for a long time. I've never stopped, just like my mother.' Then he added, 'I am tired of being I', and concluded, 'Love to you dear Pat. Keep the cord firm to the end.'

During the final weeks of his life Philip O'Connor gave up wine, complaining, 'It stinks', but he wasn't drawn to water either, which he said tasted like ink. Instead he drank herbal tea, especially vervain. On this beverage and in these circumstances, Allaye reports that Philip became positively mellow. 'We had a wonderful time,' she recalls. 'We danced. In that very cramped room. And we lay on the bed and laughed. Uncontrollably.' Philip also chose to say sorry to some of those he had hurt including Allaye's son Eli – but not to his son Patric who forgave him nonetheless. Never at any stage did he complain of the pain he was going through and he always got on well with the nurses and begged them to tell him when he was dying. Over these final days Panna ministered wonderfully to him, though sometimes coming near to breaking-point herself. And until the last day of his life, he continued to write, only stopping when he could no longer hold a pen.

On the evening of Thursday 28 May, Allaye visited her father and he told her, 'We must say goodbye.' The following morning, shortly before eleven o'clock, a nurse called Mérielle arrived for her usual stint and she and Panna raised Philip from his pillow and were trying to get him into a jersey when she told him, '*Votre heure est arrivée, Monsieur O'Connor.*' Felix was in Paris, but with Panna, Maxim and the nurse squeezed together beside the bed, Philip O'Connor died peacefully, cradled in their arms.

PART SIX

-28-

A Study of Opposites

You write such strange books.

QUENTIN CRISP TO ANDREW BARROW, 22 February 1999

I started working on this book in January 1999, though it could be said that I had been writing, thinking, or at least banging on about Quentin Crisp and Philip O'Connor for many years. In fact, though I saw both of them as 'good copy' from the start, I never planned to write at length about either of them and even when, a few months after Philip's death, I had given a party in his honour at Eldon Road, I had still not seriously considered writing a book about him. A month later, in October 1998, when I visited Quentin Crisp for the last time in New York, the thought of doing his biography was equally far from my mind.

I had by this time begun to fancy myself as a novelist, thanks to the minor success of *The Tap Dancer* and the adequate performance of its sequel *The Man in The Moon*, and planned to use Quentin and Philip as characters in a new novel. It was only when I realized that both men were larger than life and difficult if not impossible to fictionalize – didn't Anthony Powell come to the same conclusion about his brother-in-law Lord Longford? – that I formed the idea of constructing a narrative in which I, too, might play some role.

I was now fifty-three years old and had known Quentin Crisp since I was twenty-one and Philip O'Connor since I was twenty-six. The two men had played substantial roles in my life and still remained inspirations. Though both of them were performers, they also seemed less superficial than most people I knew and they had both led quite extraordinary lives, suffered acutely at the hands of different mobs. Both had had a taste of hell and both had looked life in the eye and been unintimidated by its harshest realities and darkest nightmares. With both men I felt safe – and more confident in myself. Both men had given me the feeling that I was – to borrow Mr Duffey's expression – 'doing well'.

An extra lure was that both Quentin and Philip came from a world I hardly knew, but which appealed to the condescending side of my nature. Though Philip might have liked to deny it and Quentin to exaggerate it, both came from suburban backgrounds and both had found fulfilment in the lower reaches of bohemia – a place that remains infinitely attractive to me, its squalor as alluring as its poetry. Both men belonged to the past. Both were 'period pieces'. Yet for all their cobwebbiness – or dustiness – they seemed to have been closer to the action than many more spick-and-span contemporaries. Both men had got involved with the developing media: Philip in the highbrow days of the BBC's Third Programme and Quentin with the great international circus, which eventually provided him with a website in his honour and much else besides. Both men had eventually gone abroad and both had expressed hatred of England, a country I continue to love.

But here the similarities cease. In dozens of ways, Quentin Crisp and Philip O'Connor were complete opposites, almost perfect opposites. Both had written brilliant autobiographies, both were in the 'confessional' business, but their attitudes towards other people are starkly at odds. As Professor Robinson points out, the characters in *The Naked Civil Servant* are 'shadowy and insubstantial, often reduced to a single (unattractive) feature'. In *Memoirs of a Public Baby*, even the most minor character is drawn in staggering detail and the author has a passionate relationship with everybody and everything. The tastes of the two men were also in conflict: Quentin loathes Oscar Wilde, Philip loves him. Philip is crazy about Charlie Chaplin, Quentin goes no further than acknowledging Chaplin's physical grace. For most of his life Philip O'Connor was out of control. He treated his women and, for much of the time, his children appallingly. He was insolvent, his poetry was dashed off without editing, he behaved like a drunken lunatic who could well have been locked up for more than those six months in the Maudsley. Quentin Crisp repeatedly claimed to be incompetent but was in fact highly capable, never let anyone down, always behaved impeccably and remained savagely unsentimental, his life unmarked by tantrums of any sort. From some perspectives Philip O'Connor's life seems fuller and richer than Quentin Crisp's. Madame Tillieux had introduced Philip to the human race. He had love affairs, he had children, grandchildren, friends and drinking companions. He enjoyed nature, both tramping and country walks, music, delicious food, and according to John Berger had even been an expert on wine. Quentin had never possessed what Philip describes as *une carte de visite à l'humanité* and was indifferent or actually opposed to all these things. If Philip inhabited the wilder shores of love, Quentin was right out there in the ocean, a lost soul, though very much afloat.

Putting the two lives together has been an experiment. Fans of the one man or the other may have been tempted to skip the alternating chapters on their less favourite figure and may find the structure I have imposed awkward. I would like to hope that a few readers may have found the experience worthwhile and that the yardstick each man imposes on the other strengthens the plot and highlights the identity of the other. I believe I would have found it far more difficult to write about Quentin and Philip separately, in separate volumes.

And, anyway, my narrative is not yet finished – and the writing of it is now part of the story. I started my researches guiltily, besieged by a feeling of sleaziness – some of Philip's mud had stuck – which perhaps all biographers feel as they begin to dig about in their subjects' lives. In this case the feeling was made worse by the knowledge that my attachment to both men already had a parasitical element to it. I also felt uneasy about tampering with the careful, almost lacquered image that both men had presented of themselves, particularly in their autobiographies, both of which for all their openness are extremely discreet about significant details and hard facts. I feared that in attempting to tell the story as it really was I might be doing both men no favours.

Philip O'Connor was now dead and his career had been celebrated in long obituaries in all the broadsheets, several of which had mentioned his role in the life of Quentin Crisp. His life had also been celebrated with a party in my Kensington studio, at which Anna Wing had read the poem 'Blue Bugs in Liquid Silk' and Michael Horovitz, Ian Patterson and Peter O'Connor had paid tribute to the man who touched their lives in different ways. Maria Scott was there, excited and embarrassed by the presence of two former lovers but keeping a proud distance from them. Panna Grady did not attend the event but sent a case of champagne and a case of Château de Bastet, the red wine Philip had loved in his final years. Patrick de Maré and his wife had arrived late and Tony O'Neill had not turned up at all. I had not considered mentioning the event to Quentin Crisp or gone through the motions of inviting him to it. At that time he was very likely playing to a packed audience in Cleveland, Ohio, or some other place that 'the Policeman' had sent him, his thoughts engaged on other matters altogether, such as the latest scandals engulfing President Clinton.

By the time I started work on this book, Quentin had opened his one-man show at the Intar Theatre on 42nd Street off Broadway, a six-week run which had begun on his ninetieth birthday. I waited until the middle of February 1999 to tell him of my new enterprise. He appeared unphased by the news and we talked instead about the show he had just finished and how little he had enjoyed it. 'The theatre was *so* cold and I was *so* ill.' I asked if he would appear on stage again and he said, 'I doubt it', but admitted there was a current attempt to get him to appear at the Royal Festival Hall in London. I asked if I could do anything for him and he said I could send some Germolene – 'pink and greasy, the white kind's no good' – packing it flat so it went through the letterbox. He said he had read my recent article about him and was surprised to be described as 'portly', which I justified on the grounds that this could mean 'of stately appearance'. A few days later he wrote thanking me for the Germolene and only making a passing reference to my new venture: 'You write such strange books.'

From Philip O'Connor's family I got a different sort of reaction. Most of his children and ex-wives seemed keen that I should write about him and may have even believed that I was the right person for the task. They also accepted my idea of combining Philip's life story with that of the world-famous outsider he had helped to launch, though Peter O'Connor wrote from Japan urging me to write 'a *real* book' by getting immersed in the history of the 1930s and 40s and then 'cutting savagely'.

I started my researches slowly and with mounting regrets and moments of incredulous irritation that when I knew both men well I had never asked them some of the most basic questions about their past. Why had I never asked Philip for the name of his one-legged guardian with whom he had lived for eight years? Or Quentin the name of the snobbish postal clerk he called Thumbnails? I eventually learnt the name of the guardian from the records of Dorking High School but the identity of Thumbnails, for whom I still have a sneaking admiration, remains a mystery. And why had I not explored the relationship between Philip and Quentin in more depth?

For many months I had no idea what sort of book I would write. I could have written an essay on both men and the nature of eccentricity from my own knowledge, using the very minimum of biographical detail, and this is perhaps what my publishers had in mind. On the other hand, both men were stranger than fiction and had written wonderfully unreliable autobiographies and I could not resist trying to anchor their lives in a few facts. Philip O'Connor's death had left a hollow in my life and by January 1999 Quentin Crisp's existence seemed precarious. I started to fill these real and likely voids by pursuing the minutiae of their past lives. Perhaps I was also trying to tidy up my own life and discover a pattern in it. When I started on this book I was approaching the age of Quentin and Philip when I first met them. It was high time that I cleared the decks, disposed of the past and cultivated the flowers I had planted long ago.

At the risk of sounding disingenuous, I must repeat that I felt unworthy of the task of disturbing sleeping dogs and receiving intimacies from friends and acquaintances of my two subjects. For the most part, these were what Quentin would call 'fellow hooligans', people who had once inhabited the area of London some people called Fitzrovia and Quentin himself 'the reservation'. I did not know when

QUENTIN & PHILIP

I set out that it would prove to be a magic journey into a number of private paradises. Almost everyone I met during the next two years seemed blessed or gilded by their contact with one or both of these two men. All of them were helpful, all sweet-natured. Many were artistic, had beautiful handwriting and lived in some lovely place. Some of them I already knew. Others I was meeting for the first time.

$-29-$

Private Paradises

> Quentin took me to Bertorelli's. I thought he was
> wonderful. I was actually quite in love with him. I
> used to have dreams about him. But I knew Philip
> better. I had his babies.

MARIA SCOTT TO ANDREW BARROW, 7 March 1999

I started cautiously, slowly extricating myself from other responsibilities, and made various plunges into writing the book. I had no
plan of action in mind. I hoped to see many surviving friends of
Quentin Crisp and Philip O'Connor but the order in which I did so
had no logic to it – and anyway I imagined that several significant
figures would elude my grasp. I hoped to talk to John Berger about
Philip O'Connor and to Harold Pinter about Quentin Crisp but had
no plans to get in touch with Quentin's more celebrated friends in
New York, like the pop-star Sting and the fashion model Lauren
Hutton. In Philip's circle, no one had any idea where Bobbie Battersby
was or what had become of his first wife Jean. For important structural
reasons I wanted to talk to Joan Rhodes, who had been a friend of
Quentin, Philip and my father, but she had not replied to my Christmas
cards and I had no confidence that the woman famous for tearing up
telephone directories on stage would want to see me – nor had I any
intention of pressurizing her to do so.

I began by taking a train to Lewes in East Sussex on 27 January
1999 to see Julia Ramos, whom I had met at a lunch party in Brighton
a few years earlier where she had mentioned knowing Quentin Crisp
in Chelsea in the 1950s. In her pretty house in Southover High Street

she now told me that she had not known him very well. She talked of him 'passing by' and added, 'Everyone was amazed by him and everyone liked him.' Her friend Eve Dennerhy had invited him to all her parties. Chelsea in those days, she said, was 'full of fascinating leftovers' like Isadora Duncan's brother and Agnes Joad, daughter of the notorious Professor Joad who had cheated on the railway. Another of Quentin's admirers was Peggy Thorburn, who had married the son of the famous bird-painter, but Quentin also had an enemy called Hector Freeman, an Old Harrovian whom he had hated enough to say, 'Withhold my love from Mr Freeman.' Mrs Ramos also remembered the ballet teacher Miss Lumley and believed she had come to a sticky end, diving into an empty swimming pool. Finally she urged me to get in touch with her son Tod who had recently seen Quentin in New York and reported that he was 'miserable'.

Mrs Ramos had never heard of Philip O'Connor, but the next person I saw, Ann Wolff, director of the *Captain Busby* film, had known both my subjects and had come back by Eurostar from a holiday in France to attend the party in Eldon Road. Talking in the kitchen of her large and uncluttered house in Hampstead on 13 February, she told me that her husband Heinz had met Philip at Cambridge in the mid-1930s and been delighted by his wild ways, but later grew embarrassed by him. Ann Wolff had got on well with Philip from the start but had eventually stopped keeping his letters because they were so full of complaints about people like John Berger and even – this was news to me – Saul Bellow. She also remembered Quentin Crisp's arrival at her house in Reddington Road and how she had instinctively stretched out for her mother's best tea service. While I was in the house, Ann Wolff went upstairs and started opening filing cabinets, searching for things that might help me. I heard her say the word, 'Damn!' Finally, she said it was sad the way Philip always wanted more acclaim and always tried to dine off the *Public Baby*.

A few days later I went to see Martina Thomson, widow of Philip's best friend David Thomson, at her house in Regent's Park Terrace. I had been here several times in the past, and in a snowstorm one night in February 1988 I had pinned a note on the door, learning the following morning that David Thomson had died the same night.

Martina had been involved in many of Philip's radio programmes and had also acted in *Captain Busby*. She told me that Philip got 'entirely bored' by all his programmes and it was usually left to David to finish them. She remembered Panna's house in Hanover Terrace and its 'altogether too grand' furnishings, then the incongruity of the Wimereux boarding house and the mill near Uzès where Panna slept with only a curtain dividing her from her sons while Philip had a whole large room to himself. She also remembered Philip's terrible shouting but added, 'Panna is strong in a strange way. I even wonder if she wasn't the strongest.' She also declared, 'Philip couldn't bear a joke against himself. He was absolutely humourless.' Was loneliness the basis of his persona, she finally mused, like Chaplin?

After these preliminary skirmishes I felt sufficiently in my stride to visit Maria Scott at her home at Crouch End in North London. I had been here before and had met Maria once or twice with her son Peter, and she had steeled herself to attend the party in my studio the previous autumn. On 7 March 1999, I arrived in the rain at Park Avenue South and Maria, a tiny, shy childlike figure of great grace, took my coat and laid it carefully on the radiator in the bathroom. In the basement kitchen – 'I'm a terrible tea-maker, my family tell me' – she began by talking about Quentin Crisp, telling me how much she had loved him and how surprised she was that he thought she was 'a member of the Higher Faith'. Maria used Quentin's euphemism for the homosexual community without explanation and continued, 'But I knew Philip better. I had his babies.' She told me she had not seen Philip O'Connor since he left for France in 1967. 'I was frightened of meeting him. I thought he'd say something so awful, so destructive.' As we have seen, Philip and Maria had revived their relationship by writing to each other, but Maria had steadfastly avoided seeing Philip in person. Now she added, 'Philip spoilt me for other men. I found other men very stultifying after Philip.' Of their time together she remembered particularly their poverty. 'We weren't just poor, Andrew, we were *miserably poor*.' She regretted that Philip had left school at sixteen, not gone to university. 'He was uneducated. If he'd got a degree at least he'd have been *safe*. He could have gone into literary criticism, been a lecturer . . .' But she acknowledged Panna's role in his life. 'She made his dreams come true. He always felt sorry for me, having to live in England.' She also said, 'Philip met good mothers, made babies quickly.'

My next encounter took place five days later with Patrick de Maré, whom Philip had known since they were both teenagers. Over the decades Philip had said little about de Maré, perhaps respecting him too much to mock or abuse. Is it worth relating that de Maré's late arrival at my flat the previous autumn was preceded by a telephone call to establish that the event was still in progress? Or that my visit to the house in Holly Place, Hampstead, where de Maré is still practising as a psychotherapist, was also preceded by a telephone call, saying that he would only be able to manage an hour? This air of being under pressure was reinforced when he came to the door, exclaimed 'Andrew!', and showed me into a tiny, well padded dining room and said, 'I won't be a second.' I waited for several minutes while he disposed of a patient and then followed him upstairs to another cosy room.

Patrick de Maré is a cuddly type, white-bearded, world-weary and soft-spoken, in a way that reminded me of Philip when he was shy and sober. Most of what he now told me is already in this narrative and was accompanied by remarks like 'Is this any good?' and 'Oh dear, oh dear, when one looks back' and 'Perhaps this won't be suitable?' He referred to the 'crackpot' group with whom they had first met and said of Philip's wife Jean, 'She went into a bin and never came out. I think she had a lobotomy at some point.' He told me that he and Philip had 'loved each other, in a funny sort of way' and added, 'I mean I really do think Phil was a genius. It wasn't just bullshit.' I asked him if he could define genius. '*Um. Oh. Right,*' he began and then said, 'Well, it's when you've extricated yourself from the clichés of society and established your own centre and are able to give succinct expression of the cultures around you. Something like that? Geniuses are out on a limb.' This definition would certainly embrace Quentin Crisp. Did de Maré know him too? 'Yes, I met him in the war. He was very, very nice.' After my allotted hour was over he gave me a large file of letters from O'Connor, including the last one written before his death, and did not seem to want them back. On the doorstep I asked if I could call again and he said, 'Yes, of course! *Any time!*'

Were my researches hotting up? Was the pace quickening? On the day after my visit to Holly Place, I invited Stephen Fothergill to tea. Fothergill is a famous Soho figure, who has recently published his own memoirs, nobly omitting the piece that ended up annoying Philip so much. Described by Philip as 'extremely good-looking' when they first met in the war, Fothergill is now frail and rather blind and when the appointed hour for tea was long past I went out to look for him. In a nearby street, I spotted his mackintoshed figure ambling purposefully towards me and happily guided him the last few yards. Over tea, he told me he had found Soho 'madly exciting' as a young man and still went to the Dean Street pub the French House most nights. He had met Quentin Crisp and Philip O'Connor in 1942. He remembered Quentin as 'so marvellous, so arrogant and witty. He did all the talking.' And once or twice he had borrowed half-crowns from him and to his shame never returned them. With Philip, his dealings were closer and more complicated. He described their first evening together – and Philip's robust sexual proposal – and how they'd lived together in Limerston Street and Maple Street. Fothergill's memory of Jean O'Connor was a bit vague. He called her 'too lifeless to be attractive'. He wasn't very keen on Philip's poetry or writing in general. 'I wonder why Saul Bellow liked it so much. His sentences were terribly disjointed. There was a lack of charm about his writing. An ugliness. But he was witty. I can't remember anything he said now.' On balance Fothergill had more respect for Paul Potts, whom he saw as 'a more honourable man'. When I asked if he was fond of Philip, he replied, 'I don't think I was fond of anyone in those days. I was *impressed* by him. I think he was fond of *me*.' Of Quentin Crisp's current life in New York he said, 'Apparently he's bored to death there.'

I had meanwhile been digging about in old street registers and telephoning archivists and busy local-history sections of libraries. I formed a particular bond with a lady called June Spong, a local historian based at Dorking in Surrey, where O'Connor had spent part of his childhood, returning more than once as an adult. 'I've been reading his book – what a strange character he was,' Miss Spong wrote to me that spring, going on to say that in her opinion his book was 'mostly fantasy' though conceding that he may have visited Dorking and Box Hill 'at some time in his life'.

A lot of my research was inevitably conducted on the telephone. One of the people I soon spoke to was ninety-five-year-old Norman Bradshaw, the former maths teacher at Dorking High School who furnished me with his memories of Philip O'Connor as a schoolboy. While stressing, 'He never gave me any trouble', he twice asked me in the course of a short conversation, 'Did he get into any trouble?' Another person I telephoned was the poet David Gascoyne, who remembered meeting Philip and Jean in Paris before the war. Gascoyne told me that he had thought Philip's poems were 'very, very funny' but had anticipated that he would have a difficult life.

From time to time I also spoke to Quentin Crisp in New York, but on each occasion felt that I was being a nuisance by asking him tiresome questions about his distant past when he would rather be having fun discussing the latest movie he'd seen or proposing that present-day people should be 'chopped up like parsley'. When I told him that, before they were married, his mother and father had both lived in the same street in Tooting, South London, he did not sound remotely interested – and only responded, 'My father never talked about *anything*.'

I had also rung Anna Wing and left messages on her answering machine, seeing her as another valuable link between Crisp and O'Connor as well as a character in her own right who might add zest to my book, just as she had to the party celebrating Philip's life. When she did not reply to my messages I began thinking that perhaps she wanted to keep her memories to herself and was relieved to learn, from Quentin Crisp himself, that she had been working in New York. Eventually she rang me and in her usual exuberant way told me that she had returned from America the previous day after a world tour in a Caryl Churchill play called *Blue Heart*. While in New York, she had telephoned Quentin but felt 'a little bit shy about seeing him', inhibited by 'a kind of respect', especially when he told her he was unwell, hardly able to walk down the street. I understood and shared her feelings and hesitations and did not press her when she said in an entirely friendly way that she would rather not talk about Philip. She would only say that Panna Grady and 'all the O'Connor children' were in regular touch with her. She was keener to talk about *Blue Heart*, which would be opening at the Pleasance Theatre in London the following week. I duly saw the play in which she played her small role to perfection, but after the show she was whisked out of the theatre to a waiting taxi, apparently wary of further entanglement.

I encountered no such reserve with Philip's son Patric when I visited him on 28 March in his house near Lambeth Palace; indeed the inhibition was chiefly on my part. I exclaimed 'O'Connor!' when he opened the door, but then slightly lost my nerve: I envied him the large empty room, a former garage, shared with a cat and dog and looking onto a yard full of flowers, with a staircase leading to rooms above. He told me how his father had shouted insults at him through the gate at Fontarèches the previous year, but did not seem upset about it. He told me to contact Nellie Jones, who still lived at Croesor in North Wales in the house next door to the one his parents had occupied. He also spoke of his years in Suffolk and said that 'dark things' had happened there which maybe Allaye would tell me about.

I have already indicated that I found these sorts of intimacies hard to follow through and preferred a more basic form of research. After leaving Lambeth Walk I crossed the river into Pimlico and tried to find 81 Denbigh Street, where Quentin Crisp, still then Denis Pratt, had had his first room of his own in the early 1930s. Unfortunately the street seems to have been rebuilt and the numbering changed and it was therefore impossible to identify the house or room from which the 'magical vehicle' of Quentin Crisp had first been launched.

I would continue along these lines for many weeks. I still did not know what sort of book I was writing but continued haphazard researching and ingesting the past. I smoked the pipes that Philip had given me, made more telephone calls, ordered death and birth certificates and wills of various characters in the story and pursued many red herrings. I learnt with excitement that Dr Petro who had attended Mrs O'Connor on her deathbed in 1934 was the same Dr

Petro who thirty-three years later I had seen on the David Frost TV show accused of prescribing illegal drugs on a massive scale.

Early in my researches, I also visited the BBC radio archives at Caversham in Berkshire, taking a taxi from Reading which carried a notice saying, 'If this Vehicle is Soiled by a Passenger or an Animal an extra £50 will be Charged.' Waiting for me on a large desk in a spacious room were five or six bulky dossiers bearing the name Philip O'Connor. 'There's a lot of meat there,' said the librarian Mr Summerville, and indeed I found every idea Philip submitted to the BBC between 1942 and 1972, every programme he had worked on, every memo and scribbled comment about him by his bosses and every detail of his fees and expenses. On one or two of the bundles was the tantalizing statement 'Papers of a Confidential Nature have been removed from this file' but I was able to take eleven pages of notes, many of which have found their way into this story. While on the premises I also asked if there was by any chance a file on Quentin Crisp? The indexing system quickly threw up the names of Leonard Crisp, Dorothy Crisp and Ronald Crisp and it was only after some persistence that I came across Quentin Crisp and the two stories broadcast in 1949 which I have already mentioned.

I had also begun to make further, tentative visits to places where Quentin or Philip had lived. Some of these trips were purposeful, others took place when for some other reason I happened to find myself in a particular area. One of my routes across London took me past 129 Beaufort Street and I often gazed up at Quentin's old windows as I drove by. Once there was an estate agent's board outside the house and I telephoned Foxton's to learn that there was now a flat to let in the building for £450 a week, as opposed to the six guineas a week Quentin Crisp had finally been paying eighteen years earlier. One day, after a visit to the former Forum Cinema, now part of the UGC chain, where Quentin had often gone twice in one day, I walked round the area and tried to locate the studios in Limerston Street where Philip, Jean and Stephen Fothergill had lived towards the end of the war and where Philip had spent his last night in the coal shelter before moving in with Maria in Fitzroy Street. I was disappointed to find that this part of the street had been pulled down and replaced by a dull modern block. Back in King's Road I passed the spot where Quentin had once materialized like a sprite by the wayside and made my way to the surviving branch of Lloyds Bank where in 1977 the manager had helped Quentin get his first passport.

On other days I visited Chester Square Mews, where Quentin had lived before the war, and found it untampered with, and wandered up and down Dean Street, Soho, but failed to find the cellar where Haslam Jackson had lived in the 1920s. On one of my first outings with Peter O'Connor twenty-five years earlier he had pointed out its likely site, following a visit to the street with his father, but now I could see no sign of an old-fashioned basement room and the street registers for the period did not contain the name of Robert Haslam Jackson. I also 'walked the beat' in Fitzrovia and found only its pubs had survived, though there was still a café at 91 Charlotte Street where Tony's, or Toni's, as Quentin coyly called it, once stood. And one evening in Soho, Stephen Fothergill pointed out to me the exact spot in Old Compton Street, in the middle of the road outside the former Swiss Tavern, now a notorious bar called Comptons, where he had first set eyes on Philip O'Connor. The site of the Black Cat café across the road is now occupied by a men's outfitters called Swank.

Dimly aware that this research was a way of delaying the moment when I actually got down to writing the book, I also began to explore the suburbs, justifying this on the grounds that it is where the story of both men had begun. On 31 March I went to the picturesque Clapham Library, which had impressed Philip as a boy for being 'long and vivacious and brightly lit', did some research in its local-history section and then took a bus to Longley Road, Tooting, where I found the large double-fronted house where Quentin Crisp's father had lived as a young man, and then the smaller, slightly prettier house across the road where Quentin's mother had spent part of her girlhood. The names of both houses were still faintly legible above each door and I peeped through the letterbox of the paternal home and noted the spacious hallway, which two living-in servants had presumably once kept spotless.

A few days later, on Easter Day 1999, I set off at 7 a.m. to visit Sutton in Surrey where Quentin Crisp had spent his early years. It was a fresh morning with empty streets and birdsong, daffodils in front gardens, newspaper boys scooting about and all the Edwardian pleasantness well preserved. I soon found 52 Egmont Road, the broad and spacious three-storey house where Quentin Crisp was born, but hesitated to ring the doorbell and inform the current householder of this fact, which might be a bit like telling him that a murder had once taken place here. Instead I sought out the local church, two streets away, where Quentin and his siblings had been taken in sailor suits before the First World War. Here I found Holy Communion in progress and the vicar saying, 'Christ is risen' and the congregation of about forty souls replying, 'He is risen indeed.' I then drove to Cornwall Road, where the Pratt family had lived in two different houses during the First World War, and on to Epsom where I found the much larger and grander house in Ashdown Road which the Pratts had occupied in the early 1920s: two gateways and a large garden which might still include the tennis court where Quentin Crisp had played tennis – I cannot resist repeating his phrase – 'in a hopeless sort of way'.

Epsom is only a few miles from Box Hill where, contrary to the local archivist's beliefs, Philip had spent much of his childhood. It was also exactly the sort of place Quentin's father might have taken his family for an outing in his latest old banger. That day I approached the famous beauty spot from various angles. I soon found Betchworth station, where Philip and his guardian had first disembarked in the summer of 1924 and where forty-three years later Philip had returned to film *Captain Busby*. I then drove round to the top of the chalk quarries and found an unsurfaced cul-de-sac called Fort Road, where there were mobile homes and huts galore. I felt too shy to start knocking on doors and asking questions. On the other side of the hill I found Ashmore Drive and the group of huts known as Ruskin. Was it possible that one of these pretty little chalets had been the scene of those final horrors which ended with Jean O'Connor going into hospital for the first time?

Had I made these journeys on foot, or by bicycle, I might have got closer to the spirit of Philip O'Connor, but even when travelling by car, these explorations excited me and frequently gave me a very real feeling of going back into the past, though the sense of unburying

buried lives or lifestyles continued to irk me. In the middle of April I
headed beyond suburbia into East Anglia where I had several people
and places to see. Armed with an Ordnance Survey map I found
Purton Green where Philip had lived on and off between 1948 and
1951 and which is still only accessible across fields. I soon found
the spankingly renovated and securely thatched thirteenth-century
building occupied in Philip's day by 'a lady without hair, but always
a hat', now in the safe hands of a charitable body called the Landmark
Trust, who rent it out to visitors, but there was no sign at all of the
house once known as Purton Hall or the moat or the tree of Blenheim
Oranges or of any of the other things Philip had written and brooded
about. I learnt later that Philip's former abode so vividly depicted in
The Lower View had slowly sunk into the ground and finally been
demolished in the spring of 1982. As I nosed around the place, I heard
a distant car alarm – or was it a police siren?

I retraced my steps along the edge of a field where I had left my
own vehicle and drove into Clare, a particularly charming, unspoilt
town, where Philip had attended the Labour Exchange and bought
weekly supplies from the butcher and tobacconist – 'Your darkest
flake, please.' I tried to find these shops but gave up on learning from
a lady in the queue at the town's main butchers that there had been
six butchers in the town at the date in question. Professor Chapman
of the Local History Society seemed ignorant as to the location of the
Labour Exchange and when I knocked on the door of a ninety-year-
old resident named Mr Ince with the same question in mind, I got no
reply. My next stop was Poslingford, where Annie Mygind and Denis
Lowson had lived and where Philip had often been a visitor. Clopton
Hall is, as I anticipated, a lovely and enviable house, belonging to the
past. From its open front door, on which Philip had first knocked in
1954, a young woman emerged called Lena Milbank. She had only
been living here for a short time but she already seemed to know
something about Philip O'Connor. 'I've heard nothing good about
him,' she said. 'The way he treated his wife. People round here were
very fond of her.' I drove on, failed to locate Moat Farm at Broxford
but eventually found the small thatched house at Lidgate which had

been Philip's last home with Nicolle, its name 'Brookside' freshly reprinted on a modern sign beside the road.

I spent the night in Aldeburgh with a friend who knew neither Crisp nor O'Connor but would have probably seen the point of both of them. The next day I visited David Ball and Norman Kelvin at Debenham, surviving friends of Angus McBean, whose 'only mildly sickening' photograph of the young Quentin Crisp had persuaded Tom Maschler to publish *The Naked Civil Servant*. David Ball remembered first seeing Quentin in Charing Cross Road in about 1947 and remarking to Angus McBean, 'Whatever's that?' Later that same day he had met Quentin in a flat in Rathbone Place off Oxford Street belonging to a man named Derek Neame, whose friend Johnny Noble would later become 'Gay Bishop of New York' and one of Quentin's early 'spies' or benefactors in America. These names meant nothing to me and reminded me how little I knew of Quentin's circle. McBean's friends also talked about Joan Rhodes, who had been 'around a lot' in the 1950s along with Kay Kendall and Audrey Hepburn, but it was unclear whether the last two actresses were friends of Quentin. When I asked if Quentin had ever met Danny La Rue, also 'around' in those days, David Ball said immediately, 'Mr La Rue wasn't that type' and Norman Kelvin chipped in, 'I shouldn't think so.' Then they told me about the meeting between Sir Frederick Ashton and Quentin Crisp, which I have already worked into the story.

My next East Anglian appointment was with Michael Hamburger who had known Philip O'Connor since 1942. Hamburger had written several letters explaining why he couldn't come to the party celebrating Philip's life but had responded, 'I'm so glad' when I told him that I was now writing something about Philip. Leaving the theatrical delights of Debenham behind, I drove to Hamburger's house on the edge of the village of Middleton, north of Aldeburgh. Here Hamburger, the author of over a hundred books, had darted out of the front door and shown me where to park and then ushered me into a large old house which seemed to have several sitting rooms. In one of these we soon settled, though 'settled' is not quite the right word as my host kept jumping up, lighting cigarettes, leaning over me in an excited manner. Michael Hamburger has been immensely productive as a writer – 'It's the only thing I like doing' – yet had always respected Philip in spite of his excesses. 'I was always fascinated by people who were strange,' he explained. 'Nowadays I can't cope. If I'd met him today I'd probably have avoided him.' During the Soho phase of his life Hamburger had also known Quentin Crisp and found him 'quite charming and witty'. He also told me how he had introduced Philip to Panna Grady and felt slightly sad afterwards when they 'disappeared' together to France, though Philip and he had continued to correspond vigorously. Later, Hamburger rummaged about in another large room and found a file containing copies of every letter Philip had sent him over the years, the originals now in the Brotherton Library at Leeds. These he entrusted to me and I would learn a lot from them that is now in this book. Finally Hamburger said of O'Connor, 'I couldn't write about him. He was so easily offended.'

And so it went on. My enquiries remained erratic and incomplete and so dependent on my own independent movements that many stones remained unturned. I doubt I would have visited Flackwell Heath, outside High Wycombe, where Quentin had his last taste of family life, had I not been staying nearby. And anyway here I failed to find the house called Hillcrest in Fennell's Way – several along the unsurfaced road fitted the bill – although a bit more leafing through the Voters' Register might have enlightened me. I was luckier the next day when I visited Leighton Buzzard in Bedfordshire and quickly found 25 Clarence Road, where Philip O'Connor was born in 1916 – though here again there is a possibility that the street has been renumbered, a tiresome problem which many biographers must encounter.

A few weeks later I found myself again in East Anglia and took the opportunity to call on Linda Mitchell, widow of the man Quentin had called 'the greatest television documentary maker the world has ever known'. Mrs Mitchell was still in the spacious house in Great Massingham where Quentin had stayed at Christmas 1970, never venturing out of doors and even declining a visit to the Fox and Pheasant. Linda remembered that they had got Guinness in for him and that they sat in front of a big fire and that one day Denis Forman, managing director of Granada, had dropped by to meet him. She also remembered Quentin helping her with a little home decorating, painting a lampshade for her, but she couldn't recall if he had given her a Christmas present – anyway Denis Mitchell had never given her presents. Towards the end of our conversation, I mentioned my plans to incorporate Philip O'Connor into my story – and hadn't Denis made a film with him too? At this, Linda gasped, '*You knew Philip O'Connor?*' – which gives some indication of his impact on their lives. She then described going to North Wales to make their film, holding the baby Patric sitting on her lap, and a more alarming visit from Philip to Great Massingham many years later. 'He was drunk. His mad grinning face appeared at the window. I let him in and he was immediately extremely obnoxious. My parents were there. My father said, "D'you think I ought to hit him?" '

Meanwhile, I continued to telephone Quentin Crisp in New York. Often there was no reply and I guessed that he might be out at lunch or perhaps away performing in some distant city. When I did get through to him, his mood was variable. Sometimes he sounded merry, full of friendly alertness, consciously rising to the occasion and responding keenly to a biographer's questions. On other occasions he sounded tired and vague and used the all-embracing word 'Wonderful!', which left me feeling uncomfortable and embarrassed to be bothering him. I did not tell him I had been to Flackwell Heath or Sutton, knowing that he was not interested in such things and fearing that these explorations might cast me in a bad light. He was still caught up in contemporary stunts and fanfares. On the day of my visit to High Wycombe he had appeared by video or satellite in a bizarre pop concert in the Royal Festival Hall. From time to time I managed to ask him a direct question. Who went bail for him in 1944? 'Victor Brightmore.' Where did he first meet Miss Lumley Who Can Do No Wrong? 'Oakley Street.' I dared not ask bolder questions like what was the real name of Thumbnails or who was the Czechoslovakian gentleman with the unpronounceable name? I would later discover that this latter figure was Polish not Czech, but this was as far as I got.

During the summer of 1999 I continued to gather snippets of information about both my characters, throwaway comments from many sources. At his house in Shepherd's Bush, George Melly greeted me in a toga nightgown, gave me a pink gin and described his famous meeting with Quentin in the Bar-B-Q café in King's Road where the food was so disgusting. I told him that Quentin had been surprised to be called 'portly', but when Melly started describing Quentin's 'authoritative, king-like' manner he added, *'Portly* wasn't far off.' Like thousands of others, Melly missed the point about Quentin's awful room in New York, expressing amazement that he couldn't get himself a more comfortable place. Another old friend of both Quentin and Philip, who came to see me at this time, was the poet Oliver Bernard. He spoke vividly of Quentin's courtesan-like aura but wasn't sure to which court in particular he belonged. He said, 'Quentin was able to think and speak at the same time', and added obliquely, 'I don't know why I feel so much gratitude towards him.' According to Bernard, Philip O'Connor had something in common with the equally provocative poet George Barker, but Philip was 'intellectually mixed up' whereas Barker was 'very clear, better for me, a task master, and he stayed in the same place with the same family'. Many of those I spoke to had never heard of Philip O'Connor but I was excited when the literary critic Derwent May instantly recalled him as 'a man of the gutter' and delighted when at the mention of his name Malya Woolf simply made a drinking gesture and left it at that. Many of those I spoke to were unaware of my long friendship with the two men, asking tentatively, 'Did you ever meet Quentin Crisp?' or, like Linda Mitchell, expressing utter astonishment that I had actually known Philip O'Connor in person.

Like all biographers, I also met confusion and discouragement – and occasional ribaldry. At a wedding in Chelsea Sir Christopher Bland solemnly informed me that after meeting Quentin Crisp with the Pinters he had played tennis with him, beating him in two sets. Over a drink in the Charing Cross Hotel, Paul Potts's biographer Mark Holloway said simply, 'My memory is getting very rotten', and when I asked the archivist at Newnham College, Cambridge, if any contemporaries of Philip O'Connor's wife Jean Hore might still be alive, she replied, 'It's rather a long shot, isn't it?' From Harold Pinter, to whom I had written about Quentin Crisp, I got a disappointing handwritten postcard, reading 'Dear Andrew Barrow, Sorry unable to talk about anyone at the moment. Yours Harold P.' From the Chris Beetles Gallery, whom I asked about the Mervyn Peake drawing of a cat with which Quentin had been enraptured, I got the lofty response, 'Dr Beetles doesn't know the drawing.' The Peake family were more helpful on this score, quickly sending me a coloured copy of the drawing through the post.

Some of my research required a certain amount of subterfuge. I had several conversations with the secretary of the Old Boys' Association at Denstone College, without enlightening him that the pupil called Denis Pratt had transformed himself into Quentin Crisp. He was happy to provide what little information he had and even asked me to give 'Mr Pratt' the school's best wishes, but became impatient when I enquired after the boy called Webb who had been a friend of Denis Pratt. 'May I ask why you want to know this information?' But then he back-pedalled, 'I get lots of enquiries like this. Don't worry!' Some of these episodes ended happily. A few weeks after receiving Harold Pinter's terse postcard, I met the playwright at a party in a Bayswater garden – though I was now too tongue-tied to do little more than register the great man's linen trousers and canvas gym shoes. While I gazed down in embarrassment he told me that he had known a lot about Quentin Crisp before he met him but added, 'I never really knew him very well.' Instead, he questioned me about his life in New York and asked, 'Is he lonely?' Later he said, 'Give him my best', or something like that and then, finally, almost apologetically, 'What is your name?'

The following day, 22 June, I telephoned Quentin in New York and told him of this encounter with Mr Pinter. He sounded bright and obliging and so sweet-tempered that I felt an impulse to see him again. I also managed to get a few more answers. His old employer Mr MacQueen had committed suicide. Miss Lumley did not die in a swimming pool. The pregnant actress whose cottage he'd been in when the bombardment of London started was called Catherine Morley. She had later married a Mr Reed and appeared in the audience at New-castle. No, he had never been to a St James's Street club, which was how he had described the atmosphere at Harraps, the publishing firm, and, no, he had never chopped parsley. New York, he told me, was just beginning to be hot.

I also made further trips to see people and places out of London. At the end of May I had driven in heavy rain, accompanied by the girl who had still not accepted my marriage proposal, to see Croesor. 'That's where the witches live,' said the proprietor of the hotel in the next valley where we put up for the night, and the following day we found that the remote village on the edge of Snowdonia had changed very little during the thirty-six years since Philip O'Connor's departure – and lost none of its magic. There was no sign of new buildings, the chapel was as dominant as ever and the first home Philip and Nicolle had occupied was still tucked into its side like a lean-to. Again I approached the village with a sense that there was something sordid, sad, intrusive and 'odd' about my doing so and it was not until we had started the business of knocking on people's doors that things began to go swimmingly. Most of the people Philip had described in *Living in Croesor* were still there and seemed to speak of him as if he had only just left, a few months earlier. A man called Tudur Owen, who had taken the photographs for Philip's book, began by asking, 'Do you want to know the truth, the whole truth and nothing but the truth about Philip O'Connor?' but then clammed up and spoke instead of dark troubles in some Croesor families: people killed by bulls, suicides, accidental drownings, illegitimacies. He asked of Philip, 'Was he famous? I tried to read *Memoirs of a Public Baby*. He hasn't got verbs in his sentences.'

In an attractive farmhouse a little outside the village, I found Giovanna Bloor, whose surgeon husband Kenneth had been one of the group of men who went drinking with Philip at the local inn, leaving their wives to battle with their children and the weather. 'All charismatic, dynamic, attractive men, spending money that wasn't theirs, and dying of drink-related illnesses – we fall for them, don't we?' She put me in touch with Eleanor Brooks, who lived in another lovely house in an adjacent valley and who spoke more zestfully of Philip – 'the pure brilliance of his chatter' and the 'arrogance of his bearing'. Eleanor and Jeremy Brooks had kept in touch with Philip after he left Wales – 'Philip remained slim, he never got a beer belly' – and he had been staying with them in Kentish Town when he met Panna Grady. Eleanor told me about the suitcase and the silver cup I mentioned in Chapter Fifteen.

In the village we called on Auntie Gwen, who had sent a note of sympathy to Panna the previous year, and who still lived in the same house and still possessed the eyes of 'unmatched purity' which Philip had marvelled over. We then went out of the village to Bryn Hyfrid, where Philip and Nicolle had lived for four years. There were now four cars outside this tumbledown row of cottages and a modern children's swing but otherwise the place, with its wonderful view up the mountains, can have changed very little. In the first cottage we found Nellie Jones, one of the stars of *Living in Croesor*, of which Philip had given her a copy, inscribed 'To Nellie, with love, with wonder, with respect'. She said immediately, 'I miss them. We used to get on very well' and told me quite a lot about his life there. He would drink wine at home which he got from Penrhyndeudraeth. 'On credit?' I asked. 'I don't know that they trusted him there,' she replied. She told me he had cooked a lot of shrimps. 'He was a moody fellow, always going off to London, but I got on with him all right.' Philip's cottage had now been combined with the one next door but the current occupant, a long-haired man with vaguely oriental looks showed me the upper front room where Philip had worked on his books and broadcasting ideas. After Philip's departure in 1965 the house had been rented by a writer called Thomas Blackburn, who wrote a book called *Clip of Steel*. 'He was quite different,' said Nellie. 'He talked sense.' We later took Nellie Jones for a drive round the village and to a remote farmhouse high above the village where the occupant carves fancy walking-sticks. I asked if Philip O'Connor would ever have made his way up here and Nellie replied, 'I don't think he would have had the patience, would he?'

A few weeks later, on 15 July, I had the patience, in spite of a hangover, to make a trip to Swanage on the Dorset coast to see Philip's old friend Denis Lowson, who had also come to the O'Connor celebration. Since separating from Annie Mygind, Lowson had quietly prospered as a painter and found a new wife called Marja. He had mixed feelings about Philip, spoke of his 'exploitative drunkenness' and 'innate nobility of nature'. He also described two significant journeys with Philip, the first in 1958 to enable him to conduct the interviews for *The Lower View* and the second, in northern France in 1972, to try to wean him off the bottle. When I asked Lowson if he had known Quentin Crisp in Charlotte Street, he at first denied all knowledge of him but then asked, 'Is that the man in New York with the funny hat?'

Amused by this stray remark, I drove on from Swanage to Somerset, passing through Yeovil, where I made no attempt to locate the house where Mrs O'Connor and her two children had lived briefly at the end of the First World War but long enough for her to found the Somerset Cigarette Agency, and eventually reached Evercreech at tea-time. The point of my visit to this quiet village was partly to see Barbara Markham, whom Quentin Crisp had described in *The Naked Civil Servant* as 'the greatest trouser taperer in the world'. I found Mrs Markham seated at her sewing-machine and speaking on the telephone. 'I've done *part* of your bedspread,' she was saying, 'but I haven't finished it yet.' Barbara Markham had first met Quentin in the late 1940s, introduced to him by Angus McBean's friend Esther Grant. 'I think I'd been warned by Esther what to expect,' she said. She had later done a number of sewing jobs for him, taking the tail off a shirt and relining the overcoat which he was still wearing in New York. Later, Mrs Markham and I strolled through the village to an outlying house called The Old Kennels, now the home of Esther Grant's daughter Julia and her husband Nigel Keen, whose wedding Quentin had attended in 1960. Here, we settled in the kitchen and talked about the curious people in Quentin's circle long ago, such as a man who made extremely smart, tiny sheepskin bootees with high heels. 'My mother would have talked your hind legs off,' said Julia. 'She absolutely adored Quentin. He appealed to her totally, his integrity.' As I left Evercreech I noticed that the local drama group were putting on a production of *Spinechiller* in the village hall. Wasn't that the play that had flopped at the Duke of York's before Quentin's show went on?

Back in London I continued my work in fits and starts. I ploughed through innumerable press cuttings about Quentin Crisp, which told me nothing new, and a more select handful of articles and reviews about Philip O'Connor, which told me much more. I may have been a born researcher but I was not a very thorough one. I learnt that there were letters to Philip from Cecil Day-Lewis, John Masefield, Herbert Read and others in the University of Texas but I had no intention of going through the irksome rigmarole of seeking these out. Instead I unearthed little details like the fact that Quentin Crisp's sister had left £6,040 when she died in 1976 and the fact that living in the same block in Battersea as the Pratts in 1925 was one of John Gielgud's aunts. Do such details add or detract from my story, and was it interesting that I bothered to take the same railway journey from Victoria to Sutton that Quentin's father would have taken ninety years earlier, passing the same churches, warehouses, pubs and many of the same fixtures and fittings on the railway line itself which Mr Pratt would have seen as his train trundled through Balham, Mitcham Junction and Hackbridge? And that, at the end of the journey, I would find that Sutton Town Hall, where Quentin Crisp had made his first public appearance, as a fairy in *A Midsummer Night's Dream*, had been pulled down thirty years earlier?

At the beginning of the year I had made my first attempt to see John Berger, on hearing that he was appearing in a play being staged in the unlikely environment of the Aldwych Underground station. One evening I had tried to get into the station, but could find no main entrance or stage door or sign of life, and when I tried to buy a ticket for the show I encountered only an answering machine saying that all tickets had been sold. I then rang Berger's home in the French Alps and spoke to a lady with a warm foreign voice, who said she had come in from shovelling snow. She would not give me Berger's number in London but told me to ring again in a few weeks' time. I eventually spoke to him in Paris on 20 September. The conversation was very cheerful, his voice was rich and accommodating and the trickle of water in the background suggested that he was speaking to me from a kitchen – or his bath. He cast an agreeable light on everything, made Philip O'Connor's life seem complete, triumphant, happy and worthwhile. He also praised Panna Grady, calling her 'a wonderful person who gave Philip many years of happiness'. When I asked about

Philip's qualities as a poet there were sighs and silences, but he spoke gently about the *Guardian* review that had so upset Philip, and insisted, 'I wasn't just being nice to a friend. It was sincere. I thought the book very remarkable.' Eventually he said that some people had arrived and he would have to stop.

Meanwhile, I had had an unexpected message from Stephen Fothergill telling me that he had found a telephone number for Bobbie Battersby. No one in Philip's family or circle had known Bobbie Battersby's whereabouts for many years. Philip had always talked with affection about his affair with her at the end of the war – it had produced his first son – but had made no attempt to find her. With considerable excitement I now telephoned this mystery woman at an address in Leamington Spa and was instantly struck by her vitality and enthusiasm. She immediately called me 'Darling' and agreed to see me on her next visit to London. She would make her way from Marylebone Station to Eldon Road on her fold-up bicycle.

In person Bobbie Battersby was even more high-spirited than on the telephone: a small, fit woman with long white hair, an exuberant manner and an active life. Though now eighty years old, she had recently attended the Deauville Film Festival on her magic bicycle and the previous summer she had taken part in a charity bike ride between St Petersburg and Moscow. She had also been an Aldermaston marcher and had three phases living in New York. She described herself as 'a great exhibitionist', 'an unmarried great-grandmother' and 'a lazy fucking bitch who's always been kept'. She also said that she had been 'left of the bloody Labour Party for sixty or seventy years'. Over lunch on 28 September she drank a bottle of Chablis, banged the table, raised her arms and forgot my name, but never lost the thread. 'Philip represented a great deal that I aspire to,' she said. 'I've never met anyone like him.' She was largely ignorant of the life he'd led after leaving her. 'I'd always hoped he'd become more successful. I never heard any of his broadcasts.' She described herself as 'the ugliest of his girlfriends' – and spoke of her son a few weeks younger than me, living in London but more fragile than most of Philip's children. 'Are you bored?' she asked more than once. Finally she said she would like to write to Panna Grady – 'and thank her for looking after this magnificent character, for keeping him alive, preserving him and protecting him from the stupidity of society. She must have suffered. But she suffered for love. Philip was worth keeping going.' I gave her Panna's address, went out with her, watched this unsung figure in Philip's life – 'I get no mention anywhere, darling' – unfold her bicycle and set off joyfully down the street.

Two days later I took a train to the South of France. I had not seen Panna Grady for over a year and had heard that she had not been well and had even had a spell in one of the hospitals where Philip had been, though her voice on the telephone always sounded jubilant and refreshing. I also missed that generous sweetness of which I had received so much in the past. And I was excited to be back in France, embraced by the Continent, back on Philip's territory, plugging into his magic once again.

Emerging from Avignon station on the afternoon of 30 September, I waited a while before Panna drew up. Her hair was now blondish and she wore cotton shorts. The windscreen of her car had a long crack across it which she hoped the police wouldn't notice. On the dashboard was a letter which had arrived that morning from Bobbie Battersby, reaching France in record time. In it Bobbie said that she had gone straight to the Post Office in Gloucester Road after leaving my flat, and purchased this airmail form. She admitted she was 'pissed' but praised Panna effusively for being 'faithful to a genius' and for 'keeping Philip away from the psychiatric scene'. As I digested these ideas, Panna had other thoughts to express, sometimes taking both her hands off the steering wheel in order to gesticulate more effectively.

On my visit the previous year I had stayed with Tony Daniells at his house in Flaux. By now Tony had already migrated to his house near Malaga and Panna had arranged for me to stay with Philip's daughter Allaye and her two sons, Eli and Owen, at her house in Uzès, which had several large bare rooms. Part of my reason for this trip was to talk to Allaye about her father. That night she issued vigorous instructions to her boys – 'And your bedtime is *nine*. You read till half past nine. Is that clear?' – and went out with me to a restaurant. Here she described how, at the age of fourteen, she had remet her father after a long absence. In the summer of 1973 she had been escorted to Boulogne by friends of her mother, having arranged to meet Philip at the hoverport. She had no idea what he would look like. 'He was very drunk. He was wearing a fluffy white coat. "You must be my daughter," he said. I shook hands with him. The couple with me were terribly worried about handing me over to this man but I was completely happy. My mother had agreed to this trip on condition that I paid for it myself. I had saved for it. I'd had a holiday job. It was the start of my attempt to get to know him. It took years and years and years. But I'm a very determined person. It was very painful. There were lots of tantrums. On my part.' During the evening, Allaye said nothing of the 'dark things' to which Patric had referred, but had quite a lot to say about her mother. She told me that Nicolle was 'more difficult to understand than Philip'. After Philip had left in 1967, Nicolle had never said anything unfair about him but she had banished his image, photographs of him, from the house. She had later lived with a one-legged sculptor called Cyril Winskill and had died in 1992, aged fifty-three, a victim of cancer.

The following morning Panna collected me and drove me out to Fontarèches, where I planned to rifle again through Philip's papers. I found the wooden room unchanged though the bed was now some-times occupied by Maxim or Felix when they visited their mother. Panna had found more for me to study – 'I opened this drawer. I thought it had tools in it, but *more files!*' – and I scribbled down a whole lot more stuff that has been incorporated into this story. Over the garden wall while I worked three or four lorries or tractors seemed to be preparing a new building site, certainly making noises which would have driven Philip berserk. Later, when it was quieter, I sat in the walled yard at the small round table where Philip had last held court. Panna ministered to me, as she had to Philip, suggesting I move the table further into the sun and then placing a mug containing heather in it, followed by various snacks served in beautiful duck-egg blue bowls made by her sister. 'You will join me, won't you?' I pleaded. 'You won't just serve me?' But to no avail. From inside the house came pointless cries of 'Be quiet!' as Panna wrestled with four collies. Later we went for a walk along the edge of a vast field in front of the neighbouring chateau, through picturesque ups and downs and across a road where the dogs chased a car and then a bicycle in an imbecile way. Panna continued talking, oblivious to these dramas. She told me she doesn't mind at all not being mentioned in the latest Allen Ginsberg biography, but she objects to the suggestion in Ted Morgan's book *Literary Outlaw* that she had 'pursued' William Burroughs. She asked me whom I had met on my researches. Had I seen Miss Goad? How would I interweave Quentin Crisp?

I returned to London the following evening and telephoned New York. This time Quentin Crisp picked up the telephone in that rather clumsy, clattering way that old people do – but then managed his usual full-throated '*Ohhh – yes?*' Again I attempted to ask him a few questions but his replies were discouraging – 'I can't remember. It's all so long ago' – and when I quoted some ancient witticism, he replied, 'What terrible things I said!' He then revealed that he was being forced to come to London at the end of November. I expressed horror at this idea, but was also excited by it. He said, 'I must do what the Policeman says.' I replied, recalling his threat at the end of *The Naked Civil Servant*, 'Weren't you meant to murder a policeman?' to which he managed to chortle, but I put down the telephone convinced that Quentin Crisp simply wanted to give up, to forget, to die.

$-30-$

A Significant Death

Douglas Vanner intended to carry on to the end. From
within, his position might be undermined; he would
never give way before a frontal assault. One day he
would just collapse quietly; a heap of infinitesimally
thin, brightly coloured tinsel would lie on the ground,
drift and rustle away in the wind.

ROLAND CAMBERTON, *Scamp*, 1950

Quentin Crisp had been announcing his likely demise in little bleeps
for some time. In February 1999 he had written or dictated an
article for the *Guardian* describing the blessings of death. 'By the time
you are my age you are longing for it,' he said. 'My body is dying on
me. I carry it like an old overcoat. It's horrible. You start to smell –
the smell of death. I no longer see properly. I need to wear glasses
when I go out but am far too vain. So I walk the streets blind.' And
he added, 'The absolute nothing of death is a blessing. Something to
look forward to.'

During the rest of the year, these thoughts gained momentum and
to everyone he met he made jokes about how ancient he was and how
happy he would be to be dead. 'I look forward to being extinct.' 'I've
outlived my wardrobe.' 'My siblings would be furious to think that
I'd outlived them all', 'I attribute my longevity to bad luck' and 'I
wouldn't wish eternal life on my worst enemy.' During a taxi journey
up Fifth Avenue with an interviewer named Ian Ayres he leant back,
folded his arms over his chest and said, 'I shall soon be in my coffin,
in eternal sleep. Won't that be wonderful?' There were also reports

that he had started to clear up his room. 'I don't want my relations to have to go through the garbage to get at the good stuff.'

Of course there was nothing new about Quentin's affection for the grim reaper. Even as a child he had been suicidal. During the war he had searched London for his 'own true bomb'. When I first met him in the 1960s and asked about the rumour that he planned eventually to commit suicide, he had hinted that the Beaufort Street gas-fire might do the trick. In *The Naked Civil Servant* he had written ambiguously about suicide, seeing it as either 'a gesture of frustration made by the victim of an unsuitable lifestyle' or as 'the last graceful gesture of someone whose style has been completely mastered'. A surprising number of his acquaintances had killed themselves: Mr MacQueen who'd run the advertising firm, Mr Palmer whom he'd been accused of importuning outside the Hippodrome, and even Philip O'Connor had made half-hearted attempts during his adolescence. I also remembered Quentin's admiration for a not-so-young man at the As You Like It who had thrown himself out of the window following the death of his mother. 'I'm full of praise,' he had shocked us by cooing. 'The window. Wonderful. Where else could he go?' In one of his film reviews he had given an unblinking account of this particular form of self-destruction, with body parts scattered over a wide area and the policemen wondering which bit was which, but he still found it an attractive notion or solution. In the closing months of his life he talked of his committing suicide with comic gentility – 'I *know* I should' – but blamed his inherent timidity for not doing so. The writer Clive Fisher reports him as saying, 'I can't throw myself under a car or leap from a skyscraper. It's very difficult – you see, I'm a nancy.'

He also yearned for what he called a significant death. 'I don't want to die and people to say, "I thought he was dead already." ' For many years he caused a frisson with his remark, 'It would be nice to be murdered', and now he was a bit more specific. 'My fondest hope is to die at the hands of a murderer. In America, the truly great are always murdered.' The more grisly and spectacular his death the better. At calmer moments, he also relished the idea of dying alone. 'I would have thought that was the *ideal* way to go. To die surrounded by people, you would have to die and be *polite* at the same time.'

This was all very brave, funny and very true to himself – and his reasons for wanting to die were increasing week by week. Like the character he had inspired in Roland Camberton's novel, Quentin's internal position was now 'undermined'. His body was packing up and he was suffering bouts of unbearable pain. Thanks to carpal tunnel syndrome he had completely lost the use of his left hand and even when he tried to walk a couple of blocks, he needed to pause and lean against the wall. In the afterword to the omnibus edition of his three autobiographical works he would state, 'I am now very ill with prostate cancer, an enlarged heart and eczema' and cast a dark shadow over his whole life by adding, 'My tale has not been a happy one.' In letters to England he claimed the hernia now hung down to his ankles and when friends rang him, they were sometimes met by a voice 'shrivelled in misery' and tortured cries as the telephone flew from his hand. The journalist Simon Hattenstone recalls being met with cries of 'Oh no, *oh God*, oh, oh, *oooohhhhhh*.' And another friend telephoning from England was dismayed to hear Quentin scream, '*Jesus Fucking Christ!*' I am lucky that I never got such a reception, which would have left me feeling distraught with guilt.

It says much for Quentin's willpower that he was able to surmount these terrible episodes and still present himself to most of the world with all his impish imperiousness and gorgeousness. There were certainly some good times at the end of his life and the time spent with new friends like Phillip Ward, who would later become his executor, seems to have brought him some comfort and consolation. It has also been argued that Mr Largo, 'the Policeman', added a purpose to the end of his life, by arranging for him to play to captivated capacity audiences in many parts of America. Those who saw his final performances noted the 'hushed expectation' before the performance and, though he often needed assisting onto the stage, the way he 'glowed with an extraordinary life force' once he got going. Someone somewhere will have a list of all his appearances during that final year. I only know that he appeared in St Louis in March 1999 and gave his last six public appearances at Cleveland, Ohio, in early October.

But by this time he faced the spectre he might have described as worse than death. The Policeman wanted him to undertake a six-city tour of England. During October there was a great deal of worry and confusion about the trip, which naturally increased when Quentin spent a few days in hospital and then announced, 'Not only are they sending me to England. I am being sent to dreadful places like Leeds and Manchester.' The trip was cancelled and then reinstated. Among friends who strongly advised him to cancel was Simon Hattenstone. On 31 October Crisp and Hattenstone had supper together and discussed the matter. Quentin was now in too much pain to walk to the closest restaurant but bold enough on arriving there by taxi to order chicken soup, fishcakes with mash and a glass of Scotch. Hattenstone again told him to cancel. Quentin said he couldn't let people down but became apoplectic when Hattenstone told him that at least he would be playing to adoring audiences. 'No, no, no! They hate me in England! *Hate me!* You see, this is the difference between England and America! In England, they will come because they despise you, to laugh at you! In England, they stopped me in the streets, they beat me! They *spat* at me!' The following day Hattenstone rang Quentin again and told him he must see a doctor. Quentin replied that he couldn't afford one. In confident North Country tones, Hattenstone then gave Crisp 'a good bollocking' and told him not to be 'so daft'. Crisp promised that he would consult a doctor.

To this health crisis was added a real stage drama. Earlier that autumn the popular, highbrow Bush Theatre in London announced that it would be putting on a one-man show about Quentin Crisp, starring the drag star Bette Bourne and written by the Bush's literary manager Tim Fountain. Quentin Crisp's room on East 3rd Street would be painstakingly reproduced on stage and Bourne would deliver a monologue drawn from Crisp's writings. Bourne and Fountain had visited Quentin earlier in the year and spent an amusing hour or two discussing the project and taking photographs of the room. Though he had agreed to the idea, Quentin supposedly remained ambivalent about it. He was said to have declared, 'I don't want it and I won't have it' and apparently told the *Daily Telegraph* at the end of October that he was dreading it. He predicted, 'It will be a merciless play, England is a merciless country to start with,' and explained, 'Mr Bourne has never been reverential in his life.' If he was in England, he would certainly not go and see the show, which was taking place in what he described as 'a terrible theatre in Shepherd's Bush'. Then on 5 November he was quoted in the *Evening Standard*, saying, 'Of course I don't mind at all that they are doing this play' and expressing admiration for Bette Bourne and his hope that the show would be 'a great success'.

At this stage his own tour of England was still undecided. On 6 November he was quoted as saying, 'I was coming but now I'm not' and adding beguilingly, 'I don't know whether I'm coming or going.' When it was eventually decided that he would come to England, he wrote to his niece Frances Ramsay, 'I have begged, pleaded and wept in an all-out effort not to be sent to England' and he ended his letter, 'It is true that I hoped never ever to return to England. Yours helplessly Quentin Crisp.' This sounds serious, but now, more than ever, everything Quentin Crisp said needed to be taken with handfuls of salt and the question about whether or not to come to England only echoed his much bigger dilemma about whether to live or die. At around this time he had told a reporter, 'I know that I am like a guest standing at my host's door saying that I must go – but not going.'

On 10 November the Bette Bourne show, which borrowed the title *Resident Alien* from Quentin's last book, opened at the Bush Theatre and received universally good reviews with most of the leading critics praising Bourne's performance and the tenderness of Fountain's script. I saw the show three days later and telephoned Quentin to assure him there was 'nothing fatuous' about it and that the performance by Bette Bourne was wholly respectful. Quentin now confirmed to me that he was definitely coming to England the following weekend. He sounded very perky and full-throated and cheerfully explained, 'Most of the time I shall be in a wheelchair.' I told him he would be like the late Lady Diana Cooper, whom I had seen using this form of transport in extreme old age – and he laughed loudly. He hoped he would not be staying at the Chelsea Arts Club, where the rooms were 'so cold'. I did not ask him any questions and I told him not to worry about my book, which was anyway far from finished, and though I had booked tickets for his show in London, I made no attempt to pin him down to a meeting. It was our last conversation.

Quentin's final week in New York began with him signing his will, in which he left whatever money he had in equal portions to his three nieces, and a few small legacies to their descendants. On signing this document he had apparently declared, 'Now I can die!' During the next few days he submitted himself to more interviews with English journalists, to all of whom he sounded on good, even sparkling form, especially when he spoke of his forthcoming death which he now seemed to be predicting as extremely imminent. Alan Jackson of *The Times* asked him if he had made plans for his funeral and wondered if there would be a shrine to which acolytes could flock and pay tribute. 'Oh I do hope not,' he replied giggling. 'No flowers, no candles, no long faces standing around in the rain looking down at a hole in the ground while someone drones on about how wonderful I was. I'd rather be shuffled off. Just drop me into one of those black plastic bags and leave me by the trash can.' He made the same joke to David Usborne of the *Independent* and added that he expected death to come very soon. But how soon? To Usborne, whom he saw on Thursday 18 November, he said he would like to die in New York and admitted that he had now arranged to be 'cut open' for hernia surgery the moment he returned from England, which suggested that he was by no means certain that he would die while abroad. To Gyles Brandreth, interviewing him for the *Sunday Telegraph*, he spoke about heaven where he hoped to meet some of the nastiest tyrants of the past. 'I want to meet Pol Pot and sit down with him quietly and ask him what he thought he was doing.' When Brandreth asked him about the approaching millennium, he replied, 'I won't be here. I will be hiding.'

All these reporters seem to have found Quentin Crisp looking neatly pressed and noticed that his appetite was good and that on one occasion he humped five spoonfuls of sugar into his coffee. On the Friday, a photograph of Quentin was taken by a certain Jeff Mermelstein which showed him looking bloated and ill, more like a drunken sea captain than a little old witch. That afternoon he left America on a British Airways flight from JFK to London Heathrow. He was accompanied by a young man called Chip Snell, who had escorted him on recent trips across America and knew him well. He brought with him just two small pieces of hand-luggage containing only one change of clothes. A rumour later circulated in London that the stewardesses had not recognized him and his requests for whisky were ignored, but Tim Fountain's TV film *The Significant Death of Quentin Crisp* indicates that Quentin was thoroughly pampered and took full advantage of the free drinks, lining up a row of little whisky bottles on the tray in front of him. Changing flights at Heathrow, he was recognized by other passengers in his wheelchair and waved impishly at them.

On arrival at Manchester Airport he was mobbed by a few well-wishers and greeted by Mark Ball, organizer of the tour, to whom Quentin appeared in very good form. Ball then drove him to 7 Claude Road, Chorlton-cum-Hardy, where he was scheduled to stay while appearing at Manchester's Green Room. Quentin's niece Frances Ramsay later described 7 Claude Road as 'a lovely house, warm, cosy, arty, with soothing dark colours'. On entering the house, Quentin lit up at the sight of a large open fire in the living room but shocked his hostess Emma Ferguson by his appearance. 'I expected him to look *old* but he looked *ill*.' After a glass or two of brandy, he declined supper and at about six o'clock he climbed the stairs to his bedroom. According to Fountain's film, he carried with him the three-quarters-full bottle of brandy. Also according to Fountain's film, he later raised his head from the pillow to receive a goodnight peck on the cheek from Chip Snell. If it is true that he had now come to expect this ritual, it indicates a final eleventh-hour reversal of the withdrawn behaviour he had cultivated all his long life. At 2.30 in the morning he was heard going to the bathroom.

At 8.30 on Sunday morning, 21 November, Chip Snell went into the bedroom and on failing to rouse Quentin Crisp summoned Emma Ferguson, who knew immediately that her famous guest was dead. Some pills for angina were found in his hand and the brandy bottle was mysteriously empty beside the bed, but these factors would have no bearing on the fact that he had suffered a massive heart attack. An hour or two later, the young publisher Matthew Thomas rang Claude Road from London but found the household in shock and was told nothing. By this time the police had already called – the constable's name was Cissey – and Quentin Crisp's body had already been taken to Manchester Royal Infirmary. This task had been performed by two undertakers, who were themselves homosexual and greatly honoured to perform this duty. On account of Quentin Crisp's celebrity, a post-mortem was ordered.

The news of his death broke early on Sunday afternoon. I was telephoned by my friend Mary Killen with the words 'Isn't it sad about Quentin Crisp?' and felt momentarily overwhelmed by what had happened. His death made the headlines of the six o'clock news that night, following items about the resignation of Lord Archer as mayoral candidate and the death of forty people in Sri Lanka. In America that night, Quentin's death was the second item on CNN news. The following morning's papers carried front-page stories about him and there were lengthy obituaries in all the broadsheets. The *Daily Telegraph* devoted a leading article to him under the heading 'Crisp and Courteous', and the speaker on Radio 4's 'Thought for the day' also sang his praises. In the *Independent* Clive Fisher pondered over the 'bewildered passivity' Quentin had presented when in fact he was 'self-sufficient, tenacious and determined'. The *Daily Mail* quoted Quentin as saying, 'Homosexuality is a wretched existence . . . I didn't like it, I didn't want it, I wouldn't wish it on anyone.' The tabloids also had fun – 'The Queen Is Dead' was the *Mirror*'s headline – and dramatized or sentimentalized his death by stating that he had 'collapsed and died in a chum's house', and exaggerated his latterday lifestyle by saying, 'He never paid for meals, buttonholed strangers and expected them to pick up the tabs.' He was inaccurately branded 'the gay campaigner' and the Manchester police were quoted as saying there were 'no suspicious circumstances'.

Quentin Crisp's death was registered by different people in different ways. At lunchtime the following day the actor John Hurt stepped onto the platform at the Savoy Hotel where he was presenting one of the *Evening Standard* theatre awards and begged his illustrious audience's permission to depart from his script and pay tribute to the man to whom in many ways, he said, he owed his career. His final words, 'Bless you Quentin. You're one of the greatest philosophers who ever lived', were followed by a prolonged round of applause. Hurt would later pay a further tribute in *Time* Magazine. Over at the Bush Theatre that night the show went on and Quentin was toasted in champagne at a 'wake' held after the performance.

The same day in Manchester, a post-mortem confirmed that Quentin had not committed suicide and a cremation was arranged to take place two days later on 24 November under an uncharacteristic cloak of secrecy. To avoid media attention, Quentin was cremated under the name of Bernard Smith – with all expenses being paid by the local authorities. The event was attended by Peter and Frances Ramsay, whose attempt to pick up the bill was refused, their son Tim, Chip Snell, Emma Ferguson, the show's promoter Mark Ball and a drag artiste in full regalia called Chloe Poems, who had never met Quentin Crisp. There was no hymn, no music and no priest, but Chip Snell said a few words of tribute. Afterwards there was a small gathering at Claude Road, at which several bottles of wine were drunk – 'Something out of the ordinary', according to Peter Ramsay – accompanied by muffins and Battenberg cake. Chip Snell then flew back to America first class, the empty seat beside him holding the urn containing Quentin's ashes, which would later be distributed in various parts of Manhattan.

Meanwhile, a controversy was raging about the circumstances of Quentin's demise. Several of the news stories that had accompanied the announcement of his death had questioned the suitability of making an ill old man return to the country he professed to hate. The tour's organizers made apologetic defensive statements. 'It was Quentin's choice,' said a man called Ryan Levitt. 'We gave him the opportunity to cancel four weeks ago and we strongly felt that he would, but he said he wanted to tour England one last time.' A new character of whom I had never heard called Patrick Newley emerged to declare, 'When I spoke to him two or three weeks ago in New York he was clearly not happy about coming over here for the tour. At his age it was too much. I rather think he might still be alive if he had not come across here.'

Others shared this view – which of course ignores the fact that Quentin desperately wanted to die. In a letter to the *Guardian* Judy Sproxton complained that Crisp's 'gentle readiness to acquiesce has been tragically exploited'. Others were simply incensed that Quentin had died in what they considered such an unglamorous place as Manchester, let alone Chorlton-cum-Hardy. The dramatist Bernard Kops, who had known him in the 1940s, said that it was 'tragic that this man who loved the United States had died in a Northern suburb' and even the perceptive Simon Hattenstone, himself born in a Manchester suburb, stated that Quentin would have 'hated' dying in Chorlton-cum-Hardy. Others had different views. Writing in *The Times Literary Supplement*, Patrick O'Connor argued that Chorlton-cum-Hardy was exactly the right place for someone to die 'whose notoriety owed everything to that peculiar mixture of English prurience and hypocrisy'. Back at the Bush Theatre Bette Bourne declared that Quentin Crisp 'would have laughed at his death in a Manchester suburb with the local authority having to pay for everything'.

My own views are still undecided. Sometimes I see the appropriateness of going full circle, ashes to ashes, suburb to suburb. At other times I feel that we had all – I include myself in this – got him in the end, though such a point of view assumes that the heights he had reached in Manhattan were superior to anything he had known back home. And I still cannot rid myself of the idea that he was miserable at the end of his time in New York, though putting a very brave face on it, and that it would have been 'nice', even 'cosy', had he stayed based in England all along and become an outrageously outspoken member of the British establishment. Perhaps, even, Sir Quentin Crisp.

— 3 1 —

Loose Threads

It's impossible, really, to write biographies.

TONY DANIELLS TO ANDREW BARROW, 12 February 2000

Philip O'Connor's death in his last wooden hut caused few repercussions. His cremation had quickly taken place, attended by Panna, Maxim, Felix and Allaye, but his books and possessions, even the king-size nappy under his desk, would remain untouched for weeks or months. Those who knew and loved him would not forget him and there were some who perhaps would not forgive him, but he was allowed to rest in peace. Quentin Crisp's life and death would have immediate ramifications. While floral tributes mounted outside 46 East 3rd Street, his life within the house was instantly dismantled. Boxes were removed by his executor Phillip Ward, including one of linen he had brought from England and never used. The famous telephone number was diverted to Ward's home on the Lower West Side. And the mattress on which Quentin had slept for the last eighteen years was thrown out on the street, to be quickly rescued by the fashion designer Miguel Adrover, who picked it apart, washed the material several times and turned it into a tailored suit which would cause a sensation on the catwalk and draw a paean of praise from *Woman's Wear Daily*. Within a few days the room that Quentin had made notorious had been thoroughly cleaned and there was someone else living there.

The image that Quentin Crisp had created for himself, exaggerated by make-up and fancy dress and the poses he had struck for photographers, continued to flicker in and out of the public consciousness, and his website groaned with people's reactions to his existence. Philip O'Connor's image, darker and brighter in its own peculiar way and also implemented by self-conscious poses, remained indelibly printed in the minds and memories of a small but distinguished group of friends and foes. Quentin Crisp had embraced the whole world and Philip only a very small part of it, but both men had pushed it away when it got too close.

My attempts to capture their two lives were not finished and perhaps can never finish. How and when does a biographer decide he has done enough? During the final dramas of Quentin's life, I had continued to make little stabs at research. On 15 October 1999 I had lunch with Lady Spender at her house in St John's Wood and read Philip O'Connor's letters to her husband. Stephen Spender's views on Philip, as reported by his widow, struck familiar chords: 'He was a bloody nuisance but Stephen liked people on the edge', and 'I think Stephen on the whole was rather bored by drunkenness.' The same week I had seen my old friend Niki, Philip's newly discovered niece, and taken her out to lunch where she would have pleased her grandmother by remarking, 'Good coffee is almost as irresistible as wine.' Niki had a vivid idea of her grandmother and how much she had loved Wimereux, but no photographs of her, and an equally romantic view of her grandfather, who she said had been a gambler in the habit of buying twelve shirts and twelve pairs of shoes at the same time. She also remembered being dandled on Haslam Jackson's knee when he was dying of throat cancer.

A few days later I met Niki's father, an alert and amusing ninety-two-year-old, on one of his trips to London. He told me that his late wife Desirée had always longed to live in France, just as Philip had done, and that Haslam Jackson had been 'very secretive'. He knew very little about his mother-in-law 'Winnie' and reminded me that he had never met her. After this meeting John Trethowan telephoned me and said he was sending me 'a load of stuff' about Haslam Jackson as soon as he could get to a Post Office. This included the cartoon of Jackson done when he was still affluent in 1916, a short obituary of him that had appeared in 1944, revealing that he had worked on the *Salisbury Times* at the start of the war and had been 'highly esteemed for his personal courtesy and ready help', and an undated letter that Jackson had written to Desirée from the NAAFI supply depot at Eynsham, Oxfordshire, in the middle of the war.

This sad little missive gives some indication of the distance that existed between Philip and Desirée and of the mundanity of most people's lives at that time. It begins with the observation that there were 'one or two cheery blokes of a better type' at the depot, but is mainly preoccupied with his wartime wardrobe. 'I think I shall have to have my suitcase along with pyjamas and the old suit and laundry,' he wrote. 'I have had nothing washed since I came here. I will let you know how to send it later on and also the grey overcoat as it gets bitterly cold here. Do not send it till I write again and if meantime you can get my things washed it would help.' On the telephone, I had also spoken to Philip's newly discovered cousin Patricia Portoleau, who remembered Desirée Trethowan's generosity to her as a child and various recent meetings with Philip at the end of his life. She told me she had greatly enjoyed their 'verbal ping-pong matches', but added that her cousin was, 'dare I say, as nutty as a fruitcake'.

Philip's nuttiness or veracity also came under scrutiny when on 19 November of that year I went to see Jill Goodwin, daughter of the farmer from whom Philip had rented the house at Purton Green. In *The Lower View*, Philip had given an idyllic account of his life in Suffolk and written at length about the farmer's wife Mrs Slater, attributing to her 'a schoolgirl's mind, which now and then she would flaunt like a petticoat at me in her large kitchen', and 'a nose which claimed a right to curiosity about matters cultural'. Mrs Slater's daughter, a child at the time, responded with outrage to these comments about her highly intelligent and well-read mother and added despairingly, 'Why, oh why, did he not tell my mother he was hungry? She would have fed him royally and left him alone to enjoy a good meal.' Mrs Goodwin also revealed that her father, who escapes unmentioned in *The Lower View*, later suffered from depression and, like Philip some twenty years earlier, required treatment at the Maudsley Hospital in London.

It is hardly necessary to re-emphasize that there was no rural dimension to Quentin Crisp's life – though it's worth remembering that in

1967 he had paid a long visit to Angus McBean's moated manor-house not far from Purton Green and at some later date had joyfully received half a dozen 'mammoth' eggs laid by some Suffolk hens. Though there was a strong villagey or neighbourhood element to his lifestyle and utterances, his habitat remained steadfastly urban or suburban, filmy or theatrical. In this context I still hoped to see his old friend Joan Rhodes, the only person in this story who links all its separate ingredients and whose distant starry presence had hovered over my childhood. Long before I had heard of Quentin Crisp and Philip O'Connor, I had learnt the excitingly robust name of Joan Rhodes, and thought of her extraordinary exploits on the stage of the Palladium and Metropolitan Music Hall. In December 1999 I sent Miss Rhodes a cautious Christmas card expressing my sadness at the death of our mutual friend and asking her to telephone me. Alas there was no response from Belsize Park and I turned elsewhere for inspiration.

Breakthroughs usually do not happen when one is seeking them. Early in the new millennium year I went to a party in Fulham Road and met a lively, attractive woman who told me that she had worked with Quentin Crisp in Mr MacQueen's display firm at the end of the war. This was Anne Valery, known by Quentin as Mrs Valaoritis. She was reluctant to say too much about Quentin as she was busy writing something about him, as I was, for an anthology which Paul Bailey was editing, but she did not hesitate to put me in touch with a man who had known Quentin well. John Haggarty, she said, was the original 'great unavailable dark man' about whom Quentin had often held forth. I had heard Quentin mention Mr Haggarty many years earlier, in connection with Mr Mackie, and had ascribed to him the familiarity with which Quentin had invested all his acquaintances.

John Haggarty lives in a small village near Arundel in West Sussex. He is a tall, white-bearded man, now about eighty years old, who on the occasion of my visit wore a black beret indoors and a red-spotted neckerchief. His mind is shamingly alert and bursting with illuminating ideas on many subjects. He told me of his friendship with Quentin Crisp in the late 1940s, which I have already described in some detail, and how in 1970 he approached Jonathan Cape about the film rights to *The Naked Civil Servant*, worked on the idea for many months, but felt no anger about the way the project had eventually been taken out of his hands by his friend Philip Mackie. Haggarty had a great deal to tell me about Crisp and was particularly exercised about the novel *Chog*, which he had recently reread. No one had particularly liked this when it came out and John Haggarty now described it as 'a shocking book' which contains 'nothing benign' in it and brings out 'Crisp's real shadow, in the Jungian sense; a deep, deep shadow and a King Lear rage, which only emphasizes the complexity of the man'. He went on to explain, 'Crisp's dark side was not a sexual matter – all that is in the open – but something much darker.' Haggarty still greatly admires his old friend but after reading *Chog* realized that Quentin 'deceived everyone with his marvellous glossy surface' and that 'the act' he had maintained for eighty years was 'only a suit of clothes'.

After this meeting I read *Chog* for the first time and shared John Haggarty's horror that Quentin could have written a book so misanthropic if sometimes very funny, and explored the idea that though published in 1979 it could have been written when the author had more reason for feeling black. On learning that it was in fact written after his career had taken off, I can only surmise that the freakish creature of the title, half-child, half-dog, somehow reflected his own emergence at that time as an international oddball.

By this time I had read all the other books by both Crisp and O'Connor, none of which, not even their best-known works, had I taken much trouble with before. O'Connor's works do not include a *Chog*, all the unpleasantness in his case being on the surface, if not actually worn like a feather in his cap, but in Quentin Crisp's canon there is another book, *How to Go to The Movies*, which has much to tell us about his inner and outer life. This collection of his film reviews, published in 1990, shows him at both his most callous and his most caring. In his review of *Dance with a Stranger*, the film about Ruth Ellis, the last woman to be hanged, he wishes the actual execution had been shown: 'If we could have seen her eyes bulging and her neck distended, oh, how happy we would then have been.' He also makes a number of passing swipes at sex, at one point replacing the word

partner with 'opponent', and describes kissing as 'nibbling away at' –
but this is not the whole picture. In the same book he volunteers that
Shakespeare's sonnets are 'entrancing' and slips into a review of a film
called *Ernesto* – a description of love-making of such astonishing
tenderness as to make all his jokes about sex being a 'mistake' sound
utterly false, which is perhaps how they were meant to be taken anyway.

In February 2000 I combined work with pleasure by spending a
long weekend in the south of Spain with Philip O'Connor's old friend
and neighbour Tony Daniells. For the past twenty or thirty years
Daniells has led an enviably simple life, spending the winter in a house
in the mountains near Malaga and the summers at the house near
Uzès where Philip before his final decline had been a regular caller. At
all costs Daniells avoids cities and when travelling between his two
homes uses side roads rather than the motorway. Tony Daniells is not
an eccentric. He appears healthy, happy and permanently suntanned
and paints vibrant landscapes and still lifes which he sells at an annual
exhibition in France. In some respects he is an opposite of John
Haggarty. He does not seek out people's souls or try to discover the
inner man. Confronted by questions about people's characters, he is
inclined to reply, 'I think everybody's everything' and leave it at that.
Yet his regard for Philip O'Connor had withstood the disapproval of
his friends like Lawrence Durrell and Stephen Spender and his awareness that Panna Grady had suffered on Philip's account. 'Philip barked
people off the premises. Which is a form of honesty, in a way. Because
most people *are* awful. *I'm* awful too.'

I may have learnt more about Tony Daniells on that trip than about
Philip O'Connor and I was more entertained by his comment, 'It's
impossible really to write biographies', than by his complaint about
'the rough, tough Arts and Crafts pottery mug' in which Philip served
wine. On my return to England I was immediately presented with a
larger vista of potential knowledge when I learnt from John Haggarty
that a memorial service for Quentin Crisp would be taking place in
New York on 3 March. Haggarty told me he had received his invitation
from 'the Estate of Quentin Crisp' and in a separate post had come
an invitation to a party after the event hosted by the family, which

suggested that an inner and outer circle had already formed. Haggarty couldn't go and for a while I wondered if I need make the journey. Quentin's life since leaving England had always been beyond my grasp, but I was very keen to meet any of his relations who might be there. I had still made no attempt to contact any of his family, though I had been long aware of the existence of various nieces and great-nieces and great-nephews. After some hesitation I started making telephone calls to America and soon got through to the home of Michele Crawford, the great-niece who lived in New Jersey. She told me that her mother Elaine had already arrived from Chile and her aunt Denise was on her way, and that Frances Ramsay and her husband Peter were coming from England. I said I was writing a book about Quentin and she responded that lots of people were writing books about him. A few days later I got a call from Frances Ramsay, whose voice sounded immensely reassuring, familiar, confident, friendly and chatty, and she began telling me all manner of things now in my narrative, not least that she had visited Quentin's room on East 3rd Street and found it 'rather sad'.

Having now prepared the way I decided to go to New York, flying there on 1 March and staying again at the Gramercy Park Hotel. On arrival I telephoned New Jersey and spoke to Michèle Crawford's mother, Elaine Goycoolea. She sounded foreign and full of vitality. She was baby-sitting. Her daughter and sister Denise Renner were out on the town in Manhattan with Peter and Frances Ramsay and Quentin's executor Phillip Ward. She urged me to join them and told me the address of the restaurant. Here I found Phillip Ward looking businesslike at the end of the table and the cousins exchanging repartee across it. 'I'd forgotten what a snob you are,' Frances Ramsay was telling Denise Renner. Frances is completely English, sensible, humorous and good-natured, looks a little like Quentin when she smiles. Her husband Peter seemed like an Englishman on holiday, a bit bemused by what he had got caught up in. Of the three nieces – I met Elaine later – Denise with her rather piled-up grey hair and grand features bears the strongest and most startling resemblance to her famous Uncle Denis, as they still think of him. The fact that Denise was named after her uncle certainly disproves the idea that he had been some sort of black sheep. What Quentin made of these nieces, and how he would have expressed it, would have been wonderful to know.

Two nights later, on 3 March, all these cousins, joint heiresses to their uncle's estate, assembled in the Great Hall of the Cooper Union building on East 7th Street. I arrived to find a long queue outside and a great deal of clamouring for entry. One young man was dressed as an undertaker, but the audience as a whole seemed to consist mainly of professional-looking couples, almost English in their respectability, the sort of people Quentin would have called 'cosy'. Everyone's attention was on an empty gilded armchair and a small table beside it on which stood a glass of whisky. The evening consisted of about twenty tributes, monologues by friends and admirers of Quentin Crisp. The nieces were the first onto the platform, Frances Ramsay causing a gasp of horror when she revealed that all Quentin's letters to his mother had been lost long ago. All the other speakers seemed to be people Quentin had met since his arrival in New York in 1981 and there were many moments when his life in London seemed lost and forgotten. There were also some puzzling inaccuracies. The actress Sylvia Myles announced that she had introduced Quentin Crisp to John Hurt for the first time a few years earlier in New York. Tim Fountain from The Bush Theatre was there – and so was the English style guru Peter York, dressed in a pale brown coat with a dark velvet collar similar to the one worn by Philip O'Connor in the 1970s.

Afterwards there was a party for about fifty people in a warehouse on 2nd Street where those present let their hair down and poured their hearts out. A great-great-nephew, one of Ian Quentin's older brothers, ran around with a friend, oblivious to the event but with his high cheekbones and distinctive sloping ears providing a potent living reminder of the man whose life we were now toasting with such abandon. During this part of the evening, the third niece Elaine Goycoolea, who has been married more than once and has shortish orange hair, told me that long ago her uncle had refused to allow her to sleep on the floor at Beaufort Street but stressed how kind he'd been to her later in New York, giving her two thousand dollars and saying he didn't want it back and was she sure she didn't want twenty thousand?

Tim Ramsay, son of Frances and Peter, also remembered calling at East 3rd Street, hoping to crash out on his uncle's floor, but Quentin Crisp had failed even to recognize him. Later I met Chip Snell, who had escorted Quentin to England and returned with his ashes, and heard Peter York asking Phillip Ward how much money Quentin had left. Wild rumours circulated on this score and in the heat of the moment I decided to put it about that the figure was in excess of five million dollars. The party ended with warm, friendly uncomplicated hugs and kisses of the sort that no one present had ever exchanged with Quentin himself. Except, perhaps, in the last few weeks of his life.

Back in London the next month, Quentin's life was celebrated with a season of films connected with him at the National Film Theatre. The programme on the opening night, 4 April, included Denis Mitchell's 'World in Action' portrait, followed by an interminable production of *Hamlet* in which Quentin had played Polonius, and was to conclude with Anne Wolff's film *Captain Busby*. This third item started cheerfully enough with Philip O'Connor, bearded and monocled, delivering his opening line, 'Captain Busby put his beard in his mouth and sucked it', which drew a promising burst of laughter from the audience – but then the film broke down.

I see from my diary that on 16 April I took a train to Edinburgh and spent a day in the National Library studying Philip O'Connor's letters and postcards to David Thomson. These are held in neat files held together with drawstrings and contain a fund of personal information which I have used only sparingly in this book. Many cards and letters are written 'under the influence' and during his early days with Panna he often boasts about the quality of whatever he is drinking – 'I would not – I shall not – call Pauillac '62 a superficial wine' – and simultaneously seeks forgiveness for his outpourings. Being a drinker himself, David Thomson would have sympathized with all this and one wonders how he replied to some of these missives. The letters certainly reaffirm my view that Thomson was O'Connor's closest friend.

On 10 May I went and stayed with Frances and Peter Ramsay in their comfortable bungalow overlooking the Teignmouth estuary in South Devon. I arrived in the afternoon and we had tea and then gin and tonics on a spacious verandah equipped with an electrically operated blind. Quentin Crisp never visited this house but some of the family property is there. We had tea from a silver teapot which Frances said Quentin would have known since his childhood, and inside the house is the antique dressing-table that Quentin's mother Baba brought with her when she moved to 'darkest Devonshire' in the early 1930s. Over the last few months the Ramsays had acquired more of Quentin's stuff including a pre-war portrait by Paul Drury entitled *Quentin à Sa Belle Époque*. This rather eerie etching hangs in the bungalow beside the highly stylized pen-and-ink Quentin had done of Frances's dog Walker at roughly the same period. I remarked on the tidiness of the house, compared to Beaufort Street and East 3rd Street, and questioned Frances about her attitude to such matters. She told me she *hates* housework but gets on with it and might well use some of Quentin's money to get a cleaning lady.

During dinner, the Ramsays talked about the controversial circumstances of Quentin's death – Frances said firmly, 'Really, he basically *did* like England. I think he would have been very happy to come here to die' – and about the very fair will he had left. They told me he had left well over $600,000, which was scattered among various building societies and banks. Nine hundred pounds had come to light in an account on the Isle of Man. How and when he had acquired this vast sum and how much money he had when he left England in 1981 remains a mystery. After dinner Peter Ramsay retired to bed and I sat up talking with Frances, whose calm and phlegmatic style is sometimes interrupted by a burst of slightly irreverent laughter. When I described Quentin Crisp as a star, she cheerily responded, 'In *no way* was he a star! He ran himself down far too much!' Eventually I, too, went to bed, taking with me Quentin's book *Colour in Display* published in 1938, of which I had not seen a copy since I had perused one in the British Museum more than thirty years earlier.

A few days later I saw the Ramsays again when they came to London for a celebration at the Drill Hall in Bloomsbury, where Quentin had been scheduled to make four appearances the previous November. Harold Pinter was not, as I had been told, on the stage but a programme of other tributes and short films was offered, after which Frances Ramsay unveiled a mirror in her uncle's honour and quipped that no one must ever dust it. I wondered about the people in the audience and looked around in vain for Joan Rhodes. In the interval I asked several of the older people present if they had been friends of Quentin Crisp but only got the replies 'Alas, no', and 'I'm afraid not. Wish I was.'

By now I had asked enough questions and almost come to the end of my researches. During the late summer of 2000 I visited Wimereux and found the *pâtisserie*, now in the hands of a Monsieur Laurent, still standing with almost everything about it as it must have been long before Philip O'Connor was abandoned there as a child. The three salons, the last one still private, were still there and Calais cakes and other pastries were still displayed in the left-hand window and various sweets in the right. Next door, the former pork butcher's shop now offered photographic services. In the hotel where my new wife and I stayed – in my haste to finish the story I have omitted to mention that we had at last got married – the staff remembered O'Connor as if he had only just left the town. Only Clair de Lune was a disappointment. The house that I had remembered and even written about as grand and imposing now looked small and derelict, its heart ripped out and its façade distressed.

Back in England I tied up a few loose ends or seized opportunities for further research when they arose. At the opening of the new Tate Modern Gallery I accosted Yoko Ono and talked to her about Panna Grady. Yoko shook hands with me twice and told me to give Panna her love. One Saturday morning I found myself in Beaufort Street again and rang the doorbell of Quentin's old home and was welcomed by the young woman who now occupies the whole of the first floor and uses Quentin's room as her sitting room and even has a piano in it. She had no idea that he had lived there twenty years earlier and nothing survives from those days except the window-latches. The mantelpiece has been replaced, so have the skirting-boards and the cornices and the picture rails. Doors now open to a kitchen and a bedroom. And needless to say its new owner keeps it all spotlessly clean.

During these months I made a few final telephone calls. I spoke to Crisp's one-time agent Richard Gollner, who told me only a trickle of money now comes from *The Naked Civil Servant*, and to his original agent Donald Carroll who confirmed that Philip O'Connor was 'absolutely crucial' to the story of Quentin Crisp. I went to a few more libraries – and one auction house. On 19 September forty letters from Quentin Crisp to Hermione Goacher – the relevant contents of which have been incorporated into this narrative – came up for sale at Phillips in New Bond Street. They sold for £720 to a mystery man, bidding on behalf of Trudie Styler, the wife of the pop-star Sting, who planned to give the letters to her husband as a Christmas present. The same month I visited the archives of the Bethlem Royal Hospital and sifted through crayon and pencil drawings that Philip O'Connor had done in the Maudsley during the winter of 1936–7, each item carefully preserved, mounted and stored in purpose-built boxes. The same week I also visited Reading University and consulted the Random House archives which contain bulky files on Quentin Crisp's *The Naked Civil Servant* and Philip O'Connor's *Selected Poems*, both of which were published by Jonathan Cape in 1968. Here I learnt that Tom Maschler had sent Quentin a telegram on 11 January that year reminding him that it was publication day, and that the *Pretoria News* had reviewed Quentin's autobiography under the title, 'Pathetic Misfit's Exposé of Himself'. In the file on O'Connor's book of poems I found that the same newspaper had written, 'O'Connor picks up his subject by the scruff of its neck and drops it on its face, giving it an extra push as it falls.'

Meanwhile I had at last discovered what had happened to Philip's first wife Jean. Earlier attempts to get details of her demise from the relevant Scottish authorities had proved fruitless, no death of a Jean Mary O'Connor being recorded for the likely period, and for a while I entertained the idea that Jean, to whom Paul Potts had attributed the body of a Chinese empress, might still be alive. Only when I asked the authorities to investigate more recent years did I get the information I had been seeking. Jean Mary O'Connor had died at Bangour Village Hospital near Edinburgh on 23 September 1997, after more than fifty years there. The causes of death at the age of eighty-four were given as bronchopneumonia, immobility and schizo-phrenia. God only knows what her life had been like all these years or if there had been any 'breaks in the clouds', but she had outlived her admirers Tambimuttu and Paul Potts and died only eight months before Philip.

Another long-standing matter was resolved when I returned home one night to find a recorded message from Malya Woolf, whose friend-ship with Quentin had extended over half a century, informing me that her friend Joan Rhodes would be happy to see me – and providing me with her telephone number in Belsize Park. I was excited by this news and almost equally thrilled to find that the telephone number was the same as the one I had found in my father's 1955 engagement diary. On dialling the number, I met an answering machine on which a lively voice told me to leave 'a cheerful message'. I endeavoured to do so and on the third attempt spoke to Miss Rhodes herself and arranged to have tea with her the following weekend. I asked if I should bring a cake. She said, 'Yes', and she would try to make cucumber sandwiches.

On 10 September 2000 I made my way to the same basement flat where I had called twenty-nine years earlier and which my father, or so he had told me, had visited sixteen years before that. It was also the flat where Quentin Crisp had often gone to lunch off roast lamb or play Scrabble and where, during visits from America, he had some-times stayed the night. Not everyone moves house as often as Philip O'Connor. Miss Rhodes herself opened the door to me. She is a beautiful striking woman who still does her blondish hair in the style that Laura Knight had captured in the Royal Academy portrait. She wore a flimsy outfit, bearing a leopardskin pattern, partly covered by a black coat on which was pinned an elaborate brooch. I gave her the cake and a bottle of champagne and she showed me into the sitting room where we had talked in 1971, now with its windows open onto a garden where squirrels frolicked.

Here we spent the next three hours drinking tea and eating cucumber sandwiches. Joan Rhodes remained modest or tongue-tied about her theatrical past, referring simply to her time tearing up telephone directories and breaking ten-inch nails as 'when I was working the halls' – but was voluble about Quentin Crisp. Never once, she said, had anyone insulted him when they had gone out together. She allowed me to sift through a pile of letters going back to 1945. I dared not eye them too eagerly but leafed through them casually and jotted down a few facts, which are in the story. 'I am now quite hideous,' he had written to her in 1998 and 'Where will it end?' he had asked in April 1999. She also talked a little about Philip O'Connor and remembered going to the Café Royal with him, but recalled that the outing had been spoilt by his drunkenness. I then tenderly, anxiously, asked her about my father. She remembered going to the Hampstead Golf Club very well, she said, but had no memory whatsoever of the person who had taken her there. My father had simply vanished from her mind.

This was disappointing, but the vital link or connection between my father and the chief characters in this book, between the past and the present, had been made. I left Joan Rhodes's flat expressing the hope that we would meet soon and perhaps play Scrabble together. I have not yet put this plan into action but I hope to do so soon. Other matters have deflected me. My diary records that on 27 November 2000 my wife gave birth to a baby boy, Otto, weighing eight and a half pounds, a half-brother for my teenage children Lauretta and Nicholas, who have already featured once or twice in this story. We are spending the first few weeks of Otto's life in his grandmother's house near Godalming. It is a happy time. My hands are full and messages of goodwill pour in. From the South of France, Panna Grady has sent a beautifully wrapped parcel containing two fluffy toys, a scarf and a woollen hat – and in the same post a photocopy of a blurred snapshot which I have never seen before of Philip O'Connor sitting on the steps of his hut as a boy. Maria Scott has written, sending us one of her own drawings of lost children in which she has always specialized. Anna Wing has rung and congratulated us, but still does not want to tell her side of this story. And from South Devon has come a cheery congratulations card from Quentin Crisp's niece Frances Ramsay, which I have pinned up beside Otto's cot. I do not know the bit of Surrey where we are staying, but have discovered it is not far from Dorking and only about twenty miles from Box Hill. I plan to drive over there later this morning and try to find out if the hut in which Philip O'Connor once lived is still standing.

Index

INDEX

MacNeice, Louis 222–3
MacQueen, Kenneth 154, 158, 186, 187, 508, 518, 530
Madge, Charles 121–2
Mahler, Gustav 344
Mailer, Norman 265, 267, 273, 440
Makyns, Penelope 203
Mallarmé 110
Man from the Ministry, the 105, 133, 139, 421
Mancini 58, 93
Manhattan Displays 208–9, 211
Mann, George 154, 155
Manners-Howe, Wanda 200
Manning, Olivia 102
Mansfield, Katherine 43
Marchmont Street, Bloomsbury 175–6
Marie-Therese, Wimereux butcher's daughter 52, 53, 129
Markham, Barbara 204, 208, 245, 422, 511
Mars-Jones, Adam 454
Marx, Karl 109
Maschler, Tom 241, 244, 256, 273, 295, 296, 314, 538
Masefield, John 512
Mason, Mrs 449, 457
Matisse 222
Maude, Cyril 296
Maude, Muffet 207
Maudsley Hospital 117–21, 126, 163, 181, 255, 257, 350, 352, 404, 489, 529, 538
Maugham, Syrie 10
May, Derwent 507
Mayne, Roger 237
Meadmore, Bill and Dumps 187, 192
Meaty, Mrs 57
Melly, George 7, 131, 134, 191–2, 208–9, 305, 400, 455, 406–7
Mendelson, Jacob, junk-dealer 116, 123, 143, 159, 209, 289
Menuhin, Yehudi 442
Meo, Ann 144, 190, 216
Merielle (P.O'C.'s last nurse) 483
Mermaid Theatre 227
Mermelstein, Jeff 522
Mesens, E. L. T. 122
Metropolitan Music Hall 155, 204, 286, 530
Michelangelo 100, 167

Michell, John 268, 272, 287, 335, 362, 454
Milbank, Lena 503
Miles, Bernard 227
Miller, Arthur 440
Miller, Jane 209, 211, 245–7, 295, 302
Miller, Jonathan 250, 252
Miller, Karl 245, 246
Mills, Florence 60
Mills, John, sculptor 395
Miltoh, Bo and Ruby 183
Minton, John 195
Mitchell, Denis 29, 238, 310–13, 313–15, 382, 384–6, 386, 396–7, 399, 432, 505–6, 535
Mitchell, Julian 225, 422
Mitchell, Linda 238, 311, 384–5, 396–7, 505–6, 507
Modlyn, Monty 391
Monson, Jane (P.O'C.'s grand-daughter) 479
Monteagle, Lord 46
Monteith, Charles 161, 180, 182–3, 225, 234
Montesquiou, Duchess of 404
Moore, Derry 397–8
Moore, Henry 353
Moore, Marianne 266
Morgan, Mrs 233
Morgan, Ted 266, 267, 516
Morley, Catherine 137, 508
Morris, Desmond 245
Morris, Jan 460
Mosley, Nicholas 267, 327, 368
Motion, Andrew 427
Muggeridge, Malcolm 255
Muir, Edwin 220
Murison, Estelle 101, 137
Murray, Peter 126
Mygind, Annie 178, 220, 223, 225, 227, 229, 229–30, 231, 235, 237, 250, 280, 328, 332, 369, 373, 397, 403, 408, 416, 432, 442, 503
Myles, Sylvia 534

Nabokov, Dominique 470
Neame, Derek 504
Newby, P. Howard 173–4, 174, 234
Newley, Patrick 525
Nicholson, Mavis 390
Ninn, Anaïs 265
Noble, Johnny 428, 504

INDEX